A MIDSUMMER NIGHT'S DREAM

Shakespeare Criticism

Philip C. Kolin, *General Editor*

Romeo and Juliet
Critical Essays
edited by John F. Andrews

Coriolanus
Critical Essays
edited by David Wheeler

Titus Andronicus
Critical Essays
edited by Philip C. Kolin

Love's Labour's Lost
Critical Essays
edited by Felicia Hardison Londré

The Winter's Tale
Critical Essays
edited by Maurice Hunt

Two Gentlemen of Verona
Critical Essays
edited by June Schlueter

Venus and Adonis
Critical Essays
edited by Philip C. Kolin

As You Like It
from 1600 to the Present
Critical Essays
edited by Edward Tomarken

The Comedy of Errors
Critical Essays
edited by Robert S. Miola

A Midsummer Night's Dream
Critical Essays
edited by Dorothea Kehler

A MIDSUMMER NIGHT'S DREAM

CRITICAL ESSAYS

EDITED BY

DOROTHEA KEHLER

ROUTLEDGE
NEW YORK AND LONDON

First paperback edition published in 2001 by
Routledge
29 West 35th Street
New York, NY 10001

Published in Great Britain by
Routledge
11 New Fetter Lane
London EC4P 4EE

Routledge is an imprint of the Taylor & Francis Group.

10 9 8 7 6 5 4 3 2 1

Library of Congress Cataloging-in-Publication Data

A midsummer night's dream : critical essays / edited by Dorothea Kehler.
   p. cm.
  ISBN 0-8153-2009-4 (alk. paper)
  ISBN 0-8153-3890-2 (pbk.)
  1. Shakespeare, William, 1564-1616. A midsummer night's dream.
  2. Comedy. I. Kehler, Dorothea, 1936- . II. Series: Garland
  reference library of the humanities ; vol. 1900. III. Series:
  Garland reference library of the humanities. Shakespeare
  criticism ; v. 19.
 PR2827.M544 1998
 822.3'3–dc21   97-31433
                CIP

Printed on acid-free, 250-year-life paper
Manufactured in the United States of America

FOR JESSICA

I know a bank where the wild thyme blows
Where oxlips and the nodding violet grows,
Quite over-canopied with luscious woodbine,
With sweet musk-roses and with eglantine . . .

Figure 1 (Frontispiece). Act 3, scene 1, of "A Midsummer Night's Dream," painted by H. Fuseli and engraved by R. Rhodes. Published 1794. Reproduced by permission of The Huntington Library, San Marino, California.

Contents

General Editor's Introduction   xi

Acknowledgments   xiii

I. *A Midsummer Night's Dream* and the Critics

A Midsummer Night's Dream: A Bibliographic Survey of the
    Criticism
    Dorothea Kehler   3

A Midsummer Night's Dream
    Mark Van Doren   77

Imagination in *A Midsummer Night's Dream*
    R.W. Dent   85

Titania and the Ass's Head
    Jan Kott   107

A Midsummer Night's Dream: "Jack Shall Have Jill; / Nought
    Shall Go Ill"
    Shirley Nelson Garner   127

"I Believe We Must Leave the Killing Out": Deference and
    Accommodation in *A Midsummer Night's Dream*
    Theodore B. Leinwand   145

Bottom's Up: Festive Theory in *A Midsummer Night's Dream*
    Annabel Patterson   165

Dis/Figuring Power: Censorship and Representation in
    A Midsummer Night's Dream
    Barbara Freedman   179

A Kingdom of Shadows
    Louis A. Montrose   217

Textual Theory, Literary Interpretation, and the Last Act of *A
    Midsummer Night's Dream*
    Janis Lull   241

A Midsummer Night's Dream as a Comic Version of the
    Theseus Myth
    Douglas Freake   259

Antique Fables, Fairy Toys: Elisions, Allusion, and
    Translation in *A Midsummer Night's Dream*
    Thomas Moisan   275

Disfiguring Women with Masculine Tropes:
    A Rhetorical Reading of *A Midsummer Night's
    Dream*
    Christy Desmet   299

Our Nightly Madness: Shakespeare's *Dream* Without *The
    Interpretation of Dreams*
    Thelma N. Greenfield   331

Chronotope and Repression in *A Midsummer Night's Dream*
    Susan Baker   345

Preposterous Pleasures: Queer Theories and *A Midsummer
    Night's Dream*
    Douglas E. Green   369

II. *A Midsummer Night's Dream* on Stage

A Review of Ariane Mnouchkine's *Le Songe d'une nuit d' été*
    [1968]
    Ann Fridén   401

Shakespeare at the Guthrie: *A Midsummer Night's Dream*
    [1985]
    Thomas Clayton   403

[Kenneth Branagh's] *A Midsummer Night's Dream* [1990]
    Robert A. Logan   417

Brecht and Beyond: Shakespeare on the East German Stage
    [1971-1980]
    Lawrence Guntner   421

A Midsummer Night's Dream: Nightmare or Gentle Snooze?
    [1970-1994]
    Mary Z. Maher   429

Transposing Helena to Form and Dignity [1994]
    Lisa J. Moore   453

Marion McClinton's *A Midsummer Night's Dream* at the La
    Jolla Playhouse, 1995: Appropriation Through
    Performance
    Dorothea Kehler   473

General Editor's Introduction

The continuing goal of the Garland Shakespeare Criticism series is to provide the most influential historical criticism, the most significant contemporary interpretations, and reviews of the most influential productions. Each volume in the series, devoted to a Shakespearean play or poem (e.g., the sonnets, *Venus and Adonis*, the *Rape of Lucrece*), includes the most essential criticism and reviews of Shakespeare's work from the late seventeenth century to the present. The series thus provides, through individual volumes, a representative gathering of critical opinion of how a play or poem has been interpreted over the centuries.

A major feature of each volume in the series is the editor's introduction. Each volume editor provides a substantial essay identifying the main critical issues and problems the play (or poem) has raised, charting the critical trends in looking at the work over the centuries, and assessing the critical discourses that have linked the play or poem to various ideological concerns. In addition to examining the critical commentary in light of important historical and theatrical events, each introduction functions as a discursive bibliographic essay that cites and evaluates significant critical works—essays, journal articles, dissertations, books, theatre documents—and gives readers a guide to research on the particular play or poem.

After the introduction, each volume is organized chronologically, by date of publication of selections, into two sections: critical essays and theatre reviews/documents. The first section includes previously published journal articles and book chapters as well as original essays written for the collection. In selecting essays, editors have chosen works that are representative of a given age and critical approach. Striving for accurate historical representation, editors include earlier as well as contemporary criticism. Their goal is to include the widest possible range of critical approaches to the play or poem to demonstrate the multiplicity and complexity of critical response.

In most instances, essays have been reprinted in their entirety, not butchered into snippets. The editors have also commissioned original essays (sometimes as many as five to ten) by leading Shakespearean scholars, thus offering the most contemporary, theoretically attentive analyses. Reflecting some recent critical approaches in Shakespearean studies, these new essays approach the play or poem from a multiplicity of perspectives, including feminist, Marxist, new historical, semiotic, mythic, performance/staging, cultural, and/or a combination of these and other methodologies. Some volumes in the series even include bibliographic analyses that have significant implications for criticism.

The second section of each volume in the series is devoted to the play in performance and, again, is organized chronologically by publication date, beginning with some of the earliest and most significant productions and proceeding to the most recent. This section, which ultimately provides a theatre history of the play, should not be regarded as different from or rigidly isolated from the critical essays in the first section. Shakespearean criticism has often been informed by or has significantly influenced productions. Shakespearean criticism over the last twenty years or so has usefully been labeled the "Age of Performance." Readers will find information in this section on major foreign productions of Shakespeare's plays as well as landmark productions in English. Consisting of more than reviews of specific productions, this section also contains a variety of theatre documents, including interpretations written for a particular volume by notable directors whose comments might be titled "The Director's Choice," histories of seminal productions (e.g., Peter Brook's *Titus Andronicus*) in 1955), and even interviews with directors and/or actors. Editors have also included photographs from productions around the world to help readers see and further appreciate the way a Shakespearean play has taken shape in the theatre.

Each volume in the Garland Shakespeare Criticism series strives to give readers a balanced, representative collection of the best that has been thought and said about a Shakespearean play or poem. In essence, each volume supplies a careful survey of essential materials in the history of criticism for a Shakespearean play or poem. In offering readers complete, fulfilling, and in some instances very hard to locate materials, editors have made conveniently accessible the literary and theatrical criticism of Shakespeare's greatest legacy, his work.

Philip C. Kolin
University of Southern Mississippi

Acknowledgments

The cooperation of many people made this project possible. I want to express my gratitude to the presses, journals, and individuals that granted me permission to reprint material. Special thanks to Louis Montrose for helping me secure permission to reprint his chapter, to Lisa Anne Libby for helping me to locate illustrations, and to the Huntington Library.

My thanks to San Diego State University for financial support of the anthology, to the staff of Interlibrary Loan for their prompt and kind service, to Rachel Litonjua-Witt and James Edwards of SDSU's Instructional Technology Services for their remarkably patient assistance with the preparation of camera-ready copy, and to Barbara Schloss who graciously offered to type much of the manuscript. I am also indebted to my delightful and industrious student assistants: Camille Hayes, who relentlessly checked documentation, and Nick Panissidi, whose technical expertise with computers turned an incipient nightmare into a dream. Mathew Isom was more than an assistant: the theatrical history under the rubric of Performance Criticism in the Introduction is as much his work as mine, if not more.

The general editor of this series, Philip Kolin, has been a kindly reader and mentor; my editor at Garland Publishing, Phyllis Korper, and her staff have been most supportive. I would also like to thank those who generously gave of their time to read and comment upon drafts of my introduction and essay on the McClinton production: Curtis Breight of the University of Pittsburgh, Jeanie Grant Moore at the University of Wisconsin at Oshkosh, and my colleagues Clare Colquitt and Peter C. Herman. Thanks to Marion McClinton for taking the time to speak to me at length about his production.

Above all I want to acknowledge the contributors of new essays, who have been a delight to work with, obliging in every way. Thank you, Susan Baker, Christy Desmet, Douglas Freake, Douglas E. Green, Thelma N. Greenfield, Janis Lull, Mary Z. Maher, Thomas Moisan, and Lisa J. Moore.

PART I

A Midsummer Night's Dream and the Critics

A Midsummer Night's Dream
A Bibliographic Survey of the Criticism

Dorothea Kehler

A remarkable fantasy, *A Midsummer Night's Dream* is one of the best-loved Shakespearean comedies. Probably written sometime between 1594 and 1596, that is, between *Romeo and Juliet* and *The Merchant of Venice*, *Dream* belongs to the playwright's early-middle period when Shakespeare revelled in lyricism. His poetic achievement in *Dream* may be equalled in the later works but is never surpassed. Here he creates atmosphere, in turn, charming, lush, and darkly erotic, through iterative imagery; distinguishes between character groups through elegantly patterned discourse; and employs phonic and rhythmic sound variations to make music out of language. The text, which exists in three versions differing primarily in the number of stage directions, draws on many different sources, but the delightful theatrical composite, like the poetic texture, is a triumph of originality.

The focus of *Dream* criticism has varied with the age. Restoration and eighteenth-century commentators on drama most frequently fastened on plot, nineteenth-century critics on character, and twentieth-century writers on language and theme—though in the last several decades on explicitly political issues as well. *A Midsummer Night's Dream*, while no glaring exception to trends as much socio-political as aesthetic, early evoked interest in its philosophic underpinnings. Appearance and reality, art, imagination, and above all love were central. The play has been understood as implying, platonically, that life is a dream, or, skeptically, that romantic love is a dream. The faculty of imagination, both celebrated and mocked in *Dream*, is integral to the audience as well as to the playwright; the one takes appearance—a dream of sorts—for reality, the other creates a reality from appearance. Where Shakespeare stands on the question of whether lovers are deluded by appearances or rather are receptive to a transcendant reality remains moot. The answers are apt to tell us more about the critics than about the play.

Because of the fairies, the music, the comical mistakings of the lovers, and the incomparable farce of Pyramus and Thisbe, *Dream* had often been considered especially suitable for introducing children to Shakespeare. For those unpersuaded by Jan Kott's 1960s vision of the play as cruelly, even bestially, orgiastic, no doubt it still is. But that prominent reading revolutionized criticism and stage productions. In its wake, to issues long explored, critics added often fascinating psychoanalytic and sociological excursions into the delineation of class and gender roles; of sexual maturation and preference; and most recently, of early modern but lingering racialism.

My survey of pre-twentieth-century *Dream* criticism is not subdivided into categories, since most men of letters—and they *were* men—wrote impressionistically and touched on multiple issues. As literary study became increasingly specialized, critics often chose to address a particular aspect of the play, although such thematic subjects as dream, love, imagination, and the supernatural are often linked. Analyses of *Dream*'s many complex issues are sometimes grounded in the four character groups or story lines, sometimes in a literary component such as language, sometimes in a favored critical approach. Inevitably, some essays overlap these categories, which themselves overlap.

Charting English-language twentieth-century criticism, I have for the most part proceeded chronologically within categories in order to reveal lines of development. This selective overview—*Dream* criticism is a world without end—cites some of the more important and interesting works. No census, it is also not a historical reception study, though it may invite such work. Some trends are well-known, e.g., the progression from historical backgrounding to the foregrounding practice of the various new historicisms, from a functionalist view of gender to feminist and queer theory readings. Recently, the negotiations between criticism and performance have become more visible, and performance criticism has assumed new significance. Accordingly, historicist, gender, and performance studies are the last of the critical categories, with a brief theatrical history concluding this introduction to the reprinted and new essays.

In the twentieth century, particularly the last third, as our awareness of the politics of criticism amplifies, readers are more apt to recognize whether the critic is politically and theoretically self-conscious, to ask why the critic focuses where s/he does, to speculate about whose interests are furthered by a particular piece of criticism, and about what cultural work has been achieved. For example, R.W. Dent, in his fine defense of the imagination written in the early 1960s, takes for granted that "Lysander and Hermia may not behave rationally in their flight from authority" (123,n.18); just a few years later, in the wake of the United States's civil rights movement, the sexual revolution, and the protests against the Vietnam war, political trend setters would find such behavior eminently rational and embark on a *fin de siècle* project that has transformed critical practice. We are learning, as Terence Hawkes observes, that "Shakespeare doesn't mean; *we* mean *by* Shakespeare" ("By," 3). Apropos of the meanings we bring to the play, I should mention that although this account is mainly descriptive, I have not entirely resisted editorializing about criticism whose baneful treatment of class and gender can only have a regressive influence.

A number of reference works are especially useful: D. Allen Carroll and Gary Jay Williams's annotated bibliography devoted exclusively to *Dream* (1986); the Shakespeare bibliographies compiled by Linda Woodbridge (1988), Joseph Rosenblum (1992), and Larry Champion (1993); *Shakespeare Quarterly*'s annual World Shakespeare Bibliography; and Gale Publishing's *Shakespearean Criticism* volumes on *Dream*. In his Twayne book on *Dream*, James L. Calderwood (1992) provides valuable references.

1662-1896

Given the exceptional creativity of Shakespeare in *A Midsummer Night's Dream* and the prescriptive rules which most Restoration and eighteenth-century neo-classicists upheld, it is not surprising that a work so appealing and popular today should have had to struggle for approbation in the theater, winning praise largely for the quality of the poetry or for such incidentals as Shakespeare's acquaintance with the classics. That his plays have survived the fads and biases of earlier

times is a tribute to Shakespeare. For a practical spectator like the
admiralty's Samuel Pepys (1662), who in confiding to his diary gave
posterity the first written judgment of *Dream*, it was "the most insipid
ridiculous play that ever I saw in my life." Luckily, it was not without
redeeming qualities: "I saw, I confess, some good dancing and some
handsome women, which was all my pleasure" (3: 208). An initial
problem for neo-classicists honoring the new scientism were the fairies.
Should they be depicted? *Some* should, said Dryden in 1677, by then a
major writer and arbiter of taste. He contended against excessive
restraints on writers' subject matter as he justified Shakespeare's use of
supernatural creatures; for

> Poets may be allow'd the . . . liberty, for describing things which
> really exist not, if they are founded on popular belief: of this nature
> are Fairies, Pigmies, and the extraordinary effects of Magick: for 'tis
> still an imitation, though of other mens fancies: and thus are
> Shakespeare's Tempest, his Midsummer nights Dream, and Ben.
> Johnsons Masque of Witches to be defended.

Charles Gildon, an early eighteenth-century commentator, rescued
Shakespeare for neo-classicism by commending his "beautiful
Reflections, Descriptions, Similes, and Topics," his observance of
decorum, and his apparent familiarity with Ovid and Virgil in the
original Latin; such felicities made up for the play's action, which
seemed to take less than two days and nights rather than the promised
four, a curious issue that lingered into the late nineteenth century with
Halliwell-Phillipps (1841) arguing that Shakespeare's many
inconsistencies in the play in no way "detract from the most beautiful
poetical drama in this or any other language" (5), Clapp (1885) calling
the play "unrealistic," and Furness (1895) defending it; more recently
the debate inspired Neil Taylor's 1971 note proposing a "double time-
scheme" (134) that incorporated a minimum of four nights and yet was
also timeless, and Anne Paolucci's 1977 article arguing for a *five*-day
duration.

William Duff (1770), a Scottish critic and clergyman, thought the
supernatural was Shakespeare's forte; he especially admired the
scherzo-like poetry of the fairies, "the quick returns, and (if we may
use the expression) brisk boundings of the verse" (143). Francis
Gentleman (1774), a man of the theater, also admired Shakespeare's

poetry and commended the play's characterization and originality but nevertheless regarded the plot as "puerile" and regretted the "odd mixture of incidents" and "forced connexion of various stiles" (8: 137).

One of the most important of eighteenth-century Shakespeareans, Edward Malone (1778), offers the most revealing criticism. Though he finds *Dream* splendidly imaginative, he faults the characterization and fable on grounds of decorum—that is, for not making enough of class distinctions: "Through the whole piece, the more exalted characters are subservient to the interests of those beneath them" (2: 336). Aristocrats, especially Theseus, are insufficiently distinguished from their inferiors, and any suggestion of a Saturnalian structure unnerves Malone, who concludes that this must be an early play. Presumably, had Shakespeare been older, he would have known better. That Malone, an Irish scholar who chose to live in London, writes two years after the American colonies declared their independence and little more than a decade before the onset of the French Revolution may in part account for his views. Not until the mid-nineteenth century—in the writings of Charles Knight—are class concerns addressed self-consciously and democratically.

Significant nineteenth-century criticism begins in 1808 with Shakespeare's German translator, the Romantic critic August Wilhelm Schlegel. He wisely perceived unity in the multiple plot lines, noted that the ass head literalizes Bottom's true nature, identified the tale of Pyramus and Thisbe as a burlesque of the adventures of the Athenian lovers, and regarded the entire play as a source of delight. An important English literary and theater critic, William Hazlitt (1817), liked the play no less but found that "when acted, [*A Midsummer Night's Dream*] is converted from a delightful fiction into a dull pantomime. . . . Poetry and the stage do not agree well together" (247). Of course, prior to Madam Vestris's 1840 production (see the theater history below), stagings of *Dream* played havoc with the text as was true for all of Shakespeare's plays.

The English Romantic poet and critic Samuel Taylor Coleridge (1811-12), whose Shakespeare criticism is still influential, made two points about the play. The first, that Shakespeare thought of it as "a *dream* throughout," led to further discussion later in the century (see Hudson and Brandes); the second, that Helena is guilty of "ungrateful treachery" to Hermia, served Coleridge as a springboard for misogynous maundering. Helena's betrayal of Hermia is too true a picture of the lax holds that principles have on the female heart, when opposed to, or even separated from, passion and inclination. For women are less hypocrites to their own minds than men, because they feel less abhorrence of moral evil in itself and more for its outward consequences, as detection, loss of character, etc., their natures being almost wholly extroitive [concerned with externals]. (90)

Thus are gender issues introduced into the critical canon of *Dream*. (See Lisa J. Moore's essay in this volume for an actress's take on Helena.)

William Maginn, an Anglo-Irish writer, is notable for an 1837 essay on Theseus's "the lunatic, the lover, and the poet" speech and Hippolyta's response to it. Maginn regards Theseus as Shakespeare's voice and the speech as a call for imaginative audiences. Maginn was also responsible for the first character study of Bottom—"*the* lucky man, . . . on whom Fortnne [sic] showers her favors beyond measure"(97)—who is aware only of his peers' adulation and is unfazed by the fairy queen's love. Awareness of class issues almost surfaces in Maginn's amusement at Bottom's democratizing nature: "Theseus would have bent in reverent awe before Titania. Bottom treats her as carelessly as if she were the wench of the next-door tapster" (102). Patriarchal thinking is just as soundly rooted. Maginn excuses Oberon for humiliating Titania; accidents happen: "Oberon himself, angry as he is with the caprices of his queen, does not anticipate any such object for her charmed affections [as the weaver/ass]" (99).

Hermann Ulrici (1839), like his countryman August Schlegel, was a Romantic but taught philosophy rather than literature. Linking class to platonism, Ulrici thought *Dream* organically unified in a particularly platonic way: ". . . Shakspeare has regarded human life in this play as a dream. . . ." (274). Noting class differences among the character groups, Ulrici explained what Malone considered lack of decorum through the notion of self-parody, e.g., Theseus and Hippolyta parody their station by behaving like ordinary people. Parody becomes another unifying principle which, together with platonism, constitutes the play's informing comic vision. Charles Knight (1849), a British friend of the proletariat, takes a quite different tack regarding social stratification. Replying to Malone, he argues that *Dream* demonstrates

Shakespeare's maturity as a playwright; its Thesean harmony is a product of decorum of character, the best-drawn character being Bottom. Acknowledging Bottom's self-confidence, authority, and self-love, Knight maintains, "Why, Bottom the weaver is the representative of the whole human race" (209). Knight continues by echoing Hazlitt: *Dream* is best appreciated when read rather than acted. Moreover, critical analysis of so "subtle and ethereal" a play would be reductive (213). Best that it speak for itself in the study.

In the same year, G.G. Gervinus, among the most prominent of German critics, makes a number of notable points. The play is not a dream, as Coleridge suggested; instead it is an ethical construct, an allegorical depiction of the errors of sensual love which here correspond to dream. Gervinus' notion of ethics is grounded in filial obedience: "Alike devoid of conscience, Hermia errs at first through want of due obedience to her father . . . and Lysander through mockery of his father-in-law (188)." Pyramus and Thisbe are "two lovers, who behind their parents' backs 'think no scorn to woo by moonlight'. . ." (188-89). The fairies are no better; "personified dream gods," they represent "the caprices of superficial love" (194) and lack intellect, feeling, and an ethical sense. They bring dreams and *are* dreams. This argument dissolves into orientalism, misogny, and elitism. Gervinus first locates fairy land "in the aromatic flower-scented Indies, in the land where mortals live in a half-dreamy state." Then he devalues Titania's loyalty: "Titania has no spiritual association with her friend, but mere delight in her beauty, her 'swimming gait,' and her powers of imitation"; she is also blamed for not initiating a "scene of reconciliation with her husband; her resentment consists in separation. . ." (196). Also blameworthy are "[t]he homely mechanics, who compose and act merely for gain, and for the sake of so many pence a day, the ignorant players, with hard hands and thick heads. . . ." Only Theseus, "the intellectual man" (199), is deserving of respect. Finally, like various others, Gervinus concludes that it were better not to act the play than to act it badly as has been the case in Germany.

Charles Cowden Clarke (1863), husband of Mary (*The Girlhood of Shakespeare's Heroines*), took a more becoming view of the mechanicals than Gervinus, noting both their individualization and their collective richness. Good-natured though conceited, Bottom "displays no inconsiderable store of imagination in his intercourse with the little people of the fairy world" (101). Bottom's conceit, Clarke asserts, reflects a quality inseparable from the acting profession. The comments of H.N. Hudson, an American clergyman and editor of Shakespeare (1872), are largely derivative. Hudson does perceive, however, that Shakespeare's lightness of characterization is appropriate if, like Coleridge, we understand *Dream* as a dream. Edward Dowden (1881), an Irish critic, is notable for his critique of Theseus's reflections on art. Albeit Dowden views Theseus as central to *Dream*, one of Shakespeare's "heroic men of action" like Henry V or Hector— or Essex (60)—he disputes Theseus's yoking together "the lunatic, the lover, and the poet," and the conflation of the best and the worst dramas. Only insofar as the poet must awaken his audience's imagination does Theseus speak for Shakespeare.

Henry A. Clapp (1885) returned to problems of duration (loss of a day), finding a solution "in the nature of the play, whose characters, even when clothed with human flesh and blood, have little solidity or reality" (392). A decade later, a protective Henry Howard Furness defended Shakespeare by discovering three references to dawn by means of which the playwright can both "condense time ... and expand it" (xxxiii). An American Hegelian, Denton J. Snider (1887), championed the play by faulting the stage. Like so many nineteenth-century critics, he felt that the stage could not do justice to Shakespeare's most popular comedy. Snider stressed ethics, reading *Dream* as a dialectic between understanding and imagination or between prose and poetry. His work anticipates metadramatic theory insofar as he traces three "phases or movements": the first, the "Real World" of reason; second, the "Ideal Realm" or "Fairy World" of imagination and the supernatural; and, finally, their "representation in Art," in which "the first two parts mirror themselves—the action reflects itself, the play plays itself playing; it is its own spectator, including its audience and itself in one and the same movement" (383). Unfortunately, integral to this otherwise forward-looking interpretation is an assertion of Titania's fault of caprice and deserved punishment by "a dutiful husband" (403) who says, in effect, "if you cannot live in peace with me, one of your own kind, then try the contrary, a horrid brute" (402).

Happily, nineteenth-century studies of *Dream* end on a more promising note. Denmark's George Brandes (1895-96), aside from pointing to various sources and to influences on the Romantics, looks forward to Jan Kott's significant 1964 piece (see below under Theme), though without Kott's excesses and, more broadly, anticipates psychological readings. Brandes discerns that "Oberon's magic is simply a great symbol, typifying the sorcery of the erotic imagination" (67), that Shakespeare "early felt and divined how much wider is the domain of the unconscious than of the conscious life, and saw that our moods and passions have their root in the unconscious" (71). Frederick S. Boas (1896), better known as the coiner of the label "problem play," looks at *Dream* not as an ethical treatise or psychological study but rather as a historically situated and consciously constructed entertainment which, like *The Comedy of Errors*, comes wrapped in classical trappings but nevertheless is "essentially English and Elizabethan." Boas' Theseus, therefore, is "a great Tudor noble" (184), his Helena is no morally weak betrayer but part of "a transparently clumsy device for concentrating the four lovers on a single spot" (185), and the play of Pyramus and Thisbe a parody of contemporary exploitation of classical subjects as well as a nod to a favorite Elizabethan *topos*, appearance and reality—"the relation of shadow to substance. . ." (189). This is recognizably modern criticism.

THE TWENTIETH CENTURY

Textual Criticism, Chronology, Occasion

Citations in both this section and the next are limited to contributions that generated continuing research and/or are noteworthy for their critical sophistication; see the standard editions—Brooks (1979), Foakes (1984), and Holland (1995)—for more detailed surveys. Samuel B. Hemingway (1911) reflects on chronology, arguing that *Midsummer Night's Dream* followed rather than preceded *Romeo and Juliet*, insofar as *Dream*, and especially the Pyramus and Thisbe playlet, parodied the extreme passions of the love tragedy. In a controversial study, Edith Rickert (1923) finds topical allusions to Elizabeth, James, and various aristocrats, which she offers as evidence of revision. She explains "Shakespeare's part in the political game . . . either through his friendship with Southampton . . . or through his connection with the Careys. . ." (154).

Editor and critic John Dover Wilson (1924), advanced an important revision theory. Comparing the quarto and folio texts, he argues that *Dream* was composed in three stages. In 1592 or earlier

Shakespeare first worked on the play, revising it a few years later by adding Bottom and the Puck scenes, then revising it again in 1598, perhaps for the Earl of Southampton's wedding. The poet Walter de la Mare (1935) explained lines he found bland, undifferentiated, and stylistically discordant (particularly those of the lovers) by suggesting that *Dream* was either composed piecemeal or was in part Shakespeare's revision of another playwright's work. (See Janis Lull's 1997 essay on the critical implications of Wilson's and De la Mare's theories.) Paul N. Siegel (1953), addressing the question of occasion, suggests that *Dream* having been written as a wedding entertainment, the guests were invited to consider the characters' act 5 bed-rites as betokening the appropriateness of the host and hostess consumating their own marriage. Harold F. Brooks's discussion of text, chronology, and occasion introducing the Arden edition (1979) remains a valuable summary; also see Brooks's appendices. R.A. Foakes's Introduction to the New Cambridge edition (1984) and his appended "Textual Analysis" are useful, too.

Criticism of the past decade seeks to understand the consequences of textual variation for the theater. Barbara Hodgdon (1986) examines the critical issues related to Egeus's presence at the wedding in the folio text versus his absence in the quarto, and concludes that the folio variants "complicate and enrich the performance possibilities" (541); she suspects that they reveal "Shakespeare's own revising mind" (542). Marion Colthorpe (1987) evaluates previous work on the play's occasion, considering the various weddings for which *Dream* may have been written and finding none of the speculations convincing. Invoking anthropologist Arnold Van Gennup on rites of passage, Philip C. McGuire (1989) builds on Hodgdon's work. He teases out the theatrical ramifications of Shakespeare's act 5 revisions with regard to Egeus's silence in act 4, scene 1, when Theseus allows Hermia to marry Lysander. Whether Egeus accepts Hermia or rejects her depends on whether the director follows the folio version or the quarto. A concomitant effect is the degree of cohesion between Hermia's birth family, her new marital family, and the state. Hodgdon's and McQuire's essays demonstrate the benefits of linking textual study to interpretation.

Patricia Parker (1994) and her students, in a remarkable pedagogic exercise, pondered the literary associations of "more," "moral" and "mural" in the Folio's "Now is the moral down between the two neighbors" (5.1) as opposed to the quarto's "Now is the moon used between the two neighbors," in order to determine which text to follow. In the process, they unearthed

> the sources for its play-within-a-play, from Ovid and from Golding, the network of biblical allusion that had led us to, and beyond these, both the resources of what Spitzer called "historical semantics" and, more serendipitously, the linguistic talents of the students themselves. . . . (213)

A review of research on *Dream*'s date and text can be found in Peter Holland's Introduction to the Oxford edition (1995). In the appendix, "Shakespeare's Revisions of Act 5," Holland considers the interpretive implications of Egeus's speaking Philostrate's Q1 lines.

In her "Textual Theory, Literary Interpretation, and the Last Act of *A Midsummer Night's Dream*" written expressly for this volume, Janis Lull marries textual criticism to sensitive close reading. Like Barbara Hodgdon and Philip C. McGuire, Lull is concerned with differences between the quarto and folio texts. But whereas their subject is Egeus, hers is Theseus. Lull revisits Dover Wilson's theory that Theseus's "the lunatic, the lover, and the poet" speech had been revised in order to chart its consequences for interpreting the character of Theseus and act 5 generally. Wilson's theory allows for Shakespeare's conscious fashioning of a duke who comes to appreciate the irrational, whereas the postmodern, collectivist view produces a Theseus whose ear is coarse and who mismanages language, like Bottom and Quince, albeit not as blatantly. Exploring these options, Lull concludes that "where origins remain shrouded in doubt, the juxtaposing of apparently antithetical textual theories may prove more fruitful for literary interpretation than choosing between them."

Sources, Parallels, Allusions

Source study exerts a special fascination for students of *A Midsummer Night's Dream*, conflating eras as it does, melding the classical, medieval, and Renaissance worlds in a historical synesthesia much like the bodily amalgam Bottom makes of I Corinthians 2:9. Geoffrey Bullough (1957) remains the basic repository of source materials. Bullough examines George Pettie's *The Petite Palace of Pettie His*

Pleasure for parallels to the play-within-the-play, Chaucer's *The Legend of Good Women*, and various tales of Romeo and Juliet. Kenneth Muir's *Shakespeare's Sources* (1961), actually a 1957 volume reprinted with new appendices, is especially useful for the sources of *Pyramus and Thisbe*. Roger Lancelyn Green (1962) expands upon prior folklore studies, incorporating the role of the mythological, while Madeleine Doran (1962) discusses post-Ovidian versions of the Pyramus and Thisbe story—a twelfth-century Norman lay and a sixteenth-century Italian retelling. Shakespeare, she believes, would have known just such parody-inviting versions of the story. For *Pyramus and Thisbe*'s comic inspiration, J.W. Robinson (1964) looks to hybrid plays like *Cambises*, *Damon and Pithias*, and *Histrio-Mastix*, and to the Elizabethan pre-professional acting companies. Thelma N. Greenfield (1968) finds comparable allusions and ideas in *The Praise of Folly* and *Dream*; Shakespeare may have used Erasmus as a source, since in both works the fools at least momentarily triumph, their contexts having provided "ironic but sublime hints of fleeting non-rational modes of perception. . ." (244).

Outstanding work of the '70s includes an early feminist source study by D'Orsay W. Pearson (1974) that significantly corrected received opinion. Investigating Theseus's reputation in literature from Ovid to *Dream*, she finds it other than admirable. Once past his heroic youth, Theseus became known as lecherous, faithless, and tyrannical. Moreover, many Elizabethan spectators, knowing that Theseus caused the death of his son, Hippolytus, would have found the blessing of the "best bride-bed" ironic. T. Walter Herbert's unusual and delightful book-length source study (1977) ranges over the intellectual landscape from which *Dream* derives, from the classics (Part One: The Old Learning) to the late-sixteenth century (Part Two: The New Learning and Business). Herbert reads the play from the viewpoint of a Cambridge graduate inclined to skepticism, whose response to *Dream* is great sympathy and love for his friends, himself, and his difficult world. Thomas B. Stroup (1978) was the first scholar to suggest, in a Christian reading, that Shakespeare took Bottom's name from the words "the bottom of Goddes secretes" in I Corinthians 2: 11 of the 1557 Geneva Bible, a claim disputed the following year by Robert F. Willson, Jr., but of interest to Louis Adrian Montrose (1995; 1996). Harold F. Brooks (1979), in his introduction to the Arden edition, rehearses some of the most important sources located through the late

1970s, including Spenser's *Shepheardes Calender* and the tiny fairies of Welsh folklore; he reprints sources in his second appendix.

In the 1980s and '90s, most commentators plumbed previously identified sources. Jan Kott (1981), in "The Bottom Translation," a moderated view of *Dream* unlike the chapter in his 1964 *Shakespeare Our Contemporary* (see below under Theme) explicates the play's dualism, its juxtaposing of Paul with Apuleius, of Neoplatonism with Bakhtinian carnival, by cataloguing the play's constituent myths and literary allusions. Kott now believes that *Dream* is susceptible to *light* as well as dark interpretations. John S. Mebane (1982) considers Chaucer's "Knight's Tale" the most important source for the Theseus material in *Dream*. Aside from the Theseus/Hippolyta frame, Chaucer supplies various structural characteristics and the much remarked upon *discordia concors* motif. Shakespeare's philosophic content, however, is presented more subtly than Chaucer's. Providing another summary, R.A. Foakes (1984) devotes eight pages to a discussion of sources in his introduction to the New Cambridge edition and appends "A Further Note on Sources." Hugh M. Richmond (1985) maintains in his "Shaping a *Dream*" that Shakespeare's most likely primary source for *Dream* was the ninth novella of the second decade of Cinthio's *Hecatommithi*, which includes lovers whose bonds are in flux; patriarchal authority; the supernatural; and marriage grounded, if uneasily, in romantic love. Winfried Schleiner (1985) provides a new source character: the *Pluck* of the anonymous *Most Strange and Admirable Discovery of the Three Witches of Warboys* (1593), referred to by the exorcist John Darrell in his *A Detection of that Sinnful . . . Discoverie* (1600).

In the year's most charming contribution to source study, E. Talbot Donaldson (1985) compares Chaucer's attitude toward romantic love with Shakespeare's and affirms that Shakespeare presents a grimmer and more skeptical picture. Shakespeare's Theseus is more like *Dream*'s other male lovers, who owe their "obsessive single-mindedness in love" (37) to Palamon and Arcite. Helena's and Hermia's constancy in love, which destroys their friendship, is another motif borrowed from Palamon and Arcite. Noting that Oberon and Titania derive from Pluto and his victim Proserpina in *The Merchant's Tale*, Donaldson defends Titania from the attacks of Bonnard, Brooks, and others: "Shame on you, Titania, for holding out on that nice male chauvinist King of the Fairies!" (45).

In the past decade inquiry into diverse sources persists in conjunction with a resurgence of interest in Ovid. Leonard Barkan (1986) analyzes Shakespeare's introjection and revision of Ovid's "antique fables." With love and metamorphoses as its focusing events, an Ovidian *Dream* brings together beings supernatural, legendary, and familiar. Clifford Davidson's article (1987) grows out of Robinson's 1964 study. Davidson regards the *Pyramus and Thisbe* material as a parody of the style and subject matter of pre-1585 plays for the public theater and of the amateur acting in the mysteries and moralities. Thomas Moisan (1987) compares "Solempnytee" in "The Knight's Tale," in *Dream*, and in *Romeo and Juliet*, finding them "three variants on the same experience, three re-visions of the same book, read and re-writ by Chaucer and Shakespeare with varying emphases but comparable irony" (36). Barbara A. Mowat (1989) studies Theseus, constructed out of tendentious writings on witchcraft and imagination, as one example of how Shakespeare typically employs disparate and contradictory sources to create a character.

In this decade, Anthony Brian Taylor (1990) questions the generally accepted notion that *Pyramus and Thisbe* parodies Golding's translation of Ovid; rather, Shakespeare is satirizing his own "small Latin" through Quince's misprisions. For Jonathan Bate (1993), "Shakespeare's capacity to metamorphose Ovid into a different medium is what makes his art *imitatio* of the highest form" (144). Robert L. Reid (1993) discusses the debt Shakespeare owes to Spenser's *Faerie Queene* for his conceptions of Titania and of the nature of poetry; Reid avers that Shakespeare rejects art which might "devalue common earthly passion" (25). Introducing the Oxford edition of the play, Peter Holland (1995) surveys accepted and proposed sources at length, including Renaissance notions about dreams and the allusions to dreams in Elizabethan plays.

Two contributions to this volume employ new approaches to source study. Douglas Freake analyzes the play's debts to the Theseus story while rejecting the supposed universality of mythic tales. He notes that C. Kerényi, in his account of Theseus's ancestors, the early rulers of Athens, describes conflicts over both the naming of children and women's political power. Since these accounts resonate in Oberon's and Titania's quarrel over possession of the changeling boy, Freake concludes that the Theseus myth resurfaces in *Dream* because the question of patriarchal power was as vital in Elizabethan England as it had been in classical Athens and that the comic mode to some degree cloaks an underlying social theme: women's submission to men in marriage.

Thomas Moisan addresses those most traditional subjects and approaches—textual criticism and literary allusion—as a postmodernist. In his "Antique Fables, Fairy Toys: Elisions, Allusion, and Translation in *A Midsummer Night's Dream*," Moisan relates allusion and literary translation to the elisions that mark the integration of *Dream*'s sources. These produce the conflation of boundaries and the collapsing of distinctions of time, genre, gender, and social status. He remarks that *Dream* derives much of its comic energy from that collapse, which also produces the "rude" juxtapositions that highlight its ideological resonances. To examine the elisions and distortions generated by the evoking/quoting of sources is to unexpectedly align— at least parodically—the tropics of allusion and translation with the "rude" dramaturgy of the artisans' interlude. That alignment under- scores an affinity between the workings of allusion throughout the play and hypallage—the rhetorical figure in which a symmetrical exchange of parts produces nonsense—which marks Bottom's "translation" of I Corinthians and other instances of the artisans' rhetorical mis- adventures. At the same time, to examine the shreds and patches of allusion in *Dream* is not only to interrogate the violent collocations they produce, but to consider the violence to which they are subjected. Moreover, the study of allusion clarifies the relationship between Shakespeare's own dramaturgical procedures and generic claims and the interest an authoritative figure like Theseus has in shaping the present by suppressing the past.

Atmosphere and Tone

Boas's turn-of-the-century reading of *Dream* as Tudor in its mood appeals to the well-known writer and critic G.K. Chesterton (1904), who calls "Shakespeare's description of Athens . . . the best description of England that he or any one else ever wrote." Not only is Theseus "an English squire" but so, too, are the fairies, and of course "[t]he mechanics are English mechanics, talking to each other with the queer formality of the poor" (19). Chesterton acknowledges the darker aspects of *Dream* but insists that they never dominate its sparkling tone:

The events in the wandering wood are in themselves, and regarded as in broad daylight, not merely melancholy but bitterly cruel and ignominious. But yet by the spreading of an atmosphere as magic as the fog of Puck, Shakespeare contrives to make the whole matter mysteriously hilarious while it is palpably tragic, and mysteriously charitable, while it is in itself cynical. (15)

Enid Welsford (1927) also discusses the English quality of *Dream* but in another respect. In her work on the Elizabethan court masque she notes that "Shakespeare has absorbed the scenic splendour of the masque, not only in description and picturesque language, but also in a blending of tones, a harmony of colours . . ." (326). The mechanicals provide the anti-masque, while "[t]he influence of the dance has affected not merely isolated songs and speeches, but the whole structure of *A Midsummer Night's Dream* (331). G. Wilson Knight (1932), perhaps the best-known investigator of atmosphere, finds a "tempest . . . at the heart of the play" (144) in Titania's "forgeries of jealousy" speech. Likening *Dream* to *Macbeth*, he concludes, "Darkness and fear permeate this play. It is a darkness spangled, or shot, with light" (151). Critics attuned to the music of *Dream* are more apt to agree with Welsford.

W. Moelwyn Merchant (1961), is engaged with the play's atmosphere as interpreted outside the theater as well as within it. His "Visual Re-creation" of the play, a post-Commonwealth survey of paintings, book illustrations, and costume and set drawings, reveals that "while some artists have recognized the disturbing moments of irrationality, treachery, and demonic power, rarely have these been seen as qualities which are transformable to order and grace" (184). In "The Voices of *A Midsummer Night's Dream*" (1992), Maurice Hunt locates the atmosphere of *Dream* in tonality. The characters' distinctive voices, the invective, the off-stage sounds, the cries, etc.—all are cues for the imaginative auditor to fill with meaning. When we recall that Elizabethans went to *hear*, not see, a play, Hunt's approach seems especially productive.

Structure and Formal Design

John H. Long (1955) attributes structural unity and harmony to *Dream*, qualities denied it two centuries earlier and not to be questioned for another two decades. More than any other element, music creates unity and harmony. Music lends the fairies airiness; moreover, "You spotted Snakes," the fairy song, "itself is an ayre" (85). Equally important, Oberon's call for music and a dance mark the harmonious reconciliation of king and queen, while hunting horns intimate harmony among the newly awakened lovers; the play ends with the fairies' song and dance in blessing. Shakespeare used music, says Long, "to symbolize the concord arising from the settlement of the fairy quarrel, and to foreshadow the resulting harmony between the mortals—thus emphasizing the turning point of the play" (101).

For Bertrand Evans (1960), *A Midsummer Night's Dream*, like all of Shakespeare's plays, is structured on the principle of discrepant awarenesses. Oberon, an "outside force" (34), controls events, creating a gap between the lovers' awareness and the audience's. Although Hermia and Helena, unlike the young men, sense something uncanny in their situation, only Hippolyta comes close to sharing the spectators' awareness. Their perception of Oberon's benevolence towards the lovers provides "an environment in which comic effects can flourish even in dark moments" (40). For Sheldon P. Zitner (1960), on the other hand, the play's primary structural principle is not awareness but avoidance, complications being suggested but then avoided. The consequence is "the purest of comedies without the cruelty of farce or the zeal of comedy of manners" (402).

G.K. Hunter (1962), who groups *Dream* with *Much Ado, As You Like It*, and *Twelfth Night*, holds that *Dream* is above all a patterned, dance-like play in which no single element predominates, although Theseus's "achieved self-possession" (17) is perhaps most exemplary. The structure contrasts attitudes and types of love with little regard to individuating characterization or realistic passion. For James E. Robinson (1968) the play's structure inheres in the fusion of ritual—magic and marriage—with rhetoric—love and law. The action proceeds both logically and magically within the two worlds of Athens and the forest, the one societal, the other natural, a binary opposition reproduced in the language. The interlude's styles parody "the very threads out of which the language of the play has been woven" (390).

Larry S. Champion (1970) holds that Shakespeare's most significant accomplishment in *Dream* "is primarily in structure—the arrangement of the plot strands to achieve the most effective comic perspective" (50). While we are distanced from the "virtual caricatures of lovesick youth" (47), who are manipulated by the plot, the choric subplot sharpens the play's comedic focus. Shakespeare has adapted Chaucer's "Knight's Tale" to romantic comedy.

Work on the structure of *Dream* assumed greater prominence with the assimilation of French structuralist theory. The past quarter century has seen a variety of approaches to *Dream*'s structure. Mark Rose (1972) views it diagrammatically as simple and formal, two concentric circles around a target scene. The outer circle is composed of acts 1 and 5 located in Athens, the inner circle of acts 2 and 4—the forest scenes. The central scene is 3.1, bringing Athens and the forest together in the love of Titania for Bottom. In "Comedy, Orality, and Duplicity: *A Midsummer Night's Dream* and *Twelfth Night*," Terence Hawkes (1978) conflates the comedic theories of Frye, Barber, and Bakhtin, adding his own sense of the oral, participatory nature of Elizabethan comedy; he thus uncovers the structural importance of the Pyramus and Thisbe material. For M.E. Comtois (1980) the play's structure accounts for its durability in the theater. Like Rose, she offers a diagramatic analysis. Contained within the dream concept are eight actions (one private, one public) to be effected by each of the four couples, culminating in marriage. The structure, "both graceful and tight" (311) is pyramidal, composed largely of independent scenes. Ruth Nevo (1980) also asseses the play as carefully unified: "Through his basic comic structure of initial privation or perversity, comic device both deceptive and remedial, knots of errors and final recognitions, Shakespeare has achieved . . . a complex and witty exploration . . . of the imaginative faculty itself" (96).

Like Welsford, Alan Brissenden (1981) points out the fundamental role of dance in *A Midsummer Night's Dream*: " . . . Shakespeare made dancing an essential part of the plot, a summarising action and a universal symbol [of concord] instead of merely leaving it the delectable embellishment it might have been" (43). Skiles Howard's subject is dance (1993), but she is at pains to contradict "Tillyardized" simplifications (327); the structural opposition between courtly and country dancing is not resolved into cosmic harmony, naturalizing an aristocratic patriarchal hierarchy, but rather exposes it as "provisional and man-made" (342). Whereas Howard is alert to the play's political aspects, John Wilders (1994) eschews questions of power. In a heuristic essay he suggests that performance offers a key to Shakespeare's structure, which is above all dramatic—"constructed out of hundreds of small units or sections which are to an entire play as bricks are to a house" (153-54). Wilders illustrates by showing his students the five sections of 1.1. Peter Holland (1995) discusses the play's structure under the heading *Shapes*, first by invoking role-doubling as an indicator of structure, then by exploring other facets of *Dream* through its performance history.

Susan Baker's essay for this volume discusses *Dream*'s structure as a dialogue between Bakhtinian chronotopes, which are variously attached to genres, characters, and motifs and are a function of their distinguishing historical moment. Chronotopes define genre broadly as a way of viewing and portraying society. They map how, within each genre, where and when the characters live affect their scope of action: "Any interpretation of a text, then, will set into dialogue the chronotope(s) of its original moment, the chronotopes embedded in its generic participation, and the chronotope(s) dominant in the time-space of its interpreter." Because, as Baker points out, chronotopes are in-evitably ideological, our perceptions of time and space being inseparable from our values, "chronotopes offer a (reasonably) systematic approach to observing the interanimations of form, historicity, and ideology." Her essay includes a discussion of the golden world and the green world, of the intersection of chronotopic sites that Theseus occupies, and of repressions necessary to assure the ascendence of the comic chronotope.

What all these studies have in common is that, either explicitly or implicitly, whatever their focus, all reach a similar conclusion: *Dream*'s apparent unity reveals Shakespeare's mastery of structural technique.

Language and Style

Harley Granville-Barker (1924), whose experience as playwright, director, and critic attests to his comprehensive perspective, urges that the poetry of *Dream* take precedence over stage effects. Although he discusses ways of presenting the non-realistic elements to an audience accustomed to realistic theater, he observes that meter and tone shifts are largely responsible for characterization. Mark Van Doren (1939), whose chapter on *Dream* is reprinted in this volume, provides an appealing introduction to the play's imagery. He concentrates on the unsurpassed music and on "[m]oon, water, and wet flowers," which "conspire to extend the world of 'A Midsummer Night's Dream' until it is as large as all imaginable life" (81).

In contrast to Brandes, Chesterton, and G. Wilson Knight, among others, Thomas Marc Parrott (1949) sees only charm in the play: "It is in his use of language, as in so much else in this play, that Shakespeare shows himself the master" (131). Bottom's prose, the lovers' romantic rhyme, the interlude's parody of early rhyming plays, the fluid musicality of Oberon and Titania's blank verse all contribute to the audience's sense of the play as "lyric romantic comedy" devoid of the "shadow of death or danger" (133). The variety of styles in *Dream*, which the eighteenth-century commentator Francis Gentleman lamented, is commendable in the twentieth century. Milton Crane (1951), in his analysis of Shakespeare's prose, is particularly impressed by the way Shakespeare blends prose with the several verse forms of *Dream*. Similarly, recalling Chesterton—and perhaps Leavis—B. Ifor Evans (1952) remarks on the Englishness of *Dream*. Evans sees unity in Shakespeare's fusion of the lovers' sonnet imagery, the mechanicals' realistic prose, and the fairies' lyricism into something rustic and very English. Shakespeare's poetry "is gathered up into the dominant mood of the *Dream*, where myth and romance and the gentle English scene are at one, and where all is easily intelligible, lyrical in mood and gentle" (76).

David Young's study (1966) is a major contribution to *Dream* criticism. Focusing on style and structure in the second part of his three-part book, Young calls attention to the melding of popular and aristocratic elements and to the orchestration of particular responses from the spectators. He notes that the fairies' versification and use of song are largely distinctive, Shakespeare having given Puck a sometimes light-hearted, sometimes incantatory trochaic tetrameter, while Oberon and Titania alternate between tetrameter, blank verse, and pentameter couplets; the particularity of the fairies' speech intimates "more abstract sets of opposites like illusion and reality. . ." (67). The other character groups also speak in their own styles, but without endangering the unity of the play achieved through iterative imagery, which Young calls "picturization" (75)—not a glimpse but a complete picture—panoramas providing "perspective and distance, both in the geographic and aesthetic senses of those words" (80), and a profusion of lists, which "like the reiterated images . . . serve to create a fully realized world" (83).

Many studies address a single aspect of *Dream*'s language. In the third chapter of his valuable monograph on *Dream*, Stephen Fender (1968) examines in some detail how the language of the lovers changes to reflect new experiences and new awareness: "they enter the wood speaking in a highly organised, witty, complicated manner, and leave it speaking much more simply" (36). Brian Vickers (1968) devotes himself to a rhetorical analysis of the mechanicals' speech, focusing on Bottom; Vickers demonstrates how syntax and repetition create Bottom's characterization. Thomas Clayton (1971), in an amusing essay on the wall scene, finds textual support for Wall spreading his legs (the chink) as well as his fingers, business that "would make effective dramatic and poetical sense" (101). Somewhat more—or less —broadly, René Girard (1979) attends to the animal imagery, violence, and ambiguous language, discovering a surface text (Theseus's) and a subtext (Hippolyta's). He concludes that in *Dream*, as in Shakespeare's other plays, the "basic Shakespearean relationship" is "conflictual undifferentiation" (203) and that *Dream* is informed by "a common structure of mythical meaning" (211). Wolfgang Franke (1979) notes the bawdy double meanings of the mechanicals' names and language, bawdry of which the speakers are unconscious. Their speech would not have disturbed the nobility, who accepted the physical elements of romantic love.

G.J. Finch (1981) studies Shakespearean metaphor. He points out that the very language Theseus uses contradicts his low opinion of the poet. Rather, the play is an apologia for imagination and dreaming, a celebration of the poet's ability to reveal new ways of seeing. Joan Stansbury (1982) analyzes the language of the lovers, especially their use of imagery and modes of address, observing numerous differences that account for their individuation. Deborah Baker Wyrick (1982) traces the traditions behind the figurative and punning uses of the word "ass" and their links to the play's thematic explorations of love, transformation, and imagination. Being part man, part beast, both "an animated metaphor and . . . a malapropian character" (447), Bottom figures the Apollonian/Dionysian dialectic (Theseus versus Oberon) that she claims structures *Dream*. Jay L. Halio (1990) argues that the seeming *concors* is challenged by the metaphoric language, a thesis exemplifying the skeptical interrogations of recent criticism.

Christy Desmet's 1997 essay, "Disfiguring Women with Masculine Tropes: A Rhetorical Reading of *A Midsummer Night's*

Dream," includes an extended discussion of hypallage in its study of
the play's language. Unlike earlier rhetorical analyses of *Dream*
designed to establish chronology or locate themes, Desmet's more
broadly contextualized inquiry proposes that the rich anthology of
poetic styles Shakespeare assembles in *Dream* results from the play's
exploration of humanist rhetoric as a contested site. While training in
copious speech promotes friendship within a political community of
men, rhetoricians recognize that humanist rhetoric depends on an art of
verbal ornament traditionally associated with femininity. In courtly
rhetoric, while woman and verbal ornament work together to civilize
male culture, they remain capable of disrupting masculine discourse.
Thus, Woman is the missing figure in the social economy of the verbal
arts. On all levels of the play, a struggle exists between the patriarchal
word and an intrusive feminine voice that corrects, completes, and
supplements masculine discourse with her alternative ethics and
poetics. Structurally, *Dream* operates according to the logic of
hypallage. Within the play's action, however, an alternative feminine
rhetoric operates to produce concord. While Theseus confirms the
father's right to "disfigure" his daughter at will, the women of *Dream*
disfigure masculine discourse by resisting their own erasure in the
public sphere. Hermia and Helena reduce to nonsense the male rhetoric
of erotic combat by usurping the language of the love sonnet. More
profoundly, Titania rewrites Ovidian myth to celebrate women's
friendship and sexuality, and Hippolyta articulates a feminine aesthetic
that gives meaning to the lovers' dream of mutual "transfiguration."
Finally, the interlude demonstrates comedically the folly of masculine
attempts to control and contain the feminine figures of humanist
rhetoric.

Theme: Dream, Love, Imagination, and the Supernatural

Love and imagination, the latter figured as dream and the supernatural,
are the major subjects of the play and are often treated as inseparable
(i.e., is love based on reality or an act of passionate imagining?). Critics
may bring a favored approach or explicit ideology to the play or may
unself-consciously reflect their times. E.K. Chambers (1905), an
example of the latter, distances himself from early nineteenth-century
Romanticism and looks to *fin de siècle* Symbolism. He grants that
Coleridge's notion is tenable and suggests that "taking perhaps a hint

from Lyly, Shakespeare invites us to consider the whole thing as a dream" (83). However, since the supernatural changes nothing in *Dream*, Chambers, like Brandes, feels that in this play magic represents "symbolically the familiar workings of actual love in idleness in the human heart" (84). The pansy is Chambers's *fleur de mal*, love in the comic view being characterized by caprice, infidelity, irrationality, lawlessness, and passion. This youthful aberration in humans is standard behavior for fairies.

The changes that Shakespeare did or did not ring on the folklore conception of fairies has long been the subject of one branch of *Dream* research and criticism. In 1908 Frank Sidgwick wrote on the physical nature of the fairies; by miniaturizing them, Shakespeare reshaped the popular beliefs he had initially drawn upon. Sidgwick's work was later qualified by Katherine M. Briggs (1959), who cited folklore examples of diminuitive fairies. In an extensive study of Renaissance folklore and the supernatural, Minor White Latham (1930), who devotes a chapter of her study to Robin Goodfellow, credited Shakespeare with having been the first writer to portray fairies as virtuous and non-threatening. In "The Moon and the Fairies in *A Midsummer Night's Dream*" (1955), one of two articles on *Dream* by Ernest Schanzer, the ways in which the fairies differed from each other and from the mortal characters are catalogued: Puck is malevolent; Peaseblossom, Mustardseed, and their ilk are tiny and absorbed in their duties; Oberon and Titania, paralleling Theseus and Hippolyta, are of adult human stature, and Titania is also partly informed by associations with the moon. The following year George A. Bonnard (1956) challenged Latham's reading of *Dream*'s fairies as decent creatures; rather, as bringers of dreams, they lack "all sense of responsibility, all moral impulse" (271) as we do in dreams. Stephen Fender, refined the argument by demonstrating that the fairies are capable of both vicious and virtuous action.

For H.B. Charlton (1933), as for such nineteenth-century German critics as Ulrici and Gervinus, *Dream* is a message play unified by its depiction of Titania and Oberon as irresponsible spouses, whose actions point up the beneficence of marriage as a human institution and the importance of a common-sense approach to life—which for Charlton is English country life given universal dimensions. Not surprisingly, Charlton believes that Theseus speaks for Shakespeare on the role of imagination. Basing his argument on adjectives applied to

Titania, Donald C. Miller (1940) anticipates sexualized readings in his contention that, as an inverted incarnation of Diana, she "is in love with the changeling" (69). E.C. Pettet (1949) takes a more moderate view than either Charlton or Miller, discovering in *Dream* "a correction [rather] than a criticism of romantic love," a "shaping attitude" rather than a "moral." (113). For Pettet, romantic love overlooks self-absorption and infidelity and has to do with courtship feelings rather than married fellowship.

In "The Central Theme of *A Midsummer Night's Dream*" (1951), Ernest Schanzer rejects Pettet's interpretation that blurs obsession with romance. Schanzer locates the theme in a parody of "love-madness," the form of love to which Demetrius has initially fallen victim and which is concretized by love-in-idleness. Love-madness, "as opposed to romantic love, is entirely divorced from both reason and the evidence of the senses," engendered by the imagination alone, thus bonding the lover to the lunatic and the poet. *Pyramus and Thisbe* is connected to this theme only in that, as Welsford had suggested, it provides the anti-masque to the masque of the fairies and lovers. Harold C. Goddard (1951) takes a more comprehensive view: the play self-referentially illustrates a *discordia concors* theme: the imagination bringing harmony out of its chaos of "incongruities, anachronisms, contradictions, and impossible juxtapositions. . ." (76). Bottom's awakening from materiality to spirituality—to imagination—is *Dream*'s finest moment.

Goddard's engagement with larger philosophical, aesthetic, and social subjects—binarisms that now invite deconstruction such as the relationship between reality and imagination, reason and passion, the material and the spiritual, husband and wife—was shared by many '50s critics. Like Edward Dowden in the nineteenth century, the American Poet Laureate and critic Howard Nemerov (1956) rejects the identification of Theseus's sentiments with those of Shakespeare. (Theseus's sentiments are perhaps Platonic in origin, i.e., suspicious of art.) For Theseus, the lovers' stories are fantasy; either they are liars or have been fooled; Hippolyta's view of art as transfiguring and admirable comes closer to Shakespeare's than Theseus's, which erases any distinction between good and bad art and tolerates art (if it respects authority) because entertainment promotes political stability. Ultimately, Nemerov believes that Shakespeare occupies a middle ground between Hippolyta and Theseus, though perhaps closer to the former.

Unlike Nemerov's essay, Bonnard's seems unusually dated. Bonnard celebrates the union of Theseus and Hippolyta, not for the light it casts on the nature of art but rather for its depiction of ideal love, "shorn of any romantic nonsense" (269). Theirs is "a wholly sane view of life" (270), not least because Hippolyta "will know how to keep her place, as her silence proves when he [Theseus] discusses Hermia's marriage with Egeus and the young lovers" (269-70). Theseus does not devalue imagination as long as it, too, knows its subordinate place. The amoral fairies represent imagination (for Bonnard, sensuality qualified only by taste and beauty) given full rein. Ignoring Oberon's cruelty, which might support his point, Bonnard instead offers Titania as an example of reprehensible behavior. In contrast to Hippolyta, Titania is the bad wife: "on awaking from her delusion, she feels no regret, no shame; and there is no scene of reconciliation with her husband: her resentment makes her forsake him, and they make it up in a dance; there is no trace of a real feeling in her" (271).

Paul A. Olson (1957) also reads the play conservatively, though with greater erudition. In the Renaissance, Theseus would have represented reason and right rule; his victory over Hippolyta and the Amazons is a victory for hierarchy, marriage, and love based on reason rather than passion. Titania is depicted as a wanton aspect of Diana, Oberon as a "prince of grace" (111). Olson's analysis, based on classical and Renaissance literary history, retains some prominence. Peter F. Fisher (1957) views each character group as a world with its own language, the fairies' language being song; their world of fantasy and imagination is subordinated to the court's world of reason. The lovers' world represents irrational passion; the mechanicals' world, the prosaic. The play assigns these worlds an order of precedence.

In the tradition of Pettet, John Russell Brown (1957) presents a defense of romantic love. On its surface *Dream* offers Bottom as the most reasonable character, for Bottom is not in love. Notwithstanding, "the play suggests that lovers, like lunatics, poets and actors, have their own 'truth' which is established as they see the beauty of the beloved, and . . . although it seems the 'silliest stuff' to an outsider, to them it is quite reasonable. . . ." Brown argues that our imaginative acceptance of a play as "real" is a "flesh-and-blood image of the acceptance which is

*occasion of
wild revelry or
indulgence*

*process of
relief,
relieving*

appropriate to the strange and private 'truth' of those who enact the play of love" (90).

C.L. Barber's *Shakespeare's Festive Comedy* (1959) remains an essential study of the grounding of the romantic comedies in early modern holiday customs that afford a kind of Saturnalian catharsis from frustration over social constraints. In *Dream* "[t]he whole night's action is presented as a release of shaping fantasy which brings clarification about the tricks of strong imagination." Also clarified through humor is the experience of "eros in men and women and trees and flowers" and "the tendency to take fantasy literally, whether in love, in superstition, or in Bottom's mechanical dramatics" (124). Barber sees *Dream* as occasioned by a wedding, with Theseus and Hippolyta as "stand-ins for the noble couple" (125). May games "bringing in summer to the bridal" (119), with Titania as "a Summer Lady" and Oberon as the May King, fuse various aspects of holiday, pageantry, magic, and recreational competitions. Hermia and Helena, encountering eros as they mature, change their loyalties from each other to men. Similarly, in an unconsciously masculinist reading, Titania must give up the child, now ready for "the man's world of Oberon" (137) because "nature will have its way" (131). The portrayal of the fairies, "tutelary spirits of fertility" (137), inhabiting love's wood where metamorphosis is the rule, draws on Christian as well as folk traditions. In origin largely "creatures of pastoral" which Shakespeare "varied by adapting folk superstitions" (145), they are not literal but symbolic; they "embody the passionate mind's sense of its own omnipotence" (132-33) and are imagination personified. The play's title should awaken skepticism about their reality. Discussing the ways love changes understanding, Barber examines Ovidian allusions and Shakespeare's imitative myth-making of the fairies' quarrel and the pansy's power. He suggests that "[t]he action of metaphor is itself a process of transposing, a kind of metamorphosis" (135). *Dream* is no "dream throughout," as Coleridge held but rather very much a play, parodied in *Pyramus and Thisbe*, whose prologues derive from the mummers' plays and whose ludicrousness teaches that neither playacting nor imagining can create reality. In Barber's words, "The confident assumption dominant in *A Midsummer Night's Dream*, that substance and shadow can be kept separate, determines the peculiarly unshadowed gaiety of the fun it makes with fancy" (161).

Elizabeth Sewell's discussion (1961) is unique. Treating *Dream* as part of a larger study of the relationship between art and nature, and of "the point at which forms—in nature, mind, and language—interact and interpret one another" (127), she sets Bacon's *Novum Organum* against *Dream*, arguing that Shakespeare enlarges the category of the rational by including the imaginative, with love intimating fertility and the fairies intimating myth. Sewell reads Bottom metadramatically. Shakespeare aligns himself with Bottom and the artisans, whose task of producing a wedding entertainment is also his. Their names, linked to nature as well as to their crafts, "imply the great unity of natural history, plants and trees, animals, man as body and mind, the arts" (130). Through them, Shakespeare shows the dynamic status of language, indeed, the transformative movement of all things. In no pejorative sense, she concludes that "Bottom is the human condition, the newly thinking mind subjected to natural forms and trying to make forms of its own by which to understand them" (141).

In part because of its philosophical content, Frank Kermode (1961) considers *Dream* the best of Shakespeare's comedies. Though more concerned with theme than sources, he discusses the play's debt to Macrobius, Apuleius, and Bruno, as Shakespeare explores fantasy, blind love, and—through Bottom's allusion to I Corinthians 2:9— divine love. Kermode especially commends Olson's essay.

R.W. Dent (1964), whose article is reprinted in this volume, is concerned with imagination in love and art, taking issue with such critics as Charlton, Pettet, Schanzer, and Bonnard, whose model of exemplary, because rational, love is Theseus and Hippolyta. In *Dream*, Dent argues, love is inexplicable, the offspring of imagination; it is not based on reason and need not be, as long as imagination is "controlled" (128) and love avoids "dotage" (116), Shakespearean shorthand for persisting in unrequited love (Demetrius dotes on Hermia) or loving an unworthy object (Titania dotes on Bottom). Theseus's speech opening act 5 broadens the discussion from imagination in love to imagination in art. Pointing out that Theseus is "[h]imself a creation from 'antique fable' unconsciously involved in 'fairy toy,'" (124), Dent, like Nemerov, urges the wrongheadedness of Theseus's judgment, for Theseus makes no distinction between the interlude, hobbled by the mechanicals' mistrust of their audience, whose response they fear will be either excessive or inadequate, and a masterpiece like *Dream*—

"Shakespeare's closest approximation to a 'Defense of Dramatic Poesy' in general" (129).

Among the most important, and most controversial, works on *Dream* is Jan Kott's chapter from *Shakespeare Our Contemporary* (1964), reprinted here. Kott, a Polish drama critic and professor of literature, addresses aspects of the play noted earlier by such commentators as Chesterton, Cumberland Clark, and G. Wilson Knight, but constructs a distinctive interpretation. He insists, often feverishly, on the overwhelming importance of violence and un-repressed animalistic sexuality. Lysander and Demetrius are verbally brutal, "[t]he lovers are exchangeable" (219) and objectified, the changeling is a sexual toy for Oberon, the aristocrats—mortal and immortal—are promiscuous: "The lovers are ashamed of that night and do not want to talk about it, just as one does not want to talk of bad dreams. But that night liberated them from themselves. They were their real selves in their dreams" (235).

David Young ignores Kott, while examining the play's various themes in the final section of *Something of Great Constancy* (1966), especially Shakespeare's perspective on art. But for John A. Allen (1967) Bottom symbolizes the animalistic aspect of humanity, redeemed only by Titania's maternal tenderness, which allows him to understand the love and self-sacrifice of Pyramus and Thisbe. Michael MacOwan (1968), whose preference is for John Vyvyan's Neo-platonist readings (see below), strenuously disagrees with Kott:

> Kott relies on bald, repetitive assertion rather than logical reasoning; he ignores or distorts opinions opposite to his own; he constantly manipulates facts to suit theories and colours his whole book with a pervasive, gloating salacity sometimes on the edge of hysteria (31).

Why? "Kott does not seem to be able to *hear* Shakespeare—how good is his English, I wonder?" (32).

Stephen Fender's view lies between Kott's and the traditionalists. Fender emphasizes the terrifying power of the fairies; they, not Theseus, control events. In fact, the characters, emblematic rather than realistic, are ethically ambivalent. In the wood, the lovers adapt their speech to their new situation, temporarily simplifying courtly complexities, and thus suggesting their new insights. But complexity is maintained as Theseus, Hippolyta, and Bottom offer contradictory yet in part valid reactions to the events of the midsummer night, metatheatrically implying that "[t]he real meaning of *A Midsummer Night's Dream* is that no one 'meaning' can be extracted from the puzzles with which a fiction presents its audience" (61).

Division between darker and lighter readings of the play marked the end of the decade. Philip Edwards (1968), like Dent, questions Theseus's limited view of imagination, although Theseus's sentiments are supported by *Pyramus and Thisbe* and Puck's final speech. Yet despite its ironies, *Dream* is itself a celebration of art and imagination. Michael Taylor (1969) urges recognition of the fairies' less pleasant aspects as well as their appeal and of Demetrius' nastiness before his enchantment. Taylor claims that John Russell Brown, who preceded Kott, paints too cheerful a picture. Love is painful as well as joyous, people (and fairies) often petty. *Dream* anticipates *Troilus and Cressida* and *Measure for Measure*. Herbert S. Weil (1969) shares Taylor's sense of discomfort if not of final concord. He compares *Dream* to works by Albee and Genet, particularly with regard to its open-endedness and suggests that whether or not we accept Kott's views, we be receptive to plural readings.

Despite Kott's remarkable influence, many critics of the '70s continued to favor traditional readings. R.A. Zimbardo (1970) defends imagination as the only lens through which ultimate reality can be perceived. "[P]ermanence in mutability" symbolized by the moon, and "discordia concors" (36) are basic to the play's theme of reconciliation. Since the characters are symbolic—e.g., Theseus and Hippolyta represent marriage and "a reconciliation of the seasons of nature, or the phases of time" (37) or whatever only seems separate—Hippolyta must subordinate herself to Theseus and become a matron; similarly, Titania must pass from "her motherly obsession with the changeling boy through a kind of death ... once more to be wooed and won by Oberon" (39). Just as Zimbardo, untouched by the social interrogations of the '60s, takes female subordination within obligatory marriage for granted, so, too, he accepts a totalizing view of art, that "imitates the great discordia concors, resolving in itself the conflict of what in experience appear to be opposites" (48).

James Calderwood's 1971 metadramatic treatment of *Dream* claims centrality for the exploration of dramatic illusion by blurring the boundaries between the natural and supernatural, and by depicting Oberon as "specializing in the arts of illusion as befits an illusion"

(124). Oberon is "a kind of interior dramatist," (130) responsible for Theseus overruling Egeus and bringing harmony out of discord. The lovers' identities, blurred and lost in the forest, recall actors' unstable identities; indeed, the artisans' play fails because the artisans cannot "lose their identities even imaginatively in fictional roles" (132). For Calderwood, imagination and rationality are not oppositional but exist on different levels; the play explores how art functions in our lives.

Andrew D. Weiner (1971) addresses imagination and the mysteries of marriage as testimony of God's love. Weiner states that whereas the poet's imagination creates unity by giving diverse elements form, the spectator's imagination creates unity by perceiving that form. Unity or "uniformity" alludes to eternal truths, whether perceived as Platonic or Christian. Writing in the same year, Hugh M. Richmond (1971), unlike Calderwood and Weiner, finds a warning in what he sees as the self-destructive inflections of passion that pass for love in *A Midsummer Night's Dream*: "No significant character in the play is wholly exempt from this sadomasochistic type of sexuality—unless indeed it be Bottom, who has the comparative good fortune to be chiefly devoted to himself. . ." (106). Richmond explains "the lovers' delight in an emotion heightened by conflict" (111) as part of the western tradition which, according to Denis de Rougemont, protects each lover from genuine communication and consequent disenchantment with the other. Noting the parallels between *Pyramus and Thisbe* and *Romeo and Juliet*, Richmond asks that while we "sympathize with Romeo and thus learn vicariously from his incompleteness, we might well positively admire Bottom's diverseness and emulate his poise, while laughing at his egotism" (122).

Throughout the 1970s, imagination remained a favored critical subject. Ralph Berry (1972) analyzed imagery (moon, dream, and eye) and plot elements because of their importance to *Dream's* exploration of illusion in love and art. For Berry, Shakespeare's chief concern is epistemological: "The lovers declare illusion to be reality; the actors declare reality to be illusion" (106). Ultimately reconciling these views, *Dream* vindicates imagination. Thomas McFarland (1972), who regards Kott as the victim of an overactive imagination, entitles his discussion "And All Things Shall Be Peace: The Happiness of *A Midsummer Night's Dream*," because he considers this one of the happiest literary creations of all time. The mood, established at once by the poetry, is so lovely that we cannot fear for the characters. The orgiastic eroticism Kott makes so much of provides the most minimal of subtexts.

Marjorie B. Garber (1974) sees metamorphosis as both the major subject of the play and the model for its structuring. Entering the woods is like dreaming in that the characters—and the audience— perceive differently and gain new imaginative ways of seeing. Dreams, "truer than the reality they seek to interpret and transform" (87), take priority over reason. Alexander Leggatt (1974), in a thoughtful reading, asserts that *Dream*'s grimmer elements are held at bay by the audience's sympathy for the young lovers. He singles out the fairies as the most sophisticated and unconstrained of the four character groups and proposes that the interactions between those groups are marked by contrasts that develop the comic perspective as imaginative involvement metamorphoses the playwright's experience. Ronald F. Miller (1975) advanced a philosophic, quasi-religious view of *Dream* "as a study in the epistemology of the imagination" (254) by focusing on

> the *mystery* of the fairies—the very aura of evanescence and ambiguity surrounding their life on stage—that points to a mysteriousness in our own existence, and specifically in such ambivalent earthly matters as love, luck, imagination, and even faith (255).

In Bottom's Pauline awakening speech, writes Miller, Shakespeare teases his audience with hints of an otherworldly vision.

David Bevington's essay (1975) offers one of the most appealing readings of *Dream*. Bevington finds Kott "helpful . . . though he has surely gone too far" (86). For example, while it is possible that Oberon is bisexual and desires the changeling sexually, the evidence is slight and "seems deliberately ambiguous. . . . the fairies' ideas concerning love are ultimately unknowable and incomprehensible" (90). Rather, "[t]he conflict between sexual desire and rational restraint is, then, an essential tension throughout the play reflected in the images of dark and light. This same tension exists in the nature of the fairies and of the forest" (88). The achievement of the play is its reconciliation of the tensions between the dark and the benevolent sides of love. M.E. Lamb (1979) whose essay follows David Ormerod's by a year (see Neo-platonism, below), like Ormerod compares the woods to the minotaur's

labyrinth, for Elizabethans often an allegory of sexual sin. The lovers
conquer irrational passion and find their way back. Bottom is both a
comic version of the minotaur and the "skein of thread" (480) that
guides the lovers, the myth's comic inversion holding in check
Dream's repressed tragic possibilities. Theseus as bridegroom has
conquered passion and is no longer promiscuous. The names of the
artisans also recall Daedelus, the craftsman (read playwright) who built
the labyrinth. Theseus's best-known speech intimates that the poet, if
he is to create art, must confront the irrationality he shares with the
lunatic and the lover, must accept the risks of the labyrinth. At the end
of the decade, Harold F. Brooks, reviewing the criticism for his
introduction to the Arden edition, finds desire and its culmination in
marriage at the heart of *Dream*, with other subjects—imagination,
appearance and reality—of lesser importance.

A new approach ushered in the new decade. Florence Falk (1980)
looked to the work of cultural anthropologist Victor Turner for an
interpretation of *Dream* in which traditional rites of passage trigger
development within the individual and the society. Theseus, detached
from myth (imagination), rules harshly. The lovers flee from his
structure to the *communitas* of the woods: a "spontaneous, immediate,
transitory condition"; "the abode of dream"; and "the temporary
aggregate of persons whose asocial desires require some kind of
accommodation to preserve the health of the society" (267). Here,
through a rite of passage, the asocial can be contained. Identifying
communitas with the unconscious or the dream space, with "creative
disorder," (268), Falk argues that the lovers experience release into
self-knowledge and return to a renewed Athens, albeit temporarily so.
This is *societas*, "the resolution of the dialectic between the dualism of
communitas and *structure*" (272).

Christian critic R. Chris Hassel, Jr. (1980), Germaine Greer, and
A.P. Riemer, on the other hand, return to established themes. Hassel
probes the play's Pauline allusions and references to Erasmus's *Praise
of Folly*. The experience of the lovers and of Bottom, as recounted in
his awakening soliloquy, teach them "a new humility, a healthy sense
of folly which urges that there are things that are true that can neither
be seen nor understood" (67). This lesson, says Hassel, analogizes faith
and romance. In the same vein, Theseus's speech on the lunatic, the
lover, and the poet applauds imagination but "laughs at futile attempts
to perceive, categorize, or express it" (74). According to Germaine

Greer (1980) *Dream* presents a solution to the conflict between social order and sexual passion; marriages based on respect for others (embodied in Quince's company) and raising children (suggested by the epithalamion). A.P. Riemer's focus on metamorphosis (1980) is important to later critics. The play is about transformation, the characters' metamorphoses analogizing the poet's transformative power. As opposed to comedy that holds a mirror up to folly, *Dream* presents "the essential nature of the world created by art" (207).

J. Dennis Huston (1981), like Calderwood, explores *Dream* metadramatically, maintaining that Shakespeare was "playing with the art of playwriting" (97), witness the inclusion of multiple parodies. Huston regards Bottom as a parody of Petruchio, designed to celebrate the power of the playwright over the actor. But however deflated, Bottom's awakening soliloquy tells us that "[a]rt as dream is simultaneously both illusion and revealed truth" (102). That Oberon, the most effective of Shakespeare's surrogate playwrights in *Dream*, cannot control all contingencies, draws attention to Shakespeare's own powers in this, his "most exuberantly self-reflexive comedy of play" (121).

Barry Weller (1985) also studies the interaction between imagination and the theatrical experience. Theater succeeds with an audience attuned to the difference between reality and play; e.g., *Dream*'s characters are more figurative than real, with the fairies a metaphor or "explanatory trope" (77) for both the disruption of nature and the irrationality of love. Bottom, who cannot distinguish between reality and play, is unchanged by his encounter with the supernatural, so he and the other characters "dis-figure" meaning by "undoing its figural or fictive character" (77). The play realizes itself not in the eyes of the spectators but in their imaginations. William C. Carroll, like Florence Falk, looks to Victor Turner's theories, particularly the association between liminality and the monstrous, to argue that metamorphosis—the "comic detoxification" (163) of sexuality, violence, and death, i.e., of the monstrous—is necessary before the lovers are ready for marriage, and that "the deepest metamorphic rhythms of human nature require man's yielding to a dream" (177).

One of the most innovative discussions is Terry Eagleton's deconstructive neo-Marxist reading (1986), describing the polarity between *Dream*'s erotic discourse and physical desire. Whereas the ritualistic language of love presents the would-be lover with a limited number of roles, all of which express desire in economic terms, real physical desire subverts this linguistic ritual order. Eagleton likens the capriciousness of physical desire to the irresistible flow of change in the order of signs, suggesting that Shakespeare calls attention to the "homogenizing effect" (20) of nature's initially chaotic influence. Marriage, embodying the ritual maintenance of erotic desire, is constantly mocked, the play's couplings being subject to radical reversals. The interference of the fairies demonstrates the social construction of desire (and of identity itself), ironically perceived as "natural" (22). In actuality, love consists of mutual romantic illusions, of "imaginary identification" (23). Yet Bottom's performance as himself, ass, and Pyramus suggests that the individual as a linguistic construct cannot exist outside of social exchange even when what we take for reality is grounded in fantasy and illusion.

Two years after Eagleton's *Shakespeare* appeared, William W.E. Slights (1988) proposed that the changeling, neither wholly human nor fairy and therefore indeterminate, analogizes *Dream*'s lovers. The changeling is a vehicle for an emancipating excursion to an anarchic borderland. For Peter Holland (1995) the thematic concept of dreams provides the structuring principle for an extensive and enjoyable overview of the play in his introduction to the Oxford edition.

Thelma Greenfield challenges Freudian dream theory as a key to the play in her essay written for this volume, "Our Nightly Madness: Shakespeare's *Dream* Without *The Interpretation of Dreams*." Because critics and directors have satisfied their need to ferret out the secret meanings of the dreams in *A Midsummer Night's Dream* by turning to Freudian dream psychology, what is seen on stage becomes predominantly a censoring metaphor or facade for a buried reality of sexual drives and anxieties or for Bottom's "hidden" nature.

From another perspective, rather than serving as censoring and disguising devices, dreams are valid verbal, visual, and emotional constructs—autonomous, experiential, in and of themselves—possessed of their own significance. Dreams are generated by sleep's peculiar information processes, which are unlike those operating during waking periods and which thus produce curious-seeming results. In Shakespeare's dream play, this perspective grants the audience access to the integrity of the stage image, for example, the purely metaphoric denomination of Bottom as "ass" becomes tangibly real in his wearing a visible, literal asshead. Bottom's "dream," like dreams in general, yields an extended range of experience not apt to be met with in everyday life. By respecting the autonomy of dream, we can see in this play the often-remarked connection between dream and drama, a kinship Shakespeare and his contemporaries grasped. We see Shakespeare comically exploiting the illogicality of dream experience by attaching it to the behaviors of stage figures ostensibly awake. In the play proper and in the play-within-the-play, we see his alertness to the creative role of the audience that, like the dreamer, creates, participates, and watches all at once, transcending the unbelievable illogicalities of stage illusion. Greenfield points out that, through strong images of female worlds, *Dream* opens up, at an almost mythic level, divisions between male and female that go well beyond sexual anxieties and frustrations. Only with loss, she writes, can the experiential mode of *Dream*'s dream-infused creations be sacrificed to searching out the play as a congregation of Freudian symbols.

Neoplatonism

Following Ulrici, who held that within the comic vision of *A Midsummer Night's Dream* Shakespeare was presenting a Platonic dream world, a shadow world out of which would grow a Christian future life, so too John Vyvyan (1961) regards the play as informed by Neoplatonism. He cites instances throughout, including the disorder in nature caused by the quarrel between Oberon and Titania: "it fits in with Shakespeare's wider contention—that the soul-state of his characters is objectified in their world, and that love and hate, however personal their expression, are forces that have repercussions on a cosmic scale" (80). Theseus and Hippolyta, who have turned "a war into a wedding" and "out of chaos" brought "a birth of beauty" (7) are the ideal that the other couples must attain. Order is begotten through love, when soul-mates recognize each other's divine nature, and "every betrayal of love is a movement towards disintegration" (78). As for Bottom, when Titania, under the "influence, perceives a kind of divinity in him, I fancy that she is nearer, in Shakespeare's judgement, to a true vision of him than when she sees him only as an ass" (85).

According to Peter G. Phialas's Platonic interpretation (1966), Shakespeare started with an idea, Cupid's blindness, "the inexplicable caprice of choice," then fleshed it out. The fairies are integral:

> The world which romantic lovers in Shakespeare's earlier comedies
> had created through their fancy, the spirituality which they had
> attributed to their loved ones, the otherworldliness which they had
> seen in the angelic features of their ladies—all these *A Midsummer
> Night's Dream* presents in the persons of the fairies in the enchanted
> woodland beyond Athens (114).

Their human passions, their infidelities, are remembered in Bottom's
play about passion and fidelity. The ideal in this carefully unified,
symbolically constructed play is the love of Theseus and Hippolyta—
but not because their love is founded on reason. For Phialas,
Shakespeare replies to the question "What is love?" (129) with the
mystery of Platonism, "which leads to the bosom of God" (132).

For Sidney R. Homan (1969), Oberon's fairyland is not opposed to
rationalist Athens but rather extends it to "the infinite dimensions of the
natural world" (73), a reality which only imagination can reveal—as,
for a moment, it does to the lovers and to Bottom, the artist.
Shakespeare thus echoes the Renaissance belief that "the mundane
world [is] only a dim shadow, an insubstantial microcosm of a divine
macrocosm" (82). Richard Cody (1969) analyzes the Platonic, Orphic,
and pastoral elements in *Dream*, finding a line of development from
"division into union" (134) and affirming the enhanced status of art.
Unlike Homan, David Ormerod (1978) insists on the importance of
Theseus and Athens as dialectically related to fairyland. Ormerod
interprets the play neoplatonically by looking back to the myth of the
Minotaur (the metamorphosed Bottom for whose bestial love Titania
degrades herself). In the labyrinthine woods, the lovers are deceived by
appearances; the ass head emblematizes "moral mischance" (46),
passionate love that lacks knowledge of the lover's "inner reality" (44).

Jane K. Brown (1987) discusses the connection between the
lust/love binarism illustrated by the four couples and the theme of
imagination. Both point to Renaissance Neoplatonism as the allegorical
master narrative of a play "concerned with the nature and location of
truth" (21). Most recently, in his *"The Countess of Pembroke's
Arcadia*, Shakespeare's *A Midsummer Night's Dream*, and the School
of Night: An Intertextual Nexus" (1996), Maurice Hunt claims that
whether or not Shakespeare knew Sidney's romance, both works
exemplify confidence in "the truth of identifiably Renaissance

doctrines of Neoplatonic love and knowledge in an early modern, mainly protestant, culture" (15).

Psychoanalytic Approaches

Major psychoanalytic readings of *A Midsummer Night's Dream* begin with Weston A. Gui's study (1952). Gui holds that Bottom's dream is really Shakespeare's; the Indian boy is Shakespeare's younger brother whom the playwright displaces; Bottom/Shakespeare is "an orally regressed adult" (263), and the transformed Bottom encountering Titania recalls a primal scene that hinges on anger at mother—anger for which Bottom destroys himself, stabbing that "left papp," symbolically her breast which he has psychically incorporated. Gerald F. Jacobson (1962) argues that the play also clarified "the psychosexual development of women" (22) through the relationship of the fairy king and queen and that of the lovers. The changeling could be "the little girl's fantasy of stealing mother's baby, and killing mother, as in this case the stolen child belonged to a woman who died in childbirth." Moreover, Titania is a "castrating woman who feminizes the male child" so that she "must and does give up the male child, and her claims to possess the penis, before she can once again share Oberon's bed" (23). Jacobson penetrates the secret of Hermia's preference for Lysander: in reality, Hermia loves her father's choice, Demetrius, as surrogate for her true love, Egeus. Rather than committing psychic incest, she will remain celibate. Her rivalry with Helena figures her feelings toward her mother and sister. Again the little girl's fantasy: "father really loves me; mother (sister) may love him but he does not return her love" (24). Understanding that "dreamed experiences represent an unconscious working through of infantile conflicts" (26), Shakespeare rewards each lover with a post-oedipal spouse.

    M.D. Faber's psychoanalytic essay (1972) has valuable aesthetic and social dimensions. Analyzing Hermia's dream as a disguised expression of the sexual union she desires, Faber discovers what he takes to be

> Shakespeare's basic comic strategy in the play. He suggests that the two sides of man's mind [conscious/civilized and unconscious/archaic] simply have nothing to do with one another and he

underscores this suggestion by making them have nothing to do with one another *in actuality* (186).

Thus, the love juice is an external device masking repressed desires that create unavoidable anxiety within a patriarchal society concerned with the boundaries of thought and behavior for men and women. Faber regards Theseus's past sexual experience as an asset in finding "a modus vivendi between rigid institutions and instinctual human energies" (187). He also may be the first to claim that "the problem of the *changeling* boy, a problem with homosexual overtones, explicitly focuses the problem of achieving sexual identity" (188).

Alex Aronson's Jungian interpretation (1972) posits Theseus as the conscious mind and Puck as the unconscious in the guise of a trickster-figure subservient to Oberon. Aronson follows Kott, linking unauthorized desire to fertility, symbolized by the ass and by trees. The lovers' sexual longings are symbolized by their forest encounters; they discover their true selves upon awakening. Melvin Goldstein (1973) posits that the lovers cannot return to Athens and wed until they have passed through madness (multiple disguises) and found their authentic sexual selves; for example, Helena must come to terms with her animality. Norman N. Holland (1979), in a significant essay, uses Hermia's dream to recapitulate psychoanalytic criticism, first analyzing the dream as real, as uncovering the phases of Hermia's sexual development, her search for options being a defense mechanism. Then he contextualizes the dream within the play's exploration of separation and fusion (Hermia both desires Lysander and wants to retain her virginity); this doubleness reflects "the comedy's theme of ambivalence, separations that are both loving and cruel" (12). Finally, he treats the dream transactively, relating the issues of separation/fusion and trust/betrayal to himself.

The journey to self-discovery can be mapped through a study of the characters' language as they unintentionally use words with plural, sexually revelatory meanings. Mordecai Marcus (1981), in a persuasive analysis, takes issue with Jan Kott's and Hugh Richmond's views of the conflict between Eros and Thanatos in *Dream*. Marcus seeks to demonstrate that Shakespeare "intuits the idea that love requires the risk of death and achieves force and direction from the interweaving of the life impulse with the deathward-release of sexual tension. . . ." He also proposes "that the healing force of love is connected to the acceptance of death and vice-versa" (277). Jan Lawson Hinely (1987) asserts the play's therapeutic value. Through the dreams of the lovers, of Bottom and the fairies, and of *Pyramus and Thisbe*, Shakespeare explores, releases, and transforms his characters' sexual fears, "and social harmony is reestablished" (120). Patriarchy, too, is transformed as the men offer their women "a loving equality founded on respect" (137) which, in turn, is based on trust. Most notably, Hinely holds that "Titania's loving acceptance of the assheaded Bottom . . . supplies the metaphor of basic trust that enables the warring and uncertain lovers to arrive at mature sexuality" (136). Allen Dunn (1988) is concerned with "a psychology of dramatic form," wherein the various plot strands are "*not* merely fanciful" (18) but are structured around the same concept: sexual clashes. Dunn's chief interest is in male anxiety, especially dread of oedipal revenge. Both the lovers' romance and the fairies' quarrel "present complementary versions of the father's judgment, the enabling death sentence which forces the son into the social world or . . . the symbolic order" (22). To appreciate the "fears and desires that animate the play" (18), we must read from each character's perspective.

The early 1990s saw two fine works on *Dream*. Barbara Freedman's well-received study (1991), reprinted here, considers what the play tells us about the production of dreams and ideology. In accordance with the Elizabethan notion that held the mind to be a microcosm of the great chain of being, Freedman invokes Freud and Lacan to read the playtext's psychological and ideological metaphors of authority as expressions of the repressive mechanism shaping social reality by selective deletion. Linguistic and dramatic representation also depend on the "censorship" (158) of truth to convincingly portray an organized configuration of individuals, just as graphic distortion is employed in painting to simulate perspective. According to Freedman, *Dream* justifies the ideological formation of the absolutist monarchy but not without making the maintenance process of hegemonic order visible for examination. James Calderwood (1992) offers a book-length reading for the Twayne series. His approach is primarily Lacanian, but he also draws on other psychoanalytic theories, on anthropology, and, in an expanded version of his 1991 essay on anamorphism, on Renaissance pictorial techniques. Incorporating a considerable body of contemporary criticism, particularly works having to do with gender and theater, Calderwood's book is an important and entertaining contribution.

Historicism, Class, and Race

In a sense, the predecessors of [neo]-historicist discussions of the representation of the social hierarchy and implicit class antagonism in *Dream* are earlier comments on Bottom and his fellows. Appreciation of Bottom as more than just a clown begins in the nineteenth century. While Shakespeare's audience would have been acquainted with the tradition of artisan-actors from the not yet entirely suppressed mystery plays, for Philostrate and the Athenian court spectators, mere tradesmen turning their hard hands to art is a form of disorder much like Hermia's, Titania's, or the pelting river's rebellions. The response of modern critics to Bottom and the mechanicals is still a likely index of their politics. G.B. Chesterton writes as heir to Charles Knight and Charles Cowden Clark. Among Chesterton's insights is a defense of Bottom's literary sensibilities, a predilection for sound over sense being a principal attribute of the literary mind. For J.B. Priestly (1925) Bottom is Shakespeare's first great comic character, Bottom's vanity being no more prominent than his originality and imagination. He has a "passion for the drama itself, the art of acting. . ." (7). H.B. Charlton writes, "The world is safe so long as it produces men like Bottom, for its inhabitants will never be permitted to get completely out of touch with earth, will never be allowed to forget the conditions which real life imposes on actual livers of it" (119). Also defending Bottom against the preponderate nineteenth-century opinion of him as a conceited fool is John Palmer (1946), for whom he is both a life-force and a unifying force, at home in all of *Dream*'s venues, and superior to the gentles who "cannot hold a candle to Bottom for courtesy or apprehension. . ." (106).

Taking the opposite view is George A. Bonnard, a latter-day Philostrate, whose no-nonsense concept of love and disdain for insubordinate wives (see Themes, above) go hand-in-hand with class prejudice; to support his reading of *Dream* as a play celebrating common sense, he asks, "For what is our poor uneducated artisans' ambition to act a play, and act it in the presence of the Duke, but clear evidence that, for the time being, they have lost their common sense?" (274).

Although these critics betray their sympathy—or lack thereof—for the working class, by the late '70s political and theoretical awareness were the order of the day. Left-leaning critics of *Dream* were generally divided between those who found a productively subversive message and others who argued for ultimate aristocratic co-optation. Elliot Krieger's study (1979) reads *Dream* as an exercise in subversion and containment. Theseus allows the lovers a momentary defiance of the establishment of which they are part; their flight is ineffective because his writ runs through the forest as well as the court. Ultimately, even "the forces of nature certify and bless the aristocratic predominance and autonomy" (69). Richard H. Cox's essay (1982) is a meditation not only on the play's philosophy but on its politics. Although interested in questions of appearance and reality and of *discordia/concors*, he is especially attentive to Bottom and the mechanicals (the former transformed briefly into the play's hero and Athens's savior) and to class issues among the ancient Greeks and the Elizabethans. In the past dozen years, the politics of class and theater has been addressed in some of the most useful work on *Dream*. Michael D. Bristol (1985) reads Bottom semiotically as "a temporary name assumed by a public figure whose willingness to play all parts is a comic uncrowning of limited identity and social discrimination" (174). Inadvertently transgressive, *Pyramus and Thisbe* critiques patriarchal marriage and the hierarchical class structure.

Similarly, in a neo-Marxist essay, James H. Kavanagh (1985) uses *Dream* as a brief example of Shakespeare's ideological practice. Just as rebellious women challenge patriarchy so, too, artisans bring into focus the issue of producing art that is "class-appropriate, and therefore politically acceptable" (153). Ultimately, however, Kavanagh, like Krieger, concludes that Shakespeare's language of compromise effects reconciliation and submission to the aristocracy. Theodore B. Leinwand (1986), whose new historicist piece is reprinted in this volume, draws parallels between the mechanicals and the Lord Chamberlain's Men, in that both companies sought accommodation with the aristocracy and were aware of the fine line they had to walk. Consequently, Shakespeare appears critical of the establishment in *Dream*. For Michael Schneider (1987), writing as a cultural materialist, *Dream* reflects contemporary class hostility. Bottom's brief liaison is a sexual threat as is the impropriety of the artisan's interlude. *Dream* does not end in reconciliation; rather, the mechanicals are angry and rightly so. Annabel Patterson (1988), whose work is also reprinted here, maintains that Bottom, representing the misprized underclass, is indispensable to society's festive spirit and co-operative functioning. Bottom's visionary dream honors all "mechanicals."

Class-conscious readings of the '90s follow in the same vein, though Wilson's essay has a postmodern cast and Parker's chapter is a model of language criticism. Invoking Marx, Foucault, and the artisan rioters of 1595, Richard Wilson (1993) discusses *Dream*'s inquiry into how regulation of drama by the government affected Shakespeare and authorship more generally. Marcia McDonald (1994) takes a sunnier view of the playwright's situation than do Krieger and Kavanagh. Bottom represents the Elizabethan theater; "socially marginalized" and "disruptive," he "is something like a funhouse mirror that curves and stretches what it reflects" (104). Accordingly, *Dream* is crucial to the independent role of the theater, catering to neither the nobility nor the Puritans.

Louis A. Montrose, in "A Kingdom of Shadows" (1995), reprinted in this volume and somewhat expanded in chapter 11 of his *The Purpose of Playing* (1996), describes *Dream* as a burlesque of the artisans' desire for the status of gentry. Shakespeare shares a lineage with Bottom in the artisanal "middling sort," performers of religious plays suppressed by Elizabeth's government for fear of their Catholicism and regionalism. In their place royal pageantry (e.g., the Queen's Accession Day) and the professional theater, dependent upon both patronage and the market, were encouraged. While *Pyramus and Thisbe* marks the disparity between amateurism and professionalism, subversion inheres in the audience's knowledge that Theseus, Elizabeth's surrogate and would-be controller of the hyper-imaginative—lunatics, lovers, and poets—is himself a poet's creation; moreover, the passage from I Corinthians that Bottom garbles asserts the spiritual superiority of the humble over princes. *Dream* thus ambiguates the status of the theater in England. Patricia Parker (1996), in *Shakespeare from the Margins*, also foregrounds the mechanicals, demonstrating their explicit association "with *joinery* and *joining* in particular, in ways that suggest links between the artisanal, material, or artifactual and the joinings in matrimony that form its close" (88). Parker's discussion reveals that through wordplay Shakespeare interrogates the ideology that the play ostensibly upholds.

In a postcolonialist discussion—the most recent development in *Dream* criticism—that could be seen as a long-awaited reply to the nineteenth-century commentator Gervinus, Margo Hendricks (1996) addresses the inclusion of the "Indian boy" in the cast of a University of California at Santa Cruz production. The changeling, an ethnically coded indicator of "the play's complicity in the racialist ideologies being created by early modern England's participation in imperialism" (43), was portrayed as "a rich oriental 'trifle'" (38) for the consumption of a mostly white audience. Unwittingly, the production fostered the text's "*a priori* racial ideology" (41). India, neither wholly real nor imaginary in *Dream*, is the playtext's geographic and ideological center, associated with fairyland in early modern English literature and with "an emerging racial lexicon" (43). Hendricks points to Titania's exoticized and mercantilistic description of the changeling's mother through which "India becomes the commodified space of a racialized feminine eroticism that . . . paradoxically excited and threatened the masculinity of European travelers" (53). Oberon's substitution of Bottom for the changeling is an imperialistic transaction, while the ass-headed Bottom functions as an exaggerated symbol of miscegenation, intended to draw Titania's attention to the taboo behavior embodied in the figure of the Indian boy. The inclusion of this silent "exotic" in the production revives rather than challenges the play's "fantasy of a silent, accepting native who neither speaks nor resists" (60).

Gender: Feminism and Queer Theory

As feminist criticism, established in the mid-1970s, gained ground over the years, no longer could it be assumed without textual evidence that Oberon's motives were paternal and that it was time for the changeling to leave his surrogate mother and enter a man's world. By the same token, feminist critics and their sympathizers rejected a male fantasy of Titania's "infidelity" with the changeling, which Oberon rightfully avenges. Instead, as Ruth Nevo (1980) comments, noting Titania's lines about "childing autumn" (2.1.112) and her identification with the pregnant votaress, "Oberon might mend his marriage more effectively by getting Titania with child than by trying to get Titania without child" (104). Shirley Nelson Garner (1981), in an essay reprinted here, demonstrates that the play ends with the sundering of female friendships and the patriarchal code still in place, but with heterosexuality unstable and homoeroticism suggested. David Marshall (1982), in an early feminist reading that explores the gender politics of presentation, takes issue with C.L. Barber and Paul A. Olson, who find the patriarchal ideology of marriage "luminous" (Olson's word). Are not the play's spectators being manipulated into supporting a patriarchal view they might question as readers? He notices that Hippolyta, Theseus's prisoner, barely speaks and that her few lines "are restrained and noncommital" (548). Reading her silence, Marshall observes that Hermia, too, is denied autonomy—she must look with her father's judgment—and that "[t]his struggle over vision and imagination also characterizes the dispute between Oberon and Titania" (552); Oberon uses magic to make Titania see (and love) as he wishes. The changeling (also Puttenham's term for a maladroit figure of speech) represents all the characters treated as property, changed, or exchanged, as are *Dream*'s spectators, who must "look to their eyes" (571).

Louis Adrian Montrose in "Shaping Fantasies" (1983), one of the most influential essays on *Dream*, sees the play "not only as an end but also as a source of cultural production" (61). He juxtaposes the Elizabethan court against *Dream* in order to clarify the vexed gender relations of the period and the play. The cult of the queen, whose "pervasive *cultural presence* was a condition of the play's imaginative possibility" (62), upset patriarchal hierarchy without transferring power to women. Montrose proposes that Simon Forman's dream of serving and mastering Elizabeth parallels Bottom's liaison with Titania. In both

[a] fantasy of male dependency upon woman is expressed and contained within a fantasy of male control over woman; the social reality of the player's dependency upon a Queen is inscribed within the imaginative reality of the dramatist's control over a Queen (65).

Similarly, Theseus has defeated an Amazon, Hermia is enjoined to regard "single blessedness" as a punishment, and Oberon "free[s]" (71) the changeling boy from Titania, metonymically from the maternal womb. After reviewing the extent to which Elizabeth's power was a function of her virgin maternity, her grasp of sexual politics, Montrose suggests that Theseus is less her male opposite than "her *princely surrogate*" (85). Not only do the play's incidents, its marriages and epithalamium assert patriarchalism, but metadramatically Shakespeare "contests the princely claim to cultural authorship and social authority" (86).

Jonathan Crewe (1986) uses *Dream* differently, his purpose being to demonstrate the eclectic critical approach, part aesthetic, part historicist, that he urges on the profession. Far more complex and open than *Errors* or *Shrew*, *Dream* exhibits "a complicated, historically specific sexual politics" in all the characters' relationships and in "the relationship between the play (players) and the audience" (139). D'Orsay W. Pearson (1987) interrogates the standard pre-'80s belief that male dominance ensures harmony; rather "individual male-female relationships . . . ironically show that concord is achieved by magic and 'policie'; by fiat; by achievement of feminine will; by mutual recognition of the value of intent" (26). In a postmodern piece, "Or" (1992), Terence Hawkes invokes the play's suppressed female voices to generate alternative readings of *Dream*, of its Ovidian source, and of both Elizabethan and modern patriarchal practices.

Within a larger historical context, Valerie Traub (1992) briefly but notably considers the homoerotic language of Hermia and Helena which spectators and critics have ignored, in part because of these characters' "palpable 'femininity'" (165). Posing no threat to male dominance, the homoerotic desires of the "femme" (164) could be played on stage. Kim E. Hall (1995) asserts the gendered, racist subtexts of *Dream*: "threatening female sexuality and power is located in the space of the foreign . . . the dark, feminine world of the forest, which is also replete with Indians, Tartars, and 'Ethiops'" (22). Louis Montrose, in the second part of his *The Purpose of Playing* (1996), is concerned with the way Elizabethan ideological notions about gender are represented in *Dream*. Chapters 8-10 elaborate on his 1983 essay, "Shaping Fantasies."

To a greater or lesser extent, all the essays written for this anthology suggest that gender issues are central to the play. But Douglas E. Green offers a particularly important revisionist reading of gender in his "Preposterous Pleasures: Queer Theories and *A Midsummer Night's Dream*," which does not seek to re-write *Dream* as a gay play but rather explores some of its "homoerotic significations"—moments of "queer" disruption and eruption. Green draws upon Liviu Ciulei's 1985 production for the Guthrie Theater in Minneapolis as a metatheatrical illustration of the well-known way in which this and other Shakespearean comedies represent officially

proscribed erotic possibilities, only to conclude with the naturalized
reassertion of those proscriptions. What is lost or suppressed in the
text's foreclosure of all erotic unions that do not lead to socially
sanctioned procreation, i.e., its heterosexism and homophobia, is the
subject of Green's essay. Building onto and into poststructuralist
critiques of Shakespeare, Green takes Puck as his "queer" hero because
his pleasures work against or at least challenge ideological constraints;
Puck is not only a vehicle for queering *Dream*, but he represents the
possibility of queering Shakespeare, the English Renaissance canon,
and the culture of the theaters and classrooms in which these high
humanist works are daily revived.

Performance Criticism and Theater History

An expanding circulation between the study and the stage has created
hybrid interpretations of *Dream*. For example, in his 1964 work, Jan
Kott (see Theme, above) describes a misogynous reversal in which the
"monstrous ass is being raped by the poetic Titania" (228); Kott was
the primary critical influence on Peter Brook's pivotal Royal
Shakespeare Company production that consequently actualized various
misogynous readings. Alan Howard, who played Oberon and Theseus,
explained to interviewer/editor Glenn Loney (1974) that the changeling
is Oberon's child and that Titania's humiliating liaison with Bottom as
ass is the result of Oberon's "sacrifice by allowing Titania to do
something which is very possibly in her mentality anyway" (40). Now
an important citation for performance critics, Brooks/Kott returns to the
study via Loney, Selbourne (1982), and others, fostering more biased
readings.

Another example of cross-resonances is the controversy that
developed over Kenneth Branagh's 1990 touring production of *Dream*,
in tandem with his less successful *King Lear*. Although most critics
agreed with Professor Logan, who praised the comedy (see his review
in this volume), director Charles Marowitz, in his *Recycling
Shakespeare* (1991), a *locus (anti)-classicus* for academic performance
critics, takes exception to Branagh's attempt to eliminate the director as
auteur and advance populist, accessible Shakespeare, a project that
inevitably leads to "a lifeless revival" (63). See Sinfield (1992),
especially chapter 1, and Bulman (1996) for less extreme expositions
of the value and inevitability of directorial intervention. Having

pilloried Branagh, Marowitz parodies academic criticism in his "Seeds of 'Verfremdung,'" an analysis of act 3, scene 1, the mechanical's rehearsal, as anticipating "surrealism, symbolism and even Epic Theatre" (74). While his burlesque bespeaks hostility between the stage and the study, it assumes extensive traffic between them.

Loney's 1974 book includes Brook's acting text and promptbook as well as interviews with Brook, his cast, and his production crew. David Selbourne (1982) describes the evolution of Brook's *Dream* with its weekly record of rehearsals, Brook's remarks about the play's exploration of reality and its relation to acting, and Simon Trussler's summary of Brook's work and the reception of this production. Roger Warren (1983), in his *Text and Performance* volume, devotes part 2 to productions by Peter Hall (whose interpretation Warren prefers), Peter Brook, Robin Phillips, and Elijah Moshinsky. Volume 12 of *Shakespearean Criticism* (1991) provides an account of *Dream*'s performance history and reprints reviews and commentaries. Jay L. Halio (1994), in a book-length study for the Shakespeare in Performance series, reviews important productions by Granville-Barker, Reinhardt, Bridges-Adam, Reeve, Hall, Brook, Barton, Daniels, Alexander, Moshinsky, Lapine, and Lepage, demonstrating their breadth of possibility.

Other useful sources for Shakespearean production history include Odell (1920), Trewin (1964), Babula (1981), Leiter (1986), and two books by Dennis Kennedy, *Foreign Shakespeare* and *Looking at Shakespeare*, both published in 1993. All of these served as sources for the theater history below, which maps English and American performances through the 1960s, and European productions through the 1970s. Also see the performance pieces reprinted here: Lawrence Guntner's essay (1993) on 1970s East German performances, Ann Fridén's review (1986) of Ariane Mnouchkine's 1968 production in Paris, and the essay-reviews by Thomas Clayton (1986) on Liviu Ciulei's 1985 *Dream* at the Minneapolis Guthrie theater and by Robert A. Logan (1990) on Kenneth Branagh's 1990 touring production. Not reprinted are Russell's and Bevington's reviews (both 1990); Logan's opinions are shared by Russell, but Bevington's praise is qualified.

A Midsummer Night's Dream has long been among the most popular of Shakespeare's plays, not only in English-speaking countries but throughout the world. While sometimes truncated, rearranged, or adapted into other (chiefly musical) forms, it has rarely failed to please audiences. *Dream* has been played both as a charming fantasy and, more recently, as a vehicle for representing sexual amorality. In Europe, *Dream* frequently served as a channel for protesting political abuses as well as for evoking fantasy, sexuality, and untrammeled experimentalism.

The Dream *in England*

While it is generally thought, notwithstanding a lack of hard evidence, that *A Midsummer Night's Dream* was composed for a private wedding in the mid-1590s, the first quarto edition of 1600 indicates it had already been publicly performed on several occasions by the Lord Chamberlain's Men; Ronald Watkins and Jeremy Lemmon (1974) have described their attempt at a reconstruction. *Dream*'s first expressly documented performance, however, was a production for the court in 1604, this also being the last documented performance during Shakespeare's lifetime. Thereafter, whether because of Puritan restrictions, the constraints of the patent theater system, and/or popular taste nurtured by circumstance and ideology, until the mid-nineteenth century, *Dream* appeared exclusively in adapted forms. Not only did the Puritan ban on plays encourage generic mutation, but after the Restoration, the big patent houses were preeminently suited to lavish productions—operas and ballets. The mechanicals' interlude was first detached and played as a "droll" at some time prior to 1624, when it was presented as *The Comedy of Pyramus and Thisbe*; in 1646, as the *Merry Conceited Humours of Bottom the Weaver*, it was staged at various festivals, Parliament having closed the London theaters. Thereafter, with one exception, it remained a separate piece until 1840.

Not until the twentieth century was *Dream*, originally performed under the most circumscribed theatrical conditions, once again trusted to speak unadorned to an audience. After the Puritan interregnum Thomas Killigrew re-introduced the complete text (1662) with staged dance sequences and an emphasis on physical comedy; this approach being poorly received, a series of operatic adaptations followed. The first opera, Thomas Betterton's successful *The Fairy Queen* (1692), featured a score by Henry Purcell and a script that omitted Hippolyta, reordered scenes, and distorted the verse but introduced end-of-act entertainments, the last featuring Hymen, twenty-four Chinese dancers, and six monkeys; sets were equally striking. During this period, the

Pyramus and Thisbe material, while sometimes incorporated into productions, also continued to be performed separately, in 1716 as Richard Leveridge's successful comic masque (expanded by a Mr. Lampe, a composer, in 1745), and in 1723 in Charles Johnson's *Love in a Forest, a Comedy*, as an inclusion to a version of *As You Like It*.

In 1755, David Garrick introduced *The Fairies*, a three-act opera with extraneous verse from other Shakespearean plays and from poems by Milton, Waller, Lansdowne, and Dryden, at the expense of much of the original text; the mechanicals were cut. Garrick's associate, George Colman, the elder, staged a dull five-act, thirty-three song version in 1763 that played only once. Much of Shakespeare's playtext was deleted in this longer version, too; again the mechanicals almost disappeared. The production miscarrying, Colman condensed the opera into a two-act piece called *A Fairy Tale* that became a popular after-play. So frequently did eighteenth-century adaptations excise either the mechanicals or the fairies that one might infer a distaste on the part of a class-conscious audience now shorn of its groundling component for the amorous mingling of an ethereal aristocrat with an earthy artisan.

The early nineteenth century saw more of the same with Frederick Reynolds's presentation of an operatic version of *Dream* at Covent Garden (1816), drawing on the songs from the 1755 and 1763 productions, and notable for extravagant sets and its fifth-act spectacle inspired by a *mélange* of Theseus stories. Reynolds's production achieved lasting notoriety among critics, thanks to Hazlitt's eloquent denunciations. An 1833 two-act musical version of *Dream* at Drury Lane used all the songs the play had amassed, but failed even so.

At last, at Covent Garden in 1840 after almost two hundred years, Shakespeare's playtext, essentially as written, was revived by Elizabeth Vestris and her husband Charles Matthews. Though ornately "Athenian," this romantic musical interpretation retained the play's original verse. Also noteworthy was Felix Mendelssohn's incidental music; the overture had been heard in England in 1833, and Madam Vestris, who played—and sang—Oberon expanded the Mendelsohn score. Within a few years of the revocation of the patent theaters' monopoly in 1843, Covent Garden became an opera house, but other theaters were now able to produce plays without subjecting them to generic transformation. Samuel Phelps' successful poetic staging at Sadler's Wells Theatre in 1853 made much of the moon and introduced

Figure 2. Robin-Goodfellow. Act 2, scene 2, of "A Midsummer Night's Dream." Painted by Sir Joshua Reynolds, aqua fortis by Testalini & Schiavonetti. Published 1799. Reproduced by permission of The Huntington Library, San Marino, California.

green gauze curtains and misty lighting effects, distinguishing the forest from the Athenian court. In 1856, Charles Kean premiered an elaborate *Dream* which ran for 150 consecutive performances. While faithful to the text, the production cut passages drastically. This Athens was based on up-to-date archaeological findings, but also included fantastic props, for instance, a mushroom which rose up from beneath the stage to strains of Mendelssohn, introducing Ellen Terry as a seated Puck.

For the most part, whether staged as a ballet, opera, or drama, the greatest challenge was the representation of the fairy kingdom. The opulence that became associated with *Dream* because of its Victorian productions survived in the ostentatious experimentation of later fantastic stagings. Following a revival of Phelps's production in 1870, F.R. Benson, the Stratford Globe manager, produced another extravagant *Dream* for a London audience in 1889. Theater historians remark on Augustin Daly's spectacle-oriented productions of *Dream* in 1873 and 1895-96, chiefly to censure his deletions. By the end of the century, a director who sought the respect of critics and reviewers was obliged to respect Shakespeare's text. Despite overwhelming scenic effects, the play's language finally mattered.

The tradition of romantic stagings—Decorated Shakespeare—that had its roots in Restoration and eighteenth-century Shakespearean operas continued into the twentieth century, although further abstraction and experimentation was more typical of modernists. The first significant twentieth-century production was atavistic, Beerbohm Tree's beautiful spectacle (1900) whose appeal must have seemed all the greater to a pre-film audience. Directing a "realistic" revival in 1911, Tree introduced live rabbits to the fairy forest, a much-remarked-upon innovation.

A far more significant innovation was Harley Granville-Barker's rejection of realism, more aptly termed classic illusionism, and his insistence on the theatricality of *Dream*. Breaking with the past, the 1914 Savoy production elicited mixed reactions; it featured a novel minimalist set, the court suggested by massive Egyptian columns and white silk curtains, the woods by green silk curtains. In lieu of Mendelssohn, Granville-Barker used English folkmusic, and his fairies, in gold-bronze costumes and gilded body paint, jangled as they moved. This production has been seen as a forerunner of Peter Brook's. Donald Calthrop's starkly set *Dream* (1924), was succeeded by James Agate's

Victorian extravaganza (1925), followed in turn by Harcourt Williams's staging (1929) inspired by Inigo Jones's masques. Tyrone Guthrie's 1937 Christmas-season production at the Old Vic exemplified nostalgia for the elaborate Victorian style, but his subsequent production (1951) was deliberately unadorned and abstract, with its forest of silvery bamboo, stylized Greek dress, and individualized characters, including the fairies.

Ensuing important productions were distinctly modern in conception. Michael Benthall's 1957 production implied that the play's three groups of characters were branches of a single family rather than distinct "races." Oberon was portrayed as an impulsive and capricious dictator, wholly dependent upon Puck. At the 1959 Stratford-upon-Avon Festival, Peter Hall presented Charles Laughton as Bottom in a relatively modest production, whose chief interest lay in the setting, an Elizabethan country estate, with the play comprising part of the wedding festivities. Whereas this staging stressed physical comedy over poetry, Benjamin Britten's 1960 oneiric opera captured the atmosphere of the uncanny, and Hall's 1962 revival (on which the filmed version was based) was distinguished by the beauty of its spoken verse. An important innovation of Michael Langham's 1960 production at the Old Vic was his reading of Hippolyta. She was both Other, darker than the rest of the cast, and, as her handcuffs reminded the audience, a prisoner. Although Langham kept the tone comic, an anti-romantic subtext was uncovered. Similarly, the lovers' scenes, exaggerated to the point of farce, subtextually insinuated disillusionment.

Ariane Mnouchkine had presented a circus-motif *Dream* in Paris a scant two years before Peter Brook, but his exuberantly sexual production at the 1970 Stratford-upon-Avon Festival is notwithstanding regarded as one of the most original achievements of the modern theater. Brook used a set evoking the circus in order to openly acknowledge the devices of theatre (note the influence of Brecht and Barthes as well as Granville-Barker) and thereby increase audience involvement. He doubled Theseus with Oberon and Hippolyta with Titania, to imply that the fairy kingdom is the unconscious aspect of the Athenian court. Oberon descended on a trapeze, Puck walked on stilts, and the modern tradition of masculine fairies was taken to clownish new extremes with the use of false and real moustaches. A surreal, metallic set provided "forest" scenery. Brook's post-Freudian, distinctly anti-romantic production did not please everyone. Theater critic John Simon's review (1971) is a case in point.

Mary Z. Maher's "*A Midsummer Night's Dream*: Nightmare or Gentle Snooze?" written for this volume, examines major English-speaking productions after and including Peter Brook's 1970 staging, a benchmark to which subsequent directors felt the need to respond. Some (Liviu Ciulei, Robert LePage) chose to emphasize the nightmare qualities that they perceived in Brook's work. Others (Bill Bryden, Adrian Noble) followed Shakespeare's more apparent summons and embraced comedy. Maher argues that Brook himself, although acknowledging a debt to Jan Kott's *Shakespeare Our Contemporary*, remained within the generic boundaries of comedy and that fidelity to Shakespeare's design was partly responsible for his commercial success. His chief contribution was to initiate a performance tradition receptive to the playtext's inherent sexuality. She argues, too, that productions committed to the denial of the play's comic foundations not only distort important scenes but are less successful, less a co-creation of a participative audience. Maher closes her survey with a discussion of Adrian Noble's 1995 Royal Shakespeare Company *Dream*, which comments on Brook's staging strategies twenty-five years later.

A note about some North American performances prior to Brook's: While London directors have been the trend-setters, a growing number of North American productions merit attention. The 1949 *Dream* at the Oregon Shakespeare Festival in Ashland, played in an outdoor, bare-boards theater designed as a modified reconstruction of an Elizabethan playhouse, attempted to capture the experience of a 1590s performance. Anticipating Tokyo Globe stagings, Peter Bucknell's production of *Dream* at the 1956 San Diego National Shakespeare Festival introduced Kabuki fairies with corresponding sets, choreography, and koto music.

Because of Jan Kott's influential 1964 reading of *Dream*'s carnality, by the late 1960s it had become fashionable to present the play as erotic black comedy. John Hancock's 1967 production at New York's Circle-in-the-Square employed a psychedelic set with modern lighting and optical effects: Demetrius's longings were expressed through a glow-in-the-dark codpiece, and the fairies were decorated with fluorescent paint. Mendelssohn's incidental music emanated from

a jukebox. Making comedy out of gender-role reversal, the Amazon
Hippolyta in leopardskin tights was paired with an effeminate Theseus,
and Helena was played by a transvestite. The 1968 Stratford, Ontario,
Shakespeare Festival production, directed by John Hirsch and Jean
Gascon, offended many critics. Text-based but no less erotic, it opened
with Theseus being laced into a tight corset (effeminacy again); his
booted Hippolyta carried a whip. Helena was proper, Hermia rebellious, their "cat-fight" vicious. Oberon and Titania's fairy courtiers,
predominately male and given to hissing, followed the royals across the
stage in snakelike trains to the accompaniment of rock music. Titania's
interest in the Indian boy was lustful and provoked by his ethnicity.

Most contemporary productions contribute to a dialogue of
experimentalism, in part legitimate but surely in part a concession to
spectators uneasy with Shakespeare's language but at home with sex.
While the Mendelssohn score and romantic productions of the *Dream*
have not vanished completely, a post-Brook orthodoxy has made anti-
romantic attitudes and doubled characters as common as earlier conventions. Meanwhile, performance criticism explores the extent to
which directorial intervention is legitimate, the point at which the
director displaces the author, whether that should matter, and why it
does matter to so many of us. See, for example, Marowitz (1991),
Sinfield (1992), and most recently Bulman (1996).

Two new essays are concerned with recent American productions,
representing outstanding university and regional theater. In "Transposing Helena to Form and Dignity," Lisa J. Moore relates her
challenging experience as a feminist acting Helena in a University of
Washington MFA production, conceived of by its director as a drama
of desire and disgust. Moore came to terms with the role by envisaging
Helena as having a "sense of inner dignity and deserving" despite her
fear and insecurity. In her loving persistence and lack of self-pity, she
is not entirely unlike the near-tragic Helena of *All's Well That Ends
Well*. She is, however, younger; Moore's Helena, a teen-ager, grows
from dependency on male approval to self-respect. Beautiful but
gauche, desperate but optimistic, Helena's determination to give
anything—even dogginess—her best efforts might well elicit
admiration. Unlike critics who take Hermia's and Helena's act 5
silence as symptomatic of their subordination, Moore chose to interpret
the "mute" scene as "an opportunity for Helena to assimilate her new

perspective and rejoice in her victory. No longer needing to demonstrate who she is or to garner attention, she just *is*."

Dorothea Kehler's "Marion McClinton's *Dream* at the La Jolla Playhouse, 1995: Appropriation Through Peformance" melds performance criticism with theoretical inquiry. Kehler describes a feminist-inflected production that imposed the issue of color prejudice within the African American community, thus raising the critical question of when "director's theater" enhances and when it subverts the text. Without changing the lines or the overall comic tone, director Marion McClinton supplied a reason for Egeus's choice of Demetrius over Lysander: Demetrius was light-skinned, Lysander dark. The program notes clarified the point by sketching a brief history of color prejudice within the African American community as a corollary of white racism. The essay looks to Barthes, Eagleton, and Marowitz for precepts that might validate such a seemingly extra-textual intervention. Beyond an appreciation of McClinton's production, the essay returns to the undecidable, inevitably vexed question of theatrical boundaries.

The Dream *Elsewhere*

Although the staging of *A Midsummer Night's Dream* before the Second World War was principally an Anglo-American enterprise, Tieck's 1843 German production at the Potsdam Court Theatre, with its score by Felix Mendelssohn, may well have been the single most influential nineteenth-century rendition of the play. That Tieck was not a director but a literary critic, theater historian, writer, and translator of Shakespeare is worth remarking. Other versions of the play outside England and the United States in this period rarely strayed from existing staging conventions, either emphasizing physical comedy or re-enacting the Tieck-Mendelssohn ballet.

A Midsummer Night's Dream has won enduring popularity in Germany, productions in Eastern Europe have not been uncommon, and significant twentieth-century interpretations have also been staged further afield, e.g., in Israel and Australia (both in 1978). While "traditional" stagings have not died out, continental European directors of the play in the second half of the twentieth century have exercised as much interpretive license as their Anglo-American contemporaries. Set and costume design have been variously localized and stylized, ranging from the abstract to the vehemently expressionistic—the latter epitomized by Heinz Wildhagen's flamboyantly colorful 1951 production in Flensburg, West Germany, in which the actors were dressed as tourists in tropical shirts and sunglasses. The social division of Athenians, fairies, and artisans has often been inflected politically. For example, Jim Vilé's 1978 Adelaide production relocated Athens to an outspokenly patriarchal setting, the Arab world; and "iron curtain" stagings regularly endowed the artisans with local working-class accents and vernacular speech patterns. A common tendency in modern reinterpretations of *A Midsummer Night's Dream* has been to present the play as a nightmare of lust within an ominous fairy kingdom. Whether male or female, Puck has often been painted as a demon instead of a Sprite, as in Goran O. Eriksson's 1979 Stockholm production, or Marianne Rolfe's in Bergen, Norway, 1980—an erotically sinister rendition in which Puck overshadowed Oberon.

Gustav Rudolf Sellner's 1952 production of *A Midsummer Night's Dream* at Darmstadt was an early, influential anti-romantic staging which tended toward ritual abstraction rather than sensory indulgence. The set was a simple wood platform flanked by scaffolding on both sides and adorned with huge leaves representing trees suspended above the stage. Red stage lighting distinguished the palace from the blue and green woods. The fairies inhabiting this dream were fiendish phosphorescent insects; Puck, Sellner's "Troll," was also menacing. Otherwise, the cast was less individualized than ritualized, underlining Sellner's reading of the play as a clash between human beings and the natural world. Carl Orff's score called for Bavarian folk music in the mechanicals' scenes and a threatening musical ambiance for the grotesque fairy kingdom, both synchronized with the actors' gestures and dialogue. A few members of the orchestra appeared onstage in modern dress to facilitate this interaction. The 1968 Cirque Montmartre *Dream* directed by Ariane Mnouchkine utilized the circus set that Brook was to capitalize on but downplayed comedy in favor of tragic psychological portraiture. The fairies acted out the unconscious desires of the Athenians—lust and cruelty—through rape and violence. Only the mechanicals provided humor (see Fridén's review reprinted in this volume).

Konrad Swinarski's 1970 production in Krakow was another dark reading. Though Swinarski privileged political allegory, he was not averse to sexual fantasy. Theseus and Hippolyta, as richly apparelled seventeenth-century Polish aristocrats, were starkly contrasted with the mechanicals, dressed as peasants. Aside from demonstrating the relevance of the play's themes to the reality of class structure, Swinarski evoked the omnipresence of authority in the human world with two silent bodyguards (secret police) on stage for all but the fairy sequences. The fairies were perverse distortions of humanity with extra, oddly-placed limbs and genitalia. Puck, a diabolic acrobat and drummer, precipitated and heightened an orgy among the enchanted lovers who may have represented the ruling class and/or the libido. *Pyramus and Thisbe* was played as a *commedia* in white-face and designed as a carnivalesque defiance of the establishment.

In the '70s, many productions of *A Midsummer Night's Dream* displayed the obvious influence of the Kott-inspired Brook production, which opened new modes of interpretation, still mainly psychoanalytic and political. In his "Brecht and Beyond" reprinted here, Lawrence Guntner describes significant East German stagings of the decade that drew upon Brook—Schroth's (1971), Lang's (1980), and Langhoff's (1980). Jan Kacer's 1976 production in Ostrava, Czechoslovakia, was faithful to the playtext, and balanced deep emotion with fantasy and humor. A range of theatrical conventions, from court masque and folkplay to surreal and neo-real cinema, were employed to encourage spectators to adopt multiple viewpoints. Eschewing overt politicization Kacer thematized the continuum from youth to age. Hippolyta's changeling was played by a five-year-old girl, the lover's rebellion was driven by youthful anti-authoritarianism, and Puck was played by a nearly blind actor, an impatient, work-weary old sprite. The mechanicals spoke in the dialect of the local mining community where the play was performed, thus lending the production immediacy.

While some directors followed Brook's comedic cue by employing a circus motif, others appropriated doubling. Jiri Fréhar's 1977 production in Prague portrayed the fairies as circus performers and, correspondingly, emphasized prop-comedy in their scenes. Fréhar dramatized Hippolyta's lack of independence, her emotional and political oppression, by imprisoning her in a white wooden cage. Oberon was a violinist, Puck was played by a trio of actors simultaneously, and the fairy servants were white-faced clowns who performed tricks with balloons, a bicycle, and the changeling's pram. Brook's circus motif survived through the decade. Kurt Nuotio's 1980 Finnish production made much use of acrobat-actors' swinging from ropes, and that same year in Belgium Jean-Pierre De Decker presented Puck as a ringmaster on roller skates.

Doubling the Theseus/Oberon and Hippolyta/Titania roles, another Brook hallmark, was no less common in non-English speaking countries than in England or America. In Dieter Dorn's 1978 Munich *Dream*, an exotic, tattooed Hippolyta wore a reversible garment that transformed her into Titania. A controlling character, Hippolyta/Titania spoke Puck's epilogue. Cast-doubling served to highlight the theatrical art of illusion. Kurt Josef Schildknecht's 1978 Brook-inspired production at the Schauspielhaus in Graz, Austria, was principally a Freudian reading, wherein the repressed sexuality of the Elizabethan-dressed Athenians found expression (with Puck's assistance) in their fairy alter-egos. Titania, in flesh-toned tights, was accompanied by an enticing chorus line of fairies.

Franz Marijnen's Hamburg production in the same year was abstract but, like Schildknecht's, marked by a strong sexual interest. The forest set was a shifting maze of blue balloons, and its ghost-like fairies were no more independent of supernatural influence than the "human" characters; Oberon became violently attracted to Puck upon being given love-in-idleness. In contrast to the sexuality of the forest, the white-tiled Athenian court evoked an everyday world; the privileged ate from huge bowls of ice cream, and Theseus delivered his speech on imagination with his mouth full.

Also in 1978 Oscar Fritz Schuh directed a *Dream* arresting for its neo-traditional experimentalism. Schuh's production was set in the gardens of Heilbrunn, the baroque seventeenth-century Salzburg palace. Looking back to the staging of medieval mysteries, the six-scene text was played on a processional stage of flat wagons, and juxtaposed against selected scenes, similarly staged, from Purcell's opera *The Fairy Queen* and Andreas Gryphius's *Absurda Comica oder Herr Peter Squentz*. Audience members were guided from station to station by leaf-covered fairies partially concealed in moving shrubs and sculptures.

Runar Borge's Oslo production of 1980, though unabashedly contemporary, also found a place for Purcell. The set was sparsely decorated to allow dance, but the grey "stone" backdrop pulled open to reveal a colorfully-lit fairy world. Purcell's *Fairy Queen* resurfaced in a modern arrangement with jazz and rock rhythms. Punk fairies (Puck wore a sequined T-shirt, tailcoat, and clown makeup) contrasted with classically-dressed lovers and Renaissance rulers.

Music and dance also distinguished Roberto Ciulli's much-lauded 1982 *Dream*, which played in Mülheim/Ruhr, West Germany, and elsewhere in Europe through 1984. Its contemporary staging intimated the illusory, arbitrary, and unpleasant nature of romantic love: the lovers, in modern dress, executed Latin dance steps, changing partners at the command of a female Puck's pistol shots. In a dramatization of neurosis, the quarrel scene (3.2) found them folding, and ultimately ripping up, colored papers. Going Brook one better, the actress who played Puck also played Philostrate and Quince.

Just as musical adaptations allowed *Dream* to survive from Elizabethan to Victorian times, so, too, the numerous, diverse, and eclectic international reinterpretations of the twentieth century testify to its thematic flexibility and textual durability. No single, authoritative, contemporary production standard prevails; Tieck-Mendelssohn is past. Directors today tend to be faithful to Shakespeare's playtext, but they have "re-authored" the play to an unprecedented extent by conceptual and contextual innovations in staging, preserving its themes while translating them into post-Freudian, post-modern, post-political discourses.

Postscript

After some four hundred years of commentary and performance have attached themselves like barnacles to the text, how can we not ask, whose *Dream* is Shakespeare's? Perhaps, to a greater or lesser extent, they all are. For as Alan Sinfield understands,

> [n]o story can contain all the possibilities it brings into play; coherence is always selection. And the range of feasible readings depends not only on the text but on the conceptual framework within which we address it (51).

In the same generous, pluralistic spirit, R.A. Foakes's discussion of *Dream* concludes with a prediction: "No doubt further significances will continue to be found in it, for like other great plays by Shakespeare, it appears to be inexhaustible" (41).

WORKS CITED

Allen, John A. "Bottom and Titania." *Shakespeare Quarterly* 18 (1967): 107-17.

Aronson, Alex. "Eros: Sons and Mothers: III." *Psyche & Symbol in Shakespeare.* Bloomington: Indiana University Press, 1972. 204-12.

Babula, William. *Shakespeare in Production, 1935-1978: A Selective Catalogue.* New York: Garland, 1981.

Baker, Susan. "Chronotope and Repression in *A Midsummer Night's Dream.*" *A Midsummer Night's Dream: Critical Essays.* Ed. Dorothea Kehler.

Barber, "May Games and Metamorphoses on a Midsummer Night." *Shakespeare's Festive Comedy: A Study of Dramatic Form and Its Relation to Social Custom.* Princeton: Princeton University Press, 1959. 119-62.

Barkan, Leonard. "Ovid 'Translated.'" *The Gods Made Flesh: Metamorphosis and the Pursuit of Paganism.* New Haven: Yale University Press, 1986. 251-70.

Bate, Jonathan. "Comedy and Metamorphosis." *Shakespeare and Ovid.* Oxford: Clarendon Press, 1993. 118-70, esp. 129-44.

Berry, Ralph. "The Dream and the Play." *Shakespeare's Comedies: Explorations in Form.* Princeton: Princeton University Press, 1972. 89-110.

Bevington, David. "'But we are spirits of another sort': The Dark Side of Love and Magic in *A Midsummer Night's Dream.*" *Medieval and Renaissance Studies* 7 (1975): 80-92.

————. "Singing in the Rain." *Shakespeare Quarterly* 41 (1990): 499-502.

Boas, Frederick S. "Shakespere's Poems: The Early Period of Comedy." *Shakespere and His Predecessors.* New York: Scribner's, 1896. 158-96.

Bonnard, George A. "Shakespeare's Purpose in *Midsummer- Night's Dream.*" *Shakespeare Jahrbuch* 92 (1956): 268- 79.

Brandes, George. "*A Midsummer Night's Dream*—Its Historical Circumstances—Its Aristocratic, Popular, Comic, and Supernatural Elements" [1895-96]. *William Shakespeare.* Trans. William Archer, Mary Morison, and Diana White. New York: Macmillan, 1924. 63-71.

Briggs, K.M. "Shakespeare's Fairies." *The Anatomy of Puck: An Examination of Fairy Beliefs Among Shakespeare's Contemporaries and Successors.* London: Routledge and Kegan Paul, 1959. 44-55.

Brissenden, Alan. "The Comedies I." *Shakespeare and the Dance.* Atlantic Highlands, NJ: Humanities Press, 1981. 34-48.

Bristol, Michael D. "Wedding Feast and Charivari." *Carnival and Theater: Plebeian Culture and the Structure of Authority in Renaissance England.* New York: Methuen, 1985. 162-78.

Brooks, Harold F. Introduction. *A Midsummer Night's Dream.* Ed. Brooks. The Arden Shakespeare. Cambridge, MA: Harvard University Press, 1979.

Brown, Jane K. "*Discordia Concors*: On the Order of *A Midsummer Night's Dream,*" *Modern Language Quarterly* 48 (1987): 20-41.

Brown, John Russell. "Love's Truth and the Judgements of *A Midsummer Night's Dream* and *Much Ado about Nothing.*" *Shakespeare and His Comedies.* London: Methuen, 1957. 82-123.

Bullough, Geoffrey. "Introduction to *A Midsummer Night's Dream.*"*Narrative and Dramatic Sources of Shakespeare.* Ed. Bullough. Vol. I. London: Routledge and Kegan Paul, 1957. 367-76.

Bulman, James C., ed. *Shakespeare, Theory, and Performance.* London: Routledge, 1996.

Calderwood, James L. *A Midsummer Night's Dream.* Twayne's New Critical Introductions to Shakespeare. New York: Twayne, 1992.

———. "*A Midsummer Night's Dream*: Art's Illusory Sacrifice." *Shakespearean Metadrama: The Argument of the Play In "Titus Andronicus," "Love's Labour's Lost," "Romeo and Juliet," "A Midsummer Night's Dream," and "Richard II."* Minneapolis: University of Minnesota Press, 1971. 120-48.

Carroll, D. Allen, and Gary Jay Williams. *A Midsummer Night's Dream: An Annotated Bibliography.* New York: Garland, 1986.

Carroll, William C. "*A Midsummer Night's Dream*: Monsters and Marriage." *The Metamorphoses of Shakespearean Comedy.* Princeton: Princeton University Press, 1985. 141-77.

Chambers, E.K. "*A Midsummer Night's Dream.*" 1905. Rpt. in *Shakespeare: A Survey,* 1925; rpt. London: Sidgwick & Jackson, 1958. 77-87.

Champion, Larry S. "The Comedies of Action." *The Evolution of Shakespeare's Comedy: A Study in Dramatic Perspective.* Cambridge: Harvard University Press, 1970. 12-59.

———. *The Essential Shakespeare: An Annotated Bibliography of Major Modern Studies.* 2nd ed. New York: G.K. Hall, 1993.

Charlton, H.B. "*A Midsummer Night's Dream.*" 1933. *Shakespearian Comedy.* London: Methuen, 1938. 100-22.

Chesterton, G.K. "*A Midsummer Night's Dream.*" 1904. Rpt. in *The Common Man.* London: Sheed and Ward, 1950. 10-21.

Clapp, Henry A. "Time in Shakespeare's Comedies." *The Atlantic Monthly* 55.329 (March 1885): 386-403.

Clarke, Charles Cowden. "*Midsummer Night's Dream*." *Shakespeare-Characters: Chiefly Those Subordinate*. London: Smith, Elder, 1863. Rpt. New York: AMS, 1974. 93-110.

Clayton, Thomas. "'Fie What a Question's That If Thou Wert Near a Lewd Interpreter': The Wall Scene in *A Midsummer Night's Dream*." *Shakespeare Studies* 7 (1974): 101-13.

————. "Shakespeare at the Guthrie: *A Midsummer Night's Dream*." *Shakespeare Quarterly* 37 (1986): 229-36.

Cody, Richard. "*A Midsummer Night's Dream*: Bottom Translated." *The Landscape of the Mind: Pastoralism and Platonic Theory in Tasso's "Aminta" and Shakespeare's Early Comedies*. Oxford: Clarenden Press, 1969. 127-50.

Coleridge, Samuel Taylor. "Notes on the Comedies of Shakespeare: *Midsummer Night's Dream*." *Shakespearean Criticism*. Ed. Thomas Middleton Raysor. 2nd ed. 2 vols. New York: Dutton, 1960. 1: 90-92.

Comtois, M.E. "The Hardiness of *A Midsummer Night's Dream*." *Theatre Journal* 32 (1980): 305-11.

Cox, Richard H. "Shakespeare: Poetic Understanding and Comic Action (A Weaver's Dream)." *The Artist and Political Vision*. Ed. Benjamin R. Barber and Michael J. Gargas McGrath. New Brunswick, NJ: Transaction Books, 1982. 165-92.

Crane, Milton. *Shakespeare's Prose*. Chicago: University of Chicago Press, 1951. 72-77.

Crewe, Jonathan. "Epilogue: The Way Forward." *Hidden Designs: The Critical Profession and Renaissance Literature*. New York: Methuen, 1986. 130-51.

Davidson, Clifford. "'What hempen home-spuns have we swagg'ring here?': Amateur Actors in *A Midsummer Night's Dream* and the Coventry Civic Plays and Pageants." *Shakespeare Studies* 19 (1987): 87-99.

De la Mare, Walter. Introduction. *A Midsummer Night's Dream*. Ed. C. Aldred. Scholar's Library Edition. London: Macmillan, 1935. Rpt. as "The Dream." *Pleasures & Speculations*. By de La Mare. London: Faber and Faber, 1940. 270-305.

Dent, R.W. "Imagination in *A Midsummer Night's Dream*." *Shakespeare Quarterly* 15.2 (1964): 115-29.

Desmet, Christy. "Disfiguring Women with Masculine Tropes: A Rhetorical Reading of *A Midsummer Night's Dream.*" *A Midsummer Night's Dream: Critical Essays.* Ed. Dorothea Kehler.

Donaldson, E. Talbot. "The Lunacy of Lovers: *The Knight's Tale, The Merchant's Tale,* and *A Midsummer Night's Dream.*" *The Swan at the Well: Shakespeare Reading Chaucer.* New Haven: Yale University Press, 1985. 30-49.

Doran, Madeleine. "Pyramus and Thisbe Once More." *Essays on Shakespeare and Elizabethan Drama in Honor of Hardin Craig.* Ed. Richard Hosley. Columbia: University of Missouri Press, 1962. 149-61.

Dowden, Edward. "The Growth of Shakspere's Mind and Art." *Shakspere: A Critical Study of His Mind and Art.* 3rd ed. New York: Harper, 1881. 37-83.

[Dryden, John.] "The Authors Apology for Heroique Poetry; and Poetique Licence." *The State of Innocence, and Fall of Man. The Complete Works of John Dryden.* Ed. Vinton A. Dearing. Vol. 12. Berkeley: University of California Press, 1994. 86-97.

Duff, William. "Of Shakespeare." *Critical Observation on the Writings of the Most Celebrated Original Geniuses in Poetry. . . .* 1770. Rpt. New York: Garland, 1971. 126-96.

Dunn, Allen. "The Indian Boy's Dream Wherein Every Mother's Son Rehearses His Part: Shakespeare's *A Midsummer Night's Dream.*" *Shakespeare Studies* 20 (1988): 15-32.

Eagleton, Terry. "Desire: *A Midsummer Night's Dream, Twelfth Night.*" *William Shakespeare.* Oxford: Blackwell, 1986. 18-34.

Edwards, Philip. "The Abandon'd Cave." *Shakespeare and the Confines of Art.* London: Methuen, 1968. 49-70.

Evans, Bertrand. "All Shall Be Well: The Way Found: *A Midsummer Night's Dream*." *Shakespeare's Comedies.* Oxford: Clarendon, 1960. 33-46.

Evans, B. Ifor. "*A Midsummer-Night's Dream.*" *The Language of Shakespeare's Plays.* London: Methuen, 1952. 70-77.

Evans, G. Blakemore, ed. *The Riverside Shakespeare.* Boston: Houghton Mifflin, 1974.

Faber, M.D. "Hermia's Dream: Royal Road to *A Midsummer Night's Dream.*" *Literature and Psychology* 22 (1972): 179-90.

Falk, Florence. "Dream and Ritual Process in "*A Midsummer Night's Dream.*" *Comparative Drama* 14 (1980): 263-79.

Fender, Stephen. *Shakespeare: "A Midsummer Night's Dream."* London: Edward Arnold, 1968.

Finch, G.J. "Shakespeare and the Nature of Metaphor." *Ariel: A Review of International English Literature* 12 (1981): 3-19.

Fisher, Peter F. "The Argument of *A Midsummer Night's Dream*," *Shakespeare Quarterly* 8 (1957): 307-10.

Foakes, R.A. Introduction. *A Midsummer Night's Dream*. Ed. Foakes. New Cambridge Shakespeare. Cambridge: Cambridge University Press, 1984. 1-42.

Franke, Wolfgang. "The Logic of *Double Entendre* in *A Midsummer Night's Dream*." *Philological Quarterly* 58 (1979): 282-97.

Freake, Douglas. "*A Midsummer Night's Dream* as a Comic Version of the Theseus Myth." *A Midsummer Night's Dream: Critical Essays*. Ed. Dorothea Kehler.

Freedman, Barbara. "Dis/Figuring Power: Censorship and Representation in *A Midsummer Night's Dream*." *Staging the Gaze: Postmodernism, Psychoanalysis, and Shakespearean Comedy*. Ithaca: Cornell University Press, 1991. 154-91.

Fridén, Ann. "[Ariane Mnouchkine's] *Le Songe d'une nuit d' été*." *Shakespeare Around the Globe: A Guide to Notable Postwar Revivals*. Ed. Samuel L. Leiter. 482-83.

Furness, Horace Howard. Preface. *A New Variorum Edition of Shakespeare: "A Midsummer Night's Dream."* Vol. 10. Ed. Horace Howard Furness. Philadelphia: J.B. Lippincott, 1895. v-xxxiv.

Garber, Marjorie B. "Spirits of Another Sort: *A Midsummer Night's Dream*." *Dream in Shakespeare: From Metaphor to Metamorphosis*. New Haven: Yale University Press, 1974. 59-87.

Garner, Shirley Nelson. "*A Midsummer Night's Dream*: 'Jack shall have Jill: / Nought shall go ill.'" *Women's Studies* 9 (1981): 47-63.

Gentleman, Francis. Introduction. "*A Midsummer Night's Dream*." *Bell's Edition of Shakespeare's Plays*. Vol. 8. 1774. Rpt. London: Cornmarket, 1969. 137.

Gervinus, G.G. "Second Period of Shakspeare's Dramatic Poetry: *Midsummer-Night's Dream*." *Shakespeare Commentaries*. Trans. F.E. Bunnètt. Rev. ed. 1877. Rpt. New York: AMS, 1971. 187-203.

[Gildon, Charles.] "Remarks on the Plays of Shakespear," in *The Works of Mr. William Shakespear*, Vol. 7. 1710. Rpt. New York: AMS Press, 1967. 257-444.

Girard, René. "Myth and Ritual in Shakespeare: *A Midsummer Night's Dream*." *Textual Strategies: Perspectives in Post-Structuralist Criticism*. Ed. Josué V. Harari. Ithaca: Cornell University Press, 1979. 189-212.

Goddard, Harold C. "*A Midsummer-Night's Dream.*" *The Meaning of Shakespeare.* 2 vols. Chicago: University of Chicago Press, 1951. 1: 74-80.

Goldstein, Melvin. "Identity Crises in a Midsummer Nightmare: Comedy as Terror in Disguise." *Psychoanalytic Review* 60 (1973): 169-204.

Granville-Barker, Harley. "Preface to *A Midsummer Night's Dream* [1924]." *More Prefaces to Shakespeare.* Ed. Edward M. Moore. Princeton: Princeton University Press, 1974. 94-134.

Green, Douglas E. "Preposterous Pleasures: Queer Theories and *A Midsummer Night's Dream.*" *A Midsummer Night's Dream: Critical Essays.* Ed. Dorothea Kehler.

Green, Roger Lancelyn. "Shakespeare and the Fairies." *Folklore* 73 (Summer 1962): 89-103.

Greenfield, Thelma N. "*A Midsummer Night's Dream* and *The Praise of Folly.*" *Comparative Literature* 20 (1968): 236-44.

———. "Our Nightly Madness: Shakespeare's *Dream* Without *The Interpretation of Dreams.*" *A Midsummer Night's Dream: Critical Essays.* Ed. Dorothea Kehler.

Greer, Germaine. "Love and the Law." *Politics, Power, and Shakespeare.* Ed. Frances McNeely Leonard. Arlington: Texas Humanities Research Center, 1981. 29-45.

Gui, Weston A. "Bottom's Dream." *American Imago* 9 (1952): 251-305.

Guntner, Lawrence. "Brecht and Beyond: Shakespeare on the East German Stage." *Foreign Shakespeare: Contemporary Performance.* Ed. Dennis Kennedy. 109-39.

Halio, Jay L. *A Midsummer Night's Dream.* Shakespeare in Performance. Manchester: Manchester University Press, 1994.

———. "Nightingales That Roar: The Language of *A Midsummer Night's Dream.*" *Traditions and Innovations: Essays on British Literature of the Middle Ages and the Renaissance.* Ed. David G. Allen and Robert A. White. Newark: University of Delaware Press, 1990. 137-49.

Hall, Kim E. *Things of Darkness: Economies of Race and Gender in Early Modern England.* Ithaca: Cornell University Press, 1995. 1-24, esp. 22-24.

Halliwell[-Phillipps], James Orchard. "Introduction—Title—Anachronisms." *An Introduction to Shakespeare's "Midsummer Night's Dream."* London: William Pickering, 1841. 1-5.

Hassel, Jr., R. Chris. "'Most Rare Vision': Faith in *A Midsummer Night's Dream*." *Faith and Folly in Shakespeare's Romantic Comedies*. Athens: University of Georgia Press, 1980. 52-76.

Hawkes, Terence. "By." *Meaning by Shakespeare*. London: Routledge, 1992. 1-10.

———. "Comedy, Orality, and Duplicity: *A Midsummer Night's Dream* and *Twelfth Night*." *New York Literary Forum* 5-6 (1978): 155-63.

———. "Or." *Meaning by Shakespeare*. 11-41.

Hazlitt, William. "*The Midsummer Night's Dream*." *The Round Table* [and] *Characters of Shakespear's Plays & Lectures on the English Poets*. 1817. Rpt. London: J.W. Dent, 1960. 244-48.

Hemingway, Samuel B. "The Relation of *A Midsummer Night's Dream* to *Romeo and Juliet*." *Modern Language Notes* 26.3 (1911): 78-80.

Hendricks, Margo. "'Obscured by Dreams': Race, Empire, and Shakespeare's *A Midsummer Night's Dream*." *Shakespeare Quarterly* 47 (1996): 37-60.

Herbert, T. Walter. *Oberon's Mazéd World: A Judicious Young Elizabethan Contemplates "A Midsummer Night's Dream" with a Mind Shaped by the Learning of Christendom Modified by the New Naturalist Philosophy and Excited by the Vision of a Rich, Powerful England*. Baton Rouge: Louisiana State University Press, 1977.

Hinely, Jan Lawson. "Expounding the Dream: Shaping Fantasies in *A Midsummer Night's Dream*." *Psychoanalytic Approaches to Literature and Film*. Ed. Maurice Charney and Joseph Reppen. Rutherford, NJ: Fairleigh Dickinson University Press, 1987. 120-38.

Hodgdon, Barbara. "Gaining a Father: The Role of Egeus in the Quarto and the Folio." *Review of English Studies* n.s.37 (1986): 534-42.

Holland, Norman N. "Hermia's Dream." *Annual of Psychoanalysis* 7 (1979): 369-89. Rpt. in *Representing Shakespeare: New Psychoanalytic Essays*. Ed. Murray M. Schwartz and Coppélia Kahn. Baltimore: Johns Hopkins University Press, 1980. 1-20.

Holland, Peter. "Introduction." *A Midsummer Night's Dream*. Ed. Holland. Oxford: Oxford University Press, 1995. 1-117.

Homan, Sidney R. "The Single World of *A Midsummer Night's Dream*." *Bucknell Review* 17.1 (1969): 72-84.

Howard, Skiles. "Hands, Feet, and Bottoms: Decentering the Cosmic Dance in *A Midsummer Night's Dream*." *Shakespeare Quarterly* 44 (1993): 325-42.

Hudson, H.N., Rev. "Shakespeare's Characters: *A Midsummer Night's Dream*." *Shakespeare: His Life, Art, and Characters*. Rev. ed. Vol. 1. 1872. Rpt. New York: Haskell House, 1970. 259-75.

Hunt, Maurice. "*The Countess of Pembroke's Arcadia*, Shakespeare's *A Midsummer Night's Dream*, and the School of Night: An Intertextual Nexus." *Essays in Literature* 23.1 (1996): 3-20.

――――. "The Voices of *A Midsummer Night's Dream*." *Texas Studies in Literature and Language* 34 (1992): 18-38.

Hunter, G.K. *Shakespeare: The Later Comedies*. Writers and Their Works, 143. London: Longmans, Green, 1962.

Huston, J. Dennis. "Parody and Play in *A Midsummer Night's Dream*." *Shakespeare's Comedies of Play*. New York: Columbia University Press, 1981. 94-121.

Jacobson, Gerald F. "A Note on Shakespeare's *Midsummer Night's Dream*." *American Imago* 19 (1962): 21-26.

Kavanagh, James H. "Shakespeare in Ideology." *Alternative Shakespeares*. Ed. John Drakakis. London: Methuen, 1985. 144-65.

Kehler, Dorothea. "Marion McClinton's *A Midsummer Night's Dream* at the La Jolla Playhouse, 1995: Appropriation Through Performance." *A Midsummer Night's Dream: Critical Essays*. Ed. Dorothea Kehler.

――――, ed. *A Midsummer Night's Dream: Critical Essays*. New York: Garland, 1997.

Kennedy, Dennis. *Looking at Shakespeare: A Visual History of Twentieth-Century Performance*. Cambridge: Cambridge University Press, 1993.

――――., ed. *Foreign Shakespeare: Contemporary Performance*. Cambridge: Cambridge University Press, 1993.

Kermode, Frank. "The Mature Comedies." *Early Shakespeare*. Ed. John Russell Brown and Bernard Harris. Stratford-upon-Avon Studies 3. London: Edward Arnold, 1961. 211-27.

Knight, Charles. "*A Midsummer-Night's Dream*." *Studies of Shakspere: Forming a Companion Volume. . . .* London: Charles Knight, 1849. 207-13.

Knight, G. Wilson. "The Romantic Comedies." *The Shakespearian Tempest*. Oxford: Oxford University Press, 1932. 75-168.

Kott, Jan. "The Bottom Translation." Trans. Daniela Miedzyrzecka. *Assays: Critical Approaches to Medieval and Renaissance Texts*. Vol. I. Ed. Peggy A. Knapp and Michael A. Stugrin. Pittsburgh: University of Pittsburgh Press, 1981. 117-49.

――――. "Titania and the Ass's Head." *Shakespeare Our Contemporary*. Trans. Boleslaw Taborski. 1964. Rpt. New York: Norton, 1974. 213-36.

Krieger, Elliot. "*A Midsummer Night's Dream*." *A Marxist Study of Shakespeare's Comedies*. New York: Barnes & Noble, 1979. 37-69.

Lamb, M.E. "*A Midsummer Night's Dream*: The Myth of Theseus and the Minotaur." *Texas Studies in Literature and Language* 21 (1979): 478-91.

Latham, Minor White. *The Elizabethan Fairies: The Fairies of Folklore and the Fairies of Shakespeare*. New York: Columbia University Press, 1930. Rpt. New York: Octagon, 1972.

Leggatt, Alexander. "*A Midsummer Night's Dream*." *Shakespeare's Comedy of Love*. London: Methuen, 1974. 89-115.

Leinwand, Theodore B. "'I Believe We Must Leave the Killing Out': Deference and Accommodation in *A Midsummer Night's Dream*." *Renaissance Papers 1986*. 11-30.

Leiter, Samuel L., ed. *Shakespeare Around the Globe: A Guide to Notable Postwar Revivals*. New York: Greenwood, 1986.

Logan, Robert A. "[Kenneth Branagh's] *A Midsummer Night's Dream* and *King Lear*," *MSAN: Marlowe Society of America Newsletter* 10.2 (Fall 1990): 5-7.

Loney, Glenn, ed. *Peter Brook's Production of William Shakespeare's "A Midsummer Night's Dream" for The Royal Shakespeare Company*. Chicago: Dramatic Publishing Company, 1974.

Long, John H. "*A Midsummer Night's Dream*." *Shakespeare's Use of Music: A Study of the Music and Its Performance in the Original Production of Seven Comedies*. Gainesville: University of Florida Press, 1955. 82-104.

Lull, Janis. "Textual Theory, Literary Interpretation, and the Last Act of *A Midsummer Night's Dream*." *A Midsummer Night's Dream: Critical Essays*. Ed. Dorothea Kehler.

MacOwan, Michael. "The Sad Case of Professor Kott." *Drama* 88 (Spring 1968): 30-37.

[Maginn, William.] "Characters in the Plays—Bottom, the Weaver." *The Shakespeare Papers of the Late William Maginn, LL.D.* Ed. Shelton Mackenzie. New York: Redfield, 1856. 85-104.

Maher, Mary Z. "*A Midsummer Night's Dream*: Nightmare or Gentle Snooze?" *A Midsummer Night's Dream: Critical Essays*. Ed. Dorothea Kehler.

Malone, Edmond. "An Attempt to Ascertain the Order in Which the Plays of Shakspeare Were Written: *A Midsummer-Night's Dream*." *The Plays and Poems of William Shakspeare*. Vol. 2. 1821. Rpt. New York: AMS, 1966. 333-40.

Marcus, Mordecai. "*A Midsummer Night's Dream*: The Dialectic of Eros-Thanatos." *American Imago* 38.3 (1981): 269-78.

Marowitz, Charles. "Seeds of 'Verfremdung' in *A Midsummer Night's Dream*." *Recycling Shakespeare*. 74-76.

————. *Recycling Shakespeare*. New York: Applause/Theatre Book, 1991.

Marshall, David. "Exchanging Visions: Reading *A Midsummer Night's Dream*." *ELH* 49 (1982): 543-75.

McDonald, Marcia. "Bottom's Space: Historicizing Comic Theory and Practice in *A Midsummer Night's Dream*." *Acting Funny: Comic Theory and Practice in Shakespeare's Plays*. Rutherford: Fairleigh Dickinson University Press, 1994. 85-108.

McFarland, Thomas. "And All Things Shall Be Peace: The Happiness of *A Midsummer Night's Dream*." *Shakespeare's Pastoral Comedy*. Chapel Hill: University of North Carolina Press, 1972. 78-97.

McGuire, Philip C. "Egeus and the Implications of Silence." *Shakespeare and the Sense of Performance: Essays in the Tradition of Performance Criticism in Honor of Bernard Beckerman*. Ed. Marvin and Ruth Thompson. Newark: University of Delaware Press, 1989. 103-15.

Mebane, John S. "Structure, Source, and Meaning in *A Midsummer Night's Dream*. *Texas Studies in Literature and Language* 24 (1982): 255-70.

Merchant, W. Moelwyn. "*A Midsummmer Night's Dream*: A Visual Re-creation." *Early Shakespeare*. Ed. John Russell Brown and Bernard Harris. Stratford-upon-Avon Studies 3. London: Edward Arnold, 1961. 164-85.

Miller, Donald C. "Titania and the Changeling." *English Studies* 22 (1940): 66-70.

Miller, Ronald F. "*A Midsummer Night's Dream*: The Fairies, Bottom, and the Mystery of Things." *Shakespeare Quarterly* 26 (1975): 254-68.

Moisan, Thomas. "Antique Fables, Fairy Toys: Elisions, Allusion, and Translation in *A Midsummer Night's Dream*." *A Midsummer Night's Dream: Critical Essays*. Ed. Dorothea Kehler.

————. "Chaucerian *Solempnytee* and the Illusion of Order in Shakespeare's Athens and Verona." *Upstart Crow* 7 (1987): 36-49.

Montrose, Louis Adrian. "A Kingdom of Shadows." *The Theatrical City: Culture, Theatre, and Politics in London 1576-1649*. Ed. David L. Smith, Richard Strier, and David Bevington. New York: Cambridge University Press, 1995. 68-86.

————. *The Purpose of Playing: Shakespeare and the Cultural Politics of the Elizabethan Theatre*. Chicago: University of Chicago Press, 1996.

————. "'Shaping Fantasies': Figurations of Gender and Power in Elizabethan Culture." *Representations* 1.2 (1983): 61-94.

Moore, Lisa J. "Transposing Helena to Form and Dignity." *A Midsummer Night's Dream: Critical Essays*. Ed. Dorothea Kehler.

Mowat, Barbara A. "'A Local Habitation and a Name': Shakespeare's Text as Construct." *Style* 23 (1989): 335-51.

Muir, Kenneth. "*A Midsummer Night's Dream.*" *Shakespeare's Sources. I. Comedies and Tragedies.* London: Methuen, 1961. 31-47.

Nemerov, Howard. "The Marriage of Theseus and Hippolyta." *Kenyon Review* 18 (1956): 633-41.

Nevo, Ruth. "Fancy's Images." *Comic Transformations in Shakespeare.* London: Methuen, 1980. 96-114.

Odell, George C.D. *Shakespeare: From Betterton to Irving.* 2 vols. 1920. Rpt. New York: Benjamin Blom, 1963.

Olson, Paul A. "*A Midsummer Night's Dream* and the Meaning of Court Marriage." *ELH* 24 (1957): 95-119.

Ormerod, David. "*A Midsummer Night's Dream*: The Monster in the Labyrinth." *Shakespeare Studies* 11 (1978): 39-52.

Palmer, John. "Bottom." *Comic Characters of Shakespeare.* London: Macmillan, 1946. 92-109.

Paolucci, Anne. "The Lost Days in *A Midsummer Night's Dream.*" *Shakespeare Quarterly* 28 (1977): 317-26.

Parker, Patricia. "'Rude Mechanicals': *A Midsummer Night's Dream* and Shakespearean Joinery." *Shakespeare from the Margins: Language, Culture, Context.* Chicago: University of Chicago Press, 1996. 83-115.

————. "Teaching and Wordplay: The 'Wall' of *A Midsummer Night's Dream.*" *Teaching with Shakespeare: Critics in the Classroom.* Ed. Bruce McIver and Ruth Stevenson. Newark: University of Delaware Press, 1994. 205-14 and 217-21.

Parrott, Thomas Marc. "Apprentice Work." *Shakespearean Comedy.* Oxford: Oxford University Press, 1949. 100-33.

Patterson, Annabel. "Bottoms Up: Festive Theory in *A Midsummer Night's Dream.*" *Renaissance Papers 1988*: 25-39.

Pearson, D'Orsay W. "Male Sovereignty, Harmony and Irony in *A Midsummer Night's Dream.*" *Upstart Crow* 7 (1987): 24-35.

————. "'Unkinde' Theseus: A Study in Renaissance Mythography." *English Literary Renaissance* 4.2 (1974): 276-98.

[Pepys, Samuel.] "29 September 1662." *The Diary of Samuel Pepys.* Ed. Robert Latham and William Matthews. Berkeley: University of California Press, 1970. 3: 208.

Pettet, E.C. "Shakespeare's Detachment from Romance." *Shakespeare and the Romance Tradition.* London: Staples, 1949. 101-35.

Phialas, Peter G. "*A Midsummer Night's Dream.*" *Shakespeare's Romantic Comedies: The Development of Their Form and Meaning.* Chapel Hill: University of North Carolina Press, 1966. 102-33.

Priestly, J.B. "Bully Bottom." *The English Comic Characters.* London: Bodley Head, 1925. 1-17.

Reid, Robert L. "The Fairy Queen: Gloriana or Titania?" *Upstart Crow* 13 (1993): 16-32.

Richmond, Hugh M. "Bottom as Romeo." *Shakespeare's Sexual Comedy: A Mirror for Lovers.* Indianapolis: Bobbs-Merrill, 1971. 102-22.

————. "Shaping a Dream." *Shakespeare Studies* 17 (1985): 49-60.

Rickert, Edith. "Political Propaganda and Satire in *A Midsummer Night's Dream.*" *Modern Philology* 21 (1923-24): 53-87, 133-54.

Riemer, A.P. "Emblems of Art." *Antic Fables: Patterns of Evasion in Shakespeare's Comedies.* New York: St. Martin's, 1980. 193-228.

Robinson, James E. "The Ritual and Rhetoric of *A Midsummer Night's Dream.*" *PMLA* 83 (1968): 380-91.

Robinson, J.W. "Palpable Hot Ice: Dramatic Burlesque in *A Midsummer Night's Dream.*" *Studies in Philology* 61 (1964): 192-204.

Rose, Mark. *Shakespearean Design.* Cambridge, MA: Belknap Press of Harvard University Press, 1972.

Rosenblum, Joseph. *Shakespeare: An Annotated Bibliography.* Pasadena, CA: Salem Press, 1992.

Russell, Thomas W., III. "The Renaissance Theatre Company in Los Angeles, 1990." *Shakespeare Quarterly* 41 (1990): 502-07.

Schanzer, Ernest. "The Central Theme of *A Midsummer Night's Dream.*" *University of Toronto Quarterly* 20 (1951): 233-38.

————. "The Moon and the Fairies in *A Midsummer Night's Dream,*" *University of Toronto Quarterly* 24 (1955): 234-46.

Schlegel, Augustus William, "Criticisms on Shakspeare's Comedies." *A Course of Lectures on Dramatic Art and Literature.* Ed. Rev. A.J.W. Morrison. Trans. John Black. Rev. ed. London: Henry G. Bohn, 1846. 379-99.

Schleiner, Winfried. "Imaginative Sources for Shakespeare's Puck." *Shakespeare Quarterly* 36 (1985): 65-68.

Schneider, Michael. "Bottom's Dream, the Lion's Roar, and Hostility of Class Difference in *A Midsummer Night's Dream.*" *From the Bard to Broadway.* Ed. Karelisa V. Hartigan. Lanham, MD: University Press of America, 1987. 191-212.

Selbourne, David. *The Making of "A Midsummer Night's Dream": An Eye-Witness Account of Peter Brook's Production from First Rehearsal to First Night.* London: Methuen, 1982.

Sewell, Elizabeth. *The Orphic Voice: Poetry and Natural History.* New Haven: Yale University Press, 1960 [publisher's errata correction, 1961]. 53-168.

[Shakespeare, William.] *"A Midsummer Night's Dream." The Riverside Shakespeare.* Ed. G. Blakemore Evans. Boston: Houghton Mifflin, 1974. 217-49.

Shakespearean Criticism: Excerpts from the Criticism of William Shakespeare's Plays and Poetry, from the First Published Appraisals to Current Evaluations. Detroit: Gale, 1982—. Vols. 3 (1984) and 12 (1991).

Sidgwick, Frank. Introduction. *The Sources and Analogues of "A Midsummer-Night's Dream."* Comp. Frank Sidgwick. London: Chatto and Windus, 1908. 1-68.

Siegel, Paul N. *"A Midsummer Night's Dream* and the Wedding Guests." *Shakespeare Quarterly* 4 (1953): 139-44.

Simon, John. "Spring 1971." *Uneasy Stages: A Chronicle of the New York Theater, 1963-73.* New York: Random House, 1975. 313-38.

Sinfield, Alan. *Faultlines: Cultural Materialism and the Politics of Dissident Reading.* Berkeley: University of California Press, 1992.

Slights, William W.E. "The Changeling in a *Dream." Studies in English Literature* 28 (1988): 259-72.

Snider, Denton J. *"Midsummer Night's Dream." The Shakespearian Drama: A Commentary: The Comedies.* 1887. Rpt. n.pl.: Literary School Edition, 1892. 378-427.

Stansbury, Joan. "Characterization of the Four Young Lovers in *A Midsummer Night's Dream." Shakespeare Survey* 35 (1982): 57-63.

Stroup, Thomas B. "Bottom's Name and His Epiphany." *Shakespeare Quarterly* 29 (1978): 79-82.

Taylor, Anthony Brian. "Golding's Ovid, Shakespeare's 'Small Latin,' and the Real Object of Mockery in *Pyramus and Thisbe." Shakespeare Survey* 42 (1990): 53-64.

Taylor, Michael. "The Darker Purpose of *A Midsummer Night's Dream." Studies in English Literature 1500-1900* 9 (1969): 259-73.

Taylor, Neil. "Finde out moone-shine, Finde out moone-shine." *Notes and Queries* 216 (1971): 134-36.

Traub, Valerie. "The (In)Significance of 'Lesbian' Desire in Early Modern England." *Erotic Politics: Desire on the Renaissance Stage.* Ed. Susan Zimmerman. New York: Routledge, 1992. 150-69.

Trewin, J.C. *Shakespeare on the English Stage: 1900-1964.* London, Barrie and Rockliff, 1964.

Ulrici, Hermann. *"Midsummer Night's Dream." Shakspeare's Dramatic Art: And His Relation to Calderon and Goethe.* [Trans. A.J.W. Morrison.] London: Chapman, Brothers, 1846. 270-75.

Van Doren, Mark. *"A Midsummer Night's Dream." Shakespeare.* New York: Henry Holt, 1939. 76-83.

Vickers, Brian. "From Clown to Character." *The Artistry of Shakespeare's Prose.* London: Methuen, 1968. 52-88.

Vyvyan, John. *Shakespeare and Platonic Beauty.* London: Chatto and Windus, 1961.

Warren, Roger. *"A Midsummer Night's Dream": Text and Performance.* London: Macmillan, 1983.

Watkins, Ronald, and Jeremy Lemmon. *In Shakespeare's Playhouse. A Midsummer Night's Dream.* Totowa, NJ: Rowman and Littlefield, 1974.

Weil, Herbert S. "Comic Structure and Tonal Manipulation in Shakespeare and Some Modern Plays." *Shakespeare Survey* 22 (1969): 27-33.

Weiner, Andrew D. "'Multiformitie Uniforme': *A Midsummer Night's Dream.*" *ELH* 38 (1971): 329-49.

Weller, Barry. "Identity Dis-figured: *A Midsummer Night's Dream.*" *Kenyon Review* 7.3 (1985): 66-78.

Welsford, Enid. "The Masque Transmuted." *The Court Masque: A Study in the Relationship Between Poetry & the Revels.* Cambridge: Cambridge University Press, 1927. 324-49.

Wilders, John. "Teaching *A Midsummer Night's Dream.*" *Teaching with Shakespeare: Critics in the Classroom.* Ed. Bruce McIver and Ruth Stevenson. Newark: University of Delaware Press, 1994. 152-65.

Willson, Robert F., Jr. "God's Secrets and Bottom's Name: A Reply." *Shakespeare Quarterly* 30 (1979): 407-08.

Wilson, John Dover. "The Copy for *A Midsummer Night's Dream.*" *A Midsummer-Night's Dream.* Ed. Arthur Quiller-Couch and John Dover Wilson. *The New Cambridge Shakespeare.* Cambridge: Cambridge University Press, 1924. 77-100.

Wilson, Richard. "The Kindly Ones: The Death of the Author in Shakespearean Athens." *Essays & Studies* 46 (1993): 1-24.

Woodbridge, Linda. *Shakespeare: A Selective Bibliography of Modern Criticism.* West Cornwall, CT: Locust Hill Press, 1988.

Wyrick, Deborah Baker. "The Ass Motif in *The Comedy of Errors* and *A Midsummer Night's Dream.*" *Shakespeare Quarterly* 33 (1982): 432-48.

Young, David P. *Something of Great Constancy: The Art of "A Midsummer Night's Dream."* New Haven: Yale University Press, 1966.

Zimbardo, R.A. "Regeneration and Reconciliation in *A Midsummer Night's Dream.*" *Shakespeare Studies: An Annual Gathering of Research, Criticism, and Reviews* 6 (1970): 35-50.

Zitner, Sheldon P. "The Worlds of *A Midsummer Night's Dream.*" *South Atlantic Quarterly* 59 (1960): 397-403.

A Midsummer Night's Dream*

Mark Van Doren

"A Midsummer Night's Dream" shines like "Romeo and Juliet" in darkness, but shines merrily. Lysander, one of the two nonentities who are its heroes, complains at the beginning about the brevity of love's course, and sums up his complaint with a line which would not be out of place in "Romeo and Juliet":

> So quick bright things come to confusion. (I, i, 149)[+]

This, however, is at the beginning. Bright things will come to clarity in a playful, sparkling night while fountains gush and spangled starlight betrays the presence in a wood near Athens of magic persons who can girdle the earth in forty minutes and bring any cure for human woe. Nor will the woe to be cured have any power to elicit our anxiety. The four lovers whose situation resembles so closely the situation created in "The Two Gentlemen of Verona" will come nowhere near the seriousness of that predicament; they will remain to the end four automatic creatures whose artificial and pretty fate it is to fall in and out of love like dolls, and like dolls they will go to sleep as soon as they are laid down. There will be no pretense that reason and love keep company, or that because they do not death lurks at the horizon. There is no death in "A Midsummer Night's Dream," and the smiling horizon is immeasurably remote.

Robin Goodfellow ends the extravaganza with an apology to the audience for the "weak and idle theme" with which it has been entertained. And Theseus, in honor of whose marriage with Hippolyta the entire action is occurring, dismisses most of it as a fairy toy, or such an airy nothing as some poet might give a local habitation and a name (V, i, 17). But Robin is wrong about the theme, and Theseus does not describe the kind of poet Shakespeare is. For the world of this play is both veritable and large. It is not the tiny toy-shop that most such spectacles present, with quaint little people scampering on dry little errands, and with small music squeaking somewhere a childish accompaniment. There is room here for mortals no less than for fairies; both classes are at home, both groups move freely in a wide world where indeed they seem sometimes to have exchanged functions with one another. For these fairies do not sleep on flowers. Only Hermia can remember lying upon faint primrose-beds (I, i, 215), and only Bottom in the action as we have it ever dozes on pressed posies (III, i, 162). The fairies themselves—Puck, Titania, Oberon—are too busy for that, and too hard-minded. The vocabulary of Puck is the most vernacular in the play; he talks of beans and crabs, dew-laps and ale, three-foot stools and sneezes (II, i, 42–57). And with the king and queen of fairy-land he has immense spaces to travel. The three of them are citizens of all the universe there is, and as we listen to them the farthest portions of this universe stretch out, distant and glittering, like facets on a gem of infinite size. There is a specific geography, and the heavens are cold and high.

> *Oberon.*   Thou rememb'rest
>   Since once I sat upon a promontory,
>   And heard a mermaid on a dolphin's back
>   Uttering such dulcet and harmonious breath
>   That the rude sea grew civil at her song,
>   And certain stars shot madly from their spheres,
>   To hear the sea-maids's music?
> *Robin.*   I remember.
> *Oberon.* That very time I saw, but thou couldst not,
>   Flying between the cold moon and the earth,
>   Cupid all arm'd. A certain aim he took
>   At a fair vestal throned by the west,
>   And loos'd his love-shaft smartly from his bow,
>   As it should pierce a hundred thousand hearts;
>   But I might sees young Cupid's fiery shaft
>   Quench'd in the chaste beams of the watery moon,
>   And the imperial votaress passed on,

> In maiden meditation, fancy-free.
> Yet mark'd I where the bolt of Cupid fell.
> It fell upon a little western flower. . . .
> Fetch me that flower, the herb I shew'd thee once. . . .
> Fetch me this herb; and be thou here again
> Ere the leviathan can swim a league.
>
> *Robin.* I'll put a girdle round about the earth
> In forty minutes. (II, i, 148–76)

The business may be trivial, but the world is as big and as real as any world
we know. The promontory long ago; the rude sea that grew—not smooth,
not gentle, not anything pretty or poetical, but (the prosaic word is one of
Shakespeare's best) civil; the mermaid that is also a sea-maid; the direction
west; and the cold watery moon that rides so high above the earth—these
are the signs of its bigness, and they are so clear that we shall respect the
prowess implied in Robin's speed, nor shall we fail to be impressed by the
news that Oberon has just arrived from the farthest steep of India (II, i, 69).

Dr. Johnson and Hazlitt copied Addison in saying that if there could be
persons like these they would act like this. Their tribute was to the
naturalness of Shakespeare's super-nature. Dryden's tribute to its charm:

> But Shakespeare's magic could not copied be;
> Within that circle none durst walk but he

has an identical source: wonder that such things can be at all, and be so
genuine. The explanation is the size and concreteness of Shakespeare's
setting. And the key to the structure of that setting is the watery moon to
which Oberon so casually referred.

The poetry of the play is dominated by the words moon and water.
Theseus and Hippolyta carve the moon in our memory with the strong,
fresh strokes of their opening dialogue:

> *Theseus.*Now, fair Hippolyta, our nuptial hour
> Draws on apace. Four happy days bring in
> Another moon; but, O, methinks, how slow
> This old moon wanes! She lingers my desires,
> Like to a step-dame or a dowager

> Long withering out a young man's revenue.
> *Hippolyta.*Four days will quickly steep themselves in night;
>   Four nights will quickly dream away the time;
>   And then the moon, like to a silver bow
>   New-bent in heaven, shall behold the night
>   Of our solemnities.

This is not the sensuous, softer orb of "Antony and Cleopatra," nor is it the sweet sleeping friend of Lorenzo and Jessica. It is brilliant and brisk, silver-distant, and an occasion for comedy in Theseus's worldly thought. Later on in the same scene he will call it cold and fruitless (73), and Lysander will look forward to

> Tomorrow night, when Phoebe doth behold
> Her silver visage in the watery glass,
> Decking with liquid pearl the bladed grass. (I, I, 209-11)

Lysander has connected the image of the moon with the image of cool water on which it shines, and hereafter they will be inseparable. "A Midsummer Night's Dream" is drenched with dew when it is not saturated with rain. A film of water spreads over it, enhances and enlarges it miraculously. The fairy whom Robin hails as the second act opens wanders swifter than the moon's sphere through fire and flood. The moon, says Titania, is governess of floods, and in anger at Oberon's brawls has sucked up from the sea contagious fogs, made every river overflow, drowned the fields and rotted the green corn:

> The nine men's morris is fill'd up with mud,
> And the quaint mazes in the wanton green
> For lack of tread are undistinguishable. (II, 1, 98–100)

Here in the west there has been a deluge, and every object still drips moisture. But even in the east there are waves and seas. The little changeling boy whom Titania will not surrender to Oberon is the son of a votaress on the other side of the earth:

> And, in the spiced Indian air, by night,
> Full often hath she gossip'd by my side,
> And sat with me on Neptune's yellow sands,

Marking the embarked traders on the flood. (II, i, 124–7)

The jewels she promises Bottom will be fetched "from the deep" (III,I,161). And Oberon is addicted to treading seaside groves

> Even till the eastern gate, all fiery-red,
> Opening on Neptune with fair blessed beams,
> Turns into yellow gold his salt green streams. (III, ii, 391–3)

So by a kind of logic the mortals of the play continue to be washed with copious weeping. The roses in Hermia's cheeks fade fast "for want of rain" (I, i, 130), but rain will come. Demetrius "hails" and "showers" oaths on Helena (I, i, 245), whose eyes are bathed with salt tears (II, ii, 92–3); and Hermia takes comfort in the tempest of her eyes (I, i, 131).

When the moon weeps, says Titania to Bottom, "weeps every little flower" (III, i, 204). The flowers of "A Midsummer Night's Dream" are not the warm, sweet, dry ones of Perdita's garden, or even the day-time ones with which Fidele's brothers will strew her forest grave. They are the damp flowers that hide among ferns and drip with dew. A pearl is hung in every cowslip's ear (II, i, 15); the little western flower which Puck is sent to fetch is rich with juice; and luscious woodbine canopies the bank of wild thyme where Titania sleeps—not on but "in" musk-roses and eglantine. Moon, water, and wet flowers conspire to extend the world of "A Midsummer Night's Dream" until it is as large as all imaginable life. That is why the play is both so natural and so mysterious.

Nor do its regions fail to echo with an ample music. The mermaid on the promontory with her dulcet and harmonious breath sang distantly and long ago, but the world we walk in is filled with present sound.

> *Theseus.* Go, one of you, find out the forester,
> For now our observation is perform'd,
> And since we have the vaward of the day,
> My love shall hear the music of my hounds.
> Uncouple in the western valley, let them go.
> Dispatch, I say, and find the forester.
> We will, fair queen, up to the mountain's top
> And mark the musical confusion
> Of hounds and echo in conjunction.
> *Hippolyta.* I was with Hercules and Cadmus once,

When in a wood of Crete they bay'd the bear
With hounds of Sparta. Never did I hear
Such gallant chiding; for, besides the groves,
The skies, the fountains, every region near
Seem'd all one mutual cry. I never heard
So musical a discord, such sweet thunder.
Theseus. My hounds are bred out of the Spartan kind,
So flew'd, so sanded, and their heads are hung
With ears that sweep away the morning dew;
Crook-knee'd, and dew-lapped like Thessalian bulls;
Slow in pursuit, but match'd in mouth like bells,
Each under each. A cry more tuneable
Was never holla'd to, nor cheer'd with horn,
In Crete, in Sparta, nor in Thessaly.
Judge when you hear. (IV, i, 107–31)

Had Shakespeare written nothing else than this he still might be the best of English poets. Most poetry which tries to be music also is less than poetry. This is absolute. The melody which commences with such spirit in Theseus's fifth line has already reached the complexity of counterpoint in his eight and ninth; Hippolyta carries it to a like limit in the line with which she closes; and Theseus, taking it back from her, hugely increases its volume, first by reminding us that the hounds have form and muscle, and then by daring the grand dissonance, the mixed thunder, of bulls and bells. The passage sets a forest ringing, and supplies a play with the music it has deserved.

But Shakespeare is still more a poet because the passage is incidental to his creation. The creation with which he is now busy is not a passage, a single effect; it is a play, and though this one contribution has been mighty there are many others. And none of the others is mightier than bully Bottom's.

Bottom likes music too. "I have a reasonable good ear," he tells Titania. "Let's have the tongs and the bones." So does he take an interest in moonshine, if only among the pages of an alamanac. "A calendar, a calendar!" he calls. "Find out moonshine, find out moonshine." When they find the moon, those Athenian mechanics of whom he is king, it has in it what the cold fairy moon cannot be conceived as having, the familiar man of folklore. Bottom and his fellows domesticate the moon, as they domesticate every other element of which Shakespeare has made poetry.

And the final effect is parody. Bottom's amazed oration concerning his dream follows hard upon the lovers' discourse concerning dreams and delusions; but it is in prose, and the speaker is utterly literal when he pronounces that it will be called Bottom's dream because it hath no bottom (IV, 1, 220). Nor is the story of Pyramus and Thisbe as the mechanics act it anything but a burlesque of "Romeo and Juliet."

> O night, which ever art when day is not! . . .
> And thou, O wall, O sweet, O lovely wall,
> That stand'st between her father's ground and mine!
> Thou wall, O wall, O sweet and lovely wall. (V, i, 172–7)

Shakespeare has come, even this early, to the farthest limit of comedy. The end of comedy is self-parody, and its wisdom is self-understanding. Never again will he work without a full comprehension of the thing he is working at; of the probability that other and contrary things are of equal importance; of the certainty that his being a poet who can do anything he wants to do is not the only thing to be, or the best possible thing; of the axiom that the whole is greater than the part—the part in his instance being one play among many thinkable plays, or one man, himself, among the multitude that populate a world for whose size and variety he with such giants strides is reaching respect. Bully Bottom and his friends have lived three centuries to good purpose, but to no better purpose at any time than the one they first had—namely, in their sublime innocence, their earthbound, idiot openness and charity of soul, to bring it about that their creator should become not only the finest of poets but the one who makes the fewest claims for poetry.

NOTES

*Originally published in *Shakespeare* by Mark Van Doren (New York: Henry Holt, 1939). Reprinted with the kind permission of Charles Van Doren.

+ Editor's note: all citations are from the third edition of William Allan Neilson's text prepared for The Cambridge Poets, copyright by the Houghton Mifflin Company.

Imagination in
*A Midsummer Night's Dream**

R. W. Dent

For many years editors and critics have customarily praised *A Midsummer Night's Dream* for its artistic fusion of seemingly disparate elements. Sometimes the praise involves little, really, beyond admiring the skill with which Shakespeare interwove the actions of the four lovers, the fairies, and the mechanicals in the first four acts of the play.[1] Usually, quite properly, it moves somewhat beyond this, relating this interwoven action to the thematic treatment of love in the play. But such praise has rarely concerned itself with the play's fifth act; it has tended to treat *A Midsummer Night's Dream* as essentially complete in four acts, but with a fifth act somehow vaguely appropriate in mood and content to serve as a conclusion. *Pyramus and Thisbe*, that rude offering of the mechanicals, has been briefly commended as loosely paralleling in action and theme the problems of the four lovers, and as delightful enough in itself to need no other artistic justification. Despite the consistency with which *A Midsummer Night's Dream* has been admired for its unity, in short, few critics have had much to say about the whole of the play.

The present essay seeks to reexamine the degree and kind of unity achieved by *A Midsummer Night's Dream*. Without pretending to be strikingly original, it approaches the play from a somewhat different angle, suggesting that the heart of the comedy, its most pervasive unifying element, is the partially contrasting role of imagination in love and in art. I do not mean to suggest for a moment that Shakespeare composed this play, or any play, as the result of a single governing conception to which every detail can be effectively related. But I do mean to suggest that *A Midsummer Night's Dream* has a dominant and premeditated conception. Thus, if my argument below appears guilty of the "intentional fallacy", it is so intentionally. Shakespeare's eye, in creating *A Midsummer Night's Dream,* did not "roll" in a "fine frenzy", and my point on imagination's role in the play demands my emphasis.

A prefatory word is necessary. Oversimply, to the Elizabethan the imagination ideally functioned as an essential servant to the understanding, whether as a reporter (the most emphasized function, that of transmitting accurate images of sense data, present or absent) or as a creator or inventor. When, as too frequently happened, it became dominated by passions in conflict with reason, it became a false reporter and/or inventor. In the case of passionate love, for example, one could not say that the imagination actually caused love, but rather that love so influenced the imagination as to have it misreport what it saw, thereby heightening the passion, thereby heightening the imagination, thereby ... an endless chain reaction to man's ever-increasing peril. In watching the lovers of *A Midsummer Night's Dream*, we tend to be aware of the imagination's activity only when it is thus failing in its proper function. At such times we can scarcely attribute the folly to love or imagination alone, obviously; it derives from their interaction.

Nothing is more common than the observation that *A Midsummer Night's Dream* is a play "about love", about lovers' lunacy, where "reason and love keep little company together nowadays", where the follies of imagination-dominated Demetrius and Lysander are reduced to their essential absurdity by the passion of Titania for an ass. It is for the sake of this theme, surely, that Demetrius and Lysander are given so little distinctive characterization; they cannot contrast like a Claudius and a Benedick, so that a particular pairing of lovers is demanded by the characters of those involved. For the same reason, paradoxically, Hermia and Helena are differentiated, to heighten the puzzle of love's choices (as well as to increase the potentialities for comedy in the play's middle). By all conventional Elizabethan standards, tall fair gentle Helena should be the one pursued, and when Lysander eventually boasts his use of reason in preferring a dove to a raven his argument, by those standards, is indeed rational. Our laughter stems from recognizing that it is so only accidentally, as rationalization.

According to a good many critics, Shakespeare contrasts from the start the irrationality of the lovers with what these critics regard as the admirable rationality of Theseus-Hippolyta. The latter become a kind of ideal which the lovers approach by the end of the play. If so, the role of imagination in love is simple and obvious; it is a disrupting irrational influence which must eventually be purged, and will prove in simple and total contrast to the disciplined use of imagination essential to Shakespeare's art. But I cannot see that any contrast so mechanical as this is intended.

When, thanks to Dian's bud, Lysander returns to Hermia, his "true love", the return marks a release from dotage but no return to reason as such, any more than does Demetrius' return to Helena by the pansy-juice. Love's choices remain inexplicable, and the eventual pairings are determined only by the constancy of Helena and Hermia in their initial inexplicable choices. As so frequently in Shakespearian comedy, the men fluctuate before finally settling down to a constant attachment such as the heroines exhibit from the start. Men's "fancies are more giddy and unfirm, / More longing, wavering, sooner lost and won, / Than women's are."[2] In the case of true love, once stabilized—even as in the case of mere dotage—imagination cannot "form a shape, / Besides yourself to like of"[3]; it "carries no favour in't" but that of the beloved.[4] Unlike dotage, however, it is in no obvious conflict with reason, either in its object or its vehemence. By the end of the fourth act we are assured that Demetrius and Lysander have come to stability of this kind. But the terminus, I repeat, is not a rationally determined one. Like Theseus at the play's beginning, at the play's ending Demetrius and Lysander are settled. Jill has Jack, nought shall go back, and the prospect of happy marriage is before them all.

Thus in *A Midsummer Night's Dream* the origin of love never lies in reason. Love may be consistent with reason—e.g., Lysander is undeniably "a worthy gentleman"—and a healthy imagination, although influenced by love, will not glaringly rebel against reason. But as Hermia initially indicates, her choice is dictated not by her judgment but by her "eyes", by the vision of Lysander as her love-dictated imagination reports it. As Helena says at the close of this same introductory scene, love sees with that part of the mind that has no taste of judgment. Essentially this is as true for Hermia as for the others, although her choice conflicts with parental authority rather than with sound evaluation of her beloved's merits. Despite Egeus' initial disapproval, nevertheless, her choice is eventually confirmed. She is not compelled to "choose love by another's eyes" (I.i.140), to see with her father's judgment (as Theseus at first demanded; I.i.57), nor even to convert her love to one directed by her own judgment. Her love at the end is what it was at the beginning, with the obstacles removed.

Not even Egeus accuses her of dotage, although he does think her somehow "witched" in her refusal to accept his choice rather than her own. "Dotage", in this play, appears essentially reserved for two kinds of amorous excess approaching madness: the monomaniacal pursuit of an unrequited love (thus Helena "dotes in idolatry", Demetrius "dotes" on Hermia's eyes, and Lysander dotes for Helena in the night's comedy of errors), or the ridiculous bestowal of affection upon an obviously unworthy object (most grotesquely in Titania's passion for Bottom, but also in the gross excesses of Lysander and Demetrius during their "dream").[5]

In the middle of the play, then, when dotage grows most rampant, so too does imagination. The frenzied praises and dispraises of Lysander and Demetrius are exceeded only by Titania's infatuation for Bottom, her hearing beauty in his voice, seeing beauty in his ears, and so on. Were follies so excessive in the cases of the mortal lovers, we could never end as we do in marriage and lasting love. Yet by the end of Act IV, with all obstacles to happily paired marriages removed—no thanks to the behavior of the lovers—the lovers can sound, and behave, rationally enough. Their love, however, is in its essence as inexplicable as ever.

The inexplicability of love's choices was of course a favorite topic for discussion in the age and a favorite theme for Shakespearian comedy. Why should two particular people fall in love, often at first sight? Were they so destined by the stars, like Romeo and Juliet (but not Romeo and Rosaline)? Were they marked by peculiarly "correspondent qualyties of bloud"?[6]

To this question *A Midsummer Night's Dream* perhaps suggests no kind of answer beyond the fact that such true loves do exist, are distinct from the fancy-dominated aberrations that mark inconstancy, and when properly terminating in marriage are part of the natural—and, in that sense, rational—order of things. From the start of the play, the mystery of love's choices (including the attendant male inconstancies) is stressed. Egeus, at least metaphorically, thinks Hermia "witched", and all Elizabethans would be reminded of disputes on whether love could be caused by witchcraft, or by philtres and charms, whether naturally or supernaturally administered.[7] When the fairies first appear (in II.i), and before ever they become involved with the lovers, Shakespeare skillfully prepares us for their role. First, the inexplicable fortunes and misfortunes of housewives are attributed to Puck—this may well receive first mention because it is drawn from folklore, is familiar to the audience, and this allows the easiest transition into what follows. A few lines later, all the recently experienced disorders of the English-Athenian weather are similarly attributed to temporary discord in the fairy macrocosm:

> And this same progeny of evils comes
> From our debate, from our dissension. (II.i.115–116)

For this night on which we can see fairies, we are allowed to understand, playfully, the cause for otherwise unaccountable phenomena. It is in such a context, too, that we hear the play's only reference to Theseus' well-known infidelities preceding his "true love" marriage to Hippolyta; these too are charged to fairy influence (although Titania discounts the charge). In short, aspects of the inexplicable past, familiar to the audience, have been imaginatively explained as fairy-caused.

Within the play, thus far, we have one similarly puzzling phenomenon, Demetrius' desertion of Helena to pursue Hermia, as well as the less specific mystery of love's choices generally. We have by now a hint that such mysteries—at least that of Demetrius' infidelity—may be similarly explained. The play will never say, understandably. Instead it will allow us for one single night to witness, and thereby understand, "the mystery of things, / As if we were God's spies".

The magic charm by which love is to be manipulated on this single night is quite naturally a flower potion administered on the eyes.[8] From the play's beginning we are reminded of the commonplace that although the eyes are integrally involved in the process of inspiring and transmitting love, nevertheless "love sees not with the eyes"; instead, the eyes "see" what the lover's imagination dictates. In *A Midsummer Night's Dream*, at least, this imagination does not misreport sense data, except in the sense that it selects from those data and confers value accordingly. Hermia is never imagined as tall or blonde, Bottom as hairless. Titania was "enamoured of an ass", and knew it, but her selective imagination found beauty in its "fair large ears", "sleek smooth head", even in its voice. Love, via imagination, transposes "to form and dignity" by altering the normal evaluation, either in essence or in degree. At its extreme, it sees beauty where others see "things base and vile", thus finding "Helen's beauty in a brow of Egypt".[9] Conversely, it unwarrantedly makes "base and vile" whatever object love causes it to reject. That the potion should be applied to the eyes was inevitable.

The choice of flower for the potion was almost equally so. "Maidens call it love-in-idleness." Perhaps it is foolish to labor over the implications of a flower which the play avoids calling explicitly by its most familiar name. But surely most of the audience would recognize the flower as the pansy, and "That's for thoughts", as Ophelia says, as well as for relief of the heart. Cotgrave may remind us of some of the usual associations:

> *Pensée: f.* A thought, supposall, coniecture, surmise, cogitation,
> imagination; ones heart, mind, inward conceit, opinion, fancie,
> or iudgement; also, the flower Paunsie.
> *Menues pensées.* Paunsies, Harts-ease, loue or liue in idlenesse; also
> idle, priuate, or prettie thoughts.[10]

However, although as Friar Laurence says,

> O, mickle is the powerful grace that lies
> In plants, herbs, stones, and their true qualities,

the true dispenser of grace in *A Midsummer Night's Dream* is Oberon. The flower itself, wrongly applied by Puck, can make a hell of heaven rather than a heaven of hell. Both the mispairings and the eventual proper pairings of love, on this single night, we can witness as produced by fairy influence. Oberon wishes true loves properly paired, and eventually sees that they are. Puck, while not wilfully mistaking, can delight in the consequences of his error, and we do too—the follies of mispaired doting lovers, their excessive praises and dispraises, their broken friendships, even the threat of bloodshed—potential tragedy were it not for Oberon's protection, of which we are so well aware that we can laugh at the folly they themselves take so seriously. The eventual pairings, then, are determined by Oberon, although always with the recognition that the heroines' choices are in some mysterious way right, that the pairings, to be "true loves", must correspond with their wishes. Oberon provides the remedy for the difficulties introduced at the beginning of the play and complicated by the subsequent action; the flower, like the eyes, is but his means.

The necessity of such "fairy grace" had been suggested from the start. Helena had asked in vain "with what art" Hermia won the heart of Demetrius. In love there is no art; imagination follows and encourages the mysterious dictates of the heart. Thus Lysander had appropriately wished Helena "luck" in gaining Demetrius, for only by such good fortune could she conceivably gain the man who found her every advance offensive (no more offensive, of course, than Lysander would later find Hermia, that dwarf, minimus, Ethiope). Helena had herself repeatedly lamented that her prayers were unanswered, that she somehow lacked the "grace" to be "happy", "fortunate", with "blessed and attractive eyes". On the night in the wood at last her prayers are answered. Like the rest of the lovers, including Theseus and Hippolyta, she is blessed, and an object of that "fairy grace" with which the chaos of the first four acts is ended and with which the play concludes (V.i.406).

When initially Hermia defied her father's wishes, she said she knew not "by what power" she was "made bold". In similar terms, Demetrius later acknowledges being cured of his dotage for Hermia and restored to his true love for Helena: "I wot not by what power/ (But by some power it is)". The power is perhaps that mysterious source by which Hermia swore: "that which knitteth souls and prospers loves" (I.i. 172). "Fairy grace", certainly, removes the external obstacles to marriage for Hermia and Lysander, while at least assisting in the operation of knitting souls for all four lovers.

Initially, Hermia and Lysander had lamented that the course of true love never did run smooth. In the world of tragedy, whether for Romeo or for Pyramus, it does not. "A greater power than we can contradict" thwarts the plans of Friar Laurence, just as that same Heaven hath a hand in the tragic fortunes of Richard II. Within the complex world of these tragedies written approximately at the same time as *A Midsummer Night's Dream*, the divine will plays an essential role, as critics have long recognized. Within the comic world of *A Midsummer Night's*

Dream, where Shakespeare of course avoids so sober an explanation of "events", we have "fairy grace".

In accordance with Oberon's plan, the four lovers awake harmoniously paired and think their whole experience of the night a dream,[11] although a mystifying one with (as Hippolyta says) "great constancy". We know it was no dream, at least not in the sense they regard it as one; we have witnessed its entirety and have even better reason than Hippolyta to reject Theseus' dismissal of lovers "shaping fantasies". What we have seen indeed "more witnesseth than fancy's images", partly because we are aware that we have been beholding the images of Shakespeare's "fancy" rather than that of the lovers. Yet we may well ask just how much it "witnesseth", and we may look to Bottom for a clue. When he awakes, he too thinks he has had a dream, and, as everyone knows, he soliloquizes in terms that echo *I Corinthians* ii.9–10.

> I have had a most rare vision. I have had a dream, past the wit of man to say what dream it was. Man is but an ass if he go about to expound this dream. . . . The eye of man hath not heard, the ear of man hath not seen, man's hand is not able to taste, his tongue to conceive, nor his heart to report what my dream was. I will get Peter Quince to write a ballet of this dream. It shall be call'd 'Bottom's Dream,' because it hath no bottom. . . .

> 9 But *we preache* as it is written, Things w^e eye hath not sene, & eare hath not heard, nether haue entred into mans mynde, which thinges God hath prepared for thẽ that loue hym.
> 10 But God hath opened *them* vnto vs by his Sprite, for the Spirite searcheth all thinges, yea, the botome of Goddes secretes.[12]

It used to be customary to see no significance whatever in this echo. One might merely observe, like Dover Wilson, "that Bottom was a weaver, and therefore possibly of a Puritanical turn of mind", apt to recall Scripture. Enticed by Bottom's suggestive malapropism a few minutes earlier ("I have an exposition of sleep come upon me"), it is tempting to look for more meaningful implications, ones that "expound" Shakespeare's *Dream* if not Bottom's. The lovers, of course, never saw the fairies; their "dreams" are only of the "fierce vexation" caused by Puck's mistakes in combination with their own folly. Bottom, in turn, had seen the fairies, had been the unappreciative, unimaginative object of Titania's temporary dotage and of the ministrations of her fairies.[13] Unlike either the lovers or Bottom, however, we have ourselves been admitted to a more complete vision, though we may well be asses if we seek to infer from it more than the suggestion of a mysterious "grace" that sometimes blesses true love. Unlike the lovers and Bottom, we have been witnessing a play, a creation of Shakespeare's imagination. Only a part of the time have we watched imagination-dominated "dreams"; all of the time we have watched the product of Shakespeare's own imagination. If our attitude to art is that of Theseus, we may, as the humble epilogue encourages us to do, think we

> . . . have but slumb'red here
> While these visions did appear.
> And this weak and idle theme,
> No more yielding but a dream.

But, being good Elizabethans, we may well remember that not all dreams are the product of disordered, passion-stimulated, never-sleeping imagination. Some dreams are divine revelations of truth, however difficult to expound, and we have already seen plays of Shakespeare where dreams contained at least a prophetic, specific truth, if not a universal one. Some dreams are yielding, and *A Midsummer Night's Dream*—although a poet's revelation rather than a divinity's—may be one of them.

At the same time, when we eventually hear the epilogue's modest disclaimer, we have seen much more than a treatment of "fairy grace" blessing true love. The "visions" we have beheld embrace far more than just the "visions" experienced by Titania, Bottom, and the four lovers. Our visions began with the first line of the play, and a good part of our time has been devoted to watching Bottom and his friends prepare and present a play of their own.

As I remarked at the beginning, few critics have had much to say about the relationship of *Pyramus and Thisbe* to the play as a whole.[14] Undoubtedly Shakespeare's reasons for including this farce were multiple and complex. For one thing, it is impossible to believe that *Pyramus and Thisbe* is only accidentally related to *Romeo and Juliet,* although we may never be certain which play preceded and provoked Shakespeare's contrasting treatment in the other.[15] Such considerations, however, are wholly external to our present concern with *A Midsummer Night's Dream* as an individual artistic entity. The play, if it was to be conventional, would of course include low comedy, and Shakespeare's problem was to determine what sort of low comedy would be most fitting. An ass like Bottom would serve to develop the love theme effectively, but such an ass could be easily introduced without his fellows. Why have a play-within-the-play, why give it the Pyramus-Thisbe plot, why develop it in the particular way Shakespeare employed?

To begin with, within his play for a wedding occasion[16] Shakespeare apparently saw the advantages of introducing an inept production for a parallel occasion, the wedding of Theseus. Like Biron, he recognized "'tis some policy / To have one show worse than" his own offering.[17] Of course he could not decide what sort of plot to choose for this contrasting production without at the same time considering what development he would give it. But for the moment we can consider the two aspects separately. In contrast to his own play, the mechanicals should choose for Theseus a plot thoroughly inappropriate for a wedding: love tragedy. Only their ineptitude, and Shakespeare's skill, should make *Pyramus and Thisbe* fit pastime for a wedding night, both for the newlyweds within *A Midsummer Night's Dream* and those beholding it. Secondly, the plot should be one inviting comparison with the main plot of Shakespeare's play. The moment we meet the mechanicals in I.ii we learn they are preparing a play of Pyramus and Thisbe. Even without the early reminder that Pyramus would kill himself, "most gallant, for love", the audience would at once recognize in the familiar story parallels, actual and potential, to what had begun in I.i. Like Hermia and Lysander, Pyramus and Thisbe would run off to the woods in the night, frantically hoping to escape the obstacles to their true love. Unlike Hermia and Lysander (but at this point of the play the audience cannot know of the fairy grace to come), Pyramus and Thisbe, the audience knows, will find their "sympathy in choice" brought to such sudden catastrophe as Hermia and Lysander had expressly feared (I.i.132ff.).[18]

Most critics who have related *Pyramus and Thisbe* to *A Midsummer Night's Dream* as a whole have largely confined themselves, very cryptically, to thematic implications of this partial parallel in the action. For E.K. Chambers, *Pyramus and Thisbe* is "but a burlesque presentment of the same theme which has occupied us throughout", that "lunacy in the brain of youth" which is "not an integral part of life, but a disturbing element in it."[19] For Arthur Brown, it is "an integral part of the main theme of the play, which seems to be concerned with gentle satire of the pangs of romantic love".[20]

More soberly, for Frank Kermode it "gives farcical treatment to an important thematic element; for Bottom and his friends will perform a play to illustrate the disastrous end of doting".[21] For Paul Olson, most sober of all, it "fits into the total pattern" because "it is the potential tragedy of the lovers in the woods", reminding us of the probable consequences of the "'headie force of frentick love'".[22]

Yet in the actual play as developed by the mechanicals, Shakespeare provides a focus that scarcely emphasizes any such parallel to the lovers. The thwarting parents are cast but never given even a line in rehearsal or production; they are referred to in neither Quince's argument nor in the lovers' speeches. In turn, the decision to run to the woods is presented in a single line, and the barrier wall is focused upon as farcical in itself rather than as a cause for action. Lastly, however ridiculous the love poetry of Pyramus and Thisbe, it scarcely seems focused for comic parallel and contrast to the speeches or actions of Shakespeare's four young lovers (except in one possible way, to be examined below).

For Shakespeare's actual development, few critics have much to say. They recognize such external considerations, all undeniably valid, as a possible light mocking of earlier plays, or the demonstration that a Romeo-Juliet plot could be converted to farce by its treatment, or the demands of the low comedy convention. More internally, they recognize the necessity that *Pyramus and Thisbe* be treated farcically if it is to harmonize in tone with *A Midsummer Night's Dream* as a whole.

But *Pyramus and Thisbe* is not merely a play about love with a partial resemblance to the love plot of *A Midsummer Night's Dream*. It is, as Shakespeare's original wedding audience would be inevitably aware, a play for a wedding audience. It provides a foil to the entire play of which it is a part, not merely to the portion involving the lovers. And not only Bottom's play, but his audience as well, invites comparison with Shakespeare's.[23]

It is time to turn to the principal member of Bottom's audience, and to his famous speech beginning Act V. Himself a creation from "antique fable" unconsciously involved in "fairy toys", Theseus believes in neither. His speech, without appearing improbable or inconsistent with his character, is obviously one demanded by Shakespeare's thematic development. Just as Theseus has no dramatically probable reason to refer to "fairy toys", so too he has no reason to digress on poetry while discussing the lunacy of love. But by his speech he can provide for Shakespeare a transition from the earlier emphasis of the play upon love to its final emphasis upon art. He can explicitly link the imagination's role in love with its role in dramatic poetry. For him, with his view that "the best in this kind are but shadows", pastimes to be tolerantly accepted when offered, the imagination of the poet commands no more respect that that of the lover.

Theseus' speech introduces the words "image", "imagine", "imagination", and "imagining" to the play. But of course it does not introduce the concepts involved. As we have already seen, and as Theseus reminds us, much of the play has thus far concerned the role of imagination in love. A subordinate part has similarly drawn attention to its role in drama, a role manifested by the entirety of *A Midsummer Night's Dream*.

The success of any play ideally demands effective use of the imagination by the author, the producers, and the audience. Perhaps through modesty, Shakespeare gives us little explicit encouragement to compare his own imaginative creation with that initially provided by Quince.[24] We hear nothing, strictly, of Quince's authorial problems prior to rehearsal. The sources of our laughter spring mainly from mutilation of his text in production, by additions and corruptions, rather than from the text with which the mechanicals began. Yet some measure of comparison of *A Midsummer Night's Dream* with their premutilated text is inescapable. *Pyramus and Thisbe*, with nothing demanded beyond the simple dramatization of a familiar story, could at least have been given imaginative development in action, characterization, theme, and language. It has none. The first three are less than minimal, and the language—in its grotesque combination of muddled syntax, padded lines, mind-offending tropes, ear-offending schemes—does violence even to what would otherwise be woefully inadequate. We have:

> Anon comes Pyramus, sweet youth and tall,
>> And finds his trusty Thisby's mantle slain;
> Whereat, with blade, with bloody blameful blade,
>> He bravely broach'd his boiling bloody breast,

or

> O grim-look'd night! O night with hue so black!
>> O night, which ever art when day is not!
> O night, O night! alack, alack, alack,
>> I fear my Thisby's promise is forgot!
> And thou, O wall, O sweet, O lovely wall,
>> That stand'st between her father's ground and mine!
> Thou wall, O wall, O sweet and lovely wall,
>> Show me thy chink, to blink through with mine eyne!

Contrasting in every respect we have *A Midsummer Night's Dream*, perhaps the most obviously "imaginative" of all Shakespeare's plays before *The Tempest*: we have the poetic fusion of classical and native, remote and familiar, high and low, possible and "impossible", romance and farce—all controlled by a governing intention and developed in appropriately varied and evocative language. Unlike Bottom, if not unlike the Quince who calls his play a "Lamentable Comedy", Shakespeare knows what is appropriate for his purposes. He will have infinite variety, but not merely variety as an end in itself. Bottom wishes to have a ballad written of his dream, and "to make it the more gracious" he will sing it over the dead body of Thisbe at the tragedy's end. Shakespeare, very literally "to make it the more gracious", will end his comedy with a song bestowing fairy grace. The contrast needs no laboring.

The contrast in authorial imagination, however, is not the principal cause for turning *Pyramus and Thisbe* from tragedy to farce. In the first appearance of the mechanicals, the largely expository casting scene, we get a hint of the aspect that receives subsequent emphasis: author-director Quince warns that if the lion roars "too terribly" it will "fright the Duchess and the ladies", and Bottom proposes as a solution to "roar you as gently as any sucking dove" (a remedy almost as sound as the later suggestion to "leave the killing out"). What the mechanicals fail to understand, obviously, is the audience's awareness that drama is drama, to be viewed imaginatively but not mistaken, in any realistic sense, for reality. The idea that these clowns could conceivably create a terrifying lion is in itself ridiculous, but the basic folly lies in their supposing that their prospective intelligent audience will have the naiveté of Fielding's Partridge. And it is this aspect that receives all the emphasis of the mechanicals' rehearsal scene. Except for a very few lines of actual rehearsal, enough to heighten our expectation of the eventual production as well as to allow Bottom's "translation" to an ass, the whole rehearsal is concerned with how the mechanicals abuse their own imaginations by a failure to understand those of the audience. On the one hand they fear their audience will imagine what it sees is real, mistaking "shadows" for reality; on the other, they think the audience unable to imagine what it cannot see. Paradoxically, although they lack the understanding to think in such terms, they think their audience both over- and under-imaginative, and in both respects irrational. For each error Shakespeare provides two examples. More would render the point tedious rather than delightful; fewer might obscure it. Thus, to avoid the threat of over-imagination, they resolve by various ludicrous means to explain that Pyramus is not Pyramus and that the lion is not a lion; then, to counteract the audience's under-imagination, they will create Moonshine and Wall. In a play where Shakespeare's audience has been imagining moonshine since the beginning, Bottom and Quince can conceive only of real moonshine or a character to "disfigure" it. Of course they choose the latter. So too they can think only of bringing in a real wall, weighing tons, or another disfiguring personification.[25]

Significantly, Shakespeare opens the rehearsal scene as follows:

> Bottom. Are we all met?
> Quince. Pat, pat; and here's a marvail's convenient place for our
>   rehearsal. This green plot shall be our stage, this hawthorn brake
>   our tiring house. . . .

The stage is a stage, not a green plot; the tiring house is a tiring house, not a hawthorn brake. The Lord Chamberlain's Men ask us to imagine a green plot and hawthorn brake, just as they ask us to imagine nonexistent fog or, on the other hand, imagine the invisibility of an obviously visible Oberon.[26] The play perpetually makes such demands upon us, and even greater ones. It asks us not only to accept mortal-sized actors as diminutive fairies but even to let them be bi-sized, sleeping in flowers and yet engaging in intimate association with ass-headed Bottom. Most basic of all, it asks us to enter imaginatively into a world dominated by fairies, and to accept them as the ultimate source of disharmony and of harmony, while at the same time not asking us to "believe" in them at all.

When we next see the mechanicals (except for their brief transitional appearance in IV.ii) it will be after Theseus' speech, with its condescending attitude toward poetry, and after the prefatory discussion by the court concerning the "tedious brief . . . tragical mirth" they wish to enact.[27] The emphases in the actual production—including both the production itself and the asides by the audience—are just what we have been prepared for in the rehearsal: not the follies of love but the follies of abused imagination in the theatre. When, for example, Quince concludes his Argument,

> For all the rest,
> Let Lion, Moonshine, Wall, and lovers twain
> At large discourse while here they do remain,

Theseus cannot yet believe that Quince literally means "discourse":

> *Theseus.* I wonder if the lion be to speak.
> *Demetrius.* No wonder, my lord. One lion may, when many asses do.

But before ever they hear the talking lion they listen to "the wittiest partition that ever I heard discourse", that "courteous wall" which provides the "chink to blink through", only to receive the curses of frustrated Pyramus.

> *Theseus.* The wall, methinks, being sensible, should curse again.
> *Pyramus.* No, in truth, sir, he should not. 'Deceiving me' is Thisby's
> cue. She is to enter now, and I am to spy her through the wall.
> You shall see it will fall pat as I told you. Yonder she comes.

As Theseus says, a few lines later,

> If we imagine no worse of them than they of themselves, they may
> pass for excellent men.

There is no danger of wounding the feelings of a Bottom by letting him overhear an aside. His imagination, devoid of understanding, can as easily create beauty in his own mind as it can create unintended farce on the stage. Titania's folly, if possible, was less than what we are now witnessing.

Wall's eventual exit provokes further satiric asides, followed by the primary thematic dialogue of the play:

> *Hippolyta.* This is the silliest stuff that ever I heard.
> *Theseus.* The best in this kind are but shadows; and the worst are no
>   worse, if imagination amend them.
> *Hippolyta.* It must be your imagination then, and not theirs.

While a successful production depends on the imaginative cooperation of playright [sic], producers, and audience, Bottom's group has placed the entire burden on the audience. Theseus' group quite naturally makes no effort to "amend them". The tragedy is too entertaining as farce, too fitting for their nuptial spirits, and, besides, it would take an imagination transcending Shakespeare's own to give "form and dignity" to this *Pyramus and Thisbe*.

What follows demands no further elaboration. The lion proves "a goose for his discretion"; the moon, appearing "by his small light of discretion" to be "in the wane",[28] ridiculously exits on command from Pyramus. And so on, until "Moonshine and Lion are left to bury the dead". "Ay, and Wall too."

But we may return to Theseus' comment that "The best in this kind are but shadows". In a sense he is obviously right, as Shakespeare never ceases to remind us, but his estimation of such "shadows" is consistently deprecating. A noble governor, quite willing to accept poetry for a wedding-night pastime and to acknowledge it as the well-intended offering of his faithful subjects, he at no time implies any respect for it. Shakespeare's entire play implies a contrary view, despite the humility of its epilogue.

Just how contrary a view is open to question. In his "Imagination in the English Renaissance: Psychology and Poetic",[29] William Rossky usefully surveys in detail the reasons for imagination's "general disrepute" in Elizabethan England, and the response it produced from defenders of poetry. His basic thesis is well summarized in his concluding paragraph:

Thus laboring to free the poetic imagination from the current disrepute of the faculty, Elizabethan poetic responds to the very bases of the disrepute. Although instrumental to the healthy operation of the soul, imagination, according to the psychology, is a faculty for the most part uncontrolled and immoral—a faculty forever distorting and lying, irrational, unstable, flitting and insubstantial, haphazardly making and marring, dangerously tied to emotions, feigning idly and purposelessly. And from the attempt to combat these grounds of disrepute through the adoption and adaptation of materials which were an absorbed part of every educated Elizabethan's background—materials often from the very psychology itself—there evolves a concept of poetic feigning: that poetic feigning is a glorious compounding of images beyond life, of distortions which are yet verisimilar imitations, expressing a truth to reality and yet a higher truth also, controlled by the practical purpose, the molding power, and, in almost every aspect, by the reason and morality of the poet.

The age's defenders of poetry—whether in extended defenses like Sidney's or in prefaces like Chapman's or Jonson's, or even in passing (like Hamlet's)—inevitably stressed the high moral function of poetic imagination. One seldom finds so modest a defense as that prefacing *The Shoemakers' Holiday*: "Take all in good worth that is well intended, for nothing is purposed but mirth, mirth lengthneth long life." Yet, after all, as Theseus implied, there is a time for "pastime", and only the most vigorous precisian would have denied it. *A Midsummer Night's Dream* could have been defended as indeed a pleasant pastime, especially appropriate for a wedding occasion but fitting for any moment of merriment. It could be further defended, unmistakably, as a delightful exposition of the follies produced by excessive imagination in love and the pleasures produced by controlled imagination in art. Only the most stubborn precisian could have thought poetry the "mother of lies" after witnessing Shakespeare's thematic distinction, however ambiguous in its ultimate implications, between the worlds of imagination and of "reality". Thus in offering a defense for its own existence the play simultaneously offers us Shakespeare's closest approximation to a "Defense of Dramatic Poesy" in general.

In some measure, surely, *A Midsummer Night's Dream* is such a defense, although one that expresses its view by indirection and without the emphasis upon strictly moral edification one commonly finds in more formal defenses. More legitimately than Greene, Shakespeare might well have appended to his play: *Omne tulit punctum qui miscuit utile dulci.* Theseus links lunatic, lover, and poet indiscriminately. Shakespeare, by contrasting the role of imagination in love with that in dramatic poetry, discriminates. As the play delightfully demonstrates, and lightly satirizes, the imagination in love often operates in defiance of "discretion", especially in creating beauty observable by no one but the creator. Poetic art, distinct from that of a Quince or Bottom, is in accord with discretion, and its creations are capable of universal appreciation, both as beautiful and as meaningful. In love, the ridiculous results from the dominance of imagination over reason, and the lover is unaware of his being ridiculous. In good art, the ridiculous (if it exists) is the product of imagination's cooperation with reason, occurs only when the dramatist intends it, and is subordinated to a purpose which in some degree, at the least, combines *utile* with *dulci.* Rather than being a foe to good living, poetic imagination can be its comfort and its guide, far "more yielding" than most dreams. Whether *A Midsummer Night's Dream* has an unplumbed "bottom" as well as its inescapable Bottom I hesitate to say. But it provides us "a most rare vision", one that offers us a disarmingly unpretentious defense of poetry by the greatest of England's poets.

NOTES

*Originally published in *Shakespeare Quarterly* 15 (1964), 115–29. Reprinted with the kind permission of *Shakespeare Quarterly.*

1. The frequency of such praise provoked R.A. Law's denial that the play had any organic unity whatever: "The Pre-Conceived Pattern of *A Midsummer Night's Dream*", *Texas Univ. Studies in English* (1943), pp. 5–14.

2. *Twelfth Night* II.iv.34–36.

3. To use Miranda's words, *The Tempest* III.i.56–57.

4. *All's Well That Ends Well* I.i.93–94.

5. Helena is never so doting that she cannot recognize her apparent folly. Unlike the other victims of dotage, however, her foolish behavior has its root in a true love, once reciprocated and then unaccountably rejected. Thus only Helena can be cured of dotage by Oberon's curing someone else, rather than herself.

6. Cf., for example, Boaistuau's *Theatrum Mundi* (ed. 1581), pp. 192–194, which treats both theories with equal seriousness. He concludes: "Others after that they had studyed all that euer they coulde therein, and not finding the spring and original of this so furious an euill, haue said that Loue was one, I know not what, that came I knowe not how, and burned I know not how, a thing very certain and true. . . ."

7. See Burton's voluminous annotation for *Anat. Mel.*, III.ii. V.iv, or the treatment in such familiar plays as *Endymion, Othello*, or *The Duchess of Malfi.* See also, in relation to Raleigh, Bruno, and Elizabethan preachers, T. Walter Herbert's "Dislocation and the Modest Demand in *A Midsummer Night's Dream*", *Renaissance Papers 1961* (Durham, N.C., 1962), p. 36.

8. Not surprisingly, "eyes" appears far more frequently in *A Midsummer Night's Dream* than in any other of Shakespeare's plays (with *Love's Labour's Lost* second, for comparable reasons). Like the equally abundant use of "moon", this frequency is of course partly determined by the story, but the demands of the story are in turn determined by those of the theme.

9. That the love-stirred (or hate-stirred) imagination commonly distorted in this fashion, by selection and erroneous evaluation, was a commonplace. Annotation is probably superfluous, but see *Anat. Mel.*, III.ii. III.i, or Thomas Wright, *The Passions of the Minde* (1601), pp. 92–93: "Furthermore, the imagination representeth to the vnderstanding, not only reasons that may fauour the passion [i.e., by selection], but also it showeth them very intensiuely, with more shew and apparence than they are indeede; for as the Moone, when she riseth or setteth [,] seemeth greater vnto us, than indeed she is, because the vapours or clowdes are interuerted betwixt our eyes and her[,] euen so, the beauty and goodnesse of the obiect represented to our vnderstanding, appeareth fairer and goodlier than it is, because a clowdie imagination interposeth a mist."

A useful survey of Renaissance thought on love generally, and on its relationship to imagination, appears in Chapter IV of Franklin Dickey's *Not Wisely but Too Well* (San Marino, Calif., 1957). For the present point on the love-directed distortions of the imagination it is enough to recall Sir Topas' praise of Dipsas in Lyly's *Endymion* (ed. Bond, III.iii.50–60) or the parody praise of Mopsa in Sidney's *Arcadia*, I.iii (ed. Feuillerat, I, 21).

10. Necessarily, to remedy Puck's error with Lysander, Oberon must use Dian's bud, just as he does for Titania. But the pansy influence, "Cupid's power", is clearly implied to have as lasting an effect for Demetrius as "Dian's bud" for Lysander. Witness III.ii. 88–91 and V.i. 414–415, for example. Shakespeare's working out of the love theme is perhaps a bit awkward here,

but only if we labor the play mechanically in a fashion contrary to is [sic] entire spirit. Yet we should not, I believe, do what several critics have done: treat the two flowers as representing opposed kinds of love, irrational and rational, carnal and chaste, etc.

On the association of magic flowers with Midsummer Night, see Lou Agnes Reynolds and Paul Sawyer, "Folk Medicine and the Four Fairies of *A Midsummer Night's Dream*", *SQ*, X (1959), 514–515.

11. Only Hermia has had an actual dream (II.ii. 147ff.), a prophetically accurate one to introduce the chaos into which she initially awakes. The love-threatening serpent of her dream, symbol of male inconstancy, proves more destructive than the literal "spotted snakes with double tongue" against which we have just heard the fairies sing. For spotted, double-tongued Demetrius see I.i.110, III.ii.70–73.

12. I cite the 1557 Geneva New Testament, which J.A. Bryant thinks "to have been the version that Shakespeare knew best" (*Hippolyta's View* [Lexington, Ky., 1961], p. 52). The 1557 version is like Tyndale and Coverdale in "the botome of Goddes secretes"; later 16th-century translations read "the deep things of God".

13. Two recent critics have in their different ways been especially anxious to find meaning in Bottom's echo. See Paul Olson, *A Midsummer Night's Dream* and the Meaning of Court Marriage", *ELH*, XXIV (1957), 95–119, and Frank Kermode, "The Mature Comedies", *Early Shakespeare* (Stratford-upon-Avon Studies, III, London, 1961), pp. 214–220. While very unlike one another in interpretation, Olson and Kermode agree in seeing the play as essentially serious and essentially about love, true and false, earthly and spiritual.

Kermode, p. 218, seems far-fetched in comparing Bottom's vision to that of Apuleius, who, "relieved by the hand of Isis from his ass's shape, has a vision of the goddess, and proceeds to initiation in her mysteries". Titania violently rejects her dotage when awakened, and Bottom certainly has not profited from any initiation. "Bottom's dream", Kermode argues, "is *oneiros* or *somnium*; ambiguous, enigmatic, of high import. And this is the contrary interpretation of blind love; the love of God or of Isis, a love beyond the power of the eyes. . . . Bottom is there to tell us that the blindness of love, the dominance of the mind over the eye, can be interpreted as a means to grace as well as to irrational animalism; that the two aspects are, perhaps, inseparable" (p. 219). If I understand Kermode, he appears to confuse Bottom's vision with that of Shakespeare's audience, and to make that vision a product of the "blindness of love" rather than the art of the poet.

14. Notable exceptions are Paul N. Siegel, "*A Midsummer Night's Dream* and the Wedding Guests", *SQ*, IV (1953), 139–144, and C.L. Barber, *Shakespeare's Festive Comedy* (Princeton, 1959), pp. 119–162. I am indebted to both, especially for their assuring me that my approach to the play is not wholly idiosyncratic.

15. Not merely the play by the mechanicals but aspect after aspect of *A Midsummer Night's Dream* invites comparison, and contrast, with *Romeo and Juliet*: e.g., on Cupid's arrow versus Dian's wit, on doting versus loving, on love's "infection" through the eye, on oaths, inconstant moons, and male inconstancy, on "blind love" best agreeing with night, on dreams and fairies as "begot of nothing but vain fantasy". The relationship is too complex and too tangential to pursue here, but it once again suggests the need to treat *Pyramus and Thisbe* as an integral part of *A Midsummer Night's Dream*.

16. Alfred Harbage has recently objected to interpreting Shakespeare on the basis of hypothetical occasions for which there is no external evidence ("*Love's Labour's Lost* and the Early Shakespeare", *PQ*, XLI [1962], 19–20). Nevertheless, the internal evidence that *A Midsummer Night's Dream* was either written or adapted for a courtly wedding seems to me, as to most, overwhelming.

17. *Love's Labour's Lost* V. ii. 513–514.

18. For reasons already indicated, I think Pyramus and Thisbe meant primarily to parallel Lysander and Hermia as examples of frustrated true love rather than as examples of folly. Lysander and Hermia may not behave rationally in their flight from authority, but only when misled by pansy-juice does Lysander approach the frenzied passion which so disturbed Friar Laurence. Even in that play, I believe, Shakespeare distinguishes between Romeo's doting for Rosaline and his true but frustrated love for Juliet.

19. *Shakespeare: A Survey* (New York, 1926), pp. 87, 80.

20. "The Play within a Play: An Elizabethan Dramatic Device", *Essays and Studies*, XIII (1960), 47.

21. P. 216.

22. P. 118.

23. This point of view has been excellently advanced by Siegel (see note 14 above). My own emphases are somewhat unlike his, but his essay seems to me exceptionally illuminating, rivalled only by Barber's chapter on the play. That Siegel's view has received so little attention in the past decade leads me to hope that a partial repetition of his arguments is here excusable.

24. Quince is perhaps the one who most invites contrast with Shakespeare, while his fellows contrast with the remainder of the Lord Chamberlain's Men.

Yet Bottom by his irrepressible initiative tends to usurp even the authorial role. He is indeed the play's "weaver", effectively intertwining the thematic threads of love and art in the play.

25. Shakespeare wisely avoided much use of "Antigonus pursued by a bear" on the stage of his plays, but, as several critics have pointed out, the wall for *Romeo and Juliet* II.i may have posed momentary staging problems which find their reflection here.

26. Modern productions of *A Midsummer Night's Dream*, admittedly magnificent spectacles, often seem to have more in common with the mechanicals than with Shakespeare. Such productions obscure, if not destroy, thematic implications of the kind discussed here. Readers of the play are sometimes subjected to a similar disservice by editors—e.g., the New Cambridge stage direction opening II.i: "The palace wood, a league from Athens. A mossy stretch of broken ground, cleared of trees by wood-cutters and surrounded by thickets. Moonlight[.]"

27. This includes, of course, Theseus' comments on how a noble host should accept any well-intended offering, however incompetent. Surely the host of the Lord Chamberlain's Men, especially if a greater admirer of poetry than Theseus, would recognize the implications as to how he should receive their humbly presented masterpiece.

28. It is fanciful, perhaps, to see parallel implications in the opening of Shakespeare's play, where "O, methinks how slow / This old moon wanes" before the new "moon, like to a silver bow / New-bent in heaven" can appear. Certainly while the old moon wanes we behold the inconstancies and indiscretions of lovers, the "lunatic" aspect of love. With the new moon comes harmonious marriage, and the "silver bow" with its Diana associations (witness the later *Pericles* V.i.249) may well suggest this alternative aspect of the moon, the prevalent one in the play.

29. *Studies in the Renaissance*, V (1958), 49–73.

Titania and the Ass's Head[*]

Jan Kott

> May all to Athens back again repair,
> And think no more of this night's accidents
> But as the fierce vexation of a dream.
> (*A Midsummer Night's Dream*, IV, 1)

I

The philologists long ago discovered the devilish origin of Puck. Puck is simply one of the names for the devil. His name was invoked to frighten women and children, together with the ogre and the incubus. Authors of commentaries on Shakespeare have for a long time also pointed to the similarities between Puck and Ariel, to certain repetitive situations, even lines of dialogue. Both Puck and Ariel lead wanderers astray, turn themselves into an *ignis fatuus* on the swamps:

> . . . Mislead night-wanderers, laughing at their harm (II, 1)

This has always been a favourite occupation of devils in popular folklore. Both Puck and Ariel have devoted themselves to it with great satisfaction. Ariel turns into a chimera and a harpy; it is he who bites Caliban, pricks and tickles him unbearably. George Lamming says: "Ariel is Prospero's source of information; the archetypal spy, the embodiment—when and if made flesh—of the perfect and unspeakable secret police." In my essay on *The Tempest* I have called Ariel an angel, executioner, and agent provocateur.

Shakespeare introduced such monsters in only two of his plays: *A Midsummer Night's Dream* and *The Tempest*. The *Dream* is a comedy;

The Tempest was for a long time regarded as a comedy. The *Dream* forecasts *The Tempest*, although written in a different key. Just as *As You Like It* seems to forecast *King Lear*. Sometimes one has the impression that Shakespeare in fact wrote three or four plays and kept repeating the same themes in different registers and keys, until he broke with all harmony in the *musique concrète* of *King Lear*. The storm came upon Lear and made him go mad in the same Forest of Arden where, not so long ago, in *As You Like It*, another exiled prince, another exiled brother, and a pair of lovers, had deluded themselves that they would find freedom, security, and happiness. Exiled princes are accompanied by clowns; or rather, by one and the same clown. Touchstone knows very well that the idyll of the Forest of Arden is only an illusion, that there is no escape from the world's cruelty, and that sooner or later we shall have to pass through "This cold night [that] will turn us all to fools and madmen".

The affinities between Puck and Ariel are important not only for a literary interpretation of the *Dream* and *The Tempest*. They are, perhaps, even more important for theatre productions of the two plays. If Ariel, the "airy spirit", is a devil, Prospero becomes an embodiment of Faust: like Faust he masters the powers of nature, and like Faust he loses in the end. This realization may enable one to enliven dramatically the character of Prospero, who almost invariably appears dull on the stage. Ariel, who is all thought, intelligence, and the devil, will never again appear as a ballet dancer in tights, with little gauze wings, who floats over the stage with the help of stage machinery.

But so too the conception of Puck must change, if he is to embody something of the future Ariel. He must not be just a playful dwarf from a German fairy tale, or even a poetic gremlin in the fashion of a romantic *féerie*. Only then, perhaps, will the theatre at last be able to show his twofold nature: that of Robin Goodfellow and that of the menacing devil Hobgoblin. "Those that Hobgoblin call you, and sweet Puck." The little fairy is afraid of him, wants to tame him, addresses him in endearing terms. Puck, the household brownie, suddenly takes the form of the Evil One:

> Sometime a horse I'll be, sometime a hound,
> A hog, a headless bear, sometime a fire;
> And neigh, and bark, and grunt, and roar, and burn,
> Like horse, hound, hog, bear, fire, at every turn. (III, 1)

In the 1963 production of *The Tempest* at Stratford on Avon, Ariel was represented as a silent boy with a concentrated expression. He never smiled. In the 1959 production of *The Tempest* at the People's Theatre, Nowa Huta, Ariel had a double. In the Stratford production he was accompanied by four dumb doubles. The devil is always able to multiply himself. The doubles wore masks which copied the faces of the original Ariel.

Their sense thus weak, lost with their fears thus strong,
Made senseless things begin to do them wrong;
For briers and thorns at their apparel snatch; . . . (III, 2)

This is not Ariel haunting the royal murderers on Prospero's isle. It is good-natured Robin Goodfellow chasing worthy Master Quince's troupe which has not done anybody any harm. Puck is a devil and can multiply himself too. One can easily visualize a performance where Puck will be accompanied by devilish doubles, looking like his reflections in a mirror. Puck, like Ariel, is quick as thought:

I'll put a girdle round about the earth
In forty minutes. (II, 1)

Shakespeare was not far wrong. The first Russian sputnik encircled the earth in forty-seven minutes. For Puck, as for Ariel, time and space do not exist. Puck is a quick-change artist and a prestidigitator, something of a *commedia dell'arte* Harlequin. The Harlequin as shown a few years ago by the unforgettable Marcel Moretti in *The Servant of Two Masters* at the Piccolo Teatro of Milan. He had in him something of an animal and a faun. A black leather mask with openings for eyes and mouth endowed his face with a feline and foxy expression. But above all, he was a devil, like Puck. He multiplied himself, doubled and trebled, seemed to be exempt from the laws of gravity; he changed and pupated himself, could be in several places at once. All characters have a limited repertory of gestures. Harlequin knows all the gestures. He has the intelligence of a devil and is a demon of movement.

What, a play toward? I'll be an auditor;
An actor too perhaps, if I see cause. (III, 1)

Puck is not a clown. He is not even an actor. It is he who, like Harlequin, pulls all the characters on strings. He liberates instincts and puts the mechanism of this world in motion. He puts it in motion and mocks it at the same time. Harlequin is the stage manager and director, just as Puck and Ariel are the stage managers and directors of the respective spectacles devised by Oberon and Prospero.

Puck has sprinkled the eyes of the lovers with berry juice. When at last will the theatre show us a Puck who is a faun, a devil, and Harlequin, all combined?

II

According to Shakespeare's latest biographer, A. L. Rowse, the original performance of *A Midsummer Night's Dream* took place in the old London palace of the Southampton family at the corner of Chancery Lane and Holborn. It was a spacious house in Late Gothic style, with larger and smaller galleries running on various levels round an open rectangular court which adjoined a garden well suited for walks. It is difficult to imagine more suitable scenery for the real action of *A Midsummer Night's Dream*. It is late night and the entertainment is over. All the toasts have been drunk, dancing has stopped. Servants are still holding lamps in the courtyard. But the adjoining garden is dark. Tightly embracing couples are slowly filtering through the gate. Spanish wine is heavy; the lovers have remained. Someone has passed by; the boy is waking. He does not see the girl asleep by his side. He has forgotten everything, even that he left the dance with her. Another girl is near; to reach her it is enough for him to stretch his arm. He has stretched his arm, he runs after her. He hates now with an intensity equal to that with which an hour ago he desired.

> Content with Hermia? No! I do repent
> The tedious minutes I with her have spent.
> Not Hermia, but Helena I love. (II, 2)

A feature peculiar to Shakespeare is the suddenness of love. There is mutual fascination and infatuation from the very first glance, the first touch of hands. Love falls down like a hawk; the world has ceased to exist; the lovers see only each other. Love in Shakespeare fills the entire being with rapture and desire. All that is left in the *Dream* of these amorous passions is the suddenness of desire:

> LYSANDER
> I had no judgment when to her I swore.
> HELENA
> Nor none, in my mind, now you give her o'er.
> LYSANDER
> Demetrius loves her; and he loves not you.
> DEMETRIUS (*awakes*)
> O Helen, goddess, nymph, perfect, divine!
> To what, my love, shall I compare thine eyne?
> Crystal is muddy. (III, 2)

The *Dream* is the most erotic of Shakespeare's plays. In no other tragedy, or comedy, of his, except *Troilus and Cressida*, is the eroticism expressed so brutally. Theatrical tradition is particularly intolerable in the case of the *Dream*, as much in its classicist version, with tunic-clad lovers and marble stairs in the background, as in its other, operatic variation, with flowing transparent muslin and ropedancers. For a long time theatres have been content to present the *Dream* as a Brothers Grimm fable, completely obliterating the pungency of the dialogue and the brutality of the situations.

> LYSANDER
> Hang off, thou cat, thou burr! Vile thing, let loose,
> Or I will shake thee from me like a serpent!
> HERMIA
> Why are you grown so rude? What change is this,
> Sweet love?
> LYSANDER
> Thy love? Out, tawny Tartar, out!
> Out, loathed med'cine! O hated potion, hence! (III, 2)

Commentators have long since noticed that the lovers in this love quartet are scarcely distinguishable from one another. The girls differ only in height and in the colour of their hair. Perhaps only Hermia has one or two individual traits, which let one trace in her an earlier version of Rosaline in *Love's Labour's Lost*, and the later Rosalind in *As You*

Like It. The young men differ only in names. All four lack the distinctness and uniqueness of so many other, even earlier Shakespearean characters.

The lovers are exchangeable. Perhaps that was his purpose? The entire action of this hot night, everything that has happened at this drunken party, is based on the complete exchangeability of love partners. I always have the impression that Shakespeare leaves nothing to chance. Puck wanders round the garden at night and encounters couples who exchange partners with each other. It is Puck who makes the observation:

This is the woman; but not this the man. (III, 2)

Helena loves Demetrius, Demetrius loves Hermia, Hermia loves Lysander. Helena runs after Demetrius, Demetrius runs after Hermia. Later Lysander runs after Helena. This mechanical reversal of the objects of desire, and the interchangeability of lovers is not just the basis of the plot. The reduction of characters to love partners seems to me to be the most peculiar characteristic of this cruel dream; and perhaps its most modern quality. The partner is now nameless and faceless. He or she just happens to be the nearest. As in some plays by Genet, there are no unambiguous characters, there are only situations. Everything has become ambivalent.

HERMIA
... Wherefore? O me! what news, my love?
Am not I Hermia? Are not you Lysander?
I am as fair now as I was erewhile. (III, 2)

Hermia is wrong. For in truth there is no Hermia, just as there is no Lysander. Or rather there are two different Hermias and two different Lysanders. The Hermia who sleeps with Lysander and the Hermia with whom Lysander does not want to sleep. The Lysander who sleeps with Hermia and the Lysander who is running away from Hermia.

A Midsummer Night's Dream was staged for the first time as a topical, almost "private" comedy, part of wedding celebrations. Most probably it was—Rowse's arguments sound quite convincing here—the wedding of the Earl of Southampton's illustrious mother. If so, then the young earl must have taken part in the preparation of the performance and possibly even acted in it accompanied by his admirers. All his male and female lovers and friends, all that splendid circle in which a few years before Shakespeare found himself together with Marlowe, must have come to his mother's wedding. I would have wished the "Dark Lady" of the Sonnets to be present too among the original spectators.

> I do but beg a little changeling boy
> To be my henchman. (II, 1)

If *Love's Labour's Lost*, the transparent comedy about young men who determined to do without women, is rightly considered to have been a play with a secret meaning to the initiated, how much more must this be true of the *Dream*. The stage and auditorium were full of people who knew one another. Every allusion was deciphered at once. Fair ladies laughed behind their fans, men elbowed each other, homosexuals giggled softly.

> Give me that boy, and I will go with thee. (II, 1)

Shakespeare does not show the boy whom Titania to spite Oberon has stolen from the Indian king. But he mentions the boy several times and stresses the point. For the plot the boy is quite unnecessary. One could easily invent a hundred other reasons for the conflict between the royal couple. Apparently the introduction of the boy was essential to Shakespeare for other, non-dramatic purposes. It is not only the Eastern page boy who is disturbing. The behaviour of all the characters, not only the commoners but also the royal and princely personages, is promiscuous:

> ... the bouncing Amazon,
> Your buskin'd mistress and your warrior love, ... (II, 1)

The Greek queen of the Amazons has only recently been the mistress of the king of the fairies, while Theseus has just ended his liaison with Titania. These facts have no bearing on the plot, nothing results from them. They even blur a little the virtuous and somewhat pathetic image of the betrothed couple drawn in Acts I and V. But these details undoubtedly represent allusions to contemporary persons and events.

I do not think it is possible to decipher all the allusions in the *Dream*. Nor is it essential. I do not suppose it matters a great deal either whether we discover for whose marriage Shakespeare hastily completed and adapted his *Midsummer Night's Dream*. It is only necessary for the actor, designer, and director to be aware of the fact that the *Dream* was a contemporary play about love. Both "contemporary" and "love" are significant words here. The *Dream* is also a most truthful, brutal, and violent play. Coming after *Romeo and Juliet*, as it did, the *Dream* was, as it were, a *nouvelle vague* in the theatre of the time.

The fairies' wings and Greek tunics are simply costumes; not even poetic but carnival costumes. How easily one can imagine the great entertainment that must have been given at the wedding of the brilliant countess, the Earl of Southampton's mother, or at another, equally magnificent wedding. The ball is given in stylish and fantastic costumes. In Italian courts, and later in England until the Puritan reaction, masked balls were a favourite form of entertainment and were called "impromptu masking".

But all rooms are empty now. The splendid cavalier dressed as a northern Oberon, accompanied by a retinue of boys in rough leather jackets and fur caps with stags' antlers, has departed. They went to go on drinking in a tavern on the other bank of the Thames. The boys and girls in Greek tunics left even earlier. The last to leave was Titania whose earrings made of pink pearls the size of peas aroused general admiration. The halberdiers are gone; the torches burnt out. Early in the morning, refreshed by a short sleep, the landlord goes out into the garden. On the soft grass, the entwined couples are still asleep:

> Good morrow, friends. Saint Valentine is past.
> Begin these woodbirds but to couple now? (IV, 1)

Hermia is the first to rise, though she had gone to sleep last. For her it was the craziest night. Twice she changed lovers. She is tired and can hardly stand on her feet.

> Never so weary, never so in woe;
> Bedabbled with the dew, and torn with briers;

I can no further crawl, no further go; . . . (III, 2)

She is ashamed. She does not quite realize yet that day has come.
She is still partly overwhelmed by night. She has drunk too much.

Methinks I see these things with parted eye,
When everything seems double. (IV, 1)

The entire scene of the lovers' awakening in the morning abounds
in that brutal and bitter poetry that every stylized theatre production is
bound to annihilate and destroy.

III

The metaphors of love, eroticism, and sex undergo some essential
changes in *A Midsummer Night's Dream*. They are completely
traditional to start with: sword and wound; rose and rain; Cupid's bow
and golden arrow. The clash of two kinds of imagery occurs in
Helena's soliloquy which forms a coda to Act I, scene 1. The soliloquy
is above her intellectual capacities and for a while singles her out from
the action of the play. It is really the author's monologue, a kind of
Brechtian "song" in which, for the first time, the philosophical theme
of the *Dream* is stated; the subject being Eros and Tanatos.

Things base and vile, holding no quantity,
Love can transpose to form and dignity.
Love looks not with the eyes, but with the mind;
And therefore is wing'd Cupid painted blind. (I, 1)

The last couplet is the most difficult to interpret, and it is
disturbing in its ambiguity. The imagery here shows a striking
similarity to the formulas of Florentine Neoplatonists, particularly
Marsilio Ficini and Pico della Mirandola. On the basis of the Orphic
doctrine they promulgated a peculiar *mystique* of Eros. Particularly
famous was a paradox of Mirandola's, contained in his *Opera*: *"Ideo
amor ab Orpheo sine oculis dicitur, quia est supra intellectum"*; Love
is blind, because it is above intellect. The blindness gives fulfilment
and ecstasy. Plato's *Symposium*, understood either mystically, or
concretely, was also among the favourite books of Elizabethan

Neoplatonists. But, following the Florentine example, Neoplatonism as practised in Southampton's circle, had a distinctly epicurean flavour.

Mind "seeing with an incorporeal eye" seems to mean desire. Shakespeare usually breaks through stereotypes. For the Neoplatonic dialectics of Love born through Beauty and culminating in ecstasy, "*Amor sit fruendae pulchritudinis desiderium*", Shakespeare substitutes the Eros of ugliness, born through desire and culminating in folly.[1]

Cupid, the boy who shoots his arrows blindfolded, has been evoked in this soliloquy, but only for a little while, because the imagery here is far more abstract and enters a quite different sphere of meanings:

Wings, and no eyes, figure unheedy haste. (I, 1)

In Helena's soliloquy the blindfolded Cupid has been transformed into a blind driving force, a Nike of instinct.

Schopenhauer obviously borrowed this image from the Dream. But the blind Nike of desire is also a moth. Starting with Helena's soliloquy Shakespeare introduces more and more obtrusively animal erotic symbolism. He does it consistently, stubbornly, almost obsessively. The changes in imagery are in this case only an outward expression of a violent departure from the Petrarchian idealization of love.

It is this passing through animality that seems to us the midsummer night's dream, or at least it is this aspect of the *Dream* that is the most modern and revealing. This is the main theme joining together all three separate plots running parallel in the play. Titania and Bottom will pass through animal eroticism in a quite literal, even visual sense. But even the quartet of lovers enter the dark sphere of animal love- making:

HELENA
... I am your spaniel; and, Demetrius,
The more you beat me, I will fawn on you.
Use me but as your spaniel—spurn me, strike me, ... (II, 1)

And again:

What worser place can I beg in your love . . .
Than to be used as you use your dog? (II, 1)

Pointers, kept on short leashes, eager to chase or fawning upon their masters, appear frequently in Flemish tapestries representing hunting scenes. They were a favourite adornment on the walls of royal and princely palaces. But here a girl calls herself a dog fawning on her master. The metaphors are brutal, almost masochistic.

It is worth having a closer look at the "bestiary" evoked by Shakespeare in the *Dream*. As a result of the romantic tradition, unfortunately preserved in the theatre through Mendelssohn's music, the forest in the *Dream* still seems to be another version of Arcadia. But in the actual fact, it is rather a forest inhabited by devils and lamias, in which witches and sorceresses can easily find everything required for their practices.

You spotted snakes with double tongue,
    Thorny hedgehogs, be not seen;
Newts and blindworms, do no wrong,
    Come not near our Fairy Queen. (II, 2)

Titania lies down to sleep on a meadow among wild thyme, ox-lips, musk-roses, violets, and eglantine, but the lullaby sung by the fairies in her train seems somewhat frightening. After the creatures just quoted they go on to mention long-legged poisonous spiders, black beetles, worms, and snails. The lullaby does not forecast pleasant dreams.

The bestiary of the *Dream* is not a haphazard one. Dried skin of a viper, pulverized spiders, bats' gristles appear in every medieval or Renaissance prescription book as drugs to cure impotence and women's afflictions of one kind or another. All these are slimy, hairy, sticky creatures, unpleasant to touch and often arousing violent aversion. It is the sort of aversion that is described by psychoanalytic textbooks as a sexual neurosis. Snakes, snails, bats, and spiders also form a favourite bestiary of Freud's theory of dreams. Oberon orders Puck to make the lovers sleep that kind of sleep when he says:

                    . . . lead them thus
Till o'er their brows death-counterfeiting sleep

With leaden legs and batty wings doth creep. (III, 2)

Titania's fairies are called: Peaseblossom, Cobweb, Moth, Mustardseed. In the theatre Titania's retinue is almost invariably represented as winged goblins, jumping and soaring in the air, or as a little ballet of German dwarfs. This sort of visual interpretation is so strongly suggestive that even commentators on the text find it difficult to free themselves from it. However, one has only to think on the very selection of these names to realize that they belong to the same love pharmacy of the witches.

I imagine Titania's court as consisting of old men and women, toothless and shaking, their mouths wet with saliva, who sniggering procure a monster for their mistress.

The next thing then she, waking, looks upon
(Be it on lion, bear, or wolf, or bull,
On meddling monkey or on busy ape)
She shall pursue it with the soul of love. (II, 1)

Oberon openly announces that as a punishment Titania will sleep with a beast. Again the selection of these animals is most characteristic, particularly in the next series of Oberon's threats:

Be it ounce or cat or bear,
Pard, or boar with bristled hair . . . (II, 2)

All these animals represent abundant sexual potency, and some of them play an important part in sexual demonology. Bottom is eventually transformed into an ass. But in this nightmarish summer night, the ass does not symbolize stupidity. From antiquity up to the Renaissance the ass was credited with the strongest sexual potency and among all quadrupeds was supposed to have the longest and hardest phallus.

I visualize Titania as a very tall, flat, and fair girl, with long arms and legs, resembling the white Scandinavian girls I used to see on the *rue de la Harpe* or *rue de la Huchette*, walking and clinging tightly to Negroes with faces grey or so black that they were almost undistinguishable from the night.

Thou art as wise as thou art beautiful. (III, 1)

The scenes between Titania and Bottom transformed into an ass are often played for laughs in the theatre. But I think that if one can see humour in this scene, it is the English kind of humour, *"humeur noire"*, cruel and scatological, as it often is in Swift.

The slender, tender, and lyrical Titania longs for animal love. Puck and Oberon call the transformed Bottom a monster. The frail and sweet Titania drags the monster to bed, almost by force. This is the lover she wanted and dreamed of; only she never wanted to admit it, even to herself. The sleep frees her from inhibitions. The monstrous ass is being raped by the poetic Titania, while she still keeps on chattering about flowers:

TITANIA

The moon, methinks, looks with a wat'ry eye;
And when she weeps, weeps every little flower,
Lamenting some enforced chastity.
Tie up my love's tongue, bring him silently. (III, 1)

Of all the characters in the play Titania enters to the fullest extent the dark sphere of sex where there is no more beauty and ugliness; there is only infatuation and liberation. In the coda of the first scene of the *Dream* Helena had already forecast:

Things base and vile, holding no quantity,
Love can transpose to form and dignity. (I, 1)

The love scenes between Titania and the ass must seem at the same time real and unreal, fascinating and repulsive. They are to rouse rapture and disgust, terror and abhorrence. They should seem at once strange and fearful.

Come, sit thee down upon this flow'ry bed,
While I thy amiable cheeks do coy,
And stick musk-roses in thy sleek smooth head,
And kiss thy fair large ears, my gentle joy. (IV, 1)

Chagall has depicted Titania caressing the ass. In his picture the ass is sad, white, and affectionate. To my mind, Shakespeare's Titania, caressing the monster with the head of an ass, ought to be closer to the fearful visions of Bosch and to the grotesque of the surrealists. I think, too, that modern theatre, which has passed through the poetics of surrealism, of the absurd, and through Genet's brutal poetry, can depict this scene truly for the first time. The choice of visual inspiration is particularly important in this context. Among all painters, Goya is, perhaps, the only one whose fantasies penetrated even further than Shakespeare's the dark sphere of bestiality. I am thinking of *Caprichos*.

IV

All the men are ugly, mouse- or rabbit-like, dwarfish or humpbacked. They spy on, or rather sniff at, tall girls with black shawls thrown over their shoulders; their dresses have high waists, but are long and reach down to their ankles. Sometimes the girls lift up their dresses to adjust their garters or stockings, but even in that vulgar gesture they remain inwardly absent. For the most part they sit stiffly in high chairs, contemptuous and aloof. As if on exhibition, they show themselves and their assets; they fasten the garters of their black stockings, stick out their buttocks, and expose their round breasts from under their tight bodices. Misshapen men with prominent wide noses sneak around their legs and posteriors. Sluts in black mantillas with finely dressed hair onto which tortoise-shell combs are fastened sit deep in their thoughts, looking haughtily straight ahead from behind their black fans. Beside them old women sit or walk, wearing the same sort of black shawls and tortoise-shell combs. The old hags are toothless and, perhaps, that is why their mouths are wide open in silent smiles. The sluts and the hags have a considerable likeness to each other. On examining these drawings closely one realizes that the likeness is not a chance one; that Goya deliberately and with a certain satisfaction, as it were, gives the same faces to splendid young women and to repulsive old hags. All the repellent elements in the features of those haughty girls are revealed fully when repeated in old age. Only then those elements become beastly, vulgar, ugly. All the drawings have been made with the same soft line which makes even the black spots seem warm, grey, mouse-like. For in reality, it is not only the men and the old hags that have the appearance of rats, but also all those young women, contemptuous and immovable, regal and whorish, carnal and absent at the same time.

The women are slim and tall; the men, small and looking as if they were able only to spy on and sniff at the women; as if they would have to stand up on their toes if they wanted to look them in the face. Goya must have inspired the drawings of Bruno Schulz. I still remember these drawings: small, black men with large heads like those of children ill with dropsy, watching intently the slippers, or little feet of giantesses. Schulz's drawings have the same soft line, the same warm mouse-like greyness that Goya's drawings have. Those large-headed men in bowler hats and coats too big for them, misshapen, humpbacked, crippled, yet excited almost to the point of orgasm by the little falling slipper of a giantess, are like mice.

Todos Caeran. A small withered tree with human hens in black three-cornered hats. Bird-like hen-whores with little wings stick out their round breasts and jig on their thin hen's legs. Clumsy cocks with their hackles up, also jigging ridiculously on similar thin little legs, jump on them. While other hen-whores and cocks with repulsive wrinkled old faces perch on the little withered tree.

At the bottom there are three women. Two young ones with breasts sticking out of their bodices, in ample skirts, and one very old, with hands folded as if in prayer, somehow also bird-like in spite of a big snout in place of nose and chin. The young women, excited and fluttering, drive an awl into the buttocks of a hen with an old head on a long neck. One of them holds her by the wings, the other tampers with the awl at her rump. The old woman is praying, the young ones laugh; it is an animal and sexual sort of laughter that deforms their faces and, as in the other drawings, gives them the same vulgar grimace.

La van desplumados. Four women, two young ones and two old hags, beat with brooms and chase away little bird-like men with hen's legs and the sad faces of hunchbacks. Again, we find in those sluts in mantillas the same evil glow in the eyes, the same vicious smile, a trace, or rather forecast, of future deformity in the way their mouths open, their cheeks swell.

The asses. Whole herds of asses. In white nightcaps, ugly, without any traces of good nature, inflated and conceited, they teach a young ass, his muzzle wide open, the alphabet. Their stupidity is human, not asinine. A big ass, naked, with hairy hoofs, self-satisfied and blissful, is seated comfortably in an easy chair. A hairy ape, or perhaps a man with an ape's head, plays a mandolin, while two servants hiding behind the chair laugh and clap their hands. A good-looking ass in a loose coat and long trousers, from under which hoofs are visible, is reading a book about asses. An ass-doctor, benign and smooth-faced, takes a patient's pulse. An astonishing huge, white ass, calm and understanding, is standing in front of a large blackboard, on which a hairy ape is drawing something. Tired, stooping peasants are carrying big, white, heavy, hideous asses on their shoulders. But the peasants are hideous too, hideous and ugly. They are even uglier than the asses they carry. A tall slut, her expression, as always in Goya's drawings, contemptuous and absent, is straddling a black ass with a huge muzzle. The girl's thighs are bare, and a large black comb is pinned in her hair.

Goya, or animal eroticism. Everything here is hairy, everything part of the same night. Everything has to do with squeezing, handling, sucking, sticking. Bats have the bellies and genitals of men, or women, and sometimes the flabby breasts of old women. They throw themselves on girls with protruding buttocks; they hang around old toothless hags with noses eaten away by syphilis. She-bats, with wide open fox-like muzzles and hairy female genitals, fly over a sleeping youth's head. In the second part of the series everything becomes even more animal, hairy, and nightmarish. Sometimes it is even difficult to name those half-animal, half-human, cat-like, rat-like, and fox-like beings. On the last drawings the bats become an obsession: they turn into succubi and incubi, fly with their mouths always wide open; they have the heads of imbeciles, or crawl on little, thin, and hairy legs.

In the early part of the series the animals are still symbols of stupidity, cunning, force, or debauchery, as in a medieval or early Renaissance apologue. But gradually the animals become independent, as it were, of this summary symbolism; they cease to symbolize men and are only animal variations of the human form. Goya discovers the dark sphere in which all forms—asinine, bovine, ovine, rat's, bat's, mousy, feline, male, female, young, and old—have penetrated one another and go on infecting one another with hairiness, snoutiness, with muzzles and noses, with protruding ears, with the black openings of female genitals and toothless mouths. Only occasionally, among those he- and she-bats with cat's whiskers, fox-like muzzles, and naked bellies, there appear the absent, contemptuous, carnal sluts in black mantillas with ingeniously dressed hair and black, long skirts.

One of them is dancing. She has lifted her black-stockinged leg high in the air and holds her hands above her head. Her eyes are closed. She does not see the bats sniffing at her. One of them with the head of an old baldish cat has already caught at her hair. Another with the low-hanging big head of a dwarf is already looking under her black skirt.

The girl is dancing. A third bat with a naked belly and male uncovered genitals and the head of a starved yet sexy cat has already landed on her breasts. The girl does not defend herself, does not see them; but she is dancing for them.

Titania has embraced the ass's head and traces his hairy hoofs with her fingers. She is strikingly white. She has thrown her shawl on the grass, taken the tortoise-shell comb out of her fine coiffure, and let her hair loose. The ass's hoofs are entwining her more and more strongly. He has put his head on her breasts. The ass's head is heavy and hairy.

> For she his hairy temples then had rounded
> With coronet of fresh and fragrant flowers; . . . (IV, 1)

Titania has closed her eyes: she is dreaming about pure animality.

V

The night is drawing to a close and the dawn is breaking. The lovers have already passed through the dark sphere of animal love. Puck will sing an ironic song at the end of Act III. It is at the same time a coda and a "song" to summarize the night's experiences.

> Jack shall have Jill;
> Naught shall go ill;
> The man shall have his mare again, and all shall be well. (III, 2)

Titania wakes up and sees a boor with an ass's head by her side. She slept with him that night. But now it is daylight. She does not remember ever having desired him. She remembers nothing. She does not want to remember anything.

TITANIA
My Oberon, what visions have I seen!
Methought I was enamour'd of an ass.
OBERON
There lies your love.
TITANIA
How came these things to pass?
O, how mine eyes do loathe his visage now! (IV, 1)

All are ashamed in the morning: Demetrius and Hermia, Lysander and Helena. Even Bottom. Even he does not want to admit his dream:

> Methought I was—there is no man can tell what.
> Methought I was, and methought I had—But man is but a
> patch'd fool if he will offer to say what methought I had. (IV, 1)

In the violent contrast between the erotic madness liberated by the night and the censorship of day which orders everything to be forgotten, Shakespeare seems most ahead of his time. The notion that "life's a dream" has, in this context, nothing of baroque mysticism. Night is the key to day!

> . . . We are such stuff
> As dreams are made on; . . . (*The Tempest*, IV, 1)

Not only is Ariel an abstract Puck with a sad and thoughtful face; the philosophical theme of the *Dream* will be repeated in *The Tempest*, doubtless a more mature play. But the answers given by Shakespeare in *A Midsummer Night's Dream* seem more unambiguous, perhaps one can even say, more materialistic, less bitter.

> The lunatic, the lover, and the poet
> Are of imagination all compact. (V, 1)

The madness lasted throughout the June night. The lovers are ashamed of that night and do not want to talk about it, just as one does not want to talk of bad dreams. But that night liberated them from themselves. They were their real selves in their dreams.

> . . . And sleep, that sometimes shuts up sorrow's eye,
> Steal me awhile from mine own company. (III, 2)

The forest in Shakespeare always represents Nature. The escape to the Forest of Arden is an escape from the cruel world in which the way to the crown leads through murder, brother robs brother of his inheritance, and a father asks for his daughter's death if she chooses a husband against his will. But it is not only the forest that happens to be

Nature. Our instincts are also Nature. And they are as mad as the world.

> Lovers and madmen have such seething brains,. . . (V, 1)

The theme of love will return once more in the old tragedy of Pyramus and Thisby, performed at the end of the *Dream* by Master Quince's troupe. The lovers are divided by a wall, cannot touch each other, and only see each other through a crack. They will never be joined together. A hungry lion comes to the rendezvous place, and Thisby flees in panic. Pyramus finds her blood-stained mantle and stabs himself. Thisby returns, finds Pyramus's body, and stabs herself with the same dagger. The world is cruel for true lovers.

The world is mad, and love is mad. In this universal madness of Nature and History, brief are the moments of happiness:

> . . . Swift as a shadow, short as any dream,
> Brief as the lightning in the collied night, . . . (I, 1)

NOTES

1. Compare Edgar Wind, *Pagan Mysteries in the Renaissance*, London, 1958.

A Midsummer Night's Dream
"Jack Shall Have Jill; /
Nought Shall Go Ill"*

Shirley Nelson Garner

> Jack shall have Jill;
> Nought shall go ill;
> The man shall have his mare again,
> and all shall be well.[1]

More than any of Shakespeare's comedies, *A Midsummer Night's Dream* resembles a fertility rite, for the sterile world that Titania depicts at the beginning of Act II is transformed and the play concludes with high celebration, ritual blessing, and the promise of regeneration.[2] Though this pattern is easily apparent and has often been observed, the social and sexual implications of the return of the green world have gone unnoticed. What has not been so clearly seen is that the renewal at the end of the play affirms patriarchal order and hierarchy, insisting that the power of women must be circumscribed, and that it recognizes the tenuousness of heterosexuality as well.[3] The movement of the play toward ordering the fairy, human, and natural worlds is also a movement toward satisfying men's psychological needs, as Shakespeare perceived them, but its cost is the disruption of women's bonds with each other.

I

Regeneration finally depends on the amity between Titania and Oberon. As she tells him, their quarrel over possession of an Indian boy has brought chaos, disease, and sterility to the natural world:

> And this same progeny of evils comes
> From our debate, from our dissension;
> We are their parents and original. (II.i.115–17)

The story of the "lovely boy" is told from two points of view, Puck's and Titania's. Puck tells a companion fairy that Oberon is "passing fell and wrath" because Titania has taken as her attendant "a lovely boy, stolen from an Indian king"; he continues:

> She never had so sweet a changeling.
> And jealous Oberon would have the child
> Knight of his train, to trace the forests wild.
> But she perforce withholds the lovéd boy,
> Crowns him with flowers, and makes him all her joy.
> And now they never meet in grove or green,
> By fountain clear, or spangled starlight sheen,
> But they do square, that all the elves for fear
> Creep into acorn cups and hide them there. (II.i.18–31)

Shortly afterward, when Oberon tells Titania that it is up to her to amend their quarrel and that he merely begs "a little changeling boy" to be his "henchman," she retorts, "Set your heart at rest. / The fairy land buys not the child of me." Then she explains the child's origin, arguing her loyalty to the child's mother to be the reason for keeping him:

> His mother was a vot'ress of my order,
> And, in the spicèd Indian air, by night,
> Full often hath she gossiped by my side,
> And sat with me on Neptune's yellow sands,
> Marking th' embarkèd traders on the flood;
> When we have laughed to see the sails conceive
> And grow big-bellied with the wanton wind;
> Which she, with pretty and with swimming gait

> Following—her womb then rich with my young squire—
> Would imitate, and sail upon the land,
> To fetch me trifles, and return again,
> As from a voyage, rich with merchandise.
> But she, being mortal, of that boy did die;
> And for her sake do I rear up her boy,
> And for her sake I will not part with him. (II.i.121–37)

Both accounts affirm that the child has become the object of Titania's love, but the shift in emphasis from one point of view to the other is significant. Puck describes the child as "stolen from an Indian king," whereas Titania emphasizes the child's link with his mother, her votaress. Puck's perspective, undoubtedly close to Oberon's, ignores or suppresses the connection between Titania and the Indian queen, which, in its exclusion of men and suggestion of love between women, threatens patriarchal and heterosexual values.[4]

Titania's attachment to the boy is clearly erotic. She "crowns him with flowers, and makes him all her joy," according him the same attentions as those she bestows on Bottom when, under the spell of Oberon's love potion, she falls in love with the rustic-turned-ass. She has "forsworn" Oberon's "bed and company" (II.i.62). Whatever the child is to her as a "lovely boy" and a "sweet" changeling, he is ultimately her link with a mortal woman whom she loved. Oberon's passionate determination to have the child for himself suggests that he is both attracted to and jealous of him. He would have not only the boy but also the exclusive love of Titania.[5] He needs to cut her off from the child because she is attracted to him not only as boy and child, but also as his mother's son. Oberon's need to humiliate Titania in attaining the boy suggests that her love for the child poses a severe threat to the fairy king.

Puck's statement that Oberon wants the child to be "knight of his train" and Oberon's that he wants him to be his "henchman" have led some critics to argue that the fairy king's desires to have the boy are more appropriate than the fairy queen's. Oberon's wish to have the boy is consistent with the practice of taking boys from the nursery to the father's realm so that they can acquire the character and skills appropriate to manhood.[6] But Puck describes Oberon as "jealous," and his emphasis on the "lovely boy," the "sweet" changeling, and the "lovèd boy" (II.ii.20–7) suggests that Oberon, like Titania, is attracted to the child. There is no suggestion that Oberon wants to groom the child for manhood; he wants him rather "to trace the forests wild" (l.25) with his fairy band. Those critics who attribute moral intentions to Oberon, arguing for his benevolent motives in taking the boy from Titania, overlook that Oberon has no intention of returning him to his father, with whom he, as a human child, might be most properly reared. When we last hear of the boy, Titania's fairy has carried him to Oberon's "bower" (IV.i.62).

Oberon's winning the boy from Titania is at the center of the play, for his victory is the price of amity between them, which in turn restores the green world. At the beginning, Oberon and Titania would seem to have equal magical powers, but Oberon's power proves the greater. Since he cannot persuade Titania to turn over the boy to him, he humiliates her and torments her until she does so. He uses the love potion not simply to divert her attention from the child, so that he can have him, but to punish her as well.[7] As he squeezes the love flower on Titania's eyes, he speaks a charm—or rather a curse—revealing his intention:

> What thou see'st when thou dost wake,
> Do it for thy truelove take;
> Love and languish for his sake.
> Be it ounce, or cat, or bear,
> Pard, or boar with bristled hair,
> In thy eye that shall appear
> When thou wak'st, it is thy dear.
> Wake when some vile thing is near. (II.ii.27–34)

When Puck tells him that Titania is "with a monster in love" (III.ii.6), he is obviously pleased: "This falls out better than I could devise" (l.35).

Though the scenes between Titania and Bottom are charming and hilarious, Titania is made ridiculous. Whereas her opening speech is remarkable for its lyric beauty, and her defense of keeping the Indian boy has quiet and dignified emotion power, now she is reduced to admiring Bottom's truisms and his monstrous shape: "Thou art as wise as thou art beautiful" (III.i.147). However enjoyable the scenes between her and Bottom, however thematically satisfying in their representation of the marriage of our animal and spiritual natures,

Titania, free of the influence of Oberon's love potion, says of Bottom, "O, how mine eyes do loathe his visage now!" (V.i.80). By his own account, Oberon taunts Titania into obedience; he tells Puck:

> See'st thou this sweet sight?
> Her dotage now I do begin to pity:
> For, meeting her of late behind the wood,
> Seeking sweet favors for this hateful fool,
> I did upbraid her, and fall out with her.
> For she his hairy temples then had rounded
> With coronet of fresh and fragrant flowers;
> And that same dew, which sometime on the buds
> Was wont to swell, like round and orient pearls,
> Stood now within the pretty flouriet's eyes,
> Like tears, that did their own disgrace bewail.
> When I had at my pleasure taunted her,
> And she in mild terms begged my patience,
> I then did ask of her her changeling child;
> Which straight she gave me, and her fairy sent
> To bear him to my bower in fairy land.
> And now I have the boy, I will undo
> This hateful imperfection of her eyes. (IV.i.47–64)

Oberon gains the exclusive love of Titania and also possession of the boy to whom he is attracted. But his gain is Titania's loss: she is separated from the boy and, in that separation, further severed from the woman whom she had loved. Oberon can offer ritual blessing at the play's end because he has what he wanted from the beginning: Titania obedient and under his control and the beautiful Indian boy in his bower.

II

Like the fairy king, the two men in power in the human world, Theseus and Egeus, want to attain the exclusive love of a woman and, also, to accommodate their homoerotic desires.[8] In order to do so, they, like Oberon, attempt to limit women's power, and their success or failure to do so affects their participation in the comic world.

The opening of *A Midsummer Night's Dream* puts Hippolyta's subjugation in bold relief as Theseus reminds his bride-to-be:

Hippolyta, I wooed thee with my sword,
And won thy love, doing thee injuries;
But I will wed thee in another key,
With pomp, with triumph, and with reveling. (I.i.16–19)

Capturing Hippolyta when he defeated the Amazons, Theseus has abducted her from her Amazon sisters to bring her to Athens and marry her. Though most directors play Hippolyta as a willing bride, I once saw San Francisco's Actors' Workshop, following the cues of Ian Kott, bring her on stage clothed in skins and imprisoned in a cage.[9] The text invites such a rendering, for almost immediately it sets her apart from Theseus by implying that she sides with Hermia and Lysander against Egeus and Theseus, when he sanctions Egeus's authority. After Theseus tells Hermia to prepare to marry Demetrius or "on Diana's altar to protest / For aye austerity and single life" (I.i.89–90) and then beckons Hippolyta to follow him offstage, he undoubtedly notices her frowning, for he asks, "What cheer, my love?" (I.i.122). Shakespeare heightens her isolation by presenting her without any Amazon attendants.

Though Theseus is less severe than Egeus, he is, from the outset, unsympathetic toward women. The first words he speaks, voicing the play's first lines and first image, must be taken as a sign: the moon "lingers" his desires, he tells Hippolyta, "Like a stepdame, or a dowager, / Long withering out a young man's revenue." He utterly supports Egeus as patriarch, telling Hermia:

To you your father should be as a god,
One that composed your beauties; yea, and one
To whom you are but as a form in wax
By him imprinted and within his power
To leave the figure or disfigure it. (I.i.47–51)

As a ruler, he will enforce the law, which gives Egeus control over Hermia's sexuality and embodies patriarchal order. Though he has heard that Demetrius has won Helena's heart but now scorns her, and has meant to speak to him about it, "My mind did lose it" (I.i.114). A lover-and-leaver of women himself, he undoubtedly identifies with Demetrius and forgets his duty toward Helena. He exits inviting Egeus and Demetrius to follow and talk confidentially with him, suggesting his spiritual kinship with them.

Whatever other associations Theseus had for Shakespeare's audience, he was notorious as the first seducer of Helen.[10] As early as Act II, Oberon recalls Theseus's reputation as a deserter of women.[11] When Titania accuses Oberon of infidelity, asking rhetorically why he was in Athens if not to see Hippolyta, "the bouncing Amazon, / Your buskined mistress and your warrior love" (II.i.70–71), he accuses her of loving Theseus:

> Didst not thou lead him through the glimmering night
> From Perigenia, whom he ravishèd?
> And make him with fair Aegles break his faith,
> With Ariadne and Antiopa? (ll.77–80)

It is significant that the woman whom he at last will marry is not traditionally feminine. She has been a warrior, and in her new role as the fiancée of the Athenian Duke, we see her as a hunter. Nostalgically, she recalls her past experiences:

> I was with Hercules and Cadmus once,
> When in a wood of Crete they bayed the bear
> With hounds of Sparta. Never did I hear
> Such gallant chiding; for, besides the groves,
> The skies, the fountains, every region near
> Seemed all one mutual cry. I never heard
> So musical a discord, such sweet thunder. (IV.i.113–119)

Her androgynous character appears to resolve for Theseus the apparent dissociation of his romantic life, the sign of which is his continual desertion of women who love him.[12]

Having found an androgynous woman, Theseus captures her and brings her home to be his wife. By conquering and marrying this extraordinarily powerful woman, he fulfills his need for the exclusive love of a woman while gratifying his homoerotic desires.[13] Unlike Oberon, however, he finds satisfaction for his desires merged in one person. If we imagine Hippolyta played by a male actor who, though cast as a woman, dresses and walks like a man ("buskined mistress," "bouncing Amazon"), Hippolyta and Theseus must have looked more like homosexual than heterosexual lovers. Hippolyta's androgynous appearance is further confirmed by the fact that in Renaissance fiction and drama men were occasionally disguised as Amazons, e.g., lovers, like Sidney's Zelmane, in the *Arcadia*, who wished to be near his lady.[14] Hippolyta, like Viola and Rosalind in disguise, fulfills a male fantasy, and more happily so since she is not in disguise. Because Theseus's romantic life is fortunately resolved once the young lovers have paired themselves off anew, with Demetrius loving Helena, he can sanction their preferences and ignore Egeus's persistent demand that Hermia marry Demetrius.[15]

By insisting that Hermia marry Demetrius, Egeus hopes to keep his daughter rather than lose her and to have Demetrius near him as well. Shakespeare makes Egeus's motives suspect by creating him foolishly comic, treating him more harshly than he does his other controlling and possessive fathers—Lear, Capulet, Brabantio, Shylock, Prospero. Unable to make his daughter marry where he wishes, Egeus turns to the law to enforce his will. More outrageous than Brabantio, he turns Lysander's courtship of his daughter into a series of crimes: Lysander has "bewitched the bosom" of Hermia, "stol'n the impression of her fantasy," "filched" her heart (I.i.26–38). As Shakespeare depicts the two lovers who compete over Hermia, he is careful to draw them so that Egeus's choice is irrational and not in Hermia's best interests. Lysander states his case before Theseus:

> I am, my lord, as well derived as he [Demetrius],
> As well possessed; my love is more than his;
> My fortunes every way as fairly ranked
> (If not with vantage) as Demetrius';
> And, which is more than all these boasts can be,
> I am beloved of beauteous Hermia. (I.i.99–104)

Lysander continues to accuse Demetrius of making love to Helena, who now "dotes in idolatry, / Upon this spotted and inconstant man" (ll.109–110). His accusation is evidently founded, for Theseus confesses that he has "heard so much" (l.111) and Demetrius does not deny it or defend himself. Later, Demetrius admits that he was betrothed to Helena before he saw Hermia (IV.i.172–73). Egeus chooses badly for his daughter unless he wishes to keep her for himself, as I think he does. By insisting that she marry a man whom she does not love and one who may be unfaithful to her besides, if his present conduct is a gauge, Egeus assures that she will always love her father; that she will never really leave him.

There are suggestions, as well, that Egeus has a particular affection for Demetrius. Shakespeare does not leave us to assume that Egeus's preference for Demetrius is simply proprietary, i.e., since Hermia is his, he may give her as he chooses; or that it is simply an affirmation of male bonding, like Capulet's demand that Juliet marry Paris, "And you be mine, I'll give you to my friend" (*Rom.* III.v.193). Lysander's sarcasm defines Egeus's feeling for Demetrius:

> You have her father's love, Demetrius;
> Let me have Hermia's: do you marry him. (I.i.93–94)

And Egeus immediately affirms:

> True, he hath my love,
> And what is mine, my love shall render him.

Even after Demetrius has fallen in love with Helena, Egeus continues to pair himself with him. When the lovers are discovered asleep in the forest coupled "right" at last and Lysander begins to explain what Theseus calls their "gentle concord," Egeus urges:

> Enough, enough, my lord; you have enough.
> I beg the law, the law, upon his head.
> They would have stol'n away; they would, Demetrius,
> Thereby to have defeated you and me,
> You of your wife and me of my consent,
> Of my consent that she should be your wife. (IV.i.55–60)

Egeus would draw Demetrius back to him, realigning the original *we* against *them*.

Egeus, then, has hoped to have the exclusive love of Hermia and to accommodate his homoerotic feelings by binding Demetrius to him. To give up Hermia and accept that Demetrius loves Helena would defeat him doubly. Consequently, he leaves the stage unreconciled. Had it been left to him to affirm the comic resolution, we would have none.

III

Whereas the separation of Hippolyta and Titania from other women is implied or kept in the background, the breaking of women's bonds is central in the plot involving the four young lovers.[16] Demetrius and Lysander are divided at the outset, but the play dramatizes the division of Hermia and Helena. Furthermore, their quarreling is more demeaning than the men's. And once Demetrius and Lysander are no longer in competition for the same woman, their enmity is gone. Hermia and Helena, on the contrary, seem permanently separated and apparently give over their power to the men they will marry. Once their friendship is undermined and their power diminished, they are presumably "ready" for marriage.

Hermia's fond recollection of her long-standing and intimate friendship with Helena calls attention to Helena's disloyalty, occasioned by the latter's desire to win Demetrius's thanks and to be near him. Telling her friend that she intends to run away with Lysander, Hermia recalls:

> And in the wood, where often you and I
> Upon faint primrose beds were wont to lie,
> Emptying our bosoms of their counsel sweet,
> There my Lysander and myself shall meet. (I.i.214–217)

Just as Helena breaks her faith with Hermia to ingratiate herself with Demetrius, so later she will believe that Hermia has joined with men against her. Deeply hurt, Helena chastizes Hermia:

> Is all the counsel that we two have shared,
> The sister's vows, the hours that we have spent,
> When we have chid the hasty-footed time
> For parting us—O, is all forgot?
> All school days friendship, childhood innocence?
> We, Hermia, like two artificial gods,
> Have with our needles created both one flower,
> Both on one sampler, sitting on one cushion,

Both warbling of one song, both in one key;
As if our hands, our sides, voices, and minds,
Had been incorporate. So we grew together,
Like to a double cherry, seeming parted,
But yet an union in partition,
Two lovely berries molded on one stem;
So, with two seeming bodies, but one heart;
Two of the first, like coats in heraldry,
Due but to one, and crownèd with one crest.
And will you rent our ancient love asunder,
To join with men in scorning your poor friend?
It is not friendly, 'tis not maidenly.
Our sex, as well as I, may chide you for it,
Though I alone do feel the injury. (III.ii.198–219)

In a scene that parallels in its central position Titania's wooing of Bottom, the rupture of their friendship becomes final. They accuse and insult each other, with Hermia calling Helena a "juggler," "canker blossom," "thief of love," "painted maypole"; and Helena naming her a "counterfeit" and a "puppet" (III.ii.282–296). Their quarrel becomes absurd as it turns on Hermia's obsession, taken up by both Lysander and Helena, that Lysander has come to prefer Helena because she is taller. Though no other women characters in Shakespeare's plays come close to fighting physically, Hermia threatens to scratch out Helena's eyes (III.ii.297–98). Her threat is serious enough to make Helena flee (ll.340–43). Lysander is made equally ridiculous in his abrupt change of heart; yet he and Demetrius are spared the indignity of a demeaning quarrel and leave the stage to settle their disagreement in a "manly" fashion, with swords. Even though Puck makes a mockery of their combat through his teasing, they are not so thoroughly diminished as Hermia and Helena.

In the course of the play, both Hermia and Helena suffer at the hands of their lovers. Betrothed to Helena, Demetrius deserts her for Hermia. When she pursues him, he tells her that she makes him sick (II.i.212) and threatens to rape her (ll.214–219). By doggedly following him, she maintains a kind of desperate power over him. She will not play Dido to his Aeneas. Consequently, he cannot sustain the image of the romantic rake, whose women pine and die, commit suicide, or burn themselves on pyres when he leaves them.

Disappointed in his love for Hermia, he cannot get loose from Helena.
Yet her masochism undercuts her power:

> I am your spaniel; and, Demetrius,
> The more you beat me, I will fawn on you.
> Use me but as your spaniel, spurn me, strike me,
> Neglect me, lose me; only give me leave,
> Unworthy as I am, to follow you.
> What worser place can I beg in your love—
> And yet a place of high respect with me—
> Than to be usèd as you use your dog? (II.1.202–210)

When Helena is in a position of positive power with both Lysander and
Demetrius in love with her, she cannot take advantage of it because she
assumes that she is the butt of a joke. And of course, in a sense, she is
right: she is the victim of either Puck's prank or his mistake. Hermia
must also bear Lysander's contempt. In the forest, he insists that he
"hates" her (III.ii.270, 281) and calls her outrageous names: "cat,"
"burr," "vile thing," "tawny Tartar," "loathèd med'cine," "hated
potion," "dwarf," "minimus, of hind'ring knotgrass made," "bead,"
"acorn" (ll.260–64, 328–330). While both women protest their lovers'
treatment of them, neither can play Beatrice to her Benedick. Both
more or less bear their lovers' abuses.

After the four lovers sleep and awaken coupled as they will marry,
Hermia and Helena do not reconcile. Once they leave the forest, they
lose their voices. Neither of them speaks again. Recognizing that it is
difficult for an actor to be on stage without any lines, as Helena and
Hermia are for almost all of Act V, Shakespeare was undoubtedly
aware that he was creating a portentous silence. Since Helena and
Hermia are evidently married between Acts IV and V, their silence
suggests that in their new roles as wives they will be obedient, allowing
their husbands dominance.

IV

The end of *A Midsummer Night's Dream* is as fully joyous as the
conclusion of any of Shakespeare's comedies. No longer angry with
each other, Oberon and Titania bring blessing to the human world:

Hand in hand, with fairy grace,
Will we sing, and bless this place. (V.i.398–99)

Though Oberon calls up dark possibilities, he offers a charm against them. The prospect of love, peace, safety, prosperity is as promising as it ever will be. The cost of this harmony, however, is the restoration of patriarchal hierarchy, so threatened at the beginning of the play. This return to the old order depends on the breaking of women's bonds with each other and the submission of women, which the play relentlessly exacts. Puck's verse provides the paradigm:

Jack shall have Jill;
Nought shall go ill;
The man shall have his mare again,
and all shall be well.

If we turn to some of Shakespeare's comedies in which women's bonds with each other are unbroken and their power is left intact or even dominates, the tone of the ending is less harmonious or even discordant.[17] In *The Merchant of Venice*, for example, where Portia is in control and she and Nerissa triumph over Gratiano and Bassanio, there is no ritual celebration. Portia directs the scene and carefully circumscribes her marriage with Bassanio to close out Antonio. When she and Nerissa reveal their identities as the doctor and the clerk, they make clear their extraordinary power to outwit and deceive, calling up women's ultimate destructive power in marriage and love—to cuckold. The final moments of the play move toward reconciliation, but not celebration. The last line, a bawdy joke, is spoken by Gratiano, the most hate-filled character in the play, and reminds us of men's fear of women and their need to control them: "While I live I'll fear no other thing / So sore, as keeping safe Nerissa's ring" (V.i.306–307).

In *Love's Labor's Lost*, where the women remain together and in control, there is no comic ending.[18] Echoing Puck, Berowne makes the point as he speaks to the King of Navarre:

Our wooing doth not end like an old play;
Jack hath not Jill. These ladies' courtesy
Might well have made our sport a comedy.

When the King replies, "Come, sir, it wants a twelvemonth and a day, / And then 'twill end," Berowne answers, "That's too long for a play" (V.ii.872–76). The refrains of the closing songs call forth images of cuckolding and of "greasy Joan" stirring the pot.

The pattern of these comic endings suggests that heterosexual bonding is tenuous at best. In order to be secure, to enjoy, to love—to participate in the celebration that comedy invites—men need to maintain their ties with other men and to sever women's bonds with each other. The implication is that men fear that if women join with each other, they will not need men, will possibly exclude them or prefer the friendship and love of women. This is precisely the threat of the beautiful scene that Titania describes between herself and her votaress. This fear may be based partially on reality, but it is also partially caused by projection: since men have traditionally had stronger bonds with other men than with women and have excluded women from participation in things about which they cared most, they may assume that women, granted the opportunity, will do the same. Given this possibility or likelihood, Shakespeare's male characters act out of a fear of women's bonding with each other and a feeling of sexual powerlessness. The male characters think they can keep their women only if they divide and conquer them. Only then will Jack have Jill; only then will their world flourish.

NOTES

Reprinted from *Women's Studies 9* (1981): 47–63 by permission of Gordon and Breach Science Publishers. A version of this paper was presented at a session on Feminist Criticism of Shakespeare at the Philological Association of the Pacific Coast, Berkeley, November 1980.

1. William Shakespeare, *The Complete Signet Classic Shakespeare*, ed., Sylvan Barnet (New York: Harcourt, 1972), *MND*, III.ii.461–64. Subsequent quotations from Shakespeare are from this edition.

2. C.L. Barber, *Shakespeare's Festive Comedy: A Study of Dramatic Form and Its Relation to Social Custom*, 2nd ed. (1959; rpt. Cleveland, Ohio: World, 1963), pp. 1119–124, 127.

3. In "Hermia's Dream: Royal Road to *A Midsummer Night's Dream*" *(Literature and Psychology*, 22 [1972], 188–89), M.D. Faber has observed that "the order for which the play strives is a severely patriarchal one which, by its very nature, engenders ambivalence and hostility in women and thus produces

a constant straining toward disorder." Yet Faber's insistence that Theseus, "a governor of strength and understanding," has transcended rigid patriarchal attitudes and his suggestion that women are responsible for disorder make clear that our arguments are substantially different.

4. Describing Titania's lines as "one of the most beautiful bravura speeches," Barber remarks that the moment is "a glimpse of women who gossip alone, apart from men and feeling now no need of them, rejoicing in their own special part of life's power" (pp. 136–37).

5. Some male critics regard Titania's love as Oberon's right; Melvin Goldstein writes: "We know also that Titania violates natural order by making the changeling child 'all her joy', when all her joy should be Oberon" ("Identity Crises in a Midsummer Nightmare: Comedy as Terror in Disguise," *Psychoanalytic Review*, 60 [1973], 189).

6. Goldstein argues, for example, that Titania "needs to give up the boy not only for Oberon's and for her sake, but for the boy's sake. The danger is that in her company and that of her women friends she will feminize him" (p. 189). In his introduction to the new Arden edition of *A Midsummer Night's Dream* (London: Methuen, 1979), Harold F. Brooks states, "It is perhaps (Puck may imply this) high time the boy was weaned from maternal dandling to be bred a knight and huntsman" (p. cvi).

7. Ian Kott, *Shakespeare Our Contemporary*, trans., Boleslaw Taborski (Garden City, New York: Doubleday, 1966), p. 227.

8. I use "homoerotic desires" to mean unconsummated homosexual feelings, which may or may not be recognized.

9. Allan Lewis describes John Hancock's even more extreme presentation of Hippolyta in his production of the play in Greenwich Village in 1967: she was "brought back in captivity, robed in leopard skins, was caged and guarded" ("*A Midsummer Night's Dream*—Fairy Fantasy or Erotic Nightmare?," *Educational Theatre Journal*, 21 [1969], 251).

10. References to Theseus and Helen are commonplace in the Renaissance. George Gascoigne, who uses the most ordinary classical allusions, addresses Paris in "Dan Bartholmew his first Triumpe," one of the poems from *Dan Bartholmew of Bathe*:

"Alas, shee made of thee, a noddye for the nonce,
For *Menelaus* lost hir twise, though thou hir foundst but once.
But yet if in thine eye, shee seemde a peerelesse peece,
Aske *Theseus* the mighty Duke, what towns she knew in *Greece*?
Aske him what made hir leave hir wofull aged sire,
And steale to *Athens* gyglot like: what? what but foule desire?"

(*The Posies*, ed., John W. Cunliffe [Cambridge: Cambridge Univ. Press, [1907], I.101).

11. In an excellent article, " 'Unkinde' Theseus: A Study in Renaissance Mythography" (*ELR*, 4 [1973], 276–98), D'Orsay W. Pearson outlines classical and Renaissance traditions that depict Theseus's darker side, particularly his treacherous and abusive treatment of women. Shakespeare's audience would have been familiar with these traditions. If in remembering Theseus's heroic exploits, they forgot his "unkindness," Shakespeare was careful to remind them by recalling women Theseus had loved and left. Pearson also analyzes Theseus's opening speech, describing ways in which it suggests his negative Renaissance stereotype (p. 292).

12. In his frequent desertion of women, Theseus acts similarly to men Freud describes as evincing a dissociated erotic life. See "A Special Type of Choice of Object Made by Men" and "On the Universal Tendency to Debasement in the Sphere of Love," *The Standard Edition of the Complete Psychological Works of Sigmund Freud*, trans., James Strachey (London: Hogarth, 1957), XI, 166–67, 182–83.

13. In "The Sexual Aberrations," the first of his *Three Contributions on the Theory of Sex*, Freud comments that a large proportion of male homosexuals "retain the mental quality of masculinity . . . and that what they look for in their real sexual object are in fact feminine mental traits." Their "sexual object is not someone of the same sex, but someone who combines the characters of both sexes . . . a union of both sex characteristics, a compromise between an impulse that seeks for a man and one that seeks for a woman" (VII, 144–45).

14. Celeste Turner Wright, "The Amazons in Elizabethan Literature," (*SP*, 37 [1940], 439).

15. E.K. Chambers notices that Theseus's marriage to Hippolyta evinces a change in character: "Theseus has had his wayward youth; . . . Moreover, in his passion for Hippolyta he has approached her through deeds of violence; he has 'won her love, doing her injuries.' But now, like Henry the Fifth of whom he is the prototype, he has put away childish things; he stands forth as the serene law-abiding king, no less than the still loving and tender husband" (*Shakespeare: A Survey* [London: Sidgwick and Jackson, 1925], pp. 84–85). Chambers is right in observing that Theseus has changed. I suggest that the change is not one of character but a result of altered situation: i.e., he has captured a woman who at last can fulfill his romantic needs, which until now have been disparate.

16. In considering the modification Shakespeare made in his construction of the plot involving the Athenian lovers, Chambers points especially to his "making the broken friendship that of women, not that of men" (p. 82). In Chaucer's *Knight's Tale*, which Shakespeare drew on, Palomon's and Arcite's common love of Emilia breaks their friendship. In the *Two Gentlemen of Verona*, in which the relation of Proteus and Valentine corresponds to that of Palomon and Arcite, the friendship between the two men is disrupted though two women, rather than one, are involved. Shakespeare's alteration of Chaucer's tale and variation of his former pattern in *A Midsummer Night's Dream* suggest that the disruption of women's bonds was a significant theme.

17. In a fine essay, "Sexual Politics and the Social Structure in *As You Like It*," Peter B. Erickson has argued similarly in comparing the endings of *As You Like It* and *Love's Labor's Lost*: "The ending of *As You Like It* works smoothly because male control is affirmed and women are rendered nonthreatening, whereas in *Love's Labor's Lost* women do not surrender their independence and the status of patriarchy remains in doubt." In *As You Like It*, he writes, "Festive celebration is now possible because a dependable, that is patriarchal, social order is securely in place" (unpublished paper delivered at the session on "Marriage and the Family in Shakespeare," sponsored by the Shakespeare Division, at the annual meeting of the MLA, 1979; pp. 3, 15; forthcoming in the *Massachusetts Review*).

18. See Peter Erickson, "The Failure of Relationship Between Men and Women in *Love's Labor's Lost*, this issue, *Women's Studies*.

"I Believe We Must Leave the Killing Out"

Deference and Accommodation in
*A Midsummer Night's Dream**

Theodore B. Leinwand

No sooner has the artisan weaver Bottom begun to speak with the fairy queen Titania than he takes the occasion to "gleek."[1] Observing that "reason and love keep little company together nowadays," Bottom thinks it a "pity that some honest neighbours will not make them friends" (III.i.140–141). It is at once an hilarious and a potentially subversive moment: an artisan finds himself spectacularly close to a queen. Of course, it has been noted that for all Bottom's and Titania's propinquity, "there is no communication between them: their kinds of understanding are totally different."[2] But the conception of community relations that is at the heart of Bottom's gleeking suggests that the play's artisanate and its nobility may well share certain "kinds of understanding." It is part of my purpose to show not only that the artisan-weaver is concerned with strategies of accommodation amenable to the play's nobility, but that the artisan-playwright, William Shakespeare, also accommodates himself to the aristocracy with whom he finds himself in such close proximity. The power of spectators like Theseus and Elizabeth to give meaning to command performances weighed heavily on playwrights and actors.[3] But the quality of the latter's art afforded some room for negotiation: royal interpretations of dramatic texts did not necessarily exhaust all of their meaning. Bottom envisions reason and love as two townsfolk, perhaps acquaintances, perhaps husband and wife, who are at odds. It is noteworthy that in an age now deemed notorious for litigiousness and for hate-filled interpersonal relations, Bottom looks to neighbors to adjudicate a difference.[4] His predominant conception of settlement is that of an accommodationist, not a litigant. "Honest neighbours" ought to be able to patch things up between love and reason. So too, when two seventeenth-century Yorkshire women, Emott Belton and Katherine Hodgekinson, found themselves involved in a dispute, a fellow parishioner said that she "would to God you two were frend[es], for this is not the beste meanes for neighbours one to sue another." The two women settled their differences and then "Katherine tooke the cupp and dranke the said Emotte who thanked her. . . ."[5] J.A. Sharpe documents that this settlement was only one of many indicating "a widespread attitude which regarded litigation as a breach of proper neighbourly relations, and which saw arbitration or less formal methods of reconciling those at law as an attractive method of healing such a breach."[6] To maintain harmony in their communities, villagers persuaded neighbors and "frendes att home w[i]thout chardges or trouble in Lawe" to submit to arbitration. It was not uncommon for a man like Thomas Postgate, brother to the wives of both John Buttarie and Thomas Stor, to attempt as he did in 1594 to reconcile his brothers-in-law when they were at odds.[7] Thus Bottom, always a gentle craftsman, gently reveals his layman's notion of local justice. Needless to say, his predilection for arbitration is not shared by all. Immediately after he has told Titania how "neighbours . . . make . . . friends," she commands him to remain in the woods: "Out of this wood do not desire to go: / Thou shalt remain here, whether thou wilt or no" (III.i.145–146). And in the dispute that initiates the play, Egeus turns straightaway to "trouble in Lawe." He comes "with complaint / Against my child" to Theseus (I.i.22–23); and "in this case," Theseus renders his harsh judgment as spokesman for "the law of Athens" (I.i.63 and 119). Not until IV.i, when Egeus is still begging "the law, the law upon his [Lysander's] head" (l.154), does Theseus, who earlier would by no means "extenuate" the law, arbitrate in favor of "gentle concord" (IV.i.142).

Negotiation, arbitration, and accommodation characterize Bottom's and his fellow artisans' relations with their social superiors. It is often remarked that the artisans betray a most naive understanding of the theater. Their discussions in I.ii and in III.i revolve around technical problems, obstacles that may prevent them from convincing their audience.[8] But their specific fears are resonant because they have to do with more than theatrical decorum. In particular, the players are anxious not to "fright the Duchess and the ladies" (I.ii.70–71) with their lion, or to seem to do harm with their swords (III.i.17). The artisans do not want to strike fear into the hearts of their social betters; indeed, such a reaction "were enough to hang us all." "That would hang us, every mother's son" (I.ii.73), they chorus together. To "draw a sword" is to cause "a parlous fear" (III.i.10,11), and such a fear can only cost the crew their lives. They fear for their lives because they assume that indecorous actions on their part will cause their spectators to fear for *their* lives. Bottom knows that "If you think I come hither as a lion, it were pity of my life" (III.i.40–41). And Bottom's fear is not his alone. "Lion" takes Bottom's advice and announces that he is but Snug the joiner. He then reveals his anxiety, borrowing Bottom's very words: *"For if I should as lion come in strife / Into this place, 'twere pity on my life"* V.i.220–221).

The relationship that the artisans think they have with their superiors and the attitude that they assume their superiors have toward them betray considerable anxiety. Swords, fear of hanging, and strife are a part of this interaction from first to last act. Given the players' fear of potential retribution, there is something uncannily appropriate to Theseus' response to their play: "Never excuse; for when the players are all dead, there need none to be blamed. Marry, if he that writ it had played Pyramus, and hanged himself in Thisbe's garter, it would have been a fine tragedy. . ." (V.i.342–346). The players fear for their lives, and their audience jests them into oblivion. Bottom tells Snug to announce, "I am a man, as other men are" (III.i.42–43); but during the performance, Demetrius jests that Bottom is "Less than an ace, man; for he is dead, he is nothing" (V.i.297). Performance, especially strife- and sword-filled performance, is potentially life threatening in the world of *A Midsummer Night's Dream.* No wonder Starveling opines, "I believe we must leave the killing out, when all is done" (III.i.13–14).

* * *

At least two responses to conflict or threat emerge from what I have described thus far. One might respond to drawn swords with one's own drawn sword or with the executioner's blade. Stephen Greenblatt has written brilliantly of Sidney's and Spenser's representations of such a response. Those in power crush those in revolt but manage to salvage their own honor (as well as their commitment to rhetoric over violence) in the face of engagements that threaten to darken their fame or to render persuasion ineffective.[9] When Greenblatt turns to Shakespeare's representation of a thwarted rebellion in *2 Henry VI*, he argues that property, not honor, is at stake, and that the sword used by the aristocrat (now the property-owner, Alexander Iden) can in no way be tainted by the blood of a "rude companion" (ll. 24–25). But the displacement of honor by property at the center of relations between unequal status groups also makes room for the displacement of violence by negotiation. Thus one may also respond to drawn swords and so counter provocation with arbitration and accommodation. It may be true, as Greenblatt writes, that Elizabethan "representations rarely depict the actual method most often used to punish those whom the magistrates deemed serious threats: the thousands of hangings carried out locally throughout Tudor and Stuart England" (p. 15). But it is also true (and here I take issue with Greenblatt) that Elizabethan artists might depict "the ordinary operation of the law"—instances of negotiation and accommodation through and beyond the courts that often replaced violence, and moments when it was clear that "feudal fantasies . . . of mass rebellion and knightly victories" were clearly inappropriate (p. 15). Artisans might be executed; they might also be accommodated.

Before returning to the relations between the carpenter, the weaver, the bellows-maker, the tinker, joiner, and tailor, and their betters in *A Midsummer Night's Dream*, I want to consider several occasions when actual artisans and their superiors came into conflict in Shakespeare's day. My point is not that Shakespeare was particularly alert to artisanal dissent in the counties, or that he carefully refracted such protest, or tamed it, or parodied it in his plays. Nor do I imagine that Shakespeare's response to laborers and artisans was univocal. But the demands of genre and of received history are not able to suppress entirely the tension that characterizes such apparently amicable interactions as those between, say, Bottom and Theseus, or Francis and Hal. Often distinct, but as often overlapping issues are at stake in the case of Jack Cade, in *2 Henry VI*, or in the case of Sly and the Lord in *The Taming of the Shrew* (where threats to sanity and life are also mediated by performance). For the moment, I turn to one historical context for *A Midsummer Night's Dream* to begin the sort of rewriting that Fredric Jameson calls for in *The Political Unconscious*. Jameson urges us to rewrite "the literary text in such a way that the latter may itself be seen as a rewriting or restructuration of a prior historical or ideological *subtext*, it being understood that the 'subtext' is not immediately present as such. . . ."[10] The Elizabethan subtext in this instance has been uncovered by the work of numerous historians.

Bottom's primary craft, weaving, flickers to light mainly in puns. But in 1566, a Colchester weaver declared that the "Weavers' occupation is a dead science nowadays." "We can get no work," said another, "nor we have no money; and if we should steal we should be hanged, and if we should ask no man would give us. . . ."[11] The fear of hanging expressed here was at once legitimate and exaggerated. Felonies, which included the theft of goods valued at more than one shilling, were punishable by death.[12] For Sir Edmund Coke, it was "a lamentable case . . . to see so many . . . men and women strangled on that cursed tree of the gallows."[13] But it was also true that, between 1550 and 1800, the "number of convicted actually condemned to death . . . was between 10 and 20 per cent; while the proportion of those condemned who were actually executed probably averaged about one half." Allowing for an acquittal rate of roughly one quarter to one half of all who were indicted, it would seem that "between 2.5 per cent and 7.5 per cent of those indicted for felony were actually executed."[14]

That Bottom and his crew should nonetheless have hanging on their minds may have to do with the fact that in Elizabethan Essex, for instance, tradesmen and craftsmen accounted for one quarter of all the criminals on record.[15] Coincident with the composition of *A Midsummer Night's Dream*, in the early and mid-1590s, prices soared while real wages fell markedly. Bad harvests in the period from 1592 to 1599 resulted in sustained and cruel scarcity throughout England.[16] Such economic pressures had much to do with the unusually high incidence of crime in the 1590s. The smith Thomas Bynder complained in 1595 that food was too expensive. He then threatened that "if victuals did not grow better cheap . . . twenty victuallers would be hanged at their gates."[17] Clearly the threat of hanging might alarm the "haves" as well as the "have nots." But those lowest in the social hierarchy had most to fear. Late in the Elizabethan period, gentlemen were able to avoid trial at a rate of seventy-nine percent, whereas tradesmen and craftsmen escaped only seventeen percent of the time.[18]

And even when the number of felonies was not increasing in response to deprivation, local magistrates, fearing disorder, showed themselves more willing to prosecute felons who might, in better circumstances, have been left alone. The 1590s were a decade of food shortage, and there was considerable fear on the part of those who took it upon themselves to maintain order. In the entire Elizabethan and Jacobean period, this decade saw the highest number of indictments in Essex, in Herfordshire, and in Sussex.[19]

The historian William Hunt stresses the critical nature of the 1590s: "Rhetorical promiscuity may have rendered the word *crisis* all but useless. Nevertheless, it is hard to describe English society in the 1590s without it. There was more to this crisis than inflation, bad harvests, war with Spain, and apprehensive impatience for the Queen's demise. . . . The crisis that culminated in the 1590s was brought to a peak by the conjuncture of climatic disorder ['The ox hath therefore stretch'd his yoke in vain, / The ploughman lost his sweat, and the green corn / Hath rotted ere his youth attain'd a beard' (II.i.93–95)] and military expenditure," which together "left social perceptions and public policy decisively altered."[20] The felonies (mostly thefts) that were so common a feature of this crisis are only one index to its severity. Riots also had to be dealt with. Following the collapse of the export trade in East Kent clothmaking towns in 1587, severe unemployment, bad harvests, and high food prices made for social unrest. A Sandwich weaver, Thomas Bird, talked of insurrection with Thomas Bensted, a woolcomber, and two or three other textile workers. Bird was said to have declared that they "intended to hang up the rich farmers which had corn at their own doors." On the fifth of June, the conspirators were arrested. Four were "shipped to fight in the Netherlands; Bird was also condemned to a flogging and the pillory."[21] In 1594 and 1595, artisans in the broadcloth industry in the Weald of Kent, protesting a shortage of wood due to enclosures and increased iron production, and reacting to decreasing corn supplies and wages, incited popular agitation. Several mill-working conspiracies were later discovered.[22]

One further example of artisanal dissent illustrates what might happen when conflict was not accommodated or negotiated, when it terminated in the courts or hanging. The artisans in *A Midsummer Night's Dream* agree to meet "a mile without the town, by moonlight" (I.ii.94–95) to plot their performance of "Pyramus and Thisbe." When ten men turned up at Enslowe Hill, in Oxfordshire, on the night of 21 November 1596, a different sort of plot was to be hatched. From the middle of October, 1596, until late November, the Hampton Gay carpenter Bartholomew Stere and a miller, Richard Bradshawe, planned an uprising of poor artisans. They were enduring the familiar hardships of the mid-1590s, and like many of their contemporaries, they attributed their distress to enclosures and to hoarding. Expecting to enlist some three hundred followers, Stere and Bradshawe were said to have plans to "cast down enclosures, seize goods and arms, and then cut off the enclosers' heads."[23] According to a report prepared for Sir Robert Cecil, Stere's "owtward pretense was to . . . helpe the poore cominaltie that were readie to famish for want of corne."[24] Stere's band would then march to London, join with city apprentices, and foment a general insurrection.[25] When only ten men turned up at Enslowe Hill, the artisans dispersed and abandoned further plans. But Roger Symondes, a carpenter and father of six, who initially showed interest in the plan, had already revealed the plot to a local magistrate. As a result, five men were named as "principal offenders," six were said to be "definitely involved," and nine more were implicated. The "rebels" included carpenters, weavers, millers, a mason, a bricklayer, a carter, and a baker. The principals were brought to London "under guard, with their hands pinioned and their legs bound under their horses' bellies." In 1597, a grand jury indicted three of the men for "levying war against the Queen." Only two verdicts survive: the men were to be hanged, drawn, and quartered. No indictment against Stere survives, but his brother John (a weaver from nearby Witney) is recorded as having testified that "happ what would . . . [Bartholomew] could die but once . . . he would not allwaies live like a slave."[26]

Keith Wrightson, in a judicious chapter on "Order" in Elizabethan society between 1580 and 1680, suggests one reason for juxtaposing this Oxfordshire plot with the plotting of Shakespeare's Athenian artisans: theatricality is common to both stories. Wrightson describes a Somerset crowd (also in 1596) which seized a load of cheese. They were said to be motivated by the belief that "rich men had gotten all into their hands and will starve the poor." But Wrightson doubts the seriousness of such sentiments; he thinks that "much of the drama of the government's statements and the crowd's menaces was indeed theatre. The government needed to present a stark portrait . . . to rally support . . . while the threatening postures of the poor were but a means to an end and very often no more sincere than their more accustomed postures of deference."[27] In *A Midsummer Night's Dream*, we see both the drama and the deference, but not the riot—it turns out that lawlessness has been displaced to the disobedient and violent lovers. Off the stage and in a manner akin to "honest neighbours" who would help antagonists patch up their differences, potential rioters worked to stimulate official action. Elizabethan riots were rather orderly affairs. Rioters threatened in the name of such traditional and legitimate rights as the right to eat, to buy victuals at fair prices, and to be free of hoarders and speculators. And these were rights endorsed by the authorities, particularly at the national level. As a result, argues Wrightson, "there was a strong element of negotiation in the tradition of riot which both rioters and the governing class understood."[28]

Deference and accommodation might free up the courts and slow down traffic at the gallows. In 1596, in Canterbury, rioters consulted an attorney's clerk as to the law before preventing grain from leaving the city. From below, as well as from above, there was a desire to maintain order. The central government, in the form of Parliament, the Privy Council, and Assize judges, joined with the local poor and hard-pressed artificers to respond to dearth in the 1590s. Those highest and lowest in the social hierarchy turned their attention to those in the middle. "Such marginal elements as the morally ambivalent middlemen"—badgers and enclosers—were blamed for the hardships felt by potential rioters.[29] Time after time, the poor found that the state's explanation for dearth coincided with their own. Ignoring the bad weather and consequent bad harvests, which no one could alter, magistrates and artisans agreed that villainous men, those who profited from scarcity, were the appropriate target. At the very moment when customary views of the marketplace (founded on just price and neighborly harmony) were being undermined by harsh economic realities, the state sought to reinforce such views. Dearth was blamed on the covetous and the uncharitable.[30] Therefore rather than riot, the typically depressed artisan or tradesman petitioned a government which shared what Walter and Wrightson have called his "moralistic, even medieval" economic theory. And when he did riot, the artificer contemplated not anarchy or revolution, but remedial action on the part of the state.

The structure and logic of the relations between the artisanate and those in power were based on dependence. Those with authority were able to enhance their legitimacy to the extent that they could convince poor people that they shared their concerns and could respond to them. Moralistic and paternalistic strategies permitted the poor to hold on to their sense of the legitimacy of their complaints and at the same time reduced the threat of riot. Conversely, infantilized artisans might "manipulate the fears of their betters through formal petitions and indirect threats in order to galvanize them into action, to persuade them to fulfill those moral and legal obligations in defense of the weak which legitimized their authority."[31] A comparable dynamic is diffused throughout *A Midsummer Night's Dream*. The text offers accommodation and deference, but on its margins we note raised swords and threatening gallows. Starveling would have his fellows "leave the killing out." Bottom would leave the killing in, but would devise a "prologue [a petition which would] *seem* to say we will do no harm with our swords" (III.i.13–17; emphasis added).

* * *

The paternalism inherent in Elizabethan social policy is writ large across the relationships in *A Midsummer Night's Dream*. So are deference and accommodation and the never-wholly-absent threats which follow when deference is exhausted. Theseus will patronize the artisans' play—not their labor. They are "Hard-handed men that *work* in Athens here / Which never *labour'd* in their minds till now; / And now have *toil'd* their unbreath'd memories. . ." (V.i.72–74, emphasis added). The skills which the artisans have practiced are effaced just as surely as the "battle with the Centaurs" and the "riot of the tipsy Bacchanals, / . . . in their rage" (V.i.44, 48–49). Louis Adrian Montrose notes that "these brief scenarios encompass extremes of reciprocal violence between the sexes" and so they are rejected.[32] In the context I am developing, the threat of "battle," "riot," and "rage" is equally sufficient grounds for rejection. Theseus "will hear that play" which is tendered in "simpleness and duty," for in such cases, "never anything can be amiss" (V.i.81–83). In fact, the labor to be performed here will be that of Theseus. He will have to exert himself to "take what they [the players] mistake" (l. 90). What "poor duty cannot do" (l. 91), Theseus will make up for, since he is familiar enough with the child-like inarticulateness of his inferiors. He is used to clerks who "shiver and look pale, / Make periods in the midst of sentences, / Throttle their practis'd accents in their fears" (V.i.95–97). Perhaps he is already familiar with Quince. Momentarily, the carpenter will be shivering through his mispunctuated Prologue. It is the "modesty of fearful duty" (l. 101) not "audacious eloquence" (l. 103), that Theseus looks for, arranges for, but cannot guarantee. The child-like artisan, in "tongue-tied simplicity" (l. 104) will, like Elizabethan artisans in the 1590s, perform for rulers who may defend and reward him. And Theseus, like those in power in the 1590s, will go on at length, convincing himself of the commonality between the "least," not "great clerks," and his "capacity" (I.i.93 and 105).

The performance begins with deference: *"If we offend. . . ."* However, the meaning of the prologue is rendered ambivalent by its mispunctuation in delivery. Like Elizabethan artisans who rioted not to offend, but with good will, the prologue teeters back and forth between deference and offensiveness. *"If we offend, it is with our good will"* (V.i.108), declares Quince. Harold Brooks' note in the Arden edition reminds us that malpunctuation had been used for "Machiavellian ambiguity" in *Edward II*. There is nothing Machiavellian here, but ambiguity enough for those in the actual theater audience who must make sense of this show of deference. Quince means to say that the artisans have come to content and to delight their audience; but he voices an altogether different sentiment. *"We do not come, as minding to content you,"* he proclaims; *"All for your delight, / We are not here"* (ll. 114–115). It then slips out that "the actors are at hand" that the audience may take this opportunity to "repent" (ll. 115–116). While the theater audience may hear a provocation in this, Hippolyta chooses to reassert the equation between artisan and child ("Indeed he hath played on his prologue like a child on a recorder" (ll. 122–123). Theseus, taking his cue from his betrothed's concern that the playing is "not in government," but perhaps hearing something of the prologue's challenge, adds impatiently that the "speech was . . . disordered" (ll.123, 124–125). Offense, intended or not by Prologue, evokes a response that conjoins (dis)orderly children and government. The artisans, however, have conceived their performance in another way. They envision a performance that will enrich them: "sixpence a day during . . . life," says Snug (IV.ii.19–20). Moreover if the performance goes forward, they will all be "made men" (IV.ii.18).

Though deferring, the artisans would be "men." Bottom wants Lion to "entreat" the ladies "not to fear, not to tremble" (III.i.39–40). But Snug the joiner ought also to declare, "I am a man, as other men are" (III.i.42–43). The artisans seem implicitly to recognize the degree to which they are normally infantilized (or feminized), and so throughout the play and the play-within-the-play they work to assert their manhood. Flute would rather not "play a woman" just at the moment he is becoming a man: "I have a beard coming" (I.ii.43–44). As children, they are vulnerable and betray a common fear: "That [frighting the Duchess] would hang us, every *mother's son*" (I.ii.73, emphasis added). As men, they can play the role of "a tyrant" or "play Ercles rarely . . . to make all split" (I.ii.24–26). "Every *man's* name which is thought fit through all Athens to play in our interlude" is read out by Quince in response to Bottom's request that each ought to be called, "*man* by *man*" (I.ii.2–6, emphasis added). And as each name is called, each player is identified as a worker with a particular skill: "Nick Bottom, the weaver," "Francis Flute, the bellowsmender," "Robin Starveling, the tailor." The company members assert themselves first as men, then as artificers. Their pride in their manhood, as well as their anxiety, is merely patronized by Theseus when he confidently tells Hippolyta, "If we imagine no worse of them than they of themselves, they may pass for excellent men" (V.i.211–212). For Theseus, their manhood, like their childishness, is contingent upon him.

Shakespeare's Theseus conceptualizes Bottom and his crew in much the same way North's Plutarch's Theseus thought of his Athenian workers. Plutarch's Theseus "suffered not the great multitude that came thither tagge and ragge, to be without distinction of degrees and orders. For he first divided the noble men, from husbandmen and artificers, appointing the noble men as judges and magistrates. . . ."[33] Thus Theseus promised "a common wealth . . . not subject to the power of any sole prince, but rather a popular state." But it was to be a state, like Elizabeth's, with degrees and order. Circa 1600, John Vowell, alias Hooker, enunciated a similar vision: "albeit these laborers be of the most inferior in degree yet they be liberi homines and of a free condicion."[34] Men like Quince and Bottom were seen first through their degree, as artificers, and then, perhaps, as men. Their degree insured their dependence, their impotence, and their childishness. All artificers were, for Sir Thomas Smith, among the "rascall sort" (for Puck, they are "that barren sort"—III.ii.13); and they were among the politically impotent as well.[35] But men like Smith and Hooker and William Harrison were categorizing Englishmen because they were unsure of their own power. The very business of categorization, defining degrees and roles, was a way to insure and then to ratify dependence. Imagining no worse of artificers than artificers did of themselves expressed the hope that they would not take it into their heads to imagine too well of themselves. The accommodation envisaged by both Theseuses assumes an agreement of interests: artisans or artificers will defer to judges, magistrates, and dukes who understand their values and essential needs. But in *A Midsummer Night's Dream*, it is not on the basis of their handicrafts that artisans negotiate with their superiors. Instead, they are suffered to perform a children's book version of an Ovidian tale.

Not only is this the child's version—it is a story about adolescents. The artisans who would be men dramatize "the two yong folke," not yet "man and wife," who are trying to escape their "Parents['] . . . let."[36] Whatever tragic point may attach to Ovid's Pyramus and Thisbe story is rendered ludicrous in Shakespeare's. The desolation that accompanies thwarted desire in Ovid is somewhat mitigated by Pyramus's and Thisbe's youth, if not their deaths. This desolation is mitigated precisely by their farcical deaths in the translation of the story performed in *A Midsummer Night's Dream*. Erotic confrontations involving the artisans in *A Midsummer Night's Dream* are undermined by the assertion of typically infantile artisanal impotence. There is no love story in this performance of Pyramus and Thisbe, only the "silliest stuff that ever I heard" (V.i.207). What passion there is, "and the death of a dear friend, would go near to make a man look sad" (V.i.277–278). Neither is there much of a love story in Titania's bower, where once again we are presented with an artisan not as an artisan (rather, as an ass). Bottom is treated like a child; the "tongue-tied simplicity / In the least" that so pleases Theseus is translated into Titania's command, "Tie up my love's tongue, bring him silently" (III.i.194). Perhaps it is performance and make-up which ultimately determine just how infantile or mature we find the conjunction of fairy queen and ass-headed artisan.[37] Titania issues commands, but Bottom is to share her bed (III.i.164). Whether the sexual dynamic between Bottom and Titania is pre-Oedipal, Oedipal, bestial, or adult and heterosexual, the problem of the social status of these lovers is taken up without delay. Titania sees a "*gentle* mortal" (III.i.132, emphasis added). And the attending fairies are expected to act courteously "to this gentleman" (III.i.157). It does not escape Bottom's notice that he has been translated into, among other things, a gentleman. He even expresses his concern that "cowardly giant-like ox-beef hath devoured many a gentleman of [Mustardseed's] . . . house" (III.i.185–186). Consider the translations at work here: while it was being asserted that enclosures were devouring the laboring and farming poor, an artisan weaver, now partially a beast himself, is translated into a gentleman who is concerned for the well-being of other gentlemen. On top of this, Titania has it in mind still further to translate Bottom, "to purge . . . [his] mortal grossness" (III.i.153). This does not seem to have to do with his ass-head; rather, it may have to do with elevating the "gentle mortal" weaver beyond the gentry to fairy immortality. For the moment she will treat him like a child, feeding him, doting on him, and watching over him as he sleeps.

Certainly Oberon conceives of Bottom in a more instrumental fashion than does Titania. His use of the weaver is part of the play's dramatization of statecraft, a dramatization most clearly centered on Oberon's mortal surrogate, Theseus. Duke Theseus' theory of governance might be summed up by the motto, "Our sport shall be to take what they mistake" (V.i.90). All of the mistaking, looking with "another's eyes," looking "not with the eyes," "misprision," and seeing with "parted eye" that motivates the lovers' plot, Theseus transforms and forgives magnanimously.[38] At the same time, Theseus' fairy alterego, Oberon, gives a literal twist to Theseus' motto, finding sport in taking the changeling boy that he accuses Titania of mistaking, and finding still more sport in the knowledge that Titania has mistaken an ass for a gentle lover. Theseus has already established his lordship over Hippolyta; but Oberon must reestablish his lordship over Titania ("Tarry, rash wanton; am not I thy lord?" [II.i.63]). For the moment, the "mazed world" endures a "progeny of evils": bad harvests, floods, frosts, and disease. Oberon must implement a policy that will restore order, and his instrument turns out to be Bottom. But it is unnecessary to translate the weaver-ass into a "scapegoat" whose sacrifice works "*only* to facilitate the reconciliation of those with superior social status."[39] Just as he will profit—to the tune of "sixpence a day during his life"—from his role in "Pyramus and Thisbe," so Bottom profits from his role in the reconciliation of Oberon and Titania. Newly awakened Bottom can "discourse wonders" (IV.i.28) based on his "most rare vision" (IV.i.203). Temporarily an ass, Bottom is not only made a man, but has been permitted a vision that may after all somewhat "purge . . . [his] mortal grossness."

Bottom's company takes flight at the sight of their "monstrous" fellow (III.i.99–100). But Oberon and Puck make use of this literally many-headed Elizabethan monster. Half a century later, it was said that the "many-headed monster," made up of "some turbulent spirits, backed by *rude* and tumultous *mechanic persons* would have the total subversion of the government of the state."[40] And just as Puck manipulates one of the "rude mechanicals" (III.ii.9) in *A Midsummer Night's Dream* to restore harmony in the fairy kingdom, Parliamentary leaders were not afraid "to take advantage of popular initiative" to restore justice and harmony in Caroline England.[41] But this is to allegorize and to suggest far-fetched foreshadowings in Shakespeare. It is more to the point to note that the designers of Elizabethan social policy were trying to determine the place of the poor and of artificers and husbandmen in an orderly realm. Confronted like Oberon with bad harvests and want of cheer, the Crown and Parliament tried to counter disorder with the 1563 Statute of Artificers, the Poor Laws of 1598 and 1601, the Book of Orders, issued in 1587 and 1594, and the Enclosure Act of 1598. Such statutes were meant to "take what they mistake"—to construe economic and social harmony where many poor laborers knew only cruel subsistence and chronic unemployment.

The Statute of Artificers was an attempt to control the conditions of employment for many workers, to restrict the mobility of labor, and to establish procedures to determine local wage rates.[42] Conceived of as a way to remedy the "imperfection & contrarietie" in the many existing laws, the Statute appears to protect artificers in the face of "wages and allowances . . . [that] are in divers places to[o] small, and not aunswerable to this time, respecting the advauncement of pryces."[43] But the statute goes on to fix maximum, not minimum, wages. The state sought to keep wages low, making a popular connection between large numbers of potential workers and low wages.[44] Not until 1603 did a statute order that the "assessment of minimum wages for clothmakers . . . [should] reflect the state of the economy."[45] The long apprenticeships stipulated by crafts and by law further reflect the desire for cheap labor, not the difficulty of mastering a particular skill.[46] Elizabethan labor laws, like Elizabethan poor laws, were legislated to preserve order. It was assumed that the laborers as well as the elite of England would profit from stability. The "fit" Athenian artisans in *A Midsummer Night's Dream* are rewarded for their industry and good will with the opportunity to perform for their Duke. The proximity of artisanate and nobility, the mutual celebration of aristocratic nuptials, and the expected pension for the performers make for a community of shared interests. Order is restored in Athens when all levels of society celebrate together.

Of course, those in power retain their power. They countenance the "modesty of fearful duty" (V.i.101) by bringing the artisans into their celebration. The pension in store for Bottom, "He would have deserved" (IV.ii.23). Nobles and artisans accommodate themselves to one another with ease because the latter are so obviously deserving. The English Poor Law, codified in 1598 and 1601, was the response of a ruling elite that had just made it through the difficult 1590s.[47] Those who were deemed lazy or insubordinate among the lower orders were to be punished, and the idle poor were set to work. The deserving poor were to be relieved.[48] For the most part it seems that relief measures (as well as the procedures outlined in the Statute of Artificers) were ineffective: there were few welfare or policing agencies, and few people received help. But it is important to remember that the old and orphans—the most deserving poor—never would have been a threat to social order. Artisans, freemen, and apprentices took the lead in disturbances, and they, not the poor widows and the elderly, had to be placated. Bottom is used by Oberon to counter the sort of disorder in nature that was threatening so many Elizabethan wage earners, who were worse off in the 1590s than they had been for a century.[50] Then Bottom and his company are brought into the harmonious community of the play's final act even though, as Puck knows, the "hungry lion" still roars, the "wolf behowls," and the ploughman, "All with weary task fordone," is dead tired after a day's labor (V.i.357–360).[51]

* * *

It remains to determine the extent to which Shakespeare accommodates himself, and is accommodated to, those in power. It would seem that his company was asked to perform their play at an aristocratic wedding.[52] And it has been argued by Walter Cohen that Shakespeare's theater took a "fundamentally artisanal historical form."[53] Thus an admittedly oversimplified analogy suggests itself: the Athenian artisans' play is to the dominant Athenian culture (represented by the wedding couples) as the London artisans' play is to the culture represented by the Stanleys, the Veres, Burghley, and Elizabeth. Bottom's bid to play the roles of both lover and tyrant comments upon love and tyranny in Athens. Pyramus's and Thisbe's filial rebellion and subsequent farcical-tragic fate comments upon Hermia's and Lysander's rebellion and eventual comic fate. The Athenian artisans' bid for favor and profit by means of what they take to be decorous performance comments upon the relations between high and low status groups in Athenian society. Corresponding dynamics which would correlate Shakespeare's company and play with the Elizabethan aristocracy may be sketched out. The four lovers' marriage plans in *A Midsummer Night's Dream*, and the attention these plans receive in the Athenian court, glance at marriage brokering in Elizabeth's court and her much-publicized readiness to intervene when it suited her policy or fancy. Then too, artisan players, like those in Shakespeare's troupe in the 1590s and after, were regularly forced to accommodate themselves to numerous restrictions on playing. No doubt actors and playwrights and perhaps even the likes of Philip Henslowe met to discuss proper decorum in the face of statutes forbidding comment on religious controversy, personal satire at the expense of influential persons, criticism of court policies and foreign powers, and much more. Nonetheless, play after play that survived Edmund Tilney's and then Sir George Buc's scrutiny managed to comment on the powerful, the court, and religious controversy. Playwrights deferred and yet criticized, and both City and Court responded with tolerance at one moment, imprisonment at another.

   A Midsummer Night's Dream describes relations of power in its play world that have, as we have seen, much to do with such relations in Elizabethan society. Stephen Greenblatt has argued that "Shakespeare relentlessly *explores* the relations of power in a given culture. That more than exploration is involved is much harder to demonstrate convincingly."[54] I would modify this cautious assessment, and so propose that Shakespeare criticizes the relations of power in his culture, but does so with remarkable sensitivity to the nuances of threat and accommodation which animate these relations. Walter Cohen notes that "However aristocratic the explicit message of a play might be, the conditions of its production introduced alternative effects."[55] Precisely these conditions of production are dramatized in *A Midsummer Night's Dream*, by means of the players within the play. The company that performs "Pyramus and Thisbe" reveals the company that performs *A Midsummer Night's Dream* perhaps more than the latter would care to admit. The desire to be made men but to receive a pension for life, to leave the killing out but to "gleek upon occasion"—these express the reasonable longings of artisans throughout the Elizabethan age.

NOTES

*Originally published in *Renaissance Papers 1986*, ed. Dale B.J. Randall and Joseph Porter (Durham, NC: Southeastern Renaissance Conference, 1986), 11–30. Reprinted with the kind permission of the Southeastern Renaissance Conference.

1. *A Midsummer Night's Dream*, III.i.141. All *MND* quotations are from Harold F. Brooks, *Arden Shakespeare* (London: Methuen, 1979), and will be cited in the text in parentheses.

2. Brooks, p.cxv.

3. Cf. Stephen Orgel's argument in *The Illusion of Power: Political Theater in the English Renaissance* (Berkeley: University of California Press, 1975), "that private theaters are the creation of their audiences" (p.6).

4. See Lawrence Stone, *The Family, Sex and Marriage, 1500–1800* (New York: Harper and Row, 1979), p.98: see also Stone's "Interpersonal Violence in English Society 1300–1980," *Past & Present* 101 (1983), 22–33.

5. J.A. Sharpe, "Enforcing the Law in the Seventeenth-Century English Village," in *Crime and the Law: The Social History of Crime in Western Europe Since 1500*, ed. V.A.C. Gatrell, Bruce Lenman, and Geoffrey Parker (London: Europe Publications, 1980), p.112.

6. J.A. Sharpe, "'Such Disagreement betwyx Neighbours': Litigation and Human Relations in Early Modern England," in *Disputes and Settlements: Law and Human Relations in the West*, ed. John Bossy (Cambridge: Cambridge University Press, 1983), p.175. Lawrence Stone, in his article in *Past & Present* (see above, n.4), questions Sharpe's thesis but concludes that "The evidence seems ambiguous on this point" (p.31). Stone seems to support the traditional view—that increasing litigation, even over slander, indicates "a breakdown of consensual community methods of dealing with conflict" (p.32).

7. J.A. Sharpe, "'Such Disagreement betwyx Neighbours'. . .," p.174.

8. Alexander Leggatt, *Shakespeare's Comedy of Love* (London: Methuen, 1974), p.99.

9. Stephen Greenblatt, "Murdering Peasants: Status, Genre and the Representation of Rebellion," *Representations* 1 (1983), 16–23. Further citations from this article are noted in the text.

10. Fredric Jameson, *The Political Unconscious,* p.81, cited in Louis Adrian Montrose, "'Shaping Fantasies': Figurations of Gender and Power in Elizabethan Culture," *Representations* 1 (1983), 87n.

11. J.S. Cockburn, "The Nature and Incidence of Crime in England 1559–1625: A Preliminary Survey," in *Crime in England 1550–1800,* ed. J.S. Cockburn (London: Methuen, 1978), p.61.

12. Keith Wrightson, *English Society 1580–1680* (New Jersey: Rutgers University Press, 1982), p.156.

13. Cited in Joel Samaha, *Law and Order in Historical Perspective: The Case of Elizabethan Essex* (New York: Academic Press, 1974), p.44.

14. J.H. Baker, "Criminal Courts and Procedure at Common Law 1550–1800," in *Crime in England 1550–1880,* p.43.

15. Samaha, p.27.

16. Samaha, p.168; see also Christopher Hill, *Reformation to Industrial Revolution: A Social and Economic History of Britain 1530–1780* (London: Weidenfeld & Nicolson, 1967), p.73, and D.M. Palliser, *The Age of Elizabeth: England under the Late Tudors 1547–1603* (London: Longman, 1983), pp.50 and 387.

17. Samaha, p.64.

18. Samaha, p.55.

19. Cockburn, p.55.

20. William Hunt, *The Puritan Moment: The Coming of Revolution in an English County* (Cambridge, Mass.: Harvard University Press, 1983), p.64.

21. Peter Clark, "Popular Protest and Disturbance in Kent, 1558–1640," *Economic History Review 29* (1976), 367.

22. Clark, pp.371–373.

23. Buchanan Sharp, *In Contempt of All Authority: Rural Artisans and Riot in the West of England, 1586–1660* (Berkeley: University of California Press, 1980), p.20. A comprehensive account and interpretation of this failed uprising has appeared recently; see John Walter, "'A Rising of the People?' The Oxfordshire Rising of 1596," *Past & Present 107* (1985), 90–143.

24. Edwin F. Gay, "The Midland Revolt and the Inquisition of Depopulation of 1607," *Transactions of the Royal Historical Society 18* (1904), 238.

25. In 1595, five London apprentices were executed. They had joined in riots at Tower Hill to protest the whipping and imprisonment of a few young men who had protested the price of butter. See Walter, pp.92 and 108.

26. Sharp, pp.21 and 40–41.

27. Wrightson, p.174.

28. Wrightson, pp.174–175; see also Clark, pp.378–380.

29. John Walter and Keith Wrightson, "Dearth and Social Order in Early Modern England," *Past & Present* 71 (1976), 41.

30. Walter and Wrightson, p.31; see also E.P. Thompson, "The Moral Economy of the English Crowd in the Eighteenth Century," *Past & Present* 50 (1971), 78–79 and 132.

31. Walter and Wrightson, p.32.

32. Montrose, p.75.

33. The relevant passage from Sir Thomas North's Plutarch is cited in the Arden edition of *A Midsummer Night's Dream*, p.135.

34. John Hooker, *Synopsis Chorographical of Devonshire*, cited in William J. Blake, "Hooker's Synopsis Chorographical of Devonshire," *Report and Transactions of the Devonshire Association* 47 (1915), 334–348.

35. Sir Thomas Smith, *De Republica Anglorum* (London, 1583), p.31: see also Christopher Hill, *Reformation to Industrial Revolution*, p.41.

36. Ovid, *Metamorphoses*, trans. Arthur Golding (London, 1567), Bk. 4, II. 69 and 77–78.

37. See Montrose, p.65.

38. On "misprision" in *A Midsummer Night's Dream*, see René Girard, "Myth and Ritual in Shakespeare's *A Midsummer Night's Dream*," in *Textual Strategies*, ed. Josué V. Harari (Ithaca: Cornell University Press, 1982), 189–212; and David Marshall, "Exchanging Visions: Reading *A Midsummer Night's Dream*," *ELH* 49 (1982), 543–575. Brooks notes that "Chaucer's Theseus, too, was magnanimous, forgiving. . ." (Arden editon, p.97).

39. I have conflated and given emphasis to words written by Jeanne Addison Roberts ("Animals as Agents of Revelation: the Horizontalizing of the Chain of Being in Shakespeare's Comedies," in *Shakespearean Comedy*, ed. Maurice Charney [New York: New York Literary Forum, 1980], p.85) and Elliot Krieger (*A Marxist Study of Shakespeare's Comedies* [New York: Harper and Row, 1979], p.60). Krieger's argument is, however, akin to my own. He writes that *A Midsummer Night's Dream* "dramatizes the aristocratic fantasy of, and strategy for, creating complete social poise" (p.67).

40. Christopher Hill, "The Many-Headed Monster in Late Tudor and Early Stuart Political Thinking," in *From the Renaissance to the Counter-Revolution*, ed. Charles H. Carter (New York: Random House, 1965), pp. 310–311 (emphasis added).

41. Hill, "The Many-Headed Monster. . .," p.316 and *passim*.

42. Donald Woodward, "The Background to the Statute of Artificers: The Genesis of Labour Policy, 1558–63," *Economic History Review 33* (1980), 32.

43. "An Acte Touching Divers Orders of Artificers, Laborers, Servauntes of Husbandry, and Apprentices," 5 Eliz.c.4, *Anno Quinto Reginae Elizabeth* . . . (London, 1563), C₄ᵛ.

44. See D.C. Coleman, "Labour in the English Economy of the Seventeenth Century," *Economic History Review 8* (1956), 281; and see Hill, *Reformation to Industrial Revolution*, p.41.

45. Sharp, p.54; a 1598 statute clarified the 1563 statute, making no mention of minimum wages, but tying wages to "times of plenty or scarcity."

46. L.A. Clarkson, *The Pre-Industrial Economy of England 1500–1750* (London: B.T. Batsford, 1971), p.17.

47. See Paul Slack, "Social Problems and Social Policies," *The Traditional Community under Stress* (Milton Keynes, Bucks.: Open University Press, 1977), p.98.

48. See Hunt, pp.66–79.

49. See Slack, p.100. [Editor's note: reference number missing in the original text.]

50. See L.A. Clarkson, p.212; but compare D.M. Palliser, p.159.

51. Compare Krieger, p.68.

52. James P. Bednarz makes a strong case for the Stanley-Vere wedding. See his "Imitations of Spenser in *A Midsummer Night's Dream*," *Renaissance Drama* 14 (1983), 79–102. See also Brooks, p.lvii.

53. Walter Cohen, "The Artisan Theatres of Renaissance England and Spain," *Theatre Journal* 35 (1983), 516. See also Cohen's *Drama of a Nation* (Ithaca: Cornell University Press, 1985), pp.179–185.

54. Stephen Greenblatt, *Renaissance Self-Fashioning from More to Shakespeare* (Chicago: University of Chicago Press, 1980), p.254.

55. Cohen, p.517.

Bottom's Up

Festive Theory in *A Midsummer Night's Dream**

Annabel Patterson

A Midsummer Night's Dream, as we all know, was first published in Quarto in 1600. For its other, originating boundary we have turned to one of the play's apparently topical allusions, to Titania's complaint to Oberon of what their quarrel has done to the environment:

> The ox hath therefore stretch'd his yoke in vain,
> The ploughman lost his sweat, and the green corn
> Hath rotted ere his youth attain'd a beard.
> . . . .
> The nine men's morris is fill'd up with mud,
> And the quaint mazes in the wanton green,
> For lack of tread, are undistinguishable. (II.i.93–100)[1]

This passage has situated the *Dream* in 1595–1596, a season notorious for its bad weather and bad harvests. These led to the abortive Oxfordshire rising of November 1596, when Bartholomew Stere, a carpenter, and Richard Bradshawe, a miller, had planned to "cast down enclosures, seize goods and arms, and then cut off the enclosers' heads."[2] Depositions concerning this event were still being heard in London by the Privy Council during January 1597; it was said that Stere's "owtward pretense was to . . . helpe the poore cominaltie that were readie to famish for want of corne." The handful of leaders were all artisans, and although the rising came to nothing (the leaders could find no followers), it is not implausible, as Theodore Leinwand has suggested, to see in the *Dream's* artisanal subplot, with its constant references to violence *avoided*, an imaginative version of the sad little socioeconomic farce enacted in Oxford and London and ending in tragedy for its protagonists.[3] There is surely an allusion to a time of hardship, not only in Titania's speech, but also in the name of one of Shakespeare's artisan actors, Robin Starveling. While Titania's speech, with its invocation of natural rhythms and cosmic distress, invites thought on the drama's relation to rituals connected with the seasonal cycle and the symbolization of fertility, Starveling's name and associates suggest that in this comedy Shakespeare anticipated his own later experiments in dramatizing *social* distress and in representing (in both the mimetic and political senses of that term) the under-represented underclasses.

* * *

Of all the comedies, *A Midsummer Night's Dream* offers the most powerful invitation to locate it within what is now known as festive theory. The question is, which branch of festive theory? There are three main branches to which the *Dream* has hitherto been tied, directly or implicitly. All have support from some parts of the text, but none by itself can explain the whole. Indeed, they tend partly to contradict each other, or perhaps to repeat a contest that was actually occurring in Shakespeare's day. The first and most frequently repeated, despite strenuous opposition by Richard Levin,[4] is the courtly-occasionalist premise—that because the *Dream* stages an aristocratic wedding, it must have been written to celebrate an actual marriage in the circle of Elizabeth's courtiers, and so is epithalamic in tone and function. This theory relies on the play's opening and closing emphasis on a season of "merriment" ordered by Theseus in order to change the tone of his courtship of Hippolyta from conquest to celebration, and on his goodnight speech after the artisans' play is ended:

> . . . Sweet friends, to bed,
> A fortnight hold we this solemnity,
> In nightly revels and new jollity. (V.i.368–370)

But to adopt this premise, the reader must align herself with the courtly circle around Theseus, and with what I shall call the Thesean aesthetic, which reads the entire play retroactively in the light of the Duke's all-too-frequently excerpted speech on "shaping fantasies," "aery nothing," and the power of imagination (V.i.2–27). The Thesean perspective has only one possible view of Bottom and his colleagues—the social condescension that laughs at, not with, their amateur theatricals. Yet the framing festive plot manifestly represents a strategy by which popular drama was increasingly brought under court control. By identifying Philostrate (in the list of Dramatis Personae) as "Master of the Revels" to Theseus, the Folio text of the *Dream* alludes to an office created by Elizabeth in 1581 as a strategy simultaneously for ensuring high quality in her own entertainment, for initiating the recentralization of the theater under court patronage, and for keeping it under surveillance. That there was some substance to the idea that popular drama bred subversion is attested by the records of Jack Kett's rebellion in 1549, which began as a protest against enclosures, but was actually set in motion, coincidentally or otherwise, by the staging of "a Play at Windham, by an old custome, which lasted two daies, and two nights," drawing huge audiences and producing, literally, an armed, violent, and organized demonstration.[5] Evidently the *Dream*'s artisans understand this attitude to popular theater: it keeps them jittering on the divide between terror and ambition, between fear of being hanged for frightening the ladies or drawing a sword on the stage, and the hope of being "made men," with "sixpence a day" for life.[6]

The second branch of festive theory refers not to courtly revels but to popular rituals, and assumes that the play is motivated less by the social needs of the Elizabethan court than by instincts and behavior usually interrogated by anthropologists. When C.L. Barber published his groundbreaking study of the comedies in 1959,[7] he connected Shakespeare with a large and today still expanding intellectual movement that includes the work on ritual of Durkheim, Van Gennep, and Victor Turner, and has recently merged with Mikhail Bakhtin's account of the carnivalesque. In Barber's view, the appearance in Shakespeare's plays of festive or folk elements, such as the winter season of Misrule over which Olivia's fool, Feste, presides in *Twelfth Night*, or the morris dances that appear in play after play (and are punningly alluded to in Titania's lament for the "nine men's morris . . . filled up with mud" [II.i.98]) or the May games that take the four young lovers of the *Dream* into the forest away from parental control, were part of a cultural transformation whereby the archaic and amateur forms of dramatic representation were absorbed by the mature national theater. That is to say, they were both thematized and contained.

Claiming that saturnalian impulse, "when directly expressed, ran head
on into official prohibition," Barber concluded that the transfer of
festive impulses to the theater was an enforced "shift from symbolic
action towards *symbolic* action" (p. 57):

> his comedy presents holiday magic as imagination, games as
> expressive gestures. At high moments it brings into focus, as part of
> the play, the significance of the saturnalian form itself as a
> paradoxical human need, problem and resource. (p.15)

Barber's argument generated fresh thought on the comedies but it
has serious limitations. It takes perhaps too dark a view of Elizabeth's
attitude to popular games, and too benign a view of their
Shakespearean representations. True, Feste's name points to an
allegory of festivity as "allowed fooling," permission which Malvolio,
equally standing for malevolent prohibitions, would foreclose. But
allowance within the well-regulated courtly household is, if one stops
to think about it, only another form of prohibition, more effective by
virtue of seeming to be liberal. And when Jack Cade, the leader of the
popular revolt in *Henry VI, Part 2,* is compared to "a wild Morisco, /
Shaking the bloody darts as he his bells" (III.i.346–366), Barber stops
at the point where the allusion to morris dancing invokes fertility
rituals, and misses the metaphor's social threat. In fact, Barber's theory
as a whole stops at the point where Shakespeare is declared to be, so to
speak, on top of his material, a position, it is implied, essentially
disinterested. The magic term in Barber's formulation is, not
coincidentally, the Thesean "imagination"; and the book's message
overall is that both the archaic festivals and their Elizabethan practice
functioned to reaffirm, through reconciliatory symbolic action, the
hierarchical structure of society.

The problem thus avoided was gradually articulated in the work of
Victor Turner, himself much influenced by Barber. In *The Ritual
Process* (1969), Turner developed his theory of *communitas,* or the
individual's sense of belonging, voluntarily, to a larger, cohesive, and
harmonious social group, on the idealist model of ritual action inherited
from Durkheim and Van Gennep. Thus Turner argues initially that

> Cognitively, nothing underlines regularity so well as absurdity or
> paradox. Emotionally, nothing satisfies as much as extravagant or

temporarily permitted illicit behavior. Rituals of status reversal accommodate both aspects. (p. 176)

This regulatory motive accounts for the fact, he thought, that inversion rituals occur most often "at fixed points in the annual cycle," "for structural regularity is here reflected in temporal order."[8] In Turner's later *Dramas, Fields, and Metaphors* (1974), however, inversion rituals are seen rather as motivated by some natural disaster or "public, overt breach or deliberate non-fulfillment of some crucial norm," which requires remedial rather than regulatory intervention.[9] And *communitas* is reconceived as running *counter* to the stratified and rule-governed conception of society, in the space that Turner calls *liminality*, in which social distinctions are temporarily suspended. In liminal situations, the lower social strata become privileged, and bodily parts and biological processes, conceived as the source of regenerative energy, are revalued; hence the ritual use of animal disguises, masks, and gestures. An exchange takes place, he argues, between the normative or ideological poles of social meaning, which dictate attitudes to parents, children, elders, and rulers, and the physiological poles or facts of life (birth, death, sexuality) which the norms exist to regulate; and in this exchange, as Turner sees it, "the biological referents are ennobled and the normative referents are charged with emotional significance" (p. 55), which renders them once again acceptable.

By proposing this ritual exchange between rules and energies as *occasioned* by natural disasters or unusual breaches in social relations, Turner's model seems more promising than Barber's for explaining the ritual aspects of the *Dream*, which contains as one of its festive premises the breach between Oberon and Titania that has resulted in crop failure and disrupted the natural cycle. But before developing this suggestion, I must observe that even in its late form Turner's festive theory remains, if not idealist, at least no more than meliorist. That is to say, the ultimate purpose of festive rituals is seen as social regeneration and reconciliation.

There is, of course, an alternative theory, that popular festival was essentially subversive in its motives. Deriving ultimately from Marx's view that folk misrule has historically functioned to express economic antagonisms and occasionally to sharpen them into actual conflict, this position is today represented in Shakespeare studies by Robert Weimann's brilliant account of Shakespeare's use of the popular traditions in theater, which has *almost* made available a class-conscious account of the principle of "topsy-turveydom" in Shakespeare and, by extending the analysis to the tragedies, discovered the subversive implications of porters, fools, clowns, and gravediggers. Yet Weimann's book was itself also deeply influenced by Barber. The result, ironically, was a new version of the Thesean aesthetic, by which the festive and ritual traditions became primarily the raw material for a new *formal* synthesis accomplished by Shakespeare between popular traditions and the new, learned, humanist drama. Shakespeare remains the genius at the end of the evolutionary trail, but Weimann's own insights into the subversiveness of topsy-turveydom were constrained by the orthodox Marxist position that class-consciousness was not fully available as a category of thought in Shakespeare's time. The echoes of folk misrule in the plays were, he thought, "playfully rebellious gestures," and "the contradictions between the popular tradition and the culture of the ruling classes were to some extent synthesized with the needs and aspirations of the New Monarchy and were overshadowed by an overwhelming sense of national pride and unity" (pp. 24–25). Weimann's festive theory is the only one of the three that has any explanatory force in relation to the frontal presence of the artisans in the *Dream* and the hints of popular protest in their conversations. But he finally backs down, I believe, from his own insights, his literary impulses defeating his political wishes.

Unlike Michael Bristol, who has valiantly attempted an eclectic compromise between these different festive theories,[10] I shall here argue for a synthesis posited not by the critic but by Shakespeare himself, who within the text of *A Midsummer Night's Dream* seems unmistakably to have recognized much of the thinking I have just described, and the conflicting interests it represents, then and now; and, by making the different theories critique each other, produced in the end a more capacious proposal. Within the epithalamic premise of aristocratic "revels," for instance, certain surprises are introduced. Theseus's choice of the "tragical mirth" of the artisans' play is carefully articulated as rejection of learned, humanist entertainments, and selection of the popular, the amateur, and (it turns out) the ribald— the last seldom thought of by critics as matter for a courtly audience, but rather bait for the groundlings. Yet the sexual double-entendres on holes, stones, chinks, and hair that are manifest in "Pyramus and Thisbe" and its staging, some of which a bowdlerizing editorial tradition has tried to remove,[11] would have been perfectly in keeping with the conventional bawdiness of aristocratic Renaissance weddings, which still retained archaic aspects of ancient bedding rituals—"in which," remarked George Puttenham in his courtly *Arte of English Poesie* (1589), if there were any wanton or lascivious matter more then ordinarie which they called *Ficenina licentia* it was borne withal for that time because of the matter no lesse requiring."[12]

On the other hand, the festive plot that most attracted Barber's attention, the May game that takes the four young lovers into the forest, cannot be explained merely in Barber's terms, as one of those archaic fertility rituals absorbed and contained by the transforming imagination. It is, after all, only Theseus who, finding them asleep after the confusions of identity and erotic attraction are resolved, assumes "they rose up early to observe / The rite of May" (IV.i.132–133). In fact, the motive for the transgressive excursion was escape from parental and patriarchal oppression, or, in Turner's terms, the norms of "respect for elders" and "obedience to political authorities" (*Dramas*, p.55). Barber's account of the magical doings in the forest underestimates the severity of Shakespeare's treatment of the "sharp Athenian law" (I.i.162), equally taken for granted in Elizabethan England, by which marital arrangements were based on dynastic as opposed to erotic imperatives. Yet if we look to Turner's theory for a model for the way this plot is handled, we shall be disappointed. There is no exchange between rules and energies in this tale of adolescent silliness, underlined by the very ease with which the young people's emotions are rearranged. Even Shakespeare's calendrical vagueness (is it May or Midsummer?), which evidently worries Barber,[13] is naughtily incompatible with Turner's original theory of how seasonal regularity mimics and hence reinforces social order. The callowness of the Midsummer escapees, moreover, remains when the parental and societal inhibitions have been finessed away, expressing itself in their mockery of the very play that speaks to what their own predicament was, and what its ending might have been.

And then there is the third festive plot, the one which goes deeper into the anthropological origins of Maying and Midsummer holidays, while at the same time making a more radical suggestion about contemporary Elizabethan culture than *any* of the modern theorists has posited. This is the plot of Titania's quarrel with Oberon over the changeling boy, which has caused the disastrous weather and crop failure, and which can be resolved only by the most extreme example of status inversion and misrule that Shakespeare's canon contains, the infatuation of the Queen of Fairies with a common artisan who is also, temporarily, an ass. This is the plot, also, that Louis Montrose has marvelously related to psychoanalytic conceptions of gender and power in Elizabeth's reign, and, under the aegis of Theseus's phrase for imaginative work, "Shaping Fantasies," suggested that within the fantasy of Titania's liaison with Bottom lies "a discourse of anxious misogyny" precipitated by the myth of the Virgin Queen and the pressures it exerted on male sensibilities; in other words, that Titania's infatuation is the encoded revenge of Elizabeth's male subjects.[14] There is no question that Montrose has put vital pressure on aspects of the play that Barber's benign thesis overlooked[15]—the dark pre-history of Theseus as betrayer of women, the repressed myth of Amazonian independence that Hippolyta represents, and the harshness of Theseus's treatment of Hermia (even during his own festive season). A psychoanalytic reading implies, however, that these anti-festive resonances in the play rose up from its author's and the national (male) unconscious, as distinct from being part of a conscious analytic project; and Montrose completely overlooks both the *socioeconomic* quotient in the episode that he reads as the male's revenge (the amazing suggestion that a queen could be made by magic to mate with a male from the bottom stratum of society) and the fact that its results are positive. For thanks to Bottom the Weaver, who, remarked Hazlitt, "has not had justice done to him," the crisis in the natural cycle and the agricultural economy is resolved, albeit by restoring male authority.[16]

Let us now return to Turner's proposal that rituals of status inversion or revitalization frequently make use of animal masks, and imagine with new eyes what the Elizabethan audience might have seen when Bottom appears on the stage with an ass's head replacing his own. Weimann has noted "the surprising consistency of the ass' head motif from the *mimus* down to *A Midsummer Night's Dream*" (p.50); but he assumes that it, like the calf's hide which the Elizabethan fool still wore in the Mummers' Play, was merely "the survival of some kind of mimetic magic, which, after having lost its ritual function, became alienated from its original purpose and hence misunderstood as a comic attribute" (p.31). But in the *Dream*, I suggest, the ass's head distinguishes itself from comic props and animal masks in general, and becomes part of a complex structural pun, by which the ritual exchange between rules and energies does after all take place, and the lower bodily parts, in Turner's terms, are ennobled. The name "Bottom" refers not only to the bottom of the social hierarchy as the play represents it, but also to the "bottom" of the body when seated, literally the social ass or arse. As Frankie Rubinstein observes in her dictionary of Shakespeare's sexual puns, Shakespeare and his contemporaries took for granted that *ass*, as the vulgar, dialectical spelling of *arse*, was the lexical fulcrum of a powerful set of linked concepts:

> Shakespeare . . . used "ass" to pun on the ass that gets beaten with a stick and the arse that gets thumped sexually, the ass that bears a burden and the arse that bears or carries in intercourse.[17]

And she cites as an analogy the Fool's rebuke to Lear:

> When thou clovest thy crown i' th' middle, and gav'st away both parts, thou bor'st thine ass on thy back o'er the dirt: . . . thou gav'st them the rod, and put'st down thine own breeches. (I.iv.160–174)

Here exposed bodily parts, top and bottom, crown and arse, unite in a political allegory of status inversion and corporal punishment. In the *Dream*, the structural pun on "ass" is anticipated by Puck's gratuitous bottom humor, his account of pretending to be a stool that removes itself from under the buttocks of "the wisest aunt, telling the saddest tale": "Then slip I from her bum, down topples she, / And 'tailor' cries . . . " (II.i.51–54). Here the play on "tale"/"tailer," precisely the pun, in fact, that Howard Bloch has recently explored in his rule-breaking study of the French medieval fabliaux, is an early warning signal of popular fundamentalism.[18] But the scandal of the lower bodily parts, which, as Bakhtin has also reminded us, constitute the definitive category of comic materialism,[19] has in the *Dream* a more complicated resonance than scatology for its own subversive sake. In the great medieval encyclopedia of Bartholomaeus Anglicus, translated in 1582 by Stephen Batman as *Batman upon Bartholome*, and one of Shakespeare's resources, the ass is defined as a creature in whom coalesce the meaning-systems implied by Bottom: "The Asse is called Asinus, and hath that name of Sedendo, as it were a beast to sit upon . . . and is a simple beast and a slow, and therefore soone overcome & subject to mannes service" (XIX:419). And in another text habitually cited as a source for the *Dream*, the *Golden Ass* of Apuleius, the theme of servitude symbolized by the ass is rendered fully allegorical by Apuleius. The period of slavery that the metamorphosed Lucius endures in the bakery has been recognized as "the only passage in the whole of ancient literature which realistically ... examines the conditions of slave-exploitation on which the culture of the ancient world rested."[20]

As visual pun and emblem, therefore, Bottom stands at the fulcrum of Shakespeare's analysis of the festive impulse in human social structures. Is he merely a comic figure, the appropriate butt of Thesean critical mockery, and his liaison with Titania the worst humiliation an upstart queen could suffer? Or does his (im)proper name, in symbolic alliance with his ass's head, invoke rather an inquiry into the way in which the lower social orders, as well as the lower bodily strata, function, and suggest that the service they perform and the energies they contain are usually undervalued, even to abuse? Hinting as to how this question might be answered, Shakespeare included a brilliant gloss on the multiple pun that is Bottom, keying his festive theory into the most impeccable source of ideology available to him. At the moment of his transformation back into manhood, Bottom implicates his own ritual naming in the central act of interpretation that the *Dream* demands:

> Man is but an ass, if he go about t' expound this dream. . . . The eye
> of man hath not heard, the ear of man hath not seen, man's hand is
> not able to taste, his tongue to conceive, nor his heart to report, what
> my dream was. . . . It shall be called "Bottom's Dream," because it
> hath no bottom. . . . (IV.ii.206–216)

It has long been recognized that this passage contains an allusion to I Corinthians 2.9. But so quick have most commentators been to denigrate Bottom that they focus only on his jumbling of the biblical text, rather than on its context of profound spiritual levelling. Even Weimann, who connects it to his theme of popular topsy-turveydom (p. 40), does not pursue the biblical referent to its logical conclusion, in I Corinthians 12.17–25, where the metaphor of the body is developed more fully in terms of a Christian *communitas*:

If the whole bodie were an eie, where were the hearing? If the whole
were hearing, where were the smelling? But nowe hath God disposed
the members euery one of them in the bodie at his owne pleasure. For
if they were all one member, where were the bodie? But now are
there many members, yet but one bodie. And the eye cannot say vnto
the hande, I haue no neede of thee. . . . Yea, much rather those
members of the bodie, which seeme to be more feeble, are necessarie.
And upon those members of the bodie, which we thinke most
vnhonest, put wee more honestie on: and our vncomely partes haue
more comelines on. For our comely partes neede it not: but God hath
tempered the bodie together, and hath giuen the more honour to that
part which lacked, Least there should be any diuision in the bodie:
but that the members should haue the same care one for another.[21]

In the *Dream* which has no bottom because Bottom dreamed it, the
"vncomely partes" of the social body are invested with greater honor
by their momentary affinity with a utopian vision that Bottom wisely
decides he is incapable of putting into words, at least into words in
their normal order. Shakespeare's warning to the audience is
unmistakable: prudent readers, especially those who are themselves
underprivileged, will resist the pressure to interpret the vision. Yet its
inarticulate message remains: a revaluation of those unpresentable
members of society, normally mocked as fools and burdened like asses,
whose energies the social system relies on. And if laughter is necessary
to mediate social tensions, Shakespeare's festive theory seems to argue,
then let it be a laughter as far removed as possible from social
condescension. The *Dream* imagines an ancient festive spirit deeper
and more generous than the courtly revelling that seems to have
appropriated the popular drama for its own purposes; an idea of play
and playing that could register social criticism, in Starveling's name
and the actors' fears, yet hold off the phantom of violent social protest
("let the prologue seem to say we will do no harm with our swords"
[III.i.7–18]); and a reconciliatory agenda for the national theater that,
before the turn of the century, was still, for Shakespeare, imaginable:
making the social body whole. Just over a decade later, in *Coriolanus*,
the last of the tragedies, he begins with a famine and a popular
insurrection, and with a new fable of the body in which the vital
Bottom is replaced by the empty Belly, the head has been removed

altogether, the sword has replaced the other male instrument of potency, and the real exile is not Coriolanus, but the festive spirit itself.

NOTES

*Originally published in *Renaissance Papers 1988*, ed. Dale B.J. Randall and Joseph A. Porter (Durham, NC: Southeastern Renaissance Conference, 1988), 25–39. Reprinted with the kind permission of the Southeastern Renaissance Conference.

1. All Shakespeare quotations herein are from *The Riverside Shakespeare*, ed. G. Blakemore Evans *et al.* (Boston: Houghton Mifflin, 1974).

2. Quoted from Theodore B. Leinwand, "I believe we must leave the killing out': Deference and Accommodation in *A Midsummer Night's Dream*," *Renaissance Papers* (Durham: Southeastern Renaissance Conference, 1986), p.18. The following quotation is also from Leinwand, p. 18.

3. Leinwand, pp. 11–30. While I am much indebted to this rich account of the play's social context, I am less persuaded by Leinwand's emphasis on accommodation as the goal of popular protest.

4. Levin, "The Occasionalist Scene," in *New Readings vs. Old Plays: Recent Trends in the Reinterpretation of English Renaissance Drama* (Chicago: University of Chicago Press, 1979), pp. 167–171.

5. See Alexander Neville, *Norfolkes Furies, or A View of Ketts Campe: Necessary for the Malecontents of Our Time, for Their Instruction, or Terror; and Profitable for Every Good Subject*, trans. R[ichard]. W[oods]., Minister at Frettenham in Norfolk, who describes himself "a citizen borne, who beheld part of these things with his yong Eyes" (London: 1615), B2^{r}.

6. Compare Leinwand, pp. 13–14, 20–23.

7. Barber, *Shakespeare's Festive Comedy: A Study of Dramatic Form and Its Relation to Social Custom* (Princeton: Princeton University Press, 1959).

8. Turner, *The Ritual Process: Structure and Antistructure* (Chicago: Aldine Pub. Co., 1969), p.176.

9. Turner, *Dramas, Fields and Metaphors: Symbolic Action in Human Society* (Ithaca: Cornell University Press, 1974), p. 35.

10. In *Carnival and Theater: Plebeian Culture and the Structure of Authority in Renaissance England* (New York: Methuen, 1985).

11. Neither the Quarto nor the Folio text authorizes the stage direction "Wall holds up his fingers"; it was added by Edward Capell in 1767 and is now a standard feature of modern editions, running counter to the text's bawdry and discouraging a producer from having Pyramus and Thisbe bend to reach each

other through the open legs of Snout the tinker. For an extensive defense of this as Shakespeare's intended stage-practice, see Thomas Clayton, "'Fie What a Question's That if Thou Wert Near a Lewd Interpreter': The Wall Scene in *A Midsummer Night's Dream*," *Shakespeare Studies* 7 (1974), 101–123.

12. Puttenham, *The Arte of English Poesie* (London: 1589), p. 43.

13. See Barber, *Shakespeare's Festive Comedies*, p. 120: "Shakespeare does not make himself accountable for exact chronological inferences. . . ."

14. Montrose, "'Shaping Fantasies': Figurations of Gender and Power in Elizabethan Culture," *Representations* 2 (1983), 61–94.

15. Specifically, Montrose's darker reading is directed not against Barber's concept of festive action but against that of Northrop Frye, who argued in *A Natural Perspective: The Development of Shakespearean Comedy and Romance* (New York: Columbia University Press, 1965) that the typical structure of Shakespearean comedy was to set up an opposition between "irrational laws . . . preoccupied with trying to regulate the sexual drive" and the "drive toward a festive conclusion" (pp. 73–75). It is not without interest for our purposes that Frye uses the Freudian term "drive" both for the social "law" and for its festive opposition, which ultimately, he argues, wins the contest; whereas Montrose, less sanguine, argues that the conclusion is not to liberate the sexual (or comic) drive from irrational laws, but to "fabricate a temporary accommodation between law and libido," and that "in its validation of marriage, the play is less concerned to sacramentalize libido than to socialize it" (pp. 70–71).

16. In Montrose's essay, Titania's liaison with Bottom is related not to festive inversions, but rather to the dream of Simon Forman, professional physician and amateur drama-critic, who fantasized that the Queen had made herself sexually available to him; and it is only a detail, over which Montrose does not pause, that his dream rival for the Queen's affections is "a weaver, a tall man with a reddish beard, distract of his wits" (p. 62).

17. Rubinstein, *A Dictionary of Shakespeare's Sexual Puns and Their Significance* (London: Macmillan, 1984), p. 17.

18. R. Howard Bloch, *The Scandal of the Fabliaux* (Chicago: University of Chicago Press, 1986): "In the counting of the vagina and the anus we recognize the accounting of the poet who plays upon the homophony of *con*[cunt] and *conte*[tale]" (p.106).

19. See also Bristol, *Carnival and Theater*, p. 135, and especially his salient quotation from Gregory de Rocher's translation of Laurent Joubert's 1579 *Traité du Ris (Treatise on Laughter* [Montgomery: University of Alabama Press, 1980]):

> If perchance one uncovers the shameful parts which by nature or public decency we are accustomed to keeping hidden, since this is ugly yet unworthy of pity, it moves the onlookers to laughter. . . . It is equally unfitting to show one's arse [le cul], and when there is no harm forcing us to sympathize we are unable to contain our laughter.

But Joubert's qualifier, "when there is no harm forcing us to sympathize," is equally relevant to the Shakespearean emphasis on the ass's traditional vulnerability to being beaten.

20. See Jack Lindsay, trans. *The Golden Ass* (Bloomington: Indiana University Press, 1932), p. 22. It is surely no coincidence, also, that Lucius, as ass, is alternately threatened with gelding and luxuriously rewarded for his asinine virility, which results in his eventual seduction by a beautiful aristocratic woman who covers him with perfumes, kisses, and endearments.

21. Quoted from the Geneva version (London: 1578).

Dis/Figuring Power
Censorship and Representation in
*A Midsummer Night's Dream**

Barbara Freedman

> It is precisely at the legislative frontier between what can be represented and what cannot that the postmodernist operation is being staged—not in order to transcend representation, but in order to expose that system of power that authorizes certain representations while blocking, prohibiting, or invalidating others.
>
> —Craig Owens, "The Discourse of Others:
> Feminists and Postmodernism"

I

In a recent study of Renaissance censorship, Annabel Patterson maintains that the incidents of physical torture and dismemberment we uncover are less startling than their statistical infrequency. Considering the power that a prince could wield against a playwright, what is surprising is not Queen Elizabeth's recognition of the topical implications of the 1601 revival of *Richard II* or James I's less speedy response to Thomas Middleton's *Game at Chess* but the conclusion of both productions with their players intact. Since dismemberment and trial signal the dissolution of codes governing censorship, Patterson reasons, their marked infrequency in the history of this period of drama attests to the healthy functioning of an "implicit social contract between authors and authorities ... intelligible to all parties at the time."[1]

A Midsummer Night's Dream articulates this social pact by openly celebrating the shaping vision of an aristocratic ideology. The harmless question "What hempen home-spuns have we swagg'ring here, / So near the cradle of the Fairy Queen?" (3.1.77–78)⁺ is also a question of the precise and limited conditions under which the different classes of poets and patrons can meet. And *A Midsummer Night's Dream* promptly answers that question through its fawning collaboration with state ideology. The terms governing the prince-poet relationship in *A Midsummer Night's Dream*, like those governing the husband-wife relationship in *The Taming of the Shrew*, are nostalgically tailored along the lines of an idealized pact between feudal lord and gratefully submissive servant. The play fashions itself as a mediator between court and poet as if charged with legislating their proper interaction; it genially mocks offensive playwrights while humbly requesting that they be pardoned. At the same time, the play panders to an aristocratic ideology by wreaking comic punishment on all those who defy the prince's legislation of desire. Finally, the play sets out a self-serving and conciliatory relationship between poet and prince with its gestures of flattery, apology, and self-abasement.[2] By flattering the prince as the only poet with the natural wisdom, imagination, and magnanimity to determine licensed comparisons, the play works to justify the role of the poet in the state.

A Midsummer Night's Dream's open collaboration with the aristocracy is of particular interest to the study of ideology—the means by which cultural configurations of inequitable social relationships are presented as natural and so serve the interests of a given ruling class. Critics have discovered in *A Midsummer Night's Dream* a variety of rationalizations for gender and class oppression. James Kavanagh examines how, by drawing "ideological raw materials from both insurgent bourgeois-individualist and entrenched feudal-absolutist discourses," *A Midsummer Night's Dream* subverts authoritarian rule only to pander to it, "finally trivializing any threat with a comic resolution that magically reconciles rebellious 'feminine' and individualist desire to a rigid social hierarchy of aristocratic and patriarchal privilege."[3] Louis Montrose studies how this play not only reflects but shapes culturally specific fantasies which convey ideological configurations of gender and class relationship, particularly in the context of the influence of the cult of Elizabeth on the collective political unconscious.[4] And Leonard Tennenhouse explores how the play figures the relation between queen and poet in terms of the mating of the aristocratic body and the grotesque public body.[5]

Despite the sophistication of these critiques, scholars have yet to read *A Midsummer Night's Dream* in a way that brings psychoanalytic, deconstructive, and cultural-materialist discourses together. That the play is about the mind knowing itself is hardly a new idea, although James Calderwood states the proposition most promisingly: "A major kind of knowledge made available to its audience by *A Midsummer Night's Dream* is that of the inner forms and impulses of the human mind itself—the tricks and shaping fantasies of strong imagination and the forces directing it but also the range and limits of cool reason. The mind that comes to focus on the play and especially on the drama of the forest comes to focus on itself."[6] Since *A Midsummer Night's Dream* remains one of our culture's most important theoretical texts on dreaming, it should have something to tell us about the Renaissance mind and how it organizes experience.

A reductive simplification of cultural-materialist, deconstructive, and psychoanalytic discourses is one factor that has stalled productive dialogue in this direction. Reductive versions of psychoanalysis have been partly to blame, as has the failure of literary critics to consider the more radical implications of psychoanalytic theory for literary theory. For many critics, psychoanalytic criticism is simply a helpmeet to New Criticism, and ego psychology offers a means of neatly closing up the text, like the well-analyzed personality, through "terminable" analysis. By filling in the text's blank spaces, however, these critics neglect Freud's emphasis on discovering the *laws governing the construction of blank spaces.*

Reductive versions of cultural-materialist theory are also partly to blame for the delayed production of this dramatic scene. And we can trace this tendency to the failure of much political criticism to come to terms with the deconstructive critique of representation, as evidenced in the variety of exclusionary tactics employed to invalidate deconstructive techniques. The reduction of deconstructive theory to a naive celebration of the impossibility of knowing, like the charge that deconstruction could offer any of us a safe retreat into the indeterminacy of meaning, simply doesn't hold up. Derrida's conclusion to "Structure, Sign, and Play," for example, contrasts two "interpretations of interpretation"—one denying, the other celebrating radical uncertainty—only to argue that no choice between the two is possible: "Although these two interpretations must acknowledge and accentuate their difference and define their irreducibility, I do not believe that today there is any question of *choosing* . . . because we must first try to conceive of the common ground, and the *différance* of this irreducible difference."[7]

The tendency of critics from these two camps to avoid rather than engage with one another is evidenced in the way they side with only one of Derrida's two interpretations of interpretation—or with only one of two stances on the imagination offered by *A Midsummer Night's Dream*. Critical responses to the play routinely take the form of a defense of one of its two concluding statements regarding the status of a knowledge that escapes logical proof. Theseus argues for a knowledge situated within the representable; Hippolyta's silenced voice reminds us of the conditions of repression that render such knowledge possible. Psychoanalytic critics tend to read *A Midsummer Night's Dream* through Lacanian narratives of social conditioning which privilege the wresting of the infant from the maternal as the only valid means of entry into the symbolic. They argue that to privilege Hippolyta's position or to take sides in this debate is to miss the point, precisely because psychoanalysis stresses the *interdependence* of knowledge and repression. To champion Hippolyta's cause, they claim, is tantamount to a denial of the boundaries through which knowledge is constituted. To side with Hippolyta, from this standpoint, is to deny the loss and distortion that inevitably accompany our construction in the social order.

From a cultural-materialist stance, however, the celebration of Hippolyta's vision over Theseus's law is not the result of a naive idealism that presupposes one can attain a knowledge without repression or distortion. Rather, this critical stance acknowledges the *specificity* of repression instead of universalizing its form or proclaiming its inevitability. Admittedly, we can no more deny the force of law, *in the abstract*, than we can deny the truth of that which escapes it. Yet we have a responsibility both to acknowledge the shape that repression takes against specific people and to rethink how to teach a play that celebrates this particular shaping vision. Simply because the structuralist and patriarchal assumptions of Lacanian narratives dovetail with the patriarchal ideology of *A Midsummer Night's Dream*, for example, is no reason to collaborate with those assumptions. By encouraging us to recognize how our explanatory narratives are ideologically constructed to privilege and so reinforce certain social formations, cultural-materialist approaches are finally more practical and revisionary than idealistic.

Rather than refuse to teach *A Midsummer Night's Dream* because of its colonialist fantasies or *The Taming of the Shrew* because of its overt sexism, we can learn from both. Rather than censor either work, a more productive approach would be to explore how censorship operates within them. Granted, *A Midsummer Night's Dream* stages a disturbing relationship among social formation, text, and psyche: it presents knowledge as an effect of right censorship and figures metaphor as a dangerous instrument requiring close state control. And yet precisely because *A Midsummer Night's Dream* poses the question of interpretation within this specific ideological framework, its exploration of strategies that legitimize vision can alert us to the ways in which we censor meaning today.

Since *A Midsummer Night's Dream* foregrounds a complex relationship among censorship, knowledge, and interpretation, the act of censorship serves as a conceptual lever through which ideological, deconstructive, and psychoanalytic discourses may be brought into productive dialogue. Throughout *A Midsummer Night's Dream* the audience is asked to determine the status of various imaginative experiences. Yet insofar as social conditions determine the means by which the categories of true and false, real and fantastic are figured and so licensed, these categories are always subject to change. Censorship refers to social activity that constructs the boundaries between real and imaginary; neither exterior nor interior, censorship works at the boundaries of representation in both culture and psyche.

Commenting on Freud's "Note upon a 'Mystic-Writing Pad,'" Derrida explains how censorship as a writing function mediates among text, state, and psyche:

> It is no accident that the metaphor of censorship should come from the area of politics concerned with the deletions, blanks, and disguises of writing. . . . The apparent exteriority of political censorship refers to an essential censorship which binds the writer to his own writing. . . . The "subject" of writing does not exist if we mean by that some sovereign solitude of the author. The subject of writing is a *system* of relations between strata: the Mystic Pad, the

> psyche, society, the world. . . . The *sociality* of writing as *drama*
> requires an entirely different discipline.

Derrida complains that "a psychoanalysis of literature respectful of the *originality of the literary signifier* has not yet begun, and this is surely not an accident. Until now, only the analysis of literary *signifieds*, that is, *nonliterary* signified meanings, has been undertaken."[8] New historicists such as Francis Barker and Peter Hulme point the way in their study of how discourse is "instrumental in the organization and legitimation of power-relations—which of course involves, as one of its components, control over the constitution of meaning."[9] Whether or not we seek to develop "a *history of writing*" or "a new *psychoanalytic graphology*,"[10] in question here is how to bring psychoanalytic, deconstructive, and cultural-materialist readings of dreams and of *A Midsummer Night's Dream* together. Can psychoanalytic and deconstructive approaches be aligned with a study of their complicity in social and cultural censorship? Can psychoanalytic theory prove useful to the study of the history of the signifier? And can cultural-materialist theory become more attuned to the play of meaning and repression at the level of its own discourse? If we cannot take sides in the debate between a knowledge that moves in the direction of a myth of a real and a knowledge that exposes the omissions by means of which discourses of truth and mastery operate, we can explore the politics governing the relation of these two interpretations of interpretation today.

II

Peter Quince's bungled prescription for his play aptly describes the laws governing representation in *A Midsummer Night's Dream*: "One must come in with a bush of thorns and a lantern, and say he comes to disfigure, or to present, the person of Moonshine" (3.1.59–61). By mistakenly associating presentation and disfigurement, Quince reminds us that Elizabethan playwrights whose comparisons were perceived as a threat to the status quo could be physically disfigured by the state. By punishing those who make unlawful comparisons between themselves and others, *A Midsummer Night's Dream* seeks to preserve a rigidly hierarchical social order against the threats of encroaching bourgeois individualism.

Throughout this comedy, the agreement to play one's assigned role and to accept one's social status constitutes licensed comparison, whereas the desire to change one's role or status is portrayed as a criminal act that warrants disfigurement. Hermia is condemned for seeking to play both her own and her father's parts; she expects not only to marry the bridegroom but to choose him. Helena is guilty of coveting Hermia's role as a means of winning back the love of Demetrius. She confides to Hermia: "Were the world mine, Demetrius being bated, / The rest I'll give to be to you translated" (1.1.190–91); yet she rightly attributes her plight to her jealousy: "What wicked and dissembling glass of mine / Made me compare with Hermia's sphery eyne!" (2.2.98–99). Titania's desire to play both lord and lady in questioning Oberon's control over the Indian boy is portrayed as an offense to nature itself. Bottom's desire to play every part in the production of *Pyramus and Thisby* is a comic version of the same crime. Bottom not only threatens the success of *Pyramus and Thisby* but, by extension, the success of the collaborative production we term Elizabethan social reality.

According to the terms of this play, the metaphoric language through which we map our world has clear-cut positive and negative implications. To compare love to a rose is useful only if that comparison contributes to our sense of what love is like. Order in comparison depends on a firm sense of priorities—state before individual, lord before lady, and both before the hempen homespun. When used to strengthen or extend the boundaries of the state and its power, comparison is positive. Theseus and Hippolyta, for example, speak a triumphant metaphoric discourse; secure in their vision of an ordered hierarchy, their sentences are indeed "in government." When comparisons are unlicensed, however, they threaten the social order: the four lovers lose all sense of identity in their rivalry, and in the darkness of the woods, the power to disfigure turns against these unlicensed poets with a vengeance. Comic punishment is carried out by that licensed principle of unlicensed comparisons, Puck. Puck adopts the strategy of "rope tricks" that Petruchio employed in *The Taming of the Shrew*: "He will throw a figure in her face, and so disfigure her with it" (*The Taming of the Shrew*: 1.2.113–14). Since Puck functions as a type of court fool or licensed clown, his punitive dramas are sanctioned because staged in the service of his master: "Sometime a horse I'll be, sometime a hound, / A hog, a headless bear, sometime a fire" (3.1.108–9).

Theseus lavishly employs metaphors in reprimanding Hermia and thereby parades his license to make such comparisons. What for us is an obvious case of gender ideology is for Theseus a simple matter of rational classification: as an object of meaning and value, Hermia cannot seek to determine how meaning and value function. Like words, women are merely objects to be compared and exchanged and so incapable of determining whether, how, or by whom they will be exchanged. The hempen homespuns confront the problem of unlicensed comparisons when they seek to put on a play. Their disfigured speech is described as "a sound, but not in government," "a tangled chain; nothing impair'd, but all disorder'd" (5.1.123–26). Their sole virtue is an impaired imagination that renders them incapable of effecting economic or social advancement. When they carefully inform the court that they are not to be confused with their dramatic roles, they preserve the production of Elizabethan ideology at the expense of the play at hand.

Not surprisingly, in his bid to play court propagandist Shakespeare mocks others' pretensions to advance their status as a means of advancing his own. Yet if we must castigate Shakespeare for his role in this game of comparisons, we should also acknowledge how we are implicated in the game. Given the importance of visual imagery to critics' appreciation of this play, the source of that appeal deserves examination. One of Shakespeare's most richly visual plays, *A Midsummer Night's Dream* makes us *feel* rich with its images of gold and silver, traders and merchandise, luxury and power. It continually tempts us to collaborate in fantasies of unbridled consumption. Theseus opens the play with a description of the moon as a wealthy woman who withholds her riches: "She lingers my desires, / Like to a step-dame, or a dowager, / Long withering out a young man's revenue" (1.1.4–6). Hippolyta responds with a more lucrative comparison, observing that in a speedy four days, "the moon, like to a silver bow / [New] bent in heaven, shall behold the night / Of our solemnities" (1.1.9–11). In a rush to depart, Lysander leisurely extends his discourse to describe the evening more poetically: "To-morrow night, when Phoebe doth behold / Her silver visage in the wat'ry glass, / Decking with liquid pearl the bladed grass" (1.1.209–11). Furious with Oberon, Titania conveys her decision to keep the changeling boy by describing in lush detail how she and the boy's mother used to sit and pass the time "on Neptune's yellow sands, / Marking th' embarked traders on the flood; / When we have laugh'd to see the sails conceive / And grow big-bellied with the wanton wind; / Which she, with pretty and with swimming gait, / Following (her womb then rich with my young squire) / Would imitate, and sail upon the land / To fetch me trifles, and return again, / As from a voyage, rich with merchandise" (2.1.126–34).

A Midsummer Night's Dream seduces not merely by virtue of its metaphoric language but by the precise nature of its comparisons. Is it not the silver bow and the pearls that are so beautiful, the fantasy of having trifles fetched for one that is indulgent, the spices and luxuries that are delightful? The poetry is exquisite insofar as it encourages us to enjoy colonialist fantasies with neither guilt nor obligation. Oberon knows of lush worlds we haven't seen and offers to share with us their secret powers: "I know a bank where the wild thyme blows, / Where oxlips and the nodding violet grows, / Quite over-canopied with luscious woodbine, / With sweet musk-roses and with eglantine" (2.1.249–52). With Puck's help, we can enjoy these riches without delay: "I'll put a girdle round about the earth / In forty minutes" (2.1.175–76). We can look on at others, invisible ourselves, and play pranks or indulge in fantasies of omnipotence with no concern for others' welfare. More disturbing than "how easy is a bush suppos'd a bear" (5.1.22) is how easily we first steal an Indian boy and then argue between ourselves over who deserves him. Appropriative, narcissistic fantasies of self-indulgence and power are the order of the day. Whereas *The Comedy of Errors* fascinates us with its uncanny sensibility, *A Midsummer Night's Dream* indulges us by making the strange familiar. Metaphor both appropriates and invalidates otherness by proving that everything strange can, in a moment of high narcissism, be made to reflect a part of oneself. When we imagine that everyone is like us, or can be compared to us, we are exploiting otherness as a commodity.

Metaphor not only makes a world but makes it according to certain relationships of power, since it offers precise strategies of taming and appropriating the unfamiliar. Writing on metaphor, Julian Jaynes observes that cognitive psychologists use the term *assimilation* to refer to an automatic process "where a slightly ambiguous perceived object is made to conform to some previously learned schema."[11] When the act of assimilation is conscious and intended, it is termed *conciliation* or *compatibilization*. But the act of fitting things together or making them compatible is also a strategy by means of which difference is forced into paradigms that sanction the status quo.

For Theseus, the difference between comprehension and apprehension is crucial: "Such tricks hath strong imagination, / That if it would but apprehend some joy, / It comprehends some bringer of that joy" (5.1.18–20). When we read *A Midsummer Night's Dream*, we comprehend or grasp things together; understanding is not a means of standing under something but of grabbing hold by force and assimilation. And we comprehend in the same way when we employ New Critical strategies to map out a play or piece together its parts in a hierarchical order. Walter Ong identifies as "the most fundamental stylistic difference between ancient writing and modern writing—the immeasurably greater exploitation today of visualist metaphors and of imagery which in one way or another admits of diagrammatic analysis."[12] Could it be that *A Midsummer Night's Dream* so neatly illustrates New Critical techniques because both play and critical style reflect appropriative strategies developed at triumphant points in the history of Western European hegemony?

Many of us were taught to read and to teach *A Midsummer Night's Dream* in New Critical terms that equated the discovery of meaning with the scope of our assimilative powers; the aim of literary criticism was to find the most encompassing theme, or to "find the concord of this discord" (5.1.60). In the 1960s and 1970s we followed such critics as D.A. Traversi, Philip Edwards, and David Young through various takes of the "structure and theme" variety, so that among British and American Shakespeareans the commentary on the play had indeed grown to "something of great constancy" (5.1.26).[13] And we liked to think of that line as *our* line, as the natural and well-earned product of our superior organizational skills. The prominence of Young's chapter in the anthology *Modern Shakespearean Criticism* suggested as much; here was New Criticism at its best, at everyone's disposal.

In classrooms around the English-speaking world (was there any other?) the play was diagramed on blackboards as if its coordinates were no less than the four corners of the known world. Our *Dream* not only had a bottom but a top and sides; we could neatly chart its beginning, middle, and end. We followed the characters from a harsh legalistic world, through a green world of desire, and on toward a compromise conclusion in which law is tempered by mercy and society accommodates individual desire. We located sources for this pattern in Renaissance pastorals, romances, and morality plays alike. We mapped the characters' progression from a flawed society, through a wilderness, to a new, improved society; from separation, through bewilderment, and on to reunion and harmony. We even discovered in this framework a morality pattern in which despair gave way to punishment and penance, yet ultimately led to redemption. That our critical efforts mirrored the play's treatment of how the mind organizes experience was not of concern, or of as much concern, as demonstrating the prowess of New Critical techniques. How meaning is produced or resisted, channeled or erased—for whom, when, or why—was none of our concern. This was a case of perfect dovetailing, and we didn't want to know the price of our success. We didn't want to know that the result of all our minds "transfigur'd so together" (5.1.24) was less a matter of truth than of that "something of great constancy" termed *ideology*.

Postmodernism is often described in terms of a loss of faith in Western narratives of mastery.[14] In literary theory it has taken the form of an exploration of the plurality of meanings and traditions previously repressed by traditional notions of the author, reader, work, and canon. In "From Work to Text," Roland Barthes describes this paradigm shift in terms of a move away from the single meaning of the closed, unified work in favor of an awareness of the multiple meanings, both privileged and censored, of the open text.[15] Ironically, Barthes would have us forgo the term *work* for *text* at the same time that he encourages us to focus on the real work that is involved in the performance of meaning. If the grand production that is *A Midsummer Night's Dream* has anything to do with the production of our dreams, then the collaborative work of the various parts of the mind as they legislate meaning may further clarify the relation between power and discourse on the stage of contemporary critical theory.

III

One of the paradoxes that critical theory continually confronts is the problem of figuring the mind without disfiguring it. "Perhaps the happiest moment the human mind ever knows," Stephen Booth suggests, "is the moment when it senses the presence of order and coherence—and before it realizes the particular nature (and so the particular limits) of the perception. At the moment of unparticularized perception the mind is unlimited. It seems capable of grasping and about to grasp a coherence beyond its capacity."[16] Lysander's description of the difficulty of comprehending love applies just as well to the difficulties we experience in self-apprehension: both situations yield an insight that is "momentany as a sound, / Swift as a shadow, short as any dream, / Brief as the lightning in the collied night, / That, in a spleen, unfolds both heaven and earth; / And ere a man hath power to say 'Behold!' / The jaws of darkness do devour it up: / So quick bright things come to confusion" (1.1.143–49). No sooner do we figure the mind than we disfigure it with terms of comparison.

Julian Jaynes describes how consciousness both "narratizes and conciliates . . . in a metaphorical space where such meanings can be manipulated like things in space."[17] To the extent that meanings are indeed manipulated like things in space, our descriptions of the mind are necessarily distorted by spatial metaphors. *A Midsummer Night's Dream* offers numerous descriptions of the mind meditating upon itself, but all compare the mind to some external apparatus, such as a mirror, a writing tablet, or a picture. Lysander describes the shining moon as a moment of literal self-reflection: "To-morrow night, when Phoebe doth behold / Her silver visage in the wat'ry glass" (1.1.209–10). If to know the mind is to know that it works by comparison, this is also to know that we can never properly locate the mind.

And yet the terms by which we know the mind are themselves instructive. Perhaps most striking about *A Midsummer Night's Dream* is the highly self-conscious use of metaphors to serve an aristocratic ideology. So many Elizabethan texts state as their goal the presentation of the mind as a microcosm of a divinely ordered hierarchical universe that it would be surprising indeed if cultural and psychic formations were presented as anything other than harmonious. Elizabethan authors were continually working to bring the new technology into line with prevailing ideology. Clearly the accommodation of the ideologically coercive discourses of the so-called "great chain of being" to meet and control the fantasies of a rising bourgeoisie in Shakespearean comedy is a prominent example of this trend. It is therefore reasonable to ask ourselves whether we are really uncovering political metaphors and social configurations in Renaissance descriptions of the mind or merely recovering them, since Renaissance authors were obviously serving a vested interest in depicting how text, psyche, and society could be harmoniously interrelated. In *A Midsummer Night's Dream*, for example, the real is an elaborate collaborative production, dependent upon the work of imagination which makes comparisons and the work of reason which licenses those comparisons. The mind's parts are figured as interacting according to a model of good government; the faculties of hearing and sight create the fantasies that in turn are corrected by reason.

The open acknowledgment of the limits of metaphor in modernist accounts of the mind contrasts sharply with the self-serving deployment of comparisons in Renaissance texts. For example, Freud repeatedly states his plan to "replace a topographical way of representing things by a dynamic one"[18]—and repeatedly fails in that attempt. He is continually generating models of the psychic apparatus only to realize that the aim of locating consciousness entraps him in metaphors of mirroring, picturing, and mapping which distort the thing he would describe. Caught between the desire for and the failure of metaphor, Freud describes spatial and temporal metaphors of the mind as both inevitable and impossible. The writing machine, the camera, the political process—all are metaphors that are attempted and discarded. "Strictly speaking," writes Freud, "there is no need for the hypothesis that the psychical systems are actually arranged in a *spatial* order. It would be sufficient if a fixed order were established by the fact that in a given psychical process the excitation passes through the systems in a particular *temporal* sequence."[19]

In a study of Freud's ambivalence toward his own topological models, Derrida observes that even this temporal model is based on a metaphysics of presence and so is flawed: "The text is not conceivable in an originary or modified form of presence. The unconscious text is already a weave of pure traces, differences in which meaning and force are united—a text nowhere present, consisting of archives which are *always already* transcriptions. . . . Always already: repositories of a meaning which was never present, whose signified presence is always reconstituted by deferral, *nachträglich*, belatedly, *supplementarily*: for the *nachträglich* also means *supplementary*." Even when Freud openly rejects a topological model, Derrida points out, he still cannot avoid the metaphor of psychic machinery:

> Metaphor—in this case the analogy between two apparatuses and the possibility of this representational relation—raises a question which,

despite his premises, and for reasons which are no doubt essential, Freud failed to make explicit. . . . Metaphor as a rhetorical or didactic device is possible here only through the solid metaphor, the "unnatural," historical production of a *supplementary* machine, *added* to the psychical organization in order to supplement its finitude. . . . It opens up the question of technics: of the apparatus in general and of the analogy between the psychical apparatus and the nonpsychical apparatus.

Derrida concludes that whereas Freud seeks to avoid "freezing energy within a naive metaphorics of place" and acknowledges "the necessity not of abandoning but of rethinking the space or topology of this writing," he "still insists on *representing* the psychical apparatus in an artificial model, has not yet discovered a mechanical model adequate to the graphematic conceptual scheme he is already using to describe the psychical text."[20]

As Freud becomes more convinced of the limits of topological models, he develops the hypothesis that "thoughts and psychical structures in general must never be regarded as localized in organic elements of the nervous system but rather, as one might say, *between* them, where resistances and facilitations provide the corresponding correlates." And so he finally describes psychic functioning in terms of a virtual image, using the model of a camera:

Everything that can be an object of our internal perception is *virtual*, like the image produced in a telescope by the passage of light-rays. But we are justified in assuming the existence of the [perceptual] systems (which are not in any way psychical entities themselves and can never be accessible to our psychical perception) like the lenses of the telescope, which cast the image. And, if we pursue this analogy, we may compare the censorship between two systems to the refraction which takes place when a ray of light passes into a new medium.[21]

As Freud strives to picture the psyche both as object and as process, he conveys the confusion of categories in which these descriptions are necessarily trapped. The mind is both an object to be compared and the act of comparison itself, both like a map and a mapping function of which the self is a mirage, both like a camera and itself a projection or image.

Of all Freud's models of the mind, the one most relevant to Derrida's concerns is his "Note upon the 'Mystic Writing-Pad'": "If we imagine one hand writing upon the surface of the Mystic Writing-Pad while another periodically raises its covering-sheet from the wax slab, we shall have a concrete representation of the way in which I tried to picture the functioning of the perceptual apparatus of our mind." Here Freud visibly inscribes the process of repression: "On the Mystic Pad the writing vanishes every time the close contact is broken between the paper which receives the stimulus and the wax slab which preserves the impression. This agrees with a notion which I have long had about the method by which the perceptual apparatus of our mind functions, but which I have hitherto kept to myself."[22] Elizabethan table books were also constructed of heavily waxed, erasable cardboard leaves.[23] These are the tables to which Hamlet refers, and of which Theseus speaks when figuring to Hermia her construction under a patriarchal order: "To you your father should be as a god; / One that compos'd your beauties; yea, and one / To whom you are but as a form in wax, / By him imprinted, and within his power, / To leave the figure, or disfigure it" (1.1.47–51). Is Shakespeare imagining the mind as a sort of table book? It seems oddly fitting that Freud admits to having concealed or withheld this model, that he admits to having refrained from *expressing* his theory. Since Freud's theory is riddled with the censorship that it describes, his writing pad returns us not only to Elizabethan models of repression but to Derrida's idea that "writing is unthinkable without repression."[24] Can we think of the unconscious as a trace, or an inscription that erases? Did Shakespeare?

The influence of the printing press in determining how we know exemplifies how a change in visual conventions affects basic cognitive and epistemological assumptions. Walter Ong explains:

> In many ways, the greatest shift in the way of conceiving knowledge between the ancient and the modern world takes place in the movement from a pole where knowledge is conceived of in terms of discourse and hearing and persons to one where it is conceived of in terms of observation and sight and objects. This shift dominates all others in Western intellectual history. . . . Stress on induction follows the stress on deduction as manifesting a still further visualization in

the approach to knowledge, with tactics based on "observation," an approach preferably through sight.[25]

One result of this shift was widespread ambivalence toward a growing print culture, which explains why a play like *A Midsummer Night's Dream* is so suspicious of sight and so concerned with legislating vision. We delight in Peter Quince's efforts to teach his uneducated actors to follow a play script. We laugh when he responds to Flute's "Must I speak now?" and "Ninny's tomb" with a curt "'Ninus' tomb,' man. Why, you must not speak that yet. That you answer to Pyramus. You speak all your part at once, cues and all" (3.1.89, 97, 98–100). Yet we delight even more when Peter Quince gets lost in deciphering punctuation in the Prologue to *Pyramus and Thisby*. Just as the phrase "to know" shifted from a sense of "being in the know" to a sense of being able to *envision* what one knows, so we now expect that we can *follow* another's speech according to a strict linear pattern.

Another effect of this burgeoning print culture was a tendency to think inductively, to conceive of the mind as territory that could be mapped though never seen directly. The Renaissance mind is often described as a physical container with concealed spaces: as a house with hidden rooms, a map that contains vast uncharted territories, or a perspective picture that contains hidden images. When Lysander tells Helena of his secret plans, he states: "Helen, to you our minds we will unfold" (1.1.208). Hermia speaks of her secrets with Helena as things contained within her mind and heart; she reminds Helena of the years that they have spent "emptying our bosoms of their counsel [sweet]" (1.1.216). "The mind now 'contains' knowledge," Ong explains, "especially in the compartments of the various arts and sciences, which in turn may 'contain' one another, and which all 'contain' words."[26]

Not only does the mind contain knowledge, but its manner of mediating between its various containers is distinctly political. Not surprisingly, a rigidly hierarchical society with disparate social levels envisions the mind in terms of hierarchical modes of organization according to which various parts can be interrelated yet kept strictly separate. *A Midsummer Night's Dream* figures psychological processes through acts of partitioning discrete entities between which there is no communication. The fairyland, court, and wood are clearly delineated from one another. All these realities exist simultaneously, as if nothing but imaginary walls separated them. Puck can taunt an angry

Demetrius without being caught, and Oberon can bless a house unseen. No one level of reality encompasses all the others; although the fairies can see what the mortals cannot, spirits of another sort worry Puck, and even Titania can never fully comprehend Bottom's ways.

A Midsummer Night's Dream explores the function of such partitions by showing us what happens when they break down. It encourages us to hold various "levels" of imaginative experience in our minds at once, only to confuse our sense of their priority, exclusivity, and autonomy. The play encourages us to grant equal imaginative reality to groups operating at conflicting levels of cognitive experience. As members of different groups infiltrate the others' domains, the possibility of discovering an objective standpoint from which to delineate truth from fantasy becomes increasingly less plausible. When these characters return to their usual "worlds," they have no shared language or interpretive conventions to make sense of their experience. By invalidating their own and others' perceptions, these characters lead us to question how we construct such categories as knowledge and fantasy.

IV

A Midsummer Night's Dream interrogates the status of a knowledge constructed through erasures and partitions. It stages privileged and unauthorized acts that encode and enclose knowledge, that wall it up and wall it off. *The Comedy of Errors* both figures and resists repression as its narrative moves in the opposing directions of recognition and denial, recovery and splitting. Yet by openly staging repression, *A Midsummer Night's Dream* offers a productive means of mapping both knowledge and that which escapes it. To represent censored material, *A Midsummer Night's Dream* employs a strategy similar to Freud's mystic writing pad; it visibly inscribes something only to make it appear as having disappeared. This strategy anticipates Heidegger's strategy of publishing crossed out words and so putting concepts "under erasure." To point to the inadequacy of language Heidegger writes the word "Being," crosses it out, and leaves the crossed out word in the text. The strategy of putting things "under erasure" enables us to make a mark and, without negating it, to indicate with another mark the problems such a term poses. A famous example is Derrida's phrase "The sign is that ill-named thing, the only one, that escapes the instituting question of philosophy: 'what is . . .?'"[27]

A Midsummer Night's Dream stages visions only to discredit them later, as if charming them into oblivion. Not only have we shared with Bottom and the four lovers "a most rare vision" (4.1.204–5), not only have we joined the court in witnessing a play that is not for us, but as an audience we have seen a play that questions its own status. Oberon orders Puck to stage a play only to make it later "seem a dream and fruitless vision" (3.2.371); again, at the end of *A Midsummer Night's Dream*, Puck encourages us to regard Shakespeare's play as "no more yielding but a dream" (5.1.428). Theseus seeks entertainment to "beguile / The lazy time" (5.1.40–41), and so commands Philostrate: "Say, what abridgment have you for this evening?" (5.1.39). The three hours fly by as we watch the play *A Midsummer Night's Dream*. The fairy scenes not only stage the invisible but seek to make invisible that which is already present. The fairies sing lullabies to banish all that might disturb a sound sleep: "Thorny hedgehogs, be not seen, / Newts and blind-worms, do no wrong, / . . . Weaving spiders, come not here; / Hence, you long-legg'd spinners, hence!" (2.2.10–11, 20–21). Moreover, Puck himself is an invisible creature made present only to be erased or made absent. He is "that merry wanderer of the night" (2.1.43) responsible for errors, the one "that frights the maidens of the villagery, / Skim milk, and sometimes labor in the quern, / And bootless make the breathless huswife churn, / And sometime make the drink to bear no barm, / Mislead night-wanderers, laughing at their harm" (2.1.35–39). As a visible invisible spirit, Puck makes himself invisible when he fights with Demetrius and Lysander. He removes himself as the source of the voice that commands the two rivals to "Follow my voice" (3.2.412). As a result, Demetrius and Lysander seek to conquer an absent presence that moves and so is both present and invisible. Lysander complains: "He goes before me, and still dares me on. / When I come where he calls, then he is gone" (3.2.413–14).

A Midsummer Night's Dream is filled with references to nothing—and yet these references are of two kinds. The play firmly distinguishes between the act of creating something out of nothing and the act of staging the process of repression itself. When Philostrate describes the play that he would censor as "nothing, nothing in the world" (5.1.78), Theseus responds, "The kinder we, to give them thanks for nothing" (5.1.89). Like poets, lunatics and lovers fabricate something out of nothing, Theseus explains, since "as imagination bodies forth / The forms of things unknown, the poet's pen / Turns them to shapes, and gives to aery nothing / A local habitation and a name" (5.1.14–17). Proving himself a poet, Theseus suggests that he can make something out of nothing that is the play by reminding us of his ability to read duty in silence: "Out of this silence yet I pick'd a welcome; / And in the modesty of fearful duty / I read as much as from the rattling tongue / Of saucy and audacious eloquence" (5.1.100–3). And yet the real poetry of *A Midsummer Night's Dream* derives from in [sic] its ability to embody dream, to represent the nothing or "it" of the unconscious which can only be defined as that which escapes representation.

To refuse the conventional literary critic's game of making the unseen visible is to choose the more perverse game of exploring how *A Midsummer Night's Dream* makes the visible unseen, the spoken silenced. More difficult than creating something out of nothing is the act of staging nothing itself. Herein, Foucault suggests, lies the value of psychoanalysis:

> In setting itself the task of making the discourse of the unconscious speak through consciousness, psychoanalysis is advancing in the direction of that fundamental region in which the relations of representation and finitude come into play. Whereas all the human sciences advance towards the unconscious only with their back to it . . . psychoanalysis . . . points directly towards it . . . towards what is there and yet is hidden, towards what exists with the mute solidity of a thing, of a text closed in upon itself, or of a blank space in a visible text, and uses that quality to defend itself.[28]

Is the unconscious that which is not there, that which has no locality? Lacan avows: "We don't even know if the unconscious has a being in itself, and . . . it is because one could not say *that's it* that it was named the '*it*'*[id]*. In fact, one could only say of the unconscious, *that's not it,* or rather, *that's it,* but *not for real*."[29] As the product and process of erasure that takes on a specific form, however, the unconscious is *not* "that's it, but not for real," but part of the very process of constructing "the real." *A Midsummer Night's Dream* thus moves toward what Foucault terms "a *positive unconscious* of knowledge: a level that eludes the consciousness of the scientist and yet is part of scientific discourse." Foucault adds: "We know that psychologists and philosophers have dismissed all this as Freudian mythology. It was indeed inevitable that this approach of Freud's should have appeared to them in this way; to a knowledge situated within the representable, all that frames and defines, on the outside, the very possibility of representation can be nothing other than mythology."[30] As if in response, Theseus answers: "I never may believe / These antic fables, nor these fairy toys" (5.1.2–3).

V

Derrida's stated aim in his essay "Freud and the Scene of Writing" is to prove that "the Freudian concept of trace must be radicalized and extracted from the metaphysics of presence which still retains it." The question, as he sees it, is "not if the psyche is indeed a kind of text, but: what is a text, and what must the psyche be if it can be represented by a text?" Derrida's attempts to replace a model of the unconscious as a space or place with a model of the unconscious as a trace suggest that he too is caught in the spatial and technological metaphors that he discovers in Freud. One response to his question might be to consider what the psyche must be if it can *never* be represented by a text—if it can never be represented at all. And one answer to that question is provided by Derrida's title, since his interest in figuring the psyche as text is undermined by his fascination with theatricality. Derrida's work is riddled with theatrical references—to Artaud, to the *scene* of writing, to the *staging* or *performance* of theory—and these references have serious implications for theater theory. He concludes the essay with an appropriately theatrical flair: "Thus Freud performs for us the scene of writing. Like all those who write. And like all who know how to write, he let the scene duplicate, repeat, and betray itself within the scene." Since the "scene" of writing "must be thought in the horizon of the scene/stage of the world, as the history of that scene/stage,"[31] since all Freud can do is perform for us the scene of writing, as Derrida claims, then the relationship between theatricality and writing requires closer scrutiny. If we cannot figure without disfiguring, can we not put these disfiguring processes on stage by acknowledging their role in representation?

In *The Interpretation of Dreams*, Freud advances the provocative thesis that censorship "imposes upon the dream-work *considerations of representability*" which restrict the dream "to giving things a new form." Since censorship determines representation, he reasons, dream interpretation must follow the distorting form of the dream work. Freud reproaches analysts for reductive models of interpretation that seek to retrieve an undistorted original: "They seek to find the essence of dreams in their latent content and in so doing they overlook the distinction between the latent dream-thoughts and the dream-work. At bottom, dreams are nothing other than a particular *form* of thinking. . . . It is the *dream-work* which creates that form, and it alone is the essence of dreaming—the explanation of its peculiar nature."[32] The mistake such analysts make, according to Freud, is the same error for which Derrida took literary critics to task: they adopt a simplistic model of representation which depends upon the dream of an origin, an originating wish, motive, or meaning that can be faithfully reproduced or retrieved.

Freud repeatedly acknowledges that undistorted knowledge of dreams is impossible: "Our memory of dreams is not only fragmentary but positively inaccurate and falsified." Like our memories of dreams, dream interpretation is riddled with distortions: "It is true that we distort dreams in attempting to reproduce them. . . . But this distortion is itself no more than a part of the revision to which the dream-thoughts are regularly subjected as a result of the dream-censorship." Freud concludes that "one can reconstruct from a single remaining fragment not, it is true, the dream—which is in any case a matter of no importance—but all the dream-thoughts."[33] Once Freud dismisses the importance of reconstructing the dream per se, and focuses instead on the dream work, the ontological status of both dreams and dream interpretation is, as Samuel Weber points out, radically redefined: "It [the dream] can no longer be regarded as a self-contained, fully determinable *object*, susceptible of being rendered or represented faithfully—'*dargestellt*'—by an interpretation. Rather, the dream comes to be only through a process of revision and distortion that even the best of interpretations can only hope to continue. What results . . . is a situation of interpretation that is quite different from that presumed by a hermeneutics that defines its task in terms of *explication* or of *disclosure*."[34]

Observing that Freud always considered dreams a form of distortion, of *Entstellung*—which implies both disfigurement and dislocation—Weber explains what is at stake:

The interpretation of a dream thus does indeed constitute a process of
deformation; yet far from invalidating itself, this alone constitutes,
paradoxically, its sole claim to legitimacy. For the dream "itself" is
already an *Entstellung*: not merely by virtue of what Freud describes
as "secondary elaboration" . . . but also because the specific
mechanisms of articulation that constitute the distinctive language of
the dream are all forms of *Entstellung*: a word that must be read as an
alternative to *Darstellung*, "presentation" or "exposition." . . . The
"form" of thinking peculiar to dreams . . . is that of a de-formation
that dissimulates its deformative character by creating a
representational facade. "*Darstellung*" thus becomes one of the
means by which the dream achieves its goal of "*Entstellung*."[35]

The key phrase here is "a de-formation that dissimulates its
deformative character by creating a representational facade." Is
representation always already a distortion? If "the essence of dreams"
is not to be found in some original wish but in the process of a
distorting yet constitutive inscription, if representation is a form of
dislocation or distortion, then the entire interpretive process, whether of
dreams, literature, or history, indeed must be rethought. Interpretation
is itself subsumed under the disfiguring effects of performance. Not
only is reading a reproduction that necessarily distorts the original, but
the "original" is itself a product of distortion because it too is "always
already" in representation. At the core of the dream there is no desire
that is not also a result of censorship; in essence there is no essence, no
core of the dream at all. At bottom we have reached the dream that has
no bottom. Is this critique of referentiality the limit of deconstructive
analysis?

   If there is no undistorted inscription or intent "underneath" or
"behind" the work of play or dream, how do we define the work of
critical theory today? Once Freud establishes that we can never
reconstruct the dream itself, he turns his attention to the acts of
distortion and censorship that he terms the dream work. Similarly,
rather than forgo theory, we return it to theater by rethinking meaning
as performative. In a remarkable passage, Freud directly relates
theatricality to psychoanalysis: "Condensation, together with the
transformation of thoughts into situations ('dramatization'), is the most
important and peculiar characteristic of the dream-work."[36] If the
dream work is all that we can study and if its defining characteristic is

dramatization, then the revival of theatrical terms and concepts would appear crucial to the redirection of critical theory.

Rather than conceive of the meaning of a dream or a play as a thing to be retrieved, we might rethink meaning as a social production or enactment. And theater provides an intriguing model for that production. Terry Eagleton explains: "The literary text is not the 'expression' of ideology, nor is ideology the 'expression' of social class. The text, rather, is a certain *production* of ideology, for which the analogy of a dramatic production is in some ways appropriate. A dramatic production does not 'express,' 'reflect,' or 'reproduce' the dramatic text on which it is based; it 'produces' the text, transforming it into a unique and irreducible entity."[37] The analogy of production is more than appropriate; it is necessary—which explains why Derrida must stage a scene in order to critique representation. If the literary work is displaced by the active work through which meaning is produced, we cannot avoid rethinking reading as enactment and enactment as a constitutive distortion.

The acts of staging a play that will escape censorship and producing a dream that can never be adequately translated are remarkably similar. Play production, like dream production, is a matter of a translation that effaces as it reaches toward an original. A play is, after all, a projected performance of an original that can never be retrieved or realized as such. Like a dream, the original play is "nothing, nothing in the world" (5.1.78); it can only be located as "not that," or as a simulacrum of a simulacrum, a distortion of an origin that is itself constituted by distortions. Peter Quince knows that to represent is to disfigure. Should Bottom follow up on his plans to have Peter Quince write a ballad of his dream, that ballad would also be a disfiguring translation. Censorship doesn't end with the construction of a work but continues in its reconstruction on stage and page. Dreams, like plays, are always censored translations, since presentation is a constitutive distortion of an original that is nowhere to be found.

Both dream and play production are based on "considerations of representability"—on the materiality of the signifier, on the conditions of staging, on the conventions of audience reception. Elizabethan play production, for example, was a highly collaborative activity over which no one individual maintained complete or autonomous control. Stephen Oriel observes: "The company commissioned the play, usually stipulated the subject, often provided the plot, often parcelled it out,

scene by scene, to several playwrights. The text thus produced was a
working model, which the company then revised as seemed
appropriate. The author had little or no say in these revisions: the text
belonged to the company, and the authority represented by the text—I
am talking now about the *performing* text—is that of the company, the
owners, not that of the playwright, the author."[38] Shakespeare's content
with the collaborative aspects of theatrical production, unlike the
discontent of his contemporary Ben Jonson, suggests an acceptance of
the distortion that plagues all representation.[39] Not surprisingly, Freud
stressed the collaborative and distorting nature of dream production as
well: "Each element in the content of a dream is 'overdetermined' by
material in the dream-thoughts; it is not derived from a *single* element
in the dream-thoughts, but may be traced back to a whole number."[40]
Yet Freud's focus on "considerations of representability" suggests
these distorting representations. Insofar as cultural formations
determine conditions of representability, the play of distortion is itself
limited to a local form.

VI

To what extent, then, does *A Midsummer Night's Dream* figure
interpretation as distortion or acknowledge its politics? At first glance,
A Midsummer Night's Dream follows the traditional categories of
Renaissance faculty psychology, in which reality is a collaborative
production of the hearing and the seeing senses in cooperation with
imagination and reason. Since reason must control imagination in the
production of reality, vision is "corrected" as in trick perspective
paintings. But in fact, *A Midsummer Night's Dream* differs from this
account in one important respect: patriarchal law rather than reason
actually controls perspective in this play, and its vision is depicted as
necessarily distorted and distorting. Since all power is necessarily a
distortion, the problem the play poses is not how to correct distorted
perspective but how to legitimize the distorted vision of the patriarchy.
The problem it faces is how to bring Elizabethan faculty psychology
into the service of a patriarchal aristocracy that openly employs
distortion to construct truth.

Renaissance faculty psychology was a kind of cognitive
psychology which explored how memory and judgment work with
sight and hearing. Bottom aptly describes his experience in the wood

by confusing sight and hearing in his bungled rendering of a passage from I Corinthians: "The eye of man hath not heard, the ear of man hath not seen, man's hand is not able to taste, his tongue to conceive, nor his heart to report, what my dream was" (4.1.211–14). Despite its rich visual imagery, *A Midsummer Night's Dream* keeps reminding us that the eye, the chief organ by which we know, is the most deceptive. Rather than cite the many references to erring vision in the play, consider the exceptions to the rule. The few references to erring hearing are connected to lovers' singing: Egeus charges Lysander with having bewitched his daughter not only with sight but with sound: "Thou hast by moonlight at her window sung / With faining voice verses of faining love" (1.1.30–31). When Titania is awakened by Bottom's singing, she responds: "I pray thee, gentle mortal, sing again. / Mine ear is much enamored of thy note; / So is mine eye enthralled to thy shape" (3.1.137–39). For the rest of the play, erring knowledge is figured as visual and the hearing sense is privileged.

The lengthy and seemingly irrelevant speech Hermia delivers as she discovers the erring lovers is in fact an argument concerning the limits of the seeing sense:

> Dark night, that from the eye his function takes,
> The ear more quick of apprehension makes;
> Wherein it doth impair the seeing sense,
> It pays the hearing double recompense.
> Thou art not by mine eye, Lysander, found;
> Mine ear, I thank it, brought me to thy sound.
> But why unkindly didst thou leave me so? (3.2.177–83)

Perhaps just as valid as Hermia's concluding question is why she spends such an important moment philosophizing upon the relative merits of the hearing and seeing senses.

Even the play's celebration of order is an auditory epiphany of "the musical confusion / Of hounds and echo in conjunction" (4.1.110–11). Hippolyta boasts of what she has heard, not seen, when she was with Hercules and Cadmus. What she remembers best is the sound of the Spartan hounds: "Never did I hear / Such gallant chiding; for besides the groves, / The skies, the fountains, every region near / Seem all one mutual cry. I never heard / So musical a discord, such sweet thunder" (4.1.114–18). Theseus responds boastfully that his Spartan-bred hounds bark according to a musical scale; they are "match'd in mouth like bells, / Each under each. A cry more tuneable / Was never hollow'd to, nor cheer'd with horn, / In Crete, in Sparta, nor in Thessaly. / Judge when you hear" (4.1.123–27). The question is not why Theseus employs a musical scale to champion a rigidly hierarchical social order, or even why one can judge best when one hears but not when one sees, but how right sight can be legitimized.

Shakespeare's early comedies repeatedly contrast categories of true and false perspective to stage the legislation of right perspective. *The Taming of the Shrew* carefully deletes the information upon which decisions are based in order to focus our attention on the decision-making process. It presents us with undecidable situations and then offers us a variety of alternatives through which they can be resolved. The question is never who is factually correct but which system should determine "right perspective." As in the famous scene of Kate and Petruchio's return to Padua, or as in the dispute between the Lord and First Huntsman concerning the better dog at the hunt, the emphasis is less on who is correct than on how perspective is both constructed and enforced.

A Midsummer Night's Dream is another early comedy in which the control of meaning takes precedence over any particular meaning, and in which that control is accomplished through the manipulation of sight. Theseus's reputation as a wise judge identifies him with the act of legislating right vision. He is flanked on either side by representatives of mastered fantasy; both Hippolyta and Philostrate embody imaginative forces held in check by his rule. Philostrate, as master of revels, is both the source of imaginative material and the means by which it is censored or transformed in accordance with Theseus's "right vision." Hippolyta evokes and reflects Theseus's sexual desire, which the law demands he restrain until his wedding day. When *A Midsummer Night's Dream* opens, then, the three characters on stage emblematically set out the relationship between the right vision of law and the erring vision of imagination.

The right relationship between imagination and patriarchal law is threatened when Egeus and Hermia enter and present their quarrel. By refusing to marry Demetrius, Hermia openly challenges the perspective of the Athenian patriarchy: "I would my father look'd but with my eyes" (1.1.56). Theseus upholds the "ancient privilege of Athens" (1.1.41) and responds sharply: "Rather your eyes must with his judgment look" (1.1.57). Lysander may be worthy, Theseus admits, but "wanting your father's voice, / The other must be held the worthier" (1.1.54–55). Hermia's refusal "to choose love by another's eyes" (1.1.140) has disastrous consequences: since she challenges the interpretive conventions by means of which her society measures truth, her privileges as a reader are withdrawn and her interpretation of events is discredited. Power in *A Midsummer Night's Dream* is both optical and patriarchal; patriarchal law determines perspective and operates through the control of that perspective.

Yet how valid is patriarchal perspective in this play? Consider the competing visions held by Oberon and Titania regarding the changeling boy. According to Oberon, as Puck informs us, Titania is caring for "A lovely boy stolen from an Indian king" (2.1.22). Titania, however, offers a different account: "His mother was a vot'ress of my order, / . . . And for her sake do I rear up her boy" (2.1.123,136). Since only patriarchal law legislates right vision in this play, Titania's competing perspective must be discredited. In order to place Titania in the position of an erring spectator, Oberon squeezes the juice of the flower love-in-idleness on her eyelids while chanting: "What thou seest when thou dost wake, / Do it for thy true-love take; / . . . In thy eye that shall appear / When thou wak'st, it is thy dear: / Wake when some vile thing is near" (2.2.27–28, 32–34). No sooner is Titania's viewpoint rendered distorted than Oberon's perspective is triumphantly equated with right sight. By successfully distorting Titania's perspective, Oberon presents his own interpretation of events as unerring.

An analogy for this complicated plot of competing visions is a 1638 description by Jean-François Niceron of a trick perspective in which various images, drawn from multiple points of view, are superimposed on a painting with straightforward images, so that they "represent two or three wholly different things, such that being seen from the front, they represent a human face; from the right side a death's head, and from the left something different."[41] From one perspective, Lysander and Demetrius look exactly the same—two rather uninteresting young Englishmen. Lysander points to the similarity: "I am, my lord, as well deriv'd as he, / As well possess'd; my love is more than his; / My fortunes every way as fairly rank'd / (If not with vantage) as Demetrius'" (1.1.99–102). From Egeus's standpoint, however, Demetrius appears the ideal suitor and Lysander an unrecognizable blur, whereas from Hermia's perspective the reverse is true. Again, from one standpoint, Hermia and Helena appear to be interchangeable. Helena reminds us that she and Hermia are widely considered to be of comparable beauty: "Through Athens I am thought as fair as she" (1.1.227). Yet from Lysander's perspective, Hermia appears fair and Helena disordered, whereas in the past it appears that for Demetrius the reverse was true. The problem *A Midsummer Night's Dream* presents is how to achieve not truth in vision but optical power; when Demetrius shifts his affections, he fights to stand where Lysander does. Since neither of the two will share the viewing space, each must fight to present the other's vision as distorted.

This fact alone explains why Demetrius's vision is left magically distorted at the end. Even a correction of sight is yet another distortion of sight. In *A Midsummer Night's Dream*, right vision is a social construct achieved through its own form of distortion. The play openly admits that all figuration is distortion; the problem it confronts, however, is how to legitimize the distorted vision of a patriarchal order. Oberon's manipulation of vision, however tricky, ultimately affirms a patriarchal ideology that equates men with right perspective and women with an irrational nature that defies orderly sight. Even if Titania isn't wrong, her vision is so drastically impaired by Oberon that she learns to distrust her sight. Even if Hippolyta is correct, she is silenced as speaking inappropriately and so proven incorrect in advance. Shakespeare's depiction of the relationship of the gaze to narratives of women's punishment and correction holds steady from *The Comedy of Errors* to *The Winter's Tale*. Woman is the guilty object—whether Titania or Hippolyta, Helena or Hermia, Kate or Adriana—whose erring vision, traditionally figured in her guilty sexuality, must be punished.

Similar examples of the use of distorted sight to control women are plentiful in Hollywood films of the 1940s and 1950s. At the level of narrative, these films commonly portray women as irrational, unable to see clearly and unable to trust what they see. At the level of representation, such films provide a variety of techniques for distorting, dehumanizing, and idealizing the image of woman as fetish. In Busby Berkeley's film *Dames*, the image of woman is continually distorted and then corrected in ways that deny women either individuality or humanity. . . . In one shot, a group of women lift their skirts to create an idealized image of the face of woman—in the form of the face of the film star Ruby Keeler. . . . [42] The women are seen correctly only when they have utterly effaced their individuality and merged together to form an idealized representation of Woman. Such doubling apparently reassures the male gaze: it suggests that Woman is not only the means by which we are reproduced, but an object that we can reproduce, in turn; women are nothing more than Woman—an image that can be multiplied endlessly without ever being confronted. Since women may be seen but not heard in *A Midsummer Night's Dream*, some of the most powerful productions of the play flood the stage with visions of identical women. In a Canadian Stratford production of the play with Maggie Smith, the stage was peopled with multiples of the major figures. The effect was to stage dream mechanisms, so that image distortion fed into the play's exploration of the role of censorship in the dream work. Just as uncanny repetition counteracts repression in *The Comedy of Errors*, so in this production of *A Midsummer Night's Dream* the figure of woman could not be repressed; the idea that woman should be seen but not heard was enacted with a vengeance.

Both contemporary and Elizabethan strategies of power are directly related to the control of the spectator's gaze. Jean Baudrillard claims: "Power did not always consider itself as power, and the secret of the great politicians was to know that power *does not exist.* To know that it is only a perspectival space of simulation, as was the pictorial space of the Renaissance, and that if power seduces, it is precisely— what the naive realists of politics will never understand—because it is a simulacrum and because it undergoes a metamorphosis into signs and is invented on the basis of signs."[43] Baudrillard's claim is overstated, but it aptly describes the strategies of optical power employed throughout Shakespearean comedy. The long-standing quarrel over whether Hal's "reformation" in *1 Henry IV* is real or staged exemplifies the claim that at issue is how the real is staged. That Hal's power is optical is suggested by his description of his strategy as a manipulation of others' perceptions of his image: "My reformation, glitt'ring o'er my fault, / Shall show more goodly and attract more eyes / Than that which hath no foil to set it off" (1.2.213–15). Oberon gains power, as Hal does, by presenting certain images as unquestionably distorted so that less obviously distorted images will be perceived as accurate. The curious anamorphic portrait of Edward VI . . . makes good political sense when read in the context of this strategy.[++] Just as Hal manipulates his political image by disguising himself as distorted, so

Edward's portrait physically and cognitively constrains the viewer to reject a distorted image of Edward in favor of an idealized image.

Stephen Heath reminds us that trick perspectives were less subversive than we might at first imagine, since "the 'wit' of anamorphosis is constantly a reference to a rational and stable system that it assumes in the very moment it parodies or questions and is thus always available as a final image of order."[44] And yet the rational and stable system assumed is itself presented as constructed only through distortion. The Renaissance use of distortion to construct right vision suggests that interpretation was always already a question of censorship and legitimization. *A Midsummer Night's Dream*'s exploration of the means by which knowledge and fantasy are generated is therefore less dependent upon some hidden or unconscious content per se than on the work involved in authorizing and censoring perspectives.

VII

In his early writings on dreams, Freud employs political metaphors to figure the process of representation. He maintains: "A dream-element is, in the strictest sense of the word, the 'representative' of all this disparate material in the content of the dream."[45] Further, he acknowledges the shaping role of specific social formations in the production of imaginative experience:

> A dream is not constructed by each individual dream-thought, or group of dream-thoughts, finding (in abbreviated form) separate representation in the content of the dream—in the kind of way in which an electorate chooses parliamentary representatives; a dream is constructed, rather, by the whole mass of dream-thoughts being submitted to a sort of manipulative process in which those elements which have the most numerous and strongest supports acquire the right of entry into the dream-content—in a manner analogous to election by *scrutin de liste*.[46]

The more Freud's metaphors veer away from the spatial, the local, the topological, however, the less political they become as well. Whereas Freud was reluctant to develop a politics of the unconscious, Gilles Deleuze and Félix Guattari are not. In their groundbreaking *Anti-Oedipus*, they maintain that desire is necessarily constituted by repression, and so can never be understood outside of a social context: "The law tells us: You will not marry your mother, and you will not kill your father. And we docile subjects say to ourselves: so *that's* what I wanted!"[47] By reading psychoanalysis as an ideological instrument of capitalism, Deleuze and Guattari redefine the unconscious as a social production. Rather than complain that desire can never be singled out from its representation and production, they urge us to explore how desire functions. Rather than avoid a local habitation and a name for our shaping fantasies, they encourage us to acknowledge, use, and change the metaphors we have. They urge us to stage the political and psychological problems inherent in the act of representation, to reinstate within critical discourse the materiality of the signifier by exploring the production, distribution, and circulation of meaning.

Louis Althusser's study of the relationship of ideology and psychoanalysis has been attacked on the grounds that it construes, and so constructs, ideology as a transcendental signified, as a specific form of the unknowable. But Althusser relates psychoanalysis and ideology in far more constructive ways: "It is not enough to know that the Western family is patriarchal and exogamic . . . we must also work out the ideological formations that govern paternity, maternity, conjugality, and childhood: what are 'husband-and-wife-being,' 'father-being,' 'mother-being' and 'child-being' in the modern world? A mass of research remains to be done on these ideological formations. This is a task for *historical materialism*."[48] If the conditions of representability play a major role in the construction of desire, such an analysis extends to the construction of the critic's desire, as well. *A Midsummer Night's Dream* urges its audience, as well as Hermia, to "question your desires" (1.1.67).

Further, *A Midsummer Night's Dream* offers a model for this sort of analysis. Critics have long prized Hermia's dream as a model of text and dream interpretation.[49] It suits New Critical approaches in that it can be read according to the conventional interpretive devices of imagery, theme, and structure. Yet Bottom's account of his "dream" resists this critical approach by openly acknowledging its status as an incomplete and censored translation: "I have had a dream, past the wit of man to say what dream it was," Bottom sighs, acknowledging: "Man is but an ass, if he go about [t'] expound this dream" (4.1.205–7). When Bottom finally meets up with his friends, he keeps beginning and then refusing to recount that dream in a curious act of self-censorship:

"Masters, I am to discourse wonders; but ask me not what; for if I tell you, I am [no] true Athenian. I will tell you every thing, right as it fell out. . . . Not a word of me. All that I will tell you is, that the Duke hath din'd. . . . No more words" (4.2.29–32, 34–35, 45).

Bottom's account mediates between certain knowledge and its impossibility, or between Derrida's two interpretations of interpretation, in that it conveys *certain knowledge of uncertainty.* As in discourse theory, which examines the legitimation of meaning, the focus of Bottom's account is less a particular meaning than the *performance and control of meaning itself.* Since his account of his dream is largely a record of what he cannot say, it shifts our attention away from content and onto the *legitimating process as content.* In this sense, *A Midsummer Night's Dream* suggests a model of interpretation as a socially determined activity of privileged and censored perspectives. Whereas *A Midsummer Night's Dream* does not urge us to explore the construction of an individual or personal unconscious, it does inquire into the modes of production, translation, and representation of collective imaginative experiences. It seems less appropriate, therefore, to seek to reconstruct Hermia's personal fantasies than to study the social construction of fantasy.

Even at the level of dramatic narrative, *A Midsummer Night's Dream* keeps stalling the activity of putting on a play to show us what is involved in the process. It puts representation on stage, displacing content with the disfiguring process of censorship itself. Dreams stage not only content but process as content, and what they tell us about the dream work may be more revealing than the content itself; similarly, Shakespearean comedy is to be valued for the means by which it stages its own representational strategies. The comedies resist arguments regarding the absolute certainty or uncertainty of knowledge because they study that which resists meaning as a form of knowledge. Their treatment of learned ignorance suggests an effort to understand that which escapes comprehension rather than an easy means of denying what we know. The comedies fascinate because they refuse to retreat into ignorance. They demonstrate that we can know and do know, even when we do not know. The mind may only know itself through a mirroring that displaces as it procures self-consciousness, but we can know how it unfolds through that distorting process.

A Midsummer Night's Dream may present itself to us as but another dream to be interpreted; yet we succumb to a naive form of dream interpretation indeed if we simply seek to force into place privileged signifieds, including the politics of the signifier. If *A Midsummer Night's Dream* cannot figure itself, if the mind can only know itself as not itself or through a distorting enactment, the scene of its performance nonetheless offers a kind of knowledge. Finally, *A Midsummer Night's Dream* offers a knowledge that subverts the possibility of knowledge, a knowledge that collapses neat distinctions between psyche and text, writing and censorship, or truth and distortion. We *miss* when we try to read the play from the perspective of the privileged viewer, just as we *miss out* when we assert that meaning is inaccessible. But if we follow erasures, blind spots, and distortions, we discover a different kind of truth. In "Les non-dupes errent" Lacan develops this hypothesis, and Shoshana Felman presents it concisely:

> Lacan makes it clear that we are in no way dealing with the myth of "non-knowledge" [*non-savoir*] that a superficial avant-garde used to its advantage: for not only is it not *sufficient* not to know; the very ability not to know is not granted to us, and cannot thus be taken for granted. What we are dealing with is a knowledge that is, rather, indestructible; *a knowledge which does not allow for knowing that one knows*; a knowledge, therefore, that is not supported by *meaning* which, by definition, *knows itself*. The subject can get a hold on this unconscious knowledge only by the intermediary of his *mistakes*—the effects of non-sense his speech registers: in dreams, slips of the tongue, or jokes.[50]

If it is *not* sufficient *not* to know, then the distinction between suppression and repression deserves rethinking. It is possible that the theory of repression is really a fantasy of repression—a dream of unknowingness? From this standpoint, what dreams, trick perspectives, jokes, and comedies share is a reminder of the impossibility of not knowing, of the fantasy that *is* not knowing. Since our desire to uncover the original meaning of a given work is an impossible dream, we must attend to the disfiguring processes by means of which we continually reconstruct ourselves and our knowledge. As we continue to write at the margins of representation and to posit our unknowingness, however, we do so not to reify our blind spots but to keep them on the move.

Here psychoanalytic theory and Shakespearean comedy intersect at their most puzzling and promising, as doubled discourses of non-knowledge. Riddled with meaning, both comedy and psychoanalysis set themselves the task of knowing that which they define in advance as impervious to meaning; both bear witness to what Foucault terms a "positive unconscious" of knowledge. Both stand at the limits of meaning, move by indirections to find directions out, and work through and against themselves. Between as well as within both systems is a wall. Yet it is perhaps "the wittiest partition that ever I heard discourse" (5.1.167–68), since it makes referentiality possible and representation paradoxical.

NOTES

*Reprinted from Barbara Freedman, *Staging the Gaze: Postmodernism, Psychoanalysis, and Shakespearean Comedy*. Copyright (c) 1991 by Cornell University. Used by permission of the publisher, Cornell University Press.

1. Annabel M. Patterson, *Censorship and Interpretation: The Conditions of Writing and Reading in Early Modern England* (Madison: University of Wisconsin Press, 1984), 17. In *Power on Display: The Politics of Shakespeare's Genres* (London: Methuen, 1986), Leonard Tennenhouse observes that "no other Tudor monarch maintained such tight control over the plays and players as Elizabeth" (106); he cites information from Glynne Wickham's *Early English Stages, 1300–1600* (London: Routledge and Kegan Paul, 1963), 2:75–90. In *The Politics and Poetics of Transgression* (Ithaca: Cornell University Press, 1986), Peter Stallybrass and Allon White note that Ben Jonson was arrested in 1597 for cowriting *The Isle of Dogs*, accused of treason for *Sejanus* in 1603, and imprisoned in 1605 for cowriting *Eastward Ho*; it was reported that he would have his nose and ears cut off for the latter work (74).

+ Editor's Note: All citations are from *The Riverside Shakespeare*, gen. ed. G. Blakemore Evans (Boston: Houghton Mifflin, 1974).

2. For a fascinating account of this relationship, see Frank Whigham, *Ambition and Privilege: The Social Tropes of Elizabethan Courtesy Theory* (Berkeley: University of California Press, 1984). Whigham outlines a variety of strategies employed by Elizabethan writers to further their status, including tropes of personal promotion, tropes of rivalry, and tropes of social hierarchy.

3. James Kavanagh, "Shakespeare in Ideology," in *Alternative Shakespeares*, ed. John Drakakis (London: Methuen, 1985), 155–56.

4. Louis Montrose, "'Shaping Fantasies: Figurations of Gender and Power in Elizabethan Culture," *Representations* 1 (Spring 1983), 61–94, rpt. in a shorter, revised version as "*A Midsummer Night's Dream* and the Shaping Fantasies of Elizabethan Culture: Gender, Power, Form," in *Rewriting the Renaissance: The Discourses of Sexual Difference in Early Modern Europe*, ed. Margaret W. Ferguson, Maureen Quilligan, and Nancy J. Vickers (Chicago: University of Chicago Press, 1986), 65–87.

5. Tennenhouse, *Power on Display*, 43–44.

6. James Calderwood, *Shakespearean Metadrama* (Minneapolis: University of Minnesota Press, 1971), 137.

7. Jacques Derrida, "Structure, Sign, and Play," *Writing and Difference*, trans. Alan Bass (Chicago: University of Chicago Press, 1978), 293.

8. Jacques Derrida, "Freud and the Scene of Writing," ibid., 226–27, 230.

9. Francis Barker and Peter Hulme, "Nymphs and Reapers Heavily Vanish: The Discursive Con-Texts of *The Tempest*," in *Alternative Shakespeares*, ed. Drakakis, 197.

10. Derrida, "Freud and the Scene of Writing," 230–31.

11. Julian Jaynes, *The Origin of Consciousness in the Breakdown of the Bicameral Mind* (Boston: Houghton Mifflin, 1976), 64, 65.

12. Walter J. Ong, S.J., "System, Space, and Intellect in Renaissance Symbolism," *The Barbarian Within and Other Fugitive Essays* (New York: Macmillan, 1962), 76.

13. See David Young, *Something of Great Constancy* (New Haven: Yale University Press, 1966), a section of which is reprinted in the anthology *Modern Shakespearean Criticism*, ed. Alvin Kernan (New York: Harcourt, Brace, and World, 1970), 174–89, under the title "*A Midsummer Night's Dream*: Structure." See also Philip Edwards, *Shakespeare and the Confines of Art* (London: Methuen, 1968); and D.A. Traversi, *An Approach to Shakespeare*, 3d ed. rev. (New York: Doubleday-Anchor, 1969).

14. See Craig Owens, "The Discourse of Others: Feminists and Postmodernism," in *The Anti-Aesthetic: Essays on Postmodern Culture*, ed. Hal Foster (Port Townsend, Wash.: Bay Press, 1983), 57–82, for descriptions of postmodernism. Also see the other essays in this volume, as well as Jean-François Lyotard, *The Postmodern Condition* (Minneapolis: University of Minnesota Press, 1984).

15. Roland Barthes, "From Work to Text," *Image/Music/Text* (New York: Hill and Wang, 1977), 155–64.

16. Stephen Booth, *An Essay on Shakespeare's Sonnets* (New Haven: Yale University Press, 1969), 14.

17. Jaynes, *Origin of Consciousness*, 65–66.

18. Freud, *The Interpretation of Dreams* (1900), *SE*, 5:610.

19. Ibid., 537.

20. Derrida, "Freud and the Scene of Writing," 211, 228, 212–13.

21. Freud, *Interpretation of Dreams*, 611.

22. Freud, "A Note upon the 'Mystic Writing-Pad'" (1925), *SE*, 19:232, 231.

23. See, for example, the 1581 Elizabethan table book, now in Harvard College Library, in the Riverside Shakespeare, ed. G. Blakemore Evans (Boston: Houghton Mifflin, 1974), 146.

24. Derrida, "Freud and the Scene of Writing," 226.

25. Ong, "System, Space, and Intellect," 69–70.

26. Ibid., 75.

27. Derrida, "The End of the Book and the Beginning of Writing," *Of Grammatology*, trans. Gayatri Chakravorty Spivak (Baltimore: Johns Hopkins University Press, 1976), 19.

28. Michel Foucault, *The Order of Things: An Archaeology of the Human Sciences* (New York: Random-Vintage, 1973), 374.

29. Lacan, "La méprise du sujet supposé savoir," *Scilicet* 1 (1968), 35, as translated by Shoshana Felman, in *Writing and Madness (Literature/Philosophy/Psychoanalysis)*, trans. Martha Noel Evans and the author (Ithaca: Cornell University Press, 1985), 124.

30. Foucault, *Order of Things*, xi, 374–75.

31. Derrida, "Freud and the Scene of Writing," 229, 199.

32. Freud, *Interpretation of Dreams*, 506–7.

33. Ibid., 512, 514, 517.

34. Samuel Weber, "The Blindness of the Seeing Eye: Psychoanalysis, Hermeneutics, *Entstellung*," in his *Institution and Interpretation* (Minneapolis: University of Minnesota Press, 1987), 79. I am indebted to Weber's discussion (pp. 73–84) throughout these pages.

35. Ibid., 78–79.

36. Freud, *On Dreams* (1901), *SE*, 5:653.

37. Terry Eagleton, *Criticism and Ideology* (London: New Left Books, 1976), 64.

38. Stephen Orgel, "What Is a Text?" *Research Opportunities in Renaissance Drama 2* (1981), 3.

39. See, for example, Stallybrass and White on Ben Jonson and problems of authorship in *Politics and Poetics of Transgression*, 66–79.

40. Freud, *On Dreams*, 652.

41. Jean-François Niceron, *Perspective curieuse* (1652), as quoted and translated by Ernest B. Gilman, *The Curious Perspective: Literary and Pictorial Wit in the Seventeenth Century* (New Haven: Yale University Press, 1978), 41.

42. Lucy Fischer makes this point in her fascinating essay "The Image of Woman as Image: The Optical Politics of *Dames,*" *Film Quarterly* 30 (Fall 1976), 1–10.

43. Jean Baudrillard, "Forgetting Foucault," *Humanities in Society 3* (Winter 1980), 108–9.

++ Editor's Note: When this painting, possibly by William Scrot, is viewed head on, Edward's head is elongated to the point of distortion, but when viewed obliquely the head is of a normal shape and size.

44. Stephen Heath, *Questions of Cinema* (Bloomington: Indiana University Press, 1981), 70 n. 12.

45. Freud, *On Dreams*, 1901; [*The Standard Edition of the Complete Psychological Works of Sigmund Freud*, ed. James Strachey, 24 vols. (London: Hogarth, 1953–74)], 5: 652.

46. Freud, *Interpretation of Dreams*, SE, 4:284.

47. Gilles Deleuze and Félix Guattari, *Anti-Oedipus: Capitalism and Schizophrenia*, trans. Robert Hurley, Mark Seem, and Helen R. Lane (Minneapolis: University of Minnesota Press, 1983), 114.

48. Louis Althusser, *Lenin and Philosophy*, trans. Ben Brewster (London: Monthly Review Press, 1971), 211.

49. See, for example, Norman Holland, "Hermia's Dream," in *Representing Shakespeare: New Psychoanalytic Essays*, ed. Murray M. Schwartz and Coppélia Kahn (Baltimore: Johns Hopkins University Press, 1980), 1–20, rpt. from *Annual of Psychoanalysis* 7 (1979).

50. Felman, *Writing and Madness*, 121.

A Kingdom of Shadows*

Louis A. Montrose

I

In *A Midsummer Night's Dream*, the interplay among characters is structured by an interplay among categories—namely, the unstable Elizabethan hierarchies of gender, rank and age. For example, Titania treats Bottom as if he were both her child and her lover—which seems entirely appropriate, since he is a substitute for the changeling boy, who is, in turn, Oberon's rival for Titania's attentions. Titania herself is ambivalently benign and sinister, imperious and enthralled. She dotes upon Bottom, and indulges in him all those desires to be fed, scratched and coddled that render Bottom's dream recognisable to us as a parodic fantasy of infantile narcissism and dependency. But it is also, at the same time, a parodic fantasy of upward social mobility. Bottom's mistress mingles her enticements with threats:

> Out of this wood do not desire to go:
> Thou shalt remain here, whether thou wilt or no.
> I am a spirit of no common rate;
> The summer still doth tend upon my state;
> And I do love thee: therefore go with me.
> I'll give thee fairies to attend on thee;
> And they shall fetch thee jewels from the deep,
> And sing, while thou on pressed flowers dost sleep:
> And I will purge thy mortal grossness so,
> That thou shalt like an airy spirit go. (3.1.145-6)[1]

The sublimation of matter into spirit is identified with the social elevation of the base artisan into the gentry: Titania orders her attendants to 'be kind and courteous to this gentleman' (3.1.157), to 'do him courtesies' (167), and to 'wait upon him' (190); she concludes the scene, however, with an order to enforce her minion's passivity, thus reducing him to the demeanour prescribed for women, children and servants: 'Tie up my love's tongue, bring him silently' (104).

Titania vows that she will purge Bottom's mortal grossness and will make him her 'gentle joy' (4.1.4); Bottom's own company hope that the Duke will grant him a pension of sixpence a day for his performance as Pyramus. It is surely more than dramatic economy that motivated Shakespeare to make the artisan who is the queen's complacent paramour also an enthusiastic amateur actor who performs before the Duke. Bottom is a comically exorbitant figure for the common masculine subject of Queen Elizabeth. His interactions with the Queen of Faeries and with the Duke of Athens represent distinct modes of relationship to his sovereign: in the former, that relationship is figured as erotic intimacy; in the latter, it is figured as collective homage. Within Elizabethan society, relationships of authority and dependency, of desire and fear, were characteristic of both the public and the domestic domains. Domestic relations between husbands and wives, parents and children, masters and servants, were habitually politicised: the household was a microcosm of the state; at the same time, socio-economic and political relationships of patronage and clientage were habitually eroticised: the devoted suitor sought some loving return from his master-mistress. The collective and individual impact of Elizabethan symbolic forms frequently depended upon interchanges or conflations between these domains.

Like their companion Bottom in his liaison with Titania, the mechanicals are collectively presented in a childlike relationship to their social superiors. They characterise themselves, upon two occasions, as 'every mother's son' (1.2.73; 3.1.69); however, they hope to be 'made men' (4.2.18) by the patronage of their lord, Duke Theseus. Differences *within* the mortal and faery courts of *A Midsummer Night's Dream* are structured principally in terms of gender and generation. However, by the end of the fourth act, the multiple marriages arranged within the Athenian aristocracy and the marital reconciliation arranged between the King and Queen of Faeries have achieved domestic harmony and reestablished hierarchical norms. When Bottom and his company are introduced into the newly concordant courtly milieu in the final scene, social rank and social calling displace gender and generation as the play's most conspicuous markers of difference. The dramatic emphasis is now upon a contrast between the socially and stylistically refined mixed-sex communities of court and forest, and the 'crew of patches, rude mechanicals' (3.2.9), who 'have toiled their unbreathed memories' (5.1.72) in order to honour and entertain their betters. In the coming together of common artisan-actors and the leisured elite for whom they perform, socio-political realities and theatrical realities converge. Implicated in this particular dramatic dénouement are several larger historical developments: the policies and attitudes abetting Elizabethan state formation; the enormous growth of London as an administrative, economic and cultural centre; and the institutionalisation of a professional, secular and commercial theatre with a complex relationship to the dynastic state and the royal court on the one hand, and to the urban oligarchy and the public market on the other. In the present essay, I seek to articulate some of these implications.

II

The immediate reason for the presence of Bottom and his companions in *A Midsummer Night's Dream* is to rehearse and perform an 'interlude before the Duke and the Duchess, on his wedding-day at night' (1.2.5–7). However, their project simultaneously evokes what, only a generation before the production of Shakespeare's play, had been a central aspect of civic and artisanal culture in England— namely, the feast of Corpus Christi, with its ceremonial procession and its often elaborate dramatic performances. The civic and artisanal status of the amateur players is insisted upon with characteristic Shakespearean condescension: Puck describes them to his master, Oberon, as 'rude mechanicals, / That work for bread upon Athenian stalls' (3.2.9–10); and Philostrate describes them to his master, Theseus, as 'Hard-handed men that work in Athens here, / Which never laboured in their minds till now' (5.1.72–3). In the most material way, Bottom's name relates him to the practice of his craft—the 'bottom' was 'the core on which the weaver's skein of yarn was wound' (Arden *MND*, p. 3, n. 11); and it also relates him to his lowly position in the temporal order, to his social baseness. Furthermore, among artisans, weavers in particular were associated with Elizabethan food riots and other forms of social protest that were prevalent during the mid-1590s, the period during which *A Midsummer Night's Dream* was presumably written and first performed.[2] Thus, we may construe Bottom as the spokesman for the commons in the play—but with the proviso that this *vox populi* is not merely that of a generalised *folk*. Bottom is primarily the comic representative of a specific socio-economic group with its own highly articulated culture. He is not the voice of the dispossessed or the indigent but of the middling sort, in whose artisanal, civic and guild-centred ethos Shakespeare had his own roots.[3] During his childhood in Stratford, Shakespeare would have had the opportunity and the occasion to experience the famed Corpus Christi play that was performed annually in nearby Coventry. Bottom himself, the most enthusiastic of amateur thespians, makes oblique allusion to the figures and acting traditions of the multi-pageant mystery plays.[4] Thus, Bully Bottom, the weaver, is an overdetermined signifier, encompassing not only a generalised common voice but also the particular socio-economic and cultural origins of William Shakespeare, the professional player-playwright—and, too, the collective socio-cultural origins of his craft. *A Midsummer Night's Dream* simultaneously acknowledges those origins and frames them at an ironic distance; it educes connections only in order to assert distinctions.

Recent studies in sixteenth-century English social history have emphasised that a major transformation in cultural life took place during the early decades of Elizabeth's reign, and that this cultural revolution manifested a complex interaction among religious, socio-economic and political processes. Mervyn James concludes that

> the abandonment of the observance of Corpus Christi, of the mythology associated with the feast, and of the cycle plays . . . arose from the Protestant critique of Corpus Christi, in due course implemented by the Protestant Church, with the support of the Protestant state. . . .
>
> The decline and impoverishment of gild organizations, the pauperization of town populations, the changing character and role of town societies, increasing government support of urban oligarchies, were all factors tending toward urban authoritarianism. As a result, urban ritual and urban drama no longer served a useful purpose; and were indeed increasingly seen as potentially disruptive to the kind of civil order which the magistracy existed to impose.[5]

In a study of the world the Elizabethans had lost, Charles Phythian-Adams emphasises that

> for urban communities in particular, the middle and later years of the sixteenth century represented a more abrupt break with the past than any period since the era of the Black Death or before the age of industrialization. Not only were specific customs and institutions brusquely changed or abolished, but a whole, vigorous and variegated popular culture, the matrix of everyday life, was eroded and began to perish. . . .

> If the opportunity for popular participation in public rituals was consequently largely removed, that especial meaning which sacred ceremonies and popular rites had periodically conferred on the citizens' tangible environment also fell victim to the new 'secular' order.[6]

The brilliant scholarship of these studies appears to proceed from a position that sees in the advent of the early modern Protestant state the fragmentation and loss of a pre-existing organic community. This tendency has been challenged recently in the work of Miri Rubin. Of Corpus Christi, she observes bluntly that 'a procession which excluded most working people, women, children, visitors and servants, was not a picture of the community. . . . By laying hierarchy bare it could incite the conflict of difference ever more powerfully sensed in a concentrated symbolic moment'.[7] Taking her point, I wish to emphasise a shift not from sacramental civic *communitas* to disciplinary state hierarchy but rather from a culture focused upon social dynamics within the local community to one that incorporates the local within and subordinates it to the centre.

Throughout most of the sixteenth century, the Tudor regime had been engaged in a complex process of consolidating temporal and spiritual power in the hereditary ruler of a sovereign nation-state. Consistent with this project, the Elizabethan government was actively engaged in efforts to suppress traditional, amateur forms of popular entertainment, including the civic religious drama. The Elizabethan state perceived this culture to be tainted by the superstitions and idolatrous practices of the old faith; because its traditional loyalties were local, regional or papal, it was regarded as a seedbed for dissent and sedition. Popular and liturgical practices, ceremonial and dramatic forms, were not wholly suppressed by the royal government but were instead selectively appropriated. In court, town and countryside, they were transformed by various temporal authorities into elaborate and effusive celebrations of the monarchy and of civic oligarchies; they became part of the ideological apparatus of the state. Such ceremonies of power and authority are epitomised by the queen's occasional progresses to aristocratic estates and regional urban centres; by her annual Accession Day festivities, celebrated at Westminster with pageants and jousts, and in towns throughout England with fanfares and bonfires; and by the annual procession and pageant for the lord mayor and aldermen of London, and analogous ceremonies maintained by other local, urban elites.[8]

The suppression of religious and polemical drama and the curtailment of popular festivities were policy goals vigorously pursued by the Elizabethan regime from its very inception. The custom of celebrating the queen's Accession Day began to flourish following the suppression of the northern rebellion and the York Corpus Christi play in 1569, and the promulgation of the Papal Bull excommunicating Queen Elizabeth on Corpus Christi Day 1570. The process of suppressing the mystery plays was virtually complete by 1580. As Mervyn James puts it, 'under Protestantism, the Corpus Christi becomes the Body of the Realm.'[9] At the same time, the queen's Privy Council and the court nourished the professional theatre—if only to the limited extent that it could be construed as serving their own interests. Commencing scarcely two decades before the writing of *A Midsummer Night's Dream*, resident professional acting companies, under the patronage of the monarch and her leading courtiers, were established in the vicinity of the City of London and the royal court at Westminster. Thus, the beginning of the fully professional, secular and commercial theatre of Elizabethan London coincides with the effective end of the religious drama and the relative decline of local amateur acting traditions in the rest of England.[10] As a means of entertaining the court and the people, the professional theatre seems to have been perceived by the crown as potentially if indirectly useful, both as an instrument for the aggrandisement of the dynastic nation state and for the supervision and diversion of its subjects.

The decay of Coventry's traditional civic culture during the mid- and late sixteenth century paralleled the city's economic decline. Such cultural changes were abetted, however, by the Tudor state's active suppression or cooptation of popular ceremonies and recreations. Some specific instances of this general process can provide a context for construing Shakespeare's comic representation of civic, artisanal culture and its relationship to the state. Queen Elizabeth visited Coventry on progress in 1566. In his speech of welcome, the City Recorder alluded to the role of Coventry in the overthrow of the Danes, 'a memorial whereof is kept unto this day by certain open shows in this City yearly'; the reference is to the elaborate and rowdy annual Hock Tuesday play, in which the role of women combatants was prominent. Upon her actual entrance into the city, the queen viewed the pageants of the Tanners, Drapers, Smiths and Weavers that formed parts of the Corpus Christi play.[11] Two years later, under the pressure of reformist preachers, the civic celebrations of the Hocktide shows were banned. Despite this, the queen had a subsequent opportunity to witness them at first hand. According to a putative eyewitness account, this was in 1575, during her celebrated visit to the earl of Leicester's estate at Kenilworth. Led by a mason who styled himself Captain Cox, the 'good-hearted men of Coventry' daringly presented their quaint show among the spectacular entertainments and displays with which the earl courted and counselled his royal mistress. The Coventrymen intended to make 'their humble petition unto Her Highness, that they might have their plays up again'.[12] Nevertheless, it appears that, after 1579, the citizens of Coventry ceased to entertain themselves with either their Hocktide show or their Corpus Christi play. At about the same time, in the city records for 1578, there occurs the first of a number of extant entries for payments in connection with celebrations 'on the quee[n']s holiday' (*Records of Early English Drama: Coventry*, p. 286). In these fragmentary records, we glimpse instances of the complex ideological process by which traditional ceremonial forms and events that were focused upon the articulation and celebration of the civic community itself either became occasions for the city's celebration of a royal visit, or were displaced outright by a newly instituted calendar of holidays that promoted the cult of the queen by honouring her birthday and her Accession Day.

A Midsummer Night's Dream incorporates allusions to this changed and diminished world of popular civic play forms. In its very title and in passing allusions—to the festivals of Midsummer Eve and St John's Day, to the rites of May and to St Valentine's Day—the play gestures towards a larger context of popular holiday occasions and customs that mixed together pagan and Christian traditions. In this context, it is significant that Corpus Christi, though a moveable feast, was nevertheless a summer festival, occurring between 21 May and 24 June—a circumstance that made possible its extensive open-air ceremonies and entertainments.[13] Furthermore, the institutional basis of civic ritual drama in the craft guilds survives in Shakespeare's *A Midsummer Night's Dream* in the names of the mechanicals, as enumerated by Peter Quince: 'Nick Bottom, the weaver', 'Francis Flute, the bellows-mender', 'Robin Starveling, the tailor', 'Tom Snout, the tinker', 'Snug the joiner'. The identification of the mechanicals in terms of both their particular crafts or 'mysteries' and their collective dramatic endeavour strengthens the evocation of the Corpus Christi tradition. Nevertheless, despite the conspicuous title of Shakespeare's play, and despite the oblique allusions to the guild structure of the civic community, the occasion for the artisans' play-within-the-play is not the marking of the traditional agrarian calendar, nor the articulation of the collective urban social body through the celebration of customary holidays. Neither is it the observance of the ecclesiastical calendar, the annual cycle of holy days, nor the dramatisation of the paradigmatic events of sacred history from the Creation to the Final Doom. Instead, the rude mechanicals pool their talents and strain their wits in order to dramatise an episode from classical mythology that will celebrate the wedding of Duke Theseus—an event that focuses the collective interests of the Commonwealth upon the person of the ruler.

III

As has long been recognised, *A Midsummer Night's Dream* has affinities with Elizabethan royal iconography and courtly entertainments. The most obvious features are Shakespeare's incorporation of a play performed in celebration of an aristocratic wedding, and Oberon's allusion to 'a fair vestal, throned by the west.... the imperial votaress' (2.1.158, 163)—the latter being invoked in a scenario reminiscent of the pageantry presented to the queen on her progresses.[14] From early in the reign, Elizabeth had been directly addressed and engaged by such performances at aristocratic estates and in urban centres. In these pageants, masques and plays, distinctions were effaced between the spatio-temporal locus of the royal spectator/actress and that of the characters being enacted before her. Debates were referred to the queen's arbitration; the magic of her presence civilised savage men, restored the blind to sight, released errant knights from enchantment, and rescued virgins from defilement. Such social dramas of celebration and coercion played out the delicately balanced relationship between the monarch and the nobility, gentry and urban elites who constituted the political nation. These events must also have evoked reverence and awe in the local common folk who assisted in and witnessed them. And because texts and descriptions of most of these processions, pageants and shows were in print within a year—sometimes within just a few weeks—of their performance, they may have had a cultural impact far more extensive and enduring than their occasional and ephemeral character might at first suggest. Such royal pageantry appropriated materials from popular late medieval romances, from Ovid, Petrarch and other literary sources; and when late Elizabethan poetry and drama such as Spenser's *Faerie Queene* or Shakespeare's *A Midsummer Night's Dream* reappropriated those sources, they were now inscribed by the allegorical discourse of Elizabethan royal courtship, panegyric and political negotiation. Thus, the deployment of Ovidian, Petrarchan and allegorical romance modes by late Elizabethan writers must be read in terms of an intertextuality that includes both the discourse of European literary history and the discourse of Elizabethan state power.

There is an obvious dramaturgical contrast between *A Midsummer Night's Dream* and the progress pageants, or panegyrical court plays such as George Peele's *Arraignment of Paris*. In such courtly performance genres, the resolution of the action, the completion of the form, is dependent upon the actual presence of the monarch as privileged auditor/spectator. Her judgement may be actively solicited, or, *in propria persona*, she may become the focus of the characters' collective celebration and veneration; frequently, as in Peele's play, the two strategies are combined.[15] However, there are also Elizabethan plays that do not require the queen's active participation in the action but instead refer the dramatic resolution to an onstage character who is an allegorical personage readily if not wholly identifiable with the queen. Such is the authoritative figure of Cynthia, the queen/goddess who presides over the action in both John Lyly's *Endymion* and Ben

Jonson's *Cynthia's Revels.* These formal strategies are presumably motivated in part by the practical concern to make the play playable in more than one venue, and for more than one audience. The professional players had more people to please than the monarch alone. In any case, the queen was frequently unavailable to play her part; and—as Ben Jonson discovered, having written her into *Every Man Out of His Humour* (1599)—for someone else to have explicitly personated the monarch would have been a grave offence.[16] The formal and dramaturgical responses to such manifestly practical concerns may have had larger implications. Such plays preserve the theatrical illusion of a self-contained play world. In doing so, they necessarily produce a more mediated—and, thus, a potentially more ambiguous—mode of royal reference and encomium than do those plays which open the frame of the fiction to acknowledge the physically present sovereign and defer to her mastery of acting and action. Thus, plays performed in the playhouses had a relatively greater degree of both formal and ideological autonomy than did exclusively courtly entertainments.

In royal pageantry, the queen was always the cynosure; her virginity was the source of magical potency. And in courtly plays such as Lyly's *Endymion*, such representation of the charismatic royal virgin continued to enact such a role—although the limitations and resources of dramatic representation opened up new and perhaps unintended possibilities for equivocation and ambiguity in the apparent affirmation of royal widom, power and virtue. Like Lyly's *Endymion, A Midsummer Night's Dream* is permeated by images and devices that suggest characteristic forms of Elizabethan court culture. However, Shakespeare's ostensibly courtly wedding play is neither focused upon the queen nor structurally dependent upon her actual presence or her intervention in the action.[17] Nor does it include among its onstage and speaking characters a transparent allegorical representation of the queen—a character who enjoys a central and determining authority over the action. It has often been suggested that the original occasion of *A Midsummer Night's Dream* was an aristocratic wedding at which Queen Elizabeth herself was present.[18] Whatever the truth of this attractive but unproven hypothesis, what we know for certain is that the title page of the first quarto, printed in 1600, claims to present the play 'As it hath been sundry times publicly acted, by the right honourable the Lord Chamberlain his servants'. Despite the legal fiction that public performances served to keep the privileged players of the

Chamberlain's Men in readiness for performance at court, and despite whatever adaptations may have been made in repertory plays to suit them to the conditions of particular court performances, the dramaturgical and ideological matrix of Shakespearean drama was located not in the royal court but in the professional playhouse.

Although perhaps sometimes receiving their first and/or most lucrative performances at court or in aristocratic households, all of Shakespeare's plays seem to have been written with the possibility in mind of theatrical as well as courtly performance. Certainly, this practice provides evidence for the shared tastes of queen and commoner. And, needless to say, the advertisement that a play had been performed at court or before the queen was intended to enhance the interest of Elizabeth's theatre-going or play-reading subjects, who might thereby vicariously share the source of Her Majesty's entertainment. Nevertheless, despite the broad social appeal of Shakespearean and other plays, we should resist any impulse to homogenise Elizabethan culture and society into an organic unity. The courtly and popular audiences for Shakespeare's plays constituted frequently overlapping but nevertheless distinct and potentially divergent sources of socio-economic support and ideological constraint. The writing of plays that would be playable in both the commercial playhouses and in the royal court points towards the conditions of emergence of the professional theatre at a historically transitional moment. This theatre was sustained by a frequently advantageous but inherently unstable conjunction of two theoretically distinct modes of cultural production: one, based upon relations of patronage; the other, upon market relations.

IV

In *A Midsummer Night's Dream*, the playwright's imagination 'bodies forth' the ruler and patron in the personage of Theseus. Shakespeare's antique Duke holds clear opinions as to the purpose of playing; and these opinions take two forms. One is that the drama should serve as a pleasant pastime for the sovereign, as an innocuous respite from princely care:

Come now; what masques, what dances shall we have,
To wear away this long age of three hours

> Between our after-supper and bed-time?
> Where is our usual manager of mirth?
> What revels are in hand? Is there no play
> To ease the anguish of a torturing hour?
> Call Philostrate. . . .
> Say, what abridgement have you for this evening,
> What masque, what music? How shall we beguile
> The lazy time, if not with some delight? (5.1.32–41)

The Office of the Revels had been established in the reign of Queen Elizabeth's father, and its purpose had been 'to select, organise, and supervise all entertainment of the sovereign, wherever the court might be'.[19] The expansion of the role of this court office to include the licensing of public dramatic performances as well as the provision of courtly ones indicates that the Elizabethan regime was attempting to subject the symbolic and interpretive activities of its subjects to increasing scrutiny and regulation—at the same time that it was inventing new sources of revenue for itself and its clients. In the personage of Philostrate, Shakespeare's play incorporates the courtly office of Master of the Revels, but limits it to its original charge, which was to provide entertainments for the monarch. Like the ambivalent term *licence*, Philostrate's alliterative title as Theseus's 'manager of mirth' suggests an official concern simultaneously to allow and to control the expression of potentially subversive festive, comic and erotic energies.

Of the four proffered entertainments, the first two—'The battle with the Centaurs, to be sung / By an Athenian eunuch to the harp' and 'the riot of the tipsy Bacchanals, / Tearing the Thracian singer in their rage' (5.1.44–5; 48–9)—are dismissed by Theseus, ostensibly because their devices are overly familiar. (As I have suggested elsewhere, both allude to the play's classical mythological subtext of sexual and familial violence—a subtext over which the play's patriarchal comedy keeps a precarious control.)[20] The third prospect is excluded because it smacks of social protest:

> 'The thrice three Muses mourning for the death
> Of learning, late deceased in beggary'?
> That is some satire, keen and critical,
> Not sorting with a nuptial ceremony. (5.1.52–5)

This conspicuous irrelevance has two operative points: the first, that its subject is the familiar complaint of Elizabethan cultural producers that they lack generous and enlightened patronage from the great; the second, that Duke Theseus does not want to hear about it. His taste is for something that

> is nothing, nothing in the world;
> Unless you can find sport in their intents,
> Extremely stretched and conned with cruel pain
> To do you service.

This is the play that Theseus will hear, 'For never anything can be amiss / When simpleness and duty tender it' (5.1.78–83). Thus, the other form taken by Theseus's opinions concerning the drama is that it should serve as a gratifying homage to princely power, simultaneously providing a politic opportunity for the exercise of royal magnanimity:

> Our sport shall be to take what they mistake:
> And what poor duty cannot do, noble respect
> Takes it in might, not merit.
> Where I have come, great clerks have purposed
> To greet me with premeditated welcomes;
> Where I have seen them shiver and look pale,
> Make periods in the midst of sentences,
> Throttle their practised accent in their fears,
> And, in conclusion, dumbly have broke off,
> Not paying me a welcome. Trust me, sweet,
> Out of this silence yet I picked a welcome,
> And in the modesty of fearful duty
> I read as much as from the rattling tongue
> Of saucy and audacious eloquence.
> Love, therefore, and tongue-tied simplicity
> In least speak most, to my capacity. (5.1.90–105)

The opinions of Shakespeare's Athenian duke bear a strong likeness to those of his own sovereign, as these were represented in her policies and in her own public performances. Thus, in the metatheatrical context of the play's long final scene, Duke Theseus is not so much Queen Elizabeth's masculine antithesis as he is her princely surrogate.

Theseus's attitude towards his subjects' offerings has analogues in the two printed texts that describe the queen's visit to the city of Norwich during her progress of 1578. In a curiously metadramatic speech directly addressed to Elizabeth, the figure of Mercury describes the process of creating and enacting entertainments for the queen— such as the one in which he is presently speaking:

> And that so soon as out of door she goes
> (If time do serve, and weather waxeth fair)
> Some odd device shall meet Her Highness straight,
> To make her smile, and ease her burdened breast,
> And take away the cares and things of weight
> That princes feel, that findeth greatest rest.[21]

On another occasion, as the queen returned toward her lodgings,

> within Bishops Gate at the Hospital door, Master Stephen Limbert, master of the grammar school in Norwich, stood ready to render her an oration. Her Majesty drew near unto him, and thinking him fearful, said graciously unto him: 'Be not afraid.' He answered her again in English: 'I thank Your Majesty for your good encouragement'; and then with good courage entered into this oration.

After printing the oration in the original Latin and in English translation, the account continues by describing the queen as

> very attentive, even until the end thereof. And the oration ended, after she had given great thanks thereof to Master Limbert, she said to him: 'It is the best that ever I heard.'[22]

The tone in which Theseus responds to the mechanicals' 'palpable gross play' catches the element of hyperbole in the queen's reported speech, and turns its gracious condescension towards mockery. For example, as Theseus says to Bottom: 'Marry, if he that writ it had played Pyramus, and hanged himself in Thisbe's garter, it would have been a fine tragedy—and so it is, truly, and very notably discharged' (5.1.343–7). I have suggested analogues from royal pageantry performed by children and amateurs because such performances most clearly equate to the mechanicals' performance of *Pyramus and Thisbe* within Shakespeare's play. However, the queen's attitude towards the uses of the adult, professional and commercial theatre seems to have differed little from what it was towards the uses of other forms of royal entertainment. As early as 1574, a company of professional players under the patronage of the earl of Leicester were licensed by the queen to perform in public so that they would be in readiness to play at court, 'as well for the recreation of our loving subjects as for our solace and pleasure when we shall think good to see them.'[23]

Despite the apparently indifferent attitude of the sovereign—or, perhaps, precisely because of it—in *A Midsummer Night's Dream* Shakespeare calls attention to the artistic distance between the professional players and their putatively crude predecessors; and he does so by incorporating a comic representation of such players into his play. This professional self-consciousness is the very hallmark of the play's celebrated metatheatricality—its calling of attention to its own artifice, to its own artistry. Such metatheatricality prescribes the interpretive schema of much modern scholarship in literary and theatre history, which envisions Shakespearean drama as the culmination of a long process of artistic evolution. *A Midsummer Night's Dream* parodies antecedent dramatic forms and performance styles: the amateur acting traditions that had been largely suppressed along with the civic drama by the end of the 1570s, and the work of the professional companies active during the 1570s and earlier 1580s; and it juxtaposes to them the representational powers of the Lord Chamberlain's Men and their playwright.[24] This contrast was made manifest by Shakespeare's company in the very process of performing *A Midsummer Night's Dream*. In particular, it was demonstrated in what we may presume was their consummately professional comic enactment of the mechanicals' vexed rehearsals and inept performance of *Pyramus and Thisbe*. The dramaturgical problems with which the mechanicals struggle show them to be incapable of comprehending the relationship between the actor and his part. They have no skill in the art of personation; they lack an adequate conception of playing. The contrast between amateur and professional modes of playing is incarnated in the performance of Bottom—by which I mean the Elizabethan player's performance of Bottom's performance of Pyramus. The amateur actor who wants to be cast in all the parts, the only character to be literally metamorphosed, is also the one who, despite his translations into an ass-headed monster and a fabled lover, remains immutably—fundamentally—Bottom. The fully professional collaboration between the imaginative playwright and the protean player of the Lord Chamberlain's Men creates the illusion of Bottom's character precisely by creating the illusion of his incapacity to translate himself into other parts.

The play-within-the-play device calls attention to the theatrical transaction between the players and their audience. In the process of foregrounding the imaginative and dramaturgical dynamics of this transaction, *A Midsummer Night's Dream* also calls attention to its socio-political dynamics. Shakespeare's Duke Theseus formulates policy when he proclaims that 'The lunatic, the lover, and the poet / Are of imagination all compact'; that 'Lovers and madmen have such seething brains, / Such shaping fantasies, that apprehend / More than cool reason ever comprehends' (5.1.7–8, 4–6). The social order of Theseus's Athens depends upon his authority to name the forms of mental disorder and his power to control its subjects. Theseus's analogising of the hyperactive imaginations of lunatics, lovers and poets accords with the orthodox perspective of Elizabethan medical and moral discourses. The latter insisted that the unregulated passions and disordered fantasies of the ruler's subjects—from Bedlam beggars to melancholy courtiers—were an inherent danger to themselves, to their fellows, and to the state.[25] For Theseus, no less than for the Elizabethan Privy Council, the ruler's task is to *comprehend*—to understand and to contain—the energies and motives, the diverse, unstable and potentially seditious apprehensions of the ruled. But the Duke—so self-assured and benignly condescending in his comprehension—might also have some cause for *apprehension*, for he himself and the fictional society over which he rules have been shaped by the fantasy of a poet.

Theseus's deprecation of lunatics, lovers and poets is his unwitting exposition of the scope and limits of his own wisdom. The wonderful musings of the newly awakened Bottom provide a serio-comic prelude to the Duke's set piece. Fitfully remembering his nocturnal adventure, Bottom apprehends something strange and admirable in his metamorphosis and his liaison with Titania:

> I have had a most rare vision. I have had a dream, past the wit of man
> to say what dream it was. Man is but an ass if he go about to

expound this dream. . . . The eye of man hath not heard, the ear of man hath not seen, man's hand is not able to taste, his tongue to conceive, nor his heart to report, what my dream was. I will get Peter Quince to write a ballad of this dream: it shall be called 'Bottom's Dream', because it hath no bottom; and I will sing it in the latter end of a play, before the Duke. (4.1.203–16)

Bottom's (non-)exposition of his dream is a garbled allusion to a passage in St Paul's First Epistle to the Corinthians:

And we speak wisdom among them that are perfect: not the wisdom of this world, neither of the princes of this world, which come to nought.

But we speak the wisdom of God in a mystery, even the hid wisdom, which God had determined before the world, unto our glory.

Which none of the princes of this world hath known; for had they known it, they would not have crucified the Lord of glory.

But as it is written, The things which eye hath not seen, neither ear hath heard, neither came into man's heart, are, which God hath prepared for them that love him.

But God hath revealed them unto us by his Spirit; for the Spirit searcheth all things, yea, the deep things of God.

(I Corinthians 2: 6–10; *Geneva Bible*, 1560 ed.)

This allusion has often been remarked. Insufficiently remarked, however, is the political resonance that the passage may have had for Elizabethan playgoers and readers; and the possibility that, in selecting it for parody, the playwright may have had a point to make, however oblique its expression.[26] The New Testament passage is built upon an opposition between the misconceived and misdirected profane knowledge possessed by 'the princes of this world' and the spiritual wisdom accessible only to those who humble themselves before a transcendent source of power and love. The biblical text does more than construct a generalised opposition between the profane and the sacred: it gives that abstract moral opposition a political edge by proposing an inverse relationship between the temporal hierarchy of wealth and power and the spiritual hierarchy of wisdom and virtue.

The attitude displayed by the professional playwright towards Bottom, and towards the artisanal culture that he personifies, is a complex mixture of affection, indulgence, condescension and ridicule; and the complexity of that mixture is nowhere more conspicuous than in the speech about Bottom's dream. The comical garbling of the allusion and its farcical dramatic context function to mediate the sacred text, allowing Shakespeare to appropriate it for his own dramatic ends. An opposition between sacred and profane knowledge is displaced into an opposition between Bottom's capacity to apprehend the story of the night and Theseus's incapacity to comprehend it. Shakespeare's professional theatre implicitly repudiates Theseus's attitude towards the entertainer's art precisely by incorporating and ironically circumscribing it. I am suggesting, then, that Shakespeare evokes the scriptural context in order to provide a numinous resonance for the play's temporal, metatheatrical concerns; and that these concerns are rooted in the distinction and relationship between the instrumental authority of the state, as personified in Queen Elizabeth, and the imaginative authority of the public and professional theatre, as personified in the common player-playwright. At the same time, Bottom's dream mediates the relationship of the socio-economically ascendant artist-entrepreneur to his modest roots. It is fitting that the play's chosen instrument for its scriptural message of socio-spiritual inversion is a common artisan and amateur player named Bottom—one who, earlier in the play, has alluded to the raging tyrant of the Nativity pageants in the mystery cycles (1.2.19, 36). By casting Bottom to play in 'an interlude before the Duke and the Duchess, on his wedding-day at night' (1.2.5–7), Shakespeare's play firmly records the redirection of the popular dramatic impulse toward the celebration of 'the princes of this world'. Nevertheless, Bottom's rehearsal of his wondrous strange dream is an oblique marker, an incongruous evocation, of an ethos that *A Midsummer Night's Dream* and its playwright have ostensibly left behind—a trace of social, spiritual and (perhaps) autobiographical filiation.

V

When Puck addresses the audience in the epilogue to *A Midsummer Night's Dream*, his reference to 'we shadows' (5.1.409) implies not only the personified spirits in the play but also the players of

Shakespeare's company who have performed the play. Theseus registers this meaning when he says of the mechanicals' acting in *Pyramus and Thisbe*, that 'The best in this kind are but shadows; and the worst are no worse, if imagination amend them' (5.1.208–9). The statement itself, however, is belied on two counts: on the one hand, the rehearsal and performance of the play-within-the-play invite the audience to make qualitative distinctions between the best and the worst of shadows; and, on the other hand, the onstage audience at the Athenian court refuses to amend imaginatively the theatrical limitations of the mechanicals. When Puck addresses his master as 'King of shadows' (3.2.347) the appellation recognises Oberon as the principal player in the action, whose powers of awareness and manipulation also mark him as the play's internal dramatist.[27] Although Titania has a limited power to manipulate Bottom, an artisan and an amateur actor, she herself is manipulated by this 'King of shadows', who is also her husband and her lord. Thus, in the triangulated relationship of Titania, Oberon and Bottom, a fantasy of masculine dependency upon woman is expressed and contained within a fantasy of masculine control over woman. And, more specifically, the social reality of the Elizabethan players' dependency upon Queen Elizabeth is inscribed within the imaginative reality of a player-dramatist's control over the Faery Queen.

The relationship of Shakespeare's play and its production to traditions of amateur and occasional dramatic entertainments is at once internalised and distanced in the mechanicals' ridiculous rehearsal and performance of *Pyramus and Thisbe*. And by the way in which it frames the attitudes of Theseus and the play-within-the-play's courtly audience, *A Midsummer Night's Dream* internalises and distances the relationship of the public and professional theatre to the pressures and constraints of noble and royal patronage. Its resonances of popular pastimes and amateur civic drama on the one hand, and of royal pageantry and courtly entertainments on the other, serve to locate *A Midsummer Night's Dream* in relationship to its cultural antecedents and its socio-economic context. Through the play of affinity and difference, these resonances serve to distinguish Shakespeare's comedy from both amateur and courtly modes, and to define it as a production of the professional and commercial theatre. The much noted metatheatricality of *A Midsummer Night's Dream* is nowhere more apparent and striking than in this process by which the play assimilates its own cultural determinants and produces them anew as its own dramatic effects. When I suggest that the play simultaneously subsumes and projects the conditions of its own possibility, I am not making a claim for its timelessness and universality. On the contrary, I am attempting to locate it more precisely in the ideological matrix of its original production. The foregrounding of theatricality as a mode of human cognition and human agency is a striking feature of Shakespearean drama. Such theatricality becomes possible at a particular historical moment. By this means, the professional practitioners of an immensely popular and bitterly contested emergent cultural practice articulate their collective consciousness of their place in the social and cultural order—the paradoxical location of the theatre and of theatricality at once on the margins and at the centre of the Elizabethan world.

NOTES

*Copyright Cambridge University Press, 1995. Originally published in *The Theatrical City: Culture, Theatre, and Politics in London, 1576-1649*, eds. David L. Smith, Richard Strier, and David Bevington. Reprinted with the permission of Cambridge University Press.

1. Quotations follow *The Arden Shakespeare* edition of *A Midsummer Night's Dream*, ed. Harold F. Brooks (1979), abbreviated to *MND* and cited by act, scene and line.

2. On the connection between weavers and social protest, see Theodore B. Leinwand, "'I believe we must leave the killing out": Deference and Accommodation in *A Midsummer Night's Dream*', *Renaissance Papers* (1986), 11–30, esp. pp. 14–21; also Annabel Patterson, *Shakespeare and the Popular Voice* (Oxford and Cambridge, Mass., 1989), pp. 56–7. On Elizabethan food riots, see John Walter and Keith Wrightson, 'Dearth and the Social Order in Early Modern England', *Past & Present*, 71 (1976), 22–42; Buchanan Sharp, *In Contempt of All Authority: Rural Artisans and Riot in the West of England, 1586–1660* (Berkeley, 1980); John Walter, 'A "Rising of the People"? The Oxford Rising of 1596', *Past & Present*, 107 (1985), 90–143.

3. On the playwright's social origins and his father's position in Stratford, see S. Schoenbaum, *William Shakespeare: A Compact Documentary Life* (Oxford, 1977), pp. 14–44.

4. See Clifford Davidson, "'What hempen home-spuns have we swagg'ring here?" Amateur Actors in *A Midsummer Night's Dream* and the Coventry Civic Plays and Pageants', *Shakespeare Studies*, 19 (1987), 87–99.

5. 'Ritual, Drama and Social Body in the Late Medieval English Town' (1983), rpt. in Mervyn James, *Society, Politics and Culture: Studies in Early Modern England* (Cambridge, 1986), pp. 16–47; quotation from pp. 38, 44. James emphasises the centrality of the feast of Corpus Christi to late medieval urban culture in England, and the dialectical relationship between procession and play.

6. Charles Phythian-Adams, 'Ceremony and the Citizen: The Communal Year at Coventry 1450–1550', in *Crisis and Order in English Towns, 1500–1700: Essays in Urban History*, ed. Peter Clark and Paul Slack (1972), pp. 57–85; quotations from pp. 57, 80. Also see his monograph, *Desolation of a City: Coventry and the Urban Crisis of the Late Middle Ages* (Cambridge, 1979).

7. Miri Rubin, *Corpus Christi: The Eucharist in Late Medieval Culture* (Cambridge, 1991), p. 266.

8. On the process by which cultural practices were appropriated and invented in order to aggrandise the Tudor state, see Roy Strong, *The Cult of Elizabeth* (1977); Penry Williams, *The Tudor Regime* (Oxford, 1979), pp. 293–310, 351–405; Philip Corrigan and Derek Sayer, *The Great Arch: English State Formation as Cultural Revolution* (Oxford, 1985), pp. 43–71; David Cressy, *Bonfires and Bells: National Memory and the Protestant Calendar in Elizabethan and Stuart England* (Berkeley, 1989), pp. 1–129.

9. See Mervyn James, *Society, Politics and Culture*, p. 41; Harold C. Gardiner, S. J., *Mysteries' End* (New Haven, 1946); R.W. Ingram, 'Fifteen-seventy-nine and the Decline of Civic Religious Drama in Coventry,' in *The Elizabethan Theatre VIII*, ed. G.R. Hibbard (Port Credit, Ontario), pp. 114–28.

10. Rubin points out that 'in those towns where political power and wealth were exercised through craft gilds, like York, Coventry, Beverley, Norwich, dramatic cycles were supported and presented by the crafts, expressing both the processional-communal and the sectional elements in town life ' (*Corpus Christi*, p. 275).

In some significant respects, the dramatic traditions of late medieval London differed from those of such towns. Mervyn James maintains that in London, even in the late middle ages, 'the celebration of Corpus Christi never acquired a public and civic status, and play cycles of the Corpus Christi type never developed. London had its great cycle plays; but the London cycle was performed by professional actors, and had no connection either with Corpus Christi or the city gilds ' (*Society, Politics and Culture*, pp. 41–2). Rubin appears to dispute this assertion, and presents a more complex picture of processional and dramatic elements in the capital's Corpus Christi festivities. She starts from the position that 'once we discard a view which imputes a necessary development of the Corpus Christi drama into full-cycle form we are better able to appreciate the variety of dramatic forms which evolved for Corpus Christi, and the ubiquity of dramatic creation.' (*Corpus Christi*, p. 275). She maintains that, although 'London never developed a town-wide celebration for the feast, a project which is almost unthinkable in so large and varied a city', it nevertheless sustained 'a series of processions related to parish churches, fraternities, crafts'. The most comprehensive of these was the 'great play' organised by the Skinners' Company, presented over several days 'in the form of *tableaux vivants*' (pp. 275–6).

11. See the documents printed in *Records of Early English Drama*: *Coventry*, ed. R.W. Ingram (Toronto, 1981), pp. 233–4. Also see Ingram, 'Fifteen-seventy-nine'.

12. See Robert Langham, *A Letter*, with Introduction, Notes and Commentary by R.J.P. Kuin (Leiden, 1983), pp. 52–5. The performance of the Hocktide show was preceded by a rustic brideale, complete with such village pastimes as morris dancing and running at quintain (pp. 49–52). Significantly, neither of these common and amateur entertainments is mentioned in George Gascoigne's self-promoting courtly account, *The Princely Pleasures at the Court at Kenilworth* (1576).

13. On allusions to the rites of May in *MND*, see 1.1.167, 4.1.132; on St Valentine's Day, 4.1.138. On the inseparability of St John's Day and Midsummer Night 'in the religious and folk consciousness of the sixteenth century', see Anca Vlasopolos, 'The Ritual of Midsummer: A Pattern for *A Midsummer Night's Dream*', *Renaissance Quarterly*, 31 (1978), 21–9; esp. pp. 23–6. On rites and games of May Day and Midsummer Eve and Day, also see C.L. Barber, *Shakespeare's Festive Comedy: A Study of Dramatic Form in Relation to Social Custom* (Princeton, 1959), pp. 119–24; François Laroque, *Shakespeare's Festive World: Elizabethan Seasonal Entertainment and the Professional Stage*, trans. Janet Lloyd (Cambridge, 1991), passim. On Corpus Christi as a summer festival, see Rubin, *Corpus Christi*, pp. 208–9, 213, 243, 271, 273.

14. In his Introduction to the Arden edition of *MND*, Brooks comments that 'Oberon's description of the mermaid and the shooting stars . . . reflects Shakespeare's acquaintance with the kind of elaborate courtly entertainment which combined a mythological water-pageant with fireworks, rather like those

presented to Elizabeth by Leicester at Kenilworth [1575] and the earl of Hertford at Elvetham [1591]' (p. xxxix).

15. See Louis A. Montrose, 'Gifts and Reasons: The Context of Peele's *Araygnement of Paris'*, *ELH, A Journal of English Literary History*, 47 (1980), 433–61.

16. See Helen M. Ostovich, '"So Sudden and Strange a Cure": A Rudimentary Masque in *Every Man Out of His Humour'*, *English Literary Renaissance*, 22 (1992), 315–32; Richard Dutton, *Mastering the Revels: The Regulation and Censorship of English Renaissance Drama* (Iowa City, 1991), pp. 136–7.

17. Compare G.K. Hunter, *John Lyly: The Humanist as Courtier* (London, 1962), pp. 329–30.

18. The leading contenders for the aristocratic wedding at which the play was supposedly first performed are that of William Stanley, earl of Derby, with Lady Elizabeth Vere, daughter of the earl of Oxford and granddaughter of Lord Burghley (26 January 1594/5), and that of Thomas, son of Lord Berkeley, with Elizabeth, daughter of Sir George Carey and granddaughter of Lord Hunsdon, the lord chamberlain and patron of Shakespeare's company (19 February 1595/6). For a summary of the arguments, see *MND*, liii–lvii.

19. Gerald Eades Bentley, *The Profession of Dramatist in Shakespeare's Time 1590–1642* (1971; rpt. Princeton, 1986), p. 147. On the Revels Office, also see E.K. Chambers, *The Elizabethan Stage* (4 vols., Oxford, 1923), I 71–105; Janet Clare, *'Art made tongue-tied by authority': Elizabethan and Jacobean Dramatic Censorship* (Manchester, 1990); and Dutton, *Mastering the Revels*.

20. See Louis Adrian Montrose, '"Shaping Fantasies": Figurations of Gender and Power in Elizabethan Culture', *Representations*, 2 (1983), 61–94; rpt. in *Representing the English Renaissance*, ed. Stephen Greenblatt (Berkeley, 1988), pp. 31–64. I have incorporated some passages from this earlier study into the present one; in revised form, both will be incorporated into a more comprehensive study of *MND*, the Elizabethan theatre, and the Elizabethan state.

21. Thomas Churchyard, *A Discourse of The Queen's Majesty's Entertainment in Suffolk and Norfolk* (1578), rpt. in *Records of Early English Drama: Norwich, 1540–1642*, ed. David Galloway (Toronto, 1984), p. 302.

22. B[ernard] G[arter], *The Joyful Receiving of the Queen's Most Excellent Majesty into Her Highness' City of Norwich* (1578), rpt. in *Records of Early English Drama: Norwich*, pp. 266–7,271.

23. Patent of 10 May 1574, rpt. in Chambers, *Elizabethan Stage*, II, 87–8.

24. Davidson convincingly suggests that the mechanicals' rehearsal and performance of *Pyramus and Thisbe* is designed to burlesque 'the older dramatic styles (including ... the theatrical styles of the public theatre fashionable before *c.* 1585) with their tendency toward bombastic language and clumsy use of mythological subjects'; and to conjoin this burlesque with one directed toward the acting capacities of the amateurs who performed in the civic religious drama, which had been largely suppressed by the early 1580s ('"What hempen home-spuns have we swagg'ring here?"', p. 88).

25. Among modern critical and historical studies, see Lawrence Babb, *The Elizabethan Malady: A Study of Melancholia in English Literature from 1580 to 1642* (East Lansing, Mich., 1951); Michael MacDonald, *Mystical Bedlam: Madness, Anxiety, and Healing in Seventeenth-century England* (Cambridge, 1981); Lacey Baldwin Smith, *Treason in Tudor England: Politics and Paranoia* (Princeton, 1986); Karin Coddon, '"Suche Strange Desygns": Madness, Subjectivity, and Treason in *Hamlet* and Elizabethan Culture', *Renaissance Drama*, n.s., 20 (1989), 51–75.

26. The 'context of profound spiritual levelling' implied by Shakespeare's biblical parody is noted in Patterson, *Shakespeare and the Popular Voice*, p. 68. Patterson pursues the 'genial thesis' that *MND* imagines 'an idea of social play that could cross class boundaries without obscuring them, and by those crossings imagine the social body whole again' (p. 69); accordingly, she focuses upon the integrative 'Christian communitas' suggested in I Corinthians 12: 14–15, rather than upon the obvious and immediate oppositional context of I Corinthians 2: 6–10. For another recent study of the relationship between late Elizabethan social conflict and the tensions of rank within *MND*, see Leinwand, '"I believe we must leave the killing out"'. Less sanguine than Patterson, Leinwand concludes that 'Shakespeare criticises the relations of power in his culture, but does so with remarkable sensitivity to the nuances of threat and accommodation which animate these relations' (p.30).

27. For 'shadow' as 'applied rhetorically ... to an actor or a play in contrast to the reality represented', see *OED*, s.v. 'Shadow', sense 1.6.b. The earliest usages cited by *OED* are in Lyly, *Euphues*, and Shakespeare, *A Midsummer Night's Dream* and *The Two Gentlemen of Verona*.

Textual Theory, Literary Interpretation, and the Last Act of *A Midsummer Night's Dream*

Janis Lull

A commonplace of contemporary criticism says that readers—textual scholars and editors among them—tend to reconstruct Shakespeare in the image of their own times.[1] Twentieth-century textual criticism offers many possible Shakespeares, including, at one extreme, Shakespeare the poetic individual, who exercises intentional control over all aspects of his work. On the other end of the spectrum lies Shakespeare the cultural collective, whose texts reveal such influences as social construction, multiple authorship, and even pure accident. The first of these models stresses the poet's distinctive voice. A textual critic or editor following this model attempts to separate the work of Shakespeare from any other influences that may have crept into the early printed editions. The second approach, by contrast, accepts all influences, insisting that the first editions of Shakespeare plays cannot be reduced to the intentions of the author. This essay uses mislined passages in act 5 of *A Midsummer Night's Dream*, including Duke Theseus's famous "imagination" speech (5.1.1-27), to compare some of the consequences of these two very different textual approaches for interpreting the character of the Duke.[2] A reading based on an individualistic textual hypothesis finds development in the Duke and in his relationship to Hippolyta in the final act. A reading derived from the collectivist approach, on the other hand, discovers both a more obtuse Duke and a somewhat more pessimistic ending for the play.

TEXTUAL INDIVIDUALISM AND
THE CHARACTER OF THESEUS

In the first quarto (Q1) of *Dream*, Theseus's speech and several other passages are mislined. Here is the Q1 version of the Duke's conversation with Hippolyta, with my slashes indicating the ends of regularized blank-verse lines:[3]

> *Hip.* Tis strange, my *Theseus*, that these louers speake of.
> *The.* More straunge then true. I neuer may beleeue
> These antique fables, nor these Fairy toyes.
> Louers, and mad men haue such seething braines,
> Such shaping phantasies, that apprehend / more,
> Then coole reason euer comprehends. / The lunatick,
> The louer, and the Poet / are of imagination all compact.
> One sees more diuels, then vast hell can holde:
> That is the mad man. The louer, all as frantick,
> Sees *Helens* beauty in a brow of *AEgypt*.
> The Poets eye, in a fine frenzy, rolling, doth glance
> From heauen to earth, from earth to heauen. / And as
> Imagination bodies forth / the formes of things
> Vnknowne: the Poet's penne / turnes them to shapes,
> And giues to ayery nothing, / a locall habitation,
> And a name. / Such trickes hath strong imagination,
> That if it would but apprehend some ioy,
> It comprehends some bringer of that ioy.
> Or in the night, imagining some feare,
> How easie is a bush suppos'd a Beare?
> *Hyp.* But, all the story of the night told ouer,
> And all their minds transfigur'd so together,
> More witnesseth than fancies images,
> And growes to something of great constancy:
> But howsoeuer, strange and admirable.(G2ᵛ)

The Q1 mislineations persisted in subsequent editions until they were noticed by Shakespeare's eighteenth-century editors, who simply assumed that they were mistakes. Nicholas Rowe relined "The poet's eye, in a fine frenzy rolling / Doth glance from heaven to earth, from earth to heaven" in 1709.[4] In 1714 he applied a similar correction to the lines that follow, ending with "Such tricks hath strong imagination." In 1733 Lewis Theobald completed the regularization by relining "Such shaping fantasies, that apprehend / More than cool reason ever comprehends," and the passage has stood as blank verse ever since. This is the New Arden version of the mislined verses:[5]

> Lovers and madmen have such seething brains,
> Such shaping fantasies, that apprehend
> More than cool reason ever comprehends.
> The lunatic, the lover, and the poet
> Are of imagination all compact:
> One sees more devils than vast hell can hold;
> That is the madman: the lover, all as frantic,
> Sees Helen's beauty in a brow of Egypt:
> The poet's eye, in a fine frenzy rolling,
> Doth glance from heaven to earth, from earth to heaven;
> And as imagination bodies forth
> The forms of things unknown, the poet's pen
> Turns them to shapes, and gives to airy nothing
> A local habitation and a name. (5.1.4-17)

In 1924 John Dover Wilson observed that only the mislined verses in this passage mention "the Poet," and that removing these portions would result in a coherent "first draft" about lovers and madmen:[6]

> Louers, and mad men haue such seething braines,
> One sees more deuils, then vast hell can holde:
> That is the mad man: the louer, all as frantick,
> Sees Helen's beauty in a brow of AEgypt:
> Such trickes hath strong imagination,
> That if it would but apprehend some ioy,
> It comprehends some bringer of that ioy.
> Or in the night, imagining some feare,
> How easie is a bush suppos'd a Beare?

Wilson, evidently motivated by the traditional goal of linking the early editions as closely as possible to Shakespeare as originating individual, concluded that the Q1 compositor had mislined these sections because he was confused by authorial revisions scribbled in the margins of his copy.[7] For Wilson, the mislined passages thus provided clues to the author's deliberate reshaping of the text. If so, they also show deliberate changes in the character of Theseus, who has much of the mislined verse.

Textual critics have generally rejected the idea that variations in verse quality in Theseus's imagination speech or the other mislined passages at the end of the play signal either the return of a mature Shakespeare to a much earlier draft, as Wilson holds,[8] or a Shakespearean revision of someone else's play.[9] Yet Wilson's conjecture that mislineation indicates marginal revision in the compositor's copy has been widely adopted.[10] Where eighteenth-century editors heard blank-verse cadences in Theseus's mislined speech and rearranged the lines to bring out their underlying regularity, twentieth-century textual critics, familiar with the regularized lines as touchstones of English poetry, found it easy to believe that the author had inserted the mislined portions to enhance the "draft" discovered by Wilson. Shakespeare, they thought, might very well have felt a need both to improve the Duke's verse and also to put in a good word for poets.

Wilson's case for revision, however, does not stop with the imagination speech. Six more mislined sections occur in the first part of the act, and Wilson feels that these, together with the Duke's opening speech, "contain all the beauty, all the life, all the memorable things of the passage."[11] Wilson's judgment is open to argument. If by "the passage" he means only the first eighty-three lines, where the eight major mislineations appear, he has a better case than if he allows us to go on to line 85:

> *Hip.*I love not to see wretchedness o'er-charg'd
>   And duty in his service perishing.
> *The.* Why gentle sweet, you shall see no such thing.
> *Hip.* He says they can do nothing in this kind.
> *The.* The kinder we, to give them thanks for nothing. (5.1.85-89)

This dialogue between the Duke and Duchess as they have just become (and as the Q1 speech prefixes designate them through most of the rest of the act) is certainly lively and memorable, and it must also be taken as part of the hypothetical original, since it shows none of the mislineations Wilson and others accept as signs of revision.

Somewhere between "How easie is a bush suppos'd a Beare?" and "The kinder we, to give them thanks for nothing," the Duke of "coole reason" has changed from a man who cannot believe in young lovers' dreams to one who is willing at least for a while to suspend his disbelief. While the endpoints of this transformation seem to have been established even in Wilson's supposed original, most of the details of the shift occur only in the "revised" passages.

Wilson's theory of marginal revision not only explains the sudden spate of mislineations in an otherwise carefully set play, it also singles out certain key passages that contribute to the development of the Duke during the first few conversations of his married life. If we believe that these passages are revisions, we can also see in them an authorial intelligence working to fill out the character of Theseus, rendering more plausible the Duke's rather rapid shift from rationalist to imaginationist. Under his new wife's subtle but persistent influence, Theseus becomes conscious first of the pressing importance of the irrational in his private life, then of some of the public uses of imagination in an Athenian community grounded on courtesy and reason.

The sections apparently added to the imagination speech give Theseus's lines more poetic staying power than Hippolyta's, allowing him to dominate their opening debate. Yet the revised imagination speech, just by being better verse than the original, makes Theseus celebrate poetry while trying to denounce it. Most of the other passages mislined in Q1 show the Duke gradually coming around to Hippolyta's point of view. In the next "added" passage, for example, Theseus asks "What revels are in hand? Is there no play / To ease the anguish of a torturing hour?" (5.1.36-37). Here he admits that he is as tormented by desire as any of the lovers whose perceptions he has just dismissed. In the theoretical original, he merely asks how to "beguile / The lazy time" with entertainment (40-41).

Just after the Duke confesses his sexual impatience—a motif carried over from his early appearances in the play—a further revision shows him considering how to reconcile opposites, making "concord of this discord." Encountering the full title of the rude mechanicals' play, "'A tedious brief scene of young Pyramus / And his love Thisbe, very tragical mirth,'" Theseus says, "Merry and tragical? Tedious and brief? / That is hot ice, and wondrous strange snow! / How shall we find the concord of this discord?" (5.1.56-60). As he wonders aloud how to reconcile the oxymora of the title, perhaps Theseus also suspects an analogy to his own paradoxical position as both rationalist ruler and man in love.

Philostrate, reasonable servant to a reasonable Duke, tries to reduce the oppositions to his own experience:

> tragical, my noble lord, it is.
> For Pyramus therein doth kill himself;
> Which, when I saw rehears'd, I must confess
> Made mine eyes water; but more merry tears
> The passion of loud laughter never shed. (5.1.66-70)

Having attempted to explain away the intriguingly discordant title of the play, Philostrate concludes, "my noble lord, / It is not for you: I have heard it over, / And it is nothing, nothing in the world," but the Duke insists, "I will hear that play; / For never anything can be amiss / When simpleness and duty tender it" (5.1.76-77 and 81-83).

All the passages just quoted are mislined in Q1, and thus they are all revisions by Wilson's hypothesis. Placed between the revised "lunatic" passage and the dialogue of Duke and Duchess about duty and "kindness," these additions reveal small shifts in Theseus's thinking as he moves from a repudiation of imagination to a recognition of its everyday usefulness in his courtly world. The revisions, beginning with the interpolation of the lines about "airy nothing" help create a psychological portrait of this change.

Philostrate's condemnation of *Pyramus and Thisbe* as "nothing, nothing in the world" recalls Theseus's description of how the poet "gives to airy nothing / A local habitation and a name." Both of these "nothings" count as revisions in Wilson's scheme, and both could have been added to foreshadow and emphasize the well-known "nothings" exchanged by Duchess and Duke regarding the players: "He says they can do nothing in this kind. / The kinder we, to give them thanks for nothing" (5.1.88-89). The repeated word "nothing" links the three stages of Theseus's change as he shifts from his earlier trivializing of "airy nothing" to a sense that there may be concord in discord, and at last to Hippolyta's position that minds transfigured together can transform nothing into reality. "Nothing" in this wedding comedy may also signal a sexual pun, though the wordplay here is much less explicit and its tone less harsh than it is, for example, in *Hamlet*: "*Oph.* I think nothing, my lord. / *Ham.* That's a fair thought to lie between maids' legs" (3.2.117-18).[12] Hippolyta's remarks about the power of imagination and spiritual accord to transform "nothing" into something eventually merge for Theseus with his amorous preoccupations, and together they grow to something of great constancy.

Further into the scene, Hippolyta emphasizes her triumph by testing the Duke's new commitment to imagination:

> *Hip.* This is the silliest stuff that ever I heard.
> *The.* The best in this kind are but shadows; and the worst are no
> worse, if imagination amend them.
> *Hip.* It must be your imagination then, and not theirs.
> *The.* If we imagine no worse of them than they of themselves, they
> may pass for excellent men. (5.1.207-12)

Under cover of gently mocking the play, Hippolyta plays the skeptic's role that Theseus has so lately played himself, her "silliest stuff" recalling his "fairy toys." But the Duke's response shows that he now comprehends her earlier argument: "excellent men," like excellent marriages, can be compounded of mutual imaginings as well as of cold facts. Imagination has a creative role to play in civilized life, both public and private.

Having thus made sure that the ducal couple's minds are co-transfigured, Hippolyta at last signals that their corporal desires are also in tune. Her comment, "I am aweary of this moon. Would he would change!" (5.1.242), echoes the Duke's complaint from the opening moments of the play, "O, methinks, how slow / This old moon wanes! She lingers my desires. . ." (1.1.3-4). For his part, Theseus now shows more patience: "It appears by his small light of discretion that he is in the wane; but yet in courtesy, in all reason, we must stay the time" (5.1.243-45). If the last scene of *The Taming of the Shrew* can be conceived as a knowing and ironic compact between the newly intimate Kate and Petruchio, these last conversations between Theseus and Hippolyta can be seen as similar private exchanges in a public place between another bride and groom who have come to understand each other far better than they did at the beginning of the play.[13]

If the mislined passages truly reveal authorial revision, they may also reveal Shakespeare trying out, or perhaps re-applying to Theseus, a technique of compressed character development that he also used for

Claudio in *Much Ado About Nothing*, Orsino in *Twelfth Night*, and Bertram in *All's Well That Ends Well*. The Duke joins a group of prominent last-minute learners in Shakespeare, none more successful than he. During the final moments of *Dream*, Theseus awakens to the uses of the irrational in a rational society. The first revision—ultimately a praise of poetry—heralds this change in the Duke from a character who links imagination with delusion to one who understands that imagination helps poets and others create grace and order out of what only appears to be "nothing."

TEXTUAL COLLECTIVISM AND
THE CHARACTER OF THESEUS

In spite of the vivid picture Wilson conveys of a compositor holding Shakespeare's "foul papers" and squinting at the poet's revisions jammed into the margins, no Shakespearean manuscripts are known to exist. Nobody really knows how many steps removed from authorial papers the compositor's copy for this or any other Shakespeare play may have been. Surveying this textual situation with a postmodern eye, scholars such as Michael Bristol, Margreta De Grazia, and Paul Werstine have recently recommended that instead of trying to reconstruct the master craftsman behind the early Shakespeare texts as Wilson and other traditional editors have done, critics should start treating these texts simply as the end-products of all the forces that shaped them.[14] Rather than trying to purge second-party contributions, including such presumed contributions as the compositor's mislineations of Q1 *Dream*, this contemporary approach would embrace all additions or deletions—deliberate or accidental—as parts of a collectively constructed Shakespeare. As Paul Werstine envisions it, such a method "would keep in play not only multiple readings and versions but also the multiple and dispersed agencies that could have produced the variants." Only our "desire for New-Critical unity," in Werstine's view, keeps us from admitting that Shakespeare's plays "were open to penetration and alteration not only by Shakespeare himself and by his fellow actors but also by multiple theatrical and extra-theatrical scriveners, by theatrical annotators, adapters and revisers (who might cut or add), by censors, and by compositors and proofreaders."[15] Instead of seeing the mislineations of Act 5 *Dream* as either compositor errors or evidence of a revising poet, this poststructuralist theory would simply accept them as textual facts.

In a reading based on this approach, Theseus becomes one of several characters in the play, including Bottom the Weaver and Peter Quince, who serve as vehicles of dramatic irony by mismanaging language. The Duke's lines on imagination now serve to emphasize speeches nearby that are "misarranged" in different but parallel ways. Near the end of act 4, for example, fifty lines or so before the "lovers and madmen" speech, Bottom wakes from his dream and creates a muddled rhapsody on a theme of St. Paul:

> The eye of man hath not heard, the eare of man hath not seene, mans hand is not able to taste, his tongue to conceiue, nor his hearte to report, what my dreame was. I will get *Peter Quince* to write a Ballat of this dream: it shall be call'd *Bottom's Dreame*; because it hath no bottome (G^v-G2^r; 4.1.209-15).[16]

Bottom is nowhere more likable than at this moment, as he admits he would be an ass to think he could fathom his own dream. But in spite of critics' attempts to find ingenuity or insight in Bottom's character at this point, the ingenuity resides in the language.[17] The prose figure here uses anti-parallelism to let the reader or audience see through Bottom's mismatched thoughts to a truth beyond what the character can comprehend. Bottom correctly perceives that he has been in touch with matters beyond sense. He associates his experiences vaguely with Scripture, but his speech alerts the audience to connect him and his dream specifically with the "botome of Goddes secretes" evoked, for example, in the Great Bible (1539), translated at Cranmer's behest: "The eye hath not sene, and the eare hath not heard, nether haue entred into the hert of man, the thynges which God hath prepared for them that loue hym. But God hath opened them vnto vs by hys sprete. For the sprete searcheth all thynges, ye, the botome of Goddes secretes" (1 Cor. 2.9-10).[18]

The most famous of the linguistic blunderers among the hempen homespuns is not Bottom, however, but Peter Quince as the Prologue. In a carefully prepared punctuation gag, Quince delivers a speech whose lineation and rhyme are perfect but whose pointing makes it say both less and more than he intends:

If wee offend, it is with our good will.
That you shoulde thinke, we come not to offend,
But with good will. To shew our simple skill,
That is the true beginning of our end.
Consider then, we come but in despight.
We doe not come, as minding to content you,
Our true intent is. All for your delight,
Wee are not here. That you should here repent you,
The Actors are at hand. . . . (G4ʳ; 5.1.108-16)

We can be sure that Theseus hears the intention of Quince's language through his mispunctuation, both because he says so, "This fellow doth not stand vpon points" (G4ᵛ; 5.1.118), and because he has just told Hippolyta that subjects are apt to "shiuer and looke pale, / Make periods in the midst of sentences" (G4ʳ; 95-96) and that "in the modesty of fearefull duty, / I read as much, as from the rattling tongue / Of saucy and audacious eloquence" (G4ʳ; 101-03). Theseus has sufficient sympathy, as he subsequently tells his bride, to make up for the rude mechanicals' lack of skill (Hᵛ; 5.1.208). Just as the audience of *Dream* simultaneously laughs at Bottom's errors and understands the wisdom in his inadvertent parody of Scripture, so the aristocratic audience of *Pyramus and Thisbe* simultaneously laughs at Quince's ineptitude and hears the intended compliment beneath his inadvertent insult.

Once the "mislineations" of Theseus's opening speech have been reclassified as objects for interpretation rather than errors to be explained, they can be seen to have meaning, just as Bottom's misparallelisms or Quince's mispunctuations do. Theseus speaks from old habit and without confusion when he says he "neuer may" believe in fairies and fables. But he quickly gets into trouble when he begins to theorize about people with strong imaginations:

Louers, and mad men haue such seething braines,
Such shaping phantasies, that apprehend more,
Then coole reason euer comprehends. The lunatick,
The louer, and the Poet are of imagination all compact.

Although Wilson notes correctly that only the mislined portions of the speech mention "the Poet," it is not true that only portions mentioning the poet are mislined. The mislineation begins as Theseus describes the "shaping phantasies." Significantly, his first overloaded line ends on "more," as if to demonstrate the distortion that happens when fantasy reaches out to embrace "more" than a rationalized verse form should include. Soon Theseus is making bizarre enjambments, the poetic equivalents of "periods in the midst of sentences," and cramming eight feet into a single line. Yet his deranged verse returns twice to regularity, once in the middle of the passage and once at the end. If these regular sections of the speech contain less inspired writing, they also help mark the entire passage as verse, providing a ground against which auditors, including Hippolyta, can measure the Duke's extrametrical departures.

Like Plato, Theseus is not without feeling for the poet. In the *Ion*, Socrates calls the poet "a light and winged and holy thing," but condemns poets because they speak only through inspiration rather than by rules of art.[19] So Theseus acknowledges the power of the poet to give shape to "ayery nothing," but links such inspiration with delusions of devils, wish fulfillment, and "a bush suppos'd a Beare." Yet his own lines intermittently ignore the rules of art, and when they return one last time to regularity at the end, as Walter de la Mare says, the effect is bathetic, an "abysmal *descent*."[20] Perhaps the variations in verse quality here signify a clash between the rules and the roots of art, concepts that remain as unreconciled for Theseus as for Plato.

Like Bottom's garbled Scripture or Peter Quince's mixed-up punctuation, Theseus's verse shows the audience, including the Amazonian Queen, more than the speaker can see. His language "grows to something of great constancy" even though he speaks it as an inconstant mixture of almost mechanically regular verse and verse disguised as prose. Hippolyta, like an eighteenth-century editor, harkens to the real poetry of Theseus's lines, hearing the rule-governed blank verse in his apparently jangled speech and tactfully suggesting that there is more regularity than the Duke thinks both in "the poet's eye" and in the lovers' dream. Just as Theseus hears the genuine duty beneath Peter Quince's incoherent punctuation, his bride can hear the rules of art working beneath the Duke's apparently lawless lines. If the quarto lineations are taken as "correct," however, they suggest that Theseus never does get Hippolyta's point. Passages that imply character development when emphasized by the revision hypothesis signify character stagnation when taken as meaningful mislineations.

Like Bottom and Quince, Theseus becomes a language-joke, a vehicle through which someone else can perceive meanings that remain hidden from the speaker.

Not only does Theseus never appear to recognize the orderly disorder in his own speech, his confusion also seems to contaminate those around him. At the entrance of the lovers, for instance, the Duke continues his misarranged verse and is echoed by Lysander:

> Ioy, gentle friends, ioy and fresh daies
> Of loue accompany your hearts.
>   *Lys*. More then to vs, waite in your royall walkes, your boorde,
> your bedde.
>   *The*. Come now: what maskes, what daunces shall wee haue,
> To weare away this long age of three hours, betweene
> Or after supper, & bed-time? Where is our vsuall manager
> Of mirth? What Reuels are in hand? Is there no play,
> To ease the anguish of a torturing hower? Call *Philostrate*. (G3^r;
>   5.1.29-38)

The lineation here reflects the same kind of obliviousness that afflicts Peter Quince and Bottom, except that in Theseus the lack of self-knowledge appears almost willful. His language becomes disordered when he resists full consciousness of the irrational sexual urgency he feels ("a torturing hower"), just as it does when he refuses to grant the validity of imagination. Lysander, new to the role of ducal intimate, shows signs of learning the wrong lessons from his lord, as does Philostrate, who slides into mislineation himself when describing *Pyramus and Thisbe* (G3^v; 5.1.66-70, 76-78).

The word "nothing" that echoes through these mislined passages now looks like a sign of obtuseness rather than one of dawning awareness. Theseus calls the raw material of poetry "nothing," Philostrate calls *Pyramus and Thisbe* "nothing," and the misarrangement of their lines suggests that they see no more than what they say. The quarto, like other versions, concludes its series of plays on the word "nothing" with the noble couple's stichomythic dialogue: "*Hip*. He says, they can doe nothing in this kinde. / *The*. The kinder we, to giue them thanks, for nothing" (G4^r; 5.1.89). The reader of the quarto, however, having been prepared by mislineation for an unperceptive Duke, may wonder about the sincerity of Theseus's apparently gracious attitude toward his untrained subjects, especially since he and other courtly characters make fun of the mechanicals throughout the play. And if "nothing" retains its sexual suggestiveness here, it loses the character of a shared private joke between Hippolyta and Theseus that emerges from a revisionist reading.

Mislining makes ironic hash of Theseus's remarks about finding "cōcord / Of this discord" (G3ᵛ; 5.1.70) and calls into question his professed admiration for "simplenesse and duety" (G3ᵛ; 5.1.83). The misarrangements may also cast a different light on his crucial second dialogue with Hippolyta about imagination:

> *Dutch.* This is the silliest stuffe, that euer I heard.
> *Duke.* The best, in this kinde, are but shadowes: and
> the worst are no worse, if imagination amend them.
> *Dutch.* it must be your imagination, then; & not theirs.
> *Duke.* If we imagine no worse of them, then they of the
> selues, they may passe for excellent men. (Hᵛ; 5.1.208-12)

A reading that finds Theseus essentially static in this scene will see less importance in his concessions to the imagination during the hempen homespuns' play than a reading that discovers development in the Duke's character between drafts. In all versions, Hippolyta probes to see if Theseus has broadened his view, but in the mislined text there has been no preparation for change, and so the dialogue reveals little. The Duke is willing for the moment to imagine the players as excellent men, but imagination retains for him its overtones of delusion. He only consents to imagine what the players "imagine," wrongly, of themselves. Where revision theory finds eager anticipation in the Duchess's comments in the rest of this scene, the theory of collective authorship projects resignation. Hippolyta begins to talk like her husband. Like him, she says out loud that she is bored by the play: "I am aweary of this Moone. Would hee woulde change" (H2ʳ; 5.1.242), yet like him she also musters compliments for the actors: "Well shone *Moone*. Truly, the Moone shines, with a good grace" (H2ᵛ; 5.1.256-57). Her last line shows her still in the mood of courtly mockery, yet it might also be taken as a cynical final observation on love:

> *Dut.* How chance Moone-shine is gone before? *Thisby*
> comes backe, and findes her louer.

> *Duk.* Shee will finde him, by starre-light. Here shee
> comes, and her passion ends the Play.
>   *Dut.* Methinkes, she should not vse a long one, for such a
> *Pyramus*: I hope, she will be briefe. (H3^r; 5.1.300-03)

Hippolyta has now apparently accepted a courtly code of behavior that does not require the co-transfiguring of minds, asking only that Duke and Duchess observe the outward forms of graciousness. If Hippolyta's acceptance of this code and of her new husband implies no grand passion, it at least represents a realistic accommodation to the habits and limitations of the Duke. He does not desire the "great constancy" that can come from a profoundly imaginative meeting of minds, so she meets him on his own rather superficial level. Yet one wonders if her passion will last long for such a Duke.

INTENTION AND ACCIDENT

John Dover Wilson takes an individualistic approach to the mislineations in the last act of *Dream*, constructing a single controlling consciousness that he believes revised and improved the text. Perhaps it is not a coincidence that a reading based on this hypothesis produces a better-integrated consciousness for Theseus than does the approach from collective authorship. Yet a reading of Q1 based on the latter theory, which accepts supposed "accidents" as meaningful elements of the text, can also lead to a coherent account of the Duke at the end of the play. Whereas the revision hypothesis takes the mislined passages as a separate stage in the development of the text and consequently of the Duke, the collectivist approach accepts "accidental" mislineations as legitimate features of the text, and leads to a reading that emphasizes the dramatic uses of misspeaking. Although the theory of collective authorship does not distinguish between intentional and accidental contributions to the text, it is possible to take this approach and still treat all textual elements as contributions to the artistic patterns of the play. Readings generated in this way may not discover organic unity or resolve all apparent contradictions, but, as our age knows well, neither do many intention-based readings.

There remains the question of value. Wilson stresses the poetic value of the supposed revisions in *Dream* and denigrates what he considers the original draft. Not only does he think that the mislined parts of Theseus's imagination speech were added later, he finds the "additions" far superior to the "first draft." Both Wilson in *Comedies* and Walter de la Mare read the imagination speech as patchwork, divine poetry (revised) in some places, wooden schoolroom verse in others, and both critics finally explain the discrepancies by concluding that Shakespeare worked on *Dream* only as a reviser. According to Wilson, the "jejune and insipid verse" of the first draft is the work of another author.[21] Most insipid of all for both Wilson and de la Mare is the ending of the imagination speech: "Or, in the night, imagining some fear, / How easy is a bush suppos'd a bear!" (5.1.21-22).

Wilson's theory explains the sudden rash of mislineations at the end of the quarto, and that is part of its appeal. But it also offers a possible insight into what Shakespeare may have valued in poetry, how he might have responded to passages such as the hypothetical "before" version of Theseus's speech, and what he might have done to improve such passages. To believe in Wilson's vision of Shakespeare as a carefully revising poetic craftsman is to believe not only in quality judgments about poetry, but also in the value of one individual over another, at least as far as writing is concerned.

The argument for collective authorship is precisely an argument against such value judgments about individual writers. It suggests that texts are formed by collaboration and accident as well as by individual design, and that in an old text such as the first quarto of *Dream*, there is no way to tell the difference. Nevertheless, this position need not lead to the conclusion that there is no difference between one text and another. If readers and audiences find coherent artistic effects in the mislineations of Q1, this coherence can give the text its value, regardless of whether the effects were contrived by one mind, by many minds, or by chance.

The idea of accidental or contingent authorship is interesting partly because it may represent a truth about every text, a truth that theories of textual origin focused too tightly on the conscious artistic choices of uniquely talented individuals tend to miss. Even a work clearly written by a single person may contain potentially meaningful accidents. To take a famous case, F.O. Matthiessen's praise for Melville's "soiled fish of the sea," a misprint for "coiled fish," is often cited as an example of the excesses of the New Criticism.[22] Matthiessen's reading might now be seen, however, as an instance of the poststructuralist approach advocated by Werstine and others, in which the reader accepts and interprets the text as received without inquiring into authorial intention. In addition, of course, most writers acknowledge that good writing can come from sources other than conscious artistic choice. Meaningful accidents can become integrated with authorial intention. MacDonald P. Jackson cites, in a similar connection, Malcolm Lowry's poem, "Strange Type," which begins, "I wrote: in the dark cavern of our birth / The printer had it tavern, which seems better."[23] On the other hand, as this essay has tried to suggest, most unusual interpretative strategies—such as finding meaning in mislined verses instead of regarding them as compositor's mistakes—succeed best, if they succeed at all, against a background of more orthodox practices. A reader who has never tried to understand a literary text by linking it to everyday notions about human intention will probably have a hard time making sense not only of anti-intentionalist procedures but of any kind of literary criticism whatsoever. Although innovative critical methods are often presented in opposition to older practices and practitioners, they frequently work best when used in conjunction with more traditional approaches rather than as replacements.

Given the huge number of possible causes for the mislineations in Q1 *Dream*, there is no reason to have much confidence in Wilson's revision hypothesis. But neither must readers adopt the historical atheism sometimes implied by the postmodern approach. There is a right answer to the historical question of how the mislineations got into Q1, even if we never discover it. One would like to know what that answer is, and as I have tried to show, knowing could make a difference to most readers or spectators of the play. As things stand now, however, both the source of the mislineations and their significance for interpreting the character of Theseus remain open questions. The nature of the textual evidence suggests that even if this particular puzzle were solved, we would continue to have many such questions and many such necessarily speculative answers. The point of this essay has not been to urge the superiority either of the approach from authorial intention or the approach from collective construction, but to show that in cases where origins remain shrouded in doubt, the juxtaposing of apparently antithetical textual theories may prove more fruitful for literary interpretation than choosing between them.

NOTES

1. See, for example, Gary Taylor, *Reinventing Shakespeare* (New York: Weidenfeld & Nicolson, 1989).

2. Unless otherwise noted, act, scene, and line citations refer to the New Arden *A Midsummer Night's Dream*, Harold F. Brooks, ed. (London: Methuen, 1979).

3. Citations from Q1 are taken from Michael J.B. Allen and Kenneth Muir, eds., *Shakespeare's Plays in Quarto: A Facsimile Editon of Copies Primarily from the Henry E. Huntington Library* (Berkeley: University of California Press, 1981).

4. For these early editors' changes, see Brooks, 103-04.

5. Modern-spelling quotations are taken from the New Arden edition. This text, like most modern editions, represents the play in the form Wilson believed to be the revised version.

6. "The Copy for *A Midsummer Night's Dream*, 1600," *A Midsummer Night's Dream*, The New Cambridge Shakespeare (Cambridge: Cambridge University Press, 1924), 77-100, esp. 80-83.

7. See also Wilson's "Variations on the Theme of *A Midsummer Night's Dream*," *Shakespeare's Happy Comedies* (Evanston: Northwestern University Press, 1962), 184-220.

8. Wilson, "The Copy for *A Midsummer Night's Dream*," 85-86.

9. See Walter de la Mare, *Pleasures and Speculations* (1940; rpt. Freeport, NY: Books for Libraries Press, 1969), 270-305, and Wilson, "Variations."

10. As Gary Taylor points out, the acceptance of local verbal revision in this case contrasts with a reluctance in modern criticism—recently reversed—to admit that Shakespeare may have revised whole plays between editions. See Gary Taylor, "Revising Shakespeare," *Text* 3 (1987): 285-304.

11. Wilson, "Variations," 209.

12. Quotations from Shakespeare plays other than *Dream* are taken from *The Riverside Shakespeare* ed. G. Blakemore Evans (Boston: Houghton Mifflin, 1974).

13. Many critics read the ending of *Shrew* as ironic. See, for example, Irene G. Dash, *Wooing, Wedding, and Power: Women in Shakespeare's Plays* (New York: Columbia University Press, 1981), 61-63.

14. Michael D. Bristol, *Shakespeare's America, America's Shakespeare* (London: Routledge, 1990), 109-19; Margreta De Grazia, "The Essential Shakespeare and the Material Book," *Textual Practice* 2 (1988): 69-86; Paul

Werstine, "Narratives about Printed Shakespearean Texts: 'Foul Papers' and 'Bad Quartos,'" *Shakespeare Quarterly* 41 (1990): 65-86.

15. Werstine, 86.

16. Quotations in this section are from the Allen and Muir facsimile of the Huntington Quartos. References to the line numbers in the New Arden edition follow page citations from the quarto.

17. For a reading of this passage as a revelation of Bottom's insightfulness, see Helen Peters, "Bottom: Making Sense of Sense and Scripture," *Notes & Queries* 35 (233)1 (1988): 45-47.

18. Johann Martin Augustin, ed., *The English Hexapla Exhibiting the Six Important English Translations of the New Testament Scriptures* (London: Samuel Bagster, 1841; rpt. New York: AMS Press, 1975), n. pag.

19. *The Dialogues of Plato*, trans. B. Jowett, 4th ed., 4 vols. (Oxford: Clarendon Press, 1953), 1: 108.

20. De la Mare, 304.

21. Wilson, "Variations," 212.

22. See John W. Nichol, "Melville's '"Soiled" Fish of the Sea'," *American Literature* 21 (1949): 338-39.

23. MacDonald P. Jackson, "The Year's Contributions to Shakespeare Studies: Editions and Textual Studies," *Shakespeare Survey* 42 (1990): 207.

A Midsummer Night's Dream as a Comic Version of the Theseus Myth

Douglas Freake

Myth criticism, by which I mean examinations of the relation between literary works and the myth on which they are based or to which they allude, has fallen on hard times. Poststructuralist criticism in general distrusts essentialist or trans-temporal modes of interpretation; and varieties of poststructuralism, such as new historicism, which emphasize the intricate connections between texts and their social contexts, shy away in embarrassment from the sort of literary criticism encouraged by Jung or Joseph Campbell.

A Midsummer Night's Dream, it could be argued, is of all Shakespeare's plays the most indebted to a mythic source. Yet, perhaps because it is a comedy—and therefore assumed to use myth decoratively rather than seriously—the play's mythical sources, while not ignored, have received less attention than they deserve. Although the specific episode of the Theseus story used by Shakespeare is a relatively minor one—Theseus' marriage to the queen of the Amazons—the parts of the play which make up its real action seem to become more infused with aspects of Theseus' adventures the longer one contemplates them. One notices the name Egeus (Aegeus) given to Hermia's father; the similarity of the lovers lost in the wood to the Athenian youths forced to enter the Minotaur's labyrinth; Bottom as a "monster" reminiscent of the minotaur; Bottom's craft of weaving, which recalls Ariadne's thread; Hermia's desertion which echoes

Ariadne's abandonment on Naxos; Titania as Pasiphae, in love with "sweet bully Bottom" (4.2.19)[1]; and, in Oberon, aspects of both Minos the king and judge and Daedalus the craftsman and magician, maker of labyrinths.

Reviewing some of the work that has been done on the Theseus story as it appears in Shakespeare's play, often in displaced form, I explore here the tension between an essentialist and a historicist view of myth. My hope is to suggest answers to three interrelated questions: Is it possible to reconcile these supposedly dichotomous attitudes to myth? Does *A Midsummer Night's Dream* contain or allude to a generative kernel discoverable in Greek versions of the Theseus story? Is it significant that this kernel, assuming we find it, is contained, half-hidden and half-revealed, in a *comedy*, which would therefore seem to be the best medium for preserving whatever mythic essence structures the Theseus cycle of stories?

The universalist attitude to myth always seems to assume, as Ted Hughes says in *Shakespeare and the Goddess of Complete Being*, that a myth, as an element in a literary work, operates "as a controlling, patterned field of force, open internally to the 'divine', the 'daemonic', the 'supernatural' (of which the constituent myths were the original symbolic expression), but externally to the profane, physical form and individualities of the action, to the words of the actors, and the local habitation and burden of the plot."[2] Hughes echoes Theseus' famous speech in this formulation, but he does not discuss *A Midsummer Night's Dream* in his five-hundred-page book, presumably because he does not think that the play is informed by the Great Goddess myth, although, as we shall see, such mythic residues can clearly be seen in it. Neither does he explain how, or why, the divine, daemonic or supernatural elements of myth mysteriously persist in much later literary creations. It could, I suppose, be said to reside in the narrative itself, which exists within a cultural tradition for reasons that are partly formal, partly psychological and partly accidental, but we know that thousands of ancient narratives have been lost or forgotten in spite of their "daemonic" connections.

Although he is often viewed as the most universalist of theorists, in defining myth Joseph Campbell actually allows room for historicist or 'socially constructed' factors that Hughes ignores. He claims that myths reflect

certain irreducible psychological problems inherent in the very
biology of our species, which have remained constant, and have,
consequently, so tended to control and structure the myths and rites
in their service that, in spite of all the differences that have been
recognized, analyzed, and stressed by sociologists and historians,
there run through the myths of all mankind the common strains of a
single symphony of the soul.[3]

This is as firm a statement of the universalist view as one could
imagine. Yet in the same breath, Campbell notes that traditional
functions of myth include "validating and maintaining some specific
social order, authorizing its moral code as a construct beyond criticism
or human emendation" and "shaping individuals to the aims and ideals
of their various social groups,"[4] formulations that concur with Roland
Barthes' view in *Mythologies*.

What theorists like Barthes most dislike about traditional myth
criticism is the claim that literature has inherited the universal qualities
of myth. Deconstruction has undermined all foundational ideology and
shown that claims to ongoing 'presence,' which are key to defenses of
both myth and literature, are illusory and manipulative. As Reuben
Arthur Brower has said, "Although we commonly speak of '*the*
Oedipus myth' or '*the* Hercules myth,' and although anthropologists
refer to mythical 'archetypes' or 'structures,' it can be said that there
are no myths, only versions. To put it another way, there are only texts
for interpretation. . . ."[5] Yet there is something in the study of myth that
deconstruction cannot completely dismiss. Even if myths exist only in
"versions," each version is a version of something; and even if we
allow that the 'something' can never be captured or fixed, it cannot,
either, be destroyed if the social will exists to keep it alive. Stories are
clearly remembered and retold by societies over long periods of time.
The difficult question is to explain why—without begging the question
by appeals to their concern with "irreducible psychological problems"
or to their 'greatness'—certain stories are versioned over many
centuries. Even if we can find the mythic kernel of the stories about
Theseus, we still need to explain why the story remained so popular in
European culture that it provided material not only for the Roman
dramatists but for Shakespeare and Racine as well. Perhaps some sense
of the primordial conflicts buried in the Theseus cycle and its
antecedents will explain why Shakespeare creates his idiosyncratic

version of the Theseus story as a play about marriage, intended to serve as part of a real marriage celebration.[6]

Do the episodes of the Theseus story, placed over each other like transparencies, reveal, "something of great constancy" (5.1.26)? Certainly the cycle reveals a conflict between the culture-founding, civilization-building elements of the story and more anarchic, destructive ones. In particular, it tells of Theseus' conflicts with women, suggesting, in Erich Neumann's words, that he is "the hero who conquers the symbol of matriarchal domination," that is, the minotaur.[7] Behind the Theseus myth, says Neumann, lies the conflict between the patriarchal and the matriarchal worlds and the gradual substitution of human sacrifices to animal ones in annual festivals of the renewal of kingly power.[8]

Most medieval and later retellings of the Theseus story seem far removed from such ancient rituals. Simon Tidworth, in a survey of the Theseus story in the Renaissance, remarks on "the universal popularity of the old stories and their universal accessibility. They were told not only for their own sakes but for the sake of practically any message that an author wished to impart."[9] The Theseus story was very well known in the Middle Ages and the Renaissance. It was accepted as an "antique fable," but paintings of episodes from the story suggest that it was taken as having historical validity as well. After all, Theseus appeared in Plutarch along with firmly historical figures such as Mark Antony. Moreover, like history in general, the story was seen as a repository of moral *exempla* and as having continuing significance for Christian audiences. In *A Midsummer Night's Dream*, an Elizabethan audience would see, Shakespeare is involved in *mythopoesis*, the recreation of ancient stories, transposed and given a symbolic meaning yet treated with a sophisticated self-reflexiveness. Tidworth notes that Shakespeare took a classical story and used it as the medium for his own thoughts on human conduct in "Venus and Adonis" and "The Rape of Lucrece," but that he wrote no Theseus and Ariadne, apparently from lack of interest. "Theseus appears in his conventional role as Duke of Athens in *A Midsummer Night's Dream*, but apart from that all we can gather are a few scraps of simile like 'Thou mayst not wander in that labyrinth; / There Minotaurs and ugly treasons lurk' from *Henry VI Part I*."[10]

Others have perceived in *A Midsummer Night's Dream* a more extensive use of the Theseus story, but rarely have they seen the play as dealing with conflicts present in the Greek texts. In 1979, in an admirable article, "*A Midsummer-Night's Dream*: The Myth of Theseus and the Minotaur," M.E. Lamb was the first to focus on the play's extensive use of the Theseus myth.[11] She notes that Theseus was read during the Renaissance not only as a reasonable man in control of his lower nature, but as an unkind lover and deserter of women. In spite of the fact that he and Hippolyta are happily wed at the end of the play, the audience would have known that the product of their union, Hippolytus, would eventually die because of his father's curse. This essay does not focus on the workings of "myth," in either Campbell's or Barthes' sense; instead, the dark elements in the play are seen mostly as inevitable, in the sense that fear and death reside at the heart of the labyrinth of the world, even if the comic perspective can deny them for a time.[12]

The most admired of myth critics, Northrop Frye, noted, in 1983, that *A Midsummer Night's Dream* owes a great deal to Classical mythology, and, in typically suggestive fashion, he comments that Shakepeare's play retains signs of the struggle between matriarchal and patriarchal forms of social power which Neumann saw as an essential element of the Greek myth: "It might be possible to think that the fairy world represents a female principle in the play which is eventually subordinated to a male ascendancy associated with daylight. In the background is the unseen little boy who moves from female to male company as Oberon simultaneously asserts his authority over Titania; in the foreground is Theseus' marriage to a conquered Amazon."[13]

Having had this insight, Frye immediately rejects it:

> But this seems wrong, and out of key with the general tonality of the play. Theseus' marriage will at least end his unsavoury reputation as a treacherous lover, glanced at by Oberon, and the most explicit symbol of male domination, Egeus' claim to dispose of Hermia as he wishes, is precisely what is being eliminated by the total action. The fairy wood is a wood of Eros as well as of Venus and Diana, and both sexes are equally active principles in both worlds.[14]

Frye is right to see in the play yet another version of the ascendancy of male power over the "female principle," yet all too cavalier in finding himself "wrong" and in assuming that "both sexes are equally active principles" in the world of dream and the world of political reality, if those are indeed the worlds to which he refers. His wording is in fact extremely ambiguous at this point. Are "both worlds" the world of Eros versus the world of Venus and Diana (a claim that makes little sense), or the worlds of night and day, the latter of which, at least, is not one in which both sexes are equally active "principles"? Frye's choice of such phrases as "a female principle" and "a male ascendancy associated with daylight" indicates a distaste for gender politics, which were flourishing when Frye wrote his essay. He notes a formidable tension in the play but re-represses it by an appeal to the play's genre; the "general tonality" fitting to a comedy is enough to make his potential reading unnecessary.

Louis Adrian Montrose's "'Shaping Fantasies': Figurations of Gender and Power in Elizabethan Culture," was published in 1983, the same year as Frye published the remarks just quoted. It does *not* overlook the gender politics that Frye recognizes but downplays. In discussing Elizabethan myth-making about Amazon societies supposedly being discovered in Africa and the New World, Montrose claims that Shakespeare's play reveals a similar "collective anxiety about the power of the female not only to dominate or reject the male but to create and destroy him. It is an ironic acknowledgment by an androcentric culture of the degree to which men are in fact dependent upon women: upon mothers and nurses, for their birth and nurture; upon mistresses and wives, for the validation of their manhood."[15] He has striking things to say about the central importance, in *A Midsummer Night's Dream*, of Titania's and Oberon's quarrel over a changeling boy. In a phrase reminiscent of Neumann's description of the Theseus tales, he refers to Theseus' victory over Hippolyta as "a defeat of the Amazonian matriarchate,"[16] one of many myths, he says, which recount a cultural transition from matriarchy to patriarchy. He argues that the placement of this story "at the very threshold of *A Midsummer Night's Dream*" sanctions Oberon's attempt to take the boy from Titania and "to make a man of him";[17] notices the Oedipal implications of the struggle (Oberon and the boy are rivals for Titania, who has forsworn Oberon's "bed and company" [2.1.62-63] because of their quarrel);[18] and notes perceptively that Titania's attachment to the changeling boy reflects her devotion to the memory of his mother, a devotion which Oberon destroys by forcing Titania to give the boy over to him. The play, Montrose concludes, "enacts a male disruption of an intimate bond between women: first by the boy, and then by the man."[19]

This subtle essay directs our attention to an aspect of the Theseus story which may be a key to its continuing fascination: male fear of women's procreative power and attempts to deny that power by gaining control of children, and thereby women, through patriarchal marriage and the elaborate ideology of sexual roles that accompanies it. Its argument takes us a long way towards understanding the religious and social tension that is part of both the original Greek myth cycle and of Elizabethan concerns about female power and the politics of procreation.

Validation for a reading of *A Midsummer Night's Dream* as an intersection of ancient and modern politics comes from C. Kerényi, who describes events in the myths about early Athens which resonate in the play, even though Shakespeare may not have known about all, or any, of the episodes. In his account of the early kings of Athens, the ancestors of Theseus, Kerényi records that the Athenians believed themselves to be descended not from a male primaeval being "but directly from the soft, reddish soil of Attica, which in the beginning brought forth human beings instead of wild beasts."[20] Cecrops, who was regarded as the "heroic founder" of Athens, was half-serpent, half-human: "serpent as having sprung from the earth, yet also with a share in human form and therefore *diphyes*, 'of twofold nature.'" One serpent appears in the play, in Hermia's dream, or nightmare: "Help me, Lysander, help me! Do thy best / To pluck this crawling serpent from my breast!" (2.2.144-45). In a volume on the myth of the divine child, which he wrote with Kerényi, Jung remarks that the fear of dragons and serpents points to the danger that the consciousness will be overtaken by the unconscious; "snake-dreams," he says, "usually occur . . . when the conscious mind is deviating from its instinctual basis."[21] It is hardly surprising that Hermia dreams of serpents when alone in the woods with her lover, since at that moment her consciousness is indeed threatened, by darkness, dream, and sexual desire. Her dream is not, of course, related to the story of Cecrops, but like Bottom's transformation into a half-animal creature, it does suggest that return to the womb of nature is a threat for the conscious and the social mind, a threat that Bottom can survive much more triumphantly than Hermia.

Half-animal mythical founders no doubt combine elements of chthonic origins ('the people who live here sprang from this very earth'), totem memories, and psychological aspects that link the infant or child to the uncultured beast. Bottom's name may point to ways in which, in his dual form, he is at the 'bottom' of society, in the sense of being foundational: he recalls the beast consort who may fertilize the great mother goddess, but more obviously he is a baby, almost a divine child. Kerényi comments: "Being sprung from the earth and the nurseling of the maiden goddess, Pallas Athene, her father's daughter, and formed after her mind, the picture of the primitive Athenian was first present in Kekrops."[22] The Athenians thought of themselves as autochthonous, but they worshipped Athena who, although she became a patriarchal goddess, born without a mother, was doubtless at first a mother goddess. Like Artemis/Diana, one of whose names in Ovid is Titania,[23] Pallas Athena shunned male domination, even though she became firmly placed within the Olympian hierarchy dominated by Zeus. The transformed Bottom, in his man-animal double nature, resembles Cecrops as "picture of the primitive Athenian;" in relation to Titania he seems like an indulged baby, child rather than consort of a mother goddess. He stands (or lies) in for the changeling boy, who is in fact never seen in the play. Jung's comment that in myths of the divine child "Nature, the world of the instincts, takes the 'child' under its wing,"[24] is an apt commentary on Bottom's treatment by the fairies who bring him the good things of the wood. Jung's words about the power of the child archetype uncannily capture Bottom's experience as he struggles to remember the dream that he cannot express: "Consciousness hedged about by psychic powers, sustained or threatened or deluded by them, is the age-old experience of mankind. This experience has projected itself into the archetype of the child, which expresses man's wholeness. . . . The 'eternal child' in man is an indescribable experience, an incongruity, a handicap, and a divine pre-rogative."[25] Bottom's metamorphosis is explicable, in part at least, as a vision of the child archetype.

But why would the child archetype, or, more modestly, concern with children, be part of a verson of the Theseus story? Theseus, after all, is famous for cursing and destroying his son. The issue of lineage may suggest an answer. Cecrops "discovered, as it were, the double descent of human beings, that they come not only from a mother but also from a father. He founded the institution of marriage between one man and one woman, which was to be under the protection of the goddess Athene. That allegedly was his act of foundation, worthy of a primaeval father, who was not personally the ancestor of the Athenians, although they had him to thank for their patrilineal descent."[26] The instituting of marriage no doubt marks, to some degree at least, the suppression of matriarchal customs and powers. The marriages in *A Midsummer Night's Dream*, although they are not determined by the tyrannical Egeus, nevertheless occur only with the approval of Theseus and the blessing of Oberon; moreover, "[t]hose who emphasized the point that Kekrops instituted marriage were obliged to add that men and women had mated promiscuously before his time."[27] The tradition of another status for women than that in historical Athens, where they were excluded from public life, remained in the latest form of the story of how Pallas Athena took possession of the land:

> In this version of that famous tale, the olive grew out of the earth for the first time while Kekrops reigned, and at the same time a spring appeared. The king is said to have inquired thereupon of the Delphic oracle and got the answer that the olive signified the goddess Athene, the water the god Poseidon, and the citizens were to decide after which the city was to be named. Now in those days the woman [sic] had still the franchise, and they out-voted the men by one; thus Athene was victorious and the city was named Athenai. Poseidon, as many tales teach us that he did, became angry and flooded the coasts. To pacify him, the women had to renounce their former right, and ever since then the children were not distinguished by the names of their mothers but by those of their fathers.[28]

The quarrel of Oberon and Titania causes disruptions in nature reminiscent of the floods that Poseidon visited on Athens until he was placated by the women's sacrifice of their franchise. Titania gives in to Oberon, much as the women of Athens gave up their power, for the good of the community.

These stories about the beginnings of Athens record that with the discovery of the male role in procreation came marriage, monogamy, and the 'voluntary' surrender of women's rights to political power. The aspect of Shakespeare's play that most uncannily suggests the myth of

Athen's founding is the choice of a cause for Titania's and Oberon's quarrel. Oberon wants control of a changeling boy who has been in Titania's care. It may be that Oberon is announcing the time when a boy-child should be initiated into the masculine world and that Titania is unjustifiably retarding the child's 'natural' development, but the text does not make that argument. Oberon simply says, "I do but beg a little changeling boy / To be my henchman" (2.1.120-21). The fact that he "begs" the child suggests that in spite of his later tricks, which quickly if illogically enforce Titania's compliance, he is dependent on Titania's willing gift of the child if he is to consider it his.[29]

In response to Oberon's plea, Titania presents her own little 'myth' of the boy's birth:

> His mother was a votress of my order;
> And in the spiced Indian air, by night,
> Full often hath she gossip'd by my side;
> And sat with me on Neptune's yellow sands,
> Marking th'embarked traders on the flood:
> When we have laugh'd to see the sails conceive
> And grow big-bellied with the wanton wind;
> Which she, with pretty and with swimming gait
> Following (her womb then rich with my young squire),
> Would imitate, and sail upon the land
> To fetch me trifles, and return again
> As from a voyage rich with merchandise.
> But she, being mortal, of that boy did die;
> And for her sake I will not part with him. (2.1.123-37)

Although this passage does not claim a virgin birth for the changeling boy, the simile of the "wanton wind" impregnating the sails of ships makes it appear that his mother had herself become pregnant without the help of a man. In light of Jung's remark that "like the womb of the mother, boundless water is an organic part of the image of the Primordial Child,"[30] it is striking that the changeling boy was born on the seashore. In far-off India Titania has received something close to worship ("votress of my order") from her charming follower. Their friendship is similar to that of Hermia and Helena in their girlhoods, or even to that of the Amazons. As Montrose says, for Titania the changeling boy is a token of friendship among women, who are united in part by their self-evident primacy as progenitrixes; to give him up is to submit to male power. The ignorance of early Athenians about the role of the father in conception permitted promiscuous behavior like that which the four lovers in the play are in danger of embracing. Titania's insistence on children as links between women rather than between men, as they must be in any patrilineal system, and in particular her beautiful invocation of the self-sufficiency of women, which stops just short of accepting parthenogenesis, threaten both the natural and patriarchal orders, or rather, the natural order as interpreted by a patriarchal consciousness. Compared with the mother's role, the father's is a matter of faith, dependent on the mother's 'word.' In the beginning was the word, the word of submission not only to a male symbolic order but to fatherhood as the basis of social order. The name, and law, of the father depend on the submissive word ('the child is yours') of the mother. Titania is re-stating, here, one can imagine, the attitudes to birth and female solidarity of early Athenian women and of the Amazons, including perhaps Hippolyta herself, whose protests are unvoiced, unless, as I think is reasonable, we take Titania as her alter ego.

Interestingly, in turning to thoughts of revenge Oberon uses a word employed by Theseus when, at the beginning of the play, he described his wooing of Hippolyta, who has submitted because of "injuries" done to her (1.1.17). Oberon now promises to torment Titania "for this injury" (2.1.147). He will do so by using 'love' against her, as Theseus, in a sense, has done to Hippolyta, whose loss of independence is supposedly made up for by her marriage. Titania will be forced to love, against her reason and her will, and will be shamed by that love. Oberon inserts his own Ovid-like myth at this point, explaining to Puck that the juice of the flower called "love-in-idleness" (2.1.168) "will make or man or woman madly dote / Upon the next live creature that it sees" (2.1.171-72). Ultimately Oberon uses the juice of "love-in-idleness" to effect two results connected to Kerényi's account of early Athens. After some confusion, he leads the young lovers to "marriage between one man and one woman," thereby creating a social order in which the husband's power is secured by his legalized control over his wife. He also uses the juice to bring the rebellious Titania to heel. He does this by causing her to enact a version of the Pasiphae story: Bottom is both the bull that Pasiphae lusted after and the minotaur that resulted from her lust. Although Titania does not mate with Bottom, who as I have suggested is more divine child than sexual object, she will be shamed by her desire for him. No doubt the original story of the labyrinth reflects a view of the matriarchal, or more matriarchal, religion of Crete as seen by Greeks of the patriarchal period. For them, the Cretan palace and its acrobats vaulting over the backs and horns of bulls represented a forbidding image of the mother goddess with her beast consorts, not that Greek religion, at any stage, was without its powerful goddesses. But the power of the mother goddess, except for Ceres, perhaps, who was in any case associated with the mysteries rather than with more public forms of devotion, had been reduced, by subordination to male gods and by various specializations of her power, such as patronage of love or of virginity.

The important point, of course, is that such a submission is not just generous, or inevitable, but productive of women's real social enslavement. It is hardly surprising that woman's giving up of control over the child, on many levels except that of actual care, must be seen as freely given. Myths which concentrate on this point, and many do, usually present the female submission as a gracious and 'natural' occurrence. In *A Midsummer Night's Dream*, in spite of the chaos that their quarrel has threatened, the fairy king and queen 'resolve the issue' (and here the phrase can be taken almost literally) with a suspicious haste which foreshortens the conflict and allows a comic ending, at least from the viewpoint of the patriarchal order which is thus reaffirmed. In Oberon's song in the final scene, a blessing on the children to be born to the couples that have wed that day, he refers to "issue" twice: "And the issue there [in the bride-bed] create / Ever shall be fortunate" (5.1.391-92) and "And the blots of Nature's hand / Shall not in their issue stand. . ." (5.1.395-96). The parentless changeling boy has aroused primal and dangerous conflict between Oberon and Titania, figures who, although they seem to be childless themselves, readily suggest parental power. Their conflict resonates with doubts over the origin of children which, as Kerényi shows, are bound up with the institution of patriarchal marriage. The strangely static quality of *A Midsummer Night's Dream*—the play consists of the announcement of a marriage and the celebration of a marriage, but no representation of marriage itself—suggests that the interspersed plot lines, which involve escape into night, wood, and dream, are essential to the working out of a major block to the reconciliation of Theseus and his Amazon queen. The two plot lines which 'handle' this block are that of Oberon's and

Titania's quarrel and that of the lover's night in the wood, which has been caused by Egeus' deadly willfulness, an extreme form of the position adopted by Oberon.

Although I would not claim that the story of Cecrops and early Athens is directly related to Shakespeare's play, I am impressed by the fact that it is in his great *epithalamium* that Shakespeare has chosen to recast the Theseus myth. In this recasting, he has included quarreling over the generation and control of children and, by extension, over the relative power of men and women. Oberon and Titania, in their struggle over the changeling boy and in Oberon's efforts to enforce Titania's obedience to his will, act out the sort of dream that might well trouble mortals' sleep. If the central part of the play is, among other things, a joint dream of Theseus and Hippolyta, then it is a dream that 'resolves' an underlying tension just as, according to Lévi-Strauss, and others, a myth resolves an intolerable social contradiction. Speaking of Levi-Strauss' view of myth, Ronald Schleifer has commented that "the function of mythic discourse is to create the illusory resolution of real cultural contradictions."[31] Shakespeare's play uses a version of the Pasiphae and minotaur story to create the "illusory resolution" of "real cultural contradictions." One of the most repulsive aspects of the Theseus story is transformed into a charming fantasy in which Bottom returns to nature, has his (innocent) physical and emotional desires fulfilled, and is allowed, perhaps, to indulge an appreciation of the "female principle" that the waking man can admire only when it is firmly subordinated to male supremacy. This transformation of 'repulsive' into comic material does not, however, change the underlying meaning of the plot or of the social narratives that it supports.

In what sense, then, is *A Midsummer Night's Dream* a 'mythic' version of the Theseus story? Lamb has shown us that the story informs the play as a powerful and suggestive intertext; she has also noted some of the archetypal resonances of the labyrinth and of Bottom as minotaur. Frye has noted the play's reflection of struggles between male and female principles, and Montrose has argued its involvement in the contradictions and realities of Elizabethan society. I have suggested that the play brings forward a less obvious element in the Theseus cycle of stories, namely, its somewhat veiled treatment of the conflict between the matriarchal and patriarchal orders, which in turn is connected, as Kerényi suggests, to a primordial struggle over generation.

This 'revelation' of a 'mythic kernel' need not lead us to agree with essentialist views of myth. Or at least, we must be clear about why a myth has an 'essence.' Enough stories have been significant for a time and then been forgotten to persuade us that the power of myth is dependent not on some sort of primordial 'charge' but on continuing social relevance. That is, it is not the story or myth itself that remains 'timeless,' but the social context, which in spite of great changes in particulars, can sustain a basic pattern over time. No pattern has been more sustained over time than that of male supremacy, so it is hardly surprising that uneasiness over passion and over female independence would link ancient Athens, Elizabethan England, and contemporary societies. Perhaps it makes sense to see the essentialist view of myth as a kind of metaphor pointing to particularly important ongoing concerns. Especially in the masterful hands of Jung, whose comments on the child archetype I have quoted, this metaphor can provide emotional and even logical satisfaction, as long as the historical and social contexts recorded if not explained by Kerényi are kept firmly in mind.

Although patriarchal power is explored and defended in many of Shakespeare's tragedies, its arbitrariness is nowhere more explicit than in *A Midsummer Night's Dream*. The play is a *comic* version of the Theseus story, not because it parodies the myth, nor because it transforms the minotaur into a beneficent image of the divine or archetypal child, although both of these arguments can reasonably be made. Rather, Shakespeare's playful yet haunted play of Duke Theseus is a comedy because the comic mode best allows its underlying social theme, that of women's submission to men in marriage, to pass like a dream—a dream founded on the starkest reality.

NOTES

1. All quotations from the play are taken from Harold F. Brooks' Arden edition (London: Methuen, 1979).

2. Hughes, *Shakespeare and the Goddess of Complete Being* (London: Faber and Faber, 1992), 3.

3. Campbell, "Mythological Themes in Creative Literature and Art," in *Myths, Dreams and Religion*, ed. Joseph Campbell (New York: Dutton, 1970), 141.

4. Campbell, 140.

5. Brower, *Mirror on Mirror: Translation, Imitation, Parody* (Cambridge: Mass.: Harvard University Press, 1974), 17.

6. See the introduction to the Arden edition, liii.

7. Erich Neumann, *The Origins and History of Consciousness* (Princeton: Princeton University Press, 1954; rpt. 1970), 2.

8. Neumann, 78.

9. See Tidworth, "From the Renaissance to Romanticism" in *The Quest for Theseus*, A.G. Ward *et al.* (New York: Praeger, 1970), 195.

10. Tidworth, 215.

11. Lamb, *Texas Studies in Literature and Language* 21 (1979): 478-91.

12. For further discussion of the labyrinth, see David Ormerod's "*A Midsummer Night's Dream*: The Monster in the Labyrinth," in *Shakespeare Studies* 11 (1978): 39-52. Ormerod's article uses the narrative of Theseus and the minotaur, and its allegorizations during the Renaissance, to explore the notion of "blind love" and the eventual reconciliation of opposites into "a new *discordia concors*" (39).

13. Frye, *The Myth of Deliverance: Reflections on Shakespeare's Problem Comedies* (Toronto: University of Toronto Press, 1983), 80-81.

14. Frye, 81.

15. *Representations* 1.2 (1983): 66.

16. Montrose, 71.

17. Ibid.

18. Allen Dunn follows suit in his "The Indian Boy's Dream Wherein Every Mother's Son Rehearses His Part: Shakespeare's *A Midsummer Night's Dream*," *Shakespeare Studies* 20 (1988): 15-32, especially 24-26.

19. Montrose, 71.

20. C. Kerényi, *The Heroes of the Greeks*, (1959, rpt. London: Thames and Hudson, 1974), 209; see his chapter entitled "Kekrops, Erechtheus and Theseus." I have retained Kerényi's spellings in quotations from his text but have otherwise used standard spellings.

21. C.G. Jung and C. Kerényi, *Essays on a Science of Mythology: The Myth of the Divine Child and the Mysteries of Eleusis*, Bollingen Series (1949; rpt. Princeton: Princeton University Press, 1973), 85.

22. Kerényi, 209.

23. See Frye, 80.

24. Jung and Kerényi, 87.

25. Ibid., 97-98.

26. Kerényi, 209.

27. Ibid., 210.

28. Ibid., 210-11.

29. For an interesting discussion of Elizabethan beliefs about paternity, see Montrose's article, especially 72-75.

30. Jung and Kerényi, 49.

31. Ronald Schleifer, "Structuralism," *The Johns Hopkins Guide to Literary Theory and Criticism*, eds. Michael Groden and Martin Kreiswirth (Baltimore: Johns Hopkins University Press, 1994), 700.

Antique Fables, Fairy Toys
Elisions, Allusion, and Translation in
A Midsummer Night's Dream

Thomas Moisan

PRAESCRIPTIO

In his compendious survey of the putative, not unlikely, and barely
possible textual sources of *A Midsummer Night's Dream*, Harold F.
Brooks commends Shakespeare at one point for the skill with which he
"weaves or fuses together material from a whole series of sources."[1] A
generous celebration of Shakespeare's ability to assimilate disparate
elements to forge dramatic coherence, nevertheless, in its casual elision
of "weaves" and "fuses," Brooks's remark hints both at the peculiar
"texture" and untidiness of our experience in the *Dream* and at the
ways in which that experience is complicated by the allusiveness and
textual eclecticism the *Dream* embodies. In what is to follow—and in
what bids fair to be a distinctly untidy paper—I want, on the one hand,
to ponder but a few instances of what I take to be the "unwovenness"
of the *Dream*, moments at which source materials seem unassimilated
and "fused" in such as way as to call attention to themselves as so
many textual *disiecta membra*—as *disiecta*, perhaps, as the "mangled
members" and "scattered scraps" into which the eponymous
Hippolytus is "torne" in the play by Seneca which, as Brooks contends,
looms curiously large over the *Dream*, albeit as one of its least
discussed sources.[2] To peer at the vasty deep of allusion in the *Dream*
is in part, of course, to pay homage to its intertextuality and to recall,
with Julia Kristeva, the Bakhtinian conception of "the 'literary word' as
an *intersection of textual surfaces* rather than a *point* (a fixed

meaning)."³ At the same time, to listen to the dissonant voices and competing discourses from which the *Dream* derives its inter-textuality and seemingly affirms what Barbara Mowat calls its "graven" origins,⁴ is to hear articulated another and metatheatrical discourse proclaiming the insistence of the play upon its own dramatic identity, and as something distinct from the divers texts that are its nutrients.

Indeed, any reference to "weaving" in the *Dream*—and, perhaps, a subliminal reason why Brooks modifies "weaves" with "fuses"— ineluctably evokes the lone professional weaver of the play and brings into at least parodic alignment the tropics of Shakespeare's "weaving" of his sources and the notorious adaptational labors whereby Bottom and his fellow artisans "weave" the story of Pyramus and Thisbe into the stuff of drama. In turn, though one may smile with Theseus at what he takes to be the generic indecorum in the artisans' "brief," which would elide "tragical" and "mirth" (5.1.56-60),⁵ the elision that so puzzles Theseus epitomizes the effect of the allusive collocations throughout the play, which is to elide and render precarious a great number of significant distinctions: distinctions of genre, time, and social status, distinctions between waking and dreaming, between "good fairies" and mischievous ones, and, most interestingly for our sense of the relationship of the play to its sources, between the "antique" and the "antick," an elision Theseus genially and self-interestedly perpetrates in his celebrated sortie into literary theory, when, acting as his own Lord Chamberlain, he conflates in order to dismiss "[t]hese antique fables" and "these fairy toys" as the "shaping fantasies" of "[l]overs and madmen" and their "seething brains" (5.1.3-5), thus reducing to one illusory compound the very mythography that had produced his own adverse, pre-production publicity. In this assault upon distinctions, we are reminded that this mirthful play of elisions takes as part of its "brief" the elisions to which human experience and its representation are all too susceptible. It is, then, with these elisions, and the role allusion plays in producing them, that this paper is also concerned.

I

To encounter the *Dream* with an eye and ear for the allusions Brooks and others so helpfully enumerate⁶ is, as we know, to find an admixture of discrete proverbial tags and quotations and evocations of "olden" and not so olden tales, with Chaucer and Seneca and Ovid jostling each other for verbal space with the Bible and with Shakespeare's contemporaries and folk wisdom and tales, an admixture metonymized in what seems to be an admirably multi-use, high-occupancy forest where so many activities, constituencies, and literary antecedents converge, or rather, collide. It is a forest "the character" of which, Peter Holbrook has recently noted, "is impossible to fix . . . in sociological or in any other terms: it is at once Ovidian and literary and the setting of old wives' tales, beautiful and ugly, incomparably charming and terrifying as well." [7] And, as numerous commentators have shown, it is a forest where "rude" juxtapositions notoriously transgress boundaries and elide categories simultaneously literary and social: "What hempen home-spuns have we swagg'ring here, / So near the cradle of the Fairy Queen?" (3.1.77-78), demands Puck, presently instrumental in placing the most swaggering of the homespuns *in* the royal cradle.[8] Yet, above all, the forest spatializes a central "trans"-action of the *Dream* in the degree to which it serves as a site of "translation." "Bless thee, Bottom, bless thee! Thou art translated," exclaims Quince, in helpless benediction in the face of Bottom's now formal asininity (3.1.118-19)—or, as Patricia Parker has wryly put it, "a *translatio* which . . . may involve a distinction without a difference."[9] And that the *Dream*, as Holbrook notes, is "about" translation would seem uncontroversial, especially if, with due regard for the evocations in the *Dream* of Ovid's *Metamorphoses*, "translation" is translated as "chang'd," Snout's word for the altered Bottom (3.1.114).[10]

Still, at the risk of steering towards an overly hermetic and aestheticized reading, I would suggest that the *Dream* is also "about" the metamorphoses wrought in translation as a process of verbal and artistic adaptation, a process that it persistently represents as a volatile commingling, and which, in its transgressive assault upon distinctions and partitions, makes the *Dream* for Parker, at least, a metonym for the workings of metaphor.[11] Though, for example, it would be chronologically "incorrect" for Helena to be up on her Seneca, either in its original or in John Studley's Elizabethan translation, and though it is unnerving enough for her to hear the newly awakened Lysander launch at her the avowals of amatory fealty he had most recently lavished upon Hermia, still it would only reinforce Helena's acute sense of the gender inversion to which she has been brought as a woman wooing a man (2.1.229-34, 238-42)—and, perhaps, give her due regard for the peversity of the classics—to hear in Lysander's waking promise, "And run through fire I will for thy sweet sake" (2.2.103), a close echo from the *Hippolytus*, though not of Hippolytus but of his stepmother Phaedra making her fatally improper advances.[12]

Still, as Walter Benjamin observes, "[t]ranslation is only a somewhat provisional way of coming to terms with the foreignness of languages,"[13] and "translation" in the *Dream* seems persistently "provisional," wreaking change that bears with it traces of its original, producing hybrids of the foreign and the domestic that at times render metamorphosis as something akin to transmogrification, with the products thereof rather misshapen, but not totally unrecognizable fantasies, like Lysander mouthing Phaedra's words. Thus, rather like one of his possible antecedents, the unhappy English sailor whose transformation into an ass Reginald Scot sceptically records[14] and whose restoration is achieved when he manages to kneel on his hind quarters and lift his forepaws in prayer outside a church,[15] Bottom, ass's head and Jan Kott notwithstanding, continues to be Bottom. Moreover, as Annabel Patterson has argued, Bottom is all the more socially frightening in the degree to which, contrary to the scenario of irruptive bestiality Kott envisioned,[16] Bottom's asininity is domesticated and he remains recognizable, his appetites a blend of a new craving for provender[17] and, from the perspective of the ruling classes, a socially nightmarish but all too comprehensible "bottom's up" and Simon Forman-like lust of the lower order for gentility through consummation with the queen.[18]

Indeed, the hybridity Bottom incarnates in comic *extremis* is replicated in a number of details that in their incongruity underscore their identity as translations, as borrowings from other texts more spliced onto than woven into their present surroundings. One seemingly innocuous and well-known example arises, after all, from what Patterson delicately terms the "calendrical vagueness" that would appear to ask the audience not to care that this play entitled *A Midsummer Night's Dream* suddenly acquires a May setting when Theseus, Hippolyta, Egeus, and "Train" stumble upon the sleeping quartet of lovers, an event which Theseus, never nonplussed in this play, glosses with the Theseo-centric theory that "No doubt they rose up early to observe / The rite of May; and hearing our intent, / Came here in grace of our solemnity" (4.1.132-34). Patterson notes that the ambiguity here "evidently worried" C.L. Barber,[19] who, in fact, being worried enough to deny at some length that he was worried at all, offers, instead, the disclaimer that "Shakespeare does not make himself accountable for exact chronological inferences," and then engages in some calendrical elision of his own, taking the "rite of May" as generic, and as a reference to the sort of festive May Day activity that people could perform "at various times."[20] Reasonable as this is, it is also true, as several have noted, and as I have argued elsewhere, that the coupling of Theseus with observations of the rite of May and a concern with "solemnity" effectively connect the Theseus of the *Dream* with his counterpart and antecedent in Chaucer's *The Knight's Tale*, where images of observing the May and solemnity cling to Theseus with something of the force of a signature and render him something of a walking solipsism, encased in his own ritual needs and solemnifying identity, ever construing events and individuals, as he does the supine lovers in the *Dream*, by his own pre-fixed clock and calendar.[21] And one's sense that Theseus's appearance here to observe the rite of May is an extension of a genuine pre-text that has come crashing into the *Dream* owes something to the very beginning of this scene, which commences with Theseus's reference to an "observation" just, "now," performed, the antecedents and substance of which, Barber's persuasive reconstructive efforts notwithstanding, are teasingly suppressed. In sum, the very incongruity of the reference italicizes it as a quotation and contributes to a sense of a distance between the play and the very things it quotes.

In turn, and with effects far more jarring, the sense that events and characters in the *Dream* are answerable to a variety of anterior texts gives those events their peculiar, and peculiarly arresting, illogic, while investing characters with fissionable tensions akin to schizophrenia. One thinks again, for example, of Helena, who would give almost everything to be "translated" into Hermia (1.1.191), until, of course, that translation occurs (3.2.145ff.). Introduced to us twice with epithets affiliating her as daughter and possession, respectively, of a personage, Nedar—later, Old Nedar—whom everyone in polite Athenian society seems to take for granted that they know but who is never seen (i.1.107; 4.1.130),[22] Helena shows her literary lineage to lie in the obsessivness and exquisitely inventive ability to operate against one's best interests that mark the classical, particularly in this case, Senecan heroine, displaying the rationality with which to discern the irrationality of her passion (1.1.231-39) and to acknowledge with

Phaedra in *Hyppolytus* that "[t]he thing that we should shun, we seeke,"[23] while being emotionally helpless to do anything but seek it and seek it with redoubled resourcefulness and masochistic persistence. Hence, having made a clinical assessment of Demetrius's perfidy towards her in one line, Helena determines in the very next to inform Demetrius of "fair Hermia's flight" with Lysander, so that Demetrius will "pursue" them, and she, sooner than later, Demetrius:

> And when this hail some heat from Hermia felt,
> So he dissolv'd and show'rs of oaths did melt.
> I will go tell him of fair Hermia's flight:
> Then to the wood will he, to-morrow night,
> Pursue her; and for this intelligence
> If I have thanks, it is a dear expense. (1.1.244-49)

At the same time, rather as if she were caught in a *contrapasso* from Dante, it is "Transparent" Helena's singularly bad fortune to embody the elision of two Senecan figures simultaneously; and, thus, if at first we encounter her in the forest playing Phaedra to Demetrius's Hippolytus, she soon, as we have seen, mimicks Hippolytus shunning Lysander's ventriloquized Phaedra.

If, however, it is our sense that Helena reflects the characteriological traits of a source generically at odds with the best interests and survival strategy of a romantic heroine, we find in Puck an even sharper abstract of the tendency of the play to "translate" its sources in such a way as to produce a promiscuous mingling of heterogeneous voices and impulses. Brooks has indicated a number of parallels between the *Dream* and Anthony Munday's *John a Kent and John a Cumber*,[24] a play which uses a parochial power struggle among the lords of Wales and neighboring Chester over marriage arrangements as a vehicle for pitting in sorcerous competition "white" magician John a Kent against "black" magician and nemesis John a Cumber; bringing the two necromancers and *doppelgangers* into such close proximity at times as to render them literally indistinguishable,[25] the play does little to allay popular anxieties about magic and its use as an instrument for gaining and extending power, implying in the process that the main distinction between "white" and "black" magicians is who employs whom, with "our" guy being the good magician, and "theirs" the bad one. In the *Dream* Shakespeare at once italicizes and collapses *this* distinction without a difference by making Puck the proximate cause of both kinds of magic and principal instrument in both the doing and undoing of mischief, making him at once responsive to and the agent of Oberon's "authorized" magic and the self-confessed retailer of many of the fairy pranks and "dirty tricks" contemporary English folklore had catalogued, both a significant operative and spokes-sprite for King Oberon's court, on the one hand, and "that shrewd and knavish sprite / Call'd Robin Goodfellow" (2.1.33-34), on the other.

The heteroglossia audible in the representations of Helena, Puck, and, most notoriously Theseus all play their part in making the *Dream* not simply a palimpsest, but something of an exercise in cognitive dissonance, an exercise in which the audience must exorcise or articulate an interpretative response to allusions with interpretative claims of their own that would introduce a thematic darkness into the comically sunny moonlight of the *Dream*'s central action and thereby check the drive of the play to that carnivalesque, festive, *Corriam tutti a festeggiar*, close Barber has been most instrumental in delineating.[26] How insistent these claims, and how evocative they are of contemporary socio- and psycho-cultural anxieties, have been compellingly demonstrated by Louis Montrose and Annabel Patterson, with Montrose's acutely psychoanalytical and heavily "gendered" contextualization of the play complemented and "translated" by Patterson into socio-economic terms that would have us read as symptoms of populist sentiment what Montrose would relegate, in Patterson's words, to the "author's and the national (male) unconscious."[27] Their divergencies notwithstanding, both Montrose and Patterson offer elegant accounts of the polysemous strands of the complex of allusion the *Dream* comprises. And yet, for all that they contribute to our reading of the *Dream* and to the dissection of its dissonances, both Montrose and Patterson scan the play in familiarly binary terms, representing the play of allusion in the *Dream* through couplings of contestatory polarities, subversion and containment on the one hand, hegemonic oppression and popular resistance on the other. And though Montrose's vision of Shakespeare's source materials as "the archaeological record of the texts which shaped the poet's fantasy as he was shaping his play," with references lying "sedimented within the verbal texture" of the *Dream*, does justice to the violent juxtapositions allusions produce in the *Dream*,[28] it leaves somewhat unexamined the violence the *Dream* seems to perpetrate upon allusion itself and the volatility it teases to the surface in the sources to which it alludes—their generic ambivalence, the instability and unreliability of the "history" they purport to represent. It is to these issues that I wish at once sketchily but cautiously to turn in the final section of this essay.

II

Perhaps it is because the *Dream* has not been associated with a principal literary or dramatic source—and has not even been haunted by that most ubiquitous of phantoms, the missing Ur-play—and, instead, has been parsed for its topicality and as the amalgam and intersection of a miscellany of texts and popular customs and beliefs,[29] but there is a curious sense in which the *Dream* seems at times to "enjoy" an adversative relationship with its sources, seeking, parasitically, to dissociate itself from and define itself as dramatic entity against the various textual shreds and patches that it cannibalizes. In no instance would this dissociation and declaration of theatrical independence appear to be trumpeted more volubly and with the force of a *reductio ad absurdum* than, of course, in the surgery, no, vivisection, to which Peter Quince and his colleagues subject the story of Pyramus and Thisbe, in which infelicities of script and "difficulties" of staging combine to produce not only a "most" memorably "lament-able comedy," but a travesty which thematizes the fissures between theater and the *matere* it evokes. And yet it could be argued, as E. Talbot Donaldson's close synoptic scrutiny of Quince's Ovidian and Chaucerian antecedents would suggest, that the excesses that invest the Pyramus and Thisbe production in the *Dream* with its hilarity reflect not simply an incompetent misappropriation of sources, but a fidelity to them, with the absurdities of the "rude mechanicals'" script and performances at once an evocation of their *auctors* and an illumination and elision of the fine distinctions between the pathetic and bathetic to which Chaucer and Ovid, Donaldson would maintain, wittily and yet precariously adhere.[30] After all, the wounded "pap of Pyramus; / Ay, that left pap" (5.1.297-98), seems but a demurely dry spiggot in comparison with the broken "condit" simile Chaucer employs at the corresponding moment in his rehearsal of the story in *The Legend of Good Women*[31] and with the veritable geyser Ovid, both in the original and in Golding's translation, describes in lovingly gushing and hissing detail in the *Metamorphoses*:

> cruor emicat alte;
> Non aliter, quam cum vitiato fistula plumbo
> Scinditur, et tenues stridente foramine longe
> Ejaculatur aquas; atque ictibus aera rumpit.

> the bloud did spin on hie
> As when a Conduite pipe is crackt, the water bursting out
> Doth shote it selfe a great way off and pierce the Ayre about.[32]

And if the generic premises and integrity of the story seem compromised in the artisans' "tediously brief" commingling of "tragical mirth," it is not clear that a 'straight' version of the story is to be found. Certainly a no less corrosive and self-annihilative, if subtler, playfulness inheres in Chaucer's rehearsal of the story, where the narrator, commanded by love's deity to write positively of love *and* women, seems at a loss to draw an appropriate moral for his story. Chiding Thisbe, on the one hand, for abandoning "alle hire frendes" and reposing all her trust in a man, he is unable, on the other hand, to arraign Pyramus for any failing more serious than tardiness; in fact, quite in danger of forgetting his charge and theme, the narrator offers a concluding encomium for Pyramus as a model of masculine fidelity, only to add as if in an afterthought an obligatory couplet in praise of Thisbe:

> Of trewe men I fynde but fewe mo
> In alle my bokes, save this Piramus,
> And therfore have I spoken of hym thus.
> Fir it is deynte to us men to fynde
> A man that can in love ben trewe and kynde.
> Here may ye se, what lovere so he be,
> A woman dar and can as wel as he.[33]

To the degree to which the *Dream* does, nevertheless, convey an impression of distancing itself from the sources to which it is indebted, such an impression is in large measure a result of a thematic manipulation by the two most authoritative figures in the *Dream*, Theseus and Oberon, both of whom arrogate to themselves significant parts of the direction of the narrative thread of the play and are at pains, in various ways, to insist upon their difference from the very nutrients of their definition which the play provides. "But we are spirits of another sort" (3.2.388), Oberon intones benevolently, seeking most immediately to establish a clear distance between himself and those "[d]amned spirits all" (382) whose return from their sociopathic wanderings Puck, with surely a tad of hypocrisy, has just declared to be imminent (377-87). More generally, however, Oberon may also be seeking to distance himself from everything else the audience has been told or shown in the play concerning the realm of faerie, including both his own involvement in the miscues of the night and his close association with his subordinate in mischief, Puck, to whom Oberon, like any decent administrator, has delegated tasks, and to whom, like any skillful adminstrator, he has assigned blame when the administrator's schemes have gone awry (3.2.88-91). In affiliating himself with "spirits of another sort," of course, it could be argued that Oberon is assuming that his Spenserian status as "mightie Oberon," father of Gloriana herself,[34] would be so well known as to need no gloss, though, if so, the omission represents that purest form of praeterition, in which that which can be passed over actually gets passed over! Similarly, the "spirits of another sort" could, as Brooks urges, link the Oberon of the *Dream* to his namesake, the King of the Fairies in *Huon of Bordeux*, though to think so is to suggest an association a good deal less flattering to the image of Shakespeare's Oberon than Brooks would have us believe.[35] To be sure, one principal characteristic the two Oberons share is, as Brooks notes, their tendency to define themselves by what they are not, or would have one believe they are not, namely, "bad" fairies.[36] Yet so insistent is the Oberon of *Huon of Bordeux* upon demonstrating his "white" magic and benef-icence, that there is no amount of "black" magic and torment he is unwilling to inflict in order to gain an audience and display his numinous wares.[37] Hence, to affiliate the Oberon of the *Dream* with his counterpart in *Huon of Bordeux* is to underscore the former's capacity for good *and* ill, whatever "sort" of spirit he claims to be for the nonce, and in the "momentany" space of the play. And though the Oberon of the *Dream* is at pains to dissociate his nuptial blessings, on this occasion at least, from "the blots of Nature's hand" (5.1.409) and the other deformities he recites in apophasis in his closing benediction, his very recitation effectively invokes the very spirits he would banish, rendering precarious the alterity to which he would cling and reinforcing for some members of his audience the precarious proximity of the forces of good and evil.[38]

As for Theseus, there is even more to hide, and Shakespeare is sufficiently ruthless as to allow us hints of what is being suppressed and of Theseus's own ruthlessness in suppressing it. Investing his appearances, as we have seen, in the wrappings of Chaucerian "solemnity," the play would seem to do its best to allow Theseus to project as primary the image Brooks and others have claimed for him, namely, that of "a ruler who is truly kinglike,"[39] while, as we know, marginalizing but not fully suppressing incidents from classical lore that give Theseus a more tarnished, certainly more mixed, reputation.[40] Thus, references to Theseus's pre-Hippolytan amours issue from Oberon in his ill-met and moonlit encounter with Titania (2.1.74-80), and in the process are doubly marginalized: first, since they are *not* the principal focus of Oberon and Titania's argument; and secondly, since in being rhetoricized and adduced as so much fodder in Oberon's attack and counter-attack upon Titania, they are left readily vulnerable to Titania's dismissal of them as "the forgeries of jealousy" (81).

Theseus's own part in the suppression of embarrassing allusion seems most in evidence in his self-appointed role as censor and selector of ducal entertainment, when, as if to administer some terrible object lesson on what happens in governmental funding of the arts in the absence of decent peer review processes, Shakespeare has Theseus choose the artisans' production and excuse the three alternatives. Montrose has, of course, commented on the ways in which some of the rejected material here evokes what he terms "the discourse of anxious misogyny which persists as an echo within Shakespeare's text,"[41] a discourse which Theseus's amatory notoriety might well incline him to suppress on the day of his wedding. Yet what is more to our purpose here is the degree to which aesthetic decorums and the distinction between what would make a good play and what would make a good play for the occasion get interestingly elided and enlisted in the stifling of allusion. So it is that with a cunning lack of rigor and priority Theseus's objections to the rejected scripts slide from the potentially substantive, "We'll none of that"—with uncertain inflection on the "that"—(5.1.46), to appeals to the criterion of "freshness," with variations on I've-already-told-the-story (46) and It's-been-done-before (50-51), to objections on the grounds of antiquity—"That is an

old device"(50), and socio-aesthetic incongruity—"That is some satire,
keen and critical, / Not sorting with a nuptial ceremony" (54-55).

Laboring to keep the foreground of the play clear of the less
flattering details of his *résumé*, Theseus nonetheless gives voice to
some of the very source material he would silence, opportunistically
articulating in his own criticism anxieties within that material which,
on one level, challenge its validity, and, on another, raise metatheatrical
questions about the relationship of the play to the sources to which it
alludes. Exemplary is Theseus's venture into psycho-aesthetics in
which he conflates the "lunatic, the lover, and the poet" as "of imagination all compact," and as distillers of "antique fables" "[m]ore
strange than true" (5.1.2-22). Worth noting at the outset is the gratu-
itousness of Theseus's discourse. Cued by Hippolyta's simple one-line
observation that "'Tis strange, my Theseus, that these lovers speak of"
(1), Theseus's fulsome dismissal seems disproportionate to the task of
commenting on Hippolyta's comment on the account Lysander,
Hermia, Demetrius, and Helena have presumably been offering of their
moonlit sylvan adventures, and would appear to be stalking bigger
game. And, of course, it is; given the peccadilloes attributed to him in
literary tradition, it is certainly in Theseus's interests to equate poets
and lunatics, on the one hand, and to imply that "antique" or "olden"
tales are inseparably "antic" tales, on the other. Condescending and
clearly self-serving, Theseus's speech echoes contemporary distrust of
poets and their power to provide "shapes" to "things unknown" and to
give "aery nothing / A local habitation and a name" (5.1.15-17),[42] but
more to our point, it also echoes the intermittent irritation and
petulance about the historical reliability of poetic sources to be found
in one of the main repositories of information about Theseus, and one
of Shakespeare's "likely" sources, Thomas North's Plutarch. As
Mowat has observed, "[a]t every point in Plutarch's 'Life of Theseus'
are irreconcilable stories."[43] Awash in *sunt qui*'s, and ringing changes
upon *fama est*, North's Plutarch on Theseus is a patchwork of what
"some say," and what "others write," ultimately offering a biography of
Theseus definitive in all details save those concerning his parentage,
his death, and the major events, achievements, and *faux pas* of his
life.[44] "We are not to marvell, if the historie of things so auncient, be
founde so diversely written," Plutarch rather defensively reminds his
reader, as he sedulously sets forth and weighs the contradictory claims
about Theseus's life advanced by "Historiographers" and "Poets,"

attributing a dubious claim to the "devise of Poets," anticipating Hamlet in his sense of the power of dramatic poetry in particular to make or break a public reputation. Witness the case of King Minos of Crete, who, whether deserved or not, suffered the "ill report" of Athenian dramatists:

> thereby we maye see howe perilous a thing it is, to fall in displeasure and enmitie with a cittie, which can speak well, and where learning and eloquence dothe florishe. For ever sence that time, Minos was allwayes blased and disgraced through out all the Theaters of Athens. The testimonie of Hesiodus, who calleth him the most worthie King, dothe nothing helpe him at all, nor the prayse of Homer, who nameth him Iupiters famillier friende: bicause the tragicall Poets gott the upper hande in disgracing him, notwithstanding all these. And upon their stages where all the tragedies were played, they still gave forth many ill favored wordes, and fowle speaches of him: as against a man that had bene most cruell and unnaturall.[45]

The destructive power of theater Plutarch so decries is the power inherent in poetry to create *ex nihilo*, the power to give "shapes" to "things unknown" that Theseus simultaneously disparages and exploits as he distances himself from the very materials from which he fetches his identity.

To this point the *Dream* would seem to make an easy and familiar accommodation with voicings of efforts to suppress or dissociate the play from the more unpleasant echoes that hover about and impugn its comic action: voicing the efforts at suppression, it simultaneously gives voice to what would be suppressed, establishing a subversive resonance in a minor key at an audible, but not dangerously audible, distance from Theseus's cooptive elision of the productions of theater with his interests and, by definition, those of the state. Yet, though there is little reason to acquiesce in readings of the play that would identify Theseus with Shakespeare and take as Shakespearean ventriloquism Theseus's condescending and self-serving utterances on poetry, drama, *or* love, still, in Theseus's self-interested rupture with the past, or with, at least, the texts from which his own identity proceeds, and in his effort to command the dramatic present of the *Dream*, there coincide the generic claims of the play to contemporaneity, to temporal immediacy, a coincidence established in the opening word of the play. With "Now,

fair Hippolyta, our nuptial hour / Draws on apace" (1.1.1-2), we are
introduced to Theseus's proleptic desire to collapse four days into the
immediate moment, a prolepsis which the play mirrors in its own
temporal economies, and which it echoes in its reiterative insistence on
the word "now,"[46] an insistence which, with its potential for temporal
distortion, is memorably amplified in Bottom's enactment of the
"tedious brief scene" of Pyramus's death: "Now am I dead, / Now am I
fled . . . Now die, die, die, die, die" (5.1.301-06).

Operating by its own temporal laws, the stage follows those laws,
we might infer from the *Dream*, in the incisions and excisions it makes
on the materials and discourses that are its sources. "Say, what
abridgement have you for this evening?" (5.1.39) Theseus demands of
Philostrate, and, again, his impatience for some "abridgement" with
which to shorten time happily coincides with the "abridgement" that is
the stuff and "rough magic" of theatrical translation, "abridgement"
comprising both miniaturization and excision and, thus, reserving to
itself the right to revise and distort. Hence, the operations the *Dream*
performs in its translation of its sources share a kinship with the figure
of *hyppalage* through which I Corinthians finds its way into "Bottom's
Dream" (4.1.211-13) and which surfaces in parts of Peter Quince's
script (5.1.192-93), not to mention the punctuation of his prologue
(5.1.108-17). Indeed, it is the figure George Puttenham dubs "the
Changeling,"[47] an especially apt figure with which to describe the
furtive workings of allusion in the *Dream*, where references to
disembodied personages like "Nedar" seem to come to us from
contexts not always recoverable, and where a central complication of
the "plot" is ignited by a dispute over a changeling boy whom we never
see. In fact, to square the circle, we find both the figure of *hyppalage*
and Puttenham's iconic identification of it as the changeling personified in Theseus: his representation in the play the product of theatrical
distortion, the penumbra enveloping his origins and parentage, his self-
fashioned emergence as the self-proclaimed son of a father who comes
within moments of poisoning him—it is, indeed, a wise father that
knows his own child!—and his curious status as an imitation and
substitute Hercules are all the stuff that narratives of changelings are
"made on."[48]

Yet how furtive the workings of allusion in the *Dream*, and how
complicit the interests of the play in "weaving" the past into the
"momentany" needs of the dramatic present can be with the interests of

a Theseus in suppressing that past are framed in that moment from act 4 cited above when, as if coming from "another part of the forest" and another text, and to the accompaniment of horns blowing, "Theseus, [Hippolyta, Egeus,] *and all his* Train" (4.1.102 s.d.) arrive fresh from performing their "observation" (104) and moments before discovering the still sleeping lovers (128).[49] Like so much of the action of the *Dream*, the moments Theseus and Hippolyta spend before they discover the lovers are moments in which they have nothing to do, and as at other such moments, Theseus's impulse is to "abridge" time by eliding idleness and art to produce entertainment, though how entertaining the means at Theseus and Hippolyta's disposal can be requires some thought, indeed, some imagination. "We will," Theseus directs his "fair queen, up to the mountain's top, / And mark the musical confusion / Of hounds and echo in conjuction" (4.1.109-111). That there should be a mountaintop readily available—though one which Theseus and Hippolyta are spared the necessity of having to pretend to climb by their timely discovery of the sleeping lovers—is simply another interesting feature of this well-endowed forest, though the physical distance it provides would have been essential to the aesthetic distancing required to turn the sounds of dogs on the hunt into something worth listening to, into something genuinely symphonic: "the musical confusion / Of hounds and echo in conjunction." The scene here is, of course, a moment rather like that moonlit dialogue between Jessica and Lorenzo at Belmont at the opening of the last act of *The Merchant of Venice* (5.1.1-24), in that it represents an attempt to wrest beauty from and aestheticize misery, misery made audible in this case, not simply by the hounds, however cacophonous they might be up close, but by the hunting scenes from classical lore these hounds "echo." One such scene echoed here, as Mowat reminds us, is Ovid's account of the metamorphosis and destruction of Actaeon, a story which in mythologizing the punishment wrought by Diana upon male amatory transgression—albeit of a voyeuristic sort—offers a precedent Theseus would presumably not yearn to recall on the eve of his nuptials.[50] No less dismally, the Spartan and Cretan pedigrees recalled here evoke yet another scene of canine ferocity in their recollection of, as Brooks notes, the hunting scene in the forest at the opening of the *Hippolytus*, which in its wildness, replete with "Spartayne Dogges,"[51] the pedigree Theseus proudly claims for his hounds (118), metonymizes the "confusion" of wild, destructive, and self-destructive passions that propels the tragedy of the play. Given his own sorry role in that tragedy, of course, this is hardly the sort of echo Theseus would have been interested in hearing, and, worse, his dilemma is exacerbated by the fact that in the degree to which it evokes the *Hippolytus* and, thus, the offspring of Theseus's Amazonian bride,[52] the scene looks back to the future, and to the rather unhappy events following Theseus's "nuptial hour," to the consummation of which the entire action of the play is but a prolepsis, albeit, in Theseus's view, a protracted one (1.1.3-6). Hence, in the "confusion" of Theseus's hendiatic "hounds and echo in conjunction" the past and future collide and are elided in a prismatic and allusive present, an elision quietly incarnated in the temporal ambiguities of Theseus's epithet for Hippolyta, "fair queen" (108), since Hippolyta, *regina quondam reginaque futura*, is and is not a queen, certainly not the queen she once was, nor yet even the duchess she is about to become.

Indeed, like the dialogue between Jessica and Lorenzo, this curious interlude is a moment marked by dramatic dissonances, a dissonance between, as we have seen, the pleasure Theseus derives—or expects to derive—from the symphony of hounds and their echoes and the unpleasant associations those echoes bear, a corresponding dissonance between the concord Theseus enjoys, thinks he enjoys, or aspires to enjoy with Hippolyta, and the hints of discord their discourse actually yields. Some years ago D'Orsay W. Pearson noted the evocations of marital strife that mark the pre-marital interaction of Theseus and Hippolyta throughout the play,[53] and here it would, indeed, seem that, like their subsequent "discussion" of the dramatic merits of the artisans' play, even a discussion of the merits of hunting dogs, past and present, becomes for Hippolyta and Theseus the continuation of warfare by other means. Exemplifying the fictive uses to which history can be put, allusion here becomes for Hippolyta and Theseus a thoroughfare for divergent associations and a catalyst for a curious competition. Theseus's reasonably imperative indication that "We will . . . up to the mountain's top / And mark the musical confusion / Of hounds and echo in conjunction" immediately unleashes, as it were, in Hippolyta recollection of an earlier hunting party with a canine sound show, Hippolyta makes clear, Theseus's hounds will not readily wipe from the table of her memory:

> I was with Hercules and Cadmus once,

> When in a wood of Crete they bay'd the bear
> With hounds of Sparta. Never did I hear
> Such gallant chiding; for, besides the groves,
> The skies, the fountains, every region near
> Seem all one mutual cry. I never heard
> So musical a discord, such sweet thunder. (4.1.112-18)

For numerous reasons, Theseus would not be likely to find Hippolyta's remembrance soothing. Embedded in Hippolyta's implicit challenge to the musical ability of Theseus's hounds, is, after all, a deeper, more wounding display of one-upsmanship. Surely even in liberated times hardly any prospective bridegroom is put fully at ease in hearing his prospective bride rhapsodize about the good times she had had in others' company, and the names and places Hippolyta cites might be especially unsettling. Claiming to have been "with" Cadmus "once," Hippolyta effectively pulls rank on Theseus by affiliating herself with an anterior, more mythic pre-Thesean age, an age sufficiently mythic to be even more insusceptible to historical verification than the mists of legends enveloping and mediating Theseus. In including Hercules in the party, Hippolyta only reneacts what Plutarch does repeatedly in his account of Theseus, which is, as we have noted, to associate Hercules with many of Theseus's major exploits as something of an heroic big brother and precedent setter, someone who has either gotten there first or done first what Theseus accomplishes later.[54] And in situating this hunting party in Crete, Hippolyta displaces Theseus from the very terrain of the deed for which he was accorded his greatest renown, the slaying of the Minotaur. Moreover, in calling attention to a slice of her life before Theseus, Hippolyta only calls attention to the nebula of how precisely she—or was it Antiopa?—and Theseus first came to be acquainted, whether he "woo'd" her with his sword, as he claims (1.1.16) or, as one account would have it, "by deceit and stealth," enticing her aboard his ship, only to sail away,[55] or, for that matter, whether he won her at all, or was simply given her as booty by, naturally, Hercules.[56]

Theseus's rejoinder is interesting, most obviously, perhaps, for its comic defensiveness: his hounds are also "bred out of the Spartan kind" (119), and they produce a "cry more tuneable" than anything Hippolyta, Hercules, and Cadmus could have heard in any mythic romps they might have had "[i]n Crete, in Sparta, nor in Thessaly"

(126). And Theseus's desire to suppress potentially invidious testimony from the past or the sources from which he proceeds is plainly manifest, not only in his defense of his dogs' vocal ability, but in his very anti-Wordsworthian insistence that they, and implicitly he, be judged on the basis of immediate, not recollected experience. Behind the parrying of thrusts between Hippolyta and Theseus here lies a deeper dissagreement the play allegorizes about the uses of allusion and art. If for Hippolyta art and allusion, personified in the baying of the hounds and metonymized in their echo, are a summons to memory and reflection—no matter how selective its operations—for Theseus, here and elsewhere, art and allusion are the stuff of easy listening, a "confusion" of sound and echo elided not to be sorted out, but to be used as an inducement to immediate pleasure, a position for which he has the support of dramatic exigency. "But soft! What nymphs are these?" Theseus peremptorily asks about the sleeping forms and their now properly distributed beaux we are to believe he has only just noticed (127), a dramatic irruption that suspends and rescues Theseus from a potentially unpleasant debate. And though Hippolyta's dogged recollections introduce a dissonance into the scene that Theseus would surely have preferred to suppress, the debate has the effect of keeping the past it evokes and colonizes safely aestheticized, and, for its short duration, stays at a level at which Theseus can even compete. Aestheticized, or examined as standards by which to assess the aesthetic merits of the present, the horrors of the past can be decontextualized and domesticated, displaced and trivialized as so much background noise to the reassuringly narrowed evaluative questions of whose dogs brayed better and, subsequently, why a play may or may not "work": "Judge when you hear" (4.1.126), Theseus's *credo* in this play, is an appeal to immediacy as an evaluative criterion with which the past or the testimony of sources cannot compete. In the process of allusive retrieval and translation, and through the reconciling prestidigitation of oxymoron, the "discord" of the past remains audible but audibly "musical," while its "thunder" is rendered "sweet."

NOTES

1. Harold F. Brooks, ed., *The Arden Shakespeare: A Midsummer Night's Dream* (London: Methuen, 1979), lxxxv. To demonstrate the polysemous "wovenness" through which Shakespeare's *Dream*, and the figure

of Theseus in particular, emerge from, and as, an intricate mosaic of literary sources is also, of course, the aim and accomplishment of Barbara Mowat's compelling study, "'A local habitation and a name': Shakespeare's Text as Construct," *Style* 23 (1989): 335-51.

2. Seneca, *Hippolytus*, trans. John Studley, in *Seneca His Tenne Tragedies*, ed. Thomas Newton (1581; rpt. Bloomington: Indiana University Press, 1964), 183; Brooks, lxii-iii. See also the attention paid to the *disiecta membra* of Seneca's Hyppolytus by Louis Montrose in *The Purpose of Playing: Shakespeare and the Cultural Politics of the Elizabethan Theatre* (Chicago: University of Chicago Press, 1996), 147,n.44.

3. Julia Kristeva, *Desire in Language: A Semiotic Approach to Literature and Art*, ed. Leon S. Roudiez, trans. Roudiez, Thomas Gora, and Alice Jardine (New York: Columbia University Press, 1980), 65.

4. Mowat, 335.

5. Citations of *A Midsummer Night's Dream* and *The Merchant of Venice* are taken from *The Riverside Shakespeare*, ed. G. Blakemore Evans (Boston: Houghton Mifflin, 1974) and will appear in parentheses in the text.

6. See Geoffrey Bullough, *Narrative and Dramatic Sources of Shakespeare* (London: Routledge and Kegan Paul, 1957), 1: 366-76; Kenneth Muir, *The Sources of Shakespeare's Plays* (New Haven: Yale University Press, 1978), 66-77.

7. Peter Holbrook, *Bourgeois Tragedy Literature and Degree in Renaissance England: Nashe, Shakespeare* (Newark: University of Delaware Press, 1994).

8. Besides Holbrook, ibid., 109-17, see Montrose, *The Purpose of Playing*, esp. 169-78; Jonathan Crewe, *Hidden Designs: The Critical Profession and Renaissance Literature* (New York: Methuen, 1986), 138-51; and Annabel Patterson, *Shakespeare and the Popular Voice* (Oxford: Basil Blackwell, 1989), 66-70.

9. Patricia Parker, "Anagogic Metaphor: Breaking Down the Wall of Partition," in *Centre and Labyrinth: Essays in Honour of Northrop Frye*, eds. Eleanor Cook, *et alia* (Toronto: University of Toronto Press, 1983), 46.

10. Holbrook, 109.

11. Parker, 44.

12. Seneca, 161.

13. Walter Benjamin, "The Task of the Translator: An Introduction to the Translation of Baudelaire's *Tableaux Parisiens*," in *Illuminations: Essays and Reflections*, trans. Harry Zohn (New York: Schocken Books, 1969), 75.

14. Reginald Scot, *The Discoverie of Witchcraft*, introduction by Hugh Ross Williamson (Carbondale: Southern Illinois University Press, 1964), 95-97. At the conclusion of his account of the sailor's miraculous transformation and restoration, Scot ruefully notes that "witchmongers" have derived much capital from such stories "speciallie bicause *S. Augustine* subscribeth thereunto; or at the least to the verie like," (97).

15. Ibid., 96.

16. Jan Kott, *Shakespeare Our Contemporary*, trans. Boleslaw Taborski (New York: W.W. Norton, 1974), 223-29.

17. A dietary alteration, Brooks reminds us, that Scot records in his inventory of "special" transubstantiations. See Brooks, lx; and Scot, 97. As is noted both by Muir, 68, and Brooks, lix, Shakespeare was not likely to have been unfamiliar with the story of a man's transformation to an ass in Apuleius's *The Golden Ass*, translated in 1566 by William Adlington.

18. See in particular Patterson, 64-67, on the socio-political implications.

19. Ibid., 64.

20. C.L. Barber, *Shakespeare's Festive Comedy: A Study of Dramatic Form and Its Relation to Social Custom* (Princeton: Princeton University Press, 1959), 120-21.

21. Besides Muir, 66, and Brooks, lxxxv, see Ann Thompson, *Shakespeare's Chaucer: A Study in Literary Origins* (New York: Barnes & Noble, 1978), 88-89; Thomas Moisan, "Chaucerian *Solempnytee* and the Illusion of Order in Shakespeare's Athens and Verona," *Upstart Crow* 7 (1987): 41-46; and E. Talbot Donaldson, *The Swan at the Well: Shakespeare Reading Chaucer* (New Haven: Yale University Press, 1985), 32ff.

22. To whom or what, if anything, the name "Nedar" may be an allusion has so far resisted critical detection. In *The Variorum Shakespeare: A Midsummer Night's Dream* (Philadelphia: J.B. Lippincott, 1895), 15, Horace Howard Furness dismisses the conjecture that "Nedar" is a printer's corruption of the more recognizable "Nestor"; invoking the Shakespearean source hunter's congenital predilection for an authoritative but missing dramatic original—see note #29—Furness entertains the possibility that "Nedar" is "perchance, a reminiscence of the original," but finds it "more likely [that] this familiar reference is designed merely to give vividness," a view seconded by Ernst Erler, *Die Namengebung bei Shakespeare* (Heidelberg: Carl Winter's Universitätsbuchhandlung, 1913), 46, in commenting on "*die Lebenswarheit*" the name adds. Recently, drawing interpretative capital from the penumbra surrounding the name, Terence Hawkes, *Meaning by Shakespeare* (London: Routledge, 1992), 27ff., postulates that "Nedar" is derived from a river in

ancient Greece called the "Neda" and from a nymph by the same name, which enables Hawkes to hypothesize that "[a]n 'old Neda' could easily be Helena's mother," and as such one of a cluster of "older women" whom the text of the *Dream* incorporates only to marginalize. Complicating our sense of the patriarchalist pressures at work in the *Dream*, Hawkes's inclusion of Nedar among the "missing matriarchs" has the immediate effect of exposing as an assumption the recurrent identification of "Nedar's" as a patrilinear epithet, and Hawkes's sense of "Nedar" as "an uncomplicated anagram of 'Arden', a Hellenized version of something essentially English," 15, would only underscore the relationship in the play of allusion and elision.

23. Seneca, 161.

24. Brooks, lxv.

25. Anthony Munday, *An Edition of Anthony Munday's John A Kent and John A Cumber*, ed. Arthur E. Pennell (New York: Garland, 1980), 143.

26. Paradigmatic is Barber's assertion in *Shakespeare's Festive Comedy*, that "[t]he confident assumption dominant in *A Midsummer Night's Dream*, that substance and shadow can be kept separate, determines the peculiarly unshadowed gaiety of the fun it makes with fancy" (161).

27. Montrose's reading of the *Dream*, first formulated in his influential essay, "'Shaping Fantasies': Figuration of Gender and Power in Elizabethan Culture," *Representations* 1 (1983): 61-94, has most recently appeared in expanded and even more exhaustively historicized form in *The Purpose of Playing*, 109-205. For Patterson, see *Shakespeare and the Popular Voice*, 52-70, esp., 65, for her comment on Montrose.

28. Montrose, *The Purpose of Playing*, 147.

29. Well, almost unhaunted. While prefacing his own discussion of the sources with the comment that "[t]here was probably no comprehensive source of *A Midsummer Night's Dream*," Muir, 66, then cites a reference by Thomas Nashe in 1589 to "a play about the King of the Fairies."

30. Donaldson, 18-22.

31. Hence, vowing in apostrophe to make Thisbe's gnawed wimple "feele as wel the blod of me / As thow hast felt the bledyng of Thisbe," Chaucer's Pyramus immediately stabs himself, whereupon "The blod out of the wounde as brode sterte/As water, whan the condit broken is." See Chaucer, *The Legend of Good Women*, in *The Works of Geoffrey Chaucer*, 3rd ed., ed Larry D. Benson (Boston: Houghton Mifflin, 1987), lines 848-52.

32. For the Latin original, see Ovid, *Metamorphoses*, with an English translation by Frank Justus Miller, 3rd ed., rev. G.P. Goold (Cambridge: Harvard University Press), vol.1: book 4, lines 121-24; for Golding's rendition,

see Ovid's *Metamorphoses: The Arthur Golding Translation* (1567), ed. John Frederick Nims (New York: Macmillan, 1965), book 4, lines 147-49.

33. Chaucer, *The Legend of Good Women*, lines 917-23.

34. Edmund Spenser, *The Faerie Queene*, in *The Complete Poetical Works of Edmund Spenser*, ed. R.E. Neil Dodge (Cambridge, Mass.: Riverside Press, 1936), bk. 2, canto 10, stanzas 75-76.

35. Brooks, xxv-vi.

36. Ibid., lix.

37. Thus, the heading for chapter 22 in Berners's translation in the 1601 edition aptly reads, "How King Oberon was right sorrowfull and sore displeased, in that Huon would not speake: and of the great feare that he put Huon and his companie in." See Bullough, 1: 393-94.

38. For Scot, the intellectual credulity of those who believe in the power of witches is inseparable from a spiritual deficiency that leads "witchmongers" to attribute to witches phenomena divinely manufactured. Hence, "[s]uch faithlesse people (I saie) are also persuaded, that neither haile nor snowe, thunder nor lightening, raine nor tempestuous winds come from the heavens at the commandement of God: but are raised by the cunning and power of witches and conjurors" (25-26).

39. Brooks, lxxix.

40. How "mixed" that reputation is, and how much the essential Theseus is but an amalgam of glorious attribution and inglorious allegation, all resistant to verification, are implicit in the note of *apologia* struck at the outset of Theseus's "life" in Plutarch, North's version (of Amyot's version) of whom we generally take to be Shakespeare's principal source for the classical "take" on Theseus. In an exculpatory fit of methodological petulance that might be dubbed an historian's pre-response to Sidney's *Defence of Poesie*, Plutarch prefaces his account of Theseus by lamenting the historian's dependence upon poets for biographical data: "Wherein I would wishe that the invention of Poets, and the traditions of fabulous antiquitie, would suffer them selves to be purged and reduced to the forme of a true and historicall reporte: but when they square too much from likelyhode, and can not be made credible, the readers will of curtesie take in good parte that, which I could with most probability wryte of such antiquities." See Plutarch, *The Life of Theseus*, in *Plutarch's Lives of the Noble Grecians and Romans Englished by Sir Thomas North* (1579), intro. George Wyndham (1895; rpt. New York: AMS Press, 1967), 1: 29-30.

41. Montrose, *The Purpose of Playing*, 148.

42. Mowat, 343-46, is particularly alert to the ways in which the skepticism of Theseus's discourse on things unseen is anticipated by Reginald Scot in *The Discoverie of Witchcraft*. Hence, like Theseus who sees the poet forming a triumvirate of imaginative excess with the "lunatic, [and] the lover" (5.1.7), we hear Scot recite the "miraculous actions [that] are imputed to witches by witchmongers, papists, and poets" (31-32).

43. Mowat, 337.

44. To look merely at the beginning and end of Theseus's *curriculum vitae*, his birth is enveloped in the sort of nebula reserved for figures of mythology, prompting Plutarch to liken Theseus to Romulus: "For being both begotten by stealth, and out of lawful matrimony: both were reputed to be borne of the seede of the goddes" (30). As for his death, Plutarch is certain that Theseus died of a fall from a great height on the Island of Sciros, though what precisely Theseus was doing on the island, and whether he was pushed or fell accidentally during a post-supper stroll, Plutarch admits, 65-66, are matters of differing reports.

45. Ibid., 42-43, 57; see also Plutarch's complaints about the historiographical infelicities of poets and tragedians, pp. 29-30.

46. In *Hidden Designs*, Crewe notes the "glaring and well-known temporal discrepancy" between the four days Theseus announces at the outset as the amount of time he and Hippolyta will need to wait until their wedding (1.1.1-3), and the fact that the wedding proceeds "after the single wild night that elapses in the play" (136). To be sure, that "single wild night" does not, it would appear, occur until the night of the day after the day on which the play begins, to reckon, at least, by Lysander's proposal to Hermia that they elope "[t]omorrow night" (1.1.209). The word "now" occurs, in fact, sixty-five times in *A Midsummer Night's Dream*, which makes the *Dream* just a bit above average among Shakespeare's plays in the frequency of its use of the word.

47. George Puttenham, *The Arte of English Poesie*, ed. Gladys Doidge Willcock and Alice Walker (Cambridge: Cambridge University Press, 1936), 171.

48. See the account in Plutarch's *Life of Theseus* of Theseus's nativity, 30-31; his acceptance as Aegeus's son, 39-40; and the formative role Hercules plays in Theseus's heroic "self-fashioning," 34-35.

49. In his textual note for 4.1.101 in the *Riverside Shakespeare*, 248, G.B. Evans alludes to the stage direction from F1, "Sleepers Lye still" which, immediately preceding the entrance of Theseus "and all his Train," only italicizes the jaggedness of the juxtaposition of the two pieces of stage business

and the impression of "unwovenness" that Shakespeare's admixture of his
sources in the play sometimes conveys.

50. Ovid, *Metamorphoses*, trans. Miller, vol. 3: book 3, lines 177-252;
Mowat, 341.

51. Seneca, 137-38; Brooks, lxiii.

52. Though whom precisely Theseus married is, of course, a matter of
debate. Plutarch, 55-58, claims to be following several sources in identifying
the Amazon whom Theseus "ravished" and carried away as booty by the name
Antiopa, but concedes that one "Historiographer," Clidemus, insists that it was
Hippolyta who negotiated the terms of a peace treaty with Theseus and in turn
became his bride. Landing with vigor on what he can claim with assurance,
Plutarch concludes, "Howsoever it was, it is most certain that this warre was
ended by agreement."

53. D'Orsay W. Pearson, "Male Sovereignty, Harmony and Irony in *A
Midsummer Night's Dream*," *Upstart Crow* 7 (1987): 31-33.

54. Typically, Plutarch notes, on the one hand, that Theseus is credited by
one ancient historian with having been instrumental in "the first treatie that
ever was made to recover the dead bodyes slayne in battell," only to
acknowledge immediately that "nevertheles we doe reade in the histories and
gestes of Hercules, that he was the first that ever suffered his enemies to carye
awaye their dead bodyes, after they had been put to the sword" (59).

55. Ibid., 55.

56. Ibid.

Disfiguring Women with Masculine Tropes
A Rhetorical Reading of
A Midsummer Night's Dream

Christy Desmet

For David and Dita—
the Man in the Moon and his Dog

As Felix Mendelssohn recognized, to a large extent *A Midsummer Night's Dream* is held together by music—by actual songs but also by the music of its elastic poetry. In this play, Shakespeare has compiled a rich anthology of poetic styles, ranging from the Petrarchan exchanges of the young lovers through the Senecan bombast of "Pyramus and Thisbe" to Puck's racing couplets and the unnamed fairy's lilting triplets: "Over hill, over dale, / Thorough bush, thorough brier" (2.1.2-3).[1] Critics disagree, however, about the effect of Shakespeare's verbal pyrotechnics in *A Midsummer Night's Dream*. Some have perceived a discrepancy between poetic sound and sense that subverts the play's claims for the healing power of imagination.[2] Others discover an authentic, redemptive voice beneath the artificial rhetoric and undisciplined brawling that dominates for most of the play.[3] Both schools of thought, however, confirm Father Walter Ong's feeling that "[s]ight isolates, sound incorporates."[4] In his critique of logocentrism, Jacques Derrida has challenged the primacy of an oral speech that "incorporates" over a visual writing that "isolates."[5] Yet *A Midsummer Night's Dream* cannot be reduced to a thematic opposition between

speech and writing. Rather, the play is, among other things, a study in
the promise and perils of humanist rhetoric, where spoken and written
word collide in the playful art of cataloging and generating rhetorical
figures.[6] Through the art of rhetorical ornament, *A Midsummer Night's
Dream* counters Theseus's rationalist ethics with a feminized fairy
poetics that creates indescribable visions from "musical confusion"
(4.1.110).

I. HUMANISTIC RHETORIC AND
THE GENDERED ART OF ENGLISH POESIE

A Midsummer Night's Dream depends on rhetoric in its narrowest
sense as the art of figuration. At the play's beginning, Theseus warns
Hermia that her father has created her. Having "compos'd" her beauties
as a stylist imprints soft wax, Egeus therefore retains the right to
"disfigure" Hermia (1.1.46-51). The love plot concludes with the
lovers united, their "minds transfigur'd" together to produce a vision of
"great constancy" (5.1.24, 26). The power of rhetoric to disfigure or
transfigure both individual and culture is a subject of *A Midsummer
Night's Dream*.

The art of figuration, or of verbal ornament, is part of the humanist
program for training public speakers in verbal copiousness. The goal of
rhetorical training, according to Desiderius Erasmus, is to speak with
enough facility to avoid being rendered "confused, or crude, or even
silent."[7] The characters of *A Midsummer Night's Dream* all show a
talent for copious speech. Even Bottom, who cribs his eloquence from
fustian Senecan scripts, may be confused and crude, but he is hardly
ever reduced to silence. Skill with rhetorical figures, tropes, and
schemes provides the orator with ready material for public
performance, an ability to refashion existing materials in new ways.
But as Richard Lanham has argued, rhetorical patterns can become
habits of mind that shape thought itself: "they both frame thinking and,
by their formal 'logic,' urge certain thoughts upon us."[8] In Kenneth
Burke's rhetorical lexicon, art in this case appeals through a
"conventional form."[9] It was the formal power of rhetoric as practiced
by the sophists that Plato attacked in the *Phaedrus*.

Plato's critique of sophistry and subsequent attacks and defenses
of rhetoric are conducted in gendered language that provides a context
for the ambivalent effects of rhetorical figures in *A Midsummer Night's*

Dream. Sophistry is associated with femininity. The most famous piece of sophistic rhetoric was Gorgias's encomium of Helen of Troy. Plato's dialogue about *Gorgias*, furthermore, equates rhetoric with cosmetics, the art of adorning the body with false colors. His *Phaedrus*, in reclaiming rhetoric for philosophy, repudiates the feminine by aligning "proper" rhetoric with a pederastic love between men and boys. In the *Phaedrus*, however, Plato appropriates as well as repudiates the feminine, pressing into service feminine metaphors of desire for his masculine erotic ethos.[10] In both ways, Plato contains and controls the dangerous figure of woman.

As rhetoricians have begun to discuss, Woman is the lost figure in the social economy of the verbal arts. Woman, like the Phaedra of Euripides, is a "counterfeit coin, the site of false words and deeds."[11] As Michelle Ballif argues eloquently, "*She* is never quite legitimate. As the gold standard is Man, is Truth, Woman never measures up. She is always found lacking Truth—the Truth that is man—and is thus, like Phaedra, a counterfeit coin."[12] At the outset of *A Midsummer Night's Dream*, Hermia figures as both the sign of her father's patriarchal power and as a counterfeit coin whose potential falsehood can taint the traffic in women that binds men to one another. Theseus declares that Egeus alone has created Hermia, imprinting the soft wax of her being with his own form in an act of paternal parthenogenesis:

> Be advis'd, fair maid.
> To you your father should be as a god;
> One that compos'd your beauties; yea, and one
> To whom you are but as a form in wax,
> By him imprinted, and within his power,
> To leave the figure, or disfigure it. (1.1.46-51)

By this logic, Egeus's will is divine, his prerogative undisputed. Yet Theseus's effort to affirm that power involves him necessarily in the world of rhetorical figures. As it turns out, Egeus is only "like" a God, Hermia "like" a form in wax. The sign of patriarchal power is no more than a trope, a simile weaker even than its root metaphor.

The figure of woman, as the central trope in this ritual exchange between men, disrupts the verbal economy by which Theseus's word is law and Egeus's will absolute. Egeus offers Hermia to Demetrius as a sign of the friendship between them. Demetrius has Egeus's love, "[a]nd what is mine my love shall render him. / And she is mine, and all my right of her / I do estate unto Demetrius" (1.1.96-98). If Hermia's figure can be put under erasure by paternal fiat, however, she is no true and enduring sign of male friendship but a counterfeit. Lorna Hutson has discussed how texts function in the humanist rhetoric of friendship, arguing that fictions of women become at once the textual promise and proof of the bond between men.[13] Fictions of women are objects of exchange between men, but because they are acts of persuasion as well, the evidence of friendship that they manufacture is questionable.

A counterfeit text, the feminine figure that masculine power shapes and disfigures in a type of Ovidian metamorphosis, endangers the traffic in women that bolsters the humanist rhetoric of friendship in at least three ways. First, the feminine figure is by definition false. George Puttenham's *The Arte of English Poesie*, for instance, describes many of the "auricular figures" it catalogues in terms of lies and deceptions. Counterfeits also wander; they are sexually transgressive. Many representations of Lady Rhetoric, such as that by J.B. Boudard, show her as an attractive, scantily dressed woman who reclines backward and beckons to spectators with an open hand that stands in opposition to Logic's closed fist. According to Boudard's character-ization of her, Rhetoric is a gracious, laughing woman ("*gracieuse & riante*") whose verbal displays are easy to comprehend ("*faciles à comprendre*").[14] She is therefore "untrue" in both senses of that word.

The second threat posed by the rhetorical figure of Woman involves her effect on men. She can arouse man with her eloquence (as Isabella does Angelo in *Measure for Measure*). She can emasculate man (as Helena does Bertram in *All's Well That Ends Well*).[15] In a further twist of logic, Woman can also threaten patriarchal control by her very silence: Cordelia provides an obvious example of the woman whose silence fails to signal clearly her obedience. As Ballif puts it, "Woman is the text that paradoxically cannot speak but nevertheless speaks in its silence. Her silence *is* the message; it desires to be read."[16] The seductive feminine text that courts masculine readings, like Helen of Troy, is subject to sexual theft and therefore produces violence and social collapse, in *King Lear* as in the history of Troy.

The *Arte of English Poesie* offers a series of anecdotes that illustrates, albeit covertly, the debilitating effect rhetoric can have on the conduct of masculine business. Daniel Javitch has defined two principal ways of representing rhetoric within the Western tradition that are useful for mapping woman's relation to rhetoric. The Ciceronian tradition figures persuasion as a masculine, martial battle. In an alternative, feminized model for persuasion that is best represented by Baldassare Castiglione's *The Courtier*, women and rhetoric work together to civilize man.[17] Puttenham's book belongs to the second tradition. He compares "ornament poeticall" to the costly clothing of "great Madames of honour," who wear "silkes or tyssewes & costly embroderies" rather than risk the shame of being seen in "plaine and simple apparell."[18] Despite the light touch of irony, Puttenham's poetic Lady is a dignified aristocrat: beautiful and seductive but also capable of refining masculine society. Nevertheless, the feminine art of verbal ornament exerts a price on the ethos of male orators who employ the art of verbal ornament.

Puttenham's tales illustrate the importance of using figurative language in writing and speeches but undermine his avowed enthusiasm for feminine ornament in subtle ways. In the first story, a Knight of Yorkshire, "a good gentleman and wise,"[19] delivers a speech before Queen Mary herself. Although the Knight is not unlearned, his speech comes across to auditors as an unpolished "alehouse tale."[20] The Knight's failure before Queen Mary, the silent "text" whose unspoken evaluation nevertheless begs to be read, is figured most obviously in terms of social status. The Yorkshire Knight exposes his rustic naiveté. Implicitly, however, the Knight's social failure is also a sexual one, since he reveals his lack not only of beautiful language but also of teeth.

A second anecdote involves a "Knight of the Queenes priuie chamber," a "noble woman of the Court" who is in the queen's favor, and the knight's friend, a gentleman who has lost the queen's good opinion. The "Knight of the Queenes priuie chamber" pleads with the noble woman to intercede with the queen on behalf of the friend. The powerful lady, who remains unpersuaded of the slandered gentleman's merits, replies evasively that "he"—either the Knight or his slandered friend, depending on the assignation of pronoun reference—is "to [sic] wise" to have conversation with her. She suggests instead that the friend seek legal remedy from the putative source of the slander. If the gentleman is both eloquent and innocent, the court lady implies, he should be able to persuade his detractors without the queen's interference. The Knight enigmatically replies: "had your Ladyship rather heare a man talke like a foole or like a wise man?"[21] Although the Knight is ready with a quip, the court lady successfully resists her masculine adversary, challenging his sexual and political mastery with her ambiguous speech.

Puttenham then tells of a court case involving a man and his wife, in which a doctor of the law argues that the "simple woman is not so much to blame as her lewde abbettours, who by violent perswasions haue lead [sic] her into this wilfulnesse."[22] Like Helen of Troy in Gorgias's defense of her, the shrewish wife has been conquered through language. When the judge objects to the doctor's ascription of such great power to language, the doctor tells another story about the itinerant sophist Hegesias, whose rousing speeches against the transitory nature of life persuade large numbers of Egyptians to commit suicide—"some with weapō, some with poyson, others by drowning and hanging themselues to be rid out of this vale of misery"—until Hegesias is finally banished.[23] In Puttenham's sequence of anecdotes, the feminine figures are arranged in decreasing order of stature: Queen Mary is followed by a powerful lady in Elizabeth's court, then by a caricature of the shrewish wife. In the most dazzling proof of rhetoric's scope, the Egyptian suicides, woman is no longer even present. Without the civilizing effect of feminine ornament, Puttenham implies, not only do country knights make fools of themselves but great nations can be decimated.

Within the individual vignettes, however, woman's influence on male eloquence is more equivocal. Puttenham concludes with a "pretie deuise" or emblem that Lucian claimed to have seen in the portrait of Hercules in Marseilles, "where they had figured a lustie old man with a long chayne tyed by one end at his tong, by the other end at the peoples eares, who stood a farre of and seemed to be drawen to him by the force of that chayne fastned to his tong, as who would say, by force of his perswasions."[24] The old man, by virtue of his wise age, is at once persuasive and sexually disadvantaged. The chain that binds auditors to the rhetor restrains as well his phallic tongue. Eloquence, an attribute of wise age, stands in opposition to sexual mastery. The old man, now made a text to be read rather than a speaker, becomes himself a figure of the feminine.

The third threat posed by the figure of Woman comes from her own potential to speak, to exceed her role as a written text and establish herself as a speaking subject, one who *uses* rather than *exemplifies* the orator's skills. Only one woman in Puttenham's series of stories, the court lady who enjoys Queen Elizabeth's confidence, speaks for herself. Yet by the logic of narrative, this lady's doubled speech leaves her masculine interlocutor unsatisfied and increases her own political control over the monarch's inner chamber. Although Rhetoric is usually represented as a seductive woman or more positively, as the "great Madame[. . .]" of Puttenham, in an unusual illustration ascribed to Mantegna, she appears as an emblem of the martial, Ciceronian ideal of rhetoric.[25] Chastely dressed and draped in the style of a Venus Pudica, Rhetorica nevertheless wears both helmet and sword. Reminiscent of Athena, the daughter who sprang from her father's head without maternal help, she denies her own femininity.[26] Yet Rhetorica also claims for herself the persuasive weapons of combative Ciceronian rhetoric, the high style and probable arguments of political debate. She outdoes men at their own verbal games.

George Puttenham's discussion of the value of feminine ornament to oratory and writing provides a useful guide to the verbal wars of *A Midsummer Night's Dream*. Whether or not Queen Elizabeth attended any performance of the play, "her pervasive *cultural presence* was a condition of the play's imaginative possibility."[27] She is the text whose silence is an invitation to readers and a threat to male rhetoric. The highest-ranking woman speaker in the play, although a "spirit of no common rate" (3.1.154) rather than a lady of Elizabeth's chamber, also frustrates the bonds of male friendship by withholding the changeling boy and asserting the prerogatives of female monarchy, female friendship, and female sexuality. Finally, the divorce between martial masculine rhetoric and feminine ornament nearly precipitates the kind of catastrophe that befell Egypt in Puttenham's narrative, as Lysander and Demetrius draw their swords in an effort to settle their differences with blood rather than words.

Shakespeare's play, however, foregrounds more clearly than Puttenham does the inversion of power relationships that occurs when men turn to feminine rhetoric. Women who cease to be written figures and assume their place as speaking subjects, rhetors in their own right, dominate *A Midsummer Night's Dream*. The dialectic between language that figures and disfigures takes place on two levels. In the play's own rhetorical structure, the feminine figure becomes a supplement disordering the master tropes that shape relationships in Theseus's Athens. On the level of character, the feminine figures of *A*

Midsummer Night's Dream reconceive the verbal arts in a radical way, rewriting at the same time the epistemology and ethics by which public business is conducted in Athens. In both cases, women are at once the objects of disfigurement and its subjects. They endure disfigurement at the hands of masculine orators, as Hermia does at the play's beginning, but also usurp for their own ends the arts of masculine debate, disfiguring the neat configurations of Athenian social hierarchies. Thus, the grammar of my title works in two ways.

II. HYPALLAGE OR "THE CHANGELING" AS STRUCTURE

It is a critical commonplace that *A Midsummer Night's Dream* is a highly patterned play. The plots of the lovers, the fairy lovers, and the fictional Pyramus and Thisbe replicate one another. Not only are characters doubled, but as William A. Ringler, Jr. argued long ago, characters can substitute for one another.[28] The dialectic between doubling and substitution, however, disrupts and restructures the governing patterns of the play. Puck concludes the love plot by claiming for his magic a perfectly symmetrical ending: "Jack shall have Jill; / Naught shall go ill" (3.2.461-62). Symmetry confirms and serves patriarchy, since Jack "has" Jill and the man his mare, rather than the reverse. But symmetry is also the source of the lovers' challenge to Egeus's parental prerogative. Although he describes Demetrius as a "spotted and inconstant man," Lysander's claim to Hermia rests less on his superiority to Demetrius than on their structural resemblance to one another. Lysander argues that

> I am, my lord, as well deriv'd as he,
> As well possess'd; my love is more than his;
> My fortunes every way as fairly rank'd
> (If not with vantage) as Demetrius';
> And (which is more than all these boasts can be)
> I am belov'd of beauteous Hermia. (1.1.99-104)

Lysander claims that he matches Demetrius in his lineage, possessions, and general good fortune. Helena argues as well that she is Hermia's equal in beauty, the sole quality on which female worth is calculated. Life in *A Midsummer Night's Dream* is disrupted by the rigorous logic of its own symmetry, in which one member of a structure can either double or substitute for another.

In structural terms, the comic mishaps that occur in the wood outside Athens are orchestrated by hypallage, the rhetorical figure by which a symmetrical exchange of parts creates nonsense.[29] Puttenham defines "*hipallage*" as a figure in which an exchange of words changes the "true construction and application" of a statement so that "the sence is quite peruerted and made very absurd." Puttenham's examples of hypallage are the transformation of "*tell me troth and lie not*" into "*lie me troth and tell not*"; and the transformation of "*come dine with me, and stay not*" into "*come stay with me and dine not*."[30] The most perfect example of hypallage in *A Midsummer Night's Dream* is Bottom's rendition of his dream: "The eye of man hath not heard, the ear of man hath not seen, man's hand is not able to taste, his tongue to conceive, nor his heart to report, what my dream was" (4.1.211-14). Interestingly, the examples from Puttenham's *Arte of English Poesie*, like Bottom's dream, involve sexual innuendo, a request for discreet sex ("*lie me troth and tell not*") and a tryst without the decorous formality of dinner beforehand ("*come stay with me and dine not*").[31]

In *A Midsummer Night's Dream*, Bottom is the source and symbol of hypallage or of symmetrical nonsense. But although Bottom reports his inexpressible dream with pride, the play's larger exploration of hypallage as a state of mind and a social construction is more ambivalent. In Northrop Frye's literary genealogy, which derives Shakespearean comedy from Roman New Comedy, the pairing of lovers with one another at the end of a play signals an Oedipal triumph of youth over the father.[32] Yet the symmetry of romantic exchange in *Dream*'s plot creates nonsense in a darker way. Puttenham characterizes hypallage as the "changeling."[33] In *A Midsummer Night's Dream* it is the changeling child at the root of Titania and Oberon's quarrel whose fate figures symmetry without sense. Although retained by Titania for strong and serious reasons, at the end of the play the changeling is transferred without cause into Oberon's custody. Badgered by Oberon's taunts at her love for Bottom, Titania simply gives the boy to Oberon, confirming the rights of patriarchy without either rhyme or reason. The ethos of hypallage is the ethos of Puck, to whom all Athenians look alike and whose motive may be equally malice or misprision.

Structural inversions created through hypallage make the love plot of *A Midsummer Night's Dream* unstable precisely because its ethos is unclear or even nonsensical. As she pursues Demetrius into the forest, Helena laments that for her, the Ovidian paradigm governing unrequited love is altered:

> the story shall be chang'd:
> Apollo flies, and Daphne holds the chase;
> The dove pursues the griffin; the mild hind
> Makes speed to catch the tiger. . . . (2.1.230-33)

When the Ovidian story is changed, its ethos also changes because erotic agency is transferred from Apollo to Daphne. Helena, as the aggressive female wooer of Ovidian narrative, begs to be Demetrius's spaniel. She throws herself enthusiastically into this act of meiosis, a rhetorical diminishment of her self that compensates for her assumption of leadership in the wooing game. Demetrius points out the generic dangers of such structural revolutions in the face of male resistance: violence, rape, and death. As William Keach has discussed, Renaissance stories of metamorphosis inherited from Ovid the ability to move between the comic and the grotesque.[34] *A Midsummer Night's Dream*, however, focuses on how rhetorical "translations" necessarily damage the social structures they rewrite, turning the pathos of unrequited love into dark irony or even darker tragedy. At the end of the play, Theseus disparages imagination's power to metamorphose reality:

> Such tricks hath strong imagination,
> That if it would but apprehend some joy,
> It comprehends some bringer of that joy;
> Or in the night, imagining some fear,
> How easy is a bush suppos'd a bear! (5.1.18-22)

Theseus engages in his own magisterial act of meiosis, denying the reciprocity involved in the equation between bush and bear. But as Anne Barton points out sensibly in her introduction to *Dream* for the *Riverside Shakespeare*, Theseus's theory of imagination glosses over its own structural implications. Imagining that a bush is a bear is one thing. Mistaking a bear for a bush would be much more tragic.[35]

The rhetorical symmetries that order the action of *A Midsummer Night's Dream* are intrinsically unstable because the figure of hypallage itself produces nonsense. But this effect of "nonsense" depends on the fact that the pieces in the play's figural puzzle are not altogether identical, capable of being moved from one syntactical place to another without damage to common sense. While the logic of hypallage strives to fit the play's romantic figures to its Procrustean bed, the play's female figures insist on exceeding their plots. As Ruth Nevo has noted, there exists an asymmetry in the relationships between the lovers in this play. The men exchange partners according to the elegant pattern of a dance, but the "girls, in point of fact, do not change partners at all. They are subjected to drastic changes in their lovers' attitudes, to which they bewilderedly respond, but their own attachments do not waver."[36] Even the changeling, rhetorical emblem of structural nonsense, comes equipped with a maternal lineage and a position as ward to the fairy queen that prevents him from being absorbed easily into another Ovidian plot, playing Ganymede to Oberon's Jove. The women of *A Midsummer Night's Dream*, as well, refuse to obey the generic laws of New Comedy, where they provide only an erotic backdrop to the Oedipal struggle between young lover and senex. First, the women of *Dream* usurp masculine rhetoric by speaking in the public sphere, disfiguring the patriarchal fictions that order erotic and social relationships in Shakespearean Athens. Second, they reconfigure that social rhetoric by offering alternative tropes for new ideals of love.

III. FEMININE ORATORY

A Midsummer Night's Dream opens with a courtroom drama, in which Egeus accuses Lysander of bewitching his daughter. Although Hermia does not know "by what power" she is "made bold" (1.1.59), she nevertheless forces Theseus to address her as an ethical subject with genuine choices. He delivers to her a classic kind of set speech, the persuasion to marriage that a male orator normally addresses to a masculine friend.[37] Theseus's metaphors seek to contain Hermia within a pair of classic binary oppositions: she must either "die the death" or "abjure / For ever the society of men" (1.1.65-66); alternatively, Hermia can understand her fate as a choice between life as a barren sister or as the "rose distill'd" of marital bliss (1.1.76). Already, however, the constructs that inform Athenian law have been shaken. Hermia apparently has not two choices, as Egeus claimed, but three: death, marriage, or perpetual virginity.

Patriarchal logic suffers a further blow when Theseus's elaboration on the horrors of the sisterhood inadvertently raises questions about the joys of marriage. Theseus describes the nun's life in terms of its constraints. Sisters are confined by their livery, mewed up in shady cloisters, and forced to "master so their blood" by sexual deprivation (1.1.74). Yet their "maiden pilgrimage" (1.1.75), albeit lonely, endows the nuns with metaphorical freedom to wander. Unlike future wives, they do not have to "fit" their "fancies" to a "father's will" (1.1.118). Instead, "chaunting hymns"—however "faint"—to the moon—"cold" and "fruitless" though it may be—(1.1.73), they are released out-of-doors. Married life as the "rose distilled," although depicted more obscurely than the nun's life, looks less perfect by comparison.

By involving Hermia in the humanist rhetoric of friendship, advising her to marry rather than subjecting her directly to the harsh law of the father, Theseus not only grants Hermia the status of a speaking subject, which the law itself would deny her, but he implicitly licenses her to revise the masculine tropes that configure the discourse of romantic love and marriage. In their tête-à-tête immediately following Theseus's ruling on the love quarrel, Lysander and Hermia exchange a set of highly patterned maxims, proving by simple amplification that "[t]he course of true love never did run smooth" (1.1.134). They read this "persuasion," however, in exactly opposite ways. Hermia concludes that the lovers must "teach our trial patience, / Because it is a customary cross" (1.1.152-53). Lysander, by contrast, decides that he and Hermia must elope to the house of his widow aunt, a distant seven leagues from Athens. While Hermia reads her situation as tending toward tragedy, Lysander seeks the relatively robust premises of romance. As a result, the dialogue leads not to consensus but to non-sensus, dramatizing the rhetoric of hypallage.

Joel Fineman, discussing the construction of the poetic subject in Shakespeare's sonnets, argues that the Petrarchan sonneteer lives by the proposition "I praise, therefore I am."[38] According to Fineman, in the rhetoric of love "the lover's goal is a kind of narcissistic identification or unification of subject with object, the identity or unity of which is already prefigured for him in the compact wholeness of the beloved herself."[39] But what happens when the beloved ceases to be a unified object of sight and talks back? Although only one maxim in this collaborative speech—that to "choose love by another's eyes" is "hell"—pertains directly to the situation Hermia finds herself in (1.1.140), the litany of love's impediments that she and Lysander construct is generally couched in economic language. If Hermia is "too high to be enthrall'd to low" (1.1.136), for instance, she acknowledges that a woman's value rises and falls with that of her husband and introduces the possibility of her own fragmentation. Under these premises, Hermia can be devalued, debased as a counterfeit coin through marriage to Demetrius. Furthermore, by doubling her lover's discourse, Hermia also endangers the integrity of Lysander's own self, since as Fineman points out, the value of the "I" who praises is inextricably linked to the value of the praise's object. If Hermia's price can fall, so can Lysander's.

The dissemination of sonnet rhetoric and Hermia's appropriation of it render Lysander's voice impotent. Once they are in the forest, his efforts at seduction become transparent to Hermia, and she counters his persuasions easily. When Hermia asks that he spend the night at a distance from her, Lysander resorts to improvisation, pleading his case with a variation on the myth of the hermaphrodite:

> O, take the sense, sweet, of my innocence!
> Love takes the meaning in love's conference:
> I mean, that my heart unto yours is knit,
> So that but one heart we can make of it;
> Two bosoms interchained with an oath,
> So then two bosoms and a single troth.
> Then by your side no bed-room me deny;
> For lying so, Hermia, I do not lie. (2.2.45-52)

Lysander becomes the victim of his own verbal ornament, for his concluding antanaclasis (or homonymic pun) on "lie" reduces to rubble the emblematic edifice constructed on the image of "two bosoms interchained with an oath." Lysander claims that he and Hermia are one, but his rhetoric suggests that he himself speaks with the "double tongue" of a spotted snake (2.2.9). According to the rigorous logic of hypallage that structures his "pretty" riddle, the very possibility that Lysander tells less than the whole truth ("lying so") insures that he will not "lie" next to Hermia anytime soon. In contrast to the two bosoms "interchained" with an oath, Lysander's tongue is "chained" to a recalcitrant rather than a receptive listener.

Lysander's internal division is even more profound than that of the traditional sonnet lover. In this respect, he resembles the speaker of Shakespeare's later sonnets. In sonnet 138, which subjects the rhetoric of love to heavy irony, the lover speaks self-deprecatingly of how when he and the dark lady "lie" together, "by lies we flattered be" (line 14). The dissipation of the lover's self, however, is predicated on the already doubled nature of the dark lady: he "lies" in both senses of the word because she already will and does "lie."[40] Lysander's entrapment in puns, by contrast, comes in response not so much to Hermia's doubled speech but to her plainness. Smoothly denying any insult to Lysander's integrity, Hermia nevertheless concludes:

> But, gentle friend, for love and courtesy,
> Lie further off, in humane modesty;
> Such separation as may well be said
> Becomes a virtuous bachelor and a maid. . . . (2.2.56-59)

Hermia's speech depends on nouns and a spare number of ethical adjectives. Even words such as "gentle" and "humane," which ordinarily might invite punning, offer Lysander no matter for further argument. Hermia, in fact, seems to command a wider range of rhetorical styles than Lysander does. In his Petrarchan narcissism, Lysander finally becomes a trope-producing machine, so that when he awakes under the influence of love-in-idleness juice to see Helena, Lysander instantaneously and even compulsively composes a couplet for her, picking up on her own line ending to continue the flow of poetic verse. When Helena says prosaically, "Lysander, if you live, good sir, awake," Lysander responds instantly: "And run through fire I will for thy sweet sake" (2.2.102-03).

In the case of Helena and Demetrius, the struggle for command of rhetorical tone is more pronounced; the result is a strong polarization of their language. Helena's speech is rich with ornament, Demetrius's the unmediated voice of physical menace. Helena, perhaps by virtue of her name, moves more comfortably in the world of Ovidian metamorphosis than the other lovers do. Like Oberon, she authors an etiological myth, explaining why "Love looks not with the eyes but with the mind. . ." (1.1.234). Oberon's descriptive exercise, however, is orderly, explaining the origins of "love-in-idleness" by strict laws of cause and effect and confirming his privileged perspective. As he reminds Puck, only Oberon could see the unfolding of this drama between Cupid and the virgin votaress, and thus only he can fully explain its significance. For Helena, the woman who has assumed the mythographer's authority, the myth of blind Cupid is merely instrumental, providing an excuse for betraying the confidence of Hermia and a reason for pursuing Demetrius beyond the city limits and the bounds of maiden modesty. Cupid's wings figure Helena's haste, and his blindness justifies her lack of judgment. In the democratized Athens that Helena inhabits, anyone can have access to the language of erotic love (or of etiological myth) without undergoing the rigorous training in erotic ethics that Socrates gives Phaedrus in the dialogue of that name. Helena is therefore a sophistic Lady Rhetoric, characterized by her sexually "open" demeanor and the flamboyance of her seductive speech, which is all too "easy" for Demetrius to comprehend.

For this reason, Helena's rhetoric also has an emasculating effect on Demetrius. As a spaniel, Helena claims a metaphorical place in the masculine world of the hunt. Demetrius responds to this inversion of gender hierarchy by rejecting feminine ornament altogether. While Hermia may be plain-spoken, Demetrius is "crude." To Helena's offer, he can only respond: "Tempt not too much the hatred of my spirit, / For I am sick when I do look on thee" (2.1.211-12).

In the woods, the structural nonsense that results from widespread hypallage involves the transference of martial rhetoric to an incongruously erotic context. Lysander and Demetrius woo Helena by assaulting first Hermia, and then one another. In their concerted attack on Hermia, seduction yields to violence, and the ambiguous puns of sexual persuasion give way to vituperative epithets. Hermia is labeled "cat," "bur," "vile thing," "serpent," and "tawny Tartar," "dwarf," "minimus," and finally, "bead" and "acorn" (3.2.259, 261, 263, 328-29). When Helena calls her a "puppet," Hermia correctly identifies this rhetorical identification as an act of aggression. Having "urg'd" her "tall personage," Helena has presumably "prevail'd" with Lysander in a way that combines physical threat with sexual promise (3.2.288-93). Helena's supposed eloquence, her ability to "prevail" with both Lysander and Demetrius, brings to a crisis the paradox that defines the rhetorical role of feminine figures—that is, the status of verbal ornament in persuasion. The young men, like the father Egeus before them, "disfigure" Hermia with their metaphors. At the same time, however, the feminine figure retains its own power to "disfigure," as Hermia's offer to damage Helena's eyes and face with her nails is succeeded quickly by the men's decision to abandon debate for more physical forms of combat.

Attempting to substitute martial rhetoric and deeds for the soft language of love, Lysander and Demetrius reproduce the apocalyptic conclusion to Puttenham's narrative, in which masculine rhetoric, unrelieved by feminine ornament, leads inexorably to death and destruction. Having run through their litany of Petrarchan cliches, they begin "bragging to the stars" (3.2.407) in the style of Bottom's favorite dramatic character, the tyrant. The rhetoric of praise metamorphoses into its opposite, vituperation. But ironically, the male lovers are emasculated by their abandonment of feminine rhetoric, for in choosing swords over words, they lose verbal control of the action. Puck's voice dominates in this scene. Lysander and Demetrius can only echo his threats, becoming increasingly confused and rude, until they fall into sleep and a traditionally "feminine" silence.

IV. FROM FEMININE RHETORIC TO POETICS

Women "disfigure" their male lovers in *A Midsummer Night's Dream* by usurping the public rhetoric that humanist educators fashioned to strengthen the community of men. Yet the oratory of Hermia and Helena might be considered a consequence, as well as a disruption, of masculine discourse. Rhetoric aims to establish the probability of its arguments rather than their mathematical certainty. As Arthur F. Kinney has noted, while proofs of verisimilitude can take many forms, the most popular tropes used by Tudor humanists were figures of impersonation. Most notably, the rhetors resorted to "*prosopopoeia*," a figure through which fictional individuals give voice to probable arguments.[41] In this way, the arguments achieve *energeia* or the ability to clarify abstract thought by making oral speech an object of sight. As Kinney reminds us, impersonation is used repeatedly to give persuasive speeches "their vividness, energy, and emotional conviction."[42]

The feminine figures of *A Midsummer Night's Dream* both exemplify and exploit the ability of rhetoric to fuse voice and vision. As characters inscribed within a patriarchal history, Hermia and Helena are figures of *prosopopoeia*. They speak in order to further a masterplot that ends with multiple marriages and the social regulation of aberrant individuals, to return to Northrop Frye's analysis of the play's structure. At the same time, the play's feminine figures give voice to an alternative ethics. To this extent, they produce and control the poetic "music" that shapes the argument of *A Midsummer Night's Dream*. Their voices combine in a different "musical confusion" to revise the rationalist ethics of Theseus, to whom the lover, lunatic, and poet represent all that is wrong with the world of imagination. As Kinney also notes in his analysis of "humanist poetics," the line between rhetoric and poetic can be "perilously thin."[43] In particular, the figures of impersonation cross that line. Thus, the women of *A Midsummer Night's Dream*, by stepping out of their texts and speaking up, offer a feminist poetics that transforms their political usurpation of humanist rhetoric into an ethical act.

The play's feminine ethics, an alternative to Theseus's refutation of imagination and of Oberon's exploitation of it, traces the metamorphosis of writing into voice, a transformation that gives verbal representations *energeia* or an air of plausibility. In a brilliant analysis of the rhetoric of transvestite drama that draws on deconstructive theories of writing, Lloyd Davis argues that the figure of woman on Shakespeare's stage operates according to the logic of metonymy. In the binary system that defines relationships between male and female, woman is what man is not. In terms of metaphoric structure, man has a "proper" meaning and woman is aberrant. Man is tenor, woman the vehicle. Metaphor slides into metonymy, however, because if man's meaning is "proper," "literal," and absolute, then woman is merely supplemental to masculine discourse. Her relationship to him is contingent, a metonymic accident of syntax rather than a necessary function of semantics. The figure of woman therefore calls into question the "natural" relationship between male tenor and female vehicle. Through metonymy, woman becomes "the rhetorically improper persona who may disrupt or confirm the categories of gendered ethos."[44] For this reason, "woman" becomes the supplemental term in masculine narratives that challenges those plots by its own extraneous nature, or doubleness.

The feminine narratology of *A Midsummer Night's Dream*, which operates according to the logic of metonymy or the supplement, involves a dialectic between sameness and difference. Its emblem is, appropriately, the hermaphrodite, the figure of doubleness. In the midst of the forest melee, Helena appeals to an ethic of supplementarity—one based on doubling—as a solution to the strife that now separates friends of both genders. Helena represents her past relationship with Hermia through the metaphor of the hermaphrodite as poetic creator. In their youth, Hermia and Helena were "like two artificial gods" (3.2.203) who specialized in the feminine art of needlework, creating

> both one flower,
> Both on one sampler, sitting on one cushion,
> Both warbling of one song, both in one key,
> As if our hands, our sides, voices, and minds
> Had been incorporate. So we grew together,
> Like to a double cherry, seeming parted,
> But yet an union in partition,
> Two lovely berries moulded on one stem;
> So with two seeming bodies, but one heart. . . . (3.2.204-12)

In Helena's speech the "double cherry," although "seeming parted," is in reality a "union in partition" and so exceeds its place in the anatomizing language of the masculine blazon. While Demetrius uses sonnet rhetoric to praise Helena's "ripe" lips, "those kissing cherries" (3.2.139-40), and Thisbe memorializes Pyramus's "cherry nose" (5.1.331), in Helena's version of this myth the doubled cherry stands as sign and seal of both girls' virginity. Helena poetically reconstructs an irrecoverable innocence, a time when vows were sacrosanct and emblems of doubleness had a clear, single meaning. Her virgin hermaphrodite occupies a space that predates and excludes the "hyperbolic language of salesmanship" that characterizes the masculine blazon.[45] Valerie Traub notes rightly that this passage is charged with homoerotic desire. She also points out that relegating this desire to the past contains it within a dominant heterosexuality.[46] Helena's allegory of love between female friends is indeed elegiac, but it also confronts Hermia with a present ethical imperative. Helena complains not only that Hermia has changed objects of desire but that she has betrayed a previous loyalty to Helena, a bond whose integrity is figured by an absence of the commercial language that conditions heterosexual romance. From Titania's speech, we see more explicitly how the doubled rhetoric of femininity can be put into service as both erotic and ethical discourse, successfully resisting the textual traffic in women that is sustained by sonnet rhetoric.

Titania functions as the voice of ethical commitment in *A Midsummer Night's Dream*. In her initial confrontation with Oberon, Titania also becomes involved in a courtroom drama. Although Titania and Oberon meet by chance, they quickly assume the position of adversaries. Again, the judicial cause is complex. On the one hand, Titania and Oberon are engaged in a custody battle over the changeling. Although Puck claims that Titania stole the boy from his rightful father, an Indian king, Oberon claims as well the right to make the boy "Knight" of his own "train, to trace the forces wild. . ." (2.1.25). Titania, in response, "withholds the loved boy, / Crowns him with flowers, and makes him all her joy" (2.1.26-27). The dispute between Oberon and Titania mirrors in reverse that between Hermia and Egeus. While Egeus subjects Hermia to paternal law, Oberon seeks to free the changeling boy from maternal confinement, from the protective custody in which Titania holds him and from her effeminizing crown of flowers.

The cause that sets Titania against Oberon, however, also involves sovereignty in marriage. In this respect, the plots involving fairies and lovers come together, so that Titania's voice provides an ethical context for Hermia's hermaphrodite. While the legal dilemmas that open the first two acts of *A Midsummer Night's Dream* contrast with one another by examining the relative rights of fathers and mothers, the two plots merge to offer a unified defense of female sexual sovereignty, the woman's rights over her own body and soul. Titania has forsworn Oberon's bed and company, a move that she makes herself without intervention from any ecclesiastical fairy court governing divorce from bed and board. Oberon, according to Titania's accusation, has committed at least two indiscretions, with Phillida and with Hippolyta, and has wooed Phillida under false pretenses, since he has appeared to her "in the shape of Corin" (2.1.66). Oberon, in turn, accuses Titania of adultery and of interference in Theseus's love life.

Titania's defense of her familial rights to the changeling boy provides a different perspective on her role in Theseus's sexual peregrinations. Titania, by virtue of her vaguely-defined cult, stands for the right of women to sexual independence, the same Amazonian right that Hermia claims when, despite Theseus's efforts to make her see the sisterhood from a patriarchal perspective, she prefers a life of chanting faint hymns to the cold, fruitless moon. Although Oberon implies that Titania interferes in Theseus's legitimate love affairs, the legendary record does not support him; the string of rapes and seductions that defines Theseus's love life provides a dark undertone to his Chaucerian reputation as the perfect governor and man of reason. Perigenia, daughter of a bandit, is raped in sight of her father's corpse. Antiopa, like Hippolyta herself, comes to Theseus as the spoils of war. Theseus abandons Ariadne on Naxos, where she falls prey in turn to the fickle attentions of Bacchus. Hippolyta herself is succeeded by Phaedra in Theseus's affections.[47] In leading Theseus away from these women, Titania implicitly intervenes in the master-plot of male sexual conquest. Furthermore, in her memory of her own friendship with the changeling boy's deceased mother, Titania provides an alternative to the "unwished yoke" of sexual submission.

Like Hermia, Titania defends herself to Oberon as if in a public forum. Her private memory of the changeling's mother also functions as a judicial defense based on the hierarchical relation between Titania and her votaress. While Leonard Barkan has discussed the connection between rhetoric and sodomy in the legend of Ganymede,[48] Titania's speech locates the changeling within an ethically and poetically superior matriarchy that reinforces her regal and maternal rights to him. Titania bases her right to the boy on a public duty that binds the fairy queen to her votaress. At the same time, she redefines the friendship on which that claim is based, removing herself and the votaress from the economic imagery that conditions masculine relations within kinship networks and within the humanist rhetoric of friendship. Kate's concluding speech to *Taming of the Shrew* contrasts the wife's safe life at home to the husband's "painful labor, both by sea and land; / To watch the night in storms, the day in cold. . ." (5.2.149-50). Titania and the votaress are also safe spectators of masculine commercial ventures, but unlike the tamed wife of Kate's speech, they replicate and replace the missing male presence in the family by acting as a female-female hermaphrodite. By the power of metaphor, the votaress becomes a ship, carrying the freight of her son rather than commercial cargo. The child is a burden so precious that Titania may claim with justice that "the fairy land buys not the child of me. . ." (2.1.122). Only death, not sexual infidelity or the exchange of money, can disrupt the company of women. Through her revisionary metaphor, which figures the votaress as a "big-bellied" ship, swollen with the "rich . . . merchandise" of a baby rather than with the emptiness of the "wanton wind" (2.1.129, 134) that sends merchants' ships on their way, Titania refigures her relationship to the votaress in terms of its sexual ethics. C.L. Barber recognizes that "[t]he secure quality of the play's pleasure is conveyed by having the ships out on the flood while she [the votaress] sails, safely, upon the *land*, with a pretty and swimming gait that is an overflowing of the security of make-believe."[49] Barber's definition of "play," however, unnecessarily trivializes the cultural perspective of Titania's cult. Titania's equation between woman and ship shatters the metaphoric foundations on which the traffic in women is based. From the perspective of these women on the shore, who occupy a liminal space between the patriarchal home and the uncharted oceans, woman is no longer the counterfeit coin that legitimizes masculine truth. Commercial man trades in coins, barren metal that blurs the distinction between legitimate trade and usury.[50] Furthermore, his ships are swollen with "wanton wind," suggesting both vanity and sexual infidelity. Woman, by contrast, stands for Truth as troth. Titania's matriarchy is founded on a friendship that has no price. Although Puttenham identified the figure of hypallage as "the changeling," Titania's account of the Indian changeling's genealogy denies the possibility of symmetrical exchange. If truth is troth, then Oberon cannot replace Titania as his legitimate parent.

While Hermia's myth of the hermaphrodite implicitly praises an ethics of doubleness, Titania's fairy ethics acknowledges as well the dark side of persuasion that works through figures. She alone in this play confronts and articulates the destructive power that the dialectic between figuration and disfigurement unleashes, appropriately represented by the snake with doubled tongue that the fairies banish from Titania's bower. Titania, unlike any other character in the play, balances praise for her female friendship with unflinching criticism of her own marriage. Thus, Titania's doubled discourse works ethically rather than poetically. In her own chronographia, the description of natural chaos produced by her marital quarrel with Oberon, Titania shuns the safety of etiological myth, stressing instead the material consequences of fairy strife. She takes her ethical stand by renouncing the comfort of rhetorical figures. Titania describes a world in which difference collapses into sameness, where the seasons alter and "the mazed world / . . . knows not which is which" (2.1.113-14). Metaphor becomes myth as the moon personified, "[p]ale in her anger" (2.1.104), produces physical rather than poetic disasters: sheep murrain, rheumatic diseases, and rotting crops. Even the rare personified metaphors in this speech—the young corn that rotted "ere his youth attain'd a beard" (2.1.95) or "Old Hiems," whose "icy crown" sports a mocking "chaplet of sweet summer buds" (2.1.109-10)—focus not on the poetic decorum that links tenor and vehicle but on metaphor's role in charting a series of disasters, which succeed one another by the logic of metonymy.

By engaging in rhetorical disfigurement, Titania ironically becomes the most ethical speaker in the play, for her privileged position as the figure who disfigures masculine discourse makes her also a theorist of language's violence. Like Puttenham at the end of his chapter on feminized ornament, Titania acknowledges the ambivalence that characterizes rhetorical relationships. In Puttenham's emblem the "lusty old man" is chained to his auditors as much as they are bound to him. Titania concludes her speech strongly by defining public responsibility as mutual bondage. Titania firmly, if reluctantly, affirms her connection to Oberon when she declares that "this same progeny of evils comes / From our debate, from our dissension; / We are their parents and original" (2.1.115-17). Without such bondage, there is only destruction. Within the encircling chains of persuasive rhetoric, however, the hermaphrodite becomes a figure of willing subjection as well as unity.[51]

V. DISFIGURING MOONSHINE; OR, THE RHETORIC OF COMEDY

Titania's bifurcated perspective on the arts of language becomes a theory of drama when Theseus and Hippolyta, responding to the mechanicals' performance of "Pyramus and Thisbe," articulate opposed visions of the comic genre. The main plot's successful resolution, the mental "translation" of the lovers' attitudes that untangles the nonsensical structure of hypallage or the changeling, is discussed in terms of a simultaneous figuration and disfigurement. Demetrius says that his love for Hermia "melted as the snow" (4.1.166). As a result, the events of the previous night "seem small and indistinguishable, / Like far-off mountains turned into clouds" (4.1.187-88). For Demetrius, the boundaries that define experience are erased; mountains dissolve into clouds, so that disfigurement is redemptive. Hermia, by contrast, sees double: "Methinks I see these things with parted eye, / Where every thing seems double" (4.1.189-90). Her epiphany returns Hermia to a world of rhetorical figures. It falls to Theseus and Hippolyta to characterize this imaginative "translation" in terms of poetic genre.

Theseus defines rhetorical community by division, one of Plato's favorite methods of argument. There are lovers, lunatics, and poets, and there are those of us who can resist the tricks of "strong imagination" (5.1.18). The poet's art of figuration, giving shape to things unknown and assigning to "aery nothing / A local habitation and a name" (5.1.16-17), equals the lover's fancy in its feminine frenzy.[52] Hippolyta reformulates Theseus's idea of imaginative production with a simple rhetoric of amplification, which in her hypothetical version of the night's events becomes the source of comic resolution:

> But all the story of the night told over,
> And all their minds transfigur'd so together,
> More witnesseth than fancy's images,
> And grows to something of great constancy;
> But howsoever, strange and admirable. (5.1.23-27)

Truth works not by strict categories but by a loose, baggy accumulation of stories. Thus, Hippolyta's standard for persuasion is far different from the teleological, Oedipal plot that Northrop Frye identifies as the grand pattern for Shakespearean comedy. From the perspective of her generous aesthetic, the transfiguration of the lovers' minds is an unnamed "something" that holds together with a consistency that cannot be quantified or even named.

Hippolyta's aesthetic of amplification complements Titania's ethic of responsibility. Both assume that invisible chains bind people and their narratives to one another. The looseness of such an aesthetic, its paratactic alignment of perspectives whose relation is only contingent, is necessary to translate potential tragedy into comedy. Titania's logic of responsibility depends on a spartan cause-and-effect: she and Oberon are the "parents and original" of all the natural disasters befalling humans. Hippolyta's aesthetic brings into relief the rhetorical principle of metonymy that actually structures Titania's chronographia. To speak and act ethically, we must take responsibility for chains of events whose connection is at best contingent. The supplemental quality of rhetorical accumulation, which has no necessary beginning or ending, reforms the rigid exchanges of hypallage or the changeling structure.

The concluding play of "Pyramus and Thisbe" celebrates the rhetorical contingency that makes and mars narrative constancy in the feminine comic aesthetic of *A Midsummer Night's Dream*. Although the plot of "Pyramus and Thisbe" is a tragedy governed by contingency—a missed appointment, a dropped veil, and a badly timed suicide—Bottom and his crew do their best to wrestle their dramatic material into a doggedly rational and moral pattern. They not only provide narrative background for the doomed love affair and offer metadramatic warnings protecting "Fair ladies" (3.1.39) from the lion's roar, but the actors also comment on the tragic action. Bottom as Pyramus calls on the Fates and Furies as authors of his death; Thisbe, as well, blames her death on the "Sisters Three" (5.1.336). The tragedy also has an uplifting moral, for as Bottom carefully instructs Theseus, after the double suicide of Pyramus and Thisbe, "the wall is down that parted their fathers" (5.1.351-52). He would have elaborated with an epilogue had not Theseus demanded a bergomask, instead.

Although the actors of "Pyramus and Thisbe" attempt to moralize their spectacle, their speech subverts that rationalist end with exuberant exchanges and amplification. Quince's opening prologue concludes that "[a]ll for your delight / We are not here" (5.1.114-15), forewarning spectators that the moral logic of serious drama has already been subverted by the nonsense of hypallage. Within the play's set speeches, amplification reigns also as the dominant mode of composition. Pyramus begins his lament at Thisbe's absence with exuberant parallelism and repetition of opening words (*anaphora*), exclaiming: "O grim-look'd night! O night with hue so black!" (5.1.170). But despite the existence of a written script (Thisbe speaks all of her lines at once, cues and all), Bottom is quickly at a loss for matter and resorts to simple repetition (*ploce*) to fill the iambic pentameter line: "O night, O night! alack, alack, alack. . ." (5.1.172). Thisbe's death speech comes to a similar conclusion, trailing off into simple repetition: "And farewell, friends; / Thus Thisbe ends; / Adieu, adieu, adieu" (5.1.345-47).[53]

The absurdity of "Pyramus and Thisbe's" plot, a poetic deficiency that requires the audience's imagination to mend it, becomes comedy by virtue of its amplified verse, which doubles, triples, and even quadruples the plain words of its poetic lines. In this respect the icon of the play's rhetorical standard is the person who says least in the play: Robin Starveling in his role as the "Man in the Moon." Starveling's own identity is amorphous; he may be either extremely thin or overly fat. Yet Starveling stands forth as a figure of masculine rhetoric, of plain speech and simple meanings. In the martial Ciceronian vein, Starveling as Moon stands forth to "disfigure" the play's most elusive feminine symbol, the moon (3.1.60-61). His presentation of Moon apes the sonneteer's blazon by anatomizing the moon's symbolic attributes: spherical shape, thorn bush, lantern, and dog. Starveling's courtly detractors play with the rigid logic of his representation, suggesting that the moon's horns should be on Starveling's head rather than figured by the lantern, that Starveling himself should be crushed into the lantern, and that the moon by its nature should "change" and cease its tedious oratory. Starveling responds, as Titania did before him, with plain speech that challenges the inversions of hypallage: "All that I have to say is to tell you that the lanthorn is the moon, I the man i' th' moon, this thorn-bush my thorn-bush, and this dog my dog" (5.1.257-59).

Starveling's aesthetic is deictic, pointing to objects he carries with him. Rather than represent the moon, he offers its material substitute for community acceptance. Yet Moon's rhetorical effort also relies on plenitude, on plenty of figuration. To this extent, Moon's attempt to secure audience consensus prefigures that of Puck in the play's final soliloquy. Puck seeks to avoid the "serpent's tongue" of a harsh audience by asking spectators to give him their hands, replicating the linguistic chain that ties speaker and audience. Starveling unconsciously, and Puck consciously, acknowledge that the simplest of statements—an insistence that the intractable cur is "my dog," for instance—is always a figure, inviting, demanding, and begging for declarations of rhetorical friendship. In Starveling's speech we can see the power of feminine rhetoric, like the moon itself, to permeate and transfigure its subjects.

NOTES

1. All references to Shakespeare's works are from *The Riverside Shakespeare* (ed. G. Blakemore Evans [Boston: Houghton Mifflin, 1974]), with editorial brackets omitted.

2. David Bevington, for instance, argues that a fundamental tension exists in the play "between comic reassurance and the suggestion of something dark and threatening"; "'But We Are Spirits of Another Sort': The Dark Side of Love and Magic in *A Midsummer Night's Dream*," *Medieval and Renaissance Studies 1975*, ed. Sigfried Wenzel, vol. 7 (Chapel Hill: University of North Carolina Press, 1978), 81. Jay L. Halio concludes that a poetic harmony is established in the last act of *A Midsummer Night's Dream* but only on the most superficial level: "Although the overall tone is joyful and the teasing playful, Shakespeare does not let us forget the more somber aspects of human relationships, which can and do intrude"; "Nightingales That Roar: The Language of *A Midsummer Night's Dream*," *Traditions and Innovations: Essays on British Literature of the Middle Ages and the Renaissance*, eds. David G. Allen and Robert A. White (Newark, Del.: University of Delaware Press, 1990), 147.

3. From a Christian perspective, Maurice Hunt argues that the competing voices of *A Midsummer Night's Dream* are finally orchestrated by Shakespeare's own "magical voice, marvelously fashioning an artifact of deficient and provocative voices that engage the playgoer's imagination and participation." In this way the playwright fulfills Sir Philip Sidney's claim that the poet possesses the "divine breath" of God; "The Voices of *A Midsummer Night's Dream*," *Texas Studies in Literature and Language* 34 (1992): 233. Terence Hawkes, working from a materialistic perspective, finds in the mechanicals' homely speech the commitment to community that characterizes oral culture; "Comedy, Orality, and Duplicity: *A Midsummer Night's Dream* and *Twelfth Night*" *Shakespearean Comedy*, ed. Maurice Charney (New York: New York Literary Forum, 1980), 155-63.

4. Ong, *Orality and Literacy: The Technologizing of the Word* (London: Methuen, 1982), 72.

5. Although Derrida's argument is well-known, it is laid out most completely in his *Of Grammatology*, trans. Gayatri Chakravorty Spivak (Baltimore: Johns Hopkins University Press, 1976).

6. Throughout this essay I will use rhetorical "figure" as the appropriate term to designate any structure of language that advertises itself, or is accepted as, a variation on "ordinary" speech or "literal" language. I do this without accepting the premise that "ordinary language" or "literal meaning" actually exist. I am also ignoring the Renaissance distinction between "schemes" (largely syntactic disruptions of sense) and "tropes"(semantic violations of ordinary language). A writer such as George Puttenham lists both tropes and schemes as "auricular figures," so the distinction is not absolute; *The Arte of*

English Poesie (1589; rpt. Menston: England: Scolar Press, 1968), 132-34. Readers who are interested in ways of categorizing rhetorical figures and the illogic of attempts to make absolute distinctions between figures that change a sentence's meanings and those that merely rearrange its parts may consult Richard Lanham, *A Handlist of Rhetorical Terms*, 2nd ed. (Berkeley: University of California Press, 1991), 78-80 and 154-57.

7. Erasmus, *On Copia of Words and Ideas*, trans. Donald B. King and H. David Rix, Mediaeval Philosophical Texts in Translation, 12 (Milwaukee: Marquette University Press, 1963), 17.

8. Lanham, *Analyzing Prose* (New York: Scribner's, 1983), 129.

9. Burke, *Counter-Statement*, 2nd ed. (Los Altos, CA: Hermes Publications, 1953), 126.

10. For analyses of Plato's *Phaedrus* relevant to this subject, see Marilyn Brownstein, "*Phaedrus* and Feminine Desire: Towards a Postmodern Epistemology," *Textual Fidelity and Textual Disregard*, ed. Bernard P. Dauenhauer (New York: Peter Lang, 1990), 39-54; and C. Jan Swearingen, "Plato's Feminine: Appropriation, Impersonation, and Metaphorical Polemic," *Rhetoric Society Quarterly* 22.1 (1992): 109-23.

11. Michelle Ballif, "Re/Dressing Histories; Or, On Re/Covering Figures Who Have Been Laid Bare By Our Gaze," *Rhetoric Society Quarterly* 22.1 (1992): 91.

12. Ibid.

13. See especially Chapter 2, "Economies of Friendship: The Textuality of *Amicitia*," in *The Usurer's Daughter: Male Friendship and Fictions of Women in Sixteenth-Century England* (London: Routledge, 1994), 52-85. In this chapter Hutson discusses how Renaissance humanism restructures the "traffic in women" that Gayle Rubin (following Claude Lévi-Strauss) describes as the social exchange on which culture is founded; see Rubin, "The Traffic in Women: Notes on a 'Political Economy' of Sex," *Towards an Anthropology of Women*, ed. Rayna R. Reiter (New York: Monthly Review Press, 1975), 157-210. As the humanists substitute friendship for kinship ties in the exchange between men, persuasive texts about women become the medium of that transaction. Hutson does not discuss *A Midsummer Night's Dream* specifically.

14. Boudard, *Iconologie* (Vienna 1766; rpt. New York: Garland, 1976); Logique is found in Tome Second, 159, Rhetorique in Tome Troisieme, 103. Also see the description of Rettorica by Cesare Ripa in *Iconologia* (1593; Padua, 1611 ed.; rpt. New York: Garland, 1976), 460.

15. I discuss both of these plays in "Speaking Sensibly: Feminine Rhetoric in *Measure for Measure* and *All's Well That Ends Well*," *Renaissance*

Papers 1986, ed. Dale B.J. Randall and Joseph A. Porter (Durham, NC: Southeastern Renaissance Conference, 1986), 43-51. For a discussion of the relationship between sexual decorum and rhetoric, see chapter 6 of Patricia A. Parker, *Literary Fat Ladies: Gender, Rhetoric, Property* (London: Methuen, 1987), particularly 119-25. Parker also discusses explicitly the connection between female speech and anxieties about male effeminacy in "On the Tongue: Cross Gendering, Effeminacy, and the Art of Words," *Style* 23 (1989): 445-65.

16. Ballif, 91.

17. Javitch, *Poetry and Courtliness in Renaissance England* (Princeton: Princeton University Press, 1978), especially chapter 1.

18. Puttenham, 114.

19. Ibid., 115.

20. Ibid., 116.

21. Ibid., 117.

22. Ibid.

23. Ibid., 118.

24. Ibid.

25. This plate, which appears as the frontispiece to Andrea Lunsford's *Reclaiming Rhetorica: Women in the Rhetorical Tradition* (Pittsburgh: University of Pittsburgh Press, 1995), comes from *Die Tarocchi. Zwei italienische Kupferstichfolgen aus dem XV. Jahrhundert* (Berlin: Cassirer, 1910).

26. On the iconography of Athena in the emblem tradition and the symbolic connection between the scholar (frequently Cicero) and the soldier, see examples from Geffrey Whitney's *A Choice of Emblemes* (1586) in Peter M. Daly, Leslie T. Duer, and Anthony Raspa, eds. *The English Emblem Tradition*, vol. 1 (Toronto: University of Toronto Press, 1988), 136, 201, and 327 .

27. Louis Adrian Montrose, "'Shaping Fantasies': Figurations of Gender and Power in Elizabethan Culture," *Representations* 1 (1983): 62.

28. Ringler, "The Number of Actors in Shakespeare's Early Plays," *The Seventeenth-Century Stage: A Collection of Critical Essays*, ed. Gerald Eades Bentley (Chicago: University of Chicago Press, 1968), 110-34.

29. Although her book appeared after this essay had been completed, Patricia Parker also discusses briefly the relevance of hypallage to *A Midsummer Night's Dream*; *Shakespeare from the Margins: Language, Culture, Context* (Chicago: University of Chicago Press, 1996), 100-01. Another wonderful essay that discusses the relationship of *Dream*'s structural

rhetoric and its anomalous women to the critical enterprise in general is Terence Hawkes's "Or," in *Meaning by Shakespeare* (London: Routledge, 1992), 11-41.

30. Puttenham, 143.

31. To be fair, many of Puttenham's examples of different rhetorical figures involve sexual or romantic overtones and often subject romantic relationships to irony. For an analysis specifically of hypallage in another Renaissance drama, see Ann Pasternak Slater, "Hypallage, Barley-Break, and *The Changeling*," *Review of English Studies*, n.s.34 (1983): 429-40.

32. Frye, "The Argument of Comedy," *English Institute Essays, 1948*, ed. D.A. Robertson, Jr. (New York: Columbia University Press, 1949), 58-73.

33. Puttenham, 143.

34. Keach, *Elizabethan Erotic Narratives: Irony and Pathos in the Ovidian Poetry of Shakespeare, Marlowe, and Their Contemporaries* (New Brunswick, NJ: Rutgers University Press, 1977). Shakespeare's debt to Ovid for both comic and tragic representations of metamorphosis is discussed in Jonathan Bate, *Shakespeare and Ovid* (Oxford: Clarendon Press, 1993).

35. Barton, 1974 edition, 219.

36. Nevo, *Comic Transformations in Shakespeare* (London: Methuen, 1980), 97-98.

37. Thomas Wilson, for instance, reproduces Erasmus's epistle persuading a young man to marriage (*The Arte of Rhetorique* [1553], ed. Thomas J. Derrick [New York: Garland, 1982], 95-140). Interestingly, in Erasmus's epistle the proud Titans or giants are represented as being opposed to marriage, and Titania is one of the daughters of Titan. Thus, she is outside the rhetoric of marriage that Theseus addresses to Hermia. In this light, the intertextual connections between their discourses on marriage become more interesting.

38. Fineman, *Shakespeare's Perjured Eye: The Invention of Poetic Subjectivity in the Sonnets* (Berkeley: University of California Press, 1986), 267.

39. Fineman, 18.

40. For a discussion of lies in Sonnet 138, see Fineman, 165-67.

41. Kinney, *Humanist Poetics: Thought, Rhetoric, and Fiction in Sixteenth-Century England* (Amherst: University of Massachusetts Press, 1986), 22ff.

42. Kinney, 23.

43. Kinney, 22.

44. Davis, *Guise and Disguise: Rhetoric and Characterization in the English Renaissance* (Toronto: University of Toronto Press, 1993), 134.

45. Vickers, "'The Blazon of Sweet Beauty's Best': Shakespeare's *Lucrece*," *Shakespeare and the Question of Theory*, ed. Patricia Parker and Geoffrey Hartman (London: Methuen, 1985), 97.

46. Traub, "The (In)Significance of 'Lesbian' Desire in Early Modern England," *Queering the Renaissance*, ed. Jonathan Goldberg (Durham, NC: Duke University Press, 1994), 72.

47. On Theseus's reputation as a man who seduces and abandons women, which must be pieced together from a number of sources, see D'Orsay W. Pearson's fine essay on the topic: "'Unkinde' Theseus: A Study in Renaissance Mythography," *English Literary Renaissance* 4 (1974): 276-98. See also E. Talbot Donaldson, *The Swan at the Well: Shakespeare Reading Chaucer* (New Haven: Yale University Press, 1985): "The most fully responsible character in Chaucer's *Knight's Tale* and in *A Midsummer Night's Dream* is Theseus, Duke of Athens. But while this mentor-figure is often said to be the only character that Shakespeare adopted from Chaucer without change, the second Theseus seems to me somewhat less mature, less philosophical, and a good deal more skeptical than the first" (32). Furthermore, while Chaucer suppresses Theseus's shady sexual past, "Shakespeare's Theseus is assigned an erotic activity far more specific and genuinely damaging" (34).

48. Barkan, *Transuming Passion: Ganymede and the Erotics of Humanism* (Stanford: Stanford University Press, 1991).

49. Barber, *Shakespeare's Festive Comedy: A Study of Dramatic Form and Its Relation to Social Custom* (Princeton: Princeton University Press, 1959), 137.

50. Although an extended discussion of usury is outside the scope of this essay, a discussion of the distinction between trade and usury can be found in E. Pearlman, "Shakespeare, Freud, and the Two Usuries, or, Money's a Meddler," *English Literary Renaissance* 2 (1972): 217-36. Simply put, the Renaissance defense of capitalist trade and banking ran as follows: trade is legitimate because it produces real goods (perhaps like a child); usury involves the replication of coins from other coins alone, a species of counterfeiting.

51. In chapter 9 of *The Purpose of Playing*, Louis Montrose argues that Shakespeare's plays reproduce, but also challenge the legitimacy of dominant social structures in Early Modern England:

> Within the course of a given dramatic action, representatives of opposition and difference are usually defeated, banished, converted, or otherwise apparently contained by the play's ideologically dominant forces and forms. Nevertheless, in its very representation of alternatives and resistances, the play articulates and disseminates fragments of those

socially heterodox discourses that the politically dominant discourse seeks, with only limited success, to appropriate, repudiate, or suppress. The play may try to impose symbolic closure upon the heterodoxy to which it also gives voice, but that closure can be neither total nor final. (*The Purpose of Playing Shakespeare and the Cultural Politics of the Elizabethan Theatre* [Chicago: University of Chicago Press, 1966], 144.)

Despite his careful insistence that the traces of heterodox sentiment remain visible in *Dream*, in this chapter Montrose nevertheless emphasizes the misogynistic dimension of the play's examination of Amazonomachy and stops short of assigning to the play's women the status of ethical and political subjects within the fiction of *Dream*'s plot. Bottom is his principal exemplar of heterodox forces that challenge the status quo.

52. Although working more explicitly with the contrast between Theseus's aesthetics of immediacy and his own "syncretic, bookish character" (335), derived as it is from a pastiche of printed sources, Barbara A. Mowat shows ably how in *Dream* a metaphysics of presence is undermined by the play's reliance on the written word; "'A Local Habitation and a Name': Shakespeare's Text as Construct," *Style* 23 (1989): 335-51.

53. The fact that we cannot confidently assign the poverty of Pyramus's speech to either the playwright or actor highlights the interdependence of oral and written discourse in this play.

Our Nightly Madness
Shakespeare's *Dream* Without *The Interpretation of Dreams*

Thelma N. Greenfield

A widespread and time-honored tradition regards dreams as purveyors of secret information, engineered externally or from the self and asking for ingenious decodings. The same tradition assumes that the decoder should be an expert. A priest or a wiseman might do the job or latterly a psychoanalyst. It is doubtless the bizarre nature of dream content and structure, defying as it does ordinary rational explanation, that suggests a latent significance in dreams readable by those possessed of special knowledge.[1]

Allegiance to such a concept leads many a Shakespearean (not unexpectedly) to turn to Freud for help in studying Shakespeare's handling of dream states; and with its dream title and its dark woods where swords are drawn, *A Midsummer Night's Dream* is a natural target for Freudian reading, Freud having explicitly labeled both swords and woodsy landscapes as signifiers of human genitalia.

Application of the psychoanalytic method to *Dream* is amply demonstrated in a study warmly endorsed by Maurice Charney (in his introduction to *Psychoanalytic Approaches to Literature and Film*). Charney comments on what he calls a fortunate shift from a "scientific" Freudian approach—reading characters or author biographically—to a "literary" Freudianism of theme, imagery, and structure,[2] citing as an example of what he means Jan Hinely's packed presentation of *A Midsummer Night's Dream* as Shakespeare's exploration of his characters' sexual conflicts.[3] The essay Charney refers to systematically distributes intense sexual anxieties to the young female characters, fighting as "substitute sexual consummation" to the male rivals, incestuous drives to both Egeus and Titania, and to Bottom the roles of beast, lover, and narcissistic infant (with Titania and Bottom together forming a "grotesquely tender" image of the Madonna and child). There is more in this vein; but in the end, having with negative sex drives and anxieties purged much of the laughter from the play, Hinely, too opimistically for me, undertakes to preserve the comedy by finding a happy conclusion of "mature" sexuality, trust, and merit.[4]

Marjorie B. Garber's brilliant *A Midsummer Night's Dream* chapter can serve as another excellent example of Freudian reading: ". . . somatic dreams function through the use of transformations, described by Freud as displacements and condensations, by means of which the underlying meaning is bound into an apparently fictive plot."[5] The Freudian interest in processes "subconscious and associative" and in "translation," brings Garber conveniently to the "translated" Bottom, who moves between his natural "asshood" and his visible asshood in the famous Bottomless "dream" (though, as Garber indicates, the specified processes are the critic's). At this juncture, however, we should consider a point that Garber does not: Bottom's initial natural, inborn "asshood" is, after all, a metaphoric verbal denomination, a metaphor for his over-enthusiastic self-importance, while his visible, unnatural, fairy-generated asshead is literal. To stay in the Freudian pattern, however, Garber must turn the *Dream* pattern around and designate what is seen on stage a "metaphor" for a real asshood, but one, in her Freudian word, "hidden."[6]

Other critics also read Bottom's strange new appearance as a metaphor ("Bottom [becomes a] walking metaphor, vehicle to his own tenor," writes Garrett Stewart.)[7] But the tenor itself, I reiterate, is the metaphor, and the very validity of the stage image in and of itself is important to my argument in this paper.

Further, my inclination is to find the word "hidden" surely too strong for the comic appropriateness of Bottom's translation. Here is no Freudian "mask" for something deeply concealed. What the stage does is give a visual image that compels the metaphoric verbalization applicable to Bottom's essential nature—"dumb eloquence," as Samuel Daniel might have put it. The equation is readable with comic ease.

The image insistently supplies a word Bottom will only innocently employ, however, e.g., "to make an ass of me, to fright me" (3.1.115-

16).[8] Critic's "displacement" or not, to see Bottom literally as an ass offers the audience a rhetorical-visual joke—as do Folly's ears in *Praise of Folly*. And her ears, we should remember, are quickly foisted upon the audience.[9]

For himself, Bottom, of course, skirts any articulated acknowledgement, although, as a proto-Dogberry, he comes perilously close: "methought I was—and methought I had—" (4.1.207-08). By turning his rumination into a memorably-distressed Biblical passage regarding the general confines of human perception, the play slyly turns the tables to hint at Bottom's brotherhood with those other wisely-unconfessed "patched fools"—his audience, who laugh at him. At least Bottom, though he drops the thought of having it documented in a ballad, has made to his temporary state of literal asshood a friendly accommodation, calling for literal hay and literal ear-scratching and (like King Midas, also famous for his ass's ears) preferring a decidedly inferior music.[10]

From the same perspective, Bottom's "dream" of wearing an ass's head, rather than presenting a Freudian "facade," offers him and his audience an openly self-incriminating experiential variant. The dreamer, writes Bert States, "is thus an involuntary artist who takes the labeled world to sleep and reclassifies it"—in this case from metaphor to the literal.[11] All the world is a stage, and he who would play the tyrant's, the woman's and the lion's part, not to mention the role of sweet-faced Pyramus, now involuntarily plays a more suitable role.

The integrity of image in this dream-play leads me to diverge from the usual applications of Freudian dream interpretation as far as *A Midsummer Night's Dream* is concerned. In short, I want to suggest that one can valuably see its images as "not a superficial covering for an abstract hidden world" but as possessed of a "thinglike existence" and "stand[ing] in their own right."[12] Furthermore, in my argument, the "dreams" of *Dream* (and as some dream theorists say, dreams in general) are valid verbal, visual, and emotional constructs. They are autonomous and significantly experiential in themselves, rather than "masks" or displacements of some "real" meaning that has been translated and obfuscated by a concealed operant located somewhere within the dreamer.

One must not, obviously cannot, dismiss Freud's work in dream psychology, but tillers in fields other than literary criticism have certainly not rested content with all of Freud's teaching on the subject.

For instance, Hans Christian von Baeyer can today confidently call "Freud's method of [dream] analysis ... almost frighteningly inadequate."[13] There has, in fact, always been a quarrel with Freud's insistence on the inevitable hallucinatory wish-fulfillment of dream, with the roles Freud assigns to drives, urges, and repressed infantile desires when "latent dream thought" is changed by "dream work" into "manifest dream." Beginning with attacks on his concept of dream as simultaneously a "mere facade" and a significant "hieroglyphic language,"[14] many researchers on dreaming have undertaken to extend, divert, or repudiate Freud's beliefs. Early on, this feature disturbed Jung and Adler among others. Seventy years later, an investigator such as David Foulkes, with his interest in cognitive psychology and structuralism, labels Freud's dream theories as useful in a number of ways but also riddled with error (especially in the matter of wish fulfillment). Or, for example, the Swiss dream analyst Medard Boss, a most energetic anti-Freudian exponent of the phenomenology of dream, more basically refuses the whole premise that dreams translate a "mental construct" that was "assumed to exist behind [the dream] phenomena."[15] He insists on the integrity and importance of dreaming as its own experiential state, for dreams are autonomous "modes of being" no more reducible to our waking life than waking is reducible to dream but nevertheless valuable to it.[16]

This is not to argue that dreams are rational. Duke Theseus might well have listed the dreamer in his lunatic-lover-poet linkage, for dream's mimicry of lunacy in its various guises—hallucination, psychotic delusions, delirium, and manifestations of organic brain disease—is well-known and certainly important to Shakespeare's *Dream*. Our "nightly madness" is the happy phrase applied by neurophysicist J. Alan Hobson, though Hobson is also a powerful defender of dream's healthiness and profound significance.[17] Although during dreams we are "formally delirious and demented,"[18] in Hobson's view dreams can reveal "deep aspects of ourselves," but they do so "without recourse to... disguises and censorship or ... Freudian symbols." Their bizarre character is "the normal and undistorted consequence of altered information processing" that comes with sleep—the brain then cut off from the usual waking avenues of information and proceeding on its own spontaneous neuron-enabled activity. If we try to compare it to waking experience, dream is, if you like, a "dysfunction" which includes, nevertheless, a notable effort to compensate through the imposition of a strange kind of coherence and order upon its chaos.[19]

In certain ways, today's phenomenological understanding of dreams comes surprisingly close to observations set forth by Timothy Bright in 1586 in his *Treatise of Melancholie*, "available, simple, and authoritative," says Hardin Craig, and a work Shakespeare may have read.[20] In the unlimited scope of dreams, wrote Bright, "we see . . . heare, talke, conferre, and practise what action soever, as evidently with affection of joye or sorrowe, as if the very object of these senses were represented unto us brode awake. . . ."[21] But, he indicates, dreams are free from "common" sense, from memory, from "images of outward thinges," and have their own integrity as experience. Furthermore, awake, we cannot replicate their kind of fancy, even if we try, for then "the great law of necessitie" bars the soul from the actions that busy it in sleep.[22] And finally, the dream experience, Bright remarks, tends to give us a "present," even to bringing the past and the future into that present.[23] The phenomenological view may offer too much solidity for our deconstructively-bruised understanding of what and how we know, but many of its features seem to be useful for scrutinizing how we meet Shakespeare's dramatic use of dream. Though in this case Shakespeare is not his subject, Bert O. States in *Dreaming and Storytelling* provides an example of a literary critic who pretty much sheds Freud and deals (like Boss) with dream as lived experience. Basic to States' argument is the view that the self needs to "express the possible structures of experience in imaginative terms."[24] Thus dreaming—dreaming understood as itself an autonomous experience uncontrolled by a translator and a censor—can alert one to possibilities "for existing," since at least some of the same modes of connecting with our surroundings are available to us, waking or dreaming—a sense of visual perception, of motion, of intense emotion, and the like.[25]

On such a base, I should like to pursue a little farther the experience of dreaming in *A Midsummer Night's Dream*. To put the play in context, we should remember that dreams abound in the Shakespeare corpus, often to play an important structural part or powerfully to express a tormented mind or for (sometimes wildly misread) foretellings and omens. Frequently the word "dream" itself serves in a clarifying comparison or, conversely, to represent confusion of the real and unreal. Though often ill-advisedly, many of the speakers dismiss

dreams as idle, false, foolish, quickly vanishing. And while we see
Lady Macbeth enacting her dream state, the plays ordinarily introduce
dreams through narration, though such dream-telling may be dismissed
as a useless or dangerous pastime. "You laugh," says Cleopatra, "when
boys or women tell their dreams . . . (*Ant.*, 5.2.73). "[A]re you so
choleric / With Eleanor, for telling but her dream?" (*2H6*, 1.2.51-52),
the Duchess urges deviously after her husband has recited a fearsome
one of his own. (Later in the same play, the Cardinal weightily alludes
to a dream he has had.)

A fascination with recited dreams persists throughout the canon.
"What was your dream, my lord? I pray you tell me," (*R3.*, 1.4.8),
urges the keeper to introduce Clarence's recital of his horrific sleeping
vision of drowning. All the way to Caliban, dreams are likely to enter
the plays for the telling. In *A Midsummer Night's Dream*, Hermia both
enacts and repeats her serpent dream, but Bottom perhaps remains
unique in refusing to reveal what he calls his dream, although even he
is sorely tempted to tell.

An important distinction needs to be made at the point where
Bottom draws the line. To tell a dream is to begin its transformation
into a waking narrative,[26] whereas dreaming, as has been remarked, is a
matter of experiencing—a difference Shakespeare recognized and in *A
Midsummer Night's Dream* and elsewhere, I think, demonstrated at
length. Such a recited dream as Clarence's attempts to bridge the
distinction by reconstructing the dreamer's dreamt physical anguish
while Lady Macbeth directly demonstrates the potent experiential
nature of sleep life. In its immediacy, its vividness, and its mode, in
fact, actual dreaming is much more like an enacted and watched play
than like an ordinary narrative.[27]

"The dream is pure drama," wrote Ionesco, ". . . a thought
expressed in images, and . . . always dramatic."[28] Indeed, a dream
proceeds (normally in the 'present') with the appearance of a cast of
characters, however unstable, in a place, however unlikely, and through
a sequence of events, however illogical. The dreamer, triply employed,
involuntarily creates the dream, and enters the roles of watcher and
participant at the same time.

The dreamer's creativity is actually much like the creativity of
members of a play audience. To even so dedicated a neurophysiologist
as Hobson, dreaming is a "form of creativity."[29] In the universality of

dreams, Hobson sees evidence of the universality of artistic experience (as well as the "beginnings" of art and of many a scientific discovery.[30]

When Puck at his play's end invites the audience to think they have but dreamed, he offers a reminder of the watching and creating that both play audiences and dreamers do, even as they also participate. He has already anticipated this perspective with his earlier, "What, a play toward? I'll be an auditor; / An actor too perhaps, if I see cause" (3.1.75-76). However voluntary or involuntary the involvement, Puck implies, the audience, like the dreamer, is after all at the bottom of what is created.

Shakespeare had a strong model to draw upon for his midsummer dream play. A decade before *Dream* urged its presumably high-born viewers toward accepting their part in what has happened, the court prologue to *Sapho and Phao* entreated Her Royal Highness to "imagine your self to be in a deepe dreame."[31] Lyly repeatedly insisted that his plays (filled with dream episodes) were themselves the shadows of a dream. They were also the Queen's creation: she not only determined their value—iron or bullion, swan or bat, dove or vulture—she shaped the very "waxe" they were made of.[32]

By and large, *A Midsummer Night's Dream* employs dream somewhat differently from other Shakespeare plays, though it does, as has been mentioned, share with many of them one specific, unequivocal dream episode. Perhaps with a nod toward classical belief in dream as omen, Hermia's recitation of her dream of a serpent who gnaws at her breast serves to introduce an array of confused, dreamlike experiences. (Here, Hinely and others urge a translated sexual anxiety.) In a variety of moods, dream experience becomes the whole mode of *Dream*—its language, its appearance, the manner of its action. Coleridge was surely right when he remarked that Shakespeare worked upon the play "as a *dream* throughout," his comment implying, I suppose, theatergoers as its ultimate dreamers as the action and characters are realized on the stage.[33]

Many of the play's developments repeat characteristic dream features: strange juxtapositions, strong emotional states, manifestations of figures from another world lurking in familiar settings turned strangely unfamiliar, abrupt and illogical shiftings in attitude and shape, physical movement accomplished with magical speed or frustrated by infuriating impediments, and a number of extraordinary entanglements as suddenly and unreasonably occurring as dissolved.

Even its several journeys to the forest replicate the journeys long
associated with dreaming. And Shakespeare's habit of equating night
with dream here repeats itself with the many nighttime scenes and
weighted references to darkness and moonshine.

The dream language of the play is too familiar to repeat beyond
noting that the title implicates the audience from the start and is
followed by an immediate second in Hippolyta's early "Four nights
will quickly dream away the time" (1.1.8), which equates for us
dramatic time and dream time. An hallucinatory aura provided by the
fairies, who are unseen by any but the audience and a "translated"
Bottom (3.1.113-14) persists to the end. And the lovers themselves
sense the dreamlike qualities of their woodland adventures.

All of these features blend with the much-discussed problem of the
real and unreal in dramatic art which the play reflects, though whatever
they might seem to teach us on this subject is bathed in the ambiguous
ambience provided by the ubiquitous and changeful moonshine, it, too,
immersed in complexities of reference and mode, it, too, sometimes a
passing allusion, sometimes a lyrical flight, sometimes a dramatistic
problem, and finally an actor on stage in the unprepossessing figure of
little Starveling.

F.E. Halliday, in keeping with the kind of selfhood that insentient
things can assume in dreams, calls the *Dream* moon "almost ... a
character."[34] Davis, who sees *Dream* as a "prolonged study of
dramatistic identity," finds no fewer and possibly more than six "notions of self" in the artisans' discussion of how to "disfigure" the
moon.[35] The appearance of Moonshine, however, or of a Lion as an
acted role in the artisans' play is as a stage device no more outrageous
than our seeing Bottom's actor wearing ass's ears. Philostrate's remark
on the play-within-the-play, "it is nothing, nothing in the world"
(5.1.78), applies equally to both levels. Neither is a part of our everyday waking world. The actors who play lovers with "minds
transfigur'd" (5.1.24), running about imaginary woods, belong to the
more strange than true pattern. Theseus is in part correct. The lovers'
adventures are shadows of nothingness, as are they themselves and
Theseus. And who accepts the actors as the figures they say they
represent? Who turns nothing into something? The play tells us more
than once that, as its audience, we do. It is a task ostentatiously refused
by Theseus' resistant audience who watch the mechanicals' play from
on stage. But through an alternative life—like that we experience in a

dream state—we can put aside—say—our perception of the intermediary actor on stage who plays an actor on stage playing the light of the moon, and get down to the immediate business of "seeing" Starveling attempting to be moonshine.

In "The Theatergoer as Imager," John Drummond approaches the issue of the creative experiencing of the play audience: "images are created less by the performers on stage than by the audience . . .," Drummond writes, [36] and, furthermore, the spectator "wants to make images." It is the image we "add to the specifics [sets. actors, etc.] of the play that enables drama to do its job.[37] And what we image, I would add, like Bottom's ears, is not a metaphor hiding the real thing. Akhter Ahsen puts it thus: "Images are . . . not codes" but "stand in their own right" and are not to be rejected either as metaphors or because they lack logic, memorial accuracy, or ties to what is past.[38]

Along with "translations," Freudian readings of *A Midsummer Night's Dream* pursue a strong impulse to emphasize a dark underside of the play. Indicative is such a title as Melvin Goldstein's "Identity Crises in a Midsummer Nightmare: Comedy as Terror in Disguise."[39] Indeed, we do look into prolonged dream-darkness—in the woods and at the palace. (Hearne notes the frequency of dreamers being unable to "switch on a light.")[40] But Goldstein, finding terror, madness, and "savage" sleep at the center of *A Midsummer Night's Dream*, like Hinely, at the end uncovers tameness, logic, and didacticism—in his words, "authentic selves" and "authentic society" and the "pleasures and pains of reality."[41] Insofar as we can capture the play, however, I do not find its images so horrific in its middle nor so reassuringly logical at its end.

As Parker shows us,[42] *A Midsummer Night's Dream* both approaches and delays its conclusion, with the dream-time interim building on the tensions of the loving-quarreling male-female connections, taken even as far as their correspondences in the other world of fairy and the harmonies of nature. The artisan-artists strive earnestly in the woods and at court to capture the structures of presentational art that deal with the same unsmooth path. As for what controls might work on this melange of love, defiance, jealousy, and quarrels, in this mixture of confusion and change, of parental interference and the law, even the fairies, even when their intentions are good, can bring disasters. With such hit or miss powers at work, cheerful resignation might seem a better response to the comedy than a careful search for rational therapeutic benefits.

Male and female in the play seem to have two options—loving or quarreling. Along with the comic socio-sexual conflicts, however, we glimpse striking images of an alluring world, not dark, not masking something hidden, but nostalgic, surprisingly edenic, that nevertheless allows the male-female contention much profounder roots, since its far-flung realm rules out the male or else subordinates him to an incidental role in a female domain.[43] Titania's East Indian "feminine world rich with all the mysteries of fertility, conception, pregnancy, and birth that women can treat with easy familiarity"[44] aligns itself with the invulnerable virginal sphere of the imperial vestal, throned by the west, and the similarly untouched world of Hermia and Helena, pictured as young female friends together, sewing, singing, and flourishing in "childhood innocence" (3.2.202), skillfully creating not children but an artful flower. Even the old women are allowed their kitchen community of woeful tales and mirthful wheezing. To those comfortable variant visions of female conviviality or poised solitude, of meditating, talking, laughing, singing, or sewing, we can add brief glances at the active virago world Hippolyta has known, hers an alternative realm of warfare and the joyful cries of hunting hounds ringing through "the groves, / The skies, the fountains, every region near" (4.1.114-15).

I know of nothing else in Shakespeare quite similar to this series. In contrast, the intrusive, divisive male images imposing commands and rivalries show the contentions between male and female lovers as deeply rooted in oppositional modes that admit little compromise. That the play can approach any kind of harmonious conclusion (if it does) is more miracle or accident than a logically ordered movement into firm social adjustment. Accordingly, *A Midsummer Night's Dream* comes to an uncertain end. Waking and dreaming become confused. Characters vacillate between believing and not believing, or contradict one another. Paternal and legal authorities reverse themselves. The artisans' disastrous play elicits both generosity and impatient scoffing. The action that begins in impatience ends with it.

But the audience must be patient a little longer, for the epilogue itself takes on a life of its own. One effort is aborted when Theseus, fending off more poetry, releases us from the play-within-the-play. "Never excuse," he admonishes, and opts for the Bergomask with "let your epilogue alone" (5.1.342 and 347-48). Reaching, as he always does, for an ordered world, Theseus then speaks his own epilogue, for the moment dissolving the frenzies and laughter, as we now expect from him, into a sensible division, sorting out night and day, bedtime and timely waking.

Dreams, however, are not so easily got rid of. Shakespeare, at least as a dramatist, seems basically to agree with von Baeyer, who calls dreaming "a seriously undervalued part of our lives."[45] Like Bottom springing to life after his stage death with "will it please you to see the epilogue?" (5.1.338-39), *A Midsummer Night's Dream* springs to life with intrusions from the other world after the human contingent withdraws, friendly otherworld invaders now in the very palace—the bastion of the voice of rationality—with a conclusion of song and dance and folk rites, with gruesome reminders of beasts and gaping graves mingled with blessings, and with the fairies "Following darkness like a dream" (5.1.372). They have the last word, as we, the audience, move through the uncertain, intermissive stages of awakening.

Of the five last-scene speeches any one could serve as epilogue. But all work together to shroud our own "translation" in mystery. To that end, our severance from the play is fashioned into an awareness of the distinctions between dreaming and waking states, between everyday experience and experiencing the otherworld of art. Puck's really final words tell us that one is not the other. We are also made aware of the incapacity of one fully to comprehend the other. We are told as the lovers were earlier that maybe it didn't happen. We are told to think we dreamed. We are told that maybe Puck is a teller of truth, maybe a liar. Whatever the uncertainties, however, still we know that our minds were for a time "transfigur'd ... together," although to grasp what happened during the transfiguration, you really had to be there. But there comes a time to complete our withdrawal and again it is our task. By the giving of our "hands" (5.1.423), we produce the noise that liberates us from our own spell. Now we can only talk about it, turn it into narrative, being, as Bright puts it, "unable in like sort [to] fancie being awake."

Shakespeare's *A Midsummer Night's Dream*, then, in my view, presents itself as neither representational nor symbolic but modal. Narratizing its experiential moment involves us in a process operating from a totally separate base. No continuum links them together. Neither is reducible to the other. The more rigorous the narrative we construct, the larger the gulf between. With deceptive modesty, *A Midsummer Night's Dream*, throughout, reminds us of both the validity and the elusiveness of its dreamlike experiential mode and does so in the face of our most strenuous efforts to dismiss it, or to peer underneath for rationales, or to find for it realities anywhere but in itself.

NOTES

1. See J. Allan Hobson, *The Dreaming Brain* (New York: Basic Books, 1988), 10.

2. Maurice Charney and Joseph Reppen, eds., *Psychoanalytic Approaches to Literature and Film* (Rutherford, NJ: Fairleigh Dickinson University Press, 1987), 7.

3. Ibid., 9.

4. Jan Lawson Hinely, "Expounding the Dream: Shaping Fantasies in *A Midsummer Night's Dream*, in *Psychoanalytic Approaches*, Hinely, 127 and 134. See 127-28 for Hinely's discussion of mature love.

5. Garber, *Dream in Shakespeare: From Metaphor to Metamorphosis* (New Haven: Yale University Press, 1974), 69.

6. Ibid.

7. Stewart, "Shakespearean Dreamplay," *English Literary Renaissance* 11 (1981): 46.

8. Citations from *A Midsummer Night's Dream* are taken from Harold F. Brooks' Arden edition (London: Methuen, 1979), those from other Shakespeare plays are cited from *The Riverside Shakespeare*, ed. G. Blakemore Evans (Boston: Houghton Mifflin, 1974). On the "grammatical competence" of dreams, see David Foulkes, *A Grammar of Dreams* (New York: Basic Books, 1978), 14-16.

9. Thelma N. Greenfield, "*A Midsummer Night's Dream* and *The Praise of Folly*," *Comparative Literature* 20 (1968): 236-44.

10. Ibid.

11. Bert O. States, *Dreaming and Storytelling* (Ithaca: Cornell University Press, 1993), 121.

12. Akhter Ahsen, "Odysseus and *Oedipus Rex*: Image Psychology and the Literary Technique of Consciousness," *Journal of Mental Imagery* 7 (1983): 145, 146, and 147 .

13. Von Baeyer, *New York Times Book Review*, 6 November 1994, 35.

14. Medard Boss, *The Analysis of Dreams*, trans. Arnold J. Pomeranz (London: Rider, 1957), 40.

15. Ibid., 9.

16. Paul Stern, Foreword to Medard Boss, *I dreamt last night . . .*, trans. Stephen Conway (New York: Gardner Press, 1977), xv.

17. Hobson, *Sleep* (New York: Scientific American Library, 1989), 168, 166.

18. Hobson, *The Dreaming Brain*, 9.

19. Hobson, *Sleep*, 165-66.

20. Craig, Introduction to Bright's *Treatise*, ed. Hardin Craig, Facsimile Text Society (New York: Columbia University Press, 1940), xvi-xvii.

21. Bright, 118.

22. Compare Akhter Ahsen, "Prolucid Dreaming: A Content Analysis Approach to Dreams," *Journal of Mental Imagery* 16 (1992): 56.

23. Bright, 119.

24. States, 85.

25. Gordon Globus, *Dream Life, Wake Life: The Human Condition Through Dreams* (Albany: State University of New York Press, 1987), 163 and 164; and Boss, *I dreamt last night . . .*, xv.

26. States, 7.

27. Foulkes, 14.

28. Quoted in A. Alvarez, "Let me sleep on it: Creativity and the Dynamics of Dreaming," *Times Literary Supplement*, 23 December 1994, 12.

29. Ibid.

30. Hobson, *The Dreaming Brain*, 18.

31. *The Complete Works of John Lyly*, ed. R. Warwick Bond, 3 vols. (Oxford: Clarendon, 1902), 2: 372.

32. Lyly, Epilogue to *Campaspe*, 2: 360; also see the Prologue at the Court.

33. Samuel Taylor Coleridge, *Writings on Shakespeare*, ed. Terence Hawkes (New York: Capricorn Books, 1959), 252.

34. Halliday, *The Poetry of Shakespeare's Plays* (New York: Barnes and Noble, 1964), 90.

35. Lloyd Davis, *Guise and Disguise: Rhetoric and Characterization in the English Renaissance* (Toronto: University of Toronto Press, 1993), 12-13.

36. Drummond, "The Theatergoer as Imager," *Journal of Mental Imagery* 8 (1989): 99, 101.

37. Ibid., 101-02.

38. Ahsen, "Odysseus," 147 and 149.

39. Goldstein's essay appears in the *Psychoanalytic Review* 60 (1973): 169-204.

40. K.M.T. Hearne, "A New Perspective on Dream Imagery," *Journal of Mental Imagery* 11 (1987): 78.

41. Goldstein, 197.

42. Patricia Parker, "Anagogic Metaphor: Breaking Down the Wall of Partition," *Centre and Labyrinth: Essays in Honour of Northrop Frye*, ed. Eleanor Cook et al. (Toronto: University of Toronto Press, 1983), 50.

43. See James L. Calderwood, "*A Midsummer Night's Dream*: Anamorphism and Theseus' Dream," *Shakespeare Quarterly* 42.4 (1991): 409-30.

44. Ibid., 416.

45. Von Baeyer, 35.

Chronotope and Repression in
A Midsummer Night's Dream

Susan Baker

Critics of *A Midsummer Night's Dream* have usefully discussed such Bakhtinian topics as carnival and the grotesque body.[1] Equally relevant to the play is Bakhtin's concept of the chronotope, particularly his late argument for the study of chronotopes *in dialogue* with each other. According to Bakhtin, each narrative genre has its typifying chronotope (orientation in time and space); further, in narratives characters and motifs may have their own typifying chronotopes— which are then in dialogue with each other and with the (dominant) generic chronotope. Consideration of chronotopic dialogue within *A Midsummer Night's Dream* clarifies the play's specific inflection of *genera mista* and highlights differences from Shakespeare's other green world plays. Further, considering Theseus as himself a (represented) site of chronotopic dialogue suggests that the play anatomizes a structure of repression. Throughout, I am indebted to Bakhtin's definition of *chronotope* and its implications. Several of the specific chronotopes to be discussed in this essay, however, are my own abstractions from *A Midsummer Night's Dream* and other Shakespearean plays. It is worth remembering that for Bakhtin particular points in history have their characteristic chronotopes, while particular genres carry their own chronotopes. Any interpretation of a text, then, will set into dialogue the chronotope(s) of its original moment, the chronotopes embedded in its generic participation, and the chronotope(s) dominant in the time-space of its interpreter.

I

In his discussion of "Forms of Time and of the Chronotope in the Novel: Notes toward a Historical Poetics" (dated 1937-38),[2] Mikhail Bakhtin defines the term *chronotope* and argues that the history of narrative genres can be charted as a history of changing chronotopes. In general, this approach produces a useful taxonomy for the novel, particularly its "prehistory." To my mind (and for my purposes), however, the notion of the chronotope comes into its own with Bakhtin's 1973 postscript to this discussion. In the addendum, he argues that chronotopes can be mutually inclusive: "Each such [generically definitive] chronotope can include within it an unlimited number of minor chronotopes; in fact . . . any motif may have a special chronotope of its own."[3] Further, "the general characteristic of these interactions is that they are *dialogical*"; that is, "Chronotopes are mutually inclusive, they co-exist, they may be interwoven with, replace or oppose one another, contradict one another or find themselves in ever more complex relationships."[4] I am interested in precisely such dialogue of chronotopes in *A Midsummer Night's Dream*. First, however, it will be useful to clarify my understanding of why and how the consideration of chronotopes can open methodologically rigorous inquiry into the interanimations of form, value, and contingent history.

In workaday terms, the concept of "chronotope" is easy enough to grasp. As Gary Saul Morson and Caryl Emerson put it, "the rhythms and spacial [*sic*] organization of the assembly line, agricultural labor, sexual intercourse, and parlor conversation differ markedly."[5] In typically allusive and suggestive fashion, Bakhtin introduces the notion of *chronotope* as follows: "the intrinsic connectedness of temporal and spatial relationships that are artistically expressed in literature."[6] Bakhtin's move here is to establish that chronotopes provide the arena for artistic representation. Indeed, "it is precisely the chronotope that defines genre and generic distinctions."[7] Each of the narrative genres he then discusses has its distinctive—specific and determinant— chronotope. It is important to note here what Bakhtin says of his interest in *genre*; he "tak[es] genre not in its formalistic sense, but as a zone and a field of valorized perception, as a mode for representing the world."[8] This statement comes parenthetically in a discussion of Gogol, and I would modify it somewhat. I am persuaded that genres are both formal and ideologically-saturated structures, and I am most interested in understanding precisely how form and ideology interact. Hence my focus here on the chronotope, which is at once the arena for action, a zone of *valorized* perception, and a formal determinant of representation. According to Bakhtin, "It is precisely the chronotope that provides the ground essential for the showing forth, the representablity of events. . . . All the novel's abstract elements— philosophical and social generalizations, ideas, analyses of cause and effect—gravitate toward the chronotope and through it take on flesh and blood, permitting the imaging power of art to do its work."[9] As Michael Holquist puts it, the chronotope "is a category that can comprehend the necessity of time/space as recurring elements in all perception, but which will also take into account the non-recurring particularity of any act of perception." Further, *chronotope* "is a useful term not only because it brings together time, space, and value, but because it insists on their simultaneity and inseparability."[10]

Morson and Emerson illustrate the saturation of chronotopes with values in a series of questions; those most pertinent to this essay include the following: "Are actions dependent to a significant degree on where or when they occur?"; Would it in principle be possible for the order of incidents to be different, for events to be 'reversible' or 'repeatable'?"; "What kind of initiative do people have: are they beings to which things simply happen, or do they exercise choice and control, and if so, how much and of what kind?"; "Depending on the degree and kind of initiative people have, what kind of ethical responsiblity obliges them?; "Does social context itself change, and if so, in what ways?"; "Do personal identity and character change in response to events or are they fixed?"; "How does the past impinge on the present, and what is the relation of the present to possible futures?"; "Is the greatest value placed on the past, the present, the immediate future, or the distant future?"[11] Such questions help identify and distinguish among chronotopes, but more important they help index the values (or more precisely the modes of valorizing) specific to particular chronotopes. In other words, chronotopes offer a (reasonably) systematic approach to observing the interanimations of form, historicity, and ideology.

Certainly, scholars have acknowledged (without so naming) characteristic chronotopes for Shakespearean genres, though most have attended either to time *or*, less often, to space, rather than to the conjoined time-space Bakhtin emphasizes. David Scott Kastan, for example, writes that "the plays of each genre reveal a distinct (though provisional and exploratory) conception of time and man's role within it."[12] Jeanne Addison Roberts, on the other hand, stresses place in *The Shakespearean Wild*.[13] Despite differing emphases, such descriptions as those of Kastan and Roberts point directions for defining chronotopes. Perhaps the most durable description of a Shakespearean chronotope is found in Northrop Frye's schematic outline of the argument of Shakespearean comedy: from the red and white world of history into a green world and back again.[14] Indeed, "green world" has sufficiently entered the critical vocabulary to persist quite independent of the rest of Frye's elaborate apparatus—no doubt because the green world's marginal location ungridded by quotidian time sorts well with poststructuralist concerns. (The chronotope of what we call poststructuralism is otherwise inhospitable to Frye's tidy, totalizing, and teleological system.) It will be useful here to contrast two chronotopes, which are sometimes casually confused: "golden world" and "green world." Both motifs are relevant to *A Midsummer Night's Dream*, and the following descriptions should help isolate their salient aspects as chronotopes.

The terms *golden world* and *green world* imply spatial, temporal, and value-laden dimensions. For example, as everywhere implicit in Harry Levin's classic study, *The Myth of the Golden Age in the Renaissance*,[15] *golden world* can be used to refer to a *locus amoenus* [a pleasant place, a place without pain], from which we are separated by a physical distance, a *golden age*, from which we are separated by a span of time, and a matrix of values—whether, for example, one of (as Levin suggests) "unabashed pleasure," of ignorance about good, evil, and mortality (as in the Bible), or of freedom from the evils engendered by trade (as in Book I of Ovid's *Metamorphoses*). On each count, the green and golden worlds differ; they are projections of quite different chronotopes.

First of all, the golden world is almost always conceived of as having existed in a far distant past (at the beginning of or before chronology) or as something to be attained for perpetuity in a distant future (paradise in Christianity, for example). Thus, most conceptualizations of the golden world place it at the beginning and/or the end of linear time, *in illo tempore*.[16] Although often close to the "absolute past" of epic, in its purest form the chronotope of the golden world is radically unsuited to narrative, although its memory often seems the very impulse to narration. (In Ovidian terms, I would argue that it is not the golden but the bronze age that bequeaths us epic and its heroes.) Shakespeare's green worlds, on the other hand, clearly exist—by definition—*in medio tempore*, bounded temporally on both sides, inevitably transitory for visiting protagonists. (Denizens of Shakespearean green worlds, however, can seem as static as golden-world figures; indeed, they sometimes function more as scenery than as representations of human beings.)

Neither, of course, is any of Shakespeare's green worlds entirely *amoenus*: consider the intrusion of Marcade into the park at Navarre, the bad weather in Arden, the fairies' quarrels in the woods outside Athens, the harsh love test in Belmont, Caliban's misery and his attempted rape on Prospero's island, for just a few examples critics have discussed in recent years. Green worlds offer respite from various threats of the "red and white" world, but they also contain threats of their own. In a golden earthly paradise, life would be easy, soothing, comfortable and painless—again, hardly the stuff of narrative. In contrast, the green world offers not endless static lotus-eating but rather processes of movement and change. Significantly, the specific kinds of changes represented in any given green world help encode its dialogic interaction with its surrounding generic (or dominant) chronotope. (Think, for instance, of "Athens" and "the woods outside Athens" in *A Midsummer Night's Dream* and *Timon of Athens*.) In Bakhtin's terms, Shakespearean green worlds exist in adventure-time, but I would argue that they can be set in either the adventure-time of ordeal or the adventure-time of everyday life. That is, all of Shakespeare's green worlds serve as arenas for chance and accident, for meetings achieved and meetings missed.[17] Sometimes, however, they resemble novels of ordeal in that the adventures leave no trace; other times, as in the adventure novel of everyday life, they represent characters as responsible for their actions and, indeed, move them from guilt through purification to redemption.[18] I should reiterate here that although I shall certainly refer to chronotopes Bakhtin describes at length, I shall also be coining my own descriptions for some chronotopes pertinent to *A Midsummer Night's Dream*.

II

In the play's opening lines, Theseus introduces a chronotope:

> Now, fair Hippolyta, our nuptial hour
> Draws on apace. Four happy days bring in
> Another moon; but O, methinks, how slow
> This old moon [wanes]! (1.1.1-4)[19]

Time is foregrounded here, but the image of "bringing in" carries spatial overtones, and we are immediately located in the sublunary sphere—the space of time, if you will. Certainly, we are here invited into a prenuptial space, a liminal chronotope Theseus will define further a few lines later. But observe the figure of speech the Duke of Athens employs to describe prenuptial impatience:

> She lingers my desires,
> Like to a step-dame, or a dowager,
> Long withering out a young man's revenue. (1.1.4-6)

This simile asserts two sets of competing interests: female vs. male and old vs. young; as important as gender is in this play, conflict according to age also merits attention. (Age, of course, was more definitive, more delimiting for behavior, in early modern England than today.) Oriented differently in the time span of life, a young man and a step-dame or dowager are likely to evaluate the passing of present time quite differently, and their attitudes toward past and future surely diverge as well. Further, if we assume that *revenue* in this context would refer primarily to that from land, the -tope aspect of this age-based chronotope becomes explicit.[20] We need to look closely at Theseus's next few lines as well:

> Go, Philostrate,
> Stir up the Athenian youth to merriments,
> Awake the pert and nimble spirit of mirth,
> Turn melancholy forth to funerals:
> The pale companion is not for our pomp. (1.1.11-15)

This image is one of banishing Death from the wedding banquet. Both "wedding" and "funeral" are occasions for holiday, for ritual and ritually circumscribed activity, yet they are by no means identical. Here, Theseus insists that the wedding chronotope drive out that of funeral. As specific rituals whose representations often close comedies and tragedies respectively, "wedding" and "funeral" are generically significant variations on the chronotope of ritual.[21] Of course, over the past score of years critics have observed the "impure" art of Shakespearean genres, but attention to chronotopes can help to define genres as value-laden, can underline generic mixing and ideologically-saturated generic dialogue. As we shall see, even as *A Midsummer Night's Dream* both embeds and forestalls potential tragic consequences, the play is remarkably specific about what must be repressed for "wedding" to triumph over "funeral" in a chronotopic dialogue.

The play's introductory movement concludes with Theseus's much discussed assertion:

> Hippolyta, I woo'd thee with my sword,
> And won thy love doing thee injuries;
> But I will wed thee in another key,
> With pomp, with triumph, and with revelling. (1.1.16-19)

I am tempted to rephrase as "wed thee in another chronotope," for indeed we can read these lines as placing Theseus at an intersection of chronotopes. Certainly, his classical origins (or residue) aptly suit him for this dialogic site. The Theseus of Greek and Latin literature inhabits—in various stories—at least four chronotopes:

1. Frequently, he participates in what I will call the chronotope of etiology, where places and actions are founded, inaugurated.[22] This chronotope is close to that Bakhtin ascribes to epic, an "absolute past" which is "a specifically evaluating [hierarchal] category." That is, "In the epic world view, 'beginning,' 'first,' 'founder,' 'ancestor,' 'that which occurred earlier,' and so forth are not merely temporal categories but *valorized* temporal categories, and valorized to an extreme degree."[23] As I perceive it, the etiological chronotope undergirds sites and situations in which the present claims continuity and contiguity with an absolute past.

2. In many myths, he moves in the adventure-time of ordeal Bakhtin ascribes to Greek romance; this chronotope is most obviously the wide-ranging scene of parted young lovers who are eventually reunited, utterly unchanged by intervening events; it is also the chronotope of heroic exploits, each of which *proves* but does not alter the hero.

3. In some myths, he seems closer to the variation Bakhtin calls the adventure-novel of everyday life; this chronotope is that of metamorphosis or transformation, and it utterly changes those who experience it.[24]

4. In Plutarch, especially, Theseus is placed *just prior* to historical time; he exists on the eve of history, betwixt and between the chronotopes of legend and history. In this sense, he figures the inauguration of temporality that typically marks the end of a golden world.

As a further complication, Shakespeare's Duke of Athens simultaneously moves in a chronotope the playwright and his audience could have called "a great house of today"; that is, this play portrays a very Elizabethan Athens. Finally, as is insisted upon in the metadramatics of the play's fifth act, "Theseus" also—and primarily—exists in the chronotope of performance, that luminous time and space shared by an audience, a playwright, and some actors.[25] This chronotopic multiplicity of Theseus can serve as a model for the play as an anatomy of repression. Repeatedly in watching this play we could paraphrase Shakespeare's Troilus and protest "This is and is not Theseus." And—crucially—just which Theseus we remember, which we repress, at given moments will alter our interpretation of the play, even to the point of assessing its genre, of evaluating its valorizations.

In the purest forms of adventure-time, various exploits and encounters are interchangeable; events could be rearranged, some subtracted, others added, without impact on the overall outcome of the narrative. Many of the classical tales of Theseus belong to such an adventure-time, but his assertion that he may not "extenuate" Athenian law asks us to assume that Theseus has completed his establishment of Athenian democracy before pursuing war with the Amazons; that is, the "eve of history" dominates here. Theseus—in classical literature as well as in *A Midsummer Night's Dream*—oscillates between at least two roles: hero/adventurer/rapist and wise founder, especially of Athenian democracy.[26] (Theseus is *patriarch* in many senses.) Although he won Hippolyta as violent warrior-hero, it is as civic ruler that he will wed her. He has moved from the battlefield to the agora, from an immediate present that threatens an abrupt end toward a present oriented in the direction of future consequences and, usually at least, certified by an affiliation with or reverence for a legitimating past. The *civis* has buried its dead and now looks forward to its perpetuation. To see this play as a celebration of wedding, however, as a comic representation of union and promised reproduction, we must— to some extent at least—repress the pasts of both Theseus and Hippolyta. Further, we must also repress any knowledge of their future. It is, after all, their son who will engage Theseus in yet another chronotope, that of tragedy, in which consequences are inexorable as the past weighs on the present and effaces the future. This chronotope of deadly causality everywhere haunts the play and is everywhere repressed. Repeatedly, the play raises savagely tragic possibilities and then squelches them. (Of course, in performance a director may choose to play up these possibilities, to foreground rather than recess them.)

The play wastes no time in demanding that Theseus take his place as practicing ruler. When he responds to Egeus's complaint about Hermia's defiance, Theseus enters what we can call a juridical chronotope, the time-space of administrative authority. This is the chronotope of what Northrop Frye taught us to see as "the harsh law" that opens so many Shakespearean comedies. Its place is the public square, the space of judgment, and in setting deadlines it charges time with urgency. The juridical chronotope portrays people as responsible for their actions and, further, enlists the past (precedent) to judge in the present and shape the course of a future. In placing authoritative rule above chance and in setting both temporal and spatial limits, this chronotope is nearly the polar opposite of adventure-time—so much so, it seems, that the one invokes the other, as polar terms always do in either dialectic or dialogic fashion. Repeatedly in Shakespeare's plays, judicial decree spurs characters to move into a green world.

The remainder of act 1 then focuses on getting characters into the woods. For the four young lovers, the movement into the forest is purposeful, a spatial progress oriented toward a future of fulfilled desires: Hermia and Lysander plan to enable their marriage through approaching Lysander's aunt; Demetrius hopes to win Hermia; Helena to win Demetrius. Similarly, the mechanicals gather in the woods to rehearse future actions (their play) with a quite specific goal (Theseus's patronage and thus their future security). From the perspective of all these characters time and space here are shaped as an arena for purposeful, intentional, self-initiating and self-determining action.

Immediately, we can identify some chronotopic distinctions between the wood outside Athens and some of Shakespeare's other green worlds. Consider *As You Like It*, for one example. There, courtly characters enter the Forest of Arden as a sanctuary—a place of refuge from Duke Frederick's arbitrary and capricious jurisprudence. To some extent, Hermia resembles Rosalind and Orlando in flight from a threatening authority, but the woods also offer Hermia passage toward a specific desired future, while Rosalind and Orlando escape to the forest for an unpredictable period of time and with no particular purpose beyond evading their death sentences. The secondary ingenues in each play mark a sharp contrast between values: Celia travels with Rosalind out of loyalty; Helena's entry into the woods is a betrayal of Hermia. "Loyalty" and "betrayal" are, of course, moral terms for interpersonal actions, but they also signify differing attitudes toward the past as it impinges on the present and, indeed, on the relative weighting of past obligations and future interests in the choice of present action. In other words, loyalty and betrayal represent divergent consequences of chronotopically-saturated valorizations.

Although differently motivated, the characters of both *A Midsummer Night's Dream* and *As You Like It* deliberately leave the court/agora for the green world; the distinction between them resides in the degree to which various characters are represented as free to make choices. Yet another mode of entering a green world is by way of accident—as once Prospero and Miranda, later the court party, find themselves on Prospero's island. Thus we can name at least three kinds of entry into a green world: purpose, refuge, or accident. These motives for spatial change can be restated as temporal orientations: toward the future, toward the threat of past to present, toward the pure present, respectively. As one might assume from Bakhtin's discussion, these motives can co-exist in a single play; in *The Winter's Tale*, for example, Camillo flees to Bohemia as refuge while Perdita arrives there by accident, albeit a providential one.

Of course, once the (represented) human beings of *A Midsummer Night's Dream* enter the wood outside Athens, their initial purposes dwindle under the sway of its chronotope. Now, the prevailing chronotope becomes one of coincidence. *Coincidence* is a thoroughly chronotopic term, signifying as it does an intersection or congruence of both time and space. Chance meetings and equally chancy failures to meet constitute the action in the forest. Upon entering the woods, the purposeful orientation of both Bottom and the young lovers comes into dialogue with and is (at least temporarily) overwhelmed by that of the fairies, or more precisely by those of Oberon and Titania, themselves in conflict. Overall, of course, Oberon and Titania operate in the purest sort of adventure-time; they will never grow old; nor does it seem likely that Titania's surrender of the changeling boy will more than temporarily resolve the long history of squabbling jealousies between Titania and Oberon. (Such details as Puck's spatial mobility and their past adventures with Theseus and Hippolyta confirm adventure-time as their "proper" chronotope. Indeed, recognizing that these dalliances belong to a chronotope that disallows change may, uncannily, justify the utter absence of memory about fairies that Theseus exhibits in *Dream*'s final act.) When we actually meet Titania and Oberon, however, their quarrel—which *for them* is simply one of many adventures—is clearly threatening the play's dominant (comic) chronotope. Consider Titania's famous speech specifically as a chronotopic description:

> These are the forgeries of jealousy;
> And never, since the middle *summer*'s spring,
> Met we on *hill*, in *dale, forest,* or *mead,*
> By paved *fountain* or by rushy *brook,*
> Or in the *beached margent of the sea,*
> To *dance* our ringlets to the whistling wind,
> But with thy brawls thou hast disturb'd our sport.
> Therefore the winds, piping to us in vain,
> As in revenge, have suck'd up *from the sea*
> Contagious fogs; which, falling in the *land,*
> Hath every pelting *river* made so proud
> That they have *overborne their continents.*
> The ox hath therefore stretch'd his yoke in vain,
> The ploughman lost his sweat, and the *green corn*
> *Hath rotted ere* his youth attain'd a beard.
> The *fold* stands empty in the drowned *field,*
> And crows are fatted with the murrion flock;
> The nine men's *morris* is *fill'd up* with mud,
> And the quaint *mazes in the wanton green,*
> For lack of tread, are undistinguishable.
> The human *mortals* want their *winter* here;
> No *night* is now with hymn or carol blest.
> Therefore the *moon* (the governess of *floods*),
> Pale in her anger, washes all the *air,*

That rheumatic diseases do abound.
And thorough this distemperature, we see
The *seasons* alter: hoary-headed frosts
Fall in the fresh lap of the crimson rose,
And on old *Hiems'* [thin] and icy crown
An odorous chaplet of sweet *summer* buds
Is, as in mockery, set; the *spring*, the *summer*,
The childing *autumn*, angry *winter*, change
Their wonted liveries; and the mazed *world*,
By their increase, now knows not which is which.

(2.1.81-114; italics added)

Proper place and proper time, the cycle that allows for growth and generation, rebirth and renewal, are indeed out of joint. This speech and its Ovidian origins have been much discussed, so I shall focus here specifically on its chronotopic implications. As will be remembered, Titania's discord speech (like Ulysses' analogue in *Troilus and Cressida*) explicitly imitates Book One of the *Metamorphoses*. In Ovid, these lines recount the falling away from a golden age, describe what we can call a change of chronotope. As I noted earlier, the chronotope of any golden world is one of distant stasis, ungridded for either time or space, always *in illo tempore, in illo loco*. In the *Metamorphoses*, the golden age ends precisely with the introduction of business, trade, *negotium* (neg-otium, the negation of leisure), and the concomitants of law and private property. Here, the poet anticipates the economic historian. Trade, after all, necessitates a mapping of space and a calibrating of time. Tentatively, I'd argue that one effect of this change in chronotope is to increase the value and valorizing of pragmatic knowledge while decreasing that of reverential memory.

Enter the changeling boy. For some time now, criticism has stressed the erotic and gender tensions invested in the boy.[27] Here, I would stress the differing orientation toward time he incarnates for the two fairy rulers. Quite simply, Titania loves the changeling as a memorial:

His mother was a vot'ress of my order,
And in the spiced Indian air, by night,
Full often hath she gossip'd by my side,
. . . .

> But she, being mortal, of that boy did die,
> And for her sake do I rear up her boy;
> And for her sake I will not part with him.

(2.1.123-25 and 135-37)

For Titania, the boy is the souvenir of a cherished past, one she resists ex/changing for a more harmonious present; memory here is the source of all good things, as Bakhtin suggests is typical for epic. Contrarily, Oberon is exclusively concerned with the present and future use or value of the child:

> I do but beg a little changeling boy,
> To be my henchman. (2.1.120-21)

In Bakhtinian terms, Oberon is here novelistic: he values engagement in the here and now; he demands knowledge and experience for himself and the boy. Critics have interpreted this demand in multiple ways: as the "appropriate" movement of the boy from female to male spheres; as hinting at homoerotic desire; as one move in a continuing rivalry between the fairy rulers. None of these accounts, however, rates memory as valuable.

At this point, it would seem appropriate to consider *A Midsummer Night's Dream*'s other "changeling boy," Bottom the weaver. Bottom may facilitate Oberon's humiliating sexual joke on Titania, but he also echoes Apuleius, the writer Bakhtin draws upon to characterize the chronotope of the adventure novel of everyday life. Bottom's own adventure, I would contend, leaves him unchanged, a fact counter to the expected effect of metamorphosis. One could argue, however, that the play's *audience* is here shifted into the chronotope of *The Golden Ass*, which allows for what Bakhtin calls "spying on everyday life." That is, the Athenian (read "English") workmen inject a note of homely realism into the fantastical play. Indeed, we can also consider the early-modern chronotope Bottom and the other mechanicals initially bring to the play's dialogue. The artisan's chronotope is ordinarily straightforward: the relevant space is the workshop, where time is spent processing (metamorphosing) raw materials into goods exchangeable for a livelihood in the immediate future. However aesthetically naive, these mechanicals are wise enough to reach for Occasion's forelock. (*Occasion*, as depicted in emblem books, is a spatial, embodied representation of temporal opportunity, a figure for chance charged with singularity and significance.) When we first see them, they are planning the play they hope to perform at the wedding of Theseus and Hippolyta. Their goal is straightforward: a pension from Theseus. Hence, they are seeking a place to rehearse future actions calculated to secure a future beyond the immediate. Although I wouldn't want to push this thesis too far, the mechanicals can be said to enact a transition from a quotidian chronotope of workaday production to a more distant-future-oriented one of investment for the long term.

III

With the play's final act, we enter a chronotope typical of comedy, or more precisely we see an extension of the comic harmony established at the end of act 4. That is, in terms of plot act 5 is largely superfluous to the comic resolution of the play. However, the last act of *A Midsummer Night's Dream* points to several experiential/existential possibilities that must be repressed for a dialogic victory of the comic chronotope. Another way to say this: the play catalogs what we must forget we know in order to celebrate renewal and continuity at the multiple-marriage festivities of act 5.

Repression is the psychoanalytic term for a special case of forgetting; it is a figure that fuses memory and not-memory through relegation to an unconscious. Significantly, both Freud and Lacan refer to the unconscious as "the other scene." I want to look at some "other scenes" overtly excluded from, or repressed in, *A Midsummer Night's Dream*. In the last act of the play, Theseus rejects three offered entertainments. As he does so, he explicitly forecloses the voices of anti-comic chronotopes, signalling clearly what must be repressed for a comic chronotope to prevail. But his efforts toward repression—like all such efforts—will only partially succeed. That is, as he names that which will be suppressed, he simultaneously brings it to mind. (The repressed always returns and erasure always leaves a trace.)[28]

My discussion here will depend upon reanimating Ovidian contexts for the rejected entertainments. Such use of intertextuality to argue a return of the repressed does run some methodological risks. We simply cannot know how much of the *Metamorphoses* members of Shakespeare's original audience would have recognized or remembered, though we can be sure that the sum of such recollection would have varied from person to person, with variation inflected for both rank and gender. It seems likely, however that early-modern readers knew the books they knew better than we do; they were likely to have read and owned fewer books and thus to reread more often the books available to them. Further, Ovid arranges myths thematically, increasing the likelihood that mention of one will recall the stories around it. Indeed, the following discussion could be most easily justified in an intentionalist context: Shakespeare knew Ovid well and obviously had the *Metamorphoses* much in mind during the writing of *A Midsummer Night's Dream*. Equally, however, we could argue that metonymic associations can survive the forgetting of their initiating link.

At any rate, however thoroughly or sketchily members of any audience remember Ovid, Jonathan Bate's suggestion that it seems everyone in Athens has been rehearsing an Ovidian play remains apt.[29] Specifically, prior to the selection of "Pyramus and Thisbe," three entertainments are offered: a battle with centaurs, the death of Orpheus, and a satire of the nine muses. These plays, however, offend Theseus's sense of nuptial propriety. Resituated in their Ovidian contexts, the rejected tales index a variety of repressions that enable marriage or, more precisely, enable the celebration of marriage. Michael Bristol's discussion of carnivalesque charivari, itself indebted to Bakhtin, is relevant here: "Marriage is accomplished against multiple resistance, both from the duly constituted social order that seeks to regulate the sexual pleasure of the bride and groom, and from the 'outlaw' community of bachelors whose access to sexual partners is constrained by marriage as an institutionalization of sexual exclusivity."[30] In social practice, Bristol observes, the "bride and groom, therefore, must participate in a series of games and mummings, in order successfully to negotiate these transitions."[31] In *A Midsummer Night's Dream*, I would argue, we can see represented such mummings and games not only in the Pyramus and Thisbe playlet of Act V, but also throughout the forest scenes. These scenes enact threats to the social institution of marriage, and they must be repressed in order to *celebrate* marriage.

As Bristol indicates, one threat to marriage is that of "outlaw" bachelors, and we do well to keep this fact in mind as Theseus suppresses the proffered entertainment mumming a battle with centaurs, claiming "We'll none of that: that have I told my love, / In glory of my kinsman Hercules" (5.1.46-47). This suppression is best read as the repression of any memory of outlaw bachelors, a description that certainly suits centaurs as they appear throughout both classical mythology and early-modern mythography. (Scholars debate exactly which battle with centaurs is referred to here, but I see no reason to limit the intertextual resonance to any single source.) In Book XII of the *Metamorphoses*, Ovid recounts the battle between the Lapiths and the centaurs. The scene is the wedding feast of Pirithous, where a drunken centaur seizes the bride. It is Theseus himself who attacks this outlaw and begins a battle in which the centaurs are defeated. It hardly takes a psychoanalytic critic to recognize these centaurs as representing illicit sexuality subdued by Theseus (and others) in defense of marriage. (That Ovid intends the story to be read as concerning the violation of marriage, specifically by outlaw bachelors, is underscored by the preceding stories—of the Trojan War, the result of an outrage against marriage, and of Caenis, who refused marriage only to be raped by Neptune and who chose to become a man rather than risk another rape.) In fact, despite its violence, the story of the Lapiths and Centaurs could be seen as perfectly appropriate to a wedding feast in that this violence occurs in defense of marriage.

Of course, Theseus has promised to wed Hippolyta in another key, but his apparently casual mention of his cousin Hercules may be more telling. In the Ovidian account of the battle between the Lapiths and the Centaurs, Hercules is conspicuously absent; indeed, his absence is underscored when Tiepolemus indignantly berates Nestor (who has been telling the story): "I am surprised that you have forgotten Hercules' exploits. I am sure my father often used to tell me that he had defeated those cloud-born creatures" (282).[32] Nestor admits to deliberately suppressing Hercules' role in this battle; he justifies this omission by recounting wrongs Hercules had done him and observing "who ever praised his enemy?" (272). Of course, not every member of Shakespeare's audience would remember such details, but to anyone conversant with classical mythology, the mention of Hercules and Centaurs in the same sentence is likely to evoke the memory of Nessus and the shirt steeped in his blood. Much like the Lapiths, Hercules killed the centaur Nessus in defense of his young bride, but the blood of the centaur ultimately consumed the hero in flames; iconographically, the lust Hercules thought he had conquered early in his marriage returns to destroy him. The memory of this ultimately triumphant centaur must be repressed, along with that of those defeated by the Lapiths. Indeed, this surplus of centaurs is pertinent to my reservations about the arguments of various critics that *A Midsummer Night's Dream* exorcises "the fears attendant on marriage."[33] I would argue instead that the Shakespearean comic chronotope at stake can manage only repression of such fears rather than their exorcism—some centaurs can indeed be defeated once and for all, but others eventually have their revenge. It is such revenge, I believe, such *até* that is above all repressed in the play. *A Midsummer Night's Dream* opens, it will be remembered, with a simile about a young man and a step-dame. To some of the audience, these words (which follow shortly on Hippolyta's name) will recall the story of Phaedra, Hippolytus, and Theseus's anguish. If talk of Theseus's past reminds us of his future, or if the name of the mother evokes that of the son, we may be reminded that the mature Theseus, though in this play condescending to the foolish affections of the young, has one more encounter with all-consuming passion ahead of him.

The next rejected entertainment is "The riot of the tipsy Bacchanals, / Tearing the Thracian singer in their rage" (5.1.48-49). Although Orpheus's death is described at the beginning of Book XI of the *Metamorphoses* the motive behind his murder and dismemberment by the Ciconian women harks back to the stories recounted in Book X. This book opens at the wedding of Orpheus and Eurydice—an ill-fated marriage indeed, as Hymen's gloomy presence at the ceremony foretells. Ovid describes the foreboding demeanor of the marriage god:

> His expression was gloomy, and he did not sing his accustomed refrain. Even the torch he carried sputtered and smoked, bring [sic] tears to the eyes, and no amount of tossing could make it burn. (Book X, 225)

To witness the story of Orpheus would encourage comparison of wedding celebrations, and Ovid's mournful Hymen enacts precisely that funereal melancholy Theseus first interdicted in act 1. That is, in rejecting this entertainment, Theseus echoes the command he gave Philostrate in the play's opening lines. Further, we can see here as well a repression of Hermia's dream about a biting serpent. Hymen's mourning at the wedding of Orpheus and Eurydice turns out to have been entirely appropriate:

> While the new bride was wandering in the meadows, with her band
> of naiads, a serpent bit her on the ankle, and she sank lifeless to the
> ground. (Book X, 225)

This is the first death of Eurydice; the second occurs when Orpheus
rescues her from Hades only to lose her again when she *looks back*.
"Looking back" conjoins a physical, spatial movement and a temporal
metaphor; "wedding," on the other hand, requires an orientation toward
the future and movement forward. Similarly, in order to celebrate
marriage, Hermia and Helena (and the audience) must not look back
toward Lysander and Demetrius's fickle behavior in the woods; rather,
they (and the audience) must look forward to a projected future.

Between this second death of Eurydice's and that of Orpheus,
moreover, are the remaining 676 lines of Book X, where stories of the
following are told: Cyparissus; Hyacinthus; Ganymede; the
Propoetides; the Cerastae; Pygmalion; Cinyras and Myrrha; Adonis;
Atalanta and Hippomenes. These are all stories to make Hymen weep,
for each tells of sexual energies that evade channeling into progenitive
marriage. Cyparissus and Hyacinthus are boys beloved of Apollo, and
the story of Ganymede is told briefly here as well. These tales of
homoerotic passion are appropriate enough, for Ovid tells us that after
Eurydice's death Orpheus repulsed all advances from women and
"preferred to centre his affections on boys of tender years, and to enjoy
the brief spring and early flowering of their youth" (227). And indeed,
"he was the first to introduce this custom among the people of Thrace"
(227). Further, after the story of Cyparissus, Orpheus announces he
will sing songs of "boys whom the gods have loved, and of girls who,
seized with unlawful passion, have paid the penalty for their amorous
desires" (229). The first of these girls are sisters—the Propoetides—
who deny the divinity of Venus and become the first prostitutes. It is
easy enough to read this story as an emblem of unsacramentalized sex,
particularly in that the Propoetides are associated (by locale of origin)
with the Cerastae, horned men who murder their guests. These are
stories of human intercourse alienated from numinous blessing.
Pygmalion, in turn, so loathes the wicked Propoetides that he rejects all
human women for his beautiful statue—another transgression against
the procreative order. That is, ordinarily, statues bear no children.
Venus intervenes, however, and brings the statue to life. The influence
of Venus may seem benign here, but Pygmalion and his statue are the

grandparents of Cinyras, whose daughter Myrrha develops and consummates—with the aid of her old nurse—incestuous love for her father. The child of this unlawful union is Adonis—a reminder that not even Venus herself is exempt from the arbitrary *até* of eros, any more than Titania is immune to the power of love-in-idleness. At any rate, Venus tells Adonis the story of Atalanta and Hippomenes. Venus gave Hippomenes the golden apples with which he distracts Atalanta during the footrace, but he fails to thank the goddess. (Atalanta had consulted Apollo, who told her "You have no need of a husband. . . . But assuredly, you will not escape marriage and then, though still alive, you will lose your own self" [240].) To punish this lapse in gratitude, Venus inflames Hippomenes with "an untimely desire"; he thus makes love to his wife in a cave sacred to the Mother of the Gods, a particularly holy cave filled with wooden statues of ancient gods. The Mother of the Gods punishes this (unwitting) sacrilege by turning Atalanta and Hippomenes into lions. They have transgressed both proper time and proper place.

Clearly, this group of Ovidian stories suggests at least two persistent possiblities that must be somehow forgotten, the knowledge of which must be repressed, in order to affirm the standard comic interpretation of marriage as joyful union sanctified by deities and in harmony with communal needs: erotic impulses can easily be deflected to comedically inappropriate (i.e., non-progenitive) objects, and no marriage—however mutually joyous—forecloses the vulnerability of human beings to forces outside their control. And it is "such songs as these" that the poet and lover Orpheus is singing when the Circonian women, enraged by his scorn for women, tear him apart. At the very least, echoes of these stories of destructive and transgressive passion would fit poorly into a wedding celebration.

Also rejected is the third offered entertainment, "'The thrice three Muses mourning for the death / Of Learning, late deceas'd in beggary'" because "That is some satire, keen and critical, / Not sorting with a nuptial ceremony" (5.1.52-55). Here, Theseus speaks with another voice: that of the political censor. It is true that in Ovid the Muses are associated (by juxtaposition) with yet another wedding feast disrupted by violence (that of Perseus and Andromeda). It is also true that within the story of the muses, Calliope recounts the history of Pluto and Proserpine, and a comic chronotope no doubt could be discomfited by an etiology that founds cyclical time in outrage. And it is certainly true that Theseus here refuses the imitation of funeral. But in the supression of this satire, Theseus speaks above all as a patron, one whose patronage may be as tyrannical and whimsical as his now-enforcing, now-abridging administration of Athenian justice. It is worth remembering that in the early-modern era *satire* referred almost exclusively to political or religio-political vituperation. As patron, Theseus prefers artistic ineptitude to a potentially severe critique of the hierarchal institutions he represents. Satire, after all, is chronotopically *present*, or rather it superimposes its ostensible time and place on a here-and-now, inflecting the worst of the present in hopes of amending the future. The chronotope of reform conflicts with that of sanctioned reproduction, which in some sense always prefers a comedic faith to a satiric skepticism. And Theseus's censorship of the three entertainments hints at some possibilities that must be repressed for comedic faith to celebrate its characteristic chronotope.

* * *

Theseus's rejection of the first three offered entertainments serves as prelude to a performance of "Pyramus and Thisbe," itself an Ovidian story of chronotopic disjunction—a meeting missed—whose tragic consequences Ovid describes as etiological. Similarly, in *A Midsummer Night's Dream* the multiple epilogues insist upon the wedding festivities as inaugural, as the founding action for three familial lines, as the promise of a comic chronotope. (Significantly, this comedic promise is couched as repression or foreclosure of unhappy possibilities.) In the play's final epilogue, however, Puck returns the audience to a chronotope of "present performance," which can of course be recognized as a variable; the phrase itself works as a chronotopic pronoun that can stand for any of uncounted conjunctions of time and place. As the last act of *A Midsummer Night's Dream* emphasizes, the chronotope of present performance will always intervene in the dialogue among a play's represented chronotopes.

As an analytic device, Bakhtin's notion of the chronotope is apt for the current time-spaces of Shakespeare studies, enabling systematic discussion of the interanimations between historicity and aesthetics. In *A Midsummer Night's Dream*, we can see not only multiple chronotopes but also multiple species of chronotopes. This essay has surveyed differing modes in which some chronotopes persist across changes in time and space even as they coexist with those specific to one historical situation. Adventure-time, for example, persists primarily as literary convention; in our own time, this convention serves as an artistic counterweight to the evolutionary models that have been dominant in recent western thought. In contrast, the chronotope of the artisan is, for practical purposes, lost in developed countries, although it may be imitated memorially in hobbies or in the production of luxury goods. And *A Midsummer Night's Dream* also preserves a holiday chronotope, both like and unlike today's equivalents. Each of these chronotopes organizes relationships among social and economic histories, literary histories, and aesthetic effects in distinct ways, ways which—like the events in the woods outside Athens—do and do not depend upon an observer's perspective.

NOTES

1. See, for example, Leonard Tennenhouse, *Power on Display: The Politics of Shakespeare's Genres* (London: Methuen, 1986), 40-44; and Jan Kott, *The Bottom Translation: Marlowe and Shakespeare and the Carnival Tradition*, trans. Daniela Miedzyrzecka and Lillian Vallee (Evanston: Northwestern University Press, 1987), 29-68.

2. Bakhtin, *The Dialogic Imagination*, ed. Michael Holquist, trans. Caryl Emerson and Michael Holquist (Austin: University of Texas Press, 1981), 84-258.

3. Ibid., 252.

4. Ibid.

5. Morson and Emerson, *Mikhail Bakhtin: Creation of a Prosaics* (Stanford: Stanford University Press, 1990), 368.

6. Bakhtin, *Dialogic Imagination*, 84.

7. Ibid., 85.

8. Ibid., 28.

9. Ibid., 250.

10. Holquist, *Dialogism: Bakhtin and His World* (London: Routledge, 1990), 148 and 155.

11. Morson and Emerson, 369-70.

12. Kastan, *Shakespeare and the Shapes of Time* (Hanover: University Press of New England, 1982), 7. He chooses to underweight the comedies because they make "no pretense to historicity" (7).

13. Roberts, *The Shakespearean Wild: Geography, Genus, and Gender* (Lincoln: University of Nebraska Press, 1991).

14. Frye, "The Argument of Comedy," in D.A. Robertson, ed., *English Institute Essays, 1948* (New York: Columbia University Press, 1949), 58-73.

15. Levin, *The Myth of the Golden Age in the Renaissance* (Bloomington: Indiana University Press, 1959).

16. Compare Bakhtin's discussions of "historical inversion" and eschatology. See "The *Bildungsroman* and Its Significance in the History of Realism (Toward a Historical Typology of the Novel)" in M.M. Bakhtin, *Speech Genres and Other Late Essays*, trans. Vern W. McGee, ed. Caryl Emerson and Michael Holquist (Austin: University of Texas Press, 1986), 10-25.

17. See Bakhtin, *Dialogic Imagination*, 94-95.

18. Ibid., 118; also see Bakhtin, *Speech Genres*, 10-25.

19. All citations to Shakespeare's plays are to the *Riverside* edition, G. Blakemore Evans, ed. (Boston: Houghton Mifflin, 1974).

20. In a discussion of wealth and inheritance, Lisa Jardine notes "Small wonder that Theseus... should use the lifespan of the dowager as a vivid image for the slow passing of time." *Still Harping on Daughters: Women and Drama in the Age of Shakespeare*, 2nd. ed. (New York: Columbia University Press, 1989), 85-86. Philip C. McGuire implicitly relates competing gender interests to chronotopes, particularly as he discusses different directorial decisions about the ages of Theseus and Hippolyta, their differing attitudes toward time, and their physical movements (spatial placements) *vis à vis* each other; see his *Speechless Dialect: Shakespeare's Open Silences* (Berkeley and Los Angeles: University of California Press, 1985), 1-16. Also relevant to my point is Terence Hawkes' argument that *A Midsummer Night's Dream* is "haunted by the shadowy images of older women" (*Meaning by Shakespeare* [London: Routledge, 1992], 13-15, 19-20).

21. Victor Turner remains a useful source for discussions of ritual time. See, for example, *The Forest of Symbols: Aspects of Ndembu Ritual* (Ithaca: Cornell University Press, 1967), or *The Ritual Process: Structure and Anti-Structure* (Chicago: Aldine, 1969). For the relevance of Turner to *A Midsummer Night's Dream*, see Florence Falk, "Dream and Ritual Process in *A Midsummer Night's Dream*, *Comparative Drama* 14 (1980-81): 263-79, and William C. Carroll, *The Metamorphoses of Shakespearean Comedy* (Princeton: Princeton University Press, 1985), 141-77. Also pertinent is François Laroque, trans. Janet Lloyd, *Shakespeare's Festive World: Elizabethan Seasonal Entertainment and the Professional Stage* (Cambridge: Cambridge University Press, 1991), esp. 201-43.

22. Charles and Michelle Martindale cite "aetiology" as a specific Ovidian practice of Shakespeare's in *A Midsummer Night's Dream. Shakespeare and the Uses of Antiquity: An Introductory Essay* (London: Routledge, 1990), 73-74.

23. Bakhtin, *Dialogic Imagination,* 15.

24. Again see Bakhtin, ibid., 19-24.

25. Like the novel as described by Bakhtin, drama can—perhaps must—embed other genres. Unlike novels, however, and unlike plays during a solitary reading, plays in performance have their own distinctive chronotope. Performed drama literally occurs in a specialized space (whether purpose-built or improvised) and in a delimited time. Arguably, dramatic performance always invokes a dialogue between the here-and-now of a given production and the another-time-another-place of the staged action. In *Speechless Dialect,* McGuire suggests that performances of Shakespeare's plays "defy Newtonian assumptions and procedures" (125) and are better aligned with quantum theory. McGuire focuses on questions of repeatablity, but the responses to such questions distinguish the chronotopes, the time-spaces, of classical and quantum physics (122-32).

26. See, for example, M.E. Lamb, *"A Midsummer Night's Dream*: The Myth of Theseus and the Minotaur," *Texas Studies in Literature and Language* 21.4 (Winter 1979): 478-89; and D'Orsay W. Pearson, "'Unkinde' Theseus: A Study in Renaissance Mythography," *English Literary Renaissance* 4 (1974): 276-98.

27. A few examples: Marjorie Garber, *Coming of Age in Shakespeare* (London: Methuen, 1981), 148-49; Shirley Nelson Garner, *"A Midsummer Night's Dream*: 'Jack shall have Jill; / Nought shall go ill,'" *Women's Studies* 9 (1981): 47-65; Bruce R. Smith, *Homosexual Desire in Shakespeare's England: A Cultural Poetics* (Chicago: Chicago University Press, 1991), 199-201; Phillipa Berry, *Of Chastity and Power: Elizabethan Literature and the Unmarried Queen* (London: Routledge, 1989), 144-46.

28. Interestingly, Barbara Freedman's important discussion of censorship and repression as enacted in *A Midsummer Night's Dream* ignores the proffered entertainments altogether. *Staging the Gaze: Postmodernism, Psychoanalysis, and Shakespearean Comedy* (Ithaca: Cornell University Press, 1991), 154-91.

29. Bate, *Shakespeare and Ovid* (Oxford: Clarendon, 1993), 130-31.

30. Bristol, *Carnival and Theater: Plebeian Culture and the Structure of Authority in Renaissance England* (London: Methuen, 1985), 167; also see 162-78.

31. Ibid.

32. See 282. All citations to the *Metamorphoses* are to the edition translated and introduced by Mary M. Innes (Baltimore: Penguin, 1955).

33. The quoted phrase is Carroll's, 154. For additional examples, see Harold F. Brooks' introduction to the Arden edition of *A Midsummer Night's Dream* (London: Methuen, 1979), cxxxii–cxxxiii.

Preposterous Pleasures
Queer Theories and *A Midsummer Night's Dream*
Douglas E. Green

"How happy some o'er other some can be!"[1]

Pleasure and power do not cancel or turn back against one another; they seek out, overlap, and reinforce one another. They are linked together by complex mechanisms and devices of excitation and incitement.[2]

Of all the illusions produced by performance, for me the most immediate is the illusion that performance can accommodate all of my desires at once. This is the lure of performance and, of course, its failure. And yet, like Bottom, I still go for whatever I can get.[3]

In 1985 Liviu Ciulei, artistic director of the Guthrie Theater in Minneapolis, mounted a production of *A Midsummer Night's Dream*. His version of the play was, as the program notes attest, greatly informed by modern commentary on the play, including that of such notable feminist critics as Shirley Nelson Garner.[4] This essay has its genesis in a particular aspect and effect of that production. In interludes between several scenes, accompanied by music and covered by enormous, beautiful gauze runners on a set solely of black, white, and red, some of the principal actors would join in a variety of pantomime sexual encounters—straight, gay, lesbian, bisexual, single-partner, multiple-partner, etc. As the play proceeded, these comparatively random unions rose with the confusions of the lovers and gradually sorted themselves out as the "true lovers" found each other. What I experienced at this production was a metatheatrical illustration of the well-known way in which this and other Shakespearean comedies represent disruptions of social order—ones that at times for twentieth-century viewers and readers seem liberating—only to accommodate that order, usually by reasserting some slightly modified version of it at the end.

For me Ciulei's *Dream* exposed how "it is our cultures that imagine that when heterosexual relations occur beside homosexual relations, the straight relation must win out—as if a biological destiny were asserting itself."[5] The Guthrie production suggested simultaneously the erotic possibilities (officially) proscribed by the societies of Shakespearean Athens, Elizabethan England, and Reaganite America that the text temporarily brings into play and the naturalized reassertion of those proscriptions. In so doing, Ciulei exposed one likely aspect of *Dream*'s ideological effect in our time, if not in early modern England: the play is designed to foreclose all erotic unions that do not lead to socially sanctioned (i.e., marital) procreation; in a time that had witnessed simultaneously radical feminism and the reassertion of "family values," gay rights and the cruel effects of mass paranoia about HIV and AIDS, Ciulei's production had exposed how a bit of high humanist culture like *A Midsummer Night's Dream*, despite its seeming tolerance and expansiveness, contributes to the ideological work of contemporary conservatism. If finally the text curbs the willful exercise of paternal power by Egeus, it still ends with the erasure of Amazons, the paternal sanctioning by Theseus of desired unions to ensure or enhance procreation, and the curbing too of Puckish pleasures in "those things . . . / That befall prepost'rously" (3.2.120-21).[6]

What is suppressed or lost in the text's ideological shaping of delight in such comic resolutions is the subject of this essay. Drawing on the work of Valerie Traub, I have assumed what she demonstrates: that "once the hierarchy between homoerotic and heterosexual is dissolved within the critical enterprise, homoerotic significations are everywhere—both in their expansive, inclusive modes, and in their anxious and repressed forms."[7] This essay does not (seek to) re-write *A Midsummer Night's Dream* as a gay play but rather explores some of its "homoerotic significations"—what I see as moments of "queer"[8] disruption and eruption in this Shakespearean comedy.

"Gentles, perchance you wonder at this show" (5.1.127)

> To assume that gender *predicates* eroticism is to ignore the contradictions that have historically existed between these two inextricably related yet independent systems. While they are always connected, there is no simple fit between them. Gender 1 sexuality.[9]

It is not, necessarily, that Shakespeare was a sexual radical; rather, the ordinary currency of his theater and society is sexy for us. Shakespeare may work with distinct force for gay men and lesbians, simply because he didn't think he had to sort out sexuality in modern terms.[10]

Since Frye and Barber,[11] it's no secret that comedies like *A Midsummer Night's Dream* represent temporary holiday or topsy-turvy worlds through which the discontents of civilization are mediated or negotiated, if not resolved quite so neatly as the conventional marital endings suggest. Indeed a good deal of poststructuralist criticism, especially of the new historicist and feminist varieties, has debated the ideological import of Shakespearean comedies for the construction of gender, particularly in Anglo-American culture. Feminist criticism has been particularly instrumental in exposing the hidden sexist assumptions of structuralist analyses and classical psychoanalytic interpretations. It was not so much that various feminist critical approaches denied the carnival world or topsiturviness of Shakespearean comedy but rather that they revealed the oppressive constructions of gender re-established in the endings and/or exposed the limitations, slippages, and anxieties of the carnival itself in respect to gender differences. The latter were particularly striking, given the all-male mode of early modern English theatrical production, in the case of cross-dressed heroines like Portia, Rosalind, and Viola.[12]

Though this thumbnail sketch doesn't do justice to the variety and insight of either structuralist or poststructuralist approaches to Shakespearean comedy, it does convey in miniature the character of some major shifts that have occurred in the study of Shakespeare over the last thirty to forty years. But as poststructuralist notions of ideology have generally implied, we cannot think, analyze, or write our way out of the world in which we live and work and into a utopia; there are always "blind spots."[13] In this essay, undoubtedly with its own blind spots that others will unmask, I want to help build onto and into recent poststructuralist—primarily new historicist, cultural materialist, and feminist—critiques of Shakespeare a greater awareness of heterosexism and homophobia, not to reject those poststructuralist approaches but to help open them to the further possibilities for institutional and cultural analysis and change presented by recent queer theories.[14] Just as feminist theorists, among others like postcolonial, class, and race theorists, politicize and thereby transform the methods and insights of poststructuralism in general and new historicism in particular, so I believe queer theorists can engage feminist, new historicist, and other theorists in a re-thinking at least of the terms and probably of the aims of their political commitments.[15] Thus Judith Butler, for instance, believes it now necessary "to muddle the lines between queer theory and feminism": "The relation between sexual practice and gender is surely not a structurally determined one, but the destabilizing of the heterosexual presumption of that very structuralism still requires a way to think the two in a dynamic relation to one another."[16] My efforts here are necessarily tentative and introductory and do not pretend to be comprehensive, but focusing on *A Midsummer Night's Dream*—in which "the course of true love never did run smooth" (1.1.134)— allows us to re-examine a prime site of cultural production of gender and sexuality through the new lenses of queer theory.[17]

"... past the wit of man to say what dream it was" (4.1.205-06)

Male homoeroticism can be manipulated to reinforce and justify misogyny, or it can offer itself up as the means to deconstruct the binary structures upon which subordination of women depends.[18]

Bottom's journey in *A Midsummer Night's Dream* is the queer one; through him we can see the trajectory of queer performance.[19]

Bottom's famous description of his dream constitutes a striking example of the comic way *A Midsummer Night's Dream* employs—or rather alludes to—the unthinkable that is sodomy, which Foucault calls "that utterly confused category."[20] To the extent we have it, "Bottom's Dream" (4.1.200-19) recalls but cannot identify the dreamer as the butt (literally, zoologically, anatomically) of, an elaborate dramatic paranomasia. Bottom lacks even the simplest words for any of the potential meanings of his experience—his physical and erotic transformation—though we can fill in his lacunae in a variety of ways: he thought he was "an ass" and/or "consort of the fairy queen"; he thought he had "long ears and an ass's head" and/or "a beautiful woman." But exactly what kind of ass Bottom is and even that he is one (not least of all for attempting "to expound this dream") eludes him (4.1.207). What has almost eluded us is the text's allusion to sodomy. And here we may be treading shaky linguistic ground. The *OED* distinguishes between *arse* (the rectum) and *ass* (the beast of burden associated with stupidity) as they were used and pronounced at this time and suggests further that *bottom* did not refer denotatively to a person's "bum" until the eighteenth century despite the long-standing but problematic conjecture that bum, a well-worn word by the Renaissance though of uncertain origin, is itself a contraction of bottom. One still might argue that "bottom" figuratively suggests the arse and that the association between this Bottom and an ass is enough to encourage this multi-layered visual and aural pun.[21]

Yet beyond such scatological references and imagery, which are today virtually irrepressible, the well-known synesthetic confusions with which Bottom declares the inexpressibility of his "most rare vision" bespeak the unspeakable even as they obscure it: "The eye of man hath not heard, the ear of man hath not seen, man's hand is not able to taste, his tongue to conceive, nor his heart to report, what my dream was" (4.1.204-205, 211-214). Jonathan Goldberg points out that "among the categorical confusions of the confused category 'sodomy' is categorical confusion itself— ... a denial of those socially constructed hierarchies that are taken to be natural, that social ordering that is thought to participate in and to replicate the order of being."[22] Certainly, Bottom the Weaver upsets the analogous social and natural orders in his liaison with the fairy queen, which is perhaps even more problematic once it becomes his "dream," with the hint of transgressive desire and aspiration this speech implies. Rude mechanical that he is, Bottom unwittingly exposes the sodomitical desire and act that, as we shall see, Oberon misrecognizes in relation to the changeling boy and, by extension, the anxiety that Theseus both manifests and suppresses when faced with any desire not subject to his sanction.[23]

Bottom would offer his dream of an "ass" (in what sense?) to the Duke in the "latter end" of the play-within-the-play or "Peradventure, to make it [the woman's death? the play being put on for his own preferment? the 'ballet of this dream' itself? etc.] the more gracious, at her [presumably Thisby's] death" (4.1.214-19). It is no accident that the entire entertainment Bottom and his friends offer represents the final stage of Theseus's winning and wooing the Amazon queen, thereby making her his own.[24] Moreover, it is at this moment that the representation of marriage, an institutional "deployment of alliance" that helps secure "homosocial" relations among men through an exchange of women,[25] meets the image of theater in a travesty of the cross-dressed productions of Shakespeare's day. As with the much-remarked silence of Hermia and Helena in the latter part of *A Midsummer Night's Dream*, the all-male production of the rude mechanicals and the social exchange it effects—a mirror, however parodic, of the Shakespearean theatrical enterprise itself—mark a larger elision of women's voices—and hence their power—through (and at the moment of) marriage as well as in the theater. Theseus's male subjects offer a tragedy of Babylonian lovers, in which a woman figures but does not act, in order to promote their own interests; the wedding of the Duke both masks and permits a social and economic transaction between different classes of men. Bottom's option—to sing the "ballet of this dream" at Thisby's death—thus suggests or creates a problematic link between (in this case, displaced) homoeroticism and misogyny, in which unspoken, even misrecognized sodomitical relations foster, solidify, and/or enhance the homosocial priorities of early modern England.[26]

But who is to say that the social context of the rude mechanicals' performance before the court serves so exclusively established interests among men, albeit of different classes? The Pyramus and Thisby story Bottom and his friends enact is written against the rigid system of alliance that Egeus wanted upheld at the start of Shakespeare's play; like the corrective potion, this theatrical travesty exorcises the specter of impending tragedy for the lovers that the opening scene hinted at. Yet the play-within-the-play does so without neatly corroborating an ideology of romantic love that has never succeeded—we know from our own historical moment—in dislodging patriarchal interests served by the system of alliance, any more than the weddings in *A Midsummer Night's Dream* threaten the order and hierarchy of the society the play depicts.[27] Romantic love, which can be seen as an early step in the "deployment of sexuality" that Foucault describes,[28] has its part too in leading the Babylonian lovers to the grave. And thus—at least from our historical vantage point—Bottom and his friends have "critiqued" the ostensibly companionate marriages that Theseus and *A Midsummer Night's Dream* itself commend to us. But the burlesque elements of the "love" between Flute's Thisby and Bottom's Pyramus, the metatheatricality of a performance in which even the Wall and the Moon are in drag, and the possible difference between our delight in this "poor" performance and the grudging and/or mocking *noblesse oblige* of the on-stage courtiers—"Beshrew my heart, but I pity the man" (5.1.290)—hint at desires that exceed recuperation to dominant interests. Like Quince, Flute, et al., we are glad to have our "bully Bottom" back (5.2.19): such "working-class" solidarity bespeaks feelings and motivations beyond the ken of Theseus—"If we imagine no worse of them than they of themselves, they may pass for excellent men" (5.1.215-16)—that enter the play via the social back door of Bottom and his friends. Something treasonous, or at least "transgressive," is released by Bottom's theatrical production, not to mention his encounter with Titania, that apparently for Shakespeare evokes the natural and social confusion associated in early modern England with sodomy even as the text suppresses its recognition as such.[29]

"This hateful imperfection of her eyes" (4.1.63)

Marriage is the social institution whose regulatory functions ramify everywhere. Sodomy, as Bray suggests, fully negates the world, law, nature. Hence the unlikelihood that those sexual acts called sodomy, when performed, would be recognized as sodomy, especially if, in other social contexts, they could be called something else, or nothing at all.[30]

Sinistrari observes that although moralists who treat of "this filthy vice" declare that "real Sodomy is committed between [women]," yet he has seen no one offer a credible explanation "as to how this takes place."[31]

What is it that so frightens and/or disgusts Oberon as he surveys the love-making of Titania and her Bottom? The scene enacts a crucial *méconnaissance*, really a complex series of misrecognitions by Oberon: of his own sodomitical intentions toward the changeling boy, of his own misogynistic fears of female power and desires, of the residence of his honor in Titania and of his resentment of its disposition outside himself, of Titania's "lesbianism" as bestiality and hence as sodomy, of his own desires to be desired (by Titania) and to control desires, of his own sadistic voyeurism, etc. It exposes analogically the justification for Theseus's abduction of the Amazon: what women do when not subject(ed) to men is beyond the pale. Metatheatrically, it may represent (masculine) Elizabethan incomprehension in the face of the queen, who has the power to dispose of herself and to act on her own desires—Elizabeth as sodomite, her imagined transgressiveness, whether seeking a husband or furtively fulfilling carnal desires with men (or women) not her equals.[32]

The full comic force of the scene derives precisely from the inexpressibility of the "undoings" of this moment where what is inconceivable finds its representation in what is proscribed: thus the scene may constitute from Oberon's voyeuristic position a reenactment of the unthinkable (lesbian) love of Titania for her votaress (mother of the disputed changeling boy), now displaced onto the manifest bestiality of Titania's embrace of an "ass," whose name—Bottom—may well conjure the anatomical pun, which introduces the (other) "sodomy" that is never mentioned or recognized as such but implied in Oberon's obsession with the changeling boy.[33] In this case, what Foucault says of power's masking itself in order to succeed applies as forcefully to the self-delusion of the ruler as it does to the blinding of the ruled: "power is tolerable only on condition that it mask a substantial part of itself. Its success is proportional to its ability to hide its own mechanisms."[34] Interestingly, the scene's allusion to sodomy marks multiple social frontiers. Among others, it indicates and—from and through Oberon's perspective—castigates, even negates, the possibilities of unrestrained female desires of any sort and their enactment ("Be as thou wast wont to be; / See as thou wast wont to see" [4.1.71-72]); ignores the supposedly impossible aspirations of subordinate classes and their realization, reducing them to "the fierce vexation of a dream" (4.1.69); and misconstrues and/or displaces erotic desires and practices of his own—"And now I have the boy" (4.1.62)—that he does not or cannot recognize as sodomy.

Not surprisingly, this is one of those moments of disorder in which Oberon hauls out another potion, a theatrical *deus ex machina*, to contain the explosive representations that derive originally from his own intervention in the affairs of those around him: "But first I will release the Fairy Queen" (4.1.70). We might recognize here the tension between the play's expansiveness and its containment: the very system of power relations that enables a Theseus or Oberon to intervene in and arrange the affairs of others leads to situations that belie their attempts to maintain order; the solution to those situations in turn lies with changes in the rulers themselves—a proposition at once seemingly radical in identifying the source of the problem (the rulers' having ruled poorly) and yet hopelessly contained within and supportive of the status quo.

And yet the genie cannot quite be squeezed back into the bottle. As Oberon's agent, Puck represents that slippage between power and its exercise that affords some space, however minimal, for interests, desires, pleasures, and practices other than those consonant with dominant ideology. Thus Oberon scolds Puck: "Of thy misprision must perforce ensue / Some true love turn'd, and not a false turn'd true" (3.2.90-91). Though the *OED* glosses this usage as "a misunderstanding" or "a mistake," both the legalistic sense, having to do with "a misdemeanor or failure of duty on the part of a public official," and the wholly separate substantive meaning of "scorn" or "contempt" are possible and likely operative here. Such Puckish "misprision" embodies what Dollimore calls the "paradoxical perverse," in which "the most extreme threat to the true form of something comes not so much from its absolute opposite or its direct negation, but in the form of its perversion; somehow the perverse threat is inextricably rooted in the true and the authentic, while being, in spite of (or rather because of) that connection, also the utter contradiction of the true and authentic."[35] Like Bottom, whose imagination is unfathomable and hence, if not threatening, still not ordered as Theseus would have it, Puck signals in the fairy world the possibility of disorder or, put another way, the un- or mis-recognized possibility of preposterous pleasures: "And those things do best please me / That befall prepost'rously" (3.2.120-21). If it is on such misrecognitions, on such blind spots, that the illusions of total order and control—of Oberon and, by extension, of Theseus—are constructed, it is nevertheless through the "perverse dynamic" of Puckish agency that these illusions are exposed.[36]

Nor is the space in which Titania loved her votaress so easily policed; Oberon seems to have had no more influence on their relations than on Titania's choice of love-object under the spell of the potion. If, as Bray, Goldberg, and others contend, sodomy is a category that expands to signify and contain almost every sort of disruption of natural, social, and political order, then Oberon's exercise of power through Puck bears its hybrid fruit in this scene: Oberon may succeed in degrading Titania, but his voyeurism implicates him in the bestiality he witnesses; he may have revenged himself on Titania for loving her votaress so deeply, but he can do so only by having her re-enact the supposed transgression.[37] Moreover, Oberon may fail to recognize this scene as a displacement of his own sodomitical desires for the changeling boy, but the fact that Titania's desiring Bottom effects the exchange that Oberon desires suggests that the fairy king is getting the bottom he desires, the ass he wants: "And now I have the boy, I will undo / This hateful imperfection of her eyes" (4.1.62-63; see also 4.1.57-61). Though the scene represents the moment of the fairy king's decision to end the quarrel with Titania and thereby set nature aright, it confirms sodomy not only as the paradoxically perverse sign of pervasive disruption(s) in nature and thus society but also as an unrecognized constituent of natural and social order.[38]

"So with two seeming bodies, but one heart" (3.2.212)

Moreover, it was around and on the basis of the deployment of alliance that the deployment of sexuality was constructed.[39]

Whatever other affective or social ties may be involved in a lesbian relationship—ties that may also exist in other relations between and among women, from friendship to rivalry, political sisterhood to class or racial antagonism, ambivalence to love, and so on—the term *lesbian* refers to a sexual relation, for better or worse, and however broadly one may wish to define *sexual*. I use this term in its psychoanalytic acceptation to include centrally—beyond any performed or fantasized sexual act, whatever it may be—the conscious presence of desire in one woman for another. It is that desire, rather than woman identification or even the sexual act itself (which can obviously occur between women for reasons unrelated to desire), that specifies lesbian sexuality.[40]

There is of course one famous locus of "lesbian" interpretations of *A Midsummer Night's Dream*, the "double cherry" speech of Helena (3.2.192-219). The passage bespeaks the sort of emotional and physical closeness among women in early modern England and Europe that

Lillian Faderman discusses. But the standard recuperation of what looks like a state of Donnean "ecstasy" between two girlfriends is afforded precisely by its location in the past. What we would call lesbianism or at least romantic friendship, which a poet like Katherine Phillips calls simply friendship,[41] is attributed to a same-sex loyalty typical of youth or even childhood. The very fact that Helena and Hermia have come to the woods with the men they love and are fighting about and over those men has virtually determined the context in which this speech is understood—the passage from girlhood to womanhood.[42] Whatever their current problems with their lovers and each other, most readers and critics, like Barber,[43] assume that Helena and Hermia are on the path to maturity—marriage and procreation in Renaissance terms or "compulsory heterosexuality" in ours.[44]

And herein lies the problem with the text's location of lesbianism in the irretrievable realm of youth; female "confederacy"—to appropriate the term that Helena uses for the presumed alliance of Hermia with Lysander and Demetrius (3.2.192)—is always already to be dispensed with.[45] Though Faderman notes that intense female friendships like those of Phillips in the seventeenth century were greatly admired, they were only thus regarded so long as they did not, as certain cases of female cross-dressing did, involve the assumption of male prerogative and status and thus threaten, interfere with, subvert, or replace male homosocial interests in matters like licit procreation.[46] Indeed, the idea of two women living together and forming a household in the economic, social, and political senses, if not in the sexual as we understand it, seems to have been virtually unthinkable. It therefore comes as no surprise that the Amazons and the Athenian maidens of *A Midsummer Night's Dream* are obviously expected to marry and, in any event and less obviously, to die or at least to risk dying: the Amazons through war, the marriage-resisting Athenian maidens literally in execution or figuratively in "barren" chastity (1.1.72), and the married women figuratively in the procreative act (their husbands share this sign of mortality) and actually in childbirth. It is not surprising that prior to the Fairy King and Queen's nuptial blessing against "the blots of Nature's hand" in the "issue" of these "couples three" (5.1.405-10), Puck has already put us "In remembrance of a shroud" even as he presumably sweeps away the specter of death (5.1.378, 389-90). But in this coda, as the play approaches the juncture where theater dissolves into the lives of theater-goers, the care of

...ries against the danger of death in childbirth seems indeed "No more yielding than a dream" (5.1.428).

Nevertheless, *A Midsummer Night's Dream* provides a catalog of ways in which women—really upper-class women in this play—not only comply with but also resist the mandate to marry that is designed to control their productive, particularly procreative activities (the only sex that matters), and to secure through this control the disposition of property. Thus, as is well known, Hermia's resistance to her father's will is ultimately an affair of state that calls forth the full weight of the dominant ideology: "Either to die the death, or to abjure / For ever the society of men" (1.1.65-66). But the credence Hermia gives a highly—almost ridiculously—conventionalized romantic love, "the course" of which, as Lysander states and she concurs, "never did run smooth" (1.1.134), and her naive belief that Lysander must be satisfied with adhering even in the forest to conventions of courtly honor (2.2.35-65) suggest that in throwing off one yoke she has in fact taken up another. For the conventions of romantic love between men and women are situated within other systems (familial, social, economic, political) that deploy, protect, and foster male privilege, including men's insistence on women's fulfilling male sexual desires if the situation permits; following this line, Lysander is prone to leave Hermia because she refuses to satisfy his sexual urges, while Helena can demand that Demetrius act on his male prerogative to "abuse" her.[47] Moreover, the play may suggest in Hermia's putting Lysander farther off and in her dream (*pace* Holland)[48] that her own (erotic) desires do not tend toward Lysander: is hers a coy demurral (whether maidenly or coquettish), a fear of (hetero-)sexual intercourse (of Lysander's desire, of her own, of the act itself, of its social proscription, of pregnancy as a possible consequence), or—less obvious then but more probable now[49]—a sexual disinclination to what we would call the heterosexual imperative?

For gay, lesbian, bisexual, and other "queer" readers and spectators, as well as for feminists (these categories may, of course, overlap) and perhaps others, Hermia's reluctance to sleep with or even next to the man with whom she is eloping bespeaks a lack of trust (well-founded, in light of the supernatural intervention) as well as a lack of desire. We find out that Hermia felt no reluctance about (sexual?) intimacy with her friend Helena. Moreover, a "queer" performance might build on a key sign of the depth of that relationship:

her spilling the beans to Helena about her elopement with Lysander *could* be seen as an attempt to get Helena to stop her. But is it a test of Helena's love (an "out" reading) or just reliance on intimate knowledge that Helena's abject desire to please Demetrius will likely thwart Hermia's own acquiescence in Lysander's plan (a more traditional view of the latency of the women's intimacy)? The point is not that the text *encourages* these views but that the gaps in characterological motivation the text leaves for completion need not be filled as dominant ideologies then or now would fill them—with, in varying degrees and somewhat different senses, Hermia's naive reliance on female friendship and solidarity in the face of (heterosexual) love.

Flying in the face of dominant ideological probabilities, we might see in Helena's masochistic pursuit of a man who does not love or want her (sexually or maritally) an attempt simultaneously to comply with pervasive social expectations for adult women (their procreative function in the dominant ideology) and to thwart her role in a homosocial system of marital exchange. For feminists in particular, Helena's "spaniel" masochism (2.2.203-10) has been problematic if not downright offensive. But one possible queer reading might suggest that, in a world devoid of the requisite fairy magic, Helena's apparently self-frustrating choice and strategy—a clear case of "Love's mind" lacking "of any judgment taste" (1.1.236)—is most likely to keep her, if not satisfied, at least free from the constraints of marriage as well as from the risk of death for openly resisting or, given the procreative aim of marriage, for submitting. Even Hermia's choice—against her father's will—may similarly be seen as negotiating divers unsavory social demands. Needless to say, these isolated "queer" moments result from reading consciously and conscientiously against the grain of the text; filling its gaps in ways that counter dominant and—in the case of Helena, perhaps some feminist—ideological expectations; intervening, as Sinfield would say, precisely at the points where the text is silent.[50]

But there are also other scenes, where the text "speaks," that in present circumstances may take on meanings originally unintended: the "catfight" between Helena and Hermia is notable among these. For one thing, as feminists, we might question why mutual betrayal and physical violence between women is, by convention, funny. Furthermore, I would suggest, the ostensible humor of the scene—one of the most physical up to this point in the play—is complicated by its homoerotic energy. After all, it was originally enacted by two presumably attractive boy-actors who probably disheveled or defaced their costumes and make-up—teasing audiences by foregrounding the tension between the theatrical illusion of female presence and the male bodies that produce the illusion. Though *A Midsummer Night's Dream* is not a transvestite comedy, it toys with the underpinnings of its theatrical illusion-making and attraction: that there is—for at least some members of some audiences—a homoerotic charge to a scene with two boys pretending to be women fighting seems likely, especially for those accustomed to the metatheatricality of drag.

Interestingly enough, however, this scene is one that the employment of female actors renders problematic in a variety of ways: Most obviously, the increased verisimilitude of the representation of women lends weight in our culture to the text's skepticism about the durability of female friendship as opposed to love (always assumed heterosexual). But less obviously the change in the mode of production converts the probable homoeroticism of the boy-cum-woman catfight, a representation with its own problematics of gender and sexuality, into a scene with some of the potentially pornographic effects of female mud-wrestling. Indeed, many modern productions of this scene not only presume the conventional comic view of violence between women but also rely on a sexual effect akin to the cinematic use of lesbian sex in pornography aimed at men. The implied shallowness of women's friendships, the suggestion that female bodies lack the power to do more than parody masculine combat (which, to be sure, is itself mocked later in the futility of the Lysander-Demetrius chase orchestrated by Puck), and the way in which the women depend on and/or are restrained by the men in the very moment of their confrontation—certainly such misogynistic effects constitute the conventional "joke" implicit in this scene, of which the women are the butt and the male spectators (and originally producers) are the sharers. But these effects cannot be separated from the physicality of the women in modern productions of the scene—of a Hermia being restrained by and a Helena cowering behind the men, of torn dresses that tease audiences with the revelation of the actors' female bodies, in some cases of out-and-out wrestling as part of the stage business.[51] How and for whom such scenes are erotic as well as funny in the context of modern production has a good deal to do with how we evaluate their effects: a lesbian theatrical production might or might not play up potential erotic qualities of the scene for its audiences, but in any event the term "pornographic" as a pejorative would undoubtedly not apply to such a version in the way that it *might* to a Broadway performance aimed mainly at bringing in politically, as well as socially and sexually, moderate to conservative middle- and upper-class suburbanites, tourists, and conventioneers.

Who does the seeing, who does the acting, who does the paying, and why—all these affect the erotics of this scene: feminism has led many of us to question the presumed universality of its humor and the effects of its comic conventions for the representation of gender and women in particular; additionally, queer theory suggests that this questioning can too easily subsume the erotic or sexual under the category of gender or ignore it altogether, even though the scene's erotic potentialities necessarily inform such gender analyses—all too often unconsciously. If queer theories rely on the inflated currency of the Bard in academic (and theatrical) circles, these theories—like the plurality of feminisms—also provide strategies for thwarting the uses to which dominant ideologies would put and constrain the text and for reclaiming the text for other ends, however limited in scope. Like Foucault's characterization of modern homosexual responses to the pathologizing discourse of psychoanalysis, queer literary theory and criticism constitutes a conscious and conscientious "'reverse' discourse," though hardly a monolithic one: "homosexuality began to speak on its own behalf, to demand that its legitimacy or 'naturality' be acknowledged, often in the same vocabulary, using the same categories by which it was medically disqualified. There is not, on the one side, a discourse of power, and opposite it, another discourse that runs counter to it."[52] If some queer theory risks a facile recuperation of such a classic scene, indeed of so canonical a work as *A Midsummer Night's Dream*, it also enacts from within the discursive realms of theory/criticism and literature/theater the "re-visioning"—indeed multiple re-visionings—of the literary past that Adrienne Rich calls for.[53]

"Goblin, lead them up and down" (3.2.399)

I thus put into play the following hypothesis: like all forms of desire, homoerotic desire is implicit within all psyches; whether and how it is given cultural expression, whether and how it is manifested as anxiety, is a matter of culturally contingent signifying practices.

What is culturally specific is not the fact or presence of desire towards persons of the same gender, but the meanings that are attached to its expression, and the attendant anxieties generated by its repression.[54]

Sometimes I go to queer theatre and over-identify. I write myself into the plot. Or, I want to be Bottom. I want to play all the parts: "Let me play Thisby"; "Let me play the lion too." I want to be in the representation, help produce or perform it, sometimes revise it.[55]

Anne Barton ends her introduction to the Riverside edition of *A Midsummer Night's Dream* by invoking Hippolyta's words that the lovers' story, as well as their "minds transfigur'd so together,"

More witnesseth than fancy's images,
And grows to something of great constancy;
But howsoever, strange and admirable. (5.1.24-27)

These words support Barton's view that "the play has created its own reality," one "touching our own," one beyond the "practicalities" of Theseus's common-sense view of the world.[56] As a critique of the former glorification of Theseus by critics like Hunter, Barton's reliance on Hippolyta's words as a corrective to her husband's beautiful but dismissive speech on the powers of the imagination provides a first move in dismantling the play's gender hierarchy, though she does not present it as such.[57] Hippolyta's words remind us that the tensions, the chill, of the opening scene have not disappeared entirely; marriage has transformed, perhaps even mitigated, the differences between Theseus and Hippolyta, but not eradicated them. A further problem, one might say contradiction, lies in the fact that Theseus seems better able than she to employ imagination in (mis)construing the good intentions of Bottom and his fellow-actors—albeit as a form of *noblesse oblige* that appropriates their play to his own ends as a "good" ruler. And these are just two among many "chinks" in the solidity of both the play's comic ending and the "world" it creates. If, as Barton recognizes, this is a play with more than one potential ending, what are the implications of Shakespeare's constructing "a fifth act which seems, in effect, to take place beyond the normal plot-defined boundaries of comedy"?[58] Is this generic anomaly related to the slippage in Hippolyta's words, between that constant "something"—a blank variously filled in various places and times—and its strangeness and marvelousness?[59] Why is there so much extraneous to the plot in "the latter end" of *A Midsummer Night's Dream*?

For me one answer lies in the centrality of two figures in act 5: Bottom and Puck. Though both characters are involved in the love and marriage plots, they have functioned in this regard primarily as pawns or agents in the desires of other characters. But in act 5 Bottom's exuberant imagination takes center-stage and cannot be contained by either the *noblesse oblige* of a Theseus or the mockery of other auditors; though aristocratic privilege is maintained in this scene through the interpretive practices of the elite, the "tedious brief scene" and the "very tragical mirth" of the play-within-the-play (5.1.56-57) nonetheless exceed the constraints of those practices on meaning. Furthermore, the rude mechanicals' reintroduction of tragedy and death into the final act of the play, however laughably executed, does ostensibly exorcise these elements from the play's happy marital resolution, but only at the cost of reminding us that the world is bigger than the play, that plays shape but a small part of experience through dramatic conventions and characters, and that comedy, like other genres, functions like a lens that sharpens the focus here on the social desirability and accommodation of marriage and procreation by filtering out other plots and perspectives. Quince's ill delivery of the Prologue—"All for your delight / We are not here" (5.1.114-15)—underscores the close connection between form and meaning: since "This fellow doth not stand upon points" (5.1.118), the prologue is garbled, unintentionally working against the aims of its speaker, even though both the onstage and the offstage audience can at times perceive his obscured but intended meaning. Quince's performance reveals just how slippery dramatic texts are.

The metatheater of Bottom and his friends—delivered by "many asses" (5.1.154)—reveals a textual "cranny" through which uncontainable meanings are whispered. It should remind us that if we see "sodomy," "homoeroticism," "lesbianism," or "compulsory heterosexuality" in the "aery nothing" (5.1.16) of *A Midsummer Night's Dream*, whether, how, how much, and why the text bespeaks such concerns—intentionally or unintentionally, in its time or ours, to everyone or just to some—has much to do with the place(s) of this text in the culture of early modern England, with the intersections between this text and the multiple histories of our culture(s), and with our own various relations to the politics of the present moment. Too easily dismissed as merely scatalogical buffoonery, the sodomitical elements surrounding Bottom suggest that sodomy, as a key sign in Renaissance culture of chaos and disorder, could be employed to comic effect, could—or at least can—be deployed against the aesthetic rigidities of comic form and the political ideology of the prevailing order.

And Puck? His reappearance at the end, though it puts us "In remembrance of a shroud," prepares "this hallowed house" for the entrance and procreative blessing of the fairy king and queen (5.1.378 and 388); hence it is not nearly so interestingly disruptive as his earlier appearances. But the fact that he and his words displace the fairy royals and theirs and the fact that his words bridge the space between actor and audience, calling attention to these theatrical "shadows" and "visions" (5.1.423 and 426), once again recall Puck's problematic function as the all too unreliable and often delightedly mischievous agent of Oberon. On numerous occasions, he exemplifies Dollimore's "paradoxical perverse," the glitch in Oberon's exercise of power:[60] "And so far am I glad it so did sort, / As this their jangling I esteem a sport" (3.2.352-53). Puck's proximity to Oberon, as the (in)effective agent of the latter's will, underscores the limitations of power and its practices—the quirks, the "chinks," through which its aims can be disrupted, if not countered.

Granted, Puck takes a sometimes voyeuristic, sometimes sadistic pleasure in the folly and pain of others. But unlike Oberon, who also desires the folly and shame/shaming of Titania, Puck's desires are ends in themselves, not displacements of other desires or means of asserting his own prerogatives. His engagement in the love plots—both that of the Athenian lovers and that of Oberon, Titania, the Indian boy, and Bottom—reminds us that one satisfies one's own desires almost inevitably at others' expense. Hardly a model of sensitivity to the feelings of others, Puck's obvious pleasure in mischief is a good deal more honest than Oberon's "pity" (4.1.47) for Titania after having savored her degradation and obtained from her the other object of his desires and designs.

Puck is the energy of desire itself, whatever its content; though at Oberon's service, his is an energy that cannot be fully contained within power's totalizing aims. If Bottom, who would play all the parts, is the model of Miller and Román's engagement with queer theater, Puck is my "queer" hero because his pleasures work against or at least inflect ideological constraints on desire, the very constraints he has been sent to enforce. Puck enjoys "what fools these mortals be" (3.2.115), his mistaken interventions simply adding to the vicissitudes of their fate as mortals in love and mirroring the volatility of human desire itself (3.2.92-93).

Puck is the very possibility of the perverse operating within yet against constraints, of pleasures beyond such constraints. If, as Ciulei's production implied, the text of *A Midsummer Night's Dream* attempts to exile all desires inconsistent with procreative marriage, Puck's reappearance at the end, especially as speaker of the epilogue, reinscribes the impossibility of such a program by reminding us of the play's potential for theatrical as well as ideological failure. Today we might add that how or whether these "shadows have offended" is closely tied to who is watching and what engages them (5.1.423); thus the text's enforcement of compulsory heterosexuality and procreation might commend the play to the ascendant moralists of the religious right in the U.S. today if the scene between Titania and Bottom did not theatrically signify sexual desires quite beyond fundamentalist cognizance. But such are the scenes of desire that Puck delights in and delights in making. In my view, Puck represents the possibility of queering this play, Shakespeare, the English renaissance canon, and the culture of the theaters and classrooms in which they are daily revived.

NOTES

1. All references to Shakespeare's *A Midsummer Night's Dream* are from *The Riverside Shakespeare*, ed. G. Blakemore Evans (Boston: Houghton Mifflin, 1974), 217-49. The quotation is from act 1, scene 1, line 226; hereafter such passages are cited parenthetically in the text.

2. Michel Foucault, *The History of Sexuality: An Introduction*, trans. Robert Hurley (New York: Vintage/Random House, 1990), 48.

3. Tim Miller and David Román, "'Preaching to the Converted,'" *Theatre Journal* 47 (1995): 186.

4. See Thomas Clayton's polemical review of this production, "Shakespeare at the Guthrie: *A Midsummer Night's Dream*," *Shakespeare Quarterly* 37 (1986): 229-36. Clayton praises Ciulei's *Dream* as "a major production by any measure and certainly one of the most systematically conceived," but apparently regrets the vision of Shakespeare's play as "a dark

comedy about patriarchal abuses of power in a reading Ciulei said was prescribed by the imperatives of our time" (230).

5. Alan Sinfield, *Cultural Politics—Queer Reading* (Philadelphia: University of Pennsylvania Press, 1994), 10.

6. See, for instance, Shirley Nelson Garner, "*A Midsummer Night's Dream*: 'Jack Shall Have Jill; / Nought Shall Go Ill,'" *Women's Studies* 9 (1981): 47-63. Garner holds the view "that the renewal at the end of the play affirms patriarchal order and hierarchy, insisting that the power of women must be circumscribed, and that it recognizes the tenuousness of heterosexuality," which needs, therefore, to be enforced (47). I am indebted to Garner's essay throughout, particularly for its feminist analysis of homoerotic elements in the play and of what Adrienne Rich, in "Compulsory Heterosexuality and Lesbian Existence," *Signs* 5 (1980): 631-60, calls "compulsory heterosexuality." The sodomitical import of "preposterousness" is discussed later in this essay; see Jonathan Goldberg, *Sodometries: Renaissance Texts, Modern Sexualities* (Stanford: Stanford University Press, 1992), 180-81, on the meaning of "preposterous venus."

7. Valerie Traub, *Desire and Anxiety: Circulations of Sexuality in Shakespearean Drama* (London: Routledge, 1992), 113.

8. The major pros and cons of this much-contested term are nicely outlined by Teresa de Lauretis in "Queer Theory: Lesbian and Gay Sexualities: An Introduction," *Differences: A Journal of Feminist Cultural Studies* 3.2 (1991): iii-xviii. See also Sinfield, x-xi.

9. Traub, *Desire*, 95.

10. Sinfield, 19.

11. See Northrop Frye, *Anatomy of Criticism*, (1957; Princeton: Princeton University Press, 1971), 169-71, and C.L. Barber, *Shakespeare's Festive Comedy* (1959; Princeton: Princeton University Press, 1972), 3-15 and 119-62. For a problematizing counter-view of *A Midsummer Night's Dream* and "festive theory," see Annabel Patterson, *Shakespeare and the Popular Voice* (Oxford: Basil Blackwell, 1989), 52-70 and 170-73.

12. The question of the boy-player has been central to recent discussions of these issues: see, for example, Phyllis Rackin, "Androgyny, Mimesis, and the Marriage of the Boy Heroine on the English Renaissance Stage," *PMLA* 102 (1987): 29-41; Jean Howard, "Crossdressing, the Theatre, and Gender Struggle in Early Modern England," *Shakespeare Quarterly* 39 (1988): 418-40, who provides a good summary of the scholarship on the issue; and Valery Traub, *Desire*, 117-44 and 171-75, who provides what might be called a 'queer' intervention in the feminist discussion. For bibliographies of feminist

criticism on Shakespeare and his contemporaries, see Dorothea Kehler's "A Selective Bibliography of Feminist and Feminist-Related Shakespeare Criticism, 1979-88" and Susan Baker and Lorena L. Stookey's "Renaissance Drama: A Bibliography for Feminists," in *In Another Country: Feminist Perspectives on Renaissance Drama*, eds. Dorothea Kehler and Susan Baker (Metuchen: Scarecrow Press, 1991), 261-301 and 302-24.

13. See, for instance, Jane Gallop, *The Daughter's Seduction* (Ithaca: Cornell University Press, 1982), 56-61, who deconstructs Irigaray's own "blind spot" in the French feminist's critique of Freud.

14. Though often lumped together, Sinfield identifies one of the key distinctions between new historicism and cultural materialism as the former's Althusserian "preoccupation with . . . the 'entrapment model' of ideology" (24). Most of the critics cited throughout this essay are themselves feminists, cultural materialists, and/or (new) historicists who have incorporated and/or developed queer theories or perspectives in their work; in addition to those cited elsewhere, I owe a general debt to the following authors and works: John Boswell, "Revolutions, Universals, and Sexual Categories," in *Hidden from History: Reclaiming the Gay and Lesbian Past*, eds. Martin Bauml Duberman, Martha Vicinus, and George Chauncey, Jr. (New York: NAL/Penguin, 1989), 17-36 and 478-81; Judith C. Brown, "Lesbian Sexuality in Medieval and Early Modern Europe," in *Hidden from History*, 67-75 and 495-500; James M. Saslow, "Homosexuality in the Renaissance: Behavior, Identity, and Artistic Expression," in *Hidden from History*, 90-105 and 503-506; Stephen Orgel, "Nobody's Perfect: Or Why Did the English Stage Take Boys for Women?" *Displacing Homophobia*, eds. Ronald R. Butters, John M. Clum, and Michael Moon (Durham, NC: Duke University Press, 1989); Joseph Pequigney, *Such Is My Love* (Chicago: University of Chicago Press, 1985); Gayle Rubin, "Thinking Sex: Notes for a Radical Theory of the Politics of Sexuality," in *Pleasure and Danger: Exploring Female Sexuality*, ed. Carole S. Vance (Boston: Routledge, 1984), 267-319; Eve Kosofsky Sedgwick, *Epistemology of the Closet* (Berkeley: University of California Press, 1990); Bruce R. Smith, *Homosexual Desire in Shakespeare's England: A Cultural Poetics* (Chicago: University of Chicago Press, 1991); and Bonnie Zimmerman, "Perverse Reading: The Lesbian Appropriation of Literature," in *Sexual Practice/Textual Theory: Lesbian Cultural Criticism*, eds. Susan J. Wolfe and Julia Penelope (Cambridge: Blackwell, 1993), 135-49.

15. The ongoing and salutary, if still somewhat limited, effects of the debates and critiques within feminism about race and class have, I believe, also enabled the intervention and incorporation of queer theories into

institutionalized critical practice—for example, in Jonathan Dollimore's call for the interplay of theory and history (*Sexual Dissidence: Augustine to Wilde, Freud to Foucault* [Oxford: Clarendon, 1991], 24-25) and in Diana Fuss's analysis of the debate over essentialism/anti-essentialism, especially within gay and lesbian studies themselves (*Essentially Speaking* [New York: Routledge, 1989], 97-112 and 127-29). In Shakespeare studies the intervention of queer theory was evident in a recent seminar on "Problematic Alliances: Feminism and Queer Theory in Early Modern Studies," organized and conducted by Jean Howard and Nicholas Radel, at the 1995 meeting of The Shakespeare Association of America in Chicago.

16. Judith Butler, *Bodies That Matter* (New York: Routledge, 1993), 239.

17. Whatever the shortcomings of my own eclectic application of queer theory, my conviction about its significance owes much to my former student, Linda Parriott, whose undergraduate essay on *A Midsummer Night's Dream* and *Othello* first brought home to me the function and value of a lesbian criticism ("Understanding the Fury: Subtexts of Female Homoeroticism in *A Midsummer Night's Dream* and *Othello*" [unpublished honors thesis, Augsburg College, 1993]). The play's famous line, cited here, about the bumpy "course of true love" is itself a prime site for queer re-examination, to which Valerie Traub provides a key in her brief discussion of nature's "bias" in *Twelfth Night* (*Desire*, 137-38). Though her critique does not refer directly to Stephen Greenblatt's analysis of this term from bowls, which reveals nature as "an *unbalancing* act" or "swerving" (see Greenblatt, *Shakespearean Negotiations* [Berkeley: University of California Press, 1988], 68), Traub's contention that the desires of both Sebastian and his boy-sister "obliterate the distinction between homoerotic and heterosexual—at least until the institution of marriage comes into (the) play" (*Desire*, 138)—implicitly throws into question Greenblatt's use of "bias" to describe the twist toward heterosexual object-choice as "something off-center . . . implanted in nature . . . that deflects men and women from their ostensible desires and toward the pairings for which they are destined" (Greenblatt, 68). There is in other words a presumption that the (heterosexual) object to which the lover swerves is somehow more natural than the homoerotic course or "swerving" that has led there. To be sure, the impending marital ending of this comedy ostensibly sorts out sanctioned from unsanctioned desires, but it cannot quite dispose of the homoerotic trajectories that have led to it—Antonio remains on stage and Viola is still Cesario (see Douglas E. Green, "Shakespeare's Violation: 'One Face, One Voice, One Habit, and Two Persons,'" in *Reconsidering the Renaissance: Papers from the 1987 CEMERS Conference on the Renaissance*, ed. Mario di Cesare

[Binghamton: Medieval and Renaissance Texts and Studies/SUNY Press, 1992], 336-38, especially nn. 32 and 34).

18. Traub, *Desire*, 142-43.

19. Miller and Román, 186.

20. Foucault, 101.

21. In contrast to the *OED*, Eric Partridge suggests that arse and ass are interchangeable, that the former reflects the pronunciation of the latter (*Shakespeare's Bawdy*, 3rd ed. [New York: Routledge, 1968], 59). Also, Puck's reference to the "bum" of the "wisest aunt," who has mistaken the hobgoblin for a "three-foot stool" and thus "down topples," supports the connection between bum and bottom (2.1.51-54).

22. Goldberg, *Sodometries*, 122.

23. Goldberg, citing Jonathan Crewe, makes explicit the sexual implications of Oberon's desire for the boy (*Sodometries*, 275, n. 8). James L. Calderwood discusses the analogy between the Theseus-Hippolyta sub-plot as anamorphically re-created and played out in the Oberon-Titania plot ("*A Midsummer Night's Dream*: Anamorphism and Theseus's Dream," *Shakespeare Quarterly* 42 [1991]: 409-30). See Elizabeth Pittenger, "'To Serve the Queere': Nicholas Udall, Master of Revels," in *Queering the Renaissance*, ed. Jonathan Goldberg, *Queering the Renaissance* (Durham: Duke University Press, 1994), 162-89, on "misrecognition" in regard to the problem of historical and theoretical readings of the text as evidence of "real sexual identity" and/or "real sexual practice" (168).

24. See Simon Shepherd on the contrasting images of the "warrior woman," who represents an ideal of active womanhood, and of the Elizabethan "Amazon," who is seen as lustful, disobedient, brutal (*Amazons and Warrior Women* [New York: St. Martin's, 1981], 5-17). Though his focus here is on Spenser, Shepherd's analysis suggests some of the tensions surrounding Hippolyta and her relationship with Theseus.

25. On the "deployment of alliance," see Foucault 106-11; on the term "homosocial," see Eve Kosofsky Sedgwick, *Between Men: English Literature and Male Homosocial Desire* (New York: Columbia University Press, 1985), 1-5.

26. For the possible mechanisms behind such misrecognitions, see chapter 3 of Alan Bray's *Homosexuality in Renaissance England*, 2nd ed. (London: Gay Men's Press, 1982), 58-80. In his essay on "Homosexuality and the Signs of Male Friendship in Elizabethan England," *History Workshop* 29 (1990): 1-19, Bray discusses the ways in which the signs of desirable male friendship could be (con)fused with "the profoundly disturbing image of the sodomite"

and the fearful chaos the latter represented and evoked (11). Aspiring to power and/or wealth beyond one's status or class was one of several contexts in which such confusion or deliberate accusation was likely to arise; indeed changes in the relations between masters and servingmen, which had clearly come under the notion of friendship so long as servingmen were also gentlemen, were subject to more suspicion once the retainers were not themselves "gentle" (10-15). Bottom's "dreams," in this light, constitute a rather burlesque version of suspect preferment. As Gregory W. Bredbeck points out in his discussion of Ulysses' construction of Patroclus in *Troilus and Cressida*: "sodomy and related areas of homoerotic meaning, then, do not just delineate the division between high and low—do not just make the stuff of satire; rather, they also demarcate the point at which high and low meet and may be traversed" (*Sodomy and Interpretation: Marlowe to Milton* [Ithaca: Cornell University Press, 1991], 47). On the problematic coincidence of homoeroticism and misogyny, especially in the sonnets, Traub emphasizes that exclusively homoerotic bonds could signal "anxiety about reproduction" (*Desire*, 138-43); in this light, Theseus's marriage to the Amazon queen represents a misogynistic normalization of her former autonomy. Likewise, Thisby's death suggests, among other possibilities, subtextual come-uppance for disobedience to parental will, under the guise of the tragic thwarting of true love. But it is in the "Bottom's Dream" soliloquy, as well as in the rude mechanicals' performance at the nuptial feast, that the homoerotic (Bottom's potentially sodomitical vision) and the misogynistic (the marriage of Hippolyta, which elicits a tragic play, the death of whose heroine is the occasion for a song about this dream-vision) coincide, in this case as the possible means of Bottom's elevation.

27. This section depends heavily on Foucault's formulation of "a multiplicity of points of resistance" within "power relationships": "Where there is power, there is resistance, and yet, or rather consequently, this resistance is never in a position of exteriority to power. Should it be said that one is always 'inside' power, there is no 'escaping' it, there is no absolute outside where it is concerned, because one is subject to the law in any case? . . . This would be to misunderstand the strictly relational character of power relationships. Their existence depends on a multiplicity of points of resistance: these play the role of adversary, target, support, or handle in power relations. These points of resistance are present everywhere in the power network. . . . But this does not mean that they are only a reaction or rebound, forming with respect to the basic domination an underside that is in the end always passive, doomed to perpetual defeat" (Foucault, 95-96). See Sinfield on theoretical positions that counter the

stultifying effects of the "entrapment-model of ideology and power," deriving from Althusser and some readings of Foucault, and that posit a more dynamic relation between dissidence and containment (24-27).

28. Foucault, 106-13.

29. It is tempting to posit for Shakespeare—as for his characters Bottom and, even more, Oberon and Theseus—what Goldberg calls a "dehiscence" within early modern (male) subjects around the question of sodomy. Though Goldberg and others have criticized Alan Bray's anachronistic use of the term "homosexuality" (Goldberg, *Sodometries*, 70-71), Bray describes well this "cleavage" within the subject: "For when one looks at the circumstantial details of how homosexuality was conceived of and how it was expressed in concrete social forms, it becomes obvious how very easy it was in Renaissance England—far more so than today—for a cleavage of this kind to exist, between an individual's behaviour and his awareness of its significance" (*Homosexuality in Renaissance England*, 68). Dollimore describes "transgressive reinscription" as "the return of the repressed and/or the suppressed and/or the displaced via the proximate" (33).

30. Goldberg, *Sodometries*, 19.

31. Lillian Faderman, *Surpassing the Love of Men: Romantic Friendship and Love Between Women from the Renaissance to the Present* (New York: William Morrow, 1981), 35-36. See Valerie Traub, "The (In)significance of 'Lesbian' Desire in Early Modern England," in *Erotic Politics: Desire on the Renaissance Stage*, ed. Susan Zimmerman (New York: Routledge, 1992), 150-69, for a counterargument to the usefulness of the category of sodomy for analysis of female same-sex relations, at least in England, where there were no women tried for sodomy (152). In the same article, Traub also illuminates the recuperation of "lesbian" desires and practices to the model of "heterosexual" intercourse, penetration of a woman by a man. This elision accounts for my sometimes placing the term "lesbian," among others, within quotation marks or parentheses: given the discourses on female-female relations in early modern England, the term—like homosexual and heterosexual—cannot be used without somehow signaling the historical slippage in its application. In her essay "The Straight Mind," Monique Wittig illuminates but does not resolve these problems in her analysis of the concept "woman," which "has meaning only in heterosexual systems of thought and heterosexual economic systems" (*The Straight Mind and Other Essays* [Boston: Beacon, 1992], 32).

32. I am indebted in general here to Goldberg's discussion of Puttenham (*Sodometries*, 29-61), especially the subsidiary analysis of the *Sieve Portrait* of Elizabeth (43-47). Goldberg builds on but also raises questions about new

historicist views of the anxiety elicited by the queen's sexuality and power (see, for example, Louis Adrian Montrose, *"A Midsummer Night's Dream* and the Shaping Fantasies of Elizabethan Culture: Gender, Power, Form," in *Rewriting the Renaissance*, eds. Margaret W. Ferguson, Maureen Quilligan, and Nancy J. Vickers [Chicago: University of Chicago Press, 1986], 65-87 and 329-34, and "'Shaping Fantasies': Figurations of Gender and Power in Elizabethan Culture," in *Representing the English Renaissance*, ed. Stephen Greenblatt [Berkeley: University of California Press, 1988], 31-64). See Gregory W. Bredbeck's discussion of the monarch's "two bodies" and its implications for writing (about) Edward II (50-60), especially the implicit "recognition of a space between power and person that can be narrowed or widened depending on the circumstances" (53); this space has a good deal to do, I think, with the way that through Titania concerns about the English queen's political powers are shifted to the sexual appetites of the temporal woman. Equally significant is James L. Calderwood's discussion of the double meaning of Titania's lines about the moon's "lamenting some enforced chastity" (3.1.198-200), delivered as she prepares to have Bottom hauled off to her bower (Calderwood, 421-22); the phrase, at least in its secondary meaning as compulsory chastity, calls up both the nunnery to which Hermia would be sent and the ostensible condition of the Virgin Queen herself.

33. As Bray stresses, social and economic context and power determined how sodomitical relationships were both perceived and conducted: "What determined the shared and recurring features of homosexual relationships [in Renaissance England] was the prevailing distribution of power, economic power and social power, not the fact of homosexuality itself" (Bray, *Homosexuality in Renaissance England*, 56). Traub sees a "maternal" bond between Titania and her devotee through the boy ("[In]significance," 158-59), but I would suggest that the embrace of Titania and Bottom-the-ass is a "male" metaphor for female-female relations, exchanges, and bonds. If so, was the substitution of this human ass for another woman somehow a less threatening displacement (for Shakespeare) or a sadistic, misogynistic one—a sign of confusion in the face of "lesbian" sexuality or one of anxiety? Still, I agree with Traub about Oberon's feelings of superfluousness in the face of relations that simply do not require him ("[In]significance," 159). To the extent that one does see tensions between an image of Oberon and Titania as squabbling over an adoptive son and those of the boy as embodiment of intersecting sexual relations (Titania-[votaress], Titania-boy, Oberon-boy), one might speculate also on incest as a key site of the contradiction between the family as a "deployment of alliance" and as "a hotbed of constant sexual incitement"

(Foucault, 108-109) and what that might do, if not to likely Renaissance views of the dispute over the boy, then at least to some of ours: it might suggest, among other things, incest as a sign of "perverse" desire that cannot otherwise be represented.

34. Foucault, 86.

35. Dollimore, 121.

36. According to Dollimore, "the perverse dynamic signifies the potential of those [perverse] paradoxes to destabilize, to provoke discoherence" (121).

37. Calderwood offers a good summary on the debate as to whether or not Titania or Bottom "did it" (419-25). He argues that the relationship is one of "degrading but unconsummated desire" (422). But I am assuming the text implies that, at least off-stage, something was done; at any rate, for twentieth-century interpreters, a non-sexual encounter between Bottom and Titania is almost as inconceivable as a sexual one was for the nineteenth century (see, for instance, Jan Kott, *Shakespeare Our Contemporary* [New York: Norton, 1966], 223-34). What kind of sexual act seems to me the (im)pertinent question, since for the Renaissance audience that would determine the magnitude of erotic transgression and shame the scene implies. Given the complex intertwining of gender and sexual roles in our own culture(s), the same question would have some bearing on our own categorization of the scene—as erotic, transgressive, degrading, bestial, (displaced) heterosexual, displaced homosexual, etc. One other interesting point that comes up in Calderwood's summary is the association of asses with compliant wives (419, n. 24): does Bottom then represent the wife Oberon wants, the wife Titania should be, or the wife she wants?

38. See Dollimore on the construction of "nature" and the complex interrelations between "nature" and its perversion (108-13). On matters related to "bestiality" in this and subsequent sections, see Bruce Thomas Boehrer's "Bestial Buggery in *A Midsummer Night's Dream*," in *The Production of English Renaissance Culture*, eds. David Lee Miller, Sharon O'Dair, and Harold Weber (Ithaca: Cornell University Press, 1994), 123-50, an excellent article which appeared as I was completing this essay. A new historicist, Boehrer discusses the English Renaissance "rhetoric of bestiality" (132) and the manifestations of this discourse in Shakespeare's *Dream*. Though his focus is strictly on "bestial buggery" and its representation, Boehrer makes some of the same points I am making here about the proximity of order and perversion and even the ironic dependence of the former on the latter. Interestingly, much as I do here and in the last section of this essay, Boehrer sees Puck as central to the play's ideological contradictions surrounding the 'perverse' (145-47).

39. Foucault, 107.

40. Teresa de Lauretis, *The Practice of Love: Lesbian Sexuality and Perverse Desire* (Bloomington: Indiana University Press, 1994), 284.

41. See Faderman, 65-73, on the emotional and physical bonds between women in early modern England, which includes her discussion of Phillips.

42. Traub rejects this infantilizing view of same-sex desires and friendships among women ("[In]significance," 157-59).

43. Barber, 129-30.

44. Rich, *passim.*

45. Traub, "(In)significance," 158.

46. Faderman, 67-72 and 47-54; Traub, "(In)significance," 163-65.

47. The sense that romantic love and even companionate marriage are in practice far from perfect is probably clearer and stronger for us, especially in light of modern feminist critiques, than this relative novelty, more common in fiction than in practice, was to a Renaissance audience. But Mary Astell, writing at the end of the seventeenth century, laid out early on some of the problems and pitfalls of those who marry solely for love. See Mary Astell, Selections from *Some Reflections upon Marriage*, in Vol. 1, *Norton Anthology of English Literature*, ed. M. H. Abrams et al., 6th ed. (New York: Norton, 1993), 1971-75.

48. Norman N. Holland, "Hermia's Dream," *Representing Shakespeare*, ed. Murray M. Schwartz and Coppélia Kahn (Baltimore: Johns Hopkins University Press, 1980), 1-20.

49. See Julia Creet, "Daughter of the Movement: The Psychodynamics of Lesbian S/M Fantasy," *Differences: A Journal of Feminist Cultural Studies* 3.2 (1991): 135-59, on lesbianism as the "unimaginable," especially within classic psychoanalysis (137).

50. Sinfield, 36-38.

51. Of the several professional, academic, and amateur productions I have seen since the early 1970s, most have involved some form of "striptease" as part of the fight between Helena and Hermia. Fewer have involved the intimate violence of wrestling.

52. Foucault, 101.

53. See Traub, *Desire*, 107; she employs the term "re-visioning" as defined by Adrienne Rich, in "When We Dead Awaken: Writing as Re-Vision," *College English* 34.1 (1972): 18-25.

54. Traub, *Desire*, 103.

55. Miller and Román, 186.

56. Anne Barton, introduction to *A Midsummer Night's Dream*, in *The Riverside Shakespeare*, 221 and 219.

57. See G.K. Hunter, "*A Midsummer Night's Dream*," in *Shakespeare: Modern Essays in Criticism*, ed. Leonard F. Dean, rev. ed. (London: Oxford University Press, 1967), 90-102 (especially 99-102), for a traditional glorification of Theseus and of the relationship between him and Hippolyta. In contrast, Skiles Howard, "Hands, Feet, and Bottoms: Decentering the Cosmic Dance in *A Midsummer Night's Dream*," *Shakespeare Quarterly* 44 (1993): 325-42, argues that even the play's deployment of courtly and popular dance conventions does not, as was formerly assumed, "create a timeless image of community, an imaginary unity based either on the cosmic dance or the medieval round" (342), that the tension between high and low forms here destabilizes the play's gender hierarchy, among others.

58. Barton, 219-21.

59. See the *OED* on "admirable."

60. Dollimore, 121.

PART II

A Midsummer Night's Dream on Stage

A Review of *Le Songe d'une nuit d' eté*[*]

Ann Fridén

D: Ariane Mnouchkine; TR: Philippe Leotard; P: Théâtre du Soleil;
T: Cirque Montmartre; PL: Paris; DT: 2/15/68.[+]

CAST: Members of the Théâtre du Soleil company, among them
René Patrignani as Puck. Also, two dancers, Germinal Casado and
Ursula Kubler, as Oberon and Titania, respectively.

Ariane Mnouchkine defined the subject of the *Dream* as "the
furious god" that sleeps in the hearts of men. She found nothing funny
in the text except for the delirious ending, and she made her production
into a cruel and brutal psychodrama about all sorts of love except the
divine. It thus became a nightmare rather than a dream. This nightmare
took place in a circus ring that was divided into two equal parts, one of
which was the acting area. It was covered by a carpet of goatskin,
lighter at the fringe, gradually darkening higher up, where there was a
wooden "curtain" through which the moon was seen. The spirits rolled,
ran, and slid down the slope, while the humans entered through the
gangways. Lighting was brilliant white except for the day scenes,
obscure yellow shining through foliage for the night.

The main characters were the four young lovers, conceived as
tragic. At night, their dreams became tangible. To Mnouchkine,
Titania, Oberon, and Puck were hallucinations, emotions, and
unconscious desires projected by the well-mannered young people who
managed to repress them during the day. Titania's story was not just a

fairy tale but a statement of the desire for the bestial. When she had again awakened, she was for a moment tempted to kiss the empty ass' head that she held in her hands. Puck was more of a vengeful Mephistopheles than a traditional fairy. He had a jarring laugh, and his dance was one of bacchantic leaps, agile but disharmonious. Titania and Oberon were acted by dancers that moved on the border between rhythmical running and free dance, and their physiques and fleeting movements gave an impression of their otherworldly nature. Titania's hooded attendants moved slowly around each other like sleeping insects. Apparent sadists, Oberon, Puck, and the other fauns all wore blue jeans and were stripped to the waist, with bloodstained and dirty bodies. The harshness of this world often went to extremes, as when Oberon strangled one of Titania's attendants to be able to squeeze the flower into her eyes, and raped the bewitched Hermia. The mechanicals provided the only laughs; they differed from the others in that they wore gaily colored period clothes and acted in a realistic manner. Only they had no hallucinations—Bottom did not wish his adventure, and he remembered it afterwards. These people stood out as sane and happy, but on the whole a tone of dissonance marked this Jan Kott-inspired success.

A.F.

NOTES

*Fridén, Ann. "A review of *Le Songe d'une nuit de été*," from *Shakespeare Around the Globe: A Guide to Notable Postwar Revivals*, ed. Samuel L. Leiter (1986), 482–83. Reprinted with the permission of Greenwood Press.

+Editor's note: Leiter uses the following abbreviations: D, director; TR, translator; P, producing company; T, theater; PL, city or locale of production; DT, date of production.

Shakespeare at the Guthrie
*A Midsummer Night's Dream**

Thomas Clayton

A Midsummer Night's Dream. *Presented at The Guthrie Theater,
Minneapolis, Minnesota through 20 October 1985. Director, Liviu
Ciulei; Set Design/Costumes, Beni Montresor; Lighting, Elizabeth
Smith; Sound Design, Tom Bolstad.* CAST: *Bottom, Jay Patterson;
Demetrius, Brian Hargrove; Egeus, Allen Hamilton; Flute, John
Madden Towey; Helena, Kathryn Dowling; Hermia, Katherine
Leask; Hippolyta, Lorraine Toussaint; Lysander, David Pierce;
Oberon, Peter Francis-James; Philostrate, Richard Ooms; Puck,
Lynn Chausow; Quince, Richard Howard; Snout, Robert Breuler;
Snug, Peter Thoemke; Starveling, Richard Iglewski; Theseus, Gary
Reineke; Titania, Harriet Harris.*

Shortly before the Guthrie's production of *A Midsummer Night's
Dream* opened, the director, Liviu Ciulei, resigned from his position as
Guthrie artistic director, thus making this the last of four Shakespeare
plays he will have directed during his five-year tenure. Reserving
summary comment until the end, I have resisted the temptation to treat
the production teleologically as the inevitable culmination of Ciulei's
Guthrie career (nothing is more easily foreseen than a future that is
past), a temptation understandably succumbed to by many of the
popular-press reviewers, who were also influenced, I think, by the
known fact of his impending departure.

The reviewers, at any rate, were almost unanimous in bestowing
accolades on this production, which *Times*'s William A. Henry, III,
pronounced "an idiosyncratic and brilliant *Dream* that is probably the

best since [Peter] Brook's" (26 August 1985). A major production by any measure and certainly one of the most systematically conceived, it was in effect Ciulei's "fierce vexation of a dream" (IV.i.67), a dark comedy about patriarchal abuses of power in a reading Ciulei said was prescribed by the imperatives of our time. The Guthrie press release (#676) had it that "the play's festive tone, celebrating the bliss of a wedding and the rites of summer, contrasts sharply with a male-dominated social order." The contrast was indeed apparent in this production. As reviewer Robert Collins noted,

> In [Ciulei's] view, *Dream* is the story of a power struggle that threatens the world with chaos. Oberon's fight with Titania over the changeling boy pits male against female and jeopardizes the order of the supernatural as well as the natural world. Oberon's plot to maintain control over Titania is mirrored by the Athenian court where Theseus prepares to wed the conquered Hippolyta to her evident displeasure, and where Egeus demands that his daughter obey his every command. . . . Theseus, of course, will win out over Hippolyta just as Oberon wins out over Titania, but both men are changed in the process. At play's end, patriarchy is restored but it's a less absolute, less adamant power.
>
> (KSJN Radio, 31 July 1985)

But their change was not much in evidence, and "harmonious charmingly" this vision was not, nor was meant to be.

A Midsummer Night's Dream no doubt *is* in degree "patriarchal," like the rest of Shakespeare's plays and Jacobethan society in general, but to the extent that we feel compelled to reject the social system categorically for its imperfections and injustices, dismissing it with a stigmatizing adjective, it seems pointless to attend to the period's drama, which *ex hypothesi* is merely a theatrical articulation of the sociopolitical system. We have, really, three options: to attend to the drama mainly or merely as a source of data yielding perceptions of the system's social foundations and ramifications; to read and perform it in the spirit in which its authors writ and in accordance with such ethical, social, and aesthetic values as still have currency or at least intelligibility; or to reorient it in performance or otherwise to make it say what a suitably corrected drama would say in reflecting some selection of contemporary views and values. Claiming the second (as most directors do) Ciulei in effect took the third way, giving us *A Midsummer Night's Dream* as *Lehrstück*.

I

The production subtext—or supertext—burst on the scene "up front," in an opening dumbshow antecedent to Shakespeare's *Dream* that set the production's fundamental antagonisms in bold relief. Lights came up on a stage and backwall entirely covered with stark Chinese-red vinyl. Dressed all in white, two attendants emerged from the darkened (interior black-walled) entrance at stage rear and carried a lighted brazier to the front of the stage; they strolled back whistling, until stifled by two entering representatives of Authority. Then, flanked by guards in white, a black Hippolyta in dark fatigues and with Grace Jones crewcut stalked in defiantly, high-heeled boots clicking, eyes flashing, and nostrils flaring; she stopped at midstage and glared straight ahead, into the audience. Supernumerary attendants, dress-makers, and assistants entered, again in white, scattering white mannequins and baskets of white fabric about the stage in forms and attitudes reminiscent of DiChirico. Expressionless—brain-washed?—female attendants tore off Hippolyta's fatigues, threw them on the brazier, and dressed her in a floor-length white gown and vast cape, making her a mannequin among mannequins living and inanimate. Next a condescending Theseus and his courtiers entered in white and applauded the duchess-to-be in her new clothes. Finally, with Theseus's "Now fair Hippolyta," *A Midsummer Night's Dream* began, and the pre-text was well advanced in the manner of Hippolyta's reply, "Four days will quickly steep themselves in night" speech, sarcastically half-snarled.

J.C. Trewin suggests that in viewing a production of *A Midsummer Night's Dream* we should "observe the treatment of Hippolyta. . . . There have been several notions of her: [1] tall and coffee-coloured; [2] aloofly disdainful; [3] urgently in love; [4] scuffling with Theseus on the ground; or, just as implausibly (Old Vic, 1960), [5] ironic and in manacles" (*Going to Shakespeare* [London and Boston: Allen and Unwin, 1978], p. 103). This production in effect combined 1, 2, and 5, updating *The Girlhood of Shakespeare's Heroines* with a vengeance.

The pre-textual dumbshow seemed to proclaim these sometime Elizabethan Athenians to be an antiseptic, scientistic, First-World oppressor class enslaving free and morally superior Third-World Amazons represented by their Queen Hippolyta, whose strong, mostly silent reactions were made central in the opening subscene as they had been in the dumbshow. First, dramatizing the contemptuous tone of her reply to Theseus's opening impatient-bridegroom speech, she mimed "the moon, like to a silver bow / New bent in heaven" (I.i.9–10) by drawing back an imaginary bowstring as though to hunt freely or nuke the Athenians on the spot with a sudden lunar missile, later standing with arms folded or back turned in aloof resistance. Her expression softened in sympathy for the young lovers (sharing the bond of oppressed independents); and, at Theseus's telling Hermia that she was "as a form in wax" for her father "to leave the figure or disfigure it" (ll. 49–51), Hippolyta dropped her white cape in disgust and strode toward the doorway, where she was stopped by a pair of guards. Glaring at Theseus much of the time, she guffawed derisively at Lysander's "You have her father's love, Demetrius, / Let me have Hermia's; do you marry him" (ll. 93–94). Theseus's conciliatory "Come, my Hippolyta. What cheer, my love?" (l. 122) only triggered her scornful and abrupt departure. Not an auspicious beginning for festive fifth-act nuptials. But, as Gary Reineke (Theseus) said in a discussion following a performance, if Hippolyta did not adjust to the satisfaction of the "politically astute" Theseus, he could always put her back in shackles.

For one ecstatic reviewer, Mike Steele, the production "sends your mind and emotions reeling into vertigo," but "there are *loose ends of course, the chief one here probably inherent in the script*. At play's end the glaring, icy Hippolyta does join in and adjourn with Theseus. They are not arm in arm, and we still suspect it will be an uneasy night, but she is no longer resistant, and the play gives us no reason for her change in temper" (*Minneapolis Tribune*, 29 July 1985; italics mine). Given her bondage and forced Atheniation, how *could* this Hippolyta have become Theseus's willing bride and duchess without her own— double—dose of love-in-idleness? The answer was not forthcoming in the production, which had no ready means of tying up the "loose ends" without adding threads in conclusion to complement the ones contributed at the beginning.

II

Surrounding this production was a lot of reductive rhetoric about the production choices being either Victorian gingerbread or postmodern hardtack frosted with iron filings. It is true enough that, for half a century after the important reforms of William Poel and Granville-Barker, some "Victorian" traditions of *Dream* production persisted: its resounding Mendelssohn, its twinkling, gauzy minifairies, and its pervasive fantasy—some of which, I think, is faithful enough to Shakespeare's script. Things changed drastically with Peter Hall's historico-realistic RSC production (1959) and even more so with Peter Brook's epoch-making, circus á-là-Jan-Kott *Dream*, first performed by the RSC in 1970. In 1986 the world of lace and starlight is far behind us, for the most part, and Tyrone Guthrie's "album of Victoriana" at the Old Vic in 1937 was already an obvious nostalgia trip. But whatever the setting, the festive spirit has continued central, right down to such recent British productions as Bill Bryden's eclectic one at the National Theatre (Cottesloe, then Lyttelton, 1982–83) and Sheila Hancock's RSC/Nat West Touring production (1984), and also such adaptations as Lewis Barber's Punk/Reggae musical, *The Dream*, by the "Rude Mechanicals" (1984, with the bass player, Peter Thin, doubling as Bottom). From this festive tradition Ciulei's often harsh projection of international and sexual politics was a very real departure. A usefully detailed context for comparison is provided in Roger Warren's *"A Midsummer Night's Dream": Text and Performance* (London: Macmillan, 1983), where four important recent productions are discussed: Peter Hall's (RSC, 1959–1969; Glyndebourne, 1981), Peter Brook's (RSC, 1970–73), Robin Phillips's (Stratford, Ontario, 1976–77), and Elijah Moshinski's (BBC-TV, 1981).

About Brook's modern-benchmark *Dream*, Dame Helen Gardner has expressed a view less unbalanced than either the devotees' or the deriders'. Unaware when she saw it of "the dreary absurdities and solemn nonsense with which Kott had smeared the play," she accepted it—"full of theatrical tricks and inventions"—as "a great dramatic experience," because it was "true to *the whole spirit of the play, which is a revel and a fantasy ending with general happiness*" (*In Defense of the Imagination* [Cambridge, Mass.: Harvard Univ. Press, 1982], pp. 72, 77; italics mine). Or was that but yester-Shakespeare? Remembering only the treatment of Theseus and Hippolyta, and Oberon and

Titania, in Ciulei's production, one might have thought so, and in fact a
colleague of mine judged that Ciulei had "torn the soul right out of the
play." But, even if he did exorcise some of its spirit, the balance of
Shakespeare's play asserted itself, whether by permission and
assistance or internal force deriving from the fact that so much of the
play belongs to the four young lovers and the hempen homespuns, still
more in presence and in action than in dialogue, of which the lovers
share over a third, however, Bottom and Quince a fifth. These
extensive and essential romantic and comic elements cannot be much
decentered without taking leave entirely of the script and its spirit. In
this production they were given full and effective play in recognizable
ways, and their sharing and communicating something of the heart of
Dream was evident in their typically receiving the loudest applause at
the conclusion.

All the plots are of course amatory, the fourth also a wedding gift
with a comic lion's share of the endplay, but Shakespeare's seriousness
about social as well as ethical issues solicits a thoughtful production it
has not always received. Here Ciulei bonded his chosen contemporary
issues with a dream that was a sort of allegorical nightmare giving way
to a half-awakened approach to achieved community—perhaps. By
contrast, the more usual, unequivocally festive ending makes the extra-
theatrical realities we return to—where all the world is *not* a stage—
more evidently grey, grim, and sometimes deadly, but the more worth
working to improve by virtue of a vision of the comic better part of
valor: co-operation, harmony, and community. No one needs alienation
effects to remain aware of the differences between drama and life; the
truths that life presents "straight" but also confuses in its complex of
reductive and often deluded pragmatisms, the drama mediates with
perspective, emphasis, and value. Deliberately withholding a con-
summated festive vision, and setting us as well as his characters down a
little like Christopher Sly at the end of *A Shrew*, Ciulei nevertheless, as
in his earlier productions, conceived an enthralling Rorschach test, the
provocative effect of which few denied, like it or not.

All four plots were pursued with vigor, those of the four young
lovers and Oberon-Titania with strenuousness and moments of
unmediated danger: the boys' switchblades had a realistic menace that
stage swords lack; and the paroxysms of those who were given the
mind-altering love-in-idleness, expressed by the forcible application of
a black blind-fold and apparent effects of strangulation, hardly

resembled the summer-night smiles of tranquil or desiring dreamers. Trauma was particularly vivid when Oberon pointed to Bottom on the elevated bed/platform and told Titania, "There lies your love!" and she gave a long, piercing scream, falling to the ground in convulsive shock. Such playing affects audiences by sudden and unexpected outburst alone, and for many absorbs significance in proportion to the shock value. Titania's recognition was here nearer *Alien*'s than *E.T.*'s "monster," and far at odds with the only "monster" the audience saw and knew, Bottom comically wearing on top of his head a stylized grey ass's head two feet high, held on by a chinstrap. In my view that hysterical awakening and faint were entirely off the mark of tone in Shakespeare's *Dream*, out of keeping with the general and immediate context (IV.i.75 ff.), and speciously portentous. But it had a place in a version of the story of the night concerned with the deeply irrational and disturbing elements of human nature and the social and sexual conflicts and hostilities that by inclination or compulsion we spend more of our waking and even dreaming time engaged in.

III

Some conventions come and go with theatrical fashions as well as with changing social circumstances: Granville-Barker abandoned the Victorian practice of casting women to play Oberon and Puck, but in the Guthrie *Dream* Puck was once again female, more or less, as was the Changeling "Boy," who made appearances unscheduled by Shakespeare but familiar enough in traditional production (cf. Trewin: "Titania should have, too, her 'Indian Boy'" [p. 102]). These transexualities, far from music hall and pantomime reversals, seemed dialectically at home with the production's multifarious gender probes and skewerings. Consistently mocking both Oberon and the young lovers, Puck sounded what was manifestly a production keynote in her disgusted delivery of "the man shall have his mare again, and all shall *be*, [pause] *well*—" (for the script's "all shall be well") with dismissive gestures before and a final shrug of the shoulder (III.ii.463).

In fact, Puck was centered in the production as an updated butch and punky version of *West Side Story*'s Anybodys, played as the "tomboy," skeptic, and disobedient servant, though at times she also extended to sentiment of sorts. Theseus was the post-wartime general turned "statesman" as windy bureaucrat with courtesy title, somewhat stuffy in his patronizing and cynical in noblesse oblige. He was played nearer the sometime crusading knight than sympathetic "fatherly" adviser, though he was allowed a little of the honest would-be lover and affectionate husband. Fittingly for an Amazon in earnest, Hippolyta was given some dimensions of heroic proportion. Belligerent and disdainful in the first scene, she was—at some performances— somewhat more sociable and less disagreeable in the last.

The muscular, athletic, and black Oberon's frequent vox was called upon to emphasize the contrast between the violently oppressive Oberon before contrition and the guilt-stricken and moderately reformed one after. A refined and lofty Titania had her own line in vox, especially in delivering part of "the forgeries of jealousy" speech with a grand-damning reginal bravura.

The designs for costumes, lighting, and sets forcefully emphasized primary dualities. Reviewers referred to the set as "blood red" and Ciulei was said to have thought of the color as signifying passion. The vinyl surface reflected images as though they originated within recesses of the material itself, and the warm, sometimes lurid light flushing faces, together with frantic actions, irresistibly suggested *une saison en enfer*. Color-coordinated costumes were eclectic, "timeless," significant, and allusive. The Athenians' whites were mostly loose and linen-like, suggesting oriental martial arts and, especially at the beginning, a bleached and denatured futurist society of masculist totalitarian conformity. Black was the color for the Amazon Hippolyta and for Puck, Titania, and Oberon with his six chief courtiers. Red (wet look) robes expressed the Athenian "solemnities" in V.i, the shade deliberately clashing with that of the set. The tradesman-players, as themselves in baggy, rough, and hempen-homespun grey, wore salvaged, well-worn tails in their roles as court players.

A prominent visual metaphor in this production was a long rectangular table placed crosswise at downstage center, covered with a white cloth, and set with a decanter of red wine and two glasses that were filled at either end. For reviewers it symbolized a politicians' conference table and the scene of the obstinacies of global patriarchs. As a dining table of the fashionable classes, lord and lady sat at it, a distance dividing them as much as a shared table ostensibly unites.

The central prop in several ways was a transparent plexiglass "bed"-cum-platform suspended above the stage and lowered when necessary, Ciulei's high-tech development of Brook's huge ostrich feather. Suspended, it served as a platform for Puck and Oberon to sit and watch the foolish mortals' "fond pageant" of misdirected love (III.ii), and on it Bottom slept on after Titania had been released from her spell (IV.i). It was lowered for Titania and Bottom as king-cum-ass-for-a-night to loll and romp on. Later, settled on four micropillars, it became the stage for the performance of "Pyramus and Thisby."

Director's designs inviting special comment were the related treatment of the "senior" lovers and of the social groups in the play, sometimes in conflict but not freely interrelating even when together. Ciulei chose *not* to double Theseus/Oberon and Hippolyta/Titania, as Brook and other modern directors have done, sometimes making the fairies counterparts, coming to terms in the night with matters of Theseus-Hippolyta's (and our) daytime repressions. Instead, he emphasized their differences together with their independent reality, each pair inhabiting a world with its own Weltanschauung. Robert Brustein alone of the reviewers observed that the pairs were "racially mixed couple[s]" (*New Republic*, 16 and 23 September 1985). Ciulei usually randomizes in casting black actors, making spectators color-blind—in one respect very properly. In this production race was one more obstacle to harmony between the sexes, though oppressive patriarchalism was not race-specific. *Différance* and alienation extended to other groups, notably the homespuns as players, whose unimportance to the very court they entertained was emphasized by Ciulei's business after V.i.352: here the bored courtiers left before the homespuns returned for their Bergomask, disappointed to find no audience. The worlds defined by class, race, gender, and office remained within the orbits of their separate counsels in the lunar system of this *Dream*, except as they passed in the night or drifted into conflict while going their epicyclical ways.

Ciulei made few cuts, among them jokes recoverable only by linguistic archaeology like "No die, but an ace" (V.i.299–301). In the few other textual changes, Ciulei's happy knack was seen and heard in the transposing of Helena's mid-soliloquy couplet (I.i.232–33) to make an end-of-scene capping couplet: "Things base and vile, holding no quantity, / Love can transpose to form and dignity" (placed after l. 251). The emphasizing transposition would seem to make a thematic statement, and this is what much of Shakespeare's *Dream* is all about and celebrates—but which this production consistently de-emphasized. Neither the practice nor the promise of affection was much in evidence here, where the feelings on display and in action were primarily possessiveness, resentment, or desire. This, too, was doubtless as it should be in this particular mid-eighties vision.

There was a lot of erotic byplay, in II.i–ii especially, between even the hater and the hated, as when Demetrius threatened Helen with "mischief in the wood" (II.i.235–37) and we saw "mischief" in prospect in one of several suggestive side-by-sides, general gropings, and taking-turns-on-top on the floor, innocently arrived at by scuffling but showing strong if fleeting temptations to coition. This interpretation was part of the overall fabric, and entertained the audience well in the vein of contemporary media. In these lovers, too, there was little enough scope for lower-pitched and less self-centered feelings, but there were exceptions, as in the felt delivery of Helena's protracted reverie about her youthful friendship with the now "Injurious Hermia" (III.ii.192–219), as if to say it's all *their* fault we once loving women are now at odds. The end of thought in this production was often rancors in the vessel of its peace: nostalgia, hostility, and reproach.

Often, the dialogue seemed overdramatized, slanted, and under-lyricized as a corollary to the postmodern sociologism, with an occasional jolt like that of a television commercial's coming in at double the volume of the program. A striking instance was Oberon's characteristic fortissimo delivery of his "overcast the night" speech to Puck (III.ii.354–77); with a briefly lowered tone and contrite countenance at "I'll to my Queen and beg her Indian boy, / And then I will her charmed eye release," vox returned in strident earnest with "ALL THINGS SHALL BE PEACE!"

Evidently quite deliberate (and integral), too, was the production's indifference to what admittedly seems increasingly anachronistic in our time: *Dream*'s emphasis on manners in senses of the word older than those reduced to table etiquette. Shakespeare also shows a persistent interest in "kindness," and in *Dream* specifically the "proper"— human(e)—exercise of sympathy and imagination together that makes individual and communal life not only the more harmonious but possible in the first place. In this ethical perspective, relationships between one and one, and one and more, are functions partly of individual responsibility. Such "liberal humanist" concerns were inevitably suppressed in this production, which undertook exploratory surgery nearer the jugular vein of irrepressible irrationality and power sociopolitics, as if the play had been strained through sheets of *Coriolanus*.

IV

For theatre audiences as for reviewers the production was a marked success. Some spectators and most reviewers applauded the production for its contemporaneity, some scarcely saw the reorientation. For these, after the "oddity" of the opening dumbshow the production presented a theatrically stunning enactment through which the script spoke more nearly as they had read it than as the director and his players would have had it. In such cases, it is hard to know just where to place responsibility for what—Shakespeare for a triumphant script, Ciulei for permitting and helping the script to speak for itself as well as making it speak for "us" and for him, or the audience and reviewers for their receptiveness.

Less uncritical than most of the other reviewers, Robert Brustein wrote in its favor that, although "Ciulei's new production lacks the conceptual overview of its predecessors," namely the "decade-defining" *Dream* productions of Peter Brook (1960s) and Alvin Epstein (1970s), "in freshness of approach and layered detail, not to mention a freedom from traditional ethereal delicacy, it is certainly their equal in every other respect" and "a beautiful production." But

> still, however enjoyable, something was missing from the evening. Perhaps it was . . . a unifying metaphor. One remembers details of interpretation rather than general concepts, specific meanings instead of universal themes. Brooks's [sic] *Dream* was about acrobatic vitality and high spirits, Epstein's about music and conflict. Ciulei's *Dream*—for all its scenes of sexual strife, for all its racial and feminist overtones—is largely about . . . red. (*New Republic*, 16 and 23 September 1985; Brustein's ellipses)

The success was not a case of mass "hypenosis," but hype was not conspicuous by its absence, either. Most characteristic is the assertion or implication of reviewers and others that the large-scale theatre of the late twentieth century is categorically different from and comprehensively better than that of the late nineteenth just because technology has advanced and conventional attitudes have increased and multiplied. And high-tech resources, corresponding budgets, and the intra-professional need to make it new and Mine, in conjunction with audience expectations and demands conditioned by film, teledrama, videos, all the media, are ever in danger of creating spectacle and theatrical experience that are as they are mainly for reasons independent of the thought, attitudes, and values of the script. With such meretricious materializing, theatre and patrons get each other's money's worth with neither especially the wiser, much less the better, for the commerce. When such potentialities are legion, it remains the shared and very real responsibility of director, actors, all the persons of the theatre, including audiences, to take a just measure as well as make a self-gratifying use of the contents and the contexts. And a little more willing suspension of disbelief, sometimes, would not come amiss in contemporary production of Shakespeare's plays.

V

To look back briefly at Ciulei's Guthrie years: Beginning with the concentrated comprehensiveness of *The Tempest* in 1981, Ciulei went on to the "joyous" intraterrestrial comedies, one by land and one by sea, of *As You Like It* in 1982 and *Twelfth Night* in 1984. In 1985 he returned to the world of spirits and completed his Guthrie tetralogy of Shakespearean comedies, ending with a play that in many ways completes the circle begun with his opening and Shakespeare's closing *Tempest*. To him "there are three Shakespearean plays above all that seem to contain infinite layers, this one, *The Tempest*, and *The Winter's Tale*. These are his fantasy plays and also his most poetical. By choosing a more imaginative terrain, the possibilities of associations and interpretations are vast, vast, vaster than vast. They are bottomless." This being his view, and *The Winter's Tale* having an elusive "secret," as he told me in March 1986, it is to be hoped that he may yet direct it at the Guthrie. In the meantime, his Guthrie Shakespeare plays have made a theatrically stunning tetralogy, if at last an uneasy one, exploring in comic, green-world, and variously festive but also darker and more labyrinthine terms the vicissitudes of the social human condition and some of the convolutions and recesses of the human heart, head, and, for lack of a better word, soul, a serviceable seat for those acts of imagination that become art, excellence, and virtue even if, or *because*, all these are conceptual as well as phenomenal, "for there is nothing either good or bad but *thinking* makes it so."

For me personally, it is *Twelfth Night* that lingers most insistently, most affectingly, in the memory. Backstage it was said that Ciulei thought the circus setting and Shakespeare's script never really came together, whereas they did in *A Midsummer Night's Dream*, though Brustein thought otherwise, as I did. What *Twelfth Night* specially had, I think, was a seasoned and imaginative exploitation of all the resources of the Guthrie stage, a sympathetic but never infatuated reverence for the text, and ultimately a generous measure of universality in depth of address to the condition of the "human mortals" with a delicate balance of the fallible, the risible, the elegiac, the ultimately transient yet memorably vital. Something approaching the heart of the stuff that dreams are made on, dreams that have not only grief but sweetness, and, finally, more than a little something of great constancy.

Ciulei brought to the Guthrie a fresh and deeply committed internationality of perspective and production that for nearly five years made this midwestern Twin Cities theatre an undisputed major center for theatrical exploration and achievement in ways new to the Guthrie, where earlier mentors had come primarily from either the British or the American theatrical worlds. These are of course not necessarily "worse," but they *are* different—or to be more accurate they are *not* so different, since in tradition they are us or nearer us. By contrast Ciulei brought a range of interests and experience that are especially Continental, Eastern European, and withal more broadly internationalistic and extending to Far Eastern, than the Guthrie and its audiences have been used to. Some of what he brought to entertain us and compel us to rethink has outraged some, no doubt, and a reviewer of *A Midsummer Night's Dream*, dissenting from the majority, went so far as to say that "I, for one, am tired of going to that theater and seeing Eastern European intellectualism passed off as high art" (Steven LaVigne, KFAI Radio, 8 August 1985). But few on reflection will charge Ciulei or his guest directors and designers with wantonly vandalizing the scripts or plundering them for commercial ends, even if the reconstructions sometimes seemed gratuitously willful or the attitudes less relevant to our condition than to their places of origin and the preoccupations of their architects.

Or are they? A standing question, to elicit diverse answers. Certainly these theatrical productions were conceived and performed with inventiveness, scope, conviction, and intensity. Originality of vision and obliqueness of address for a time destabilized our theatre and made it more vital as well as disconcerting. The returns on this epoch's vigorous activity will take some time to collect and assess in the round, "but howsoever, strange and admirable" theatre has been Liviu Ciulei's half-decade's heritage at the Guthrie, most emphatically and I think least disputably in his own Shakespearean productions. He will be missed, and he goes with well-earned gratitude and good wishes.

NOTE

*Originally published in *Shakespeare Quarterly* 37 (1986): 229–36. Reprinted with the kind permission of *Shakespeare Quarterly*.

[Kenneth Branagh's]
A Midsummer Night's Dream[*]

Robert A. Logan

Presented at the Elgin Theatre in Toronto. June 11 . . . 1990. Directed
by Kenneth Branagh.

Whatever one's conceptions of *A Midsummer Night's Dream*, Kenneth
Branagh's production is likely to provide some surprises and fresh
insight. To begin with, there was a single set, a large, raked, circular
disk with a two-thirds, semi-circular moat a bit back from the curving
ramp at the front of the stage. The floor of the disk consisted of what
appeared to be red and purple flakes. The aluminum walls were the
luster and color of pewter with imploded star-shaped holes of various
sizes and, at stage right on the wall, a moon-shaped fixture, hung
authoritatively. Apart from the moat, there were three openings for
entrances and exits, one at each side of the stage and one at the back;
the latter had the appearance of an armoire or wardrobe and it opened
inwardly toward the audience. Jenny Tiramani's set was suggestive and
evocative, rather than defined or realistic. Often the lighting of Jon
Linstrum was used to make it theatrically engaging. That the audience
was called upon to respond to the set with an active imagination not
only held to the spirit of Renaissance staging but identified the agent
largely responsible for the strength and pleasure of our response. Our
participating imagination became significant in another way, too; for,
even as Shakespeare dramatized his view of the transforming power of
the imagination, we were called upon to experience it. The result was

that our felt experience validated and enriched our perceived experience.

I have never been one to look with less than skepticism upon gimmickry in Shakespearian productions. Thus, the mix of what passed for ancient Athenian garb among those figures who appeared at court, the Halloween costumes of the fairy folk, and the 1990s garb of the mechanicals might have seemed to offer grounds for complaint. But it did not. The costuming simply aided in pulling out all the audience's imaginative stops and in providing more sources for comic incongruity. At the play within the play, for example, Peter Quince, dressed in an ill-fitting tuxedo with a scarlet bow tie, acted the over-zealous emcee for his troupe of actors, at once comically foolish in his exaggerated attempts at theatrical propriety and touching in his paternalistic concern for his troupe. The costume enabled us, even as it evoked our mirth, to perceive through a visual symbol his confusion and intense earnestness.

Throughout the performance of *A Midsummer Night's Dream*, most immediately and permanently enjoyable was the actors' command of the language and their confidence in their understanding of it (the Scottish burrs of some of the actors notwithstanding). The inflection and interpretation of their lines indicated that they always knew whereof they spoke and, ultimately, that they found the center to the play in the mysterious powers of the imagination, a faculty as easily the source of darkness as of light. Of particularly impressive note were Francine Morgan who managed to make Hermia into a flesh-and-blood character instead of a caricature; Emma Thompson who made Helena's mix of wit and witlessness comic, touching, and thoroughly likeable, and who invested the soliloquy at the end of the first scene with philosophical meaning without losing its psychological significance as part of her own humanity; and Simon Roberts who, although at times too effeminate as Theseus (if not as Oberon), gave a reading to Theseus' well-known speech at the beginning of Act V that indicated the ruler's individual generosity of spirit as well as the reasoning, authoritative voice of society.

Giving coherence to the production was director Branagh's sense of the thinness of the line that separates comedy from tragedy. A case in point was Hippolyta's concern with and evident displeasure at the Athenian law's tough pronouncement on Hermia's love for Lysander. Another indication, although less obvious, came from the characterizations. The characters had depth and were not simply the stock or flat characters from comedy. I was particularly taken with the conception of Demetrius who, more overtly nasty than in the usual conception of him, paid for his intense emotional stress by having to use techniques of meditation as both an anodyne and a soporific. Another example was in the characterization of Nick Bottom who, although splendidly comic, was less singlemindedly egocentric, more vulnerable, and less of a blusterer than one is used to. Still another was conveyed by the campy, erotic words and actions of a raspy-voiced Titania, giving the fairy queen just the right blend of naturalness and artificiality. She could be overbearing and a bit menacing, but she was also a comic delight.

Of the members of the company who stood out for their acting ability, the mechanicals as a whole can easily be commended. This was especially true of Richard Briers who managed to invest Nick Bottom with humanity without slighting the role's opportunities for exhibiting a superb comic sense. I would also point to the fine ensemble acting of Kenneth Branagh as Peter Quince, sometimes officious, often befuddled, but always energetic and well-intentioned; Gerard Horan as an awkward, lumbering Francis Flute and, in the play put on by the mechanicals, a comically oafish, firmly male Thisby dressed incongruously in a flowing white bridal gown; Karl James as the perplexed but always helpful Snug; and Bryan Kennedy as the largely bewildered, silent Tom Snout. The one weak major characterization was that of Puck, played and overplayed by Ethna Roddy. The conception of Puck as a raucous, squealing female ninny is a bit puzzling, but I suspect had something to do with Branagh's notion of the dark side of the imagination and his intention, through the portrayals of the fairy folk, not to eschew it.

Most impressive, I think, was the genuineness of the fun and the good humor of this production. I have never known an audience, including myself, to be so truly convulsed with laughter at a production of this play. And with good reason. The mechanicals inspired humor through their many incongruities of language, action, and dress. Their play within a play ended with an all-out song and dance routine reminiscent of "The Lambeth Walk" from *Me and My Girl*: the laborer-actors spurred on the three pairs of aristocratic lovers to join in with their singing and dancing in a grand pastiche of a Broadway musical show-stopper. The tradition of the royal audience and the actors joining in on a dance at the climax has authenticity as part of the tradition of the production of Renaissance court masques and may have actually taken place at the first performance of the play, if in fact it was written as an entertainment for a wedding. Branagh's sense of the play as musical comedy worked especially well, even if the show-stopping conclusion to the play within the play somewhat undercut the climax of the play itself. Moreover, at times (e.g., during Theseus' speech at the beginning of Act V) Patrick Doyle's music was intrusive. In all, however, out of the dozen or so productions of *A Midsummer Night's Dream* that I have seen, this was easily the most enjoyable.

NOTE

*Originally published as "*A Midsummer Night's Dream* and *King Lear*," *MSAN: Marlowe Society of America Newsletter* 10.2 (Fall 1990): 5–7. Reprinted with the kind permission of *MSAN*.

Brecht and Beyond

Shakespeare on the East German Stage[*]

Lawrence Guntner

Whereas Shakespeare performance in the 1960s had centered on the tragedies and histories, plays concerned with the conflict between humanistic ideals and a repressive social order, the role of the masses in shaping history, and the use and abuse of political power, Shakespeare performance in the 1970s focused on plays like *A Midsummer Night's Dream* and *Romeo and Juliet*, plays concerned with the conflicts between social duty and individual self-fulfillment, obedience to public authority and personal happiness, plays about young men and women who defy parental and state authority for the sake of love. *A Midsummer Night's Dream* is also about the role of theatre in society, a theme which played an important role in various productions.

There were a series of *Dream* productions which rejected the romantic illusionism of the Max Reinhardt tradition, still very much alive on the East German stage, in favor of highlighting the conflicts and contradictions in the play in the manner of Jan Kott and Peter Brook. In 1971 Christoph Schroth directed a production in Halle which highlighted the theme of the struggle for individual freedom in a rigid and restrictive society rather than celebrating a world of romantic harmony.[1] The script was a new translation by Maik Hamburger which foregrounded the theatrical *gestus* of Shakespeare's language rather than its "literary" qualities. Attention was paid to translating the emotional and social situation into physical expression which the players could perform. The woods were seen as "a mythologically alienated, distorted reflection of the Athenian court,"[2] and the roles of

Thesus [sic] and Oberon were played by the same actor, Hippolyta and Titania by the same actress, an idea made popular by Peter Brook, but unknown to Schroth at the time. This production suggested that whereas the rigid authority of the court stifled individual self-fulfillment, the unbridled passion of the woods confused it. In the woods the male lust for domination was unrestricted and Oberon himself had to intervene to prevent the young men from killing each other.

On stage the Athenian court was depicted by broad white strips of cloth hung vertically in the back and on the sides to suggest rows of Greek columns, and when the scene shifted to the woods these strips of cloth were brought into a disarray through which the lovers staggered. The similarity between Theseus and Oberon became visible in act 4, scene 1 when Theseus, Duke of Athens, entered wearing a hunting outfit similar to the costume of Oberon, King of the Fairies, and even imitating Oberon's gestures. In this production the exact distinction between the two worlds remained unclear, and thus the woods always retained a dreamlike quality, which was emphasized by the color-fulness of the costumes. In keeping with the undefined border between the two worlds, Bottom was not totally transformed into an ass but remained an enchanted human being, and Titania's caresses contained a visible element of passion and desire. Bottom, as a member of the lower orders, was aggressive and unpredictable but also had a great capacity for love. Continuing in this vein, the "harmony" of the final scene in Athens was undercut by the behavior of the members of Thesus' court, including the young lovers, who ridiculed and laughed at the mechanicals' crude but well-meant amateur performance of "Pyramus and Thisbe," for Schroth the only true love story in the play. The young lovers had attained their niche in the restrictive social order of Athens, and in act 5 they could afford to laugh at notions of equality and freedom of choice in matters of love so important to them in act 1. This performance implied not only a criticism of how the state was treating its young people but was also a sad commentary on the official treatment of theatre by the East German government.

The decade of *Dream* performances culminated in two simultaneous productions in 1980 in Berlin: at the Deutsches Theater directed by Alexander Lang and at the Maxim Gorki Theater directed by Thomas Langhoff. Obviously influenced by Jan Kott in his dramaturgical concept, Lang rigorously cut or understated any passages which might suggest sweetness or harmony. The basic motif of Lang's production is summed up best by Lysander's remarks after being drugged:

For, as a surfeit of the sweetest things
The deepest loathing to the stomach brings;
Or as the heresies that men do leave
Are hated most of those they did deceive. (2.2.136–9)

For Lang, directing the play in Max Reinhardt's own theatre, Shakespeare's "dream" was on closer inspection a nightmare: Theseus' Athens an oppressive patriarchy, and Puck's love potion, "love in idleness," translated into German as "love in madness" (*Liebe im Wahnsinn*), a forcibly administered narcotic to insure the totalitarian power of the state.[3] In this performance Puck and Oberon, like muggers from a gangster film, chloroformed Demetrius and Lysander, who could only struggle sleepily against what was being done to them. When they awoke, they discovered in themselves not only new passion but also brutal aggression, and the utopian garden of delights became an arena of sexual violence in which Hermia and Helena were the victims. Gradually the narcotic took effect, however, and the four lovers ended up anesthetized, swaying back and forth, arms and legs entwined, barely able to mutter their lines. Lang rejected the traditional "poetic" Schlegel-Tieck translation in favor of the rough-hewn eighteenth-century translation by Johann Joachim Eschenburg, which lacks the lyrical qualities of Shakespeare's original and Schlegel's romanticism.[4] Gero Troike's set, a simple three-sided box of red paper, may have suggested the confinement of a restrictive East German society, yet it also emancipated the actors from illusionistic stage decorations and provided them with an almost Shakespearean "empty space" in which to perform. Here the influence of Brook's *Dream* on Lang became visible (Lang had seen it in Warsaw); however, the roles of Theseus/Oberon, Hippolyta/Titania were not doubled. This production explored the problems of authority on different levels of the dramatic action rather than dealing with character. Both levels—court and wood—were social orders of absolute male dominion and both stifled love and creative fantasy.

The performance opened with Theseus in ermine cape fondling his captive Hippolyta (Johanna Schall) who was obviously suffering. She also wore an ermine cape which had been quickly flung over her tight-fitting black amazon pants suit. . . . Oberon (Jürgen Hentsch) in a black plastic coat (as was Puck) was, like Theseus (Otto Mellies), also a symbol of male dominion but aware of its price for his subjects. Titania (Katja Paryla), in an attempt at emancipation, wore the attire of a Hollywood vamp: tight-fitting off-the-shoulder dress, high-heeled shoes, blond wig, and coat with fur collar, but as with Hippolyta's ermine cape, it seemed to be a crude attempt to assume a role rather than an attempt to signify her real self. In the end, it was Bottom, not a plebeian craftsman but an amateur actor, in beat-up hat and baggy, broad-checked knickerbockers who, in his innocent and exuberant affirmation of immediate experience and enthusiasm for role-playing, was Lang's antidote for Theseus' oppressive "harmony." For her night with Bottom, Titania shed her blond wig, coat, and high heels, and when awakened, she cried and clung so tightly to her animal lover that Oberon and Puck had to extract her forcibly from his arms. With Bottom she had abandoned her assumed role to discover her true self, and having experienced this was reluctant to return to role-playing again in the harsh reality of Oberon's kingdom. . . .

Lang's critique was directed less at a romantic illusionistic theatre tradition than at an official government policy of papering over contradictions and unresolved conflicts in contemporary East German culture and society for the sake of an illusory social harmony. The officially proclaimed dream of self-fulfillment and personal happiness had become a nightmare for a younger generation in a restrictive society ruled by old men, and this was brought out in this performance. The rude mechanicals were not Brecht's plebeian craftsmen but tired actors struggling to be heard in an indifferent society. While they struggled with "Pyramus and Thisbe" in the rear, the young men lay disinterestedly on cushions on the forestage, between the players and the audience, and fondled their now silent fiancées. Now integrated into the Athenian establishment, the young lovers, like the rest of the court, were no longer interested in the issues of free choice in matters of love. From this perspective, with the courtiers between them and the players, the audience slowly realized how actors felt when they performed Shakespeare's innocent travesty of *Romeo and Juliet* for an officialdom not interested in theatre. Theseus interrupted their Bergomask dance and called for a song to disperse winter before the court tore down the paper walls of the set and went off to bed.

Thomas Langhoff's production of *A Midsummer Night's Dream*, like Lang's, celebrated the creative flexibility and regenerative capacities of theatre in general and Shakespeare in particular. However, Langhoff, also influenced by Peter Brook, had little quarrel with the Reinhardt tradition and tried to do justice to the amplitude of the play: to all three plots as well as the various levels of meaning and style. The roles of Theseus/Oberon and Hippolyta/Titania were doubled. The emphasis was on physical forms of theatrical expression, and little attention was given to the recitation of blank verse. Although Langhoff's Athens was less restrictive than Lang's, it too had little patience with a Hippolyta whose clothing (a mixture of amazon and late-hippie) did not match the Athenian norm. "Love in idleness" was not translated as "love in madness" but as "love in delusion" (*Liebe in Wahn*). In this production it was the wonderfully delusory power of love which drove young people to defy parental and state authority, disregard the social hierarchy of Athens, and probe their physical and emotional limits. This was celebrated with exuberance from the beginning of the performance. When they reached the woods by breaking through the paper walls of the stage decorations, the lovers entered a foggy, circus-like world inhabited by bizarre aberrations: a bald-headed Titania, a sex-crazed, Pan-like Oberon, a wrestler, gnome-like Puck, a world in which nothing was stable, predictable, or dependable. The wood flooring suddenly became a trampoline on and off which the lovers and the fairies bounced and were bounced. The emphasis on the physicality of the performance freed the actors from the "literary" text and provided space for them to experiment with playful physical forms of theatrical expression. Back in Athens, when the dream was over, the flooring became stable again, and the young lovers were reincorporated into the world of adult social convention. In this performance, however, "Pyramus and Thisbe," acted with passion by the amateur players, was not ridiculed but was convincing to the members of the court. Theseus and Hippolyta changed back into the costumes of Oberon and Titania on stage, and contradicting Lang's production, Puck, not Theseus, had the final word.

All three productions shared basic presuppositions about East German society and the role of theatre within it: that society was rigid and restricted young people or anyone else who did not fit the social norm, that the official representatives of this society were not particularly interested in theatre, that a cultural policy which expected

Thomas Langhoff's production of *A Midsummer Night's Dream*, like Lang's, celebrated the creative flexibility and regenerative capacities of theatre in general and Shakespeare in particular. However, Langhoff, also influenced by Peter Brook, had little quarrel with the Reinhardt tradition and tried to do justice to the amplitude of the play: to all three plots as well as the various levels of meaning and style. The roles of Theseus/Oberon and Hippolyta/Titania were doubled. The emphasis was on physical forms of theatrical expression, and little attention was given to the recitation of blank verse. Although Langhoff's Athens was less restrictive than Lang's, it too had little patience with a Hippolyta whose clothing (a mixture of amazon and late-hippie) did not match the Athenian norm. "Love in idleness" was not translated as "love in madness" but as "love in delusion" (*Liebe in Wahn*). In this production it was the wonderfully delusory power of love which drove young people to defy parental and state authority, disregard the social hierarchy of Athens, and probe their physical and emotional limits. This was celebrated with exuberance from the beginning of the performance. When they reached the woods by breaking through the paper walls of the stage decorations, the lovers entered a foggy, circus-like world inhabited by bizarre aberrations: a bald-headed Titania, a sex-crazed, Pan-like Oberon, a wrestler, gnome-like Puck, a world in which nothing was stable, predictable, or dependable. The wood flooring suddenly became a trampoline on and off which the lovers and the fairies bounced and were bounced. The emphasis on the physicality of the performance freed the actors from the "literary" text and provided space for them to experiment with playful physical forms of theatrical expression. Back in Athens, when the dream was over, the flooring became stable again, and the young lovers were reincorporated into the world of adult social convention. In this performance, however, "Pyramus and Thisbe," acted with passion by the amateur players, was not ridiculed but was convincing to the members of the court. Theseus and Hippolyta changed back into the costumes of Oberon and Titania on stage, and contradicting Lang's production, Puck, not Theseus, had the final word.

All three productions shared basic presuppositions about East German society and the role of theatre within it: that society was rigid and restricted young people or anyone else who did not fit the social norm, that the official representatives of this society were not particularly interested in theatre, that a cultural policy which expected actors to recite "literary" masterpieces paralyzed actors as well as Shakespeare's text, that there were real social conflicts and contradictions in East German society which should not be covered up for the sake of a superficial harmony, and that these unresolved conflicts prevented a communion between actors and audience at the end of the performance. All three *Dream* productions had exposed the contradictions in the societies ruled by Theseus and Oberon, but none provided an ending or interpretation which suggested that the social conflicts represented in the past by Shakespeare had been resolved in the present by Socialism. This was in marked contrast to the majority of Shakespeare productions in the 1960s. Although these three directors were more immediately influenced by the work of Peter Brook and Benno Besson than Bertolt Brecht, their approaches to Shakespeare performance were, nevertheless, the continuation of Brecht's ideas in that they did not simplistically resolve the social conflicts of Shakespeare's past in terms of the East German present but provoked their audiences to reexamine assumptions about their own time.

NOTES

*Copyright Cambridge University Press. Originally published in *Foreign Shakespeare: Contemporary Performance*, ed. Dennis Kennedy (1993), 122–28. Reprinted with the permission of Cambridge University Press. Notes are renumbered for the reader's convenience.

1. Maik Hamburger, "New Concepts of Staging *A Midsummer Night's Dream*," *Shakespeare Survey* 40 (1988): 52ff; Armin-Gerd Kuckhoff, "Theaterschau," *ShJ [Shakespeare Jahrbuch]* 109 (1973): 174–6; other productions were staged in Magdeburg 1972 (Dir.: Werner Freese), Dresden 1974 (Dir.: Klaus-Dieter Kirst), and Rudolstadt 1976 (Dir.: Klaus Fiedler).

2. Hamburger, "New Concepts," 52.

3. Martin Linzer (ed.), *Alexander Lang Abenteuer Theater* (Berlin: Henschel, 1983), 92.

4. On the Lang and Langhoff productions, see Hamburger, "New Concepts," 55–8; Martin Linzer, "*A Midsummer Night's Dream* in East Germany," *TDR* 25.2 (Summer 1981): 45–54; "Tag-Träume," *ThdZ [Theater der Zeit]* 35.7 (1980): 38–42; "Nacht-Träume,'" *ThdZ* 35.12 (1980): 13–15; *Alexander Lang*, 69–100; Armin-Gerd Kuckhoff, "Zur Shakespeare-Rezeption in der DDR (1945–1980)," *ShJ* 118 (1982): 117ff; and "Theaterschau," *ShJ* 118 (1982): 142–51.

Figure 3. The Straight-Arm Phallus. Peter Brook's production, 1970. Bottom (David Waller), borne by fairies, with Titania (Sara Kestelman) in the foreground. Photograph by David Farrell. Used with permission.

A Midsummer Night's Dream: Nightmare or Gentle Snooze?

Mary Z. Maher

A Midsummer Night's Dream is filled with invitations. From Titania's enticing Oberon to "go with us" (2.1.141)[1] to Puck's requesting audience approval with his "Give me your hands, if we be friends" (5.1.437-38), the playtext is filled with solicitations. Hamlet's caveat to "let those that play your clowns speak no more than is set down for them" (3.2.38-40) is absolutely null and void in this context: the *Dream* is a summons to a high order of creation in the comic mode. Peter Brook recognized this and responded. Thereafter, the torch of invention was passed from director to director in a new and exuberant way.

The play reads like a primer in actualizing theories of comedy. Susanne K. Langer recalls that from the ancient fertility rites of Greece, comedy has always been "erotic, risque, and sensuous if not sensual, impious and even wicked."[2] What first comes to mind is the fairy queen, part-human and part-sprite, sleeping with Bottom, part-human, part-animal. Indeed, the fairy kingdom maintains a moratorium on conventional sexual mores, an attitude soon adopted by the Athenian lovers during their night in the wood. Henri Bergson lists among the chief comic devices "something *mechanical* encrusted upon the living"[3] in the creation of characters. He adds that physical mishap, repetition, puns, and wordplay are laughable. When Freud says we feel a sense of superiority over a comic person in a funny situation,[4] we are reminded of the wit-crackers' comments during the mechanicals' scenes. Such behavior is ungenerous but we've all been there, watching an entertainment and making what we imagine to be the cleverest remarks. This is standard audience behavior at a comedy; for laughter, Bergson asserts, is social and contagious.[5]

It is the mechanicals' play-within-the-play that effectively issues the invitation to improvisation. Here are local tradesmen enacting an ambitious but ill-chosen entertainment, a heavy piece of turgid tragedy where we sense the playwright's hand cueing us to possibilities of laughter that the hempen homespuns do not see. It is their fate to take themselves seriously, and this absolute sincerity of purpose (especially in Bottom's case) is necessary in grounding the play, because comic characters are funny in proportion to their own lack of self-knowledge: taking oneself seriously is the first step in the portrayal of an effective comic persona, the first step in becoming "mechanical." The scene is saturated with humorous devices which act as an enticement or lure to improvisation and invention.

Just sample Peter Quince's Prologue, his invitation to the interlude. What seems like an impossibly convoluted communication turns out to be a sophisticated theater in-joke. As an amateur, Quince has committed the sin of pausing at the end of each metric line and not bothering to figure out the sense of the line (i.e., finding the subject and the verb) before he memorized the line. The result is chopped-up sense, run-on sentences, and an obscure speech made even more so. (Actually, it's a bit like reading a deconstructionist critic.)

There is comedy of language peppered throughout the dialogue— mispronunciations like "Thisne" (1.2.52), misplaced verbs in "I see a voice . . . I can hear my Thisby's face" (5.1.192-93), and hideously overwrought poetic devices fitfully phrased: "with bloody, blameful blade,/ He bravely broach'd his boiling, bloody breast" (5.1.146-47). Most actors would not pass over the opportunity of an alliterative riff like that one. Thisby in a 1964 video version (Bottom played by Benny Hill) referred to "Pinnaminnimus," surely a streak of creative lightning to couple "minimus" with "Pyramus."[6] The history of both stage and film productions of the play is replete with comic ideas that have flowered where Shakespeare planted the seed.

There is ample comedy of character. Snout, Snug, and Flute are comic stereotypes of earnestness, innocence, and downright cantankerousness. Not one but two comic deaths are provided, both vying in poetic flights of soulfulness and both enough to bring tears of mirth to Philostrate's eyes. The wedding feast itself invites comic celebration. So, there is comedy of situation, of character, of language, of gesture.

Although the visual image of *A Midsummer Night's Dream* in the nineteenth century was the gauzy-winged fairy, the immediate icon of the late twentieth century was the up-thrust arm between Bottom's legs, the oversized ass's penis created by two actors positioned to show arousal in Peter Brooks' 1970 staging of the play. These two mental photographs are metaphorical of the changes that have occurred in the production of this play from Brook to the present. A quarter of a century later, it is appropriate to survey—in a suggestive rather than exhaustive way—productions on the English-speaking stage after Peter Brook. It is clear that cultural and theatrical barriers were significantly dislodged by this director's airborne flights of imagination. The program note to the 1995 Royal Shakespeare Company production of *Dream* at the Barbican Centre in London states that "the impact of Brook's *Dream* has allowed subsequent productions to display a greater awareness of the play's darker elements." Although many writers discuss how Brook's production drew inspiration from the gloomy prurience of Jan Kott's vision[7] and emphasized the sex in the play in a non-traditional way, that description is misleading and inaccurate. In fact, the performance was permeated with lightness, physicality, laughter, comedic insights, even sight gags. Furthermore, there were far darker *Dream*'s earlier than Brook's: Ariane Mnouchkine directed a "cruel and brutal psychodrama" in 1968,[8] also using the circus as a production metaphor. John Hirsch, at the Stratford, Ontario festival in the same year, was experimenting with what he felt were the more disturbing elements of the play.[9]

Peter Brook's staging of the play was a shifting point: after 1970, all sorts of productions exploded out of the imaginations of highly inventive directors. Notably, few directors ever totally abandoned comedy. Brook's production was influential partly because it had many lives and was performed in front of many audiences. It opened in August 1970, subsequently went to London, and then on to a world tour through 1974 which included the British Isles, Australia, both eastern and western Europe, Japan, Canada, and major cities in the United States.[10] Furthermore, the production took place during one of the most important socio-cultural revolutions of the twentieth century. We are still dealing with the "afterlife"[11] of this particular set of performances, necessarily a series of phenomenal impressions rather than a single documentable event. Yet to say that Brook's play dealt with the dark side of *A Midsummer Night's Dream* is to miss the point of the production entirely.

Jonathan Miller claims that when a Shakespearean play is staged, there are so many possible internal themes or strands or messages it is impossible to play all of them: a director must choose. The obverse of this coin is selectivity and sensitivity: " . . . I admit that [the plays] are not totally malleable and should not be subject to an infinite number of possible interpretations."[12] What Brook did was corrective; he was re-inserting and re-issuing the seminal strand of sexuality into the mainstream of the play's production history.

Brook accomplished this by displacing the traditional climax of the play, the mechanicals' scene, with Titania taking Bottom off to her bower at the end of act 3, scene 1. The scene was sexual but also joyous and exuberant. According to David Meyer, at the moment the famous fist appeared between Bottom's legs,

> Bottom looked in surprise and horror at it, and Titania had this 'Oh, FABULOUS!' reaction on her face. The fairies flung paper plates and confetti and streamers came from the onstage balcony. The Wedding March from Mendelsohn boomed out on loudspeakers, an ironic theatre joke which lifted the moment into celebration and triumph, not into something raunchy or destructive. It was a huge post-modern pun and it also resoundingly signalled the act break![13]

Brook's treatment of Titania's obsession differs substantially in tone from Kott's: Brook treated the incident with relish and humor ("it never failed to produce a huge explosion of joy from an audience"[14]) whereas Kott saw violence and victimization: "The monstrous ass is being raped by the poetic Titania, while she still keeps on chattering about flowers."[15] Indeed, the atmosphere of Brook's *Dream*, played in bright white light and featuring the antics of actors as circus entertainers, was a distinct relief from the mysogynistic, nightmare images of Kott's vision. It was as if a theatre artist had picked up the brushes of Bosch and painted like Matisse. Kott was an inspiration but not a straitjacket.

Moving the comic climax of the play necessarily affected the mechanicals' scene. Brook emphasized the reality of the characters, asking that the actors imagine the seriousness of their situation. These hard-handed men could be punished for not pleasing the court; thus the wit-crackers' comments during the play-within-the-play became meaner. Nevertheless, the mechanicals won over with their bumbling sincerity, and audiences willed the traditional laughter back into the scene. David Selbourne describes a preview performance of the production:

> The audience seems almost literally to love it.... And this love... is requited. For there is much more happening now than a mere exchange of actors' jokes and spectators' laughter. The mechanicals are in fact confiding in the audience. Anxiously, and ludicrously, they are entrusting their technical problems... to the groundlings who surround them.[16]

The comic characters taking themselves seriously is funnier and more natural than comedy induced from the aristos patronizing the plebs or from forcing irrelevant humor into the scene. Even Snug the Joiner's lion mask was a mark of his profession, a snugly-joined and well-carved square box of wood.

In fact, the darkest segment of Brook's production was enacted when the lovers awoke in the wood. Threateningly, fairies in the galleries jiggled giant slinkies on wires, slashing them against the walls. No one was hurt and the violent movement emphasized the confusion onstage.[17] The funniest section, according to John Kane, who played Puck, was a wonderful bit of schtick:

> In the lover's quarrel, Lysander attempted to leave to go after Helena. Mary Rutherford could, as Hermia, simply have barred the way. With practice Lysander and Hermia perfected the business. Lysander started for the door set into the back wall. Hermia ran from the lower right diagonally up left and after about five steps dived forward, timing it so that Lysander caught her as she reached the door. Hermia held her body rigid in his arms parallel with the floor so that she formed a sort of plank which prevented him getting through the door. He tried twice or thrice, banging her on the side of the door and bouncing back—still holding her parallel and stiff in his arms and then shaking her to the floor. It seldom failed to win applause and was the perfect example of that theory of comedy that says people are comic when they behave like objects or machines.[18]

Brook's unprecedented innovation, his iconoclastic act of creativity, was that he proposed to change the nature of the theatre event. He wanted to bring the audience into the play in an interactive capacity, so that they drove the production and their expectations became part of the energy charge that spurred the actors. Selbourne explained, "the spectators thus become additionally conscious of themselves as an audience . . . as knowing accomplices of the action. If not actors themselves, they [were] no longer passive either."[19]

More importantly, Brook initiated this process on the first day of rehearsal, determined to wipe out time-encrusted images of playing Shakespeare and, particularly, of traditional ways of speaking each line. Early rehearsals were workshops, exercises and improvisations which prodded the actors to discover what each scene was really about and to motivate the lines afresh out of original dramatic improvisations. John Kane told a poignant story of a young actor being schooled in this new method:

> . . . that morning after the performance at the Birmingham Arts Centre, Peter actually said to the gathered company something like "I was delighted with the progress and the choices you made last night. It seems to me that everyone has taken a major step forward. All except you." And to my horror, he was looking at me. He then went on to say how I had thrown away all the work I had accomplished during rehearsals and had taken the easy options playing to the audience. I have no difficulty remembering his exact words—"a cheap end-of-pier comic." This was a low blow because he happened to know that only seven years previously I had been, at the age of 17, exactly that. I don't think I have ever felt unhappier in my life. It was probably necessary however, as it made me wary of falling back on the old performance tricks . . . and forcing me to search and delve ever and ever deeper for the truth in what I was doing.[20]

The appropriate mode of participation between the actors and the audience was not automatic. It was closely choreographed and willed into being. If the bond happened, there was magic; if it did not, there was deadly theatre. This production was an important step in Brook's ongoing search for a transactional connection between audience and actors. Brook wanted these two entities to co-create the phenomenon of "two hours' trafficke" each night on the stage. The closing of the performance, as told by a cast member, illustrated the magus at work:

> For the wedding-celebration, the aristocrats had donned robes. After the "iron tongue at midnight" speech when Theseus tells everyone to go to bed, the cast found themselves in a straight line upstage with their backs to the audience. At this point, the cloaks were let fall and everyone turned around and moved downstage toward the audience. At the same time, the lights came up so that house lights and stage lights merged. Theseus became someone halfway between Theseus and Oberon and all the characters began to be in this limbo of your character dropping away from you and your real self, David Meyer, standing on the edge of the stage looking at the audience whom you'd been busy entertaining for the last couple of hours. Puck's lines, "If we shadows have offended" became the recognition that we were all human beings and the wall between player and audience, watcher and performer, speaker and listener, was beginning to melt.
>
> You could feel a surge of energy come up in the audience as they looked at you. (Roy Kinnear would always mutter, "Fooled 'em again!") On "give me your hands," two sets of drums crashed in the background, everyone cheered, and we actually shook the audience's hands. It was all carefully orchestrated— and some players in the first wave would slip out the back doors, nip round to backstage and burst back through the stage doors waving at people so that the circle of energy was kept high with no hiatus.
>
> And that was the "secret play," that process of being taken away from yourself and into the understanding of someone else's pain and anger, a journey made by the audience. If asked what the play was about, it was about *love*—that's the bottom line.
>
> This is why people were breaking into the windows of the dressing rooms in Warsaw in order to sit on the gangway and watch the production.[21]

Brook thus affected the afterlife of the play for generations to come. For one thing, critics subsquently began reviewing productions by classifying them into two seemingly dichotomous categories: non-traditional, anti-romantic, not always terribly funny, and "Brookian;" or traditional, romantic, funny and fun-loving and "non-Brookian." Oddly enough, the original production had gotten assigned to the wrong box, and an examination of subsequent productions shows many more gradations of individuality than these labels permit. However, one basic distinction continually asserted itself and that was about genre. If a director saw the *Dream* as a parable of domination including maltreatment of women, then it was difficult to find the mechanicals risible and the fairies usually became malign.

The dark strains of the play seem to have been explored primarily by American directors after Brook. Arthur Holmberg reported on a series of "Erotic Dreams"[22] which began in 1975 and ended in 1990. All of these productions "eroticized" the play, and that meant that love was merely amorous but sex was murky and threatening and *relevant*: "This uninhibited celebration of the play's sensuality—and an attendant willingness to plumb its shadowy, even menacing depths— has carried us beyond Brook to a distinctively American vision of Shakespeare's fantasy."[23] Holmberg stated that each of these stagings offered "different solutions to the fairy problem."[24] It is significant that the fairies have somehow become a problem (indeed, that might be news to Shakespeare) and that these creatures offer only a slightly lesser challenge for presentation than do the mechanicals. In fact, productions which emphasize the dark side of the *Dream* often have to declare a kind of lacuna during the performance where all the black magic gets banished so the audience can enjoy the mechanicals' interlude, the one scene everyone agrees should be amusing.

Alvin Epstein directed a production at the American Repertory Theatre which opened in 1975 and was re-staged in 1980. Epstein readily admits that his metaphor was nude (later we shall see that Liviu Cuilei's was *red*), a device that translated into "push[ing] the sexual explorations to the point of menace" and "explor[ing] Freudian depths or Jungian reflections."[25] A.J. Antoon's 1988 production for the New York Shakespeare Festival was set in Brazil and emphasized the strands of domination in a colonial world. One critic sighed with relief that the director "rode his concept lightly," and was pleased to find that both lovers and mechanicals were actually allowed to be funny within the confines of the production design.[26] Mark Lamos' production at the Hartford Stage Company found the director declaring that the fairies could partake of both light and dark worlds: "I wanted my fairies to be a cross between Grimm's fairy tales and Dante's Inferno"[27] in a mounting that Holmberg terms a "sprawling, darkly philosophic phantasmagoria."[28] In all of these presentations, Titania waked and straightway copulated with—not loved, not doted on—but copulated with—an ass. By far the most attention was directed toward a *Dream* originally directed by Liviu Ciulei at the Guthrie Theater in Minneapolis, a production which featured sex, drugs, and very little rock and roll. The lovers duelled with switchblades and the closing stage picture was a blood-red wine stain spilled on a white linen tablecloth, a remnant of the wedding party. The tone of the production was set with a scene choreographed to open the play. Against a red vinyl back wall, a proud and militant black Hippolyta was led onstage for her first speech (she mimes the "silver bow" as a real weapon), then stripped of her army fatigues and dressed in white by female attendants to stand alongside other white manikins. She reacted to the ensuing scene with contempt, with sympathy for the lovers, and finally with scorn for Theseus. In fact, critics felt that she would never consent to become his wife. There were strong notes of bitterness, domination, and edginess in the production. When Oberon showed Titania the creature she had slept with, she let out a piercing scream and fell to the ground in convulsive shock. The design concept was hard-edged and geometrical, the music by Philip Glass. Although local newspaper critics were ecstatic about the theatre experience they'd witnessed, University of Minnesota's Professor Thomas Clayton was troubled by Ciulei's revisioning of the script:

> *A Midsummer Night's Dream* no doubt *is* in degree "patriarchal," like the rest of Shakespeare's plays and Jacobethan [sic] society in general, but to the extent that we feel compelled to reject the social system categorically for its imperfections and injustices . . . it seems pointless to attend to the period's drama. . . . We have, really, three options: to attend to the drama mainly or merely as a source of data yielding perceptions of the system's social foundations and ramifications; to read and perform it in the spirit in which its authors writ and in accordance with such ethical, social, and aesthetic values as still have currency or at least intelligibility; or to reorient it in performance or otherwise to make it say what a suitably corrected drama would say in reflecting some selection of contemporary views and values.[29]

Ciulei chose to re-orient. Clayton attempted to be objective, yet he clearly felt that Ciulei was making a serious error in terms of the contract theatre artists have with playwrights, which is to at least respect the spirit of the original work.

Margaret Tocci, reviewing for *Shakespeare Bulletin*, opined that there wasn't much rescue for the mechanicals' playlet and noted that "[the director] could not overlap the rest of the play's violent, gloomy moods with the play-within-a-play's hilarious sprightliness."[30] When a director has appeared to violate the tone of the original artwork in the guise of "relevance," audience members finally decide if these changes were effected as gimmickry, interpretative clarification, or the overwhelming need to be different. Given the shock-value tactics used in Cuilei's production, one tends toward the latter opinion. This attitude toward staging Shakespeare invites a question about the scope of creativity Shakespeare summons in his play: is there a hidden invitation to re-invent theme, tone, and even genre?

A summary look at the reviews of American productions in *Shakespeare Bulletin* from 1970 to 1994 reveals that American festivals and regional theatres around the U.S. were about evenly divided between traditional and non-traditional productions. Many festivals chose to take advantage of local woodland settings and to characterize the fairies as creatures connected with nature. The play continued to be a popular venue, with a production materializing about every six weeks.[31] Furthermore, in Great Britain the trend appeared to be energetically retro, toward a whole-hearted celebration of the comic spirit.

After a brief hiatus of *Dream*s after Brook's at the Royal Shakespeare Company, John Barton took up the challenge in 1977 and produced a thoroughly traditional staging, complete with woodland sprites, Elizabethan lovers, and mechanicals playing themselves very straightforwardly, using the lines and little added humor. This was followed in 1981 by a Victorian *Dream*, a concept which may have been distantly related to the RSC's successful *Nicholas Nickleby*. Director Ron Daniels conceived of the fairies as Dickensian wooden puppets held by actors dressed in black; they were threatening creatures although somewhat softened by their Punch-and-Judy resemblances. Daniels doubled Hippolyta with Titania and Theseus with Oberon (as had Brook); this couple looked like figurines one might find on a shelf in a Victorian parlor. The golden costume of the Indian boy fit in with the decoratif art that swept Britain in her Imperial era. It is notable that any references to colonialism beyond the design concept were scrupulously absent. There was a serious air about the whole production; Oberon was threatening, the fairies spooky, and the presence of the Jack-the-Ripper underworld of the period tended to dampen comic high spirits in the mechanicals' scenes.

Bill Bryden produced a *Midsummer Night's Dream* at the Royal National Theatre's Cottlesloe in 1982 which imitated Ron Daniel's in one regard: it was set in the Victorian period. Beyond that, it was most decidedly a flight of joyous fantasy. Bryden elected to highlight the fairyland overall, to give it due weight and prominence, to feature it as a main strand.[32] The production concept was that the play was taking place in an Elizabethan home haunted by Elizabethan fairies at the turn of the century. Although the aristocracy and the mechanicals wore bowlers and crinolines, the fairies (some young, some old) remained earthy, lusty, and physical, "certainly not delicate nor floating but non-ethereal and they got rigorously and vigorously played."[33] In fact, the fairies propelled the action and were the energizing source in the production. They were costumed in raggedy moss-colored doublets and skirts and wore shock wigs. Fairy king and queen Paul Scofield and Susan Fleetwood took full responsibility for their quarrel, "guiltily conscious of the universal repercussions of their row."[34] Titania's "forgeries of jealousy" speech demonstrated how ashamed she was about the disturbances in nature.

Bryden wanted the various worlds inside the play to intermingle. Michael Billington stated, "The key moment in this production comes, I suspect, when four of the fairies steal out of darkness to plant a kiss on the newly-reconciled lovers."[35] The fairy world was clearly benevolent and nurturing rather than hostile and malignant. Bryden decided that the world of the play should also intermingle with and include the audience. The audience sat on cushions surrounding the stage at the Cottlesloe (indeed, one critic complained endlessly about his sore bum)[36] and were brought into the action; when Demetrius was lost in the forest, he stumbled among the observers, making use of them in his performance.

The mechanicals were honest Edwardian tradesman who were not condescended to nor made maudlin but had their own dignity. Snout (as Wall) was covered with bricks almost as if he were a clothesline hung with them; he also wore brick *cothurni*, a clever costume joke. Music in the play was a combination of Edwardian and Elizabethan. The musicians had been coached by a professor whose specialty was early wind instruments. The play opened with a musical pun to the strains of "Beautiful Dreamer." The Bergomask was a sand dance in the cheerful style of Wilson, Keppel, and Betty.

Overall, Bryden's was a *Dream* which generously acknowledged its comic roots. It was "populist, well-beloved by audiences, and got lots and lots of laughs. People left the theatre having very much enjoyed it.[37] The production opened in November 1982, went on tour to Bath and other English locales, then returned to London and re-opened in the Lyttleton in April 1983. Critic Nicholas Shrimpton described it as ". . . full of good ideas and rich performances but without any particular ax to grind."[38]

Cheek by Jowl, one of the freshest and most inventive of the fringe theatre groups in London, emerged with a modern concept that delighted audiences during its run in the spring of 1986. The company is known for minimal staging and experimental techniques such as using cast members not onstage (stored around the acting area or in the stalls) to provide sound, music, and other special effects for the performance. Ten cast members doubled parts to play all the roles. Hippolyta and Theseus were obvious send-ups of Princess Diana and Prince Charles, with "frightfully-frightfully" accents betraying their upper-class status. The lovers followed along as Sloanies, Hermia and Lysander sporting backpacks and sleeping bags and Helena negotiating the woodlands in high heels and a Burberry raincoat. The mechanicals were translated into two women and a man, pillars of the local drama society. Playing the overly fussy director in pink was Miss Quince, aided by actress Miss Flute, who concentrated on warm-ups and seriously looked for her motivation. Bottom was the local vicar in a bottle hat, sweet but fatuous. Thus was class-consciousness lightly touched upon, juxtaposing jet-set aristocrats against middle-class "proles" rather than the usual lower-class bumpkins. More than one critic felt the group was truant from an Ayckbourn play.[39]

Reviews for the production were uniformly approving, a rarity in British theatre. The troupe took a refreshing point of view and coupled that with imagination, good ensemble work, and energy. The audience was literally " . . . choking, groping, and crying with laughter."[40] The production invited the audience to laugh at prevailing pretensions, reflecting current interests in the tabloids and in contemporary British novels. The concept fulfilled one of the oldest roles of comedy: that of a social corrective, with the actors serving as the abstract and brief chronicles of the time.

This *Dream* was selected by the British Council to tour to India and South America. It also won Laurence Olivier award nominations for "Best Comedy of the Year" and "Best Director of the Year." The director was the very imaginative Declan Donnellan, one of the founders of the company, whose aim continues to be to "democratise the classics" without the clouds of academic fustiness nor the posturing of high culture.[41]

In 1993, an event began to take shape which had great promise. Richard Eyre hired Canadian Robert LePage to direct *A Midsummer Night's Dream* at the Royal National Theatre. LePage had an interesting background as an actor and director of unusual performance pieces and was, at that time, artistic director of the French Theatre of the Canadian National Arts Centre. He was a proponent of bringing cultures together, fostering *rapprochement* by developing working relationships between the politically divided artists of French Canada and English Canada. LePage endorsed Peter Brook's ideas, especially about observers: "I believe in the intelligence of the audience, I believe that the audience wants to create."[42]

Since LePage had a reputation for experimental ideas, he worked very openly with actors. He liked to use creative play to find opportunities to sense the forward movement of an idea and to guide it to completion rather than imposing a pre-conceived notion over the top of a script, as British directors did.[43] *A Midsummer Night's Dream* was his second Shakespearean play in English:

> Dealing with Shakespeare we're dealing with an avalanche of resources, a box of toys to be taken out. There are some authors that are so infinitely rich and give so much permission. . . . I think he offers a lot of permission to the actor, the translator, the director.[44]

Beginning with this attitude, LePage created a production that was set in a pool of black, swampy water transported onto the huge stage of the Olivier Theatre. The Athenian lovers were dressed in white cotton nightgowns and pajamas. Titania looked like an East Indian queen and Puck was played by a contortionist. The mechanicals were dressed like homeless indigents, and one had a live dog with him onstage.

This production was memorable for me as one of the lengthiest and most uncomfortable evenings ever spent in the theatre. Since the play opened in a mud puddle and stayed in a mud puddle, there was little differentiation among the worlds of the play. The front row of spectators were provided with plastic raincoats to protect their clothes. Actors waded through grit and mud and spent a great deal of time pushing around a steel bedstead. There were electric lightbulbs hanging over the set and Titania herself hung upside-down for twenty minutes (I forget why). The water splashed just enough to mask out parts of the dialogue. The mechanicals' scene was not funny but sad, even pathetic.

These were insurmountable problems. First, audience members empathized with the apparent discomfort and potential dangers posed for actors. Second, the technical challenges of sound, smell and chill actually prevented an observer from involvement with the story onstage. Almost all of the reviewers mentioned the difficulties, even if they were generous and critiqued the production well. Pity and compassion are great enemies to comedy; however, comedy did not appear be paramount within the concept.

Ultimately, the set design was too controlling a metaphor. Although an interesting multicultural strand began to emerge, almost as ooze from the slime, the idea never truly took shape. The theme of domination was explored—among the lovers, between Hippolyta and Bottom—but it became bogged down in technical problems created by the physical environment, among them that everybody began to look dirty and helpless after a while.

As a theatrical experience, the performance was a failure. Nevertheless, true creative spirit was evident in the one place most directors would not welcome it. As an invitation to wit, cleverness, and journalistic repartee, not a few critics rose to the occasion:

Mud, mud, glorious mud, nothing quite like it for cooling the blood . . . A Mudsummer Night's Dream . . . .[45]

The danger facing the cast would seem to be swamp fever.[46]

. . . Titania writhes in a sexual frenzy in the pond as if looking for her frog prince. . . .[47]

[the lovers] are almost unrecognizable in their mudpacks.[48]

... Bottom, a fatuous twerp trying to be a cool medallion man, seems, in these water-logged conditions, to have made an inspired fashion choice in his platform shoes.[49]

Again, how can anybody be appalled by Titania's affair with Bottom when viler creatures are all around?[50]

Lepage has little time for the text, though, since he goes to great lengths to distract you from it ... one thing the production teaches you that it's impossible to slosh silently.[51]

For addicts of mud-wrestling, the production is a must.[52]

But where Brook was all light and air, this is earth and water.[53]

As Helena rightly puts it: "O long and tedious night."[54]

A critic approaching Robert LePage's eagerly awaited production of Shakespeare's dream play must tiptoe warily between the whirlpool of philistinism and the jagged rocks of over-enthusiasm.[55]

Doubtless some gullible loon will claim this production is as big a breakthrough as Peter Brook's landmark 1970 Stratford *Dream*.[56]

Well, it wasn't a loon but a Nightingale, Benedict by name, who voiced the minority opinion: " ... the most original *Dream* since Peter Brook's version two decades ago, and the most strange and disturbing since—but there I have no memory to match it."[57] (Whatever he means by that.) At least a half dozen reviewers mentioned "the wet dream," and I began to think there was some psychological truth in that. In any event, the opportunity for LePage to don Brook's mantle had evaporated.

In July 1994, Adrian Noble directed a production of *A Midsummer Night's Dream* which transferred to the Barbican in the summer of 1995 and subsequently toured the United States. It appeared in many ways to be a quotation of Brook's staging of the play, almost an anniversary performance updated with softer edges, more technology, and computer magic from the 1990's. There were a number of similarities. As the audience entered the theatre, they faced a large box placed on a wide stage, red with a blue splash of light on the apron. It was the white box brightly color-washed. Theseus/Oberon and Hippolyta/Titania were doubled, but Noble went further than Brook and doubled the fairies with the mechanicals. Titania and Bottom coupled noisily and with relish in a bower flown in from above; it was pillow-lined in hot pink, which brought out the red ostrich feathers trimming the petal-like hem of Titania's costume, a design touch reminiscent of the red bower in Brook's *Dream*. The performance acknowledged all kinds of sexual play with hints of a relationship between Oberon and Puck. Puck mimed humping the fairies and also allowed Oberon to pluck a black ostrich feather from his flirtatious underwear. At the end of the production, the cast came to the edge of the stage and threw golden glitter at the audience.

The music was immediately familiar, its electronic, new-age boinging sounds surrounding the audience, the same music (also developed by the Royal Shakespeare Company) used to highlight futuristic special effects at the Cirque de Soleil in Las Vegas (another correspondence to Brook, whose central metaphor was "circus"). The sound supported the setting: a jewel-like neon fantasy-land where not just Bottom but indeed all the creatures existed on the cusp of human and surreal.

Costumes were executed in clear primary colors, Hermia in a simple orange sundress, Helena in purple, and Lysander and Demetrius in shirts of blue and green silk. Puck wore bright yellow oriental silk trousers. Bottom was dressed like a motorcyclist from the 1940's and the other mechanicals were in workaday costumes. Bottom the Ass grew giant horsey teeth as two ears emerged from his motorcycle cap. The lighting dappled pure color on the stage floor in clear reds, blues, turquoises, yellows. Glowing lightbulbs suspended from the flies on long cords rose and fell, twinkling atmospherically. The green-haired fairies in their lustrous spandex costumes were fanciful creations.

The mechanicals were played broadly; Thisby became a leading comic role featuring inventive sword tricks. Bottom was outsized and given to physical comedy. The low characters were at the comic core of the play. The lovers were equally physical. When Helena begged to be used as a spaniel, she crawled on all fours. When Demetrius said, "I will not [pause, with a look at her] . . . STAY . . . " (2.2.235), Helena responded like a dog by heeling.

The programme contained a selection of quotations about dreams as revelations. Dreams were not nightmares but natural entities which free us to play, to resolve, to role-play, and to interpret. Adrian Noble's combination of scenic spectacle and creative characterizations was

1990's magic; it harked back to Brook but looked forward to the future. This was an adult fantasy *Dream*, a bit liberated for a "schools-play" but definitely warm at heart. Dark shadows, Boschian or Goyaesque horrors were banned, and although the production ran for three hours, the audience expressed pure joy.

Jay Halio suggests that the performance issues in *Midsummer Night's Dream* include the treatment of the fairies, the amount of differentiation among the lovers, the kind of music used, the doubling of roles, the forest setting, and the relationship between Theseus and Hippolyta.[58] However, one question basic to all these others must be resolved as rehearsals begin, and that is the question of genre. Contemporary directors have shown a predilection for tracing strands of misogyny, colonialism, family conflict, and marital discord through a play we once labelled a comedy. This is nothing new in the twentieth century. There was, after all, a ten-year fashion of playing *Twelfth Night* à la Chekhov even though no one dares deconstruct *Macbeth* into a midnight thriller starring Gene Wilder.

There is a siren call in the *Dream*. Critics have hearkened, obeying the irresistible urge to be cute, resorting to the comedy of bad manners. Actors have gone overboard and hammed it up. Directors have teased a dark thread out of the weaving, then ignored the tapestry. Peter Brook's success was based on focusing on solving problems he posed as a director rather than on essaying the definitive production. His success was the result of an unobstructed intelligence which fired his invention and shaped his achievement.

The years after Brook's production have showcased imagination and energy in directors who presented *A Midsummer Night's Dream*. It would be as impossible to examine every production or to quantify the number of traditional versus non-traditional interpretations of the play as it would be unfair to say that a particular population prefers one treatment over another.

However, so many fairies have flitted to the bottom of our Ardens since Peter Brook that we must ask: do theatre artists and audiences today care about the text's comic design? If we are to take Brook, Jonathan Miller, and most modern theatre practitioners at their word, the answer is "probably not." Most would insist that the director of Shakespeare becomes an *auteur* and can do whatever s/he likes with the text. Certainly there are no Script Police to give Interpretation Citations when the spirit of the play has been violated. For some, the performance text seems so radically separate from the literary text that a director may do as s/he so desires. I would argue, however, that the literary text and the performance text are not different, and that the written text should guide the performance text. In fact, the written text provides the foundation for the performance text.

A major clue to the playwright's conception is genre. If artists create from the substructure of the written text, *A Midsummer Night's Dream* sustains its identity as a comedy. Despite the experimentation with shadowy, nightmare dreams, the center has held. The text of the play can support Romantic Comedy, Dark Comedy, and perhaps Black Comedy, but it does not support emptying the play of its basis in humor.

Some non-traditional interpretations risk confusing the audience. In comedy, context is overpowering. If a comic device is set in a somber frame, it won't play as well, and sometimes it won't play as comedy at all. In the regional areas of the United States, productions can be a spectator's first experience (or early experience) with Shakespeare in the theatre, and those spectators need guidance with the storyline. I've taken students to productions of *Dream* that left them hopelessly confused because the lovers, the aristocrats, and the fairies all looked like members of a Blade-Runner Punk Underground. The play juxtaposes four different narratives, and novices need help identifying each of the play's worlds.

It is my contention that there are many different right interpretations and many different wrong ones.[59] Brook acknowledged bestiality, cruelty, and the whimsical interchangeability of love relationships in the *Dream*, yet he remained faithful to the comic context. Clive Barnes was talking about an affinity for the play's center, about a movement toward its underpinnings and mass, about respect for the play's design, when he described Brook's common-sense approach toward play production:

> He has taken this script and staged it with regard for nothing but its sense and meaning. He has collaborated with Shakespeare, not twisted his arm or blinded his senses, not tried to be superior, but just helped him out to get this strange play on the stage.[60]

Ultimately, collaboration is part of accepting an invitation to invent. The playwright is a member of the team that completes the theatrical enterprise. Playwrights may be long departed, but their spirits live on in their work. An invitation is a lure and an enticement, but it is also a request and a summons—for respecting the maker as well as the life-giving potential in a work of art.

NOTES

1. All Shakespeare citations are taken from *The Riverside Shakespeare*, ed. G. Blakemore Evans (Boston: Houghton Mifflin, 1974).

2. Langer, *Feeling and Form: A Theory of Art Developed from "Philosophy in a New Key"* (New York: Charles Scribner's Sons, 1953), 349.

3. Bergson, "Laughter," *Comedy: "An Essay on Comedy" [by] George Meridith / "Laughter" [by] Henri Bergson*, Introduction and Appendix by Wylie Sypher (Baltimore: Johns Hopkins University Press, 1980), 92, italics added.

4. Sigmund Freud, *Jokes and Their Relation to the Unconscious*, excerpted in *Comedy: A Critical Anthology*, ed. Robert W. Corrigan and Glenn M. Loney (Boston: Houghton Mifflin, 1971), 753.

5. Bergson, 64-65.

6. *A Midsummer Night's Dream*, videocassette distributed by Video Yesteryear, 1991. Original production shown on 24 June 1964, in Great Britain by Rediffusion Network Television.

7. Kott, "Titania and the Ass's Head," *Shakespeare Our Contemporary* (New York: Anchor Books, 1966), 213-36.

8. Michael Mullin, "*A Midsummer Night's Dream*" in *Shakespeare Around the Globe*, ed. Samuel Leiter (New York: Greenwood, 1986), 482.

9. Ibid., 483-84.

10. Glenn Loney, ed., *Peter Brook's Production of William Shakespeare's 'A Midsummer Night's Dream' for the Royal Shakespeare Company: The Complete and Authorized Acting Edition* (New York: The Dramatic Publishing Company, 1974), 104.

11. The term is extensively discussed in Jonathan Miller's *Subsequent Performances* (London: Faber and Faber, 1986), 23-74.

12. Miller, 35.

13. I interviewed actor David Meyer on 27 June 1995, in London. He played Moth and later Demetrius in the world tour of Brook's production.

14. John Kane, who played Puck in the original production, wrote a letter to me about the production on 25 July 1995.

15. Kott, 228.

16. Selbourne, *The Making of "A Midsummer Night's Dream": An Eye-Witness Account* . . . (London: Methuen, 1982), 295.

17. Interview with David Meyer, 27 June 1995.

18. Letter from John Kane, 25 July 1995.

19. Selbourne, 297.

20. From a subsequent letter regarding the production from John Kane to me, 31 July 1995.

21. Interview with David Meyer, 27 June 1995.

22. See Holmberg's article by that title in *American Theatre*, April 1989, 12-17.

23. Holmberg, 14.

24. Ibid.

25. Holmberg, 17.

26. Richard Hornby, "Shakespeare in New York," *Hudson Review* 41 (Summer 1988): 340.

27. Lamos is quoted in Holmberg, 14.

28. Holmberg, 17.

29. See Clayton's "Shakespeare at the Guthrie: *A Midsummer Night's Dream*" in "Theatre Reviews," *Shakespeare Quarterly* 37 (Summer 1986): 230.

30. Margaret Tocci, "Regional Theatre Reviews," *Shakespeare Bulletin* 4 (1986): 14.

31. This is a conservative estimate produced by Stanley Wells in his article "'A Midsummer Night's Dream' Revisited," *Critical Survey* 3 (1991): 14.

32. I am indebted to actor David Rintoul, who played Demetrius, and who provided information about this production in a telephone call on 15 July 1995. I did not see the production.

33. Ibid.

34. Ibid.

35. Billington, review in *The Guardian* shortly after the play opened on November 25, 1982; quoted from *London Theatre Record* 2 (1982), 273.

36. Ironically, he was named Jack Tinker. Quoted from a review in the *Daily Mail*, reported in *London Theatre Record* 3 (1983): 663.

37. Telephone conversation with David Rintoul, 15 July 1995.

38. Nicholas Shrimpton, "Shakespeare Performances in Stratford-upon-Avon and London, 1982-83," *Shakespeare Survey* 37 (1984): 168.

39. See Nicholas de Jongh, who reviewed the play on 30 March 1986 for *The Guardian*, and Martin Hoyle, who reviewed the play on the same day for *The Financial Times*; quoted in *London Theatre Record* 6 (1986): 272.

40. Mary Harron in a review from *The Observer*, 23 March 1986; quoted in *London Theatre Record* 6 (1986): 271. I saw a production a week later and audiences reacted in the same way.

41. *City Limits*, 24 March 1986, 33.

42. "Directors: Stephen Daldry, Nicholas Hytner, and Robert LePage," *Platform Papers, No. 3*, (London: Publications Department of the Royal National Theatre, 1993), 28.

43. See Robert LePage interviewed by Christie Carson, "Collaboration, Translation, Interpretation," 31-34, *New Theatre Quarterly* 14 (February 1993): 31-33.

44. "Directors," *Platform Papers, No. 3*, 29.

45. Michael Coveney, review, *The Observer*, 12 July 1992; quoted in *London Theatre Record* 12 (1992): 822.

46. Benedict Nightingale, review, *The Times*, 12 July 1992; quoted in *London Theatre Record* 12 (1992): 821.

47. Maureen Paton, review, *Daily Express*, 12 July 1992; quoted in *London Theatre Record* 12 (1992): 822.

48. Ibid.

49. Paul Taylor, review, *Independent*, 11 July 1992; quoted in *London Theatre Record* 12 (1992): 823.

50. Benedict Nightingale, review, *Times*, 11 July 1992; quoted in *London Theatre Record* 12 (1992): 821.

51. Paul Taylor, review, *Independent*, 11 July 1992; quoted in *London Theatre Record* 12 (1992): 823.

52. Jack Tinker, review, *Daily Mail*, 7 July 1992; quoted in *London Theatre Record* 12, (1992): 824.

53. Robert Hewison, review, *Sunday Times*, 12 July 1992; quoted in *London Theatre Record* 12 (1992): 825.

54. Paul Taylor, review, *Independent*, 11 July 1992; quoted in *London Theatre Record* 12 (1992): 823.

55. Steve Grant, review, *Time Out*, 7 July 1992; quoted in *London Theatre Record* 12 (1992): 821.

56. Michael Billington, review, *The Guardian*, 7 November 1992, quoted in *London Theatre Record* 12 (1992): 822.

57. Nightingale, review, *The Times*, 11 July 1992; quoted in *London Theatre Record* 12 (1992): 821.

58. See Jay L. Halio, *A Midsummer Night's Dream*, Shakespeare in Performance Series, eds. J.R. Mulryne and J.C. Bulman (New York: Manchester University Press, 1994), 1-8.

59. I am not speaking of the design concept (the costumes, lighting, sound and the setting) as separate interpretations in and of themselves; hopefully, the design concept will support and clarify the directorial vision.

60. Loney, 13.

Figure 4. The University of Washington's School of Drama production. Act 3, scene 2. Clockwise from the left: Lysander (Mario Burrell), Helena (Lisa Moore), Demetrius (Gillen Morrison), and Hermia (Stephanie Stephenson). Reproduced courtesy of the University of Washington.

Transposing Helena
to Form and Dignity

Lisa J. Moore

The delicious challenge of playing Helena was recently mine in a 1994 production of *A Midsummer Night's Dream* at the Playhouse Theater in Seattle, Washington. Describing in language the indefinable experience of acting is my challenge here, and, although something is lost in the translation of stage experience to the printed page, I can nevertheless describe the choices I explored in the rehearsal process that ultimately revealed my portrayal of Helena. Presented by the University of Washington's Professional Actor's Training Program (PATP) under Steve Pearson,[1] the production itself was in the hands of Seattle director Mark Jenkins, who chose to explore the dark side of the frequently produced play. It was to be, as he put it, a dramatization of desire, and its flip side, disgust, with emphasis on the sensual, dark, and more sinister elements in the play.[2] The world of the fairies, for example, was to be sexual and malevolent.

From this departure point, cast, crew, and director journeyed through many variations and antitheses in our attempt to create a production. In any rehearsal period, as many ideas are always thrown out as are kept, and in this production many concepts changed up until the day we opened. The performance is not a product, nor is the process of creating a production linear: the preparation for the play is not separate from the moment of performance but rather is the performance itself. All the discarded choices, design revisions, text work, arguments and flubbed lines (as well as the conscious selection of choices and moments) resonate in the moment of performance.

Indeed, the opening night does not mark the end of the process, for the show is not a finite, definable, static piece but always a string of ever-changing responses to a set of actions, as varying and changing as the actors fulfilling the roles. This is true for the individual actor as well, for the discovery of the character continues long after the run has started. The play is never the same but is always informed by traces of its past.

I.

The designers for our production proposed a world in which modern elements were interwoven with the architecture and costumes of the court of Athens. The set consisted of three large rustic stone platforms descending to the main part of the large thrust stage, which served as the Court as well as the forest. Stage right, stood an enormous tree made up of a Greek column, steel bars, and tree bark. The only other suggestions of foliage were a small tree stump and a Doric column cut to resemble a tree stump. The conscious omission of the lush greenery ordinarily associated with *A Midsummer Night's Dream* generated a spare effect. A brick wall behind the playing area presented a billboard-sized image of lovers kissing, muted except for the woman's bright red lips. This provided the backdrop for the moon, a large circle cut out of a moveable, back-lit black panel that moved slowly across the back wall as the "Dream" unfolded. Down center in the midst of the forest was a storm drain. The lighting design juxtaposed the brilliantly lit Court of Athens scenes against those of the dark and shadowy forest. The fairies were elegant, glamorous, and scantily clad in strange but modern dress. Although the mortals wore traditional Athenian garb, certain details were modern. For example, the lovers' chitons were trimmed with Nike, Prudential, and other recognizable logos, and "Moon" carried a Coleman camping lamp for his lantern. It was within this world of incongruity and sexuality that I had to create my Helena.[3]

My initial Helena was rife with incongruities. From the outset I wanted not only her angst and insecurity to register but her self-possession and strength as well. Desperate, she appears undignified in her pursuit of Demetrius, and yet Helena is not without a sense of inner dignity and deserving. That Demetrius does not love her makes no sense to her. While she endures insult, injury, and outright abuse making the torturous journey to reclaim him, she rejects useless self-pity. And, while much of the humor arises out of her desperation, it is her struggle to maintain dignity and her hopeful perseverance that makes us love Helena even as we laugh at her.[4]

But these incipient concepts and the actual enacting of them onstage are worlds apart. Considering the amount of character development necessary for creating a role, the onstage moments are relatively few. Whether a large or small role, an actor has a finite number of words to speak and actions to perform. Helena's five scenes, two soliloquies, and mute Court scene at the end are her only opportunities to present herself to the audience. However tempting, one can't add lines, run back onstage to explain, or publish program notes justifying one's interpretation. In the limited time a character is onstage the audience compiles her character. No finite Helena, no Platonic form is essentially *her*. Observing the brief moments of specific action and response between Lisa/Helena and the other actors/characters as the play unfolds, the spectators themselves form their pictures of the character. An extreme position holds that the perfect play is one in which the audience watches a bare stage and makes up the play themselves. Because the character is being created to some degree in the minds of the audience, it is not effective to batter them with generalized emotions. "I am as ugly as a bear" (2.2.94)[5] spoken with a pout in woe-is-me tones leaves nothing up to the audience. I find that when I concentrate on making the character's situation clear and specific to myself, the actor, spectators will engage with the unfolding drama and create many Helenas in their minds. Rather than one generalized Helena, I am as many different possible Helenas as there are audience members. I am not in control of producing the character; the audience does that from my choices. And the more specific my choices, the more interesting the Helena they can create. Specificity and clarity about what I (the character) want are of the utmost importance.

When the play is Shakespeare's, actors confront an entirely new set of hurdles. How to unlock the complex poetry to allow a living being to emerge on stage? How to simultaneously honor the text, the director, the audience and the actor herself? How to avoid playing a stuffy notion of what Shakespeare "should" be? How to *connect* with poetry that supports huge passions and idea? Luckily, in some ways Shakespeare's plays are a do-it-yourself acting kit: instructions (scansion, breath stops, etc.) are included, some assembly required.[6]

The text abounds with information, both explicit and implicit. As John Barton remarks, "Shakespeare's text is full of hidden hints to the actors. When an actor becomes aware of them, he will find that Shakespeare himself starts to direct him."[7] Academic resources are also useful when creating a role, although achieving an appropriate balance between intellectual information and the actual creation of character remains a challange. However intriguing, critical theory, textual analysis, and historical information serve the actor only as they can inform specific theatrical decisions. In fact, many actors and directors are wary of over-analyzing, apprehensive about getting too "in your head," too cerebral, at the expense of becoming the character. In my own process, however, the basic "table work" of analyzing text, paraphrasing it in modern language, looking up words in the *OED,* and examining Shakespeare's rhetorical strategies can be invaluable. In this stage—functioning as one's own dramaturge—current critical views can be enlightening. Stanislavski describes the effective *secondary* use of intellectual analysis: "In art it is the feeling that creates, not the mind; the main role and the initiative in art belong to feeling. Here the role of the mind is purely auxiliary, subordinate. The analysis made by an artist is quite different from one made by a scholar or a critic. If the result of a scholarly analysis is thought, the result of an artistic analysis is feeling. An actor's analysis is first of all an analysis of feeling, and it is carried out by feeling."[8]

II.

An essential undertaking is to determine what my character wants in each scene as well as in the play as a whole. What Elizabethan actors connected with naturally, a modern actor must consciously approach by analyzing the text, fully using breath and voice, and creating specificity, since the more specific and crucial an actor makes what she has at stake, the more interesting she will be to watch. For instance, because in our time broken engagements are commonplace, Helena's level of desperation may be difficult for a modern actress to identify with, but it arises out of a genuine and powerful need. I knew that if I made Helena's need specific enough for myself, the audience would buy it.

Before I could begin to do that, however, I had to consider the director's expectations of Helena. Many directors gear their notes towards a certain desired quality or end-result, and leave it to the actor to bridge the gap between action/intention and end-result. Mark, however, repeatedly warned me against general desperation, anxiety, or self-pity as a state of being for Helena. "Get your intentions specific, and play against those despairing feelings—they are obstacles to getting what you want." If I gave in to self-pity, it was tantamount to saying I had already lost. I think Helena is still very much "in the game." I decided the best way for Helena to avoid the self-pity trap was to struggle to be optimistic about her efforts working. I would be dauntless. I would insist, in the face of humiliation, that Demetrius still loved me. I would intelligently, doggedly, relentlessly pursue him in the hope that I could win him back. Mark also suggested pinpointing Helena's action/intention by creating a verb to express her struggle in each scene. In exploring and clarifying my overall objective—to recover Demetrius' affection—I wrote down some ideas about seeking adoration as a form of love after having been rejected. Demetrius, after betraying me, would have to swear even more persuasive oaths of love to win me back. Mark responded with a written note:

Helena—To seek adoration is on the right track, but why? Let us suppose the following. When Demetrius first courted you something changed radically. You were no longer autonomous. You no longer existed independently. Demetrius introduced to you the concept of your own beauty. Before that you were innocent of yourself, a child. But now with Demetrius' gaze on you, his desire, you became beautiful. You looked in his eyes, saw yourself as he saw you and it was beautiful and it became all that was important to you. Narcissus looking into the pool saw himself and fell in love with the image. You did that too. Demetrius is the pool. But then he took his gaze from you and put it on Hermia. With his gaze went your beauty, and now that beauty is all you became, he takes you from yourself. You now only exist in hunger. Only to get back your beauty. To retrieve yourself. But he has it. Without receiving his gaze, his affirmation, you are ugly, you don't really exist but as a shadow, a vapor. Like any organism you must survive. So you go after the gaze. Then what happens is this: You receive Lysander's gaze. He sees you the way you need to be seen. But it's bogus. It doesn't work. It's not authentic. (And it isn't, you intuit accurately. It's drug induced. It's temporary.) You will have none of it. Then Demetrius gazes on you

again but it isn't authentic either. It doesn't reflect back on you as
beauty. It instead mocks you. The pool of Narcissus is muddy,
distorted. Then a wonderful thing happens. You accept your lack of
beauty. Something more important takes its place and a self-reliant
self emerges. Below the beauty or lack thereof, there you find a
dignity. You value truth, honesty, above your own needs for
affirmation. When Hermia joins the conspiracy, you see her as a
betrayer of your dignity, your individuality, and of your gender. You
try to turn them all on each other so you can escape and live sadder,
wiser, and stronger. After you sleep and dream, Demetrius gazes on
you yet again and this time with his original love, flattery, and image
of your beauty. You will take it. You will take him. But you get to
choose and he can no longer define you.

Even though my own feminist perspective was markedly different in
many ways from Mark's views, I liked his description of an inner
transformation from a self defined by beauty to a self defined by
dignity. Although my Helena would undergo such a transformation,
she was stronger and more resilient from the beginning. I had to
integrate my own ideas with Mark's so that I could come up with
something we both thought of as Helena. I had to make it work in both
of our terms, (or—like Helena—change the man's mind).

Thinking about Mark's ideas also helped me focus on various
cultural issues concerning beauty and their bearing on Helena. Any
woman in our society (or that of ancient Greece or Renaissance
England) can get caught in the trap of being valued and rewarded for
her beauty, of being admired to the degree to which she is revered by
men. So encultured and powerful is the reward for beauty that once a
woman has evoked adoration, it is difficult for her to remember the self
that existed before being perceived and defined by her looks. It is
hardly surprising that Helena frequently wonders if her physical
appearance is the problem.

Many productions of this play present Helena as the homelier of
the two Lovers. I don't think the text supports that interpretation. More
of a problem for Helena (and hence "juice" for the actress) is created if
Demetrius' rejection of her is random and unfounded. Also, if Helena's
beauty equals Hermia's (which equals power in their society), Helena
is less of a victim; she is still in the fight. Helena says she is thought to
be as fair as Hermia in Athens, an assumption supported by Demetrius'

original preference. When Hermia is as attractive as Helena, Demetrius' infidelity undergoes a more rigorous interrogation, and the whimsical nature of love, one of the issues of the play, is emphasized.

Women are taught in any age by the culture that looks are an effective way into a man's heart. This power of being seen as beautiful is fleeting and can be reclaimed by the viewer at any time. Helena's sense of her own beauty exists within her and had once been independent of Demetrius' admiration. Her self-doubt stems from the fear that he won't be able to see her beauty, rather than that she's plain. She isn't a cool confident beauty, careless of how she is perceived, but she does have a sense of herself, of deserving, of hoping that he will see what she knows is true—that she is beautiful. Clinging to the belief that external beauty is what determines love is adolescent. If only it were as simple as having the right hair color or "stature." It would almost be easier for Helena to face Demetrius' rejection of her, were it due to her appearance, than an abandonment far more capricious and uncontrollable. Helena's journey through the play takes her from this adolescent ordering of the universe to womanhood, where other people's perceptions of her do not determine her value. During the course of the play, as Helena puzzles over what went wrong, she looks beyond herself as the sole source of answers: she wonders about the nature of love, but most specifically about men. She is perplexed—why are they fickle? She is solving a mystery: what is now different about me that your feelings should change? She has faith that if she can hit upon the key to the problem, she will regain Demetrius's love. This is the key to avoiding the common trap of Helena's lapsing into passivity, victimization, and self-pity. Her dauntless optimism, underlying all her actions, is the quality that keeps her strong (and funny). She faces obstacles: her own self-esteem, magic, men! It is her fight against those obstacles that is interesting for an audience to watch.

III.

I've been talking in terms of a general conception of Helena that evolved from a long and personal process of rehearsal as I played with different ideas, theories, and approaches. Now I would like to describe some specific choices that I made in this process by focusing on particular problems in each scene and the ways I attempted to find my Helena through the solutions.

If acting is a process of answering questions, for me the answers come when I get specific. Background research can help, as can non-academic or even fictional avenues to specificity. What does my bedroom (where I dream about Demetrius being mine again) look like? How many dresses do I own and which one does he like the best? Where were we when he proposed? Broke it off? One of my favorite exercises is to go through the play line by line and write down in three columns 1) everything everyone in the play says about the character 2) everything the playwright says about her, and 3) everything that the character says about herself. Of course, it's also necessary to determine who is lying and when. But the rehearsal process is much more than an intellectual analysis: rehearsal is really a way of brainstorming on one's feet. Playing as well as thinking enables the process of physicalizing Helena—the way I would carry myself, the level of self-consciousness I would feel, the adrenalin that would be present in my body as a result of intense attraction. Sometimes that free and imaginative play was a part of offstage exercises as well. For instance, I write stream-of-consciousness inner monologues to marry my own experience and associations to those of the play. One of these writings led me to consider my own situation: I happened to be five months pregnant during rehearsals, and although we were not suggesting a pregnant Helena as part of the production, I privately used the idea of having the secret that I was pregnant to fuel my desperate need to win Demetrius back. However unlikely a part of Shakespeare's original concept, it gave me a way to center on Helena's agony.

In act 1, scene 1, Helena is mentioned several times, so the audience is introduced to her before they actually see her. A picture of Helena is already in each audience member's mind, a picture which, obviously, was not "my" Helena. Because the first moment I appeared would be a challenge to that preconceived notion, it was important for me to find a way to announce her "essence" with that first entrance. Since Helena is, in my opinion, hilarious, and because she seems to have a knack for getting stuck in awkward situations, I wanted that first entrance to capture her brand of comedy and, at the same time, intimate her dignity and beauty. To accomplish that, it was especially important to be clear about where I was going and where I was coming from so that the entrance could be specific. It probably does not matter that the audience know where Helena has just been or where she is going, but it matters to Helena and will greatly affect the way the audience perceives her. The text doesn't specify a purpose for Helena's comings and goings, so I had to create specificity in my "memory," using clues from the text. I finally settled on the place I would be going and the reason for going there: I supposed that I knew Demetrius was at the Court that morning, and that I was on my way to stop him somehow from asking for Hermia's hand. In the process of rehearsal, I had tried and discarded many ideas for motivation: that I was looking for him to show off a new dress and freshly washed hair (fear/belief that he loves me for my looks and that they may or may not win him over), that I was going to provoke guilt (he was misguided and would reconsider if reminded of his commitment to me), that I had rehearsed a new, more convincing argument (he was logical and would listen to reason), or that I was going to throw myself on the mercy of the Court and expose his "bigamy" (I would force him to marry me or at the very least prevent Hermia from getting him).

After many trial-and-error rehearsals, I decided that as I made my first entrance, I would be on the way to the court to confront Demetrius and to plead my case myself, but as I rushed there, I stumbled into the scene between Hermia and Lysander. In my surprise at intruding on their love scene, I did a multiple take, standing for a second like a deer caught in the headlights, trying to speak, then running away. Hermia's "Godspeed, fair Helena! Whither away?" (1.1.180) was what drew me back into the scene. It worked well, but most importantly, it helped me key into one aspect of Helena: that feeling of being the one whose knee socks always fall down, the one who steps on gum, the one who walks in on her best friend and boyfriend when she has no one. That way I could hear Hermia's question and still not understand what she meant. FAIR Helena? Is she referring to me as FAIR? Jealousy, confusion, martyrdom, despair—all came into play in that first reaction from Helena.

When interacting with Hermia, Mark wanted me to try an almost scary, passive-aggressive attack. Helena is so effusive in her admiration of Hermia that he viewed her behavior as a kind of reverse jealousy. He wanted the lines, "My ear should catch your voice, my eye your eye, / My tongue should catch your tongue's sweet melody" (1.1.188-89) to be a study of how to actually snatch those body parts away from Hermia in order to get Demetrius. If I had a knife I might lop off that tongue and try it for my own. My own version of that moment revealed my absolute fascination with what she looked like and sounded like, as

I made the keenest examination of our differences so that I could rectify the situation and get him back. I let that maniacal quality Mark wanted result from my intense concentration on Hermia, trying to see what Demetrius saw in her, rather than any ill will toward her. It so happened that the costume Hermia wore in the play was one that (if I hadn't been pregnant) I would have much preferred to my own. I was able to call upon that feeling in the scene: I would look at her costume if I needed to refuel my desire to have what she had. If I had her dress or her eyes or her voice, I could win Demetrius back. I didn't, however, take myself out of context or substitute anything. I took the jealousy from what I saw before me, the actor I was working with. Concentrating on the dress was a way of staying present to the Hermia I saw before me on the stage each night and not to my preconceived idea of Hermia. I can't act with a pretend Hermia when I have a real one in front of me, so I wanted to use the combination of her appearance and the specific history I had worked out between our two characters.

The stichomythia that follows my plea to "teach me how you look, and with what art / You sway the motion of Demetrius' heart" (1.1.192-93) is an almost foolproof comic sequence if the actors use the set-ups Shakespeare has provided. Mark wanted a real reproach on "None but your beauty" (1.1.201). I tried to play the entire scene flattering Hermia insincerely to get what I wanted. I tried using the words in the text in a way that would threaten and intimidate her. I tried laying on guilt and evoking pity to get her to stay away from him, but here was a Helena trap that Mark had warned me about: sounding self-pitying. I ultimately made quite a different choice, for I discovered that what worked better was being very much in earnest. She had information I wanted, and I was desperate to have her let me in on the "secret" to his heart. Although residues of discarded choices probably remained, the objective that worked best was to earnestly seek her help and carefully study her moves. This follows from my image of Helena as an optimist who believes, in the face of logic, that if she can hit upon the right strategy, she will be successful. If I could just figure out the magic word, action, deed, look, I could have him back.

And then came Helena's famous (loaded) first soliloquy.[9] Anytime I handle "charged" text (e.g., "To be or not to be," or "Lord what fools these mortals be") I have a superior "toff" Shakespearean voice sounding the text in my head. So there was that to overcome, and of course soliloquies in general are difficult for several reasons: justifying the audience's presence; determining who the audience is; determining where they are. Although one could argue that the audience is not really present in the play, they are, physically, sitting there, so an actor cannot just ignore them. Also, to whom is the actor speaking? The actor can't decide to speak the words to no-one; she must speak either to the specific people in the audience—are they allies, foes, or confidantes?—or to herself. Helena is the only one of the Lovers who soliloquizes. What does that mean to me as I play Helena? A soliloquy must be justified, the emotions or stakes behind it must be so strong that the thoughts have to be spoken aloud; only song requires more justification. Soliloquies are also revealing. The character stands in front of people with her deepest emotions, thoughts, fears, unmasked. Another problem with this particular soliloquy is that Helena keeps the argument turning back on herself. Also, the argument or images would be unfamiliar to most audience members, and making their sense clear is crucial. If the audience doesn't understand what she is saying (or at least what she is trying to do), the actor is just standing alone onstage babbling. Mark reminded me that Shakespeare writes the way people think, not the way they talk, so I tried to let the sense of Helena's thought process dominate my work with the text. This is once again an opportunity to fall into the pity pot. True, Helena complains and feels sorry for herself, but playing only such emotions while alone onstage is death. I tried again, this time attempting active reasoning with the soliloquy. Shaken though she is by the sight of Hermia and Lysander "having it all," Helena takes a moment to reconnoiter, to shore herself up and allow Plan B to materialize. I saw the speech not as a plaintive recounting of her woes but rather as another attempt to figure out the key to winning back Demetrius. I do think, though, that Helena in that moment needs an ally, a partner in crime. Her best friend is abandoning her by leaving with Lysander. Hermia is also, in some sense, betraying her by getting what Helena herself so desperately wants, and finally by (however unwittingly) casting her spell over Demetrius. I used the soliloquy and the audience to replace my best friend. I needed to talk something out to devise an effective strategy, I needed support, I needed sympathy, and I needed validation. In the soliloquy I tried to get all of that from the audience.

The first beat, "How happy some o'er other some can be!" and the famous line, "Through Athens I am thought as fair as she" (1.1.226-27) are worlds apart, and making that jump is difficult. The Cupid references are hard for the audience to understand, and I had to be clear on the exact path of the argument. However, having a discovery onstage rather than filling the audience in is always the more interesting choice, so I let the Cupid argument occur to me piece by piece, and indeed Shakespeare makes the text build on itself there. He lets you figure it out like a math problem. Oohhh, *that's* why Cupid is said to be a child! Because he in choice he is so oft beguiled! The parts of the speech that get most interesting are where Helena fails to rationally unravel the Demetrius mystery and falls into anger, indignation, despair, and self-loathing. The argument became more personal, and passion broke through at "For ere Demetrius look'd on Hermia's eyne" (1.1.242); the "heat from Hermia" (1.1.244) was the second time I vented blame on Hermia, even more strongly. I allowed myself a big wash of disgust and despair at the climactic "showers of oaths did melt" (1.1.245). Mark wanted me to actually "feel" the memory of those oaths all over me, and I had a difficult time doing so. Finally, I got what he wanted at the dress rehearsal, I think because I wrote out the very words Demetrius had used when he wooed me and then had someone say them to me. When they turned out to be hollow oaths, I felt Helena's loss of innocence; the faith I felt in his promise turned to disgust with his fickleness and my own naivete. I let the oaths melt on my body and attempted to shake them off my dripping hands. Out of this failed attempt at reasoning with its corollary, a lapse into bitterness and despair, came a new, mischievous plan. I saw it as means to my end, yes, but there was also a secret delight in upsetting Hermia's plans. I let the thought of the consequences (losing their friendship) sober me as I mused, "[A]nd for this intelligence / If I have thanks, it is a dear expense (1.1.248-49). I hung poised in indecision for a moment, and then succumbed to the overwhelming need to have Demetrius (and with him my own sense of self-worth and identity) back. With adrenalized determination I ran offstage.

In Helena's next scene, the audience sees her problem played out for the first time. The problem posed by this scene is also its key: Helena's dauntlessness in the face of Demetrius' relentless rejection. I needed to let his cruelty affect me but still make lines like "I am your Spaniel" (2.1.203) seem plausible and not pathetic. The trick was finding that split second where the verbal kick-in-the-face could hit me before casting it off. Helena isn't stupidly deaf to his rejection, and it hurts. However, her only hope is to keep trying. Shakespeare begins her speech with the line, "You draw me, you hard-hearted adamant" (2.1.195), and Demetrius does seem to have some magically irresistible pull that ensnares Helena. She doesn't understand it herself, but she is powerless over her need to follow him. I wanted to feel that tangible pull of Demetrius reining me in. Centering techniques helped me ground myself and locate my center. I imagined a laser beam emanating from my "center" which was connected to Demetrius. Whenever he moved onstage, I was aware of the way it pulled me. I could play with when and where I resisted the pull, when I gave in, and when I pulled him. During the scene I was always in electric relationship with him. It was easy, then, to let that force pull me onstage.

This idea of magnetic forces also plays into the concept of a Doppleganger, or shadow self. I rehearsed with the idea that Helena herself was moving my body and propelling me through the scene. This way, I could divorce myself from my own movement patterns and let Helena's movement come through. Physical "brainstorming" played a large part in shaping my movement decisions.[10] I wanted her physicality to come out in this scene in particular, because it is her first descent into desperation as she tries to make her plan work. She is struggling to restrategize as her plan backfires. The "moment before" is a crucial detail of which actors must be aware. The scene, and indeed most scenes in *Dream*, start offstage or mid-scene. The chase had to be in progress before the audience could see us. The staging problem was that Demetrius entered down on a shallow thrust stage while speaking his first lines, and I felt that I reached him far too quickly. I wanted him to actually reel me in on my line "You draw me" (2.1.195), and I often said it with an added innuendo. At any rate, I had to cheat my progress across the stage without stalling the momentum of the chase. I had Helena take the tactic of the quiet and patient stalker. If I didn't break into Demetrius' preoccupation, I wouldn't upset the balance and therefore would not be cast off before the opportunity presented itself to win him back. This helped me move slowly and quietly to cover less ground and yield the stage on his entrance, but still keep the urgency bubbling inside. One can't let that inner ball of need or "fire" drop, lest the energy deflate and disappear from the performance. To keep that energy buzzing, I did some physical training exercises and stomping just before entering the scene.[11]

Quick thinking on her feet makes Helena a powerful figure in this scene. That is how I ultimately got around the "Spaniel" bit and made it work for me. As a feminist (or merely a human being), at first I had a hard time saying those lines and meaning them. By the time we opened, however, I loved that bit and looked forward to it every night. There is great humor here; and I even tried it a few times as if cajoling Demetrius into laughter. Although Helena can be fumbling and ungainly, she comes up with some stellar arguments and tactics: guilt, reason, seduction, threats, shaming—she tries them all. Any idea that Helena comes up with in this scene comes from adrenalized inspiration, and some are bound to be bowzers. She goes for everything full force, however, and once I fully surrendered to dogginess, it seemed like a viable tactic. I modeled myself after my own desperate-for-affection dog, complete with nosing the master's hand to be petted and performing a self-gratifying act on the master's leg. I love the fact that Helena (and Shakespeare) go to extremes: it's not just "I love you" for Helena—she'll "die upon the hand [she] loves so well" (2.1.244).

If some of the content of her arguments needs work (e.g., the spaniel ploy is not adroit), the verbal agility and persistence Helena displays make up for the deficiency, for she quick-wittedly takes anything that Demetrius says and reshapes it to her own ends. Helena returns every potential ace Demetrius deals her. She is incredibly creative and clever; thus, instead of merely deflecting insults, she transforms them into new tactics:

> Demetrius: For I am sick when I do look on thee.
> Helena: And I am sick when I look not on you. (2.1.212-13)

This line, incidentally, provides a good example of how I might use an academic resource—rhetorical analysis—in conjunction with acting tools. Normally one would never stress the word "not" or any negative. However, Helena's line is a translation of Demetrius's, and for the argument to come across as the clever re-shuffling it is, one must emphasize the negative. The scansion supports the acting choice, and the acting choice arises from knowledge of text. Helena's power lies in re-organizing Demetrius' words. She can break through the arguments, and therefore his resistance, by re-ordering his words/thoughts. She can be almost cheerful in the exhilaration of successfully rebutting every line he has. Her power lies in her mastery of language and her ability to better him in this stichomythic tennis match. Her patterns of speech support the choice of doggedly pursuing her man. Anapests, associated with military march verse and energetic movement, really helped me become resolute and strong: "And even for that do I love you the more" (2.1.202). Since Shakespeare gives her the last word, I used that moment as a statement of determination. Demetrius took his last few lines as he exited and was out of sight by the time I got to those lines. I therefore took the lines as a vow to fuel my resolve: "I'll follow thee" (2.1.243) became my oath rather than my threat.

In these central scenes, Helena is playing her own romantic moonlit scenario, but Demetrius, annoyingly, keeps butting in with his agenda and ruining hers. His rejection seems only to fuel her determination. This also made me consider the mysterious syndrome in which the unrequited lover becomes even more enamored of the very one who rejects that love, and made me wonder if Helena was more in love with Demetrius now than before his attentions strayed. At any rate, attaining the unattainable becomes an active challenge to which she continues to rise.

Mark thought, just as Helena wants to grab an tongue or eye from Hermia, so she wants to grab Demetrius but in a much more sensual way. He wanted the physical/sexual need to be at a rolling boil in Helena, her physical desire for him aroused. This worked very well for me, because it played into the physicality I was exploring with her. I would fixate on Demetrius' ear lobe or his fingers and think about what would happen if I just took a bite out of them.

My Demetrius, Gillen Morrison, was perhaps more gentle than the Demetrius in my own mind. Here lies another problem: how to reconcile my own images with what is actually happening onstage, and how then to have that affect me in a way that makes sense for the play. I saw this as a crucial scene to "win" the audience's affection and empathy, which meant I couldn't feel sorry for myself. After all, for whom does one feel sorry, the woman bemoaning her luck and saying "poor me" or the woman out striving to change the situation in the face of rejection?

Act 2, scene 2, was the next step in Helen's descent into humiliation. Helena has nearly lost her dignity and seems at a loss to regain it. As this is Helen's last-ditch effort before the tides change, I wanted her to really be a mess. Preparing for "O, I am out of breath in this fond chase" (2.2.88), I literally ran around backstage (sometimes playing chase with my Demetrius actor) to heighten my breathlessness. Once I set up an imaginary backstage obstacle course: pretend rocks to stumble over, streams to leap or wade through, ferns and cobwebs to brush against that would catch in my hair, twigs to break underfoot. I loosed several tufts of hair from my upswept style, and flapped my feet as I ran. If Helena has attempted to control Demetrius with appearances in the past, by this scene she has moved on. She doesn't give a thought to her appearance as she speeds through the forest. I was so hell-bent on catching him that I might have tackled him had I gotten close enough. This is sheer will and adrenaline operating, and it sets up her self-disgust for the "I am as ugly as a bear" line (2.2.94) as well as for her immediate suspicion of the suitors in the following scenes. If there is a scene where Helena feels sorry for herself, this is it! But I did think that the dizzy chase had to give way to a surprise realization/discovery of what she looked like for the "ugly as a bear" line. In the lines that follow, Helena faces reality and virtually surrenders: "What wicked and dissembling glass of mine / Made me compare with Hermia's sphery eyne" (2.2.98-99). This is the only moment when Helena feels defeated. It is precisely at this moment that the discovery of Lysander complicates the plot, setting the chaos in motion.

The huge scene with all four lovers seemed to work by itself because the preceding scansion had been observed. This scene to me is about traffic. The slapstick choreography and wild pitch of the humor required a tremendous amount of energy, but by that point, the passions required had been inspired by actual interactions onstage. The difference in Helena's state of mind was readily apparent in the text. Whereas in previous scenes the lines had been fairly regular and the breath stops plentiful, now the meter varies widely, and the verse provides few full stops. Helena, though extremely agitated and truly confused, manages to regain dignity and control in this scene. Without becoming whiny or ill-tempered, Helena must reject and reproach her suitors and face the ultimate betrayal from Hermia. The deeper the feeling, the more the heat of the moment intensifies, the further into the text an actor must go, because Shakespeare has built the emotion into the text through the poetics of meter, images, and alliteration.

Because *A Midsummer Night's Dream* is a play with several distinct populations, our rehearsal process was unusually segregated. As one of the lovers, I was barely aware that the world of the fairies existed. We rehearsed separately and, in some theatrical ways (say costuming), were in entirely different worlds. Nor had we any awareness of the mechanicals. For the most part, like typical self-absorbed young lovers, we were unaware that anyone else in the world of the play existed. There was, however, one major exception to this isolation. To underscore his original concept of desire and dark sensuality, Mark added a choreographed scene in which the lovers, as well as Titania and Bottom, performed a slow motion, erotic dance. It took place in the middle of act 4, scene 1, as we all lay sleeping on the forest ground after Titania has entwined drowsy Bottom in her arms. To dissonant, exotic strains of music, the lovers mimed a fairly graphic representation of an orgy. The initial partners in the scene were Helena and Demetrius, and Hermia and Lysander, but these pairings dissolved as we switched partners. Another slow-motion movement led to homosexual pairings and then, ultimately, to a foursome. Across the stage, Bottom and Titania performed a similar erotic dance, which was comical as well as disturbing. In staging a voyeuristic Puck above the scene, Mark insinuated that the fairies played an important role in undoing the last of civilization's constraints, as the desire explicit in the movement of the dance metamorphosed into a manifestation of the darkness of the fairy world. The choreographed expression of desire was a unifying moment for the play, intensifying as it did the moment of connection among the otherwise isolated groups of characters. The sexual moment for Helena revealed the depth of her desire for Demetrius as well as a more sensual side of her that we sense underlying her wish for Demetrius but don't otherwise openly encounter in the play. Including it at this point also helped me make Helena's last important transition in what I see as her journey from a self struggling against being defined by externals such as beauty, to a mature and whole woman, self-confident and self-defined.

In the confusion and sorting out which follows the lovers' awakening the next morning, Helena is in suspense as to what her lot will be. During the exchange between Theseus, Egeus, and Demetrius, I finally surrendered my need for Demetrius and resigned myself to his loss. Although that resignation lasted only a moment, it was crucial to Helena's regaining her personhood. When Demetrius did extend his hand to me and declare his love, I could receive it as an equal and as a mature and deserving woman.

This growth, the regaining of self and dignity, was also important to survive what Hermia and I referred to backstage as our "mute" scene. (Did Athenians cut out the woman's tongue during the wedding ceremony?) Perhaps one of the most difficult moments in acting comes when you are onstage with no lines. Even more difficult are those moments when you are not central to the action, and still more difficult are those when your character has already achieved victory over her super-objective. I needed a new and strong objective for this scene, one that would allow a way to confront the seeming sexism inherent in the text. I had to assume that the omission of lines for Helena and Hermia was deliberate and make a reason for myself to be onstage. I decided that Helena's journey had taken her out of the "Lord what fools these mortals be" category and had elevated her to a new wisdom. I let the celebration scene be an opportunity for Helena to assimilate her new perspective and rejoice in her victory. No longer needing to demonstrate who she is or to garner attention, she just *is*.

For the viewer of the play, Helena's union with Demetrius is apt to make love seem no less whimsical, insofar as it rests after all on his drug-induced state. But if my portrayal of Helena succeeded, perhaps some viewers entertained another possibility: however tenuously balanced on the incongruities of the play, Helena's relationship with Demetrius marks the moment of triumph for Helena, who can, from her perspective, claim that in the outcome of her fate at least she exerted some *agency*.

NOTES

1. The University of Washington's program is now ranked as one of the top three in the United States, the others being Yale's and New York University's. Pearson is responsible for many of the acting techniques and values I discuss.

2. Jenkins, now a faculty member in the Professional Actor Training Program, was following Jan Kott's 1960s reading of the play more closely than had Peter Brook.

3. The greatest influence on my performance was Emma Thompson's uproarious and, in my opinion, flawless portrayal for Kenneth Branagh's Renaissance Theatre Company's touring production. Other notable Helenas include Irene Worth in the 1951 Tyrone Guthrie production, Vanessa Redgrave at the 1959 Stratford-upon-Avon Festival, and Diana Rigg at the 1963 Royal Shakespeare Company production at the Aldwych. These last two stagings

were both directed by Peter Hall; the Rigg version was filmed as a television video.

4. J.C. Trewin points out that Helena was first played as a comic rather than purely romantic role by Audrey Carten at the Royal Court in 1920 and Edith Evans at Drury Lane in 1924 ; *Going to Shakespeare* (London: George Allen & Unwin , 1978), 101.

5. All quotations from *A Midsummer Night's Dream* have been taken from *The Riverside Shakespeare*, ed. G. Blakemore Evans (Boston: Houghton Mifflin, 1974).

6. Cicely Berry, voice coach for the Royal Shakespeare Academy, discusses using the meter, rhythm, and structure of Shakespeare's text to inform acting choices; *The Actor and the Text* (New York: Applause Books, 1992. Kristin Linklater (*Freeing Shakespeare's Voice: The Actor's Guide to Talking the Text* [New York: Theatre Communications Group, 1992] has also worked extensively with the Royal Shakespeare Company. Another helpful source is John Barton's *Playing Shakespeare* (London: Methuen, 1984).

7. Barton, 13.

8. Constantin Stanislavski, *Creating a Role*, trans. Elizabeth Reynolds Hapgood, ed. Hermine I. Popper (New York: Theatre Arts Books, 1961), 8.

9. Berry provides helpful exercises for tackling this difficult speech; ibid., 180-82.

10. For exercises to assist the search for a character's physicality, see Michael Chekhov, *To the Actor: On the Techniques of Acting* (New York: Harper and Row, 1953).

11. My physical regimen derives from the intense actor-training methods of Tadashi Suzuki, a renowned Japanese theater director; see *The Way of Acting: The Theatre Writings of Tadashi Suzuki*, trans. J. Thomas Rimer (New York: Theatre Communications Group, 1986).

Figure 5. Act 3, scene 2, of Marion McClinton's production, 1995. Lysander (Malcolm-Jamal Warner) and Demetrius (Duane Boutté) vie for Helena (Lisa Louise Langford). Photograph by Ken Howard. Used with permission.

Marion McClinton's *A Midsummer Night's Dream* at the La Jolla Playhouse, 1995
Appropriation Through Performance

Dorothea Kehler

Cast: Bottom, Wendell Pierce; Demetrius, Duane Boutte; Egeus/Quince, Mark Christopher Lawrence; Hermia, Carla Harting; Helena, Lisa Louise Langford; Hippolyta/Titania, Loretta Devine; Lysander, Malcolm-Jamal Warner; Puck/Philostrate, Akili Prince; Theseus/Oberon, Keith Randolph Smith.

Designers: Costume, Paul Tazewell; Lighting, Christopher Akerlind; Set, Robert Brill; Sound, Michael Bodeen; Movement, Marvette Knight.

Speaking for innovative theatrical practitioners world-wide, Richard Foreman—director, playwright, and performance critic— acknowledges, "When directing, I'm actively engaged in deciding, from moment to moment, whether the staging should reinforce the overt meaning of the text, or if it should contradict it in some way."[1] Contradiction is no arbitrary, self-aggrandizing gesture on the part of the director. Rather,

> The task is to create a complex composition that helps the spectator realize that many different meanings are available in any chosen perceptual experience. We abide by cultural directives that urge us:

clarify each thought, each experience, so that you can cull from them their single, dominant meaning and, in the process, become a responsible adult who knows what he or she thinks. But what I try to show is the opposite: how at every moment, the world presents us with a composition in which a multitude of meanings and realities are available, and you are able to swim, lucid and self-contained, in that turbulent ocean of multiplicity.[2]

If we subscribe to Foreman's views, Marion McClinton is to be commended for underscoring gender issues and introducing racial issues that, by enhancing multiplicity in *A Midsummer Night's Dream*, extend its range of signification. But for those who come to Shakespeare through the printed page rather than the theater, Foreman raises questions: when does a director's Shakespeare cease to be Shakespeare? That is, how far behind can performance leave the work, as we have come to know it, and still lay claim to Shakespearean authorship? May *any* issues be introduced into the production? May they be ahistorical? Need the text offer the director a plausible point of entry? Are constraints on "director's theatre" advisable? If the pursuit of relevance takes us outside the text, is the price of our engagement too high? Should fidelity to the text outweigh its creative appropriation? Such questions are fundamental to Shakespeare studies, albeit our answers will of necessity be tentative and unenforceable. I propose to consider these issues in the context of McClinton's production of *A Midsummer Night's Dream* that both builds upon and runs counter to earlier interpretations by critics and directors.

THE PRODUCTION

The La Jolla Playhouse on the campus of the University of California, San Diego, enjoys the reputation of a distinguished regional theatre. Founded in 1947 by Gregory Peck, Dorothy McGuire, and Mel Ferrer, operations were suspended after eighteen summer seasons. When the Playhouse reopened in 1983, it soon became known for its imaginative productions including *The Tempest, As You Like It, Twelfth Night*, and, in the summer of 1995, Marion McClinton's *Dream*.[3] While *Dream* was his directorial debut as a Shakespearean, McClinton is no newcomer to the theatre. A well-produced playwright and prize-winning director, his work has been seen throughout the United States.

McClinton's aesthetic was formed less by his college studies in the '70s, when the theorizing of social concerns was in the air but perhaps not in the classroom, than from conversation, reading, and, above all, theater itself. Though he now believes that actors and directors alike are bound to profit from experience with Shakespeare, prior to seeing Cuilei's production of *Dream* for the Guthrie he had found the plays more vivid on the page than in performance. But Cuilei helped McClinton go beyond the stories and the poetry he loved. Recalling Cuilei's shackled, resentful Hippolyta, McClinton saw the contemporaneity of *Dream*: "the play seemed new to me."[4] The issue of male domination was one that a decade later McClinton, too, was to explore in *Dream*, linking gender to another problematic construction—race—in a theatrical coup.

A man who laughs easily and chats volubly, who greatly enjoys challenges, theatre, and Shakespeare, McClinton explained that he chose to subsume *Dream*'s vital social issues under the theme of "attempts, always unsuccessful, to control love." This broader perspective allowed him to fill what he sees as a hunger on the part of audiences for art that clarifies life. "People want to understand on the human level," he asserts. "They don't want messages in Big Red Letters." Believing that the public may miss many of the subtleties that *Dream*'s complex text offers a responsive director, McClinton urges an initial focus on the intersection between love and power as central and revelatory. Refusing to draw fine lines between the universal and the socially constructed, he compares Shakespeare's grasp of human behavior with Chekhov's and applauds both playwrights as masters of the exquisitely balanced *genera mista*. He notes that in the seemingly frothy *Dream*, references to death, violence, and killing outnumber those to love by some three to one, and that the tale of Pyramus and Thisbe also delineates the possible fate of the Athenian lovers while evoking the tragedy of Romeo and Juliet. A key motif in his company's discussions of the play was the line "So quick bright things come to confusion" (1.1.149).[5] Thus, for example, in the duet over the catastrophes in wait for lovers, nothing short of Lysander's soothing kiss could restore Hermia, who had been driven to comic hysteria by the threat of "confusion." Yet despite a somber undercurrent within the text, the production's sight and sound gags evoked a rollicking mood. Denied a place beside the chaste Hermia, Lysander disappointedly covered himself with a roll of pre-planted grass turf. As Lysander and

Demetrius sought to comfort a tearful Helena by pressing their handkerchiefs upon her, they mistakenly hugged each other. Puck sometimes lapsed into an amusing southern accent, though not, as in his epilogue, when the poetry sings. And the "mechanicals" were superbly funny. As the suicidal Pyramus attempted to weep—"Come, tears, confound," (5.1.295)— Moon thoughtfully spit at Bottom. Pyramus died at great length, pulling out a red scarf to denote blood. Once dead, he refused to relinquish his sword to Thisbe (who sang her adieus), at first denying her a suicide weapon. "The director of Shakespeare, like the playwright, must keep the balance between serious themes and comedic tone." *Dream*, says McClinton, "is a delicate fabric." In his Athens, despite the serious issues which surface, genre escaped violation and the play consistently entertained.

To that end, the first image presented the audience was Akili Prince, a silken Puck reminiscent of *Porgy*'s Sporting Life: a ballroom dancer, his rhinestone-studded zoot suit sparkling, yellow from bowler hat to crepe shoes, playing jazz trumpet astride a crescent moon in a starry sky. At the suggestion of Max Roach,[6] McClinton's production was set in New Orleans, a cultural crossroads, and looked back to the stage show with Louis Armstrong, *Swingin' the Dream*. McClinton feels that jazz can create an appropriately festive atmosphere for the twentieth century much as Mendelssohn did for the nineteenth. The "rude mechanicals" entered in the likeness of a high-stepping Dixieland jazz band, which Peter Quince, clad in the authority of business suit and hat, "directed" from a second-story window of the *Vieux Carré* Rooming House.[7] Appropriately, the mechanicals left the stage playing their jazz bergamasque.

The '20s and voodoo, the preferred form of magic, contributed to the costuming; Titania and Oberon, in furs, feathers, and sequins, were tended by female flapper fairies and male fairies attired as '20s gangsters, who groomed Oberon with combs hitherto concealed in violin cases. Gangster attendants were apt, for without compromising the play as comedy, McClinton sought to undermine Oberon's appeal and to intimate that "the contention over the changeling boy is not merely a sexual issue; rather, it is about power and priority." *Dream*'s forest, a New Orleans cemetery, was similarly evocative. Two above-ground tombs, the one crested by a Greek statue of a reclining woman, the other by a cross, appeared to emblematize flesh versus spirit. Capitalizing on the fame of New Orleans cemeteries, McClinton not only provided a dual sylvan/urban milieu but also reminded the audience of the not entirely dispelled patriarchal death threat hovering over Hermia.

McClinton's "New Orleans of the imagination" owed as much to the 1950s as to the '20s. Puck's vignette was followed by a formal dance at Theseus' court, with Hermia and Helena in bouffant cocktail dresses. Hermia roamed the cemetery in her ball dress, saddle shoes, and athletic jacket, carrying a pink overnight case; she slept in a strapless bra and crinoline. Helena, too, was a bobby-soxer in a sweater, circle skirt, and sneakers. While the '50s look wasn't restricted to the teenagers, their appearance made a point about gender. McClinton intended these "feminine" girls of the benighted '50s to anticipate femin*ists*, in that their emotional strength leads them to defy propriety and custom for love and control over their own lives. Humorously, emotional strength went hand in hand with physical strength. Hermia, though given to walking into walls, displayed anger at her father and drew a sword against Demetrius, threatening to castrate him for what she deemed mock-love. "[N]ymph" Helena (3.2.137) pushed Lysander and kicked Demetrius, twisting his arm, wrestling him to the ground, and rolling him over. Through farcical action McClinton allowed Hermia and Helena to contest predetermined social roles and interrogated an old misogynous stereotype: who's the weaker vessel? *A Midsummer Night's Dream* ends happily, but for McClinton that ending is open:

> Granted, that these lovers love absolutely as young people do, and that finally Demetrius sees in Helena what he had earlier seen in Hermia. But the question remains: will their love succeed? These lovers are trying for a second time, and now with neither a potion nor adversity to hold them together. Are Lysander and Demetrius up to dealing with the "new women" they have married?

Like Hermia and Helena, the director's Hippolyta and Titania also make a feminist point. In light of the play's often doubled roles (Theseus/Oberon, Hippolyta/Titania) McClinton found a strong contrast between Theseus's growth as a lover and Oberon's destruction of whatever feeling Titania may have had for him. Loretta Devine as Hippolyta was suited up for combat in camouflage fatigues, an ammunition belt across her chest, a cigarette in her mouth. An outsider,

the Amazon queen would neither dance nor kiss Theseus; instead,
restlessly she *patrolled* the dance floor, recalling her status as a prize of
the spear. When Theseus agreed with Egeus (a Creole aristocrat) that
Hermia must "die the death," Hippolyta was exasperated; Theseus,
himself exasperated by Hippolyta's quick judgment, softened Egeus's
demand, offering Hermia the alternative of a single life—an alternative
that the Amazon queen, if not Hermia, could only find attractive. It was
this offer, which McClinton reads as indicating Theseus' fundamental
fairness, that awakened the possibility of affection in Hippolyta.
Understandably, their development as lovers was a slow process: for
example, in the musical hunt scene, their competitive claims, although
accompanied by Mozart's lovely clarinet quintet, furnished the scene's
"discord" (4.1.118). At one point Hippolyta threatened Theseus with
her bow. But McClinton maintains that Theseus's wrongheaded speech
on "the lunatic, the lover, and the poet" (5.1.7) is defensive. Theseus is
growing emotionally, though perhaps without understanding what is
happening to him. He learns to love, an experience beyond Oberon;
and by the last act, the director rewards Theseus with a queen, elegant
in scarlet gown and diamonds, who appears at home in the court of
Athens. Theseus kissed Hippolyta just before the Bergamasque and
pursued her as teasingly she ran off-stage.[8]

Theseus' fairy counterpart entered the moon-lit cemetery from
above, a *deus ex machina* on a piano, his entrance heralded by a storm.
Titania and her changeling, a red-cheeked college boy in a pinstriped
suit and white gloves, occupied the roof of a mausoleum. The argument
between Oberon and Titania drew comical screeches from her, malice
from him as he wished her a beast lover. A visual irony was introduced
when, as he intoned "Be it ounce, or cat, or bear" (2.2.30), fairies
attentively curried *his* furry cloak. Fifties swing accompanied the
descent of Titania and Oberon into their monument, while Bottom
arrived in sartorial resplendence: a red Hawaiian shirt, striped knickers,
and cowboy boots. As captivated by the baby-voiced, lusty, bossy
Titania as she was by him, rather than merely succumbing he courted
her, wagging his tail as irresistibly she crooned *a cappella*, "I love thee
now and for eternity."[9]

But Bottom was also attracted to the flapper fairies, Titania's
bower being revealed as a bordello. (Among the few textual changes
"Monsieur" became "mo-dom.") "Tie up my lover's tongue" (3.1.201)
was Titania's equable if peremptory way of dealing with Bottom's

heavy breathing. However, when Titania's right vision was restored and she saw Bottom as an ass, she screamed in horror. Because Oberon only laughed, vastly amused by the orgy in which he had involved her, in a fury Titania hurled lightning at Oberon, who reciprocated with a stronger bolt that left her wilted and obedient. The scene concluded as Oberon, still laughing inordinately with Puck, rewarded the sole male fairy (pimp?) among Titania's attendants, who had given Puck the opportunity to enchant Titania. That lowly fellow was beaten by the flappers in a sexually charged dance through which they enacted the anger Titania could no longer show. Meanwhile the king escaped, his power intact but not his image. McClinton's Oberon, by degrading his wife, had made something worse than a brothel of his home. "It is not enough that Oberon wins," observes McClinton. "He must humiliate Titania by showing her the beast she loved. Perhaps he's jealous of the comfort, the easy relationship she had with Bottom, and not with him. Puck thinks it's all a scam. He just wants more fun, but Oberon is vindictive."

McClinton wanted to show that Oberon not only annihilates any chance of a loving marriage (at the end of the play Titania remains distant) but that the changeling is psychologically destroyed by Oberon's prank. Life in a caring bordello fairyland hasn't disturbed him, but bestiality does: "The loss of innocence that Titania had feared and was able to protect him from occurs: the child goes emotionally dead." Availability and financial considerations[10] led to the choice of a young man rather than an actual child to play the changeling—a role in itself a directorial addition, being absent from *Dream*'s *dramatis personae*. McClinton didn't regret this piece of casting; he felt that a child couldn't show such a transformation as clearly. Concerned, nevertheless, to keep the comic tone, McClinton elicited laughter with Puck's costume change; Puck entered in a butcher's apron after having restored Bottom's identity by carrying out Oberon's command: "Robin, take off this head" (4.1.80). The mood turned lyrical as Bottom found the flower love-in-idleness and wistfully recalled fragments of his dream. His incoherence mirrored McClinton's sense that not all experiences can or should be related.

The most important aspect of this production, however, was an issue that McClinton imposed upon *Dream*—racism within the black community—an issue that made this production a theatrical first. Whereas on its surface the text implies an interchangeable Lysander and Demetrius and an irrational Egeus (or one whose power is sustained through his choice of beneficiary, thus defending against aging and death), for those spectators attuned to the implications of the multi-racial but not "color-blind" casting, McClinton supplied a reason for Egeus' preference: Demetrius was played by a light-skinned African American; Lysander was darker. Egeus, an African American southerner, wants a light (near-white) son-in-law. The set and costumes that opened and closed the play were generally black and white—racial metonyms. Aside from a splash of red, the set for Theseus' ball in act 1 employed a white backdrop and contrasting black floor planks.[11] Hermia, Helena, and Lysander wore black and white throughout the play, while Demetrius, a Marine officer, initially wore a white dress uniform, though later in the forest, regulation tans. The point of the set and costumes—and of the deliberate color-based casting—was to underscore a racial theme. This racial motive supplements and emphasizes the text's concern with social stratification and the domination of women by men. "'Do you marry him' [1.1.94] isn't just a joke line," says McClinton; in effect, a marriage of attitudes exists between Egeus and Demetrius.

With the introduction of this new issue, we become aware of the contest that performance, to a greater or lesser degree, establishes between author and director. Yet, despite his thematic expansion of the play, McClinton's respect for its poetry was evidenced in his minimal textual additions, none concerning race.[12] Instead, program notes recounted for the audience the history of prejudice on the part of America's mulatto elite:

> After the Civil War the mulatto elite no longer had the distinction of freedom to separate them from the dark-skinned masses. Many mulattoes, disenfranchised by the war effort, suffered not only from the loss of property, business, and wealth but also from the backlash of White Southerners, some of whom had previously supported them. To preserve their status this colored elite began to segregate themselves into a separate community. In the process they actively discriminated against their darker-skinned brethren. . . . The elitism that had begun before the Civil War became further entrenched after it, and still remains evident today in the color gap in power and privilege that divides the Black community.

Mulatto elite social clubs like the Bon Ton Society of Washington, D.C., and the Blue Vein Society of Nashville were formed during Reconstruction, when southern cities were flooded with the "sot-Free," Negroes freed by the Emancipation Proclamation. The elite group of those who had been free before the war, in many case [sic] for generations, called themselves the "bona fide" free and reacted to the upheaval by forming exclusive social clubs based on color and class, which provided an effective way to maintain the old hierarchy. Membership was considered an honor, and the "blue veiners" and "bon tonners" were thought to have the finest of bloodlines. In practice, however, admission to a blue vein society depended not on family background but on skin color. An applicant had to be fair enough for the spidery network of purplish veins at the wrist to be visible to a panel of expert judges. Access to certain vacation resorts, like Highland Beach on Chesapeake Bay, was even said to be restricted to blue-vein members.[13]

Consequently, successive generations of the elite sought to breed their children lighter, thus attempting to insure not merely enhanced prestige among blacks and social acceptance by whites but the economic opportunites accessible to those who looked more white than black. McClinton explained that Carla Harting (Hermia) and other white actors and actresses at Theseus' ball were intended to represent the light-skinned black elite. That the dark-skinned Lysander of this production calls the white-appearing Hermia "Ethiop" (3.2.257) and "tawny Tartar" (3.2.263) reflects the insidious, socially defined, non-perceptual nature of racism. Lysander sees the biases in his own mind and gives them a name—Hermia. He is indeed "under the influence" in more ways than one. Allied to color is social image. The light-skinned Demetrius was costumed as a spit-and-polish officer, a "safe" quasi-white image, the military suggesting political conservatism and offering the prospect of significant advancement. Lysander wore a glitzy jacket to the ball and took to the woods in black leather, his weapon a knife. At the ball, sedate rococo music played as Hippolyta, the outsider, appeared contemptuous of the bi-racial elite's identity choices. In the last act the stars and stripes colored yellow, maroon, and green bedecked the back wall, while the lovers reappeared in their black and white formals. Visually, the stage became a metaphor for black society in a nation that still countenances racism as our "peculiar institution."

THE DIRECTOR AS READER

Roland Barthes's familiar distinction between the "work" and the "text" avers the former static, "author"-itative, closed; the latter plural, actively productive, inviting expansion. The former can be read with pleasure but not rewritten; the latter makes a co-author, a collaborator of the reader.[14] In his essay "The Death of the Author" Barthes enlarges on the text:

> a text is made of multiple writings, drawn from many cultures and entering into mutual relations of dialogue, parody, contestation, but there is one place where this multiplicity is focused and that place is the reader, not, as was hitherto said, the author. The reader is the space on which all the quotations that make up a writing are inscribed without any of them being lost; a text's unity lies not in its origin but in its destination. . . . the birth of the reader must be at the cost of the death of the Author.[15]

Shakespeare's "textuality" is evidenced by the sheer quantity of interpretations the plays have elicited, even though most critics have been, and many still are, intentionalists, eager to speak for Shakespeare. Understandably, when the author of a text is iconic, his "death" at the hands of every reader is problematic. Therefore, rather than figuring the author as perpetually erased as his art is consumed, let us think, when we examine the McClinton production with an eye to the boundaries of author and reader, that the force sustaining both author and text is nothing less than our own involvement.

Given that Greek and Elizabethan dramas are apt to lend themselves to more varied productions than do their realist (or rather, classic illusionist) successors, in shaping their production today the director is the reader, the *dominant* reader, who creates meaning through interaction with these comparatively open texts. Drama, other than closet drama, is dependent on collaborative and penetrable texts, or *play-texts*, and so invites invasiveness as does no other genre, eliciting the magnification of directorial privilege. For some, the Barthian director, like the Barthian reader/critic, is hedonistic, his objective, *jouissance*, an irresponsible eroticism.[16] There is, however, an ethically oriented facet of *jouissance*, in keeping with Barthes' political ideals. Barthes defines the "[t]ext of bliss" as "the text that imposes a state of loss, the text that discomforts . . . unsettles the reader's historical, cultural, psychological assumptions, the consistency of his tastes, values, memories, brings to a crisis his relation with language."[17] Arguably, McClinton's production qualifies as a text of bliss by virtue of its engagement with Egeus' preference. The sensitive spectator, i.e., the reader of the director's text, is encouraged to recognize that a racist society distorts the self-image of the oppressed, leading its victims to see themselves through the oppressors' eyes,[18] and to take as a primary marker of self whatever facet of identity the oppressor chooses as key—here color. In McClinton's *Dream*, patriarchalism feeds racism as the father urges the death of his daughter to prevent her from breeding children visibly akin to him. At the least he is willing to sacrifice her happiness in marriage, not merely because of the social benefits a racist society offers the lighter skinned but because of the color prejudice he himself has introjected. Surely, it is unsettling for the many white American "spectators" appalled by racism to realize that the color prejudice of the black "actor" could not be diminished by a presidential Proclamation, a constitutional amendment, a legislative act. To diminish and to restore self-esteem are, in Portia's words, "distinct offices, and of opposed natures" (*MV*, 3.1.61-62). McClinton demands that his audience—predominantly if not exclusively white—admit that they cannot fix what has been broken, cannot atone. In this sense McClinton's *Dream* "imposes a state of loss . . . discomforts . . . unsettles the reader's historical, cultural, psychological assumptions. . . ." *Jouissance*, which may jolt some viewers into this awareness, resides in the abrupt power with which McClinton invests Egeus' demand.

Yet while we are sympathetic to race and gender issues, the question remains: is there a point at which the "multiplicity" that Barthes finds in the text of bliss, that Foreman urges on the director, and that McClinton actualizes in his production, supplants "Shakespeare," however loosely we construe that unstable authorial, editorial, theatrical enterprise? To explore the basic divergence of opinion regarding this question, I set the analysis of a literary critic against the stance of a director, both interested in Shakespeare, neither hidebound. Terry Eagleton, discussing the relationship of dramatic text to dramatic production, asserts that the function of the production is not to "express," "reflect," or "reproduce" the dramatic text; rather, "Text and production are incommensurate because they inhabit distinct real and theoretical spaces."[19] The production doesn't bring the text to life; it is not "the soul of the text's corpse." Since the text has its own space and materiality, "the life of the text is one of literary significations, not a typographical 'ghosting' of the flesh of production." The work done by the actor to "produce" a role suggests that "The relation between text and production is a relation of *labour*: the theatrical instruments (staging, acting skills and so on) transform the 'raw materials' of the text into a specific product, which cannot be mechanically extrapolated from an inspection of the text itself." Thus, Eagleton continues, the "same" text can result in very different productions.[20] Notwithstanding this initial argument for separation of text and production, Eagleton balks at ahistoricity. The text imposes constraints on the director: "In studying the relations between text and performance, then, we are studying a mode of determination which is precise and rigorous, yet which cannot be accounted for in terms of a 'reflection' or 'reproduction'. We are examining, in short, the conditions of a *production*."[21] Because the text is marked by historical pressures, the production—"the *production of a production*" (67)—can interpret the text as a product of its time, reading its suppressions and mystifications as well as its awarenesses. In fact, it is the director's business to interrogate the text as a historical product.

Eagleton occupies a fairly traditional position. He avoids strait-jacketing the director (the production is allowed some degree of autonomy) but confines the director to dealing with the text as a *historical artifact*, whether to endorse or undermine it. Paradoxically, Eagleton's theatrically conservative stance derives from opposition to the politically conservative reputation of the classics, subjected to the explicit and/or implicit censorship of patrons and expositors. "The 'aesthetic' is too valuable to be surrendered without a struggle to the bourgeois aestheticians, and too contaminated by that ideology to be appropriated as it is," he writes.[22] Even so, I would think that on his view, although England had been engaged in the slave trade for some half a century by the 1590s, and blacks were by that time living in London, as a historical artifact *Dream* does not support McClinton's introduction of black racism.

Charles Marowitz's position on the director's prerogatives is in some ways similar, in others widely divergent. At the least, for Marowitz, who acknowledges a debt to Jan Kott and Peter Brook, a "true" director "is someone who challenges the assumptions of a work of art and uses *mise-en-scène* actively to pit his beliefs *against* those of the play" (my emphasis);[23] intellectual engagement with the play, he says, entails no less. Arguably, then the "true" director, praiseworthy for "insinuating rather than uncovering ideas,"[24] is—historicity aside— not that different from Eagleton's ideal director who "read[s] its suppressions and mystifications as well as its awarenesses." But Marowitz's preferred position transcends all vestiges of restraint imposed by the author:

> what is essential in the better works of William Shakespeare is a kind of imagery-cum-mythology which has separated itself from the written word and can be dealt with by artists in isolation from the plays that gave it birth. And, by insisting on the preservation of the Shakespearian language, as if the greatness of the plays were memorialized only there, the theatre is denying itself a whole slew of new experiences and new artefacts which can be spawned from the original sources, in exactly the same way that Shakespeare spawned his works from Holinshed, Boccaccio, Kyd, and Belleforest. The future of Shakespearian production lies in abandoning the written works of William Shakespeare and devising new works which are tangential to them. . . .[25]

Paradoxically, performance, the very activity that keeps Shakespeare alive in our visually oriented era, is most capable of destroying the text. It is for each of us to decide where "Shakespeare" ends and Shakespearean adaptations or spin-offs begin. There are, of course, such praiseworthy examples of these categories as *West Side Story* and *Rosencrantz and Guildenstern Are Dead*, which make no pretense to being anything other than Shakespeare-inspired Bernstein and Stoppard—"new works which are tangential" to their source. The challenging case is one that credits Shakespeare as playwright but reduces him to joint author—where a subtext is allowed to overwhelm the surface (Foreman's "overt meaning"); where, as is most prevalent, a conspicuous number of speeches are truncated or excised in favor of action or visual images; where genre is no longer a constant, governing the mood of the production. For such radical revisions, or autonomous versions, Shakespeare's name is less a signifier of authorship than a reliable come-on to attract spectators. My concern is, basically, with truth in advertising. The name Shakespeare creates audience expectations—not of particular meanings but rather of dazzling language and complex but consistent characterization. If these expectations are disappointed, the well-versed are apt to be alienated, the less well-versed deceived, taking the latter-day "improver" for Shakespeare.[26] Surely, both playwright and audience deserve better. One line in the program—"*adapted* from Shakespeare's play"—would alert the audience to a production's divided authorship and go a long way toward reconciling the hands-off "work" with the scriptible "text."

Marowitz's term "insinuation," is a fair description of Egeus' color-based preference in McClinton's production, which makes a thought-provoking point about a major social problem without pitching the language overboard as Marowitz urges, or even changing the words to clarify the new subject. (It should be noted that spectators who didn't read the program notes could easily have missed the visual cues to this social problem.) Moreover, despite the seriousness of the issue of black racism, the genre of *Dream* remains unchanged. As Barthes and Eagleton propose, such diverse interpretations as these are evoked by the multiplicity—and corollary ambiguity, or undecideability—of the Shakespearean text. One evocative question in *Dream* is *why* Egeus insists on Demetrius as his choice. Is it because Demetrius is *not* Hermia's choice? Is forcing a marriage on Hermia Egeus' way of displaying his continuing power, his potency, despite advancing age? Is the unwanted marriage an attempt to keep his daughter's affections for himself by assuring that Hermia will not love her husband? Is Egeus another datum for Puck, perversely, another mortal fool for love? Is his aim to spite Hermia for preparing to leave him by reaching womanhood? Did Demetrius woo and win Egeus, the real object of his regard?[27] Or should we read Egeus as merely irrational, that being the mortal condition?

But suppose Egeus' choice is not dictated by familial politics or desire and is not irrational. Egeus might have a pragmatic social reason for preferring Demetrius if Lysander's evaluation of his comparative worth is unreliable:

I am, my lord, as well deriv'd as he,

As well possess'd . . .
My fortunes every way as fairly rank'd
(If not with vantage) as Demetrius'. . . . (1.1.99-102)

Could there be some factor that Lysander is not taking into account but Egeus is? Lysander, after all, being invested with subjectivity that the Chorus in *Romeo and Juliet* lacks—"Two households both alike in dignity" . . . (Prologue, 1)—is therefore less trustworthy. A socially disadvantaged Lysander extends the play thematically, creating a new subtext. The patriarch need not be a psychic sufferer. He need not be arbitrary, illogical, or unaware of Demetrius' betrayal of Helena. (Egeus may have caused that betrayal by wooing Demetrius as a prestige-conferring son-in-law.) Egeus could be played as a would-be enforcer of a hierarchy that Lysander is unaware of or refuses to acknowledge. Given McClinton's use of an American setting and modern dress (a directoral recontextualization so common as to be unexceptional), the insinuation of color as a determinant of status within the black community can be viewed as a legitimate analog to the role of class and gender in Shakespeare's England.[28] Moreover, this particular manifestation of prejudice in America acts as a reminder of the racist practices that, along with magnificent drama, are part of our Elizabethan heritage. Both then and now, as Walter Benjamin wrote, "There is no cultural document that is not at the same time a record of barbarism."[29]

McClinton's fantasy, *his* dream, is perhaps less fantastic for being rooted in our time rather than a legendary era, and for locating its interpretation of Shakespeare at the intersection of misogynous patriarchalism and racism as they still affect the politics of marriage. McClinton deserves praise for the light touch with which he highlights these issues and uncovers new critical cruxes while respecting the language and preserving the festive tone of the play. For although one could argue that in the strictest sense every production is an adaptation, I believe that most spectators would rightly regard the La Jolla *Dream* as "Shakespeare," the thing itself.

NOTES

1. Foreman, *Unbalancing Acts: Foundations for a Theater*, ed. Ken Jordan (New York: Pantheon Books, 1992), 50.

2. Ibid., 52-53.

3. The production ran from 20 June 1995, the first preview, through 16 July 1995.

4. McClinton was equally impressed by Cuilei's *The Tempest.* Throughout this essay I paraphrase and quote from a telephone interview with McClinton (24 July 1995).

5. All quotations are cited from *The Riverside Shakespeare,* ed. G. Blakemore Evans (Boston: Houghton Mifflin, 1974).

6. Roach, who played with Miles Davis, had collaborated with George Ferencz on a well-received jazz *Dream* for the San Diego Repertory Company in 1987.

7. At one performance, McClinton was unexpectedly called upon to play Quince and Egeus, which he did with verve; as a fictional director, he was a gentle soul eager to please his company; however, in act 1, scene 2, in order to silence the unduly demanding Bottom, McClinton/Quince found it necessary to choke him. During the rehearsal Quince was himself carried away by the appeal of artistic creation, his speech becoming delightfully foppish. A courtly Quince read the act 5 prologue to *Pyramus and Thisbe* in a tuxedo jacket and lavender sequin cummerbund.

The effect of Egeus' anger in act 4 was qualified by the comical appearance of a hunter's red-checked jacket, but anger was especially appropriate because the doubling of Quince with Egeus excludes Egeus from the act 5 wedding festivities (as in Q1 but not the Folio text) and therefore suggests his lack of reconciliation with Hermia.

8. McClinton's reading is supported by Dover Wilson's theory of marginal revision; see Janis Lull's "Textual Theory, Literary Interpretation, and the Last Act of *A Midsummer Night's Dream,*" in this volume.

9. Devine can be seen in the film *Waiting to Exhale.*

10. In fact, limited funding allowed McClinton and his cast, few of whom had played in Shakespeare previously, only two months to prepare the production.

11. The color scheme may have doubled as a tribute to Cuilei, who used the same three colors.

12. The most conspicuous was having the mechanicals read a notice containing some new phrases and transposed Shakespearean lines; it advertised a need for wedding entertainments and promised the six-pence pension.

13. Program note from *Performing Arts: La Jolla Playhouse 1995 Season,* Southern California ed., 29 (July 1995), 7, quoted from Kathy Y. Russell, Midge Wilson, and Ronald Hall, *The Color Complex: The Politics of Skin*

Color Among African Americans (New York: Harcourt Brace, 1992), 24-25; the program also quotes from Wallace Thurman's novel, *The Blacker the Berry* (1929; rpt. New York: Arno Press, 1969), 29, an early exploration of color prejudice within the black community. McClinton's play *Police Boys* and his in-progress Shakespeare spin-off *Othello Moore* deal with similar themes.

14. Roland Barthes, "From Work to Text," in *Image-Music-Text*, trans. Stephen Heath (New York: Hill and Wang, 1977), 155-64.

15. Barthes, *Image-Music-Text*, 148. Barthes' proposition is interesting, not least for its Eurocentrism. Chinua Achebe has pointed out that in traditional African societies, rather than contention for dominance among the literary trinity (words, *griot*, and audience), "there is a generally shared understanding that all three of these elements must be present for the poem to be realized; what begins as a crowd becomes a community; poem, poet, and public interact to produce a new and living organism"; I quote Bill Moyers discussing Achebe in the introduction to Moyers' *The Language of Life: A Festival of Poets* (New York: Doubleday, 1995), xiii.

16. See, for example, Terry Eagleton, *Literary Theory: An Introduction* (Minneapolis: University of Minnesota Press, 1983), 82-83.

17. Barthes, *The Pleasure of the Text*, trans. Richard Miller (New York: Hill and Wang, 1975), 14.

18. W.E.B. Du Bois made this point eloquently in *The Souls of Black Folk* (1903), reprinted in *The Oxford W.E.B.Du Bois Reader*, ed. Eric J. Sundquist (New York: Oxford University Press, 1996), 102:

> After the Egyptian and Indian, the Greek and Roman, the Teuton and Mongolian, the Negro is a sort of seventh son, born with a veil, and gifted with second-sight in this American world,—a world which yields him no true consciousness, but only lets him see himself through the revelation of the other world. It is a peculiar sensation, this double-consciouness, this sense of always looking at one's self through the eyes of others, of measuring one's soul by the tape of a world that looks on in amused contempt and pity.

19. Eagleton, *Criticism and Ideology: A Study in Marxist Literary Theory* (London: NLB, 1976), 64. Eagleton's purpose here is to draw an analogy to the relationship between ideology and the literary text.

20. Ibid., 65. W.B. Worthen clarifies this point, observing that in contrast to the authoritative Barthean *work*,

> [b]oth texts and performances are materially unstable registers of signification, producing "meaning" intertextually in ways that deconstruct notions of intention, fidelity, authority, present meaning. At the same

time, texts and performances retain the gesture of such semiosis, and discussions of both text and performance remain haunted by a desire for authorization.

("Disciplines of the Text/Sites of Performance," *TDR: The Drama Review*, 39.1 [1995]: 23). Also see Worthen's "Staging 'Shakespeare': Acting, Authority, and the Rhetoric of Performance," in *Shakespeare, Theory, and Performance*, ed. James C. Bulman (London: Routledge, 1996), 12-28.

21. Eagleton, 67.

22. Ibid., 187.

23. Marowitz, *Recycling Shakespeare* (Houndmills, Basingstoke, Hampshire: Macmillan, 1991), 3.

24. Marowitz, 12.

25. Marowitz, 15.

26. For example, Thomas Clayton quotes a Twin Cities newspaper reviewer who, despite his admiration for Ciulei's *Dream*, wondered why the fiercely resistant Amazon had become compliant by act 5. Concluding that the fault likely lay with Shakespeare, the reviewer explained to his sizeable reading public, "there are loose ends of course, the chief one here probably inherent in the script" (*Minneapolis Tribune*, 29 July 1985); quoted in Clayton, "Shakespeare at the Guthrie: *A Midsummer Night's Dream*," *Shakespeare Quarterly*, 37 (1986): 231.

27. James L. Calderwood offers these last two suggestions in his delightful *A Midsummer Night's Dream* for Twayne's New Critical Introductions to Shakespeare series (New York: Twayne, 1992), 13-14.

28. Class concerns, linked to racism in regard to Egeus' preference, also surfaced in McClinton's treatment of the artisans. Their good fellowship and mutual respect were prominently contrasted with the dissension and deceit at higher levels of society. McClinton suggested the development of a sense of self-worth through the characterization of Robin Starveling, at first so shy that he hid behind his tuba. Yet in act 5, perhaps emboldened by his role as Moonshine, he responded with anger to the aristocrats' mockery. "When all is said and done," explains McClinton, "they [the mechanicals] weren't intimidated. They didn't give up, but did what they set out to do—as best they could." McClinton believes that Shakespeare mocks and celebrates himself through these stage-struck artisans.

29. Benjamin, "Edward Fuchs, Collector and Historian," *One-Way Street*, trans. Edmund Jephcott and Kingsley Shorter (London: NLB, 1979), 359.